MW00620755

Paleopathology at the Origins of Agriculture

Bioarchaeological Interpretations of the Human Past: Local, Regional, and Global Perspectives

University Press of Florida

Florida A&M University, Tallahassee
Florida Atlantic University, Boca Raton
Florida Gulf Coast University, Ft. Myers
Florida International University, Miami
Florida State University, Tallahassee
New College of Florida, Sarasota
University of Central Florida, Orlando
University of Florida, Gainesville
University of North Florida, Jacksonville
University of South Florida, Tampa
University of West Florida, Pensacola

Participants in the Paleopathology at the Origins of Agriculture Conference, April 25–May 1, 1982. *Front row, left to right*: Clark Spencer Larsen, Douglas H. Ubelaker, Michael S. Nassaney, Christopher Meiklejohn, Jane E. Buikstra, Della Collins Cook, Mark N. Cohen, David N. Dickel (on knees). *Middle row, left to right*: Marvin J. Allison, Alan H. Goodman, Claire Monod Cassidy, Ann M. Palkovich, George J. Armelagos (holding volley ball), J. Lawrence Angel, C. Jean DeRousseau, Kenneth A. R. Kennedy; *standing in middle row*, Paul R. Nickens, Barbara A. Burnett. *Back row, left to right*: Anthony J. Perzigian, Patricia Smith, Anna C. Roosevelt, Robert A. Benfer, Enrique Gerszten, Ted A. Rathbun, Jerome S. Cybulski, Mark W. Blaeuer, Andrew Sillen, Jerome C. Rose, Christy G. Turner II, Mahmoud Y. El-Najjar. Not pictured: Lynette Norr.

Paleopathology at the Origins of Agriculture

Edited by Mark Nathan Cohen
and George J. Armelagos

Foreword by Clark Spencer Larsen

University Press of Florida
Gainesville · Tallahassee · Tampa · Boca Raton
Pensacola · Orlando · Miami · Jacksonville · Ft. Myers · Sarasota

Printed in the United States of America on acid-free paper

First cloth printing, 1984, by Academic Press, Inc.
First paperback printing, 2013, by the University Press of Florida

A record of cataloging-in-publication data is available from the Library of Congress.
ISBN 978-0-8130-4489-7

The University Press of Florida is the scholarly publishing agency for the State University System of Florida, comprising Florida A&M University, Florida Atlantic University, Florida Gulf Coast University, Florida International University, Florida State University, New College of Florida, University of Central Florida, University of Florida, University of North Florida, University of South Florida, and University of West Florida.

University Press of Florida
15 Northwest 15th Street
Gainesville, FL 32611-2079
http://www.upf.com

In memory of T. A. Cockburn and A. T. Sandison, who were pioneers in paleopathology, and Marty Baumhoff, an archaeologist who first proposed the use of skeletal pathologies (Harris lines) as a direct test of the relative merit of various prehistoric economic strategies.

Contents

Foreword

It is an honor for me to write this foreword to the reprinted version of this important book. Many disciplines outside of anthropology have come to know the book, and it is at the top of every bioarchaeologist's reading list. I well recall my excitement back in the autumn of 1980 when I received the letter from Mark Cohen and George Armelagos inviting me to a special conference "to discuss the changing patterns of health and nutrition which precede and accompany the transition from hunting and gathering to agriculture in various parts of the world. Our proposal is fairly specific: we are interested in having individuals who have worked with archaeological human populations in terms of known (putative) indices of health (demographic characteristics, stature, dimorphism, incidence of various classes of pathologies or stress indicators, trace element concentrations, etc." At this early stage of my career, I was thrilled to be invited. Several months before receiving the invitation, I had defended my doctoral dissertation dealing with the health and behavioral outcomes of the foraging-to-farming transition on the Georgia coast and was just starting my second year as a faculty member at a small university located outside of New Bedford, Massachusetts. I was especially excited to be invited to an event that would provide a wonderful comparative basis for my own work on the foraging-to-farming transition. I, of course, was familiar with the research and writing of both Cohen and Armelagos, prominent figures in the discipline. In their letter, they also provided me with a list of the invitees: just about anybody who was anybody working on human remains from archaeological settings was included.

The weeklong conference, held in the spring of 1982 at the State University of New York Plattsburgh's Valcour Conference Center, located on the western shore of Lake Champlain, was everything I hoped that it would be—and more. In putting together the entire record from various settings, the health outcomes described by conference participants (see photograph) were patterned: In general, evidence of morbidity increased in tandem with the shift to farming. By and large, the results strongly suggested that there were negative health outcomes once people became farmers. Some parameters in the regions discussed at the conference showed no change or even improvement, but the general pattern that we all observed in presentation after presentation was striking. As a group, we were testing the hypothesis that health declines with a lifeway change involving the adoption of a diet involving more carbohydrates and living in sedentary circumstances with more crowded conditions. For many of the papers, the expectation was met.

Invigorated with new ideas and plans, I went home excited to finish writing my chapter for the volume. Cohen and Armelagos collected and edited the submissions, and the book was published in a timely fashion by Academic Press, *Paleopathology at the Origins of Agriculture*.

The response to the volume was overwhelmingly positive, and it set off a series of debates and discussions that have shown no sign of abating. The volume encouraged a whole new generation of bioarchaeologists to apply lessons learned from the conference and its follow-up book, especially consideration of sampling and what the various pathological conditions mean in broad perspective. Even broader questions were being asked, such as *What is health? How can health be measured in an archaeological setting from a collection of skeletons? What are the strengths and limitations of such a record?*

The conference and the volume, now reprinted here, played a central role in the development of research programs that I have directed or co-directed over the past three decades. The volume created a basis for the development of new and continuation of existing bioarchaeological research programs with a focus on regional variation around the world. As one might have predicted, it also provided an essential platform for collaborations by many of those who participated in the conference and other bioarchaeologists since. It reconfirmed the general commitment to the notion that archaeological and other contexts are essential elements of learning about past human adaptations. Finally, the volume set the foundation for much of the great work being done decades later, contributing to the vibrancy of modern bioarchaeology and its growing diversity in research strategies, including health and adaptation viewed in contexts of climate, social change, stratification, population movement, conflict, and interpersonal violence. What a field it has become, and what a great future it holds, in many ways owing to this remarkable book.

Clark Spencer Larsen
Series Editor

Preface to the 2013 Edition

George J. Armelagos and Mark Nathan Cohen

When this book was first published in 1984, it had an impact far beyond what we (or the reviewers of the time) expected. It contained a good deal of data that are still relevant. But far more important, the book established a number of precedents in uses of paleopathology to address archaeological issues and interpretations of prehistory. The conference resulted from the confluence of two areas of research that previously had had little interaction. The first was the statement of a new interpretation of prehistory and particularly the emergence of sedentary agriculture as demand driven, rather than propelled by a new "invention," and involving reluctant adoption of novel but inferior economic patterns (Cohen 1977). The second area of research occurring concurrently with the changes in archaeology was the development in biological anthropology that incorporated the interaction between cultural and biological systems (Armelagos and McArdle 1976). The emergence of bioarchaeology became a significant feature of biocultural anthropology, providing a means for measuring the cause and effects of the origins of agriculture.

Thoughts on the Archaeology of the Origins of Agriculture

The argument in *The Food Crisis in Prehistory* (Cohen 1977) grew in large part from the perception that extant theories of agricultural origins erred in a number of directions. They focused on identifying particular "hearths" where agriculture was independently invented and from which the various crops diffused. The commonly assumed hearths included Egypt, the Fertile Crescent, Mexico, Peru, possibly China and India, and the eastern United States. In the 1960s, many of us as students aspired to be the one who finally identified the earliest "true" hearths.

A common assumption was that the "fortuitous" invention led to improvements in life, health, and longevity by permitting populations to settle in one place, accumulate new technologies, and store resources. It also permitted communities to grow, opening the doors to civilization. In fact, progress as a largely undifferentiated monolithic pattern was generally assumed (e.g., Childe 1951, 1965).

Moreover, the origins of agriculture of many initial hearths were consistently explained in terms specific to the particular region in question (e.g., Reed, ed. 1977). Yet the adoption of agriculture and the pattern of the evolving Mesolithic or Archaic strategies that preceded it occurred in a remarkably parallel and synchronous manner in the few hearths then identified (and, as it turns out, in many more locations discovered around the globe). In fact, the number of such independent hearths recognized has expanded in recent years (Barker 2006) to perhaps a dozen.

A proposed explanatory variable has to match the distribution of the events it attempts to explain, a seemingly obvious principle necessary to establish causation in any science. Local explanations of local adoptions of agriculture, while introducing variations, simply are and were not adequate to explain such a general phenomenon occurring on a nearly global scale. As the number of potentially independent centers of agriculture adoption increased, the need for a general explanation became more important.

In *The Food Crisis in Prehistory* Cohen's primary goal was to identify a variable of sufficient geographical breadth to explain the general phenomenon. The only hypothesis capable of explaining the economic changes on a world scale, he argued, was the pressure of population on food resources. Cohen defined the concept of population pressure as "nothing more than an imbalance between population, its choice of foods, and its work standards, which forces the population either to change its eating habits or to work harder and which if no adjustment is made can lead to the exhaustion of various resources." In fact, all three happened.

The need to increase labor and/or alter diet, not a fortuitous invention, would result in economic change. And the presumed carrying capacity of the environment was elastic, since what is now referred to as niche or diet breadth (Laland and Brown 2006) could expand as needed. This argument remains largely valid, although in retrospect, Cohen placed too much emphasis on population growth. Recent work (Richerson et al. 2001) has suggested a larger role than Cohen believed for worldwide climate changes at the end of the Pleistocene as a factor that changed the conditions for potential agriculture. Climate change had to have been complementary to, not exclusive of, population pressure as evidenced by the sequences of temporal change. Although the post-Pleistocene climate may have improved conditions for agriculture, it clearly lessened the value of natural habitats for hunter-gatherers, forcing them into reduced circumstances before sedentary farming was adopted. (For various takes on this theme, see Cohen, ed. 2009.)

The Food Crisis in Prehistory also helped set up a model of evolving ecology, economic choice, and diet breadth among foragers that clarified the impact of these changes on the adoption of sedentary farming, which anticipated later work in "optimal foraging" and "human behavioral ecology" (see Kennett and Winterhalder, ed. 2006).

The "population pressure" hypothesis was not new except as to the time period and geographical breadth to which Cohen applied it. The most important statement regarding population pressure was made by Ester Boserup (1965), who applied the concept to developmental stages of modern and historic agricultural systems. She argued that increasing populations would have necessitated more and more "intensive" food production, increasing caloric output per unit of land. More intensive food production necessitated the adoption of the hoe, the plow, fertilizer, irrigation, and other features of technology.

Boserup's major contribution was her enormously important deconstruction of the concepts of efficiency and progress. She made it clear that neither existed in the singular but only in distinguishable constituent forms. Efficiency, for example, might be measured along many axes not necessarily correlated with one another. In particular, she argued that increasing efficiency in the use of land (intensification) actually reduced the efficiency of labor. The two measures were mutually opposed much as miles per gallon and miles per hour. She claimed then that populations of increasing density forced increased intensity (production per unit of land) at the expense of the caloric efficiency of labor. Individual applications of these ideas were made by a number of authorities (Dumond 1965; Binford 1968; Flannery 1969, 1973, Smith and Young 1972, and others).

Cohen's contribution was to turn the arguments to explain prehistoric, pre-farming economic change. It is important to note at this juncture that although the compromised, bruised, battle-weary title of Cohen's book referred to a food "crisis," it was clear that the actual text referred rather to thousands of years of evolving food economies, with no crises, no abrupt breaks, and no revolutions. The proposition of "population pressure"—that population growth caused innovation rather than merely reacting to it—could not be tested directly, but two of its subsidiary propositions could. First, the theory predicted that the efficiency of labor would decline; labor costs would rise, providing a clear disincentive to voluntary adoptions of new strategies as populations moved toward sedentary agricultural economies. This measure has been more formally stated by researchers working in optimal foraging theory or human behavioral ecology as the balance of calories out (food produced) to calories in (work effort). Studies of this measure from ethnographic populations throughout the world have repeatedly confirmed that the ratio of calories out/calories in would have gotten smaller (i.e., demanded more labor per unit of food, not less) as hunter-gatherers adopted first Mesolithic/Archaic economies and then sedentary agriculture. Agriculture with very low productivity per unit of labor, at least in its early stages, would kick in only when the returns from wild resources had become so small that growing one's own would appear attractive (see Kennett and Winterhalder, eds. 2006).

The second subsidiary proposition was that health and nutritional quality would also decline rather than improve as populations approached and adopted each new strategy. Cohen (1989) has argued that three independent lines of evidence suggest that this was the case: uniformitarian arguments about parasite life cycles and nutrient distributions that would enable us to predict probable health patterns in the past; studies of health among ethnographic populations actually partaking of different lifestyles; and the evidence from paleopathology. The triangulation of the three legs of the tripod appears to reinforce one another. It was the possibility of using paleopathology in bioarchaeological contexts as an analytic tool related to this goal and of testing alternative hypotheses that framed the organization of the April 1982 symposium supported by Wenner-Gren that became *Paleopathology at the Origins of Agriculture*.

The Bioanthropological Background

The intellectual journey to *Origins* required a significant transformation in method and theory in skeletal biology. Three decades earlier, Sherwood Washburn (1951, 1953a, 1953b) had introduced the "new physical anthropology." Washburn argued that for physical anthropology to transform from a descriptive science into an analytic science there must be changes in method and theory. Typology and description, the hallmark of traditional anthropology, should be replaced with the analysis of process with a focus on hypothesis testing that would become the objective of the discipline. Even with Washburn's emphasis on shifting to process and hypothesis testing, for the next two decades skeletal biology remained typological and descriptive. Physical anthropology continued to play its role as a "handmaiden to history" with its typological emphasis used to reconstruct cultural history (Lasker 1970). The typological emphasis in skeletal biology was not surprising, since even genetics, which was thought to introduce population analysis to the discipline, remained mired in typology. For example, blood group gene frequencies and other traits were used to reconstruct racial history.

Thirty years after Washburn's manifesto, Armelagos and colleagues (1982) still characterized skeletal biology as a descriptive endeavor that was in a "moribund" state. Their harsh assessment further described skeletal biology as "methodologically sterile" and "theoretically impoverished." In its role as a "handmaiden to history," racially typed crania were still being used to reconstruct cultural history. Similarities in morphology were evidence of cultural relationships. In paleopathology, diagnosing a disease and determining its chronology and geographic boundaries were the only objectives.

Four theoretical developments set the stage for the production of the synthesis seen in *Paleopathology at the Origins of Agriculture*. The first was the application of population perspective (Armelagos 2008; Larsen 1997) involving quantitative studies of the frequency of certain pathologies rather than their mere identification. Second was the realization that culture (the technology, social organization, and ideology) were key environmental variables that influenced the disease process (Armelagos 2003; Bates 1953). Third, instead of focusing on single pathological conditions, skeletal biologists began looking at multiple rather than individual indicators. The fourth development began when paleopathologists undertook inter-population comparisons of the pattern of multiple pathologies to assess temporal changes in health (Buikstra 1977; Larsen 1997).

Some research in the 1970s was designed to document the role that agriculture played in improving health. However, the results from Dickson Mounds, Illinois (Goodman et al. 1984; Lallo et al. 1978; Rose et al. 1978) produced counterintuitive findings that indicated that agricultural populations were experiencing significant increases in nutritional deficiencies and infectious disease. The increase in infectious disease was expected. The increase in nutritional deficiencies were so unexpected that they demanded further analysis in other populations that might help to clarify the role that population pressure may have played in the origins. Following up on this work, we invited scholars working in various areas to a rather brief, intense, somewhat overcrowded and underbudgeted conference to compare results relevant to the proposition of health changes with agriculture in various parts of the world. The 1982 symposium considered case studies in which a transition from preagricultural economies or horticulture to intensive agriculture occurred and in which the health status of nineteen populations that experienced the transition were evaluated.

The populations from the Eastern Mediterranean (Angel), Western Europe

(Meiklejohn et al.), the Levant (Smith et al.), Iran and Iraq (Rathbun), South Asia (Kennedy), Sudanese Nubia (Martin et al.), lower Illinois River valley (Buikstra, Cook), Dickson Mounds, Illinois (Goodman et al.), central Ohio River valley (Cassidy), Ohio River valley (Perzigian et al.), Georgia Bight (Larsen), lower Mississippi valley (Rose et al.), American Southwest (Palkovich), central California (Dickel et al.), lower Central America (Norr), Equador (Ubelaker), Peru and Chile (Allison), and Paloma Valley, Peru (Benfer) made the corpus of the study.

The geographical area samples are limited. Only six sites are from the Old World (two in Europe, two in the greater Levant, single sites in Asia and Africa). Central America and South America were the locations of four studies. The United States was the most extensively surveyed with nine studies in the Illinois, Ohio, and Mississippi River valleys and along the Georgia coast.

The volume utilized multiple stress indicators (1984, chapter 2) and included patterns of growth based on subadult and adult long bone lengths and morphology, cranial lesions such as cribra orbitalia or porotic hyperostosis (thought to indicate anemia), trauma, arthritis, sexual dimorphism, Harris lines, dental attrition, antemortem tooth loss, enamel hypoplasia, and enamel microdefects. It also included trace element analyses and incipient work in stable isotope analyses to facilitate the reconstruction of diets. There were a number of interesting findings that emerged from the transition to agriculture that were reported in *Paleopathology at the Origins of Agriculture*. To begin with, it appears that whether the population was practicing agriculture or not, the onset of sedentism was the precursor to an increase in infectious diseases. This increase was not solely dependent on the practice of agriculture. In California some groups were so successful in collecting acorns that a sedentary pattern of living became possible (Dickel et al. 1984). Similarly, gatherer-hunters from the northwest coast were living in such a resource-rich environment (Cybulski 1994) that they were also able to maintain a large sedentary population. In both of these cases, the development of sedentism increased the infectious disease load. However, if and when sedentary populations incorporated intensified agriculture, a rise in nutritional deficiencies would also become apparent. Our widely varied results demonstrated clearly that a "progress" metaphor could not cover the realities of the transitions; rather, we identified irregular patterns of ups and downs (mostly downs) in health through time.

The conference and resulting book had many effects on the scope of paleopathological research. Among its accomplishments, the conference and resulting volume helped to reinforce and consolidate the population-based approach, comparative methodology in paleopathology, and it reinforced the fledgling use of quantitative, population-oriented paleopathology for documenting and interpreting adaptive shifts in prehistory—a technique that subsequently spread widely in the Old World as well as the New; and it demonstrated the utility of "controlled comparison" both to establish broad parallels among regions and to call attention to the outliers. In this manner, it became clear that the outliers were areas in which health did not decline. The problem as much as any other was how to explain why health did *not* decline in some regions but did so in others.

Some Challenges

While the approach used in *Origins* was state of the art thirty years ago, there are significant limitations to many areas. A number of criticisms of the 1984 volume have been offered: The way in which agriculture was defined in *Origins* represented a major shortcoming (Cohen and Crane-Kramer 2007a; Cohen 2009; Pinhasi and Stock 2011; Steckel and Rose 2002). Most of our samples actually involved regions in which some degree of agriculture was already present and the level of subsistence varied. In actuality, most of the populations in *Origins* were dependent on some domesticated plants, often for millennia.

At the time, no clear standards of diagnosis or measurement of the various pathological conditions had been established. Buikstra and Ubelaker (1994) proposed more narrowly defined standards. However, the question has subsequently been raised (Danforth et al. 1993) whether, even with these new standards, interobserver error can be eliminated. The response of Cohen and Crane-Kramer was to argue that the best comparisons were between studies done in one area by one team, rather than cross-regionally or by different teams.

In a number of settings, the samples utilized were too small, too irregular, and too scattered in time and space because of the limited samples that existed with only a few comparable populations that had been excavated at that time. There were few available samples from the entire Old World, and most of the limited comparable studies existed in the New World. The *Origins* conference stimulated the study of more skeletal series globally to broaden the sample.

Moreover, paleopathological studies worked with "opportunity samples" that were few and far between. As we pointed out in *Origins,* they were occasional and scattered snapshots of ongoing processes, and the "pictures" in each sequence were different. The results from other studies turned out to be mixed.

For example, the transformation to agriculture as in the Valley of Mexico did not always show the expected increase in disease and nutritional deficiencies (Hodges 1987; for summary, see Cohen 2007b).

Some techniques reported in *Origins* are no longer considered useful. The application of trace-element analysis to evaluate diet has been criticized in extensive fashion. Isotopic techniques other than that reported by Norr (present volume) were in their infancy with few standards in how to apply or interpret them. The use of DNA to identify ancient peoples, their movements, and their diseases was not known. Another area of criticism has been the use of life tables or life expectancy estimates that do not consider the role of fertility and may be useful only on a gross scale.

Perhaps the most important issue was the meaning of pathological conditions and their frequencies in cemetery populations. It was argued by some that pathology frequencies in the cemetery population may not reflect the pathology frequencies in the once-living population. Ortner (1991) argued that it took relatively good health in life to allow a pathology time to develop in bone. Given this scenario, skeletal pathology might perversely be a sign of good health; the absence of pathology may be the result of rapid death, not the lack of insult. Ortner featured the research of Stuart-Macadam (1991, 1992), who claimed that cribra orbitalia was a positive adaptation showing that slight iron deficiency anemia protected against bacterial infections that require iron. In actuality, this was a testable hypothesis, and it was demonstrated by using life tables to show cribra orbitalia increased mortality from two to six months in the first ten years of life (Armelagos and Van Gerven 1993).

Virulent viral infectious diseases and acute bacterial infections, unlike chronic infections, kill before the bones have an opportunity to respond to a degree that they leave a signature on the bone. But such epidemics are confined to large and densely distributed post-Neolithic urban populations. The fact that they are invisible in the skeleton but occur late in prehistoric time suggests that the gradient toward an increasing disease burden was even steeper than skeletal pathologies alone indicate (as reflected perhaps in health and longevity statistics for seventeenth- to early-nineteenth-century Europe (Cohen 1989).

The same argument was echoed in "The Osteological Paradox" (Wood et al. 1992), which argued in effect that pathology frequencies in an archaeological population bore no predictable relationship to pathology in the once-living population. This idea has been criticized on several grounds by, among others, Cohen (2007a), Cohen et al. (1994), Goodman (1993), and Steckel and Rose (2002). Cohen (2007b) demonstrated on both empirical and theoretical grounds that the paradox did not apply to large-scale comparisons of *relative* pathology frequencies when two or more large skeletal populations are used directly to read the health of populations. First, they showed that despite the warnings of paradox, a direct reading of comparative pathology frequencies most commonly accords with the results from other sources. As noted, the cross-validating techniques discussed in Cohen (1989 and 2007b) found that comparisons of skeletal markers matched the patterns of the other two methods. Cohen also summarized various studies of paleopathology differentiated by social class, demonstrating that the direct readings of pathology frequencies were as predicted by class distinctions, confirming the superior health of higher-class individuals. Cohen (2007a) also argued that factors not accounted for in the assumptions of the "paradox" would tend strongly to make stress markers in skeletons a fair representation of relative population health when two or more populations were compared. Defects in enamel hypoplasia (Armelagos et al. 2009) further demonstrated the problems with the osteological paradox.

Subsequent Work

The largest and in many ways most important collection post–1984 was presented in Steckel and Rose (2002), whose results largely reinforce our own. Their study involved more than 12,500 individuals from sixty-five sites in the Western Hemisphere making significant strides toward standardizing techniques and creating an index permitting comparisons of overall health. One of the criticisms of *Origins* was the issue of sampling. The large samples help to "smooth" the problems of quality of excavation and curation. The *Backbone of History* included a large corpus of remains from the sites in the New World. The editors developed and applied the "Mark I Index," a tool for systematically and objectively comparing populations. The index incorporates three features: multiple stress indicators, age adjustment, and a measure of the severity of the lesion. The lesions that are included in the index affect both children (linear enamel hypoplasia, stature, anemia) and adults (dental deficiencies, degenerative joint disease), and two affect all classes (trauma and infection).

While the individual is the unit scored, the unit of analysis can be the individual or groups of individuals. Because of difficulties using the individual-level index, the comparisons reported in that volume include groups of Native Americans, European Americans, and African Americans. An interesting aspect of the "Mark I" index is the ability to provide age-specific measures of each of its components. In addition, the researcher can compute estimated quality-adjusted life-years that provide a means to measure the impact of pathology in ways that have not been previously available.

There are a number of problems with computing the index that are inherent in the analysis of all skeletal populations. Skeletons only rarely show evidence of acute diseases that quickly cause death. In addition, incomplete skeletons are problematic when computing the Mark I index. Since the number of complete skeletons varies between sites (half of the 12,500 skeletons in the present study were incomplete), it was necessary to aggregate the data for each site. The application of Mark I in this volume "represents one of the first attempts to develop a tool for systematically and objectively comparing populations" (Steckel and Rose 2002:596). We have some concerns about the use of the index. Our concern is that some researchers will see the computation of the Mark I index as an end in itself. Other researchers may compute the index and "quit early" by not doing what Steckel and Rose describe as the "microanalysis." It is the microanalysis of the values of the index that will reveal what the numbers mean by comparing it with the index in other populations. In addition, the index does not reveal the mortality cost of childhood lesions.

In subsequent studies, Cohen and Crane-Kramer (2007) added to the sample from the New World, including several reinvestigations of North American regions, as well as Mesoamerica, Peru, and Chile. Old World studies came from England, Portugal, India, South Africa, Bahrain, the UAE, China, Mongolia, Thailand, and Malaysia. These studies demonstrated patterns of ups and downs (but mostly downs) in health.

There are also the studies of specific indicators that have been evaluated since *Origins*. Mummert and coworkers (2011) described patterns of decreasing stature following the transition to agriculture. Fourteen of their twenty-one studies (two cases showed no change and five found an increase), demonstrated a decline in stature after the shift to agriculture. A trend toward decreasing adult height and a reduction of overall health following the shift to primary food production that we noted remains valid. The subsistence change was accompanied by decreasing stature in populations across the globe (Europe, Africa, the Middle East, Asia, South America, and North America) regardless of the temporal period during which agriculture was adopted. Cohen (1989) demonstrated that the pattern of declining health continued during the process of urbanization and even into modern recorded history. This represents an added value to the methods used in *Origins*.

New theoretical approaches to origins of agriculture have received considerable attention (Cohen, ed. 2009). There are regional differences in the time and type of agricultural difference that have to be described in each case study with European contact and colonization. The Valley of Mexico experienced an increase in infectious disease and nutritional deficiencies. A pattern was found in other areas of contact and conquest (Larsen 1994)

The most recent study of agriculture transition, *Human Bioarchaeology of the Transition to Agriculture* (Pinhasi and Stock 2011), featured the use of new techniques to analyze the origin and spread of primary food production. Their contributors rely heavily on stable isotopic analysis to determine subtle and yet complex aspects of the shift to agriculture in Europe. The complexity of agricultural transformation has become apparent since Ammerman and Cavalli-Sforza's first assessment over forty years ago with their simple "wave of advance theory" (Ammerman and Cavalli-Sforza 1971). The findings are now more complex with no pattern emerging (Armelagos and Harper 2005). Pinhasi and Stock do agree that the notion of the adverse effects of agriculture were not a universal feature of the transformation. When we conceived the symposium that led to *Origins*, we were not interested in finding a universal outcome of subsistence transformation. We were championing a method (multiple stress indicators) to test hypotheses. If that goal was met, we have succeeded.

One of the most interesting new issues raised has been a refinement of demographic processes that defined the transition to agriculture. Despite declining health, agriculturalists were able to increase population size by reducing birth spacing (Armelagos et al. 1991). The best (and necessary) estimates of the growth rate of population (reasonable variations on these estimates change very little) required to increase very small prefarming populations to about (widely estimated) 10 million to 20 million from 100,000 to 10,000 BP must have been not very different from zero. Estimates are that a world population of perhaps 10 million people at the dawn of settled agriculture perhaps 10,000 years ago grew to 500 million at the end of the fifteenth century AD. The growth rate of compounding still must have been trivial, suggesting that whatever events took place, mortality and fertility rates still tracked one another almost perfectly. If fertility increased, then mortality must have increased and life expectancy declined. If survivorship increased, then fertility must have declined (Cohen, ed. 2009).

There is a growing consensus that fertility and birthrate increased for a variety of reasons, including changes in infant carrying and breast feeding practices as well as a change from negative to positive feedback with regard to the size of population, which suggests some increase in fertility with sedentism and farming (cf Bentley et al. 2001). The clear implication is that mortality also increased.

The stability of the Paleolithic populations raises another issue about the factors that controlled population growth during the millions of years of hominid existence. Demographic Transition Theory (DTT) conceived by Warren Thompson (1929) and developed by Davis (1945), Notestein (1945), and Coale (1973) argued that prior to industrialization there was maximum fertility and very high mortality that created balanced populations that remained quite low. With industrialization, mortality was controlled and fertility remains high with populations growing rapidly. Eventually the birthrate declined, returning the population to a balance with lower fertility and lower mortality. This scenario is intuitively appealing; however, mounting evidence supports another explanation. Studies of populations adopting agriculture resulted in substantial increases in infectious and nutritional diseases, countering DTT. Paleopathological evidence indicates that mortality rates increased as populations adapted to an agricultural subsistence base. Thus Neolithic fertility rates must have also increased in order for population sizes to expand to meet the increase in mortality. In this model, agriculture ushered in elevated fertility to increase the population as it faced higher mortality rates. According to DTT, human populations were already at their maximum fertility rates and therefore not able to increase fertility to meet the increased mortality.

Lambert (2009) sees a conflict between physiological fitness and reproductive fitness. We would disagree. In evolutionary terms, the measure of success is reproductive fitness. Physiological fitness when compromised is the biological cost of that adaption. For example, the reduction in birth spacing and the change to an agricultural subsistence pattern can result in considerable biological costs to segments of the population, with women of reproductive age, infants, and children bearing the burden (Goodman and Armelagos 1989). Cohen (2009) has also argued that reproductive fitness is an ultimate cause reflected in more obvious and salient proximate variables such as health so that reproductive fitness would not actually have figured in reproductive decisions.

Ongoing Research Looking at the Origin of Agriculture and Health

Paleopathology in particular and bioarchaeology in general have made considerable strides in the past three decades. We can now measure (a) the long-term trends in patterns of trauma and violence (Martin and Frayer 1997; Martin et al. 2012), (b) the origins and impact of inequality (Goodman et al. 1995; Goodman 1998), (c) the impact of aging on health (Martin and Armelagos 1979), (d) health during the rise and fall of civilizations (Cohen 1989), (e) geographic patterns of health (Baker and Armelagos 1988), including general patterns (Larsen 1995), (f) the impact of activity on degenerative joint disease and work (Bridges 1991; Larsen and Ruff 2011), (g) the analysis of population genetics and migration patterns using ancient DNA (Renfrew 2010), and (h) the use of DNA from specific pathogens to study the co-evolution of humans and pathogenic processes (Donoghue et al. 2005; Ingram et al. 2009; Itan et al. 2010). (For a list, see Steckel and Rose 2002.) Steckel and Rose suggest that the next advance in paleopathology will come with the use of multiple stress indicators that exist at different levels of analysis (ecosystem, population, individual, organ, tissue, cell, or skeletal constituents such as collagen, apatite, and DNA).

Conclusion

There remain two primary areas of discussion regarding Cohen (1977) and Cohen and Armelagos (1984, this volume): the significant paradigm shifts in our understanding of history that have occurred in which these works have played a pivotal role. The first is the shift from an invention/supply side image of economic growth to a demand-based model. Human populations have pushed carrying capacity and required new technologies that were adopted as needed, not "invented." We know that many new technologies including those in food production were understood long before they were implemented; the latter occurred only as need arose.

In fact, demand (largely synonymous with population size) would have pushed economic change up to the point when population size and demand were decoupled. With the beginning of "civilizations" or markedly stratified societies maintained by force, the bulk of the population could no longer exert economic demand and were fed only at the whim of the rich. At that point Malthusian reasoning applies because population density no longer motivates economic change. The latter becomes a matter of fortuitous invention by those with plenty of food. That principle still applies in the twenty-first century. The massed poor may want food, but without economic clout they create no economic demand for it, so it is not produced. If they had the economic means to purchase it, it would be produced. The problem is not lack of supply; it is lack of demand.

The second is a shift from assumptions of steadily improving health through human history to one of irregular and most often declining health, a decline reversed in the West only in the mid-nineteenth century (Cohen 1989; Cohen and Armelagos 1984). In effect, we echo Boserup in deconstructing both "efficiency" and progress. The efficiencies have many more axes along which to be measured, foremost the efficiency with which human health issues are addressed, another efficiency which often runs counter to our normal interpretation of the word. This efficiency is largely neglected. "Progress" has been purchased at a very high human cost.

Given the importance of farming in the development of civilization, there are those who claim it is the bane of human existence and represents a maladaptation (Manning 2004) and "childhood's end" (Bar-Yosef 2004). It has been described by Jared Diamond (1987) as "the worst mistake in the history of the human race," since it is the basis for malnutrition, starvation, infectious disease, and social inequalities. Diamond is the latest in a long list of those that criticize the transformation to agriculture. Criticisms of agriculture also come from some unexpected sources. In the Indian epic *Ramayana* (Sen 1976), agriculture is seen as a curse on mankind (Mehta 2001).

> In the Golden Age, agriculture was abomination. In the Silver Age, impiety appeared in the form of the agriculture. In the Golden Age, people lived on fruits and roots that were obtained without any labor. For the existence of sin in the form of cultivation, the lifespan of people became shortened. (Sen 1976)

Even the Bible despairingly describes agriculture as the penalty for original sin. Humans were driven from the Garden of Eden where all their needs were being met because of that first moral transgression, and they were ordained to toil the weed-filled land forever when God decreed:

> I have placed a curse on the ground. All your life you will struggle to scratch a living from it. It will grow thorns and thistles for you, though you will eat of its grains. All your life you will sweat to produce food, until your dying day. Then you will return to the ground from which you came. For you were made from dust, and to the dust you will return. (Genesis 3:17–19)

Notwithstanding these criticisms, agriculture provided the lever for the advances that characterize human civilization. While the adverse biological and cultural consequences of agriculture have been documented, we would hardly be engaged in this discussion without it. We do not expect that these criticisms will convince many of us to return to a life of hunter-gatherers, but it does raise the question as to why *Homo sapiens* adopted agriculture as a means of subsistence in the first place. We have become such "Neolithic chauvinists" that to even raise the question seems misguided. For most students of human evolution, it seems incredible that *Homo sapiens* took so long to "discover" agriculture. As we have shown, there are varied responses to the transformation in subsistence that will provide grist for the researchers' mill for decades to come.

References Cited

Ammerman, A. J., and L. L. Cavalli-Sforza
1971 Measuring the Rate of Spread of Early Farming in Europe. *Man* 6:674–688.
Armelagos, George J.
2003 Bioarchaeology as Anthropology. In *Archaeology Is Anthropology*, edited by S. D. Gillespie and D. Nichols, 27–40. Archaeological Papers of the American Anthropological Association Series, Arlington.
2008 Biocultural Anthropology at Its Origins: Transformation of the New Physical Anthropology in the 1950s. In *The Tao of Anthropology*, edited by A. J. Kelso, 269–282. University of Florida Press, Gainesville.
Armelagos, George J., and Kristin N. Harper
2005 Genomics at the Origins of Agriculture, Part Two. *Evolutionary Anthropology* 14(3):100–121.
Armelagos, George J., and Alan McArdle
1976 The Role of Culture in the Control of Infectious Disease. *Ecologist* 6(5):179–182.
Armelagos, George, and Dennis P. Van Gerven
1993 Paleopathologist as Detective: Disease and Death in Prehistory. In *Ela'Qua: Essays in Honor of Richard Woodbury*, edited by R. B. Thomas and J. W. Cole. University of Massachusetts, Amherst.
Armelagos, George J., David S. Carlson, and Dennis P. Van Gerven
1982 The Theoretical Foundation of Development of Skeletal Biology. In *A History of Physical Anthropology, 1930–1980*, edited by Frank Spencer, 305–328. Academic Press, New York.
Armelagos, George J., Alan H. Goodman, and Kenneth Jacobs
1991 The Origins of Agriculture: Population Growth during a Period of Declining Health. "Cultural Change and Population Growth: An Evolutionary Perspective," a special issue of *Population and Environment* 13(1):9–22.
Armelagos, G. J., Alan H. Goodman, Kristin N. Harper, and Michael L. Blakey.
2009 Enamel Hypoplasia and Early Mortality: Bioarcheological Support for the Barker Hypothesis. *Evolutionary Anthropology: Issues, News, and Reviews* 18(6):261–271.
Baker, B. J., and G. J. Armelagos
1988 The Origin and Antiquity of Syphilis: Paleopathological Diagnosis and Interpretation. *Current Anthropology* 29(5):703–38.
Bar-Yosef, Offer
2004 Guest Editorial: East to West—Agriculture Origins and Dispersals into Europe. *Current Anthropology* 45 S:S1-S3.

Barker, Graeme
2006 *The Agricultural Revolution in Prehistory: Why Did Foragers Become Farmers?* Oxford University Press, Oxford.
Bates, Marston
1953 Human Ecology. In *Anthropology Today*, edited by A. L. Kroeber, 700–713. University of Chicago Press, Chicago.
Bentley, Gillian, Richard Paine, and Jasper Boldsen
2001 Fertility Changes with the Prehistoric Transition to Agriculture. In *Reproductove Ecology and Human Fertility*, edited by Peter T. Ellison, 203–231. Aldine de Gruyter, New York.
Binford, Lewis Roberts
1968 Post-Pleistocene Adaptations. In *New Perspectives in Archeology*, edited by S. R. Binford and L. R. Binford, 313–341. Aldine, Chicago.
Boserup, Ester
1965 *The Conditions of Agricultural Growth: The Economics of Agrarian Change under Population Pressure*. Earthscan, London.
Bridges, P. S.
1991 Degenerative Joint Disease in Hunter-Gatherers and Agriculturalists from the Southeastern United States. *American Journal of Physical Anthropology* 85(4):379–91.
Buikstra, Jane E.
1977 Biocultural Dimensions of Archaeological Study: A Regional Perspective. In *Biocultural Adaptation in Prehistoric America*, edited by R. L. Blakely, 67–84. University of Georgia Press, Athens.
Buikstra, Jane E., and Douglas H. Ubelaker
1994 Standards for Data Collection from Human Skeletal Remains. Arkansas Archaeological Survey Research Series 44. Fayetteville, Arkansas.
Childe, V. Gordon
1951 *Man Makes Himself*. New American Library, New York.
1965 *Man Makes Himself*. Watts, London.
Coale, A. J.
1973 Demographic Transition. In *Proceedings of IUSSP International Conference*, 1:53–73. International Union for Scientific Study of Population, Liege.
Cohen, Mark Nathan
1977 *The Food Crisis in Prehistory: Overpopulation and the Origins of Agriculture*. Yale University Press, New Haven.
1989 *Health and the Rise of Civilization*. Yale University Press, New Haven.
2007a Appendix. In *Ancient Health: Skeletal Indicators of Agricultural and Economic Intensification*, edited by M. N. Cohen and G.M.M Crane-Kramer, pp. 345–348. University Press of Florida, Gainesville.
2007b Introduction. In *Ancient Health: Skeletal Indicators of Agricultural and Economic Intensification*, edited by M. N. Cohen and G.M.M Crane-Kramer, pp. 1–9. University Press of Florida, Gainesville.

2009 Introduction: Rethinking the Origins of Agriculture. *Current Anthropology* 50(5):591–595.

Cohen, Mark Nathan (editor)

2009 Introduction: Rethinking the Origins of Agriculture. *Current Anthropology* 50(5):591–712.

Cohen, M. N., and G. M. M. Crane-Kramer (editors)

2007a *Ancient Health: Skeletal Indicators of Agricultural and Economic Intensification.* University Press of Florida, Gainesville.

2007b Editors' Summation. In *Ancient Health: Skeletal Indicators of Agricultural and Economic Intensification*, edited by M. N. Cohen and G. M. M. Crane-Kramer. University Press of Florida, Gainesville.

Cohen, M. N., J. W. Wood, and G. R. Milner

1994 The Osteological Paradox Reconsidered. *Current Anthropology* 35(5):629–637.

Cybulski, J. S.

1994 Culture Change, Demographic History, and Health and Disease on the Northwest Coast. In *In the Wake of Contact: Biological Responses to Conquest*, edited by C. S. Larsen and G. R. Milner, 75–86. New York: Wiley-Liss.

Danforth, M. E., K. S. Herndon, and K. B. Propst

1993 A Preliminary Study of Patterns of Replication in Scoring Linear Enamel Hypoplasias. *International Journal of Osteoarchaeology* 3(4):297–302.

Davis, K.

1945 The World Demographic Transition. *Annals of the American Academy of Political and Social Science* 237:1–11.

Diamond, Jared

1987 The Worst Mistake in the History of the Human Race. *Discover Magazine*, May, 64–66.

Dickel, David M., P. D. Schulz, and H. M. McHenry

1984 Central California: Prehistoric Subsistence Changes and Health. In *Paleopathology at the Origins of Agriculture*, edited by M. N. Cohen and G. J. Armelagos, 439–461. Academic Press, Orlando.

Donoghue, H. D., A. Marcsik, C. Matheson, K. Vernon, E. Nuorala, J. E. Molto, C. L. Greenblatt, and M. Spigelman

2005 Co-infection of Mycobacterium Tuberculosis and *Mycobacterium leprae* in Human Archaeological Samples: A Possible Explanation for the Historical Decline of Leprosy. *Proceedings of the Royal Society of London—Series B: Biological Sciences* 272(1561):389–94.

Dumond, D. E.

1965 Population Growth and Cultural Change. *Southwestern Journal of Anthropology* 21(4):302–324.

Flannery, Kent V.

1969 Origins and Ecological Effects of Early Domestication in Iran and the Near East. In *The Domestication and Exploitation of Plants and Animals*, edited by P. J. Ucko and G. W. Dimbleby, 73–100. Aldine, Chicago.

1973 The Origins of Agriculture. *Annual Review of Anthropology* 2(1):271–310.

Goodman,Alan H.

1993 On the Interpretation of Health from Skeletal Remains. *Current Anthropology* 34(5):281–288.

1998 The Biological Consequences of Inequality in Antiquity. In *Building a New Biocultural Synthesis: Political-Economic Perspectives on Human Biology*, edited by A. H. Goodman and Thomas L. Leatherman, 141–169. University of Michigan Press, Ann Arbor.

Goodman, Alan H., and George J. Armelagos

1989 Infant and Childhood Morbidity and Mortality Risks in Archaeological Populations. *World Archaeology* 21(2):225–243.

Goodman, Alan H., John Lallo, George G. Armelagos, and Jerome C. Rose

1984 Health Changes at Dickson Mounds (AD 950–1300). In *Paleopathology at the Origins of Agriculture*, edited by M. N. Cohen and G. J. Armelagos, 271–305. Academic Press, Orlando.

Goodman, A. H., D. L. Martin, and G. J. Armelagos

1995 The Biological Consequences of Inequality in Prehistory. *Rivista di Antropologia* 73.

Hodges, D. C.

1987 Health and Agricultural Intensification in the Prehistoric Valley of Oaxaca, Mexico. *American Journal of Physical Anthropology* 73(3):323–332.

Ingram, Catherine, C. A. Mulcare, Y. Itan, M. G. Thomas, D. M. Swallow

2009 Lactose Digestion and the Evolutionary Genetics of Lactase Persistence. *Human Genetics* 124(6):579–591.

Itan, Yuval, Bryony L. Jones, Catherine J.E. Ingram, Dallas M. Swallow, and Mark G. Thomas

2010 A Worldwide Correlation of Lactase Persistence Phenotype and Genotypes. *BMC Evolutionary Biology* 10(1):36.

Kennett, Douglas J., and Bruce Winterhalder (editors)

2006 *Behavioral Ecology and the Transition to Agriculture*. University of California Press, Berkeley.

Laland, K. N., and G. R. Brown

2006 Niche Construction, Human Behavior, and the Adaptive-Lag Hypothesis. *Evolutionary Anthropology: Issues, News, and Reviews* 15(3):95–104.

Lallo, John W., Jerome R. Rose, and George J. Armelagos

1978 Paleoepidemiology of Infectious Disease in the Dickson Mounds Population. *Medical College of Virginia Quarterly* 14(1):17–23.

Lambert, Patricia M.

2009 Health versus Fitness: Competing Themes in the Origins and Spread of Agriculture? *Current Anthropology* 50(5):603–608.

Larsen, Clark Spencer

1994 In the Wake of Columbus: Postcontact Native Population Biology of the Americas. *Yearbook of Physical Anthropology* 37:109–154.

1995 Biological Changes in Human Populations with Agriculture. *Annual Review of Anthropology* 24:185–213.

1997 *Bioarchaeology: Interpreting Behavior from the Human Skeleton*. Cambridge University Press, Cambridge.

Larsen, Clark Spencer, and Christopher B. Ruff

2011 "An External Agency of Considerable Importance": The Stresses of Agriculture in the Foraging-to-Farming Transition in Eastern North America. In *Human Bioarchaeology of the Transition to Agriculture*, edited by Ron Pinhasi and Jay T. Stock, 293–315. Wiley-Blackwell, Chichester.

Lasker, Gabriel W.

1970 Physical Anthropology: Search for General Processes and Principles. *American Anthropologist* 72:1–8.

Manning, Richard

2004 *Against the Grain: How Agriculture Has Hijacked Civilization*. North Point Press, New York.

Martin, Debra, and George J. Armelagos

1979 Morphometrics of Compact Bone: An Example from Sudanese Nubia. *American Journal of Physical Anthropology* 51(4):571–579.

Martin, Debra L., and D. W. Frayer (editors)

1997 *Troubled Times: Archaeological and Osteological Evidence for Violence in Past Populations*. Gordon and Breach, New York.

Martin, Debra L., Ryan P. Harrod, and Ventura R. Pérez (editors)

2012 *The Bioarchaeology of Violence*. University Press of Florida, Gainesville.

Mehta, Narendra G.

2001 Did Agriculture Reduce Human Lifespan? *Nature* 409:131.

Mummert, A., E. Esche, J. Robinson, G. J. Armelagos

2011 Stature and Robusticity during the Agricultural Transition: Evidence from the Bioarchaeological Record. *Economics and Human Biology* 9(3):284–301.

Notestein, Frank W.

1945 Population: The Long View. In *Food for the World*, edited by T. W. Schultz, 36–57. University of Chicago Press, Chicago.

Ortner, Donald J.

1991 Theoretical and Methodological Issues in Paleopathology. In *Human Paleoopathology: Current Syntheses and Future Options*, edited by D. J. Ortner and A. C. Aufderheide, 5–11. Smithsonian Institution Press, Washington, D.C.

Pinhasi, R., and J. T. Stock

2011 Human Bioarchaeology of the Transition to Agriculture. Wiley, Oxford.

Reed, Charles A. (editor)

1977 *The Origins of Agriculture*. Mouton, The Hague.

Renfrew, Colin

2010 Archaeogenetics—Towards a "New Synthesis"? *Current Biology* 20(4):R162-R165.

Richerson, P. J., R. Boyd, and R. L. Bettinger
2001 Was Agriculture Impossible during the Pleistocene but Mandatory during the Holocene? A Climate Change Hypothesis. *American Antiquity* 66:387–411.
Rose, Jerome. R., John W. Lallo, and George J. Armelagos
1978 Histological Enamel Indicator of Childhood Stress in a Prehistoric Population. *American Journal of Physical Anthropology* 49(4):511–516.
Sen, M. L. (translator)
1976 *The Ramayana of Valmiki 602*. Munshiram Manoharial, New Delhi.
Smith, P. E., and T. C. Young
1972 *The Evolution of Early Agriculture and Culture in Greater Mesopotamia: A Trial Model*. MIT Press, Cambridge.
Steckel, R. H., and J. C. Rose (editors)
2002 *The Backbone of History: Health and Nutrition in the Western Hemisphere*. Cambridge University Press, Cambridge.
Stuart-Macadam, Patty
1991 Porotic Hyperostosis: Changing Interpretations. In *Human Paleopathology: Current Syntheses and Future Options*, edited by D. Ortner and A. Aufderheide, 36–39. Smithsonian Institution Press, Washington, D.C.
1992 Porotic Hyperostosis: A New Perspective. *American Journal of Physical Anthropology* 87(1):39–47.
Thompson, Warren
1929 Population. *American Journal of Sociology* 34:959–975.
Washburn, Sherwood L.
1951 The New Physical Anthropology. *Transactions of the New York Academy of Sciences* 13(2):258–304.
1953a The Strategy of Physical Anthropology. In *Anthropology Today*, edited by A. L. Kroeber, 714–727. University of Chicago Press, Chicago.
1953b The New Physical Anthropology. *Yearbook of Physical Anthropology* 7:124–130.
Winterhalder, Bruce, and Douglas Kennett
2006 Behavioral Ecology and the Transition from Hunting and Gathering to Agriculture. In *Behavioral Ecology and the Transition to Agriculture*, edited by D. J. Kennett and B. Winterhalder, 1–21. University of California Press, Berkeley.
Wood, John W., G. R Milner, H. C. Harpending, and K. M. Weiss
1992 The Osteological Paradox: Problems of Inferring Prehistoric Health from Skeletal Samples. *Current Anthropology* 33(4):343–370.

Preface to the First Edition

This volume contains revised papers from a 1982 Wenner-Gren-sponsored symposium utilizing data from human skeletal analysis and paleopathology to measure the impact on human health of the Neolithic Revolution and antecedent changes in prehistoric hunter–gatherer food economies. The symposium developed out of our perception that many widely debated theories about the origins of agriculture had testable but untested implications concerning human health and nutrition and our belief that recent advances in techniques of skeletal analysis, and the recent explosive increase in data available in this field, permitted valid tests of many of these propositions.

We asked specialists to prepare syntheses of archaeological and skeletal data comparing the health of prehistoric human populations before, during, and after the Neolithic Revolution in different parts of the world. Because we were interested in generalizations about processes of cultural evolution and their impact on human life, rather than merely in local archaeological sequences per se, the conference and this volume were arranged in a format of "controlled comparison" in which regional sequences are prepared and presented in a manner parallel to one another as much as posible to facilitate comparative analysis. This format was designed to facilitate identification of health trends common to the various world regions or to recognizable subsets of these regions.

This volume is the first such synthesis of paleopathological data from around the world focusing on changing patterns of health among human populations rather than the diagnosis of particular pathologies or the interpretation of the history of specific diseases. It also represents the first attempt to apply these data to the testing of theories of culture change other than at the local level.

In the studies presented, a number of common patterns emerge with sufficient clarity to provide striking answers to several long-debated questions concerning the impact of this one major technological revolution on human health. The conclusions that we have drawn are discussed in our own final chapter, while an independent analysis is offered by Anna Roosevelt. The individual regional chapters that make up the bulk of the volume, and which cover essentially all regions of the world for which reasonably good data could be obtained, provide an up-to-date synthesis of existing data on changes in human health associated with the transition. They also provide a data set from which other investigators can test their own theories or evaluate our conclusions independently, and state-of-the-art examples of the application of recently developed techniques in skeletal analysis and paleopathology. The language of these applications has been standardized insofar as possible to facilitate easy comprehension and comparison. An introductory chapter by Goodman *et al.* provides a nontechnical summation of the techniques utilized and the pathologies commonly discussed. Chapter bibliographies direct the reader to more technical descriptions of research techniques as well as more complete presentations of regional data.

The book is designed primarily as a reference and sourcebook for scholars and students in the fields of economic and ecological prehistory, skeletal analysis, and paleopathology. However, the book addresses issues concerning the impact of progress and civilization that have been of broad scholarly and popular interest at least since the writings of Hobbes, Rousseau, and Francis Bacon. Moreover, because it is necessary that the data from skeletal analysis be comprehensible to nonspecialists if those data are to be used to test theories of culture change, and because it is necessary for individual archaeological sequences to be comprehended easily by prehistorians working in different regions, we have put a great deal of editorial effort into making each contribution readily comprehensible by a reader with only a modest background and with a general interest in the issues discussed. As such, the book should be of value and interest not only to professionals and students in immediately related fields but also to a range of laymen, students, and professionals interested in a host of related fields: history and medical history, subsistence economics, culture change, nutrition, epidemiology, the philosophy of science, and the history of technology.

The conference on which the book is based was held at the Valcour Conference Center of the State University of New York College at Plattsburgh and was sponsored jointly by the Wenner-Gren Foundation for Anthropological Research and the Hudson Symposium Fund of SUNY College at Plattsburgh. We wish to thank Dean Charles Warren and Acting Dean Houng Liu, Mr. Robert Moll, Ms. Bette Brohel, Mrs. Katie Covey, and Mrs. Jamesena Moore as well as the faculty and students of the Department of Anthropology, SUNY College at Plattsburgh, for their assistance in running the conference.

AN INTRODUCTION TO THE SYMPOSIUM

Mark Nathan Cohen

Department of Anthropology
State University of New York
College at Plattsburgh

A long-standing debate among prehistorians concerns the impact of early "improvements" in food-related technology on human health and well being. A traditional view (Childe 1951), still popularly held, argues that the adoption of agricultural economies, which occurred at various places around the world between 5000 and 10,000 years ago (and earlier in a few isolated instances), generally resulted in the improvement of human health, improvements in the quality and reliability of human food supplies, and the overall lessening of labor demands in the food quest. Similar arguments are commonly offered concerning earlier technological changes in the human food quest, such as the adoption of marine foraging, the intensive processing of wild seeds, and the hunting and gathering of small game, all of which appear or become intensified relatively late in the human archaeological record, near the end of the Pleistocene. In recent articles, Hayden (1981a,b; see also Butzer 1982) has suggested that these changes in human foraging economies generally had the effect of improving the buffering of human groups against periodic food crises while simultaneously reducing labor costs.

Beginning in the 1960s, however, an alternative view of prehistory was put forward, inspired in large part by the theoretical models of economist Ester Boserup (1965) and by widely reported research on the !Kung San of the Kalahari by Richard Lee and his associates (Lee 1968, 1969; Lee and Devore 1976) as well as research on other foraging groups (Lee and Devore 1968; Sahlins 1972; Woodburn 1968). Boserup proposed that advances in agricultural technology historically had been accompanied by diminishing returns to labor as new systems were adopted to feed increasing numbers of people. Lee and his colleagues described the foraging !Kung San as working less hard than most farmers, yet as better nourished, more reliably provisioned, and generally healthier than their agricultural neighbors. Armed with Lee's data, a number of prehistorians offered theories extending Boserup's model back into prehistory to encompass the origins of agriculture as well as its later intensification (Binford 1968; Cohen 1977; Flannery 1969; Meyers 1971). Agriculture, they argued, should be viewed as an economic strategy necessitated by high population densities among hunter-gatherers and/or by declining wild resources. According to this theory, farming permitted more mouths to be fed without necessarily increasing leisure time or lessening the demands of the food quest, while resulting in a general decline in the quality and desirability of food. At least one of these studies, by one of the editors of this volume (Cohen 1977), argued that changes in hunter-gatherer food-getting strategies through the Pleistocene before the origins of agriculture also might be viewed in Boserupian terms (i.e., that the adoption of marine foraging and small seed processing, like the later adoption of farming, represented a compensation for growing population rather than technological "progress").

During the past two decades, the issue has also expanded to include arguments by scientists in a range of related fields. Nutritionists (Barnicot 1969; Yudkin 1969; see also Yesner 1980b) have argued that the diets of foragers, in theory, should have been relatively healthy, offering more and better quality protein and a better balance of other nutrients than the diets of farmers that became focused heavily on cereals or root crops. Arguments from ecological theory have been brought to bear suggesting that, contrary to long-standing assumptions about the security of domesticated food supplies, the relatively narrowly focused, artificial agricultural economy might be more vulnerable to failure than foraging economies and that farmers might therefore be more prone to episodic starvation than hunter-gatherers (Gall and Saxe 1977). Cross-cultural surveys have attempted to assess the relative reliability of the two economies (Gaulin and Konner 1977).

In addition, epidemiologists have argued that the small populations and mobility of most hunter-gatherer groups not only should have protected them altogether from many of the acute, epidemic crowd diseases known to civilization, but also should have reduced the risk and probable parasite load resulting from many other, more chronic diseases of types likely to have plagued larger, sedentary early farming communities (Armelagos and Dewey 1970; Black 1975; CIBA 1977; Fenner 1970; Polgar 1964).

The latter theoretical arguments have been embraced by a range of prehistorians, including some who would argue against a Boserupian model of culture change but who would agree that the adoption of farming, whatever the motivating conditions, posed a number of new health risks (Hassan 1981). Several demographic histories of our species have at least speculated about whether the adoption of farming despite its undoubted positive effects on the growth rate of the population, actually may have had a negative effect on human life expectancy (Coale 1974; Dumond 1975; Hassan 1981).

However, the extrapolation of these arguments into the prehistoric past, in the general absence of good data from which they can be tested directly, has generated a great deal of debate. The Boserupian model has been widely argued (Bronson 1975; Cowgill 1975; Hassan 1981; Spooner 1972). The quality of life of the !Kung San and of other hunter-gatherers has been debated (Handwerker 1983; Harding and Teleki 1981; Harpending and Wandsnider 1982; Hawkes and O'Connell 1981; Howell 1979). Actual studies of the health of modern hunter-gatherers have produced mixed results (compare, for example, Heinz 1961 and Price *et al.* 1963). Moreover, the question has been raised repeatedly whether the !Kung or any other contemporary hunting and gathering groups should be considered truly representative of prehistoric populations. Many scholars still assume that prehistoric hunter-gatherers faced a highly hostile environment. A high rate of exposure to episodic stresses including starvation has been offered as one explanation of the low overall growth rates of hunting and gathering populations (Ammerman 1975; Hayden 1981a). Moreover, despite speculations about a possible decline in longevity associated with early agriculture, reconstructions of the demographic history of the human species have generally recognized a slight positive slope in human life expectancy as technology advanced (while noting that most of the increase in life expectancy we now enjoy is of very recent origin) or have conservatively argued for an irregular pattern with no clear trends until the very recent upsurge in longevity (Acsadi and Nemeskeri 1970; Deevy 1960; Hassan 1981; Howell 1976; Weiss 1973). Handwerker (1983) suggests specifically that the increase in population growth rates in the Neolithic reflects reduced mortality.

In addition to these major theoretical issues about the relative quality of hunter life, there are a number of other, more specific, unresolved issues concerning hunter-gatherer health and nutrition: whether, as has been claimed, hunter-gatherers were and are indeed relatively nonviolent (see Ember 1978); whether the shift from hunting and gathering to farming affected the work load, relative health, and status of women (Draper 1975); whether apparent latitudinal variations in hunter-gatherer diets are indeed representative of prehistoric conditions (Lee 1969; compare Ember 1978); whether a decline over time in the percentage of meat in the human diet and an increase in vegetables (particularly small seeds and vegetable starches) and of seafoods, which are apparent in the archaeological record (Cohen 1977; Hayden 1981a; Yesner 1980a), are real or an artifact of preservation (see Kamminga 1981); and whether the emergence of trade networks and incipient political centralization had positive or negative effects on health.

During the last two decades, a number of new techniques and perspectives have emerged in the field of skeletal analysis that promise to test some of these propositions by affording the means to make resonable comparative analyses of the length and quality of life and of the quality and quantity of the diet of populations actually participating in the economies of the prehistoric past. These trends include (1) the integration of paleopathology with paleoecology; (2) a new, quantitative, population-oriented rather than specimen- or disease-oriented perspective in paleopathology; (3) the recognition and increasing use of generalized, quantifiable indicators of biological stress (as measured by patterns of growth and the disruption of growth in the skeleton), which supplement the description of specific pathologies and make interpopulation comparisons more meaningful; and (4) the use of an array of new chemical and atomic indexes of nutritional variables (see Buikstra and Cook 1980).

In recognition of the potential of these emergent techniques in paleopathology to help resolve issues concerning the impact of prehistoric economic change on human life, we (the editors of this volume) arranged a symposium of paleopathologists to discuss issues concerning the relative health of prehistoric hunter-gatherers and farmers. We proposed to collect and compare data on health trends in different regions of the world at the time of the adoption of agriculture.

We asked each participant to act as a synthesizer of paleopathological data from a particular region of the world and to offer those data in the form of comparisons between populations representing different periods and economies. To maximize comparability, we asked them to arrange their data distinguishing early and late preagricultural populations (roughly analogous to the distinction between Paleolithic and Mesolithic populations in the Old World or between Paleoindian and Archaic populations in North America); transitional or incipient agricultural populations; and later (fully or intensively agricultural) populations. These regional syntheses then were to be presented as much as possible in a manner parallel to one another to permit comparison and the isolation of significant common trends. The participants were asked to make comparative statements about the occurrence of as many as possible of a common set of indexes of health, diet, and pathology derived from recent summaries of paleopathological techniques (Buikstra and Cook 1980; Huss-Ashmore *et al.* 1982). Specifically, we asked that they collect information, as available, on the following:

1. Life expectancies for different age and sex classes of each population
2. The occurrence, frequency, and age and sex distribution of indicators of (unspecified) stress sufficient to disrupt childhood growth patterns (such as growth arrest lines or Harris lines of long bones and linear enamel hypoplasias of teeth)
3. The occurrence, frequency, and age and sex distribution of both generalized lesions of infection (periostitis, osteitis, osteomyelitis) and of specific infections such as tuberculosis
4. The occurrence of changes in bone growth (such as cortical bone thinning, poor mineralization, or delayed growth) considered indicative of generalized, chronic malnutrition

5. The occurrence of indicators suggesting specific nutritional deficiencies
6. Changes in stature and sexual dimorphism putatively linked to nutrition and work load
7. Caries of teeth and other oral pathologies
8. The occurrence, location, and sex and age distribution of trauma, differentiating if possible between accidental and violence-related trauma
9. Muscular development and arthritic degeneration suggestive of high work load and physical stress
10. Trace element and isotopic analysis of bone, indicative of the composition of the diet
11. Such other indications of changing diet and health as the individual saw fit to report or that were reported and utilized in a comparative manner by published studies concerning the region under discussion.

Our goal was to come as close as possible to a good controlled comparison of many separate instances of the economic transition from hunting and gathering to farming. We set up this controlled comparison of different regions based on the belief that only by summarizing many independent local sequences would we get a general sense of prehistoric trends in diet and health. We reasoned that, given the vagaries of human nature, individual prehistoric cultures might have followed idiosyncratic pathways, alternately subjecting themselves to unwonted stresses for cultural reasons and fortuitously protecting themselves against more likely risks. The literature on the health and ecology of contemporary groups, as well as any simple look at our own decision-making processes, makes it clear that the presence or absence of specific stresses in any particular culture is often a function of idiosyncratic habits that may not be readily reconstructed from archaeological remains and that may not be predictable from our necessarily limited knowledge of the economies and cultures involved. Hence, any one prehistoric sequence, like any one modern culture, might present a misleading picture of the general consequences of the economic shift. We felt that the comparison of many sequences would permit us to weed out and isolate the idiosyncratic while identifying the systematic consequences of economic change through the identification of parallel trends. Thus, we hoped to be able to get a sense of common patterns and thereby isolate the exceptional occurrences for special analysis.

We chose participants with three factors (not entirely mutually compatible) in mind: (1) their work in regions with available data of appropriate quality and time depth, (2) their demonstrated willingness to produce the kind of population-level description, synthesis, and comparison that we required, and (3) the global distribution of their study areas. Despite our efforts to fulfill the third criterion, the results are heavily skewed geographically. For example, although we contacted several individuals working with recent human skeletal remains in sub-Saharan

Africa, no relevant work could be identified from this region. Similarly, no work could be identified from South America outside the Andean region (Ecuador to Chile). Most of North, Central and East Asia are also unrepresented by appropriate data. Conversely, North America, and particularly the continental United States, contains more local sequences and more scholars than could be accommodated.

Final representation of the results reported in this volume is as follows: There are eight regional sequences from the United States, including California (Dickel *et al.*), Ohio (Perzigian *et al.*), Kentucky (Cassidy), Georgia (Larsen), the lower Mississippi (Rose *et al.*), the Southwest (Palkovich), and two studies from Illinois (Goodman *et al.*; Buikstra and Cook). The New World is further represented by one study from Central America (Panama and Costa Rica by Norr); one from Ecuador (Ubelaker), and two from Peru-Chile (Benfer, Allison). Two sequences are reported from Europe (Western Europe by Meiklejohn, *et al.* the Mediterranean by Angel), two are reported from the Middle East (the Levant by Smith *et al.*; Iran and Iraq by Rathbun), one from South Asia (Kennedy), and one from North Africa (Nubia by Martin *et al.*).

The comparison of the sequences provides a number of problems. Each sequence, because it is based on comparison of several distinct populations, represents in effect a series of snapshots of a continuous process of economic evolution in the region. Each reflects only a small sample of the populations involved. Moreover, because of the vagaries of archaeological preservation and recovery, each represents a slightly different series of snapshots, so that it is difficult to isolate precisely equivalent stages of transition for comparison between regions. Each sequence involves its own unique series of confounding factors in the form of changing meteorological or political climate. In each sequence the interaction of changing diet, population growth, population nucleation, and sedentism (factors that might exert independent effects on health) is unique.

The studies themselves suffer from the facts that skeletal populations are almost always skewed representations of living groups and that the skewing may not be the same in any two instances. They suffer from the fact that different analyses have been performed in different regions and often on different populations from the same region, making both interregional comparisons and interpopulation comparisons within a region more difficult. They suffer from the fact that comparable analyses were not always performed in a comparable manner in different regions or among different populations in a region, further complicating the problem of analysis. For these reasons, the best comparative results tend to be those in which a single individual or team has carried out the analysis or at least has inspected first hand all of the populations compared. Where regional synthesizers have had to compare the published reports of others, the meaning of intergroup differences is hard to interpret and the synthesizers have been appropriately cautious about drawing comparative conclusions. For the same reason we caution the reader against comparing absolute numbers from one chapter to the next.

Perhaps the most important limitation of the studies as a whole, from the point of view of the questions that inspired the work, is the difficulty of identifying and describing skeletal remains of truly early, mobile hunter-gatherers, which are rarely found in large numbers. In most of the studies cited, such early hunter-gatherers (Paleolithic or Paleoindian populations) either are unrepresented or are represented only by scattered, often fragmentary finds. Most statements about hunter-gatherers offered here, therefore, reflect relatively late preagricultural groups that may have adopted features such as sedentism, class stratification, and relatively large population aggregates that usually are considered more typical of farmers. Only tantalizing glimpses are offered of the earlier groups, and conclusions about hunter-gatherer lifestyles must be tempered accordingly (although the existing data often show clear trends that might be extrapolated back into the past).

A further problem is that skeletal populations occasionally lack association with organic archaeological refuse sufficient to permit neat discriminations between stages of economic change. In a few instances, associated economies are postulated almost entirely from associated artifacts and site distributions supplemented by data from skeletons themselves (including data on tooth caries frequencies or the trace element and isotopic composition of bone considered indicative of diet). Even at best, quantified estimates of diet are generally unavailable.

Finally, several of the sequences involve populations demonstrably on the fringe of, and to varying degrees influenced, for better or--more often, apparently--for worse, by nearby polities. The variable of external political influence and the possible skewing of skeletal populations through variables related to social class add an additional cautionary note to the interpretation of results.

These caveats notwithstanding, the studies that follow suggest a number of consistent (and in some cases not altogether expected) trends that contribute to the resolution of several of the questions posed above and that point the way to additional work that would resolve them further. Following a chapter by Armelagos and associates, which provides background information on the interpretation of indicators of health and pathology, these studies are presented in geographical succession from Old World to New. A discussion is offered by Roosevelt. In the final chapter, we (Cohen and Armelagos) offer our sense of the trends observable in the combined studies.

REFERENCES

Acsadi, Gy., and J. Nemeskeri
1970 *History of human lifespan and mortality*. Akademiai Kiado, Budapest.

Ammerman, A. J.
1975 Late Pleistocene population dynamics: An alternate view. *Human Ecology* 3:219-234.

Armelagos, G., and J. R. Dewey
1970 Evolutionary responses to human infectious diseases. *Bioscience* 157:638-644.

Barnicot, N.
1969 Human nutrition: Evolutionary perspectives. In *The domestication and exploitation of plants and animals*, edited by P. J. Ucko and G. W. Dimbleby, pp. 525-530. Duckworth, London.

Binford, Lewis
1968 Post-Pleistocene adaptations. In *New perspectives in archaeology*, edited by L. R. Binford and S. R. Binford. Aldine, Chicago.

Black, F. L.
1975 Infectious diseases in primitive societies. *Science* 187:515-518.

Boserup, Ester
1965 *The conditions of agricultural growth*. Aldine, Chicago.

Bronson, B.
1975 The earliest earliest farming: Demography as cause and consequence. In *Population ecology and social evolution*, edited by S. Polgar, pp. 53-78. Mouton, The Hague.

Buikstra, Jane, and Della Cook
1980 Paleopathology: An American account. *Annual Review of Anthropology* 9:433-470.

Butzer, Karl
1982 *Archaeology as human ecology*. Cambridge University Press, Cambridge.

Childe, V. G.
1951 *Man makes himself*. Mentor, New York.

CIBA
1977 *Health and disease in tribal societies*. Elsevier, Amsterdam.

Coale, A.
1974 The history of human populations. *Scientific American* 231:41-51.

Cohen, M. N.
1977 *The food crisis in prehistory*. Yale University Press, New Haven.

Cowgill, G.
1975 On the causes and consequences of ancient population changes. *American Anthropologist* 77:505-525.

Deevy, E.
1960 The human population. *Scientific American* 204:194-204.
Draper, Patricia
1975 !Kung women: Contrasts in sexual egalitarianism in the foraging and sedentary contexts. In *Toward an anthropology of women*, edited by R. Reiter, pp. 77-109. Monthly Review Press, New York.
Dumond, Don
1975 The limitation of human population in natural history. *Science* 187:713-721.
Ember, Carol
1978 Myths about hunter gatherers. *Ethnology* 17:439-448.
Fenner, Frank
1970 The effects of changing social organization on the infectious diseases of man. In *The impact of civilization on the biology of man*, edited by S. V. Boyden, pp. 48-68. Australian National University, Canberra.
Flannery, K. V.
1969 Origins and ecological effects of early agriculture. In *The domestication and exploitation of plants and animals*, edited by P. J. Ucko and G. W. Dimbleby, pp. 73-100. Duckworth, London.
Gall, Patricia, and A. Saxe
1977 The ecological evolution of culture: The state as predator in succession theory. In *Exchange systems in prehistory*, edited by T. Earle and J. Ericson, pp. 255-268. Academic Press, New York.
Gaulin, Steven, and M. Konner
1977 On the natural diet of primates, including humans. In *Nutrition and the Brain* (Vol. 1), edited by R. I. and J. J. Wurtman, pp. 1-86. Raven, New York.
Handwerker, W. P.
1983 The first demographic transition: An analysis of subsistence choices and reproductive consequences. *American Anthropologist* 85:5-27.
Harding, R. S. O., and G. Teleki (editors)
1981 *Omnivorous primates*. Columbia University Press, New York.
Harpending, H., and L. Wandsnider
1982 Population structures of Ghanzi and Ngamiland !Kung. In *Current developments in anthropological genetics*, edited by M. Crawford and J. Meilke, pp. 29-50. Plenum, New York.
Hassan, Fekri
1981 *Demographic archaeology*. Academic Press, New York.
Hawkes, K., and J. O'Connell
1981 Affluent hunters? Some comments in light of the Alyawara case. *American Anthropologist* 83:622-626.
Hayden, Brian
1981a Research and development in the stone age. *Current Anthropology* 22:519-548.
1981b Subsistence and ecological adaptations of modern hunter/gatherers. In *Omnivorous primates*, edited by

R. S. O. Harding and G. Teleki, pp. 344-422. Columbia University Press, New York.

Heinz, H. J.
1961 Factors governing the survival of the Bushmen worm parasites in the Kalahari. *South African Journal of Science* 57:207-213.

Howell, Nancy
1976 Toward a uniformitarian theory of human paleodemography. *Journal of Human Evolution* 5:25-40.
1979 *Demography of the Dobe !Kung*. Academic Press, New York.

Huss-Ashmore, R., A. Goodman, and G. A. Armelagos
1982 Nutritional inference from paleopathology. *Advances in Archaeological Method and Theory* 5:395-474.

Kamminga, J.
1981 Comment (on Hayden 1981a) *Current Anthropology* 22:535-536.

Lee, R. B.
1968 What hunters do for a living or how to make out on scarce resources. In *Man the hunter*, edited by R. B. Lee and I. Devore, pp. 30-43. Aldine, Chicago.
1969 !Kung Bushman subsistence: An input-output analysis. In *Ecological studies in cultural anthropology*, edited by A. Vayda, pp. 47-49. Natural History Press, Garden City.

Lee, R. B., and I. Devore (editors)
1968 *Man the hunter*. Aldine, Chicago.
1976 *Kalahari hunter gatherers*. Harvard University Press, Cambridge.

Meyers, J. T.
1971 The origins of agriculture: an evaluation of hypotheses. In *Prehistoric agriculture*, edited by S. Streuver, pp. 101-121. Natural History Press, Garden City.

Price, D. L., G. V. Mann, O. A. Roels, and J. M. Merrill
1963 Parasitism in Congo Pygmies. *American Journal of Tropical Medicine and Hygiene* 12:383-387.

Polgar, S.
1964 Evolution and the ills of mankind. In *Horizons of anthropology*, edited by S. Tax, pp. 200-211. Aldine, Chicago.

Sahlins, M.
1972 *Stone age economics*. Aldine, Chicago.

Spooner, B. (editor)
1972 *Population growth: Anthropological Implications*. MIT Press, Cambridge.

Weiss, K. M.
1973 Demographic models for anthropology. *Society for American Archaeology Memoir* No. 27.

Woodburn, J.
1968 An introduction to Hadza ecology. In *Man the hunter*, edited by R. B. Lee and I. Devore, pp. 49-55. Aldine, Chicago.

Yesner, David
1980a Maritime hunter-gatherers: ecology and prehistory. *Current Anthropology* 21:727-750.

1980b Nutrition and cultural anthropology. In *Nutritional Anthropology*, edited by N. W. Jerome, R. F. Kandel, and G. H. Pelto, pp. 85-116. Redgrave, Pleasantville, New York.

Yudkin, J.
1969 Archaeology and the nutritionist. In *The domestication and exploitation of plants and animals*, edited by P. J. Ucko and G. W. Dimbleby, pp. 547-554. Duckworth, London.

CHAPTER 2

INDICATIONS OF STRESS FROM BONE AND TEETH

Alan H. Goodman[1]

Department of Anthropology
University of Massachusetts-Amherst

Debra L. Martin

School of Natural Science
Hampshire College

George J. Armelagos
George Clark

Department of Anthropology
University of Massachusetts-Amherst

INTRODUCTION: MODELING DISEASE IN PREHISTORIC POPULATION

The purpose of this chapter is to review current uses of skeletal and dental evidence[2] in reconstructing patterns of health in prehistoric human populations. This brief overview may be supplemented by reference to a variety of recent publications. For more detailed discussions of the diagnosis of disease in prehistoric populations, the reader should consult volumes by Ortner and Putschar (1981) and Steinbock (1976). Information on nutritional and physiological stress can be obtained from Buikstra and Cook (1980), Huss-Ashmore et al. (1982), Wing and Brown (1980), and Mielke and Gilbert (1984).

[1]*Present address: Department of Orthodontics, University of Connecticut Health Center, Farmington, Connecticut 06032.*
[2]*See Allison et al. (Chapter 20 this volume) for soft tissue analysis.*

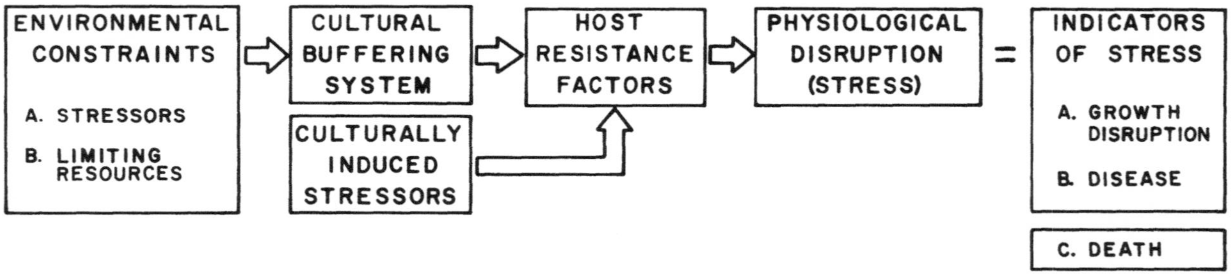

FIGURE 2.1 Model for interpretation of stress indicators in paleoepidemiological research.

This overview is organized around a model of the causes and results of physiological disruption or stress (see Figure 2.1). This perspective has emerged out of a desire to answer processual questions. The severity, duration, and periodicity of a disease may be as important to understanding biocultural process as the identity of the particular pathogenic agent. In theory, if two different diseases are equal in the severity and duration of physiological disruption that they cause, the impact on the individual and the population should be equal.

Stress is a product of three sets of factors which are represented schematically in Figure 2.1: environmental constraints, cultural systems, and host resistance. Environmental constraints include both limiting resources and stressors. These may vary over time and space. If uncorrected, these constraints will result in increased physiological disruption. Cultural systems may act to buffer the impact of environmental constraints. For example, our technological society has effectively buffered cold stress by the invention and use of central heating systems. However, cultural systems may also magnify existing stresses or produce novel ones. For example, while intensification of subsistence systems may allow for greater population density, subsistence intensification may result in a lower quality of diet for each person and amplify interpersonal strife as access to quality nutrients is limited.

If stress is not adequately buffered by extraindividual means, its effects may be buffered only by individual host resistance. Host resistance varies by age and sex. Genetic factors also play an important role in resistance to certain diseases; however, these are difficult to trace in the archaeological record.

When host resistance and environmental constraints are held constant, variation in stress levels may be related to cultural differences. The primary purpose of this volume is to determine changes in health associated with culture change where environmental and host resistance factors are presumed constant.

Physiological disruption cannot be directly measured in skeletal remains. However, stress does leave a series of indicators in bone and teeth. A primary goal of paleopathology is to 'read' these indicators of stress.

In this chapter indicators of stress are organized under three major headings: (1) indicators of general, cumulative stress; (2) indicators of general, episodic stress; and (3) indicators of stress associated with specific diseases. These groupings are somewhat arbitrary; it could be argued that there is a continuum of indicators from most to least general and most to least episodic. Other grouping schemes are also possible but may not be as useful in understanding underlying similarities in the causes of stress. General indicators are based on the organism's nonspecific response to noxious stimuli (Selye 1950, 1971). Cumulative indicators provide a summation of the amount of stress over long periods of time while episodic indicators are more precise and confined in the time at which stress occurred.

General, cumulative indicators include mortality measures and growth assessments. Under stressful conditions the growing organism will either slow growth or cease to grow since its available nutrients are better put to combating the stress (Acheson 1960). Since stress generally results in the release of catabolic hormones (those which release energy) the anabolic process of growth is inhibited (Cannon 1932; Tanner 1978). Therefore, indicators of growth may be indicative of stress of a general nature.

Periodic indicators of stress provide information on the age at which stress episodes occurred. Two common examples of general, periodic indicators are Harris lines (disruptions in linear bone growth) and enamel hypoplasias (disruption in tooth enamel matrix formation).

Finally, some diseases or disease classes may leave more specific indications of stress on bone and teeth. This is true for trauma and degenerative pathologies, and for some infectious diseases and nutritional deficiencies.

To summarize the model, stress is a result of environmental constraints, cultural filters, and host resistance factors. While stress is not directly measurable in skeletal remains, it may be inferred from a series of indicators. When host resistance and environmental constraints are held relatively constant, variation in stress may be attributed to cultural differences. Increasing levels of stress may also act as a cause of changes in cultural patterns. An ultimate goal of paleopathology is to understand the process by which cultures may both cause and respond to stress.

GENERAL AND CUMULATIVE STRESS INDICATORS

Mortality

Mortality data for skeletal populations derive from assessment of individual ages at death (see Ubelaker 1978 for an overview of methods of skeletal age determination). Traditional presentations of mortality data involve either the direct estimation of life expectancy at birth (based on the mean age at death) or the construction of life tables. In addition to estimating life expectancy at birth, life tables provide estimations of life expectancy, probability of dying, and survivorship for all age classes (see Swedlund and Armelagos 1976: Appendix A for method of computation).

Two types of criticisms have been voiced against measurements of mortality and specifically against the use of life tables in paleodemography. The first concerns the appropriate method of presentation and use of mortality data from archaeological populations. Angel (1969) argues that life tables are too sophisticated a tool for limited available paleodemographic data. However, where population sizes are sufficiently large and appear to be well represented, life tables may provide a series of meaningful and valid statistics (Acsadi and Nemeskéri 1970; Moore et al. 1975; Swedlund and Armelagos 1969).

More fundamental criticisms of life tables concern the various assumptions which are inherent in the method. The construction of these tables assumes that a skeletal sample is truly representative of a real population; that no population growth is occurring; that there is little stochastic fluctuation in the population's size; and that individual ages-at-death are accurately determined. Moore et al. (1975) have determined that undernumeration of infants, the principal source of skewing in archaeological samples, has little effect on mortality estimates except in the youngest age classes. Stochastic fluctuation may introduce errors in very small populations. However, this error may be estimated. Similarly, growth or decline in population size introduces error. However, the error is small under conditions close to equilibrium. These same authors provide a reminder that mortality statistics are probability statements and should be regarded as having ranges of reliability (Moore et al. 1975). Under normal conditions the estimated errors in paleodemographic data are small. Finally, it has recently been proposed that paleodemographic analyses are seriously flawed due to inaccuracy in age determination (Bocquet-Appel and Masset 1982). However, Van Gerven and Armelagos (1983) have argued that serially aging the skeletal series reduces this error.

Part of Van Gerven and Armelagos's argument in favor of the use of life tables includes an assessment of the validity of life table data in specific contexts. Life table analysis has frequently led to interpretable and meaningful conclusions in paleodemographic analyses. For example, Green et al. (1974) show a decrease in life expectancy in Sudanese Nubians who are buried without superstructures and in those who died while their village was in decline.

We believe that the major limitations of the paleodemographic method are practical ones. These include the representativeness and size of the sample and the ability to provide accurate assessment of developmental age (Lovejoy et al. 1977). Age at death stands as perhaps the most important single indicator of stress. Age at death is of additional importance as other stress indicators are related to it. If other stress indicators are associated with decreased ages at death, then this supports their validity as indicators of stress.

Growth Assessment

Growth assessment is a common tool for analysis of the degree of environmental stress in prehistoric populations. Assessments may include the construction of growth curves based on measured length and width of long bones for each age category of subadults; the measure of attained length and width from adult long bones; the estimation of stature derived from adult long bone lengths; and the determination of sexual dimorphism derived from male-female differences in selected anthropometric measures.

These indicators are based on the theoretical proposition that the slowing or cessation of growth is a logical response by an organism to increased stress (Cannon 1932). However, all growth comparisons must consider the importance of genetic factors affecting size and shape. When genetic variables are controlled, the experimental and clinical literature strongly suggests that delayed or decreased growth may be reflective of physiological disruption (Acheson and Fowler 1964; Dickerson and McCance 1961; Engfeldt and Hjertquist 1961; Himes 1978; Johnston 1976; McCance and Widdowson 1962; Platt and McCance 1964; Stewart 1975; Tanner 1977, 1978).

Subadult Long Bone Length and Width Curves

The analysis of growth in subadult long bones is based on the fact that dental development is less affected by stressful conditions than skeletal growth (Garn et al. 1959, 1965; Lewis and Garn 1960). Provided that a large population of subadults is available for study with intact long bones and dental ages, long bone growth may be plotted against dental age.

Such growth curves have been constructed by Sundick (1978) and Ubelaker (1978), among others, for archaeological populations. The growth curves of prehistoric populations generally differ from modern standards in two principal ways. The first is a reduced rate of growth between the ages of approximately 2 and 5 years and the second is a delay in the timing of the adolescent growth spurt. The decrease in rate of growth at ages 2-5 relative to modern standards (Maresh 1955) may be indicative of undernutrition or other stress acting on that segment of the population. For example, Cook (1976) interprets such a disease in growth rate in a prehistoric population from Illinois to be due to a poor weanling diet. The delay in the adolescent growth spurt may be the result of chronic undernutrition or other chronic stresses. Frisancho and Garn (1970) attribute such a growth delay in Quechua Indians living on the Peruvian altiplano to chronically low nutrient availability. The view that this delay is adaptive in the face of limited calories is supported by Thomas (1973), who demonstrates that the delay in growth significantly reduces the energy needs of the population.

While comparison of prehistoric growth curves with modern standards may be illustrative, Buikstra and Cook (1980) warn against overinterpretation. Prehistoric data are not strictly comparable to modern data; age estimates for prehistoric individuals are based on developmental criteria (tooth eruption) whereas modern individuals are usually aged by the calendar.

Moreover, prehistoric data are cross-sectional (different individuals dead in different age classes) rather than longitudinal (the same individuals progressing from age class to age class).

In light of these limitations, perhaps the most valid use of prehistoric growth curves involves comparisons of curves from genetically similar populations. An example of this approach is Lallo's (1973) study of long bone growth curves from Dickson Mounds populations (also see Goodman et al., Chapter 11 this volume). Lallo is able to demonstrate a statistically significant secular decrease in mean tibial length for individuals of ages 5-10 when comparing the Dickson Middle Mississippian to earlier Dickson populations.

Similarly to the above, long bone width, circumference, and cortical thickness may be plotted against dental age. Lallo (1973) has also demonstrated a secular decrease in tibial circumference relative to age which parallels the length decrease mentioned above (also see Goodman et al., Chapter 11 this volume).

Huss-Ashmore (1981) in an analysis of juveniles from prehistoric Sudanese Nubia has shown that long bone growth in length may be maintained at the expense of cortical thickness (also see Garn et al. 1964). Thin cortices in growing children are a clear indication of stress, but in a sense may also represent an adaptive response. Decreased bone mass in growing children permits continued growth of bones in length as well as the liberation of minerals and nutrients to aid in the maintenance of soft tissue systems in which nutrients are most required. Comparison of long bone widths and length curves may provide a hierarchy of growth responses to stress (Huss-Ashmore et al. 1982). Width is first affected. But if stress is severe and long lasting, then length increase may also slow or stop.

Adult Long Bone Length and Width

The measurement of size and shape of adult long bones is among the most standard of procedures in anthropometric and skeletal analysis. Many researchers have provided data on adult long bone width and length in prehistoric samples and have derived stature estimates from these data. (See Ubelaker 1978, for stature formulas.) Comparison across populations again introduces problems in interpretation as it is difficult to estimate the degree of genetic involvement in size and shape differences. Size and shape differences in adult skeletons may be more easily related to environmental conditions and physiological disruption if there is relative genetic homogeneity in samples. The relative genetic continuity of successive samples provides the basis for the interpretation of recent secular increases in height within a country or defined geographic area (Acheson and Fowler 1964; Craig 1963). These secular increases have most frequently been interpreted as being due to a decrease in infant-childhood disease and elimination of nutritional stresses (Dobos 1965:77-79; Huber 1967). Similar interpretations may be applied to similar patterns in prehistory if genetic continuity can be postulated or proved. See, for example, Larsen (1982 and Chapter 14 this volume), who demonstrates a decrease in adult long-bone length in successive populations on the Georgia coast.

While long bone length yields information on group adaptation, analysis of long bone thickness, width, and histological structure can reveal patterns of metabolic activity and physiological disruption in adults. Because cortical bone is in a constant state of remodeling by resorption and deposition, introduction of any stress which seriously affects metabolism may alter the rate of remodeling (Stout and Simmons 1979). When rates of bone remodeling are in disequilibrium, bone can be lost instead of maintained. Conditions resulting in osteoporosis (bone loss) include metabolic disturbances, systemic disease, and nutritional stress (Garn 1970; Huss-Ashmore et al. 1982; Martin and Armelagos 1979; Ortner 1976).

Cross sections of bone shafts can be analyzed by calculating the percentage of the cortical area (bone thickness versus bone marrow cavity) and plotting this by age and sex (Garn 1970). Thin sections can also be made and viewed under a bright field microscope to reveal its microstructure (Martin et al. 1984). These measures assess the amount and quality of the cortical bone present and reflect the nutritional and health status of the individual. Huss-Ashmore and co-workers (1982) have demonstrated the usefulness of cortical bone analysis in the assessment of the quality and quantity of diet. Age-controlled samples from temporally sequential populations have been used to equate bone loss and increase remodeling activity with nutritional stress (Martin 1983; Richman et al., 1979; Stout 1979).

Sexual Dimorphism

Though common, analyses of the degree of sexual dimorphism are difficult to interpret for archaeological populations. In theory, a decrease in sexual dimorphism should be indicative of increased stress since the growing male is more susceptible to stress than the growing female (see Stini 1969, 1972, 1975). However, analysis of sexual dimorphism is confounded by potential genetic variation in the degree of dimorphism among populations and the likelihood that males are more protected from stress in many societies. Furthermore, in archaeological analysis the same traits which are used to determine sex are often used to access the degree of dimorphism, thus engendering circularity.

The standard method for assessment of sexual dimorphism involves the determination of male to female ratios for stature or for various measures of skeletal width and robusticity. More detailed multivariate analyses of sexual dimorphism have been performed by Van Gerven (1972) based on femoral measures and by Gustav (1972) based on pelvic measures.

While comparison of the degree of sexual dimorphism both among and within populations may prove to be useful, at present the results are difficult to interpret. For example, Larson (1982, Chapter 14 this volume) argues that an *increase* in sexual dimorphism is associated with increased stress. This results from the increased physical work load placed on females, which decreases their growth.

Other Cumulative Indicators of Stress

Other skeletal indicators may prove to be useful in providing data on cumulative levels of stress in archaeological populations. Angel (1978, 1982, and Chapter 3 this volume) argues that skull base height and pelvic inlet form are indicative of growth efficiency and nutritional stress. Angel may be correct in this assessment. However, his arguments should be supported by experimental data which at present are sparse. And, as with other growth assessment, the degree of genetic control must be considered.

Dental crowding should be indicative of nutritional or other chronic, severe stress since teeth will be less affected by chronic stress than alveolar bone size. Widdowson and McCance (1964) have demonstrated this effect in undernourished piglets and Trowell and co-workers (1954) have noted increasing crowding and impacted molars in severely malnourished children. Increased dental crowding may be indicative of severe and chronic stress in archaeological populations. However, we are unaware of the use of this potential indicator in any evaluation of health in prehistory.

Guargliardo (1982) has recently presented an argument that tooth size variation within a skeletal population may be indicative of environmental stress. This proposition is based on his observation that decreased tooth size is often associated with a mean earlier age at death. Individuals who are most stressed die earlier and their teeth fail to grow to their genetically determined potential size.

Fluctuating or random asymmetry refers to size differences in a bilateral organism in which one side is larger than the other, but in which no consistent pattern occurs (where, for example, some teeth on the right are larger and some smaller than their counterparts on the left; see Buikstra and Cook 1980, and Huss-Ashmore et al. 1982 for more detailed reviews of asymmetry). Asymmetries in long bone lengths and especially in dental crown measures have been used by a variety of authors as an index of stress in both living and prehistoric populations (cf. Bailit et al. 1970; DiBennardo and Bailit 1978; Niswander and Chung 1965; Perzigian 1977; and Perzigian et al., Chapter 13 this volume). Dental asymmetry is generally greater in populations which are under the greatest stress (Bailit et al. 1970). However, populations may also vary in the degree to which they are genetically predisposed to increased asymmetries (Niswander and Chung 1965). If asymmetries are due to stress, then the critical period is likely to be in utero during the development of tooth buds (Bailit 1975). The postnatal environment may affect tooth size, causing asymmetries, but how this effect is produced is unclear. As noted, this condition frequently has been used as a measure of stress on a populational level. Its use likely will increase as the mechanisms by which asymmetries develop are better understood.

INDICATORS OF GENERAL AND EPISODIC STRESS

Harris Lines

Harris (1926, 1933) was one of the first researchers to study the mechanisms and causes of Harris lines. Harris lines, which consist of dense transverse lines visible in longitudinal sections or radiographs of longbones, are also referred to as "transverse trabeculae" (Platt and Stewart 1962), "transverse lines" (Park and Richter 1953), "radiographic transverse lines" (Harris 1933), and "lines and bands of increased radiopacity" (Garn et al. 1968). While the latter label is the most accurate description of the phenomena, we will refer to them as Harris lines or transverse lines for brevity and in agreement with the prevailing convention (Figure 2.2).

The mechanism by which Harris lines are formed involve a reduction in the thickness of the epiphyseal cartilage plate with increased resistance of the immature cartilage cells to capillary and osteoblastic penetration. Subsequently, a thin osteoblastic layer (primary stratum) is formed and replaces the more mature cartilage cells below the plate. Finally, horizontally oriented trabeculae are formed by the osteoblasts of the primary stratum (Garn et al. 1968; Park 1964; Park and Richter 1953; Steinbock 1976). Once formed, Harris lines may resorb and disappear. There is little agreement on how, when, and where resorption occurs. Hence, resorption introduces a potential source of error into analyses of Harris lines as indicators of past stressful experiences (cf. Garn et al. 1968; Park 1964).

There is little consensus about the cause of Harris lines (see Buikstra and Cook 1980; Huss-Ashmore et al. 1982, and Martin et al. in press for discussions on the meaning and use of Harris lines in paleoanthropology). The mechanisms of line formation require a period in which growth is arrested, followed by a period of growth recovery (Acheson 1959; Steinbock 1976). This process may take place within approximately one week (Steinbock 1976). Thus Harris lines should be indicative of stresses of approximately this duration. However, the clinical and experimental literature show only a weak association between known stressors and Harris line formation (see Marshall 1967). Published correlation

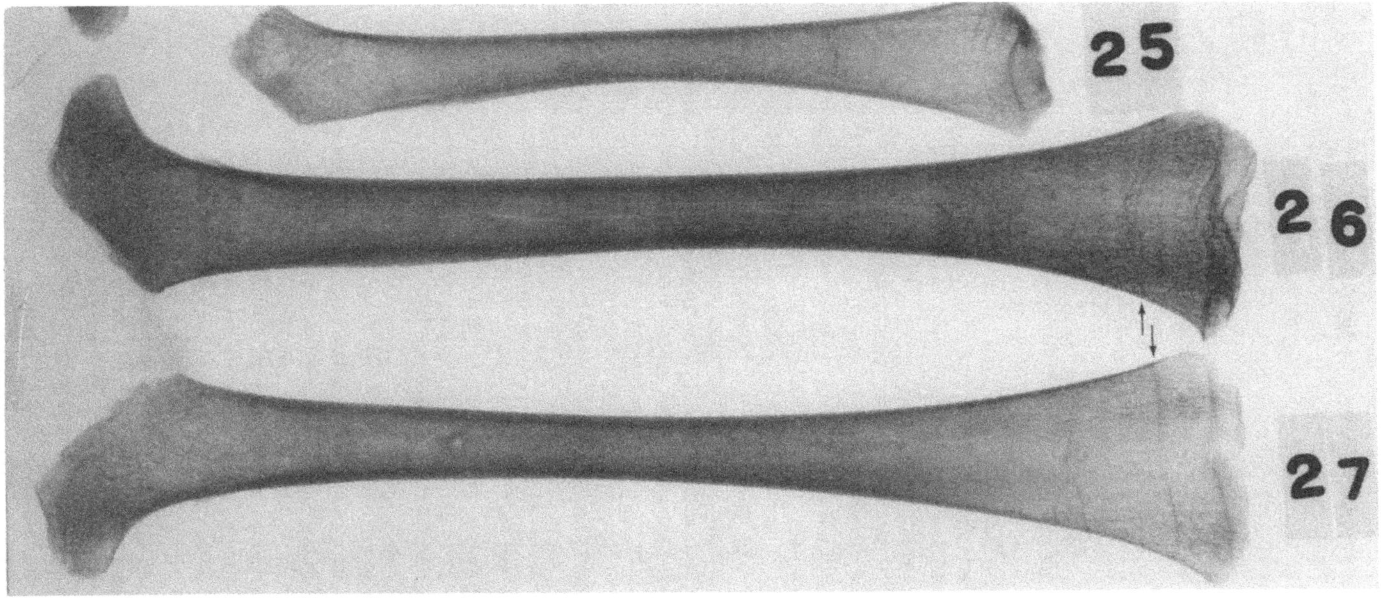

FIGURE 2.2 Harris lines in the distal femur of subadults from the Pueblo period at Black Mesa, Arizona (numbers are for identification).

coefficients for the associations between Harris lines and diseases range from .03 to .30 (Mensforth 1981).

Despite these low correlations, Harris line analyses have been common in paleopathology since Wells (1967) hailed the method as an exciting "new approach to paleopathology." The enthusiasm of Wells and others (Allison et al. 1974; Clarke 1978; Cook 1979; Goodman and Clark 1981; Gray 1967; McHenry 1968; and Woodall 1968) is likely to be a function of the ease of the method and the potential for gaining chronological information about episodic stresses. Harris line frequencies have been used to measure gender differences in stress (Wells 1967), interpopulation differences in stress (Goodman and Clark 1981), periodicity of stress (Cook 1979), and the chronology of stress during development (Clarke 1978). If Harris lines are a valid indicator of stress, then they are likely to indicate acute and episodic stress in contrast to the previously noted indicators of cumulative stress.

The standard method for analysis of Harris lines involves the production of radiographs of long bones in anterior-posterior position. Lines may be rated for thickness, degree of opacity, and amount that they traverse the diaphysis. However, we are unaware of a highly replicable method for scoring either the presence or absence or the quality of a line.

Chronologies of the time of development of lines have been developed based on the position of lines relative to the mid-shaft using established chronologies for the growth in length of long bones (see Goodman et al., Chapter 11 this volume). These chronologies can be adjusted for variations in growth as a function of age, sex, and body part but can not account for individual and population level variations in growth. Harris line analysis for adult long bones may provide a chronology of stress during the complete period of long bone growth. Analysis of subadult long bones may yield a chronology up to the age at death.

Interpretation of Harris line data must be undertaken with caution. Differences in frequency may be interpreted as a function of variation in degree of episodic stress. However, one must be aware of the low correlations between Harris lines and known stressors in the clinical and experimental literature as well as a series of inverse relationships between Harris lines and other stress indicators in paleopathological studies (Goodman and Clark 1981; McHenry and Schulz 1976). Similarly, Harris line chronologies may be useful in pointing to the distribution of stress over the growing years. However, interpretation of chronologies is also dependent on one's faith in the meaning of lines as well as a consideration of age-related host resistance and growth phenomena. Finally, evaluation of the frequency of Harris lines across studies is cautioned against because data concerning Harris lines are known to vary by observer, radiographic material and method employed, long bone observed, and age of sample (Martin et al. 1984). Harris lines are potentially an excellent source of data obtainable in no other way, but their interpretation should be supported by parallel analyses of other stress indicators.

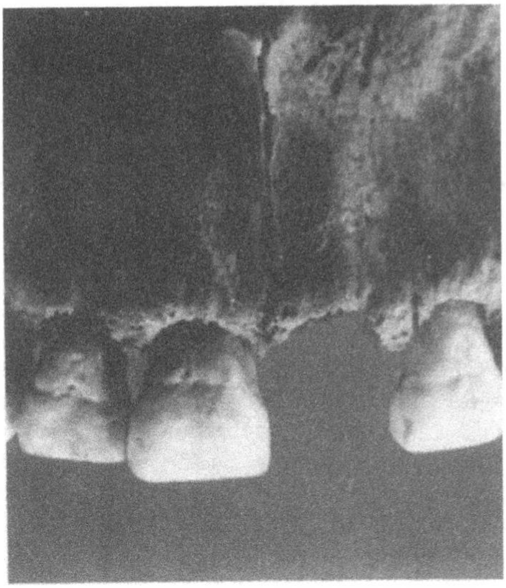

FIGURE 2.3 Enamel hypoplasia of the maxillary central and lateral incisors in an adult from the Pueblo period at Black Mesa, Arizona.

Enamel Hypoplasias

Enamel hypoplasia (chronologic or linear hypoplasia or aplasia) is a deficiency in enamel thickness resulting from a cessation in amelogenesis (Sarnat and Schour 1941). Enamel hypoplasias are visible on tooth crown surfaces as lines, bands, or pits of decreased enamel thickness (Goodman et al. 1980; see Figure 2.3).

The mechanisms by which enamel hypoplasias develop is without controversy (Kreshover 1960; Osborn 1973; Rose et al. in press). Enamel matrix is formed by secretory ameloblasts. If these ameloblasts are disrupted to a degree that they lose their functional ability, then less matrix will be formed and the resulting enamel will be reduced. Since amelogenesis, the process of matrix formation, occurs along a coordinated front whose shape and timing have been determined, the age of development of hypoplasia may be deduced (Sarnat and Schour 1941). Finally, since enamel, once formed, is not resorbed or remodeled during life, it provides a permanent and unaltered chronologic memory of stress during its development.

The experimental basis for relating hypoplasias to periods of stress is a strong one. Hypoplasias have been associated with a wide variety of diseases and nutritional deficiencies (see Kreshover 1960; Pinborg 1982; Rose 1973; Rose et al. 1984).

With little variation, the associations with known stresses are high, with r^2 values around .5. Unexplained variation may be related to host resistance and methodological difficulties (Rose et al. 1984).

Hypoplasias have been examined for both deciduous and permanent dentition in prehistoric populations. The frequency of hypoplasias in the deciduous dentition is generally low, perhaps reflecting intrauterine protection (Blakey 1981; Sciulli 1977). The advantage of studying deciduous teeth is that they provide a record of stresses during their unique time of development--the first year of life and the last 5 months of prenatal development.

Enamel hypoplasias of the permanent dentition in prehistoric populations have been studied by a variety of authors in recent years (see Buikstra and Cook 1980; Huss-Ashmore et al. 1982; Rose et al. 1984). The usual method of analysis involves the recording of defects on a single tooth, usually the canine. Goodman and co-workers (1980) have shown that the canine may be a particularly good choice as it is highly susceptible to stress and has a long developmental period (Condon 1981; Rose et al. 1984).

Hypoplasia analysis includes a recording of the available enamel surface for observation and the position of hypoplasias on the enamel crown. Observation of hypoplasias may be aided by use of a binocular microscope. While hypoplasias differ in width, depth, and continuity (pits versus lines or bands), such characteristics are infrequently recorded. There is no standard definition of the minimum requirement for scoring a hypoplasia. The position of hypoplasias on the enamel crown may be recorded as distance from the cemento-enamel junction (in mm) and/or by estimation of the relative position of the defect on the crown.

An alternative to the single tooth analysis has been provided by Swärdstedt (1966), who studied all available permanent teeth except for the highly variable third molar. The two main advantages of this method are (1) an ability to check that the underlying stress is systemic rather than local in origin by showing that the same episode is recorded on different teeth, and (2) an extension of the chronology by use of teeth developing at slightly different times. The main disadvantage of this method is that it requires more time than the single tooth analysis. Goodman and co-workers (1980) proposed a compromise to the above with a "best teeth" analysis which includes the use of the maxillary central incisor and mandibular canine. In the Dickson Mounds study, 95% of systemic stresses were recorded on one or both of these teeth.

Hypoplasia frequencies have been used in archaeology to compare the frequency of stress by gender (Swärdstedt 1966), by status group (Cook 1981; Goodman et al. 1983), and by age class (Cook 1981; Goodman and Armelagos 1980; Swärdstedt 1966), as well as to compare populations (Cook 1976; Goodman et al. 1980). The comparison of age groups is of particular interest as authors have found that individuals with more hypoplasias die at an earlier age.

These data are evidence that hypoplasias record childhood events which are important to the survival of the individuals.

Hypoplasias have been used to reconstruct the chronological distribution of stress. Swärdstedt (1966) notes a peak period of stress around age two to four in a Swedish medieval population while Schulz and McHenry (1975) note a peak at age four to five in their California Amerindian sample. Goodman and co-workers (1980) noted that hypoplasias are more often separated by a year than by a half year. This is given as evidence of an annual cycle of stress.

In summary, enamel hypoplasias are a relatively valid and replicable indicators of infant-childhood stress. Further experimental work and more agreement on the minimum requirement for scoring defects would benefit interpretation. At present hypoplasias are a valuable method for evaluation of general stress occurring at early ages.

Enamel Microdefects

Enamel microdefects (pathological striae of Retzius, Wilson bands) are observable in longitudinal sections of teeth as a line or band running relatively perpendicular to enamel prisms which exhibits abnormal shape and prism bending (Rose et al., 1984) (Figure 2.4).

A microdefect is the result of a temporary disruption in amelogenesis. Matrix formation has a natural periodicity and under normal conditions will result in a series of incremental lines in enamel (Yaeger 1980). However, if the metabolism of the active, secretory ameloblasts is disrupted, then the matrix formed may be altered in thickness, prism direction, and protein content. The observable result of this disruption is a microdefect. Microdefects have been associated with a wide variety of disease and nutritional disturbances in clinical (Massler et al. 1941; Watson et al. 1964) and experimental studies (Rose and Pasley 1980). Though less research has been done on microdefects as compared to hypoplasias, the results are similar. It is likely that these two defects are different levels of analysis of the same disruption (Condon 1981). Hypoplasias may be associated with the severest grade of microstructural disruption.

Methods for analysis of microdefects include the preparation of undecalcified longitudinal sections through tooth crowns. Recorded information is similar to that for hypoplasias (available enamel and location of defects relative to the cemento-enamel junction). A variety of operational definitions of microdefects have been employed (Rose et al. 1984) which vary mainly in their definition of the point at which a band is no longer considered to be due to normal processes. Rose's (1977) advocation of the term *Wilson bands* provides the most restricting definition of a microdefect. Wilson bands include a radical change in prism direction

FIGURE 2.4 Wilson band from a permanent canine (160×). Note the trough-like appearance of the band (Condon, 1981).

and abnormal prism structure. Condon (1981) and Rudney (1981), however, believe that a change in prism direction is sufficient to indicate systemic disruption.

In recent years a variety of studies have emerged on the appearance of microdefects in prehistoric populations (Clarke 1978; Condon 1981; Cook 1981; Jablonski 1981; Rose 1973, 1977, 1979; Rose et al. 1978; Rudney 1981). An exemplary series of studies of microdefects has been provided by Rose (1977) and co-workers (Rose et al. 1978). They demonstrate an increased frequency of Wilson bands in Dickson Mounds versus Gibson Mounds populations, a peak frequency of defects around 2 years of age, and an inverse relationship between Wilson bands and age at death.

Microdefect analysis is likely to increase in popularity in paleopathology. With a biologically meaningful and agreed upon minimum criteria for scoring a defect, microdefects provide a particularly sensitive indicator of stress. In comparison to hypoplasias, microdefects may record more disruption, including less severe and long-lasting ones. The major drawbacks of this method include the need to sacrifice teeth and the time and costs involved in the study.

Other Episodic Stress Indicators

Teeth provide a series of other episodic stress indicators which are less frequently used but may provide important information on stress. While enamel hypoplasias and microdefects are due to disruption in enamel matrix formation, enamel hypocalcifications are defects which result from a disruption in maturation of enamel (Yaeger 1980). These are visible as increased opacities in enamel and are often found in consort with hypoplastic defects (Blakey 1981). The common occurrence of hypoplasias and hypocalcifications is indicative of their being the result of the same metabolic disruption.

Dentin development is similar to enamel development. Dental matrix (predentine) is first formed and is quickly calcified (Avery 1980). Incremental lines (lines of von Ebner) are observable in dentin. Contour lines of Owen are accentuations of the normal incremental pattern and may be used to indicate metabolic stress (Avery 1980). Molnar and Ward (1975) have provided an overview of the potential application of dentin microdefects in anthropology. In theory, dentin should yield a set of indicators of stress which are as valid as enamel defects. However, dentin defects have been studied far less frequently, perhaps because there is no means of studying them without making histological thin sections.

INDICATORS OF SPECIFIC DISEASE STRESS

Porotic Hyperostosis

Porotic hyperostosis (lesions of the frontal, parietal, and occipital bones of the cranium) and cribra orbitalia (lesions on the superior border of the orbits) are manifest as a widening of the spongy diploe with a corresponding thinning of the outer dense cortical bone resulting in the appearance of surface porosity (see Figure 2.5). In severe cases, there is total obliteration of the bone surface with a lattice of trabecular overgrowth (see Figure 2.5). Mensforth and co-workers (1978) have presented the most thorough discussion of porotic hyperostosis in archeological populations. Steinbock (1976) provides information that is useful in the differentiation of the various factors which cause the lesion to be present in humans.

First described by Welcher in 1885, the condition has been attributed to a number of factors including thalassemia, hereditary anemias, sickle-cell anemia, and iron deficiency anemia (Moseley 1963). The alteration in skeletal tissue from these anemias is caused by the increase in red blood cell production which takes place in the marrow cavities of long bones and the diploe of flat

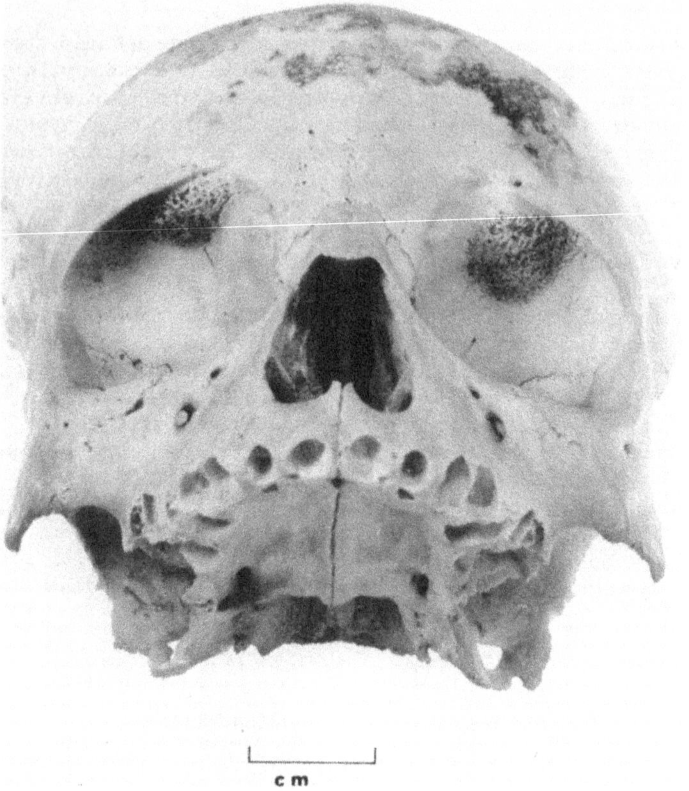

FIGURE 2.5 Porotic hyperostosis (cribra orbitalia) of the orbital surface.

bones. Because the cranial bones are so thin, they are often affected. As the diploe expands, the outer layer of bone becomes very thin and the inner trabecular bone is exposed. The thickened and porous bone has a sieve-like appearance.

In a landmark study, Hengen (1971) analyzed 459 human crania from various time periods and geographic areas and discussed the various possible explanations for the occurrence of porotic lesions. After casting out those explanations which did not fit most cases, he suggested that iron deficiency anemias fit most examples and that the lesion could be traced to the dietary habits. He further proposed that iron deficiency acted synergetically with infectious and parasitic diseases. Differential diagnosis could be made by examining the location of the lesion, its severity, and the age distribution of affected individuals. Numerous researchers have argued that porotic hyperostosis is due to nutritional stress in most cases in the New World since other explanations (malaria, hemoglobin derived anemias) can not be applied to New World populations (El-Najjar et al. 1976; Lallo et al. 1977; Mensforth et al. 1978).

Carlson and co-workers (1974) furthered Hengen's hypothesis by suggesting that the interaction of cultural, environmental, and biological factors could account for the incidence of the pathology in prehistoric Sudanese Nubian populations. This study emphasized a consideration of the lesion with respect to age and found a higher incidence of lesions among infants and females of child-bearing ages. At about the same time El-Najjar and co-workers (1976) reached similar conclusions for two prehistoric Southwestern Amerindian populations. Both these studies suggest that porotic hyperostosis is a nonspecific pathology that reflects an anemic condition. High frequencies of infectious disease, a diet low in iron or one that inhibits iron absorption, and cultural factors such as weanling diarrhea, all increase the potential for porotic hyperostosis.

Studies conducted by Lallo and co-workers (1977) and Mensforth and co-workers (1978) expanded the previous research by examining the frequency and distribution of the lesions within specific age categories. Through the use of refined age categories, the clustering of lesions in younger children was shown to reflect the increased need for iron metabolism during periods of rapid growth and development. In addition, the evidence of healing of the lesion can provide important information on its impact on mortality. The evidence from remodeling (healing) suggests that the individual has survived the initial episode. Mensforth and co-workers (1978) were able to demonstrate that a large percentage of individuals did survive early stresses, while Huss-Ashmore and co-workers (1982) demonstrated that individuals with active porotic hyperostosis show a slight increase in mortality during early childhood.

The association of porotic hyperostosis and infectious diseases should also be considered. When both pathological conditions occur together in an individual, the infectious lesions are usually more severe (Lallo et al. 1977). Through the use of refined age categories and diagnostic distinctions of healed and unhealed lesions of both porotic hyperostosis and infectious reactions, Mensforth and co-workers (1978) were able to demonstrate that for the Libben population, infectious diseases were the initial pathological response which made individuals more susceptible to porotic hyperostosis.

Analyses of porotic hyperostosis have often been hindered by failure to consider the physical quality of the lesion (healed versus unhealed), failure to define precise and narrow categories, and failure to consider the synergistic relationship between host resistance, diet, and other variables such as infectious disease. However, when all factors are considered, and when the narrowest biologically meaningful age categories are used, porotic hyperostosis is a valuable marker of nutritional stress in skeletal populations.

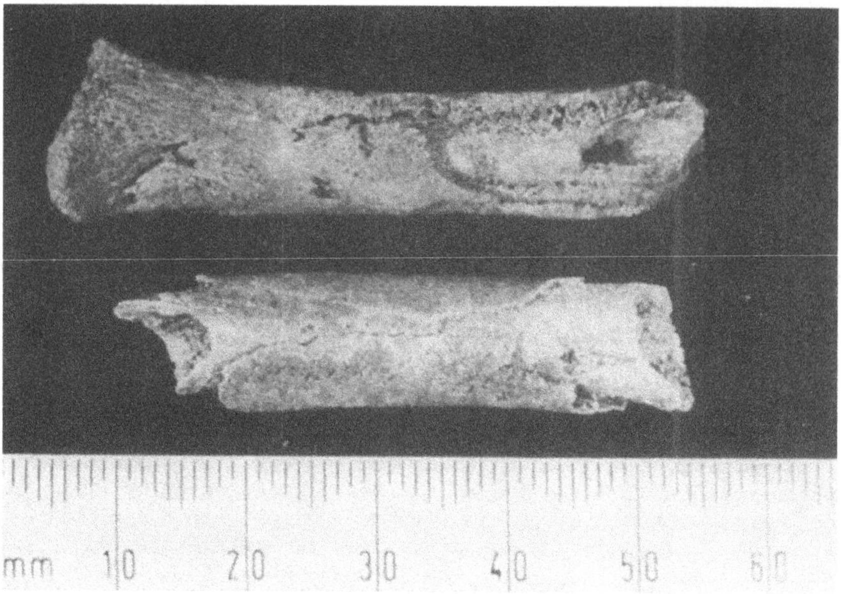

FIGURE 2.6 Periosteal reactions involving the long bone shafts.

Infectious Disease

Most examples of infectious disease in prehistoric skeletal remains are nonspecific; that is to say the lesions are caused by various kinds of microorganisms, but their exact etiology is unknown. Specific infectious diseases such as treponema (yaws/syphilis), tuberculosis, and leprosy, which can be differentially diagnosed, are much rarer (refer to Buikstra 1981; Ortner and Putschar 1981; Steinbock 1976). Nonspecific infectious lesions on bone are referred to as *periosteal reactions* (when the lesion is confined to the outer periosteal surface of bone, Figure 2.6) and *osteomyelitis* and *osteitis* (when the reaction courses throughout the bone tissue involving both the marrow and cortex). The latter reaction can be diagnosed only via radiographs; but the localization of the inflammatory process rarely occurs and there is usually some degree of involvement of all the anatomical components (Steinbock 1976).

Severe osteomyelitis and osteitis are caused by the spread of the microorganisms of *Staphylococcus* and *Streptococcus*. Periosteal reactions may also be caused by the organisms but other factors can result in a periosteal reaction (Greenfield 1975; Kunitz 1970). Depending on the virulence of the microorganism and the resistance of the host, the infectious reaction may be an acute and localized one, or chronic and systemic (appearing simultaneously on many bones).

Periosteal reactions result from an elevation of the fibrous outer layer of the periosteum due to the compressing and stretching of blood vessels (Jaffee 1972). Subperiosteal hemorrage occurs which in turn reduces the blood supply to the bone. If the physiological disruption is severe and long term, the periosteal bone tissue will die (necrosis); otherwise, the periosteum will resume normal growth when the disruption is stopped.

Periosteal reactions account for a great majority of pathological alterations found in early human and animal bones (Steinbock 1976). In the New and Old World, infections may be found in every archaeological horizon and geographic location (refer to Jarcho 1966; Ortner and Putschar 1981; Steinbock 1976). Recent research has emphasized the synergistic interaction which infectious disease has with nutritional and degenerative disease. Often one pathophysiological state will predispose an individual to one or several other diseases.

Because infectious disease is so common in archaeological specimens, the interpretation of its meaning will be clear only when it is viewed within the larger cultural context and with respect to analysis of several indicators of stress. Thus, an effective analysis of infectious diseases of nonspecific origin requires several important considerations.

1. The narrowest biologically meaningful age categories should be used because broad age categories will obscure the range of susceptibility.
2. The analysis of the skeletal lesions should distinguish degrees of severity (light, moderate, and severe reactions), describe their location (single bone versus many bones, diaphysis versus epiphysis, long bones versus flat bones), and note any evidence of healing.
3. Consideration should be given to the synergistic reaction between infections, poor nutrition, and cultural factors.
4. The distribution of lesions across sex and age categories should be noted, as should differences in the age of onset, patterning, and frequency among cultural subgroups.
5. The distinction should be made between nonspecific periosteal reactions or osteomyelitis and specific disease entities such as tuberculosis and syphilis.
6. The lesions of infectious disease should be analyzed in conjunction with other stress indicators rather than being interpreted in isolation.

Lallo and co-workers (1978) examined the frequency of infectious disease for 595 burials from Dickson Mounds. They demonstrated that the incidence of infectious diseases increased dramatically as the group changed from a hunting-gathering economy to one based more fully on agriculture. The explanation of this increase rested on the fact that there was an increase in population density which increased the number of potential hosts and facilitated the transmission of disease within a population. Further, reliance on a maize diet reduced nutritional adequacy. A synergistic interaction between malnutrition and infectious diseases resulted in a higher rate of morbidity and mortality.

Infectious disease can be a powerful indicator of physiological stress in a population, but its meaning in a broader sense can only come from an analysis considering the cultural and ecological context and employing several indicators of stress.

Trauma

Traumatic lesions have been classified by Ortner and Putschar (1981) as belonging to four major types: (1) fractures, (2) dislocations and displacements, (3) deformity induced artificially, and (4) disruption in nerve or blood supply. These types of injury are primarily caused by physical force or by contact with blunt or sharp objects. The cause of trauma can often be determined by analyzing the intensity and direction of the force. Interpretations concerning trauma are straightforward if the age, sex, and health status of the individual are known. If the traumatic lesion occurs with periosteal reaction and infectious inflammation, a severe condition which involves the soft tissue as well as the bone is implied. Steinbock (1976) has stated that simple fractures which do not break through the soft tissue and skin rarely become infected. The degree to which a trauma has healed provides a clue to the relationship between the traumatic event and the death of the individual.

Specific types of trauma often provide a direct inference about specific behavior patterns. Certain activities predispose individuals to certain types of accidental trauma. Moreover, various forms of interpersonal violence (warfare, scalping, mutilation, lacerations) and of surgical intervention (trephination, amputation) may be specifically identified (Ortner and Putschar 1981).

Fractures are the most common traumatic injuries encountered in archaeological populations. The response of bone to a fracture is immediate; vascularization and new bone formation begin within a few days after a break is made. Calcium salts are released from dead bone fragments and also from the living bone and are used in calcifying the callous matrix which forms a binding and connecting sheath around the two bone ends. Within two weeks, calcification is underway, and the internal remodeling and reorganization of the bone callus begins. The process can last for months or years, depending on the severity of the break (Steinbock 1976). Even a poorly aligned bone will eventually mend itself if infection does not set in. The rate of this repair is modified by age, type of fracture, degree of vascularization, amount of motion between the broken ends, and presence of infection (Steinbock 1976). Infection at the site of the bone can seriously hamper repair, and the determination of the timing of the fracture on archaeological specimens is rarely possible without determining the nature of the healing process.

One of the most thorough analyses of fractures at the population level is presented by Lovejoy and Heiple (1981) for the Libben skeletal collection. A quantitative approach to the analysis of long bone fractures was shown to be valuable in interpreting various behavioral aspects of the population. These authors found that most fractures occurred as a consequence of accident; the fracture rate was highest in the 10-25 and 45+ age grou; that care of patients was skillful; and that the chance of fracture was largely determined by accumulated years of risk in the population.

Degenerative Conditions

Osteoarthritis is among the oldest and most commonly known diseases afflicting humans. However, the paleopathological diagnosis is sometimes complicated. Measuring the amount of arthritic involvement with skeletal remains is problematic, but numerous researchers have attempted to assess it systematically (refer to Jurmain 1977; Ortner and Putschar 1981). While many factors may contribute to the breakdown of skeletal tissue, such as nutrition, genetics, and even viral infections, the primary cause of osteoarthritis is related to biomechanical wear and tear and functional stress. Biomechanical stress is most apparent at the articular surfaces of long bone joints and is referred to as *degenerative joint disease*. The patterning of degenerative joint disease has been linked to behavioral factors. Individuals who habitually engage in activities which put strain on the joint systems are more likely eventually to show degeneration (refer to Aegerter and Kirkpatrick 1968).

Degenerative joint disease is defined by changes in the articular surface areas of joint systems. Following the exposure of subchondral bone, the articular surface regions become pitted, with marginal lipping and erosion; eventually eburnation takes place. Eburnation is the formation of a very hard callus on bone surfaces which are rubbing together without being cushioned by lubricating fluids. Degenerative joint disease is not an inflammatory disease, but develops on the basis of aging changes and breakdown of the cartilage and lubricating fluid. The condition is slowly progressive, but is not found to occur in all older adults in the same form. Thus, the condition probably is the accumulation of years of alterations of the articular cartilage and breakdown of the joint system. Lifestyle and activity repertoire play an important role in either buffering an individual from arthritis or enhancing the chance that the condition will appear.

The analysis of degenerative joint diseases should consider the severity of the condition, distinguishing slight involvement from severe. There are numerous sets of criteria published to assist the researcher in devising a graded scale of severity of involvement (Aegerter and Kirkpatrick 1968; Jurmain 1977; Martin et al. 1979; Steinbock 1976). In addition, degenerative joint diseases are rarely confined to a single joint complex. The weight-bearing joints such as the hips and knees and those joints exposed to chronic trauma such as the shoulder and elbow are most frequently affected (Jurmain 1978; Martin et al. 1979). The pattern, distribution, severity, and onset by age class and sex in adults can be used to interpret the role of cultural activity in the etiology of degenerative joint disease.

Vertebral osteophytosis is another form of degeneration which is characterized by marginal lipping on the vertebral bodies, and has been associated with changes in the intervertebral disc (Chapman 1973). Commonly found in prehistoric and modern populations, this degeneration typically begins at 30 years of age and affects almost all individuals by 60 years of age (Steinbock 1976). The marginal lipping may range from a slight sharpness to complete fusion of the vertebral bodies. When the degree of osteophytosis is assessed, each vertebra should be divided into four quadrants and each quadrant assessed on both the superior and inferior margins using a scale which ranges from no lipping to extreme bony ridges and eversion at the margins (Chapman 1973). The bony ridges, or osteophytes, can grow to a great size.

As with other pathological processes in bone, maximum information can be obtained regarding the cultural implications of a disease if it is combined with analyses of other stress indicators. A preliminary study correlating the incidence of degenerative joint disease, osteophytosis, and periosteal reactions was undertaken for the Dickson Mound population (Martin et al. 1979). Individuals with multiple joint involvement showed a statistically higher percentage of periosteal reactions. Both infectious lesions and degenerative joint disease appeared to be a function of age, and the more severe arthritic involvements consistently showed more severe infectious reactions.

Dental Pathologies

Dental pathologies are frequently found in prehistoric populations. Among those which are most common are caries, periodontal disease, excess or abnormal attrition, abscessing, excessive calculus, and premortem loss (see Brothwell 1972 for standard scoring techniques and Ortner and Putchar 1981 for illustrations).

Dental pathologies are often interrelated. For example, periodontal disease (measured by degree of alveolar resorption), caries, attrition, and abscessing all may cause premature loss of teeth. Attrition and caries patterns are often interrelated

(Turner and Machado 1983). Both may be a result of diet and eating habits. However, the rate of attrition may affect the rate of caries formation (Armelagos 1969).

An increase in rate of caries through time has been cited as invariably associated with a shift to high carbohydrate and then to refined carbohydrate diets. Based on this relationship, some archaeologists and physical anthropologists have begun to use caries rates as an indicator of carbohydrate consumption where archaeological evidence for diet is insufficient (see Rose et al., Chapter 15 this volume). Turner and Machado (1983) have presented a similar argument for attrition patterns. These interpretations, however, may introduce circularity to the analysis. If caries or attrition are used to help determine dietary changes, then they certainly can not be used to assess the impact of the change.

Finally, while dental pathologies may be common, it is uncertain as to how much they add to the disease load of prehistoric populations. While some conditions may cause temporary pain and others may decrease chewing efficiency, it is likely that they are generally of less consequence to population level adaptation than most of the previously mentioned conditions.

Isotopic and Trace Element Studies

New chemical methods have recently been developed and tested which offer hope for more precise indication of dietary contents than has hitherto been possible. Trace element analysis may provide the most direct information concerning diet of individuals prior to death (Schoeninger 1979; Zurer 1983). From observations of differing amounts of trace elements such as iron, calcium, magnesium, lead, zinc, copper, and strontium, it may be possible to deduce the presence of dietary insufficiencies (Gilbert 1977).

Stable carbon isotopic analysis can provide an assessment of the principal dietary components (Schoeninger et al. 1983; Sillen and Kavanaugh 1982). These studies will contribute to current analyses of dietary change by establishing the presence of certain cultigens such as maize in the diet, segregating groups of individuals with differential access to these cultigens, and determining the proportion of specific cultigens, animal protein, and other foodstuffs in the diet (Bumsted 1981; Smith et al., Chapter 5 this volume; Norr, Chapter 18 this volume). Such analyses, however, are just beginning to make a contribution to paleonutrition research.

CONCLUSIONS: PATTERN, PROCESS, AND MULTIPLE INDICATORS OF STRESS

The purpose of this chapter has been to present a model for the interpretation of skeletal indicators of stress and to provide an overview of the use and meaning of a series of commonly used indicators. The various indicators may have partially overlapping etiologies; but they are not identical or equally useful. For these reasons, coupled with the inherent uncertainty of archaeological research and paleopathological diagnosis, we advocate the use of several indicators (and thereby multiple confirmations) of stress.

Multiple stress indicators may be used to determine the degree and pattern of stress in populations. Is stress primarily chronic or acute, affecting children or adults, related to increased mortality or unrelated to mortality? By evaluating the pattern of stress within populations we may be able to better understand the conditions which are causative of the stress and evaluate likely responses to the stress.

The pattern and severity of stress can also lead to inferences about the causal conditions. As an example, the accumulation of indicators of stress occurring around the ages of two to four has lead Cook (Chapter 10 this volume) to an evaluation of weanling diet. Her conclusion is that the weanling diet in her maize agriculturalists was inadequate and led to the onset of a variety of stresses.

From an examination of a population's total stress load one may begin to make inferences about long-term consequences for culture and behavior. For example, mortality is traditionally high in the younger and older age segments of preindustrial populations. However, this mortality has little impact on a population's ability to maintain itself. If the middle age segment of a population shows signs of increased morbidity and mortality, however, then reproduction and production may be severely affected.

The skeleton is an important artifact or source of information. We have tried to illustrate the fact that bone and teeth may provide an important and interpretable record of events in individuals' lives and their responses to these events.

ACKNOWLEDGMENTS

We wish to acknowledge the following sources of financial support: NIDR Grant No. T-32-DE07047 (A.H.G.), NIH Biomedical Support Grant No. RR07048-17 (D.L.M. and G.J.A.), and NIH Biomedical Support Grant No. 632-509 (G.J.A. and G.C.).

REFERENCES

Acheson, R. M.
1959 The effects of starvation, septicaemia and chronic illness on the growth cartilage plate and metaphysis of the immature rat. *Journal of Anatomy 93*:123-130.
1960 Effect of nutrition and disease on human growth. In *Human growth*, edited by J. M. Tanner, pp. 73-92. Pergamon Press, New York.

Acheson, R. M., and G. B. Fowler
1964 Sex, socio-economic status and secular increase in stature. *British Journal of Preventative Social Medicine 18*:25-34.

Acsádi, G., and J. Nemeskéri
1970 *History of human life span and mortality*. Akademei Kiadó, Budapest.

Aegerter, E., and J. A. Kirkpatrick
1968 Orthopedic diseases (second ed.). W. B. Saunders, Philadelphia.

Allison, M., D. Mendoza, and A. Pezzia
1974 A radiographic approach to childhood illness in pre-Columbian inhabitants of southern Peru. *American Journal of Physical Anthropology 40*:409-415.

Angel, L. J.
1969 The basis of paleodemography. *American Journal of Physical Anthropology 30*:427-438.
1978 Pelvic inlet form: A neglected index of nutritional status. *American Journal of Physical Anthropology Abstract 48*:378.
1982 A new measure of growth efficiency: Skull base height. *American Journal of Physical Anthropology 58*:297-305.

Armelagos, G. J.
1969 Disease in ancient Nubia. *Science 163*:255-259.

Avery, J.
1980 Dentin. In *Orban's oral histology and embroyology* (ninth ed.), edited by S. N. Bhaskar, pp. 107-179. C. V. Mosby, St. Louis.

Bailit, H.
1975 Dental variation among populations. *Dental Clinics of North America 19*(1):125-139.

Bailit, H., P. L. Workman, J. K. Niswander, and C. J. MacClean
1970 Dental asymmetry as an indicator of genetic and environmental stress in human populations. *Human Biology 42*:626-638.

Blakey, M.
1981 An analysis of hypoplasia and hypocalcification in deciduous dentition from Dickson Mound. In *Biocultural adaptation comprehensive approaches to skeletal analysis*. University of Massachusetts Department of Anthropology Research Reports No. 20, pp. 24-34.

Bocquet-Appel, J. P., and C. Masset
1982 Farewell to paleodemography. *Journal of Human Evolution* *11*:321-333.

Brothwell, D.
1972 *Digging up bones* (second ed.). Trustees of the British Museum, London.

Buikstra, J. (editor)
1981 *Prehistoric tuberculosis in the Americas.* Northwest University Archeological Program, Evanston, Illinois.

Buikstra, J., and D. Cook
1980 Paleopathology: An American account. *Annual Review of Anthropology* *9*:433-470.

Bumsted, M. P.
1981 The potential of stable carbon isotopes in bioarcheological anthropology. In *Biocultural adaptation comprehensive approaches to skeletal analysis*, University of Massachusetts, Department of Anthropology Research Reports No. 20, pp. 108-126.

Cannon, W. B.
1932 *The wisdom of the body.* W. W. Norton, New York.

Carlson, D. S., G. J. Armelagos, and D. P. Van Gerven
1974 Factors influencing the etiology of cribra orbitalia in prehistoric Nubia. *Journal of Human Evolution* *3*:405-410.

Chapman, F. H.
1973 Osteophytosis in prehistoric Brazilian populations. *Journal of Man* *8*:93-99.

Clarke, S. K.
1978 Markers of metabolic insult: The association of radioplaque transverse lines, enamel hypoplasias and enamel histopathologies in a prehistoric skeletal sample. Unpublished Ph.D. dissertation, Department of Anthropology, University of Colorad, Boulder.

Condon, K. W.
1981 Correspondence of developmental enamel defects between the mandibular canine and first premolar. Unpublished M.A. thesis, Department of Anthropology, University of Arkansas, Fayetteville.

Cook, D. C.
1976 Pathologic states and disease process in Illinois woodland populations: An epidemiologic approach. Unpublished Ph.D. dissertation, Department of Anthropology, University of Chicago.
1979 Subsistence based on health in prehistoric Illinois valley: Evidence from the human skeleton. *Medical Anthropology* *4*:109-124.
1981 Mortality, age-structure, and status in the interpretation of stress indicators in prehistoric skeletons: A dental example from the lower Illinois valley. In *The archeology of death*, edited by P. Chapman and K. Randsborg, pp. 133-144. Cambridge University Press, London.

Craig, J. O.
1963 The height of Glasgow boys: Secular and social influences. *Human Biology 35*:524-539.
DiBennardo, R., and H. Bailit
1978 Stress and dental asymmetry in a population of Japanese children. *American Journal of Physical Anthropology 48*: 89-94.
Dickerson, J. W., and R. A. McCance
1961 Severe undernutrition in growing adult animals: 8. The dimensions and chemistry of long bones. *British Journal of Nutrition 15*:567-576.
Dubos, R.
1965 *Man adapting*. Yale University Press, New Haven.
El-Najjar, M., D. J. Ryan, C. Turner, and B. Lozoff
1976 The etiology of porotic hyperostosis among the historic and prehistoric Anasazi Indians of Southwestern United States. *American Journal of Physical Anthropology 44*: 477-488.
Engfeldt, B., and S. Hjertquist
1961 Vitamin D deficiency and bone and tooth structure. *World Review of Nutrition and Dietetics 2*:187-208.
Frisancho, A. R., and S. Garn
1970 Childhood retardation resulting in reduction of adult body size due to lesser adolescent skeletal delay. *American Journal of Physical Anthropology 33*:325-336.
Garn, S. M.
1970 *The earlier gain and later loss of cortical bone in nutritional perspective*. C. C. Thomas, Springfield.
Garn, S. M., A. B. Lewis, and R. S. Kerewsky
1965 Genetic, nutritional and maturational correlates of dental development. *Journal of Dental Research 44*:228-242.
Garn, S. M., C. G. Rohman, M. Behar, F. Viteri, and M. A. Guzman
1964 Compact bone deficiency in protein-calorie malnutrition. *Science 145*:1444-1445.
Garn, S. M., A. R. Lewis, and D. L. Polacheck
1959 Variability of tooth formation. *Journal of Dental Research 38*:135-148.
Garn, S. M., F. N. Silverman, K. P. Herzog, and C. G. Rohman
1968 Lines and bands of increased density: their implication to growth and development. *Medical Radiography and Photography 44*:58-89.
Gilbert, R.
1977 Applications of trace element research to problems in archeology. In *Biocultural adaptation in prehistoric America*, edited by R. Blakely, pp. 85-100. University of Georgia Press, Athens.
Goodman, A. H., G. J. Armelagos, and J. C. Rose
1980 Enamel hypoplasias as indicators of stress in three prehistoric populations from illinois. *Human Biology 52*: 515-528.

Goodman, A. H., and G. A. Clark
1981 Harris lines as indicators of stress in prehistoric Illinois populations. In *Biocultural adaptation comprehensive approaches to skeletal analysis*, University of Massachusetts Department of Anthropology Research Reports No. 20, pp. 35-46.

Goodman, A. H., N. A. Rothschild, and G. J. Armelagos
1983 Social status and health in three prehistoric populations from Dickson Mounds, Illinois. *American Journal of Physical Anthropology 60*(2):199 (abstract).

Gray, P. H.
1967 Radiography of ancient Egyptian mummies. *Medical Radiography 43*:34-44.

Green, S., S. Green, and G. J. Armelagos
1974 Settlement and mortality of the Christian site (1050 A.D.-1300 A.D.) of Meinarti (Sudan). *Journal of Human Evolution 3*:297-311.

Greenfield, G. B.
1975 *Radiology of bone disease* (second ed.). Lippincott, Philadelphia.

Guargliardo, M.
1982 Tooth crown size differences between age groups: A possible new indicator of stress in skeletal samples. *American Journal of Physical Anthropology 58*(4):383-390.

Gustav, B.
1972 Sexual dimorphism in the adult boney pelvis of a prehistoric human population from Illinois. Unpublished Ph.D. dissertation, Department of Anthropology, University of Massachusetts, Amherst.

Harris, H. A.
1926 The growth of long bones in children, with special reference to certain bony striations of the metaphysis and to the role of the vitamins. *Archives of Internal Medicine 38*:785-806.
1933 Bone growth in health and disease: The biological principles underlying the clinical, radiological and histological diagnosis of perversions of growth and disease in the skeleton. Oxford University Press, London.

Hengen, O. P.
1971 Cribra orbitalia: Pathogenesis and probable etiology. *Homo 22*:57-75.

Himes, J. H.
1978 Bone growth and development in protein-calorie malnutrition. *World Review of Nutrition and Dietetics 28*:143-187.

Huss-Ashmore, R.
1981 Bone growth and remodeling as a measure of nutritional stress. In *Biocultural adaptation comprehensive approaches to skeletal analysis*. University of Massachusetts Department of Anthropology Research Reports No. 20, pp. 84-95.

Huss-Ashmore, R., A. H. Goodman, and G. J. Armelagos
1982 Nutritional inference from paleopathology. *Advances in Archeological Method and Theory* 5:395-474.

Jablonski, K. A.
1981 Enamel calcification patterns of the Averbuch site (40DV60), Nashville, Tennessee. Unpublished M.A. thesis, department of Anthropology, University of Tennessee, Knoxville.

Jaffee, H. L.
1972 *Metabolis, degenerative and inflammatory disease of bone and joints.* Lea and Febiger, Philadelphia.

Jarcho, S. (editor)
1966 *Human palaeopathology.* Yale University Press, New Haven.

Johnston, F. E.
1976 Hereditary and environmental determinants of growth in height in a longitudinal sample of children and young of Guatemalan and European ancestry. *American Journal of Physical Anthropology* 44:469-476.

Jurmain, R. D.
1977 Stress and the etiology of osteoarthritis. *American Journal of Physical Anthropology* 46:353-365.
1978 Paleoepidemiology of degenerative joint disease. *Medical College of Virginia Quarterly* 14:45-56.

Kunitz, S.
1970 Disease and death among the Anasazi. *El Palacio* 76:17-22.

Kreshover, S.
1960 Metabolic disturbances in tooth formation. *Annals of the New York Academy of Sciences* 85:161-167.

Lallo, J.
1973 The skeletal biology of three prehistoric American Indian populations from Dickson Mounds. Unpublished Ph.D. dissertation, Department of Anthropology, University of Massachusetts, Amherst.

Lallo, J., G. J. Armelagos, and R. P. Mensforth
1977 The role of diet, disease and physiology in the origin of porotic hyperostosis. *Human Biology* 40:471-483.

Lallo, J., G. J. Armelagos, and J. C. Rose
1978 Paleoepidemiology of infectious disease in the Dickson Mounds population. *Medical College of Virginia Quarterly* 14:17-23.

Larsen, C. S.
1982 The anthropology of St. Catherines Island. 3. Prehistoric human biological adaptation. *Anthropology Papers of the American Museum of Natural History* 57(3).

Lewis, A. B., and S. M. Garn
1960 The relationship between tooth formation and other maturational factors. *Angle Orthodontics* 30:70-77.

Lovejoy, C. O., and K. G. Heiple
1981 The analysis of fractures in skeletal populations with an

example from the Libben Site, Ottowa County, Ohio. *American Journal of Physical Anthropology 55*:529-541.

Lovejoy, C. O., R. S. Meindl, T. R. Prysbeck, T. S. Barton, K. G. Heiple, and D. Kotting
1977 Paleodemography of the Libben site, Ottawa County, Ohio. *Science 198*:291-293.

Maresh, M.
1955 Linear growth of long bones of extremities from infancy through adolescence. *American Journal of Diseases of Childhood 89*:725-742.

Marshall, W. A.
1967 Problems in relating the presence of transverse lines in the radius to the occurrence of disease. In *The skeletal biology of earlier human populations*, edited by D. R. Brothwell, pp. 245-261. Pergamon Press, Oxford.

Martin, D. L.
1983 Paleophysiological aspects of bone remodeling in the Meroitic, X-Group and Christian populations from Sudanes Nubia. Unpublished Ph.D. dissertation, Department of Anthropology, University of Massachusetts, Amherst.

Martin, D. L., and G. J. Armelagos
1979 Morphometrics of compact bone: An example from Sudanes Nubia. *American Journal of Physical Anthropology 51*: 571-578.

Martin, D. L., G. J. Armelagos, and J. R. King
1979 Degenerative joint disease of the long bones in Dickson Mounds. *Henry Ford Hospital Medical Journal 27*:60-63.

Martin, D. L., A. H. Goodman, and G. J. Armelagos
1984 Skeletal pathologies as indicators of quality and quantity of diet. In *The analysis of prehistoric diet*, edited by J. Mielke and R. Gilbert, in press. Academic Press, New York.

Massler, M., I. Schour, and H. G. Poncher
1941 Developmental pattern of the child as reflected in the calcification pattern of the teeth. *American Journal of Diseases of Childhood 62*:33-67.

McCance, R. A., and E. M. Widdowson
1962 Nutrition and growth. *Proceedings of the Royal Society of Britain 156*:326-337.

McHenry, H.
1968 Transverse lines in long bones of prehistoric California Indians. *American Journal of Physical Anthropology 29*: 1-17.

McHenry, H., and P. Schulz
1976 The association between Harris line and enamel hypoplasias in prehistoric California Indians. *American Journal of Physical Anthropology 44*:507-512.

Mensforth, R. P.
1981 Growth velocity and chondroblastic stability as major factors related to the pathogenesis and epidemiological

distribution of growth arrest lines. *American Journal of Physical Anthropology* Abstract *54*:253.

Mensforth, R. P., C. O. Lovejoy, J. W. Lallo, and G. J. Armelagos
1978 The role of constitutional factors, diet and infectious disease in the etiology of porotic hyperostosis and periosteal reactions in prehistoric infants and children. *Medical Anthropology* *2*(1):1-59.

Mielke, J., and R. Gilbert (editors)
1984 The analysis of prehistoric diets. Academic Press, New York, in press.

Molnar, S., and S. Ward
1975 Mineral metabolism and microstructural defects in primate teeth. *American Journal of Physical Anthropology* *43*:3-17.

Moore, J., A. Swedlund, and G. J. Armelagos
1975 The use of life tables in paleodemography. *American Antiquity Memoirs No. 30*:57-70.

Moseley, J. E.
1963 The paleopathologic riddle of "symmetrical osteoporosis." *American Journal of Roentgenology* *95*:135-142.

Niswander, J. D., and C. S. Chung
1965 The effects of inbreeding on tooth size in Japanese children. *American Journal of Human Genetics* *17*:390-398.

Ortner, D. J.
1976 Microscopic and molecular biology of human compact bone: An anthropological perspective. *Yearbook of Physical Anthropology* *20*:35-44.

Ortner, D. J., and W. G. Putschar
1981 Identification of pathological conditions in human skeletal remains. *Smithsonian Contributions to Anthropology*, No. 28.

Osborn, J. W.
1973 Variations in structure and development of enamel. *Oral Science Review* *3*:3-83.

Park, E. A.
1964 The imprinting of nutritional disturbances on the growing bone. *Pediatrics* (Supplement) *33*:815-862.

Park, E., and S. Richter
1953 Transverse lines in bone: the mechanics of their development. *Bulletin of The Johns Hopkins Hospital* *93*:234-248.

Perzigian, A.
1977 Fluctuating dental asymmetry: Variation among skeletal populations. *American Journal of Physical Anthropology* *47*(1):81-88.

Pinborg, J. J.
1982 Aetiology of developmental enamel defects not related to fluorosis. *International Dental Journal* *32*(2):123-134.

Platt, B. S., and R. A. McCance
1964 Severe undernutrition in growing and adult animals. *British Journal of Nutrition* *18*:393-408.

Platt, B. S., and R. J. C. Stewart
1962 Transverse trabeculae and osteoporosis in bones in experimental protein-calorie deficiency. *British Journal of Nutrition 16*:483-495.

Richman, G. A., D. J. Ortner, and F. P. Schulter-Ellis
1979 Differences in intracortical bone remodeling in three aboriginal American populations: Possible dietary factors. *Calcified Tissue Research 28*:209-214.

Rose, J. C.
1973 Analysis of dental micro-defects of prehistoric populations from Illinois. Unpublished Ph.D. dissertation, Department of Anthropology University of Massachusetts, Amherst.
1977 Defective enamel histology of prehistoric teeth from Illinois. *American Journal of Physical Anthropology 46*:439-446.
1979 Morphological variations of enamel prisms within abnormal stria of Retzius. *Human Biology 51*:139-151.

Rose, J. C., G. J. Armelagos, and J. Lallo
1978 Histological enamel indicators of childhood stress in prehistoric skeletal samples. *American Journal of Physical Anthropology 49*:511-516.

Rose, J. C., K. W. Condon, and A. H. Goodman
1984 Diet and dentition: developmental disturbances. In *The analysis of prehistoric diets*, edited by J. Mielke and R. Gilbert, in press. Academic Press, New York.

Rose, J. C., and J. N. Pasley
1980 Stress and dental development: An experimental paleopathological model. *American Journal of Physical Anthropology 52*:272 (abstract).

Rudney, J.
1981 The paleoepidemiology of early childhood stress in two ancient Nubian populations. Unpublished Ph.D. dissertation, Department of Anthropology University of Colorado.

Sarnat, B. G., and I. Schour
1941 Enamel hypoplasia (chronological enamel aplasia) in relation to systemic disease: A chronologic, morphological and etiologic classification. *Journal of the American Dental Association 28*:1989-2000.

Schoeninger, M. J.
1979 Diet and disease states in Calcatzingo: Some empirical and technical aspects of strontium analysis. *American Journal of Physical Anthropology 51*:295-310.

Schoeninger, M. J., M. J. DiNiro, and H. Tauber
1983 Stable nitrogen isotope ratios of bone collagen reflects marine and terrestrial components of prehistoric diet. *Science 220*:1381-1383.

Schulz, P. D., and H. McHenry
1975 The distribution of enamel hypoplasia in prehistoric California Indians. *Journal of Dental Research 54*(4):913.

Selye, H.
1950 *Stress: The physiology and pathology of exposure to systemic stress.* Acta, Inc., Montreal.
1971 Hormones and resistance, part 1. Springer, New York.
Shore, L. R.
1935 Polyspondylitis marginalis osteophytica. *British Journal of Surgery 22*:850-863.
Sciulli, P. W.
1977 A descriptive and comparative study of the deciduous dentition of prehistoric Ohio Valley Amerindians. *American Journal of Physical Anthropology 47*:71-80.
Sillen, A., and S. Kavanagh
1982 Strontium and paleodietery research: A review. *Yearbook of Physical Anthropology 25*:69-90.
Steinbock, R. T.
1976 *Paleopathological diagnosis and interpretation.* C. C. Thomas, Springfield, Illinois.
Stewart, R. J. C.
1975 Bone pathology in experimental malnutrition. *World Review of Nutrition and Dietetics 21*:1-74.
Stini, W.
1969 Nutritional stress and growth: Sex differences in adaptive response. *American Journal of Physical Anthropology 31*:417-426.
1972 Reduced sexual dimorphism in upper arm muscle circumferences associated with protein-calories deficient diet in South American populations. *American Journal of Physical Anthropology 36*:341-352.
1975 Adaptive strategies of populations under nutritional stress. In *Biosocial interactions in population adaptation*, edited by E. S. Watt, F. E. Johnston, and G. W. Lasker, pp. 19-39. Mouton, The Hague.
Stout, S. D.
1979 Histomorphometric analysis of archeological bone. Unpublished Ph.D. dissertation, Department of Anthropology, University of Washington.
Stout, S., and D. J. Simmons
1979 Use of histology in ancient bone research. *Yearbook of Physical Anthropology 22*:228-249.
Sundick, R. I.
1978 Human skeletal growth and age determination. *Homo 29*:228-249.
Swärdstedt, T.
1966 *Odontological aspects of a Medieval population in the province of Jamtland/Mid-Sweden.* Tiden-Barnangen Tryckerien, Stockholm.
Swedlund, A. C., and G. J. Armelagos
1969 Une recherche en Paleodemographie: La Nubie Soudanaise. *Annales Economies Societies Civilisations* Ser. 4 *24*:1281-1298.

1976 *Demographic anthropology.* W. C. Brown, Dubuque, Iowa.

Tanner, J. M.
1977 Human growth and constitution. In *Human biology*, (second ed.), edited by G. H. Harrison, J. S. Weiner, J. M. Tanner, and N. A. Bannicot, pp. 301-385. Oxford University Press, New York.
1978 Fetus into man. Harvard University Press, Cambridge, Massachusetts.

Thomas, R. B.
1973 Human adaptation to a high Andean energy flow system. Pennsylvania State University Occasional Papers in Anthropology No. 6.

Trowell, H. C., J. N. Davies, and R. F. Dean
1954 *Kwashiorkor.* Arnold, London.

Turner, C., and L. M. Machado
1983 A new dental wear pattern and evidence for high carbohydrate consumption in a Brazilian Archaic skeletal population. *American Journal of Physical Anthropology 61*(1): 125-130.

Ubelaker, D. H.
1978 *Human skeletal remains: Excavation, analysis and interpretation.* Aldine, Chicago.

Van Gerven, D.
1972 Sexual dimorphism in the adult human femur. Unpublished Ph.D. dissertation, Department of Anthropology, University of Massachusetts, Amherst.

Van Gerven, D. P., and G. J. Armelagos
1983 "Farewell to paleodemography?" Rumors of its death have been greatly exaggerated. *Journal of Human Evolution 12*: 353-360.

Watson, A., M. Massler, and M. Perlstein
1964 Tooth ring analysis in cerebral palsy. *American Journal of Dentistry 107*:370-384.

Welcher, H.
1885 Cribra orbitalia. *Archive für Anthropologie 17*:1-18.

Wells, C.
1964 *Bones, bodies and disease.* Praeger, New York.
1967 A new approach to paleopathology: Harris lines. In *Disease in antiquity*, edited by D. R. Brothwell and S. T. Sandison, pp. 390-404. Thomas, Springfield, Illinois.

Widdowson, E. M., and R. A. McCance
1964 Effects of nutrition and disease on growth. *British Dental Journal 117*:326-330.

Wing, E. S., and A. B. Brown
1980 *Paleonutrition: Method and theory in prehistoric foodways.* Academic Press, New York.

Woodall, J.
1968 Growth arrest lines in long bones of the Cases Grandes population. *Plains Anthropologist 13*:152-160.

Yaeger, J. A.
1980 Enamel. In *Orban's oral histology and embryology* (ninth ed.), edited by S. N. Bhaskar, pp. 46-106. Mosby, St. Louis.

Zurer, P. S.
1983 Archeological chemistry. *Chemical Engineering News 61*: 26-44.

CHAPTER 3

HEALTH AS A CRUCIAL FACTOR IN THE CHANGES FROM HUNTING TO DEVELOPED FARMING IN THE EASTERN MEDITERRANEAN

J. Lawrence Angel

Department of Anthropology
National Museum of Natural History
Smithsonian Institution

INTRODUCTION

To be healthy is to race death successfully.

In terms of energy for individuals and populations to survive and multiply, health has two aspects: physical growth, and sufficient longevity for birth of children and for survival of parents to the point that they, interacting with others, can bring up their children to be vital people. The expansion of the human population reflects our success in this race. The prehistoric pattern of human deaths shows only a 20-30% loss at and right after birth, compared to the 60-80% loss among the offspring of wild creatures (Angel 1971; cf. Lack 1967). The human pattern also shows a few individuals living past the end of reproductive life. The lengthening of life was a major human evolutionary adaptive change (see Angel 1975; Mann 1975) promoting fertility and population growth.

Yet the causal networks between environment and culture on the one hand, and health, growth, reproduction, and longevity on the other are not simple ones. There is expectable feedback between growth in population density and both cultural and biological success. Moreover, even biological success involves some costs. A healthy population can and does carry a large load of disease. It is important to establish how much poor health a society can endure without collapse, and it is important to identify those aspects of poor health that actually impede successful adaptation by the population. For example, Tuchman (1978) shows that in fourteenth-century Europe, the complex pattern of wars, famines, and disease exerted Malthusian controls on population. Did these factors play a similar role during the transition from hunting to farming?

INDICATORS OF HEALTH

For overall health, the simplest indicator is adult longevity. In addition, growth and nutrition can be measured by (1) the degree of arching or vertical growth (supporting weight against gravity) of the pelvic inlet (Angel 1978a) and the base of the skull (Angel 1982; Angel and Olney 1981); (2) stature as estimated from the lengths of long bones; (3) the roundness of shafts of long bones as a reflection of bone mineral available (Adams 1969; Angel 1971; Buxton 1938); and (4) trace elements in bone derived from minerals in food (cf. discussion by Goodman et al., Chapter 2, this volume). Moreover, adequate protein in childhood, plus adequate intake of vitamins (vitamin D and A precursors (DeLuca 1980), and vitamin C) will ensure proper formation of tooth enamel as well as bone. Adult dental lesions in part reflect inadequate protein and vitamin intake in childhood (Sognnaes 1956). Growth arrest lines on booth enamel (linear enamel hypoplasias) and in long bones reflect growth stress from malnutrition or from disease (cf. discussion by Goodman et al., Chapter 2, this volume).

In addition, patterns of occurrence of specific stress indicators such as porotic hyperostosis or the lesions of bony tuberculosis can provide an indication of the overall health and success of the group. Production of children can be estimated by comparing the number of births, derived from female pelvic birth scars (Angel 1972), with the number of juvenile deaths (Angel 1975), allowing estimates of population change (Angel 1971, 1972). The successful admixture of populations through migration and interbreeding can be measured through changes in Howells' sigma ratio (Angel 1975). This chapter will provide a comparative assessment of such indicators for populations from the Paleolithic through the early Iron Age in the region of the Eastern Mediterranean.

THE REGION

The Eastern Mediterranean is defined for the purposes of this chapter as including Greece and western Turkey. Problems of archaeological sampling, however, prevent the making of meaningful comparisons entirely from within this region. Therefore, for Upper Paleolithic and Mesolithic hunter-gatherers (ca. 15,000-7000 B.C.) the focus is broadened to include the Balkans (Vlasac and Lepenski Vir at Iron Gate on the Danube), the Ukraine (Kostenki and Dnieper bend sites Vasilievka and Voloschkoyo), and North Africa and Israel (Taforalt, Afalou, the Nile sites of Jebel Sahaba and Wadi Halfa in Nubia, and the Natufians). These sites supplement data available from samples in the main study area (Hotu on the Caspian, Kara'In in Turkey, and Franchthi in Argolis).

The region has not always experienced genetic continuity between periods. The early farming populations of the seventh and sixth millennia B.C. at Çatal Hüyük, Nea Nikomedeia, Franchthi Cave, and Lerna, for example, include migrant descendants of Semitic-speaking Africans and of Balkan riverine populations (Angel 1973b). But the regional focus minimizes the effects of genetic change in later periods.

Ecology

The Eastern Mediterranean rainless summer is long and hot, above 26° C. Hence vegetation consists of drought-resistant maritime pines, juniper and evergreen oaks, olives, pistachio, and maquis (Angel 1971; Shay and Shay 1978). Coniferous forests and meadows with wild cereals occur in the mountains. Soils vary from podzols and the acid red earths of the karst basins to arid steppe, flysch, marls, and especially volcanic soils rich in trace elements and excellent for cultivated olives and grape vines. In addition, calcareous and stony silts provide good soils for cattle- and horse-meadows and for wheat and barley (Maull 1922). These silts were critical for nutrition because, for geological reasons (Angel 1971, 1975), mountains and sea diminish the cultivable area (even with terracing) to only 20-25% of the lands, and lack of climatic contrasts limits chemical renewal. The stony, lime-rich soil therefore demanded (1) shallow cultivation with the scratch plow or ard and (2) frequent manuring, plowing in of legumes, fallowing, and burning-over. It cannot stand overuse (see Angel 1971, 1975; Butzer 1970, 1971).

Changes in sea level, which helped to deposit these silts by affecting river flow, also were critical in affecting the disease environment of early populations. Coastal and riverine (as well as inland basin) marshes allowed anopheline mosquitos (*A. sacharovi* and *A. superpictus*) to move in at the end of the Pleistocene and spread malarias, including the new (and relatively lethal) mutant *Plasmodium falciparum* (Angel 1966, 1975, 1978b). But the latter also were dependent on temperature and on the density of human populations for their success.

TABLE 3.1a Chronological Change in Health Indicators (Growth, Bone Minerals, Variability, Length of Life, Fertility, Population Density) Related to Ecology, Culture, and Diet, Upper Paleolithic to Bronze Kings Period[a]

P e r i o d	Paleolithic	Mesolithic	Early Neolithic	Late Neolithic	Early Bronze	Middle People	Bronze Kings
	30,000 9000	7000	5000	3000	2000		1450
Skull base height (aur.-bas.) (mm)	22.4	20.4	18.7	18.0	20.7	18.6	24.0
N	46	82	19	9	84	51	7
Pelvic inlet depth index (ap/tr) (%)	97.7	86.3	76.6	75.6?	85.	78.8	82.6?
N	3+	5	10	1	27	23	2
Stature (Trotter-Gleser fm.), male (cm)	177.1	172.5	169.6	161.3	166.3	166.1	172.5
N	35	61	39	6	83	83	14
Stature (Trotter-Gleser fm.) female, (cm)	166.5	159.7	155.5	154.3	152.9	153.5	160.1
N	28	35	31	13	72	54	3
Femur platymeric shaft roundness index	78.2	80.0	72.9	75.4	75.0	76.4	82.4
N	101	70	70	28	285	116	13
Teeth lesions per mouth, caries, abscess, loss	2.3	1.3	3.5	2.6	5.0	6.0	1.2
N	54	75	105	26	202	123	20
Enamel growth arrests, continuous scale	1.1	1.2	1.2	1.4	1.1	1.7	1.5
N		ca. 70	90	21	111	108	20
Strontium/calcium site-corrected ratio	(low)[b]	.74[c]	(high?)[b]	.679[b]	.606[b]		
N		17		10	354		
Zinc in bone (μg/g				?175.7?[b]	153.7[b]		
N	(high?)[b]			10	354		
Porotic hyperostosis, continuous scale	1.1-	1.2	1.5	1.2	1.1+	1.1+	1.1-
N		6	165	63	332	169	20
Variability, sigma ratio (%)	(ca. 100)	110	121	109	109	128	120
N							
Adult length of life, male, (years)	35.4	33.5	33.6	33.1	33.6	36.5	35.9
N	59	120	106	32	184	107	22
Adult length of life, female, (years)	30.0	31.3	29.8	29.2	29.4	31.4	36.1
N	53	63	157	43	206	94	5
Births (pelvic scars)/adult female	(4.5)	4.+?	4.5	4.0?	4.1	5.0	
N			25	3	45	27	
Survivors to age 15/adult female	2.1?	2.1??	2.2	2.0?	2.1	2.4	
Population density estimate (persons/km²)	.1	.15	1.5	7 -	10	18 -	
	Rivers cutting	M a r s h y			Less m a r s h y		
C l i m a t e	-5° C colder than today	Warming	Warmer than today	Warmest +2.5 °C / Cooler & drier	Warmer Dry		
and	W ü r m	Pre-Boreal to Boreal	drier	Wetter Atlantic	S u b - b o r e a l		
S e a - l e v e l relative to today	Fluctuating -100 m	-50 to	Rise -10 to + 2	Average + 2 to 0 / Reversal 0 to + 2	lower again + 1 m		

TABLE 3.1b Chronological Change in Health Indicators (Growth, Bone Minerals, Variability, Length of Life, Fertility, Population Density) Related to Ecology, Culture, and Diet, Late Bronze Age to Imperial Roman Period[a]

Period	Late Bronze (1450–1150)	Early Iron (1150–650)	Classic (650–300 B.C.)	Hellenistic (300 B.C.–120 A.D.)	Imperial Roman (120 A.D.–600)
Skull base height (aur.-bas.) (mm)	17.6	18.6	19.3	18.7	18.2
N	102	82	98	95	87
Pelvic inlet depth index (ap/tr) (%)	79.5	80.6	83.5	86.6	84.6
N	16	18	23	11	9
Stature (Trotter-Gleser fm.), male (cm)	166.8	166.7	170.5	171.9	169.2
N	56	42	52	23	18
Stature (Trotter-Gleser fm.) female, (cm)	154.5	155.1	156.2	156.4	158.0
N	41	53	30	20	19
Femur platymeric shaft roundness index	76.8	77.1	77.5	79.6	82.5
N	98	98	93	40	42
Teeth lesions per mouth, caries, abscess, loss	6.7	6.8	4.1	5.2	6.1
N	134	106	138	114	91
Enamel growth arrests, continuous scale	1.4	1.4	1.4	1.2	1.2
N	71	83	103	85	39
Strontium/calcium site-corrected ratio	1.012	.801	.941	.466	.777
N	85	31	28	77	9
Zinc in bone (μg/g	146.0	143.5	147.8	147.3	138.6
N	85	31	28	77	9
Porotic hyperostosis, continuous scale	1.1	1.1-	1.1-	1.2-	1.3-
N	215	114	151	138	100
Variability, sigma ratio (%)	108	111	104	105	108
N					
Adult length of life, male, (years)	39.6	39.0	44.1	41.9	38.8
N	182	105	146	103	79
Adult length of life, female, (years)	32.6	30.9	36.8	38.0	34.2
N	120	90	84	50	51
Births (pelvic scars)/adult female	4.6	3.5	5.0	3.4?	4.0?
N	10	17	15	5	9
Survivors to age 15/adult female	2.1	1.3	3.2	1.2?	2.0?
Population density estimate (persons/km²)	30	20	36	33	25?
Climate and	Warm	Cooling Droughts vs. Rainy	Average Maritime		Wetter Warming Marshy
Sea-level relative to today	Falling 0 to -2m	+1	-2m	Sub -1m	-Atlantic +1

TABLE 3.1c Chronological Change in Health Indicators (Growth, Bone Minerals, Variability, Length of Life, Fertility, Population Density) Related to Ecology, Culture, and Diet, Medieval Greece to Modern (U.S. White) Period[a]

Period	Medieval Greece	Byzantine Constantinople	1400 Baroque	1800 Romantic	1920 Modern U.S. White
Skull base height (aur.-bas.) (mm)	19.0	20.4	19.6	20.8	20.9
N	63	11	45	176	175
Pelvic inlet depth index (ap/tr) (%)	85.9	87.9	84.0	82.9	92.1
N	3	19	4	8	113
Stature (Trotter-Gleser fm.), male (cm)	169.3	169.8	172.2	170.1	174.2
N	30	68	46	151	92
Stature (Trotter-Gleser fm.) female, (cm)	157.0	154.9	158.0	157.6	163.4
N	27	16	30	88	68
Femur platymeric shaft roundness index	83.4	84.3	84.7	82.7	87.6
N	16	71	38	163	159
Teeth lesions per mouth, caries, abscess, loss	6.6	3.4	5.5	12.3	15.7
N	71	163	45	194	170
Enamel growth arrests, continuous scale	1.5	2.0	1.4	1.6	1.6-
N	48	33	14	77	111
Strontium/calcium site-corrected ratio		.442			
N		35			
Zinc in bone (μg/g)		125.0			147.1
N		35			40
Porotic hyperostosis, continuous scale	1.2-	1.1-	1.5	1.4	1.0+
N	87	120	53	200	181
Variability, sigma ratio (%)	110	114	110	102	105
N					
Adult length of life, male, (years)	37.7	46.2	33.9	40.0	71.0
N	65	100	29	216	census
Adult length of life, female, (years)	31.1	37.3	28.5	38.4	78.5
N	28	32	26	33	
Births (pelvic scars)/adult female	(4.0)	2.8	2.7?	(3.8)	2.4
N	est.		3	est.	
Survivors to age 15/adult female	1.4?	.5?	.9?	2.0?	2.2
Population density estimate (persons/km²)	20	ca. 200	10	25	20-60
Climate	Fluctuating then cooling	New	silt: soil recovery Cool then warming		
and	Drier				
Sea-level relative to today	Fluctuating +1 to 2	0	Little Ice Age Falling 0 to -1	Modern 0	Level 0

Footnotes to Table 3.1

[a]*I use standard United States methods of determining age at death for all skeletons that I study--examination of the pubic symphysis (Todd, also Stewart and McKern, Gilbert), scapula (Graves), vertebral column, and other joint exostoses (Stewart); more cautiously, endocranial skull sutures (Todd and Lyon), tooth eruption, and relative wear. I use and publish the centers of my ranges--i.e., 22-36 = 29. In the skeleton we see physiological age, while our aim is to determine chronological age. See Angel 1971 and Stewart 1979 for references on aging and sex differences.*

For data on bone chemistry see Sillen (1981) and Bisel (1980). For data on Upper (Late) Paleolithic sites of Kostenki (Ukraine), Afalou, Taforalt (North Africa), Jebel Sahaba (Nubia), Hotu (Iran), and Kara'In (Turkey) see Debets (1955a), Ferembach (1962), Anderson (1968), Angel (1952) and unpublished. For data on Mesolithic (Epipaleolithic) sites of Vlasac and Lepenski Vir (Iron Gates), Vasilievka and Voloschkyo (Ukraine), Franchthi Cave (Greece), Shukbah, Nahal Oren, Mallaha, Erg-el-Ahmar, and other Natufian sites (Israel), Zawi Chemi Shanidar (Iraq), and Wadi Halfa (Nubia) see Nemeskeri and Szatmary (1978) (in Garasinin), Nemeskeri in Srejović (1972), Konduktorova (1957), and Debets (1955b), Angel (1969), Keith (1931), and Ferembach (1961, 1977), Ferembach (1970), and Greene and Armelagos (1972).

[b]*Data of Bisel (1980).*

[c]*Data of Sillen (1981).*

SEQUENCES OF CULTURE AND HEALTH

Table 3.1 shows two differing breakdowns of health with subsequent advances. First, there was a fairly sharp decline in growth and nutrition during the confusions and experiments of the transformation from hunting to farming (Cohen 1977), with its many inventions and increasing trade (Jacobs 1969) and disease (Cockburn 1967) between about 10,000 and 5000 B.C. Partial recoveries and advances in health occurred during the Bronze Age rise of civilization; then real advance (e.g., a 7-11-year increase in longevity) occurred with the rise of Hellenic-Roman culture. Second, there was an increase in disease and crowding during the decline and religious metamorphosis of the Roman Empire, eventually leading to an irregular breakdown of general, but not nutritional, health under a complex disease load, from about A.D. 1300 to 1700 (Ackerknecht 1965). The near doubling of life expectancy and improved nutritional health (except dental) of the twentieth-century Western world does reflect both scientific and technological input. But otherwise, technological advance does not neatly correlate with good health, as Cohen (1977) has pointed out. The extent to which technological and ecological factors modify each other's effects on demographic (i.e., health) changes remains to be worked out.

UPPER PALEOLITHIC AND MESOLITHIC TIMES

Upper Paleolithic hunters in the Eastern Mediterranean were a sparse population. They avoided the cold and partly glaciated mountains, 3-5° C below today's temperatures, and probably had coastal camps that are now mostly under water. More sheltered places like Franchthi Cave (Jacobsen 1969) were also for temporary occupation. The hunters lived in cold, temperate open woodland and could gather many root plants, nuts (pistachio, almond, hazel), fruits (apple), herbs, and mollusks. They hunted and ate a variety of medium to large game (Butzer 1970, 1971; Jacobsen 1969; Stephanos 1884). In Egypt, and possibly elsewhere, they were using wild grain (Reed 1977a,b) and perhaps were starting to domesticate barley (Wendorf et al. 1979). They had neither the great herds of wild ungulates nor the intense winter cold of the North African or Eurasian steppes or tundra. Population was denser in the Upper Paleolithic than in Mousterian times (Cohen 1977). Hunting was equally skilled, with a long tool list based on the long flint blade (rarely the sharper obsidian) and including mortars and pestles (Reed 1977a,b). There is evidence of leisure for art and religion.

Four innovations mark the transition to Mesolithic hunting culture: development of composite tools for harpoons and arrows and sickles; the bow to propel arrows (partly replacing atlatl and spear or harpoon); the domesticated dog as pet and/or hunting assistant; and harvesting of stands of wild grains for food.

With first the Allerod and then the pre-Boreal climatic warmings in the ninth to eighth millennia B.C., at the start of postglacial times, there was a great spread of woodland, a 100 m rise in sea level eventually above the present norm, a change in fauna (more deer and pig), and a change in disease. This involved especially a northward spread of malarias into unadapted populations. These forces tended to restrict migration and to promote local settlements on the edge of sandy heaths, lakes, rivers, marshes, and the sea.

Obsidian demonstrates distant trade. Mesolithic microliths for new composite tools (including sickle blades with silica polish) are often of obsidian derived from the Aegean island of Melos, the Hasan Mountains east of Çatal Hüyük on the Konya plain, and Armenia. Use of obsidian helped to maintain the trade, which later on spread the ideas and techniques of farming from their various centers of invention (Jacobs 1969). Trade with Melos encouraged development of sailboats in the Aegean, which in turn facilitated the catching of big sea fish as at Franchthi Cave before the end of the eighth millennium B.C. (Jacobsen 1969).

Health and Culture

Paleolithic

In Upper Paleolithic times nutritional health was excellent. The evidence consists of extremely tall stature from plentiful calories and protein (and some microevolutionary selection?); maximum skull base height from plentiful protein, vitamin D, and sunlight in early childhood; and very good teeth and large pelvic depth from adequate protein and vitamins in later childhood and adolescence. With upper femur shaft index (A-P/transverse thickness) at 78, the long bone shafts were well rounded, considering the extra lateral stresses on the hip area caused by hunting and moving from summer to winter camp over rough trails.

Adult longevity, at 35 years for males and 30 years for females, implies fair to good general health. Because of the extra stresses of pregnancy and dangers of childbirth (combined with shifting camp, carrying burdens, and presumably doing much of the food collecting and cooking), females died younger.

There is no clear evidence for any endemic disease. Modern hunting populations at a comparable level have no really serious endemic or epidemic diseases (Jadin 1938; Yesner 1980), the latter because populations are too small and scattered. The best explanation for relatively short life span is the combination of stresses of nomadism, climate, and warfare. The latter is especially clear in the Jebel Sahaba population, where projectile wounds affecting bone are very common (Wendorf 1968) and "almost half the population probably died violently [p. 993]."

Mesolithic

Similar violence and fighting occurred in Mesolithic times. For evidence, there are the archery battle scenes in Spanish caves (Maringer and Bandi 1953; 133) and the two almost circular depressed skull fractures made at or around the moment of death on the left frontal of *1 Fr* from Franchthi Cave (Angel 1969), a man apparently killed in his middle twenties. Violence is a social disease.

Since hunting on a reasonable scale continued through the Mesolithic (and into the Farming Transformation), it is not surprising that meat and fish protein and vitamin D precursors were enough to keep growth efficient in early childhood (evident in good skull base height and dental health) and good in late childhood (evident in deep pelvis and intermediate long bone roundness). At Vlasac and other Iron Gate sites on the Danube (Nemeskeri and Szatmary 1978; Srejović 1972; Živanović 1975) and Dnieper river sites (Debets 1955b; Konduktorova 1957) deer and river fish maintained this Upper Paleolithic growth level. Sillen's (1981) site-corrected strontium/calcium (Sr/Ca) ratio of .74 at Hayonim Cave is intermediate; Natufians ate a balance of plants and meat. Nevertheless, a sudden drop in stature occurs in the Mesolithic at some sites: Franchthi, 157 cm (2 males) and 138 cm (2 females); Natufians, 164 cm (10) and 155 cm (6) (Ferembach 1977; Keith 1931); Zawi Chemi Shanidar, 1964 cm (5) and 154 cm (1) (Ferembach 1977). In addition, signs of seasonal growth arrests occur at Franchthi Cave, specifically.

Likely causes of decreased stature are new endemic diseases causing anemias (malaria, hookworm) or local decline in calories. Some substitution of fish and seafood for meat (cf. Cohen 1977) tended to lower calories. In addition, three of six skeletons from Franchthi cave have porotic hyperostosis (marrow-space thickening and porosity) indicating anemia (Angel 1969). Probably this is heterozygous thalassemia selected by endemic falciparum malaria after that plasmodium's origin by mutation at least three or four millennia earlier. The occurrence of infants with extreme anemia (i.e., homozygotes killed by thalassemia) is critical evidence for this diagnosis, of course. There is some porosity at Vlasac on the Danube. Greene and Armelagos (1972) note no severe anemia at Wadi Walfa in Nubia. Farther north, at Iron Gate and Dnieper river sites, endemic malarias are unlikely even at the thermal maximum. It is striking that the Western Mesolithic reduction in general health, seen in shortening of adult longevity, did not occur in our area. Population apparently did not increase in density strikingly (cf. Cohen 1977). The increased settling down of Mesolithic bands promoted health and longevity, especially of females, by reducing migration stress. But settling close to water or marsh facilitated the malarias and other diseases.

NEOLITHIC TIMES

Many different theories attempt to explain the actual start of agriculture (Cohen 1977; Flannery 1965; Reed 1977a,b) in western Asia and other centers after the end of the most recent glacial retreat. It is a transformation far too irregular, deeply rooted, and gradual to be called a revolution.

There is no sign of a unified center for the start of early farming. In the highlands of western Asia, ancestral wheat (*Triticum aegilopoides*) and two-row barley spread as far east as Turkestan and west to Israel and Thrace (Helbaek 1960); people began to plant as well as to gather these before 7000 B.C. By 9000 B.C. wild sheep of several varieties and wild goats were being domesticated (Butzer 1971; Reed 1977a,b). Cattle and pigs came soon after, each at different sites from Khuzistan to Turkey to Greece. The plant and animal domestication and all the technological inventions of sickle, hoe, threshing equipment (hot stones for parching, flail, later the doğen), grindstones, effective waterproof houses and pit granaries, storage containers (skin, basketry, stone, and later pottery), and production of copper tools occurred at very different places and times within the matrix of early farming and settlement.

The trading and the rapid spread of ideas and of products (obsidian and other worked stone, ornaments, pottery, bitumen, foods, later wool) was facilitated by the rise in sea level above today's and the 7° C (Boreal and Atlantic) climatic warming during the entire Mesolithic to Late Neolithic sequence. Sites display increasing permanence related to improved food storage. Increasing population strained the productivity of any one site (Reed 1977a,b), resulting in further colonization. The rise in sea level (Rapp et al. 1978) and the spread of forests enhanced crowding in existing settlements. But the actual force for change to farming had to be psychological: over-response to the challenge of raising families at a time when living in settlements restricted hunting and gathering but also allowed women enough security in pregnancy to bear and raise more children (see Table 3.1).

By the sixth millennium B.C., Early Neolithic culture was richer than anything earlier (Mellaart 1967), especially at the sites that give us skeletons. Frescoes and sculpture displayed both naturalistic and symbolic ceremonial art. Technology also went well beyong the Upper Paleolithic in shaping stone and bone tools, in polishing obsidian mirrors, and in the start of metallurgy. Wood-framed houses were developed, often adobe walled, and towns were walled for defense.

Populations were 10 to 50 times as dense as in the Paleolithic. At Çatal Hüyük, Todd (1976) estimates a density of about 75 persons/km^2 for the town and its supporting area. A fair overall estimate for the Eastern Mediterranean is, therefore, 2-5 persons/km^2, taking into account the density of sites (Angel 1972). New cereal crops supported this expansion. Todd (1976) further estimates that if half the surrounding area (78.5 km^2) at Catal Hüyük were in grain and half fallow or in legumes for support of herds, there would be food enough for 5000-75000 people, at 300 kg of grain/person annually. Grain could be stored. For meat, such a population would consume 3 head of cattle daily or almost 1100 annually (Angel 1971). This would be difficult to attain even with Todd's optimum estimate of herds of 3750 plus hunting. I believe (Angel 1971) that the meat eaten would have been only 10-20% of the Upper Paleolithic optimum.

We do not know when properly baked bread first appeared. If cereals were consumed in the form of improperly baked, unleavened bread, *maza*, bulgur, or porridge, they would contain phytate; this can bind iron and zinc and interfere with gastrointestinal absorption of protein and calcium (Bisel 1980; Reinhold 1972). Crucifers, nuts, and fruits should have provided enough fats and vitamins B and C. In late winter there may have been minimal shortages of vitamins A and D.

The main disease stresses were those of crowded settlement: hookworm, dysenteries including amebiasis, the malarias caused by the frequent location of sites near marshes or streams clear of woodland (Angel 1978b), and perhaps occasional personality clash or depression.

Health and Culture: Early Farming

With the beginning of farming, some stabilizing of general health occurred, with at least maintenance of female longevity near the hunting period norm. This promoted a slight excess of survivals over deaths in juveniles and a consequent fairly rapid population increase (Table 3.1). There are two obvious reasons. First, the absolute end of nomadism meant less stress during pregnancy and also, for the whole population, a more certain food supply (from stored grain) during winter and early spring. Second, postnatal adjustment and genetic adaptation of each population to endemic infections occurred, especially to the malarias, through the balanced polymorphic increase of genetically determined abnormal hemoglobins, allowing antibody formation with just enough iron and zinc in the diet.

The largely cereal diet supplied enough calories for maintenance of stature at a subadequate level--none of the slight Upper Paleolithic to Mesolithic stature loss was regained. (Only in our upper classes have we yet returned to the Upper Paleolithic level.) Owing to poor diet throughout childhod, the dimensions of the skull base, pelvic inlet, and long bone shafts, as well as general dental health, were depressed below any reasonable health norm. This growth depression came (1) from insufficient protein (especially essential amino acids from red meat) and (2) from restriction of blood calcium or of vitamin D precursors. Schoeninger (1981) finds site-corrected strontium levels about the same at Iranian prepottery Neolithic sites as at Natufian sites (except where seafood complicates the picture). We have no data on indicators in bone of protein and zinc absorbtion in our area until the early fourth millennium B.C. Chalcolithic at Kalinkaya (Bisel 1980) in Anatolia near Boghazköy, where a very high site-corrected strontium level indicates a diet poor in animal protein.

The Neolithic population as a whole is low in general health and at the low point of nutritional health, with signs of the muscular effort and fatigue necessary in farming. Yet energy remained for considerable cultural achievement, partly derived from the fairly high level of variability (a preamble to genetic mixture) seen in Table 3.1. The balance with society was a wavering positive feedback.

BRONZE AGE

From earliest Neolithic to Classical times, population density increased steadily from about 2 to just under 40 persons/km^2. Hence soils, forests, and minerals were under increasing pressure of use. Technological advance sometimes slowed and sometimes accelerated this ecological stress. By the Early Bronze Age in the third millennium B.C., sailing and oared ships for trade, exploration, and warfare were made possible in part by better axes and adzes. Increasingly these tools and weapons were made of the new bronze. Over the two millennia from 3500 to 1500 B.C. bronze was developed through alloying copper with arsenic and later with tin. Extensive exploration for tin (Wertime 1978), indispensable for its hardening effect on copper, led in time to vastly expanded zones and lines of trade, by sea and by land, and brought silver and gold into the heart of civilization. Bronze cutting weapons, and later armor, made warfare an instrument of the emerging city-states.

The new food base consisted of improved grains, including emmer and early bread-wheat, fava beans, fig and other fruit trees, domesticated grapes, and the olive (Chadwick 1976; Hopf 1962; Rapp et al. 1978). These were cultivated with irrigation, fertilizing, and use of the new Early Bronze Age ard drawn by oxen. The now diminishing meat supply was much more domestic than wild and was a minor part of diet (Gejvall 1969; Shay and Shay 1978). Bees were domesticated to produce honey.

In the latter half of the third millennium B.C., various groups of Indo-European speakers (with ox-drawn wheeled wagons) intruded into the Near East and South Europe, producing stimulating mixtures of peoples and of genes. There was an accompanying gradual shift to patriarchal systems. By Late Bronze times, over a half millennium later, "cities" in Hittite, Minoan, and Mycenean zones expanded into almost feudal city-states (cf. Chadwick 1976). Horse-and-chariot warfare demanded huge stone defense walls. Elaborate metallurgy and textile production, once centered in

Mesopotamia and Egypt, expanded and flourished. At Kultepe in Anatolia, Assyrian merchants had established systems of trade in tin, cloth, etc., with credit and written tablets (cuneiform). Record-tablets in Linear B script show the self-consciousness of a true developing civilization and the need to record resources as population pressures, disputes, and wars developed all over the Mycenean-dominated Aegean world.

Improvement again in mixed farming is implied in detail in the tablets (Chadwick 1976; Ventris and Chadwick 1956) and is fairly clearly recalled in Homer (see Seymour 1908). As sea level lowered, the Myceneans undertook some massive marsh- and lake-drainage projects; for example, of the Copaic basin. These and the drier climate kept malaria down. But the population was dense enough for childhood epidemics to begin. According to arrest lines on teeth (Table 3.1), epidemics probably started after 2000 B.C., in the Middle Bronze Age. Diet grew more varied as more sea fish and probably ducks were added, but in the Late Bronze Age it still included unleavened cakes or pita (Seymour 1908) rather than leavened bread. Some "slaves," specifically weavers, got a daily ration of wheat and figs. They had to collect their own greens, but the tablets do not mention their having meat. Diet for the rulers is not specified on the tablets (Chadwick 1976). Living conditions did not really improve much for the farmers.

EARLY IRON AGE

The Homeric epics belong to the succeeding, rather brief "Dark Age" epitomized in migrations from overpopulation, local depopulations, droughts, piracy, and local autonomy in the interval of oral history between the syllabic writing of the Linear B tablets and the invention of the Greek alphabet from West Semitic (Gelb 1963). As usual in a time of quick change, there were several inventions. The chief of these was the smelting and forging of iron, and the carburization of iron to give steel. Iron brought about the efficient metallizing of the tools of agriculture, once stone or bronze, such as the tip of the wood plow, and the sickle--though flint or obsidian backed blades continue down to the present in the doǧen or threshing-sled. Iron freed the more expensive bronze for more special uses than tools or weapons and spread widely a metallic economy. But use of iron also brought a crisis in wood-based energy throughout the Mediterranean.

HEALTH AND CULTURE: EARLY BRONZE AGE TO CLASSICAL TIMES

From the basic low point in the Neolithic, nutritional health (Table 3.1) continued in a straight and only slightly fluctuating equilibrium for almost five millennia until the immense total health advance of Classical times. Skull base height was about 15% and pelvic depth and stature about 7% below the Upper Paleolithic norm, and dental disease three or four times more severe. We have site-corrected strontium values at medium to high levels indicating less than adequate red meat, but zinc values about the same as modern, suggesting some zinc sources other than meat. In the Late Bronze Age particularly, a human to sheep-goat Sr/Ca ratio of about 1.00 shows that people were getting more strontium than was possible only from plants. The obvious source is sea fish, since a fish diet tends to raise both zinc and strontium. Both levels go down in the Early Iron Age, suggesting disturbance of fishing by piracy, migrations, or custom change. It is puzzling that skull base height, pelvic inlet depth, and stature all remain below normal, especially since stress from malaria had vanished (Table 3.1). Part of the explanation is the continued absorption of phytate from unleavened and coarse bread (*maza*) still in use through the Early Iron Age (Seymour 1908; Tannahill 1973), as well as somewhat low caloric levels, partly from population pressure (McDonald and Simpson 1961).

Regional Variation: Lycia Versus Greece

The people at Early Bronze Age Karataş, in ancient Lycia in southwest Anatolia, show better nutritional health than their contemporaries in Greece (mainly from Hagios Kosmas in Attica, Corinth, and Hagios Stephanos in southeast Peloponnesus). The Karataş sample has a higher skull base (21 mm [N = 172] versus 19 mm [N = 12]), apparently a deeper pelvis (inlet index of 85% [N = 27]), and greater stature (153.1 versus 148.8 cm [N = 5] for females, 166.5 versus 162.2 cm [N = 5] for males). In dental health (5 lesions/mouth [N = 175]) and in longevity (29.5 years [N = 191] for females and 33.7 [N = 159] for males) the Karataş people fit the general Bronze Age norm. Their adult plus child incidence of porotic hyperostosis is a little lower than the 20% at Middle Bronze Age Lerna (Angel 1971), and the occurrence at Karataş of extremely anemic children implies that there were thalassemia homozygotes. Falciparum malaria must have had some selective microevolutionary effect as it had at Lerna later.

These observations suggest good nutrition at Karataş, especially in childhood. The site-corrected Sr/Ca ratio at .60 (N = 322) is low enough to indicate plentiful meat protein. The Karataş bone zinc level of 148 μg/g matches the modern United States level of 147 (Bisel 1980, personal communication, 1982). Karataş soil zinc is low. There is a puzzling difference between the sexes in zinc level; it is significantly lower in females by over 20 μg/g (female 137.0 [N = 173], male 161.0 [N = 149]). Individual differences are very high. The presence of immigrants may explain in part some high values in males. Females dying young, in childbirth on the evidence of 0-2 births/pelvis (N = 12), have significantly low zinc values at 122 μg/g compared with 191.4 in females having 6-10 births (N = 12).

Stature does not correlate with Sr/Ca or zinc. Only in skull base height is an effect seen. Twenty-three people with low skull bases have significantly higher Sr/Ca ratios than 60 people with average and high bases (.71 versus .60). Their zinc levels are lower, too, but not significantly.

Class Variation: Mycenean Royalty

During the latter part of the Middle Bronze Age in Greece, the "royalty" at Mycenae (Table 3.1) differ so greatly from the general population that we exclude them from the overall statistics. In longevity they fit the Bronze Age norm. They show the same striking diversity of morphology (and implied origins) as the general population, then in the process of absorbing Indo-European and other new settlers, including some from Africa. However, the 4% increase in stature and in pelvic depth and the 30% increase in skull base height in the royalty, their thicker and more rounded long bones, and the five-fold improvement in their dental health all show nutritional improvement that must involve more meat protein than the average citizen got. The only non-bone indicator of this high protein diet is the occurrence of gallstones in one man (Angel 1973a: plate 249). From Homer comes the historical implication that rulers were better fed and ate more meat.

Regional Variation: Athenians versus Nichorians

In the Late Bronze Age there is a puzzling regional contrast in health between Athenians and southwest Peloponnese Nichorians (Angel et al. 1980a; Bisel 1981). At Athens the site-corrected Sr/Ca ratio is 1.21 (N = 59) as compared to .55 (N = 26) at Nichoria; Bisel infers from this that much more meat, and no sea fish, were eaten in the southwest Peloponnese. Sloan and Duncan (1978) find almost no fish bones at Nichoria. It is ecologically logical to assume that less meat was eaten at Athens, and the Sr/Ca ratio higher than 1.00 there proves consumption of sea fish. Mycenaean Greeks were still eating unleavened bread with some phytate. The Athenian bone zinc at 157.2 μg/g (N = 59), therefore, is below the value expected in a population with high fish diet.

Nichorians, whose diet was virtually fishless, have a low zinc value at 120 μg/g. It is quite possible that the phytate and fiber of coarsely ground flour and oatmeal or porridge bound and prevented absorption of zinc, as well as iron (not directly measured).

Overall Health

With a decrease in malarias preceding the late Bronze Age decline in porotic hyperostosis, general health improved enough for a 2-year increase in adult longevity (more for males), and consequent increase in births and population. This lasted until the slight health decline of the Early Iron Age. Important is the successful absorption of the various groups of Indo-European-speaking intruders whose presence and beginning mixture raised incredibly the variability of the Middle Bronze Age population. The approximately 500-year time of mixture, with consequent reduction of variability by 20% or more by the Late Bronze Age, was a most creative time culturally. The Early Iron Age represented a brief interruption and then strengthening of this creativity.

SUMMARY OF HUNTING TO FARMING SHIFTS

In ecology there was a marked sequence of changes, first climatic and then man made. Pleistocene cold mountain forest, steppe plateau, or long foreshore with maquis vegetation and few marshes gave way to more deciduous forest and crowded shores, developing with a postglacial temperature rise of 4 or 5° C and a rise in sea level to a point higher than today's. Then, after necessary use of marshy river bank areas for early farming, a gradual expansion of farmland occurred to 20% of total land area, as forests were gradually used in houses, for boats, and for metallurgy. Because of population pressure from about 1500 B.C. onward, there developed the strong challenge of overuse of soils.

In health and disease the changes were paradoxical, with general health and nutritional health moving in generally opposite directions. The apparent stability in female longevity during first Mesolithic and then early farming fixed settlements allowed population increase, probably starting before farming began and helping to create a need for it. Because of the population density, nomadism became impossible except for specific groups of traders, tinkers, mountain hunters, shepherds, etc.

Nutrition became progressively, not suddenly, poorer with early farming. This applied especially to protein from red meat needed for adequate childhood growth against gravity in skull, pelvis, and long bones (stature). An increase in disease was also involved.

Although intergroup fighting continued from the Upper Paleolithic through the Bronze Age and increased as civilization "advanced," there was also a great deal of successful and creative population mixture. The position of women apparently declined but social health was adequate until slavery developed.

Disease effects were minor in the Upper Paleolithic except for trauma. In postglacially hot areas, porotic hyperostosis (anemia) increased in Mesolithic and reached high frequencies in Neolithic to Middle Bronze times. Apparently this resulted mainly from thalassemias, since children show it in long bones as well as their skulls. But porotic hyperostosis in adults had other causes too, probably from iron deficiency from hookworm, amebiasis, or phytate, effect of any of the malarias. The thalassemias necessarily imply falciparum malaria. This disease may be one direct cause of short stature.

The other pressure limiting stature and probably also fertility in early and developing farming times was deficiency of protein and of iron and zinc from ingestion of too much phytic acid in the diet. In addition, new diseases including epidemics emerged as population increased, indicated by an increase of enamel arrest lines in Middle Bronze Age samples. The earliest vertebral tuberculosis, in a 15-year-old girl at Argos, dates at about 900 B.C. in the Early Iron Age. Cancer metastases occur in one Late Bronze Age example.

The most striking finding is local site variability at all periods. The site variability means (1) that we have to pool populations to get a broad picture and large enough samples, and (2) that the causal network of disease-health-culture-environment must be untangled at the local level. Broad correlations are suspect without references to single sites.

We can conclude that farmers were less healthy than hunters, at least until Classical to Roman times. We cannot state exactly how much less healthy they were, however, or exactly how or why.

ACKNOWLEDGMENTS

Support of field work came from fellowships or grants from Harvard University, the University of Minnesota, the Smithsonian Institution, Bryn Mawr College expedition, the American School of Classical Studies at Athens, Jefferson Medical College, the National Institutes of Health (A-224), the American Philosophical Society, and the Guggenheim and Wenner-Gren foundations.

I am most grateful to the above institutions, to the many individuals associated with them, to Greek and Turkish archaeological services, and to many archaeologists for providing dated skeletons; also to Sara Bisel, Gloria Yedynak, and A. Sillen for unpublished data used; Sara Bisel, Jennifer O. Kelley, Alan Mann, Theodore A. Wertime, and Andrew Sillen for critical reading of the manuscript; Peggy Angel for invaluable field assistance; and Katharine Holland for painstaking typing and retyping of the manuscript.

REFERENCES

Ackerknecht, E. H.
1965 *History and geography of the most important diseases.* Hafner, New York.

Adams, P.
1969 The effect of experimental malnutrition on the development of long bones. *Bibliotheca "Nutritio et dieta" 13*:69-73.

Anderson, J. E.
1968 Late Paleolithic skeletal remains from Nubia. In *The prehistory of Nubia* (Vol. II), edited by F. Wendorf, pp. 966-1040. Southern Methodist University, Dallas.

Angel, J. L.
1952 The human skeletal remains from Hotu, Iran. *Proceedings of the American Philosophical Society 96(3)*:258-269.
1966 Porotic hyperostosis, anemias, malarias and marshes in the prehistoric Eastern Mediterranean. *Science 153*:760-763.
1969 Human skeletal material from Franchthi Cave. *Hesperia 38*: 343-381.
1971 *The people of Lerna.* Am. School of Classical Studies at Athens and Smithsonian Institution, Washington, D.C.
1972 Biological relations of Egyptian and Eastern Mediterranean populations during Pre-dynastic and Dynastic times. *J. Human Evolution 1*:307-313.
1973a Human skeletons from grave circles at Mycenae. Appendix in *The grave circle B of Mycenae* (in Greek), by G. E. Mylonas, pp. 379-397. Archeological Society in Athens, Athens.
1973 Early Neolithic people of Nea Nikomedeia. In *Die Anfänge des Neolithikums vom Orient bis Nordeuropa*, edited by E. Schwidetzky, pp. 103-112. Böhlau, Köln.
1975 Paleoecology, paleodemography and health. In *Population, ecology and social evolution*, edited by S. Polgar, pp. 167-190. Mouton, The Hague.
1978a Pelvic inlet form: A neglected index of nutritional status. *American Journal of Physical Anthropology 48*: 378 (Abstr.).
1978b Porotic hyperostosis in the Eastern Mediterranean. *Medical College of Virginia Quarterly 14(1)*:10-16.
1982 A new measure of growth efficiency: Skull base height. *American Journal of Physical Anthropology 58*:297-305.

Angel, J. L., and L. M. Olney
1981 Skull base height and pelvic inlet depth from Prehistoric to modern times. *American Journal of Physical Anthropology 54*:197.

Angel, J. L., S. Bisel, and S. Dietz
1980a Det mykenske menneske. *Saertryk of National museets Arbejdsmark*, pp. 1-13.

Bisel, S. L. C.
1980 *A pilot study in aspects of human nutrition in the ancient East Mediterranean, with particular attention to trace*

minerals in several populations from different time periods. Ph.D. thesis, University of Minnesota, Minneapolis.
1981 Nutrition in Late Bronze Age Greece, as indicated by bone mineral analysis. *American Journal Physical Anthropology 54*:201 (Abstr.).

Butzer, K. W.
1970 Physical conditions in Eastern Europe, Western Asia and Egypt before the period of agricultural and urban settlement. In *Cambridge Ancient History I* (3rd ed.), edited by I. E. S. Edwards, C. J. Gadd, and N. G. L. Hammond, pp. 35-69. Cambridge University Press, Cambridge.
1971 *Environment and archeology: An introduction to Pleistocene geography (second ed.).* Aldine, Chicago.

Buxton, L. H. D.
1938 Platymeria and Playtycnemia. *Journal of Anatomy 73*:31-36.

Chadwick, J.
1976 *The Mycenaean world.* Cambridge University Press, Cambridge.

Cockburn, A.
1967 *Infectious diseases: Their evolution and eradication.* Thomas, Springfield.

Cohen, M. N.
1977 *The food crisis in prehistory. Overpopulation and the origins of agriculture.* Yale University Press, New Haven.

Debets, G. F.
1955a Paleoanthropological find in Kostenki. *Sovetskaya Etnografiya 1*:43-53.
1955b Skeletons in the Epipaleolithic (Mesolithic) cemetery at Voloschkoyo. *Sovetskaya Etnografiya 3*:62-73.

DeLuca, H. F.
1980 The control of calcium and phosphorus metabolism by the Vitamin D endocrine system. *Annals of the New York Academy of Sciences 355*:1-17.

Ferembach, D.
1961 Squelettes du Natoufien d'Israel, étude anthropologique. *L'Anthropologie 65*:46-66.
1962 *La Nécropole Épipaléolithique de Taforalt (Maroc Oriental).* Centre National de la Recherche Scientifique, Rabat.
1970 Étude Anthropologique des ossements humains Proto-Neolithiques de Zawi Chemi Shanidar (Irak). *Sumer* No. 1-2, pp. 21-65.
1977 Les Natoufiens de Palestine. *Eretz-Israel 13*:241-252.

Flannery, K. V.
1965 The ecology of early food production in Mesopotamia. *Science 147*:1247-1256.

Gejvall, N.-G.
1969 *Lerna 2.* The fauna, American School of Classical Studies at Athens, Princeton, New Jersey.

Gelb, I. J.
1963 *A study of writing* (revised ed.). University of Chicago Press, Chicago.

Greene, D. L., and G. Armelagos
1972 The Wadi Halfa Mesolithic population. *Department of Anthropology, University of Massachusetts, Amherst Research Report* No. 11.
Helbaek, H.
1960 The paleoethnobotany of the Near East and Europe. *University of Chicago Studies in Oriental Civilization* No. 31, pp. 99-118.
Hopf, M.
1962 Nutzpflanzen von Lernäischen Golf. *Jahrbuch der Römisch-Germanischen Zentralmuseums Mainz 9*:1-19.
Jacobs, J.
1969 *The economy of cities*. Random House, New York.
Jacobsen, T. W.
1969 Excavations at Porto Cheli and vicinity, preliminary report II: The Franchthi Cave, 1967-1968. *Hesperia 38(3)*: 343-381.
Jadin, J.
1938 Aperçu sur l'état sanitaire des pygmies de l'Ituri. *Anthropologie (Prague) 16*:69-83.
Keith, Arthur
1931 *New discoveries relating to the antiquity of man*. Williams & Norgate, London.
Konduktorova, T. C.
1957 Paleoanthropology materials in the Mesolithic Cemetery Vasilievka I. *Sovetskaja Antropologia 2*:189-210.
Lack, D. L.
1967 *The natural regulation of animal numbers*. Oxford University Press, London and New York.
Mann, A. E.
1975 Paleodemographic aspects of the South African Australopithecines. *University of Pennsylvania Publications in Anthropology*, No. 1.
Maringer, J., and H.-G. Bandi
1953 *Art in the Ice Age*. Praeger, New York.
Maull, O.
1922 *Griechisches Mittelmeergebiet*. Hirt, Breslau.
McDonald, W. A., and R. H. Simpson
1961 Prehistoric habitation in Southwestern Peloponnese. *American Journal of Archaeology 65*:221-260.
Mellaart, J.
1967 *Çatal Hüyük. A Neolithic town in Anatolia*. McGraw-Hill, New York.
Nemeskeri, J., and L. Szatmary
1978 Anthropology section. In Vlasac: A Mesolithic settlement in the Iron Gates (Vol. II), edited by Milutin Garasanin. *Serbian Academy of Sciences and Arts Monographies* Vol. DXII, Dept. of Historical Sciences 5:67-284.
Rapp, G., S. E. Aschenbrenner, and S. C. Kraft
1978 The Holocene environmental history of the Nichoria region. In *Excavations at Nichoria in SW Greece I, Site, environs*

and techniques, edited by G. Rapp and S. E. Aschenbrenner, pp. 13-25. University of Minnesota Press, Minneapolis.

Reed, C. A.
1977a A model for the origin of agriculture in the Near East. *Origins of agriculture*, edited by C. A. Reed, pp. 543-567. Mouton, The Hague.

Reed, C. A. (editor)
1977b *Origins of agriculture*. Mouton, The Hague.

Reinhold, J. G.
1972 Phytate concentrations of leavened and unleavened Iranian breads. *Ecology of Food and Nutrition 1*:187-192.

Schoeninger, M. J.
1981 The agricultural 'revolution': Its effect on human diet in the Middle East. *American Journal of Physical Anthropology 54*:275 (Abstr.).

Seymour, T. D.
1908 *Life in the Homeric Age*. Macmillan, New York.

Shay, J., and C. T. Shay
1978 Modern vegetation and fossil plant remains. In *Excavations at Nichoria in SW Greece I*, edited by G. Rapp and S. E. Aschenbrenner, pp. 41-59. University of Minnesota Press, Minneapolis.

Sillen, A. B.
1981 Strontium and diet at Hayonim Cave. *American Journal of Physical Anthropology 56*:131-137.

Sloan, R. E., and M. A. Duncan
1978 Zooarchaeology of Nichoria. In *Excavations at Nichoria in SW Greece I*, edited by G. Rapp and S. E. Aschenbrenner, pp. 60-77. University of Minnesota Press, Minneapolis.

Sognnaes, R. F.
1956 Histologic evidence of developmental lesions in teeth originating from paleolithic, prehistoric, and ancient man. *American Journal of Pathology 32*:547-577.

Srejović, D.
1972 *New discoveries at Lepenski Vir*. (Transl. L. F. Edwards) Stein and Day, New York.

Stephanos, C.
1884 Grèce. Geographie Médicale. In *Dictionnaire Encyclopédique des Sciences Médicales* (Vol. X), edited by A. Dechambre, Sect. IV. P. Asselin, Paris.

Stewart, T. D.
1979 *Essentials of forensic anthropology*. C. C Thomas, Springfield, Illinois.

Tannahill, R.
1973 *Food in history*. Eyre Methuen, London.

Todd, I. A.
1976 *Çatal Hüyük in perspective*. Cummings, Menlo Park, California.

Tuchman, B. W.
1978 *A distant mirror: The calamities of the 14th century*. Knopf, New York.

Ventris, M., and J. Chadwick
1956 *Documents in Mycenaean Greek.* Cambridge University, Press, Cambridge.
Wendorf, F.
1968 Site 117: A Nubian final Paleolithic graveyard near Jebel Sahaba, Sudan. *The Prehistory of Nubia* (Vol. II), edited by F. Wendorf. *Southern Methodist University Contributions in Anthropology* No. 2, pp. 954-985.
Wendorf, Fred, R. Schild, N. El Hadidi, A. E. Close, M. Kobiesiewicz, H. Wieckowska, B. Issawi, and H. Haas
1979 The use of barley in the Egyptian Late Paleolithic. *Science 205*:1341-1347.
Wertime, T. A.
1978 The search for ancient tin: The geographic and historic boundaries. In *The search for ancient tin*, edited by A. D. Franklin, J. S. Olin, and J. A. Wertime, pp. 1-6. Smithsonian Institution, Washington, D.C.
Yesner, D. R.
1980 Nutrition and cultural evolution, patterns in preshitory. In *Nutritional anthropology*, pp. 85-115. Redgrave, Pleasantville, New York.
Živanović, S.
1975 A note on the anthropological characteristics of the Padina population. *Zeitschrift für Morphologie und Anthropologie 66*:161-175.

CHAPTER 4

SOCIOECONOMIC CHANGE AND PATTERNS OF PATHOLOGY AND VARIATION IN THE MESOLITHIC AND NEOLITHIC OF WESTERN EUROPE: SOME SUGGESTIONS

Christopher Meiklejohn
Catherine Schentag
Alexandra Venema

Department of Anthropology
University of Winnipeg

Patrick Key

The KEY Company, Inc.
Williston, North Dakota

INTRODUCTION

A total synthesis of paleopathological trends in Europe from the end of the Upper Paleolithic through the developed Neolithic is beyond the scope of a single paper. Indeed, the published data do not permit the comprehensive collection of such material. As seen below, it is clear that the collection of available data yields as many questions as answers.

This synthesis started with material from the Mesolithic period in western Europe, defined here as Scandinavia (except Finland), the Benelux nations, the United Kingdom, Ireland, France, Switzerland, Italy, Spain, and Portugal. Constraints of time prevented synthesis of the Upper Paleolithic materials. The constraints on the reliability of the Mesolithic data base also would have been more problematic for the Upper Paleolithic, where total sample size is smaller by an order of magnitude.

A survey was also made of published analyses of Neolithic remains with emphasis on recent work with larger samples in an attempt to obtain reliable frequency data. Time constraints limited regional coverage primarily to the Benelux and France.

The Mesolithic data base used here has been subject to rigorous evaluation of provenience by Newell et al. (1979; see also Bouville et al. 1984; Constandse-Westermann and Newell 1984; Constandse-Westermann et al. 1984; Larsson et al. 1981). One hundred and eighty-six sites with skeletal material referred to as Mesolithic were evaluated by these authors for stratigraphic and archaeological provenience and absolute dating. From this base, 76 sites had skeletal material of assured Mesolithic age. One new site has now been added to the sample, Skateholm in southern Sweden (Larsson 1980, 1981, 1982). Three sites previously regarded as being of indeterminate status have been demonstrated to contain Mesolithic material: Viste (Norway), Hohlestein (West Germany), and Uzzo (Italy). Thus, the sample for this report is based on 80 sites. However, the majority of sites consist of materials that either are single burials or are highly fragmentary (see Larsson et al. 1981). Only 7 sites have sample sizes greater than 10 (Moita do Sebastião, Cabeço da Arruda, and Cabeço da Amoreira in Portugal, Höedic and Teviec in France, Vedbaek-Bøgebakken in Denmark, and Skateholm in Sweden[1]).

Similar control of the Neolithic sample is not yet possible. No rigorous study of provenience for this period has been attempted. For this study, material from 51 sites has been synthesized (see Appendix 1), of which 23 have sample sizes of over 10 and 6 have sample sizes of over 50.

CULTURAL UNITS AND ECONOMIC TRENDS

The cultural base for this discussion must begin with the Upper Paleolithic. This period in western Europe is among the best known in the Old World (see recent syntheses by Campbell 1977; de Lumley 1976; Laville et al. 1980).

In brief, the Upper Paleolithic of western Europe is usually divided into earlier and later cultural groups, succeeding the Middle Paleolithic Mousterian complex. The early Upper Paleolithic begins with dates of circa 33,000 B.C. (this and all other ^{14}C-based dates in this chapter are uncalibrated). The most parsimonious model has sequentially replacive Chatelperronian, Aurignacian, and Perigordian industrial complexes, with boundaries at circa 32,000 and 26,000 B.C., ending about 18,000 B.C. Evidence shows a broad-based hunting economy as seen by the presence of a number of large herd mammals in the faunal record (Spiess 1979). Environmental reconstructions suggest that, though tundra and scrub tundra dominated regions near the glacial ice front, sheltered localities as far north as the Perigord region harbored temperate tree species.

Between 19,000 and 17,000 B.C. the terminal Perigordian was replaced by the Solutrean industry, which was in turn replaced by the Magdalenian, spanning the period from the late glacial maximum

[1] *Ofnet (BRD), San Teodoro (Italy), and Arene Candide (Italy) are considered to be Upper Paleolithic in age, as are all Azilian materials.*

to the end of the terminal Younger Dryas oscillation, circa 8300 B.C.

The Magdalenian provides the population base for the succeeding Mesolithic period. Cultural and faunal evidence suggests a specialized hunting economy, with heavy exploitation of key game resources. Although local variation occurs, related to local ecology, most faunal assemblages are dominated by reindeer (Spiess 1979). Evidence for exploitation of secondary resources is limited (Meiklejohn 1978), apparently related to the observation that in periglacial environments, low species diversity is a correlate of environmental instability (Slobodkin and Sanders 1968).

Current evidence supports neither models of high population size and density nor long-term sedentary aggregations during the Upper Paleolithic (Burch 1972; Meiklejohn 1977, 1978; Spiess 1979). The evidence fits with Wobst's (1976) estimate of 0.05 persons/km^2 as an upper limit. Higher figures require evidence for semipermanent settlement, that, while suggested on the basis of data from reindeer, can be shown to be based on imprecise methodology (Binford 1973; Spiess 1979). Evidence supports a model analogous to the pattern of modern arctic and subarctic hunters, with seasonal site occupation, considerable mobility, and low population density (Meiklejohn 1977, 1978; Spiess 1979).

A consequent question concerns the shape of the Upper Paleolithic growth curve. A calculated steady-state growth rate for the Upper Paleolithic would be in the order of 0.01%/annum (compare with a modern rate of 2.0%/annum) (Meiklejohn 1978). Within the life span of an individual, this is not significantly different from a zero growth rate. Doubling time approaches 20,000 years. A sawtooth model may, however, better fit the facts. If this is correct, then environmental instability, channeled through resource availability, is heavily implicated (Burch 1972). Mechanisms for a steady-state mechanism are far harder to pinpoint. It does seem clear, however, that overall Upper Paleolithic growth rates are considerably below those of the Mesolithic (see below).

The Mesolithic, as defined here, begins at the Younger Dryas-Preboreal boundary, circa 8300 B.C., also the normally defined Pleistocene-Holocene boundary. North of the Mediterranean, this marks the debut of climatic conditions with annual temperatures near the modern mean, accompanied by a forest succession beginning with pine-birch dominance and leading towards a climax oak forest. Even in the Mediterranean basin there are major ecological changes, though not so drastic (Newell et al. 1979).

Mesolithic industries are dominated by microlithic assemblages (for recent syntheses see de Lumley 1976; Gramsch 1981; Kozlowski 1973; Mellars 1978; Rozoy 1978). Typologically differentiated areas have been identified, though these do not necessarily mark major population boundaries (Newell and Anderson 1982; Newell et al. 1982). The Mesolithic lasts from the Preboreal until the appearance of farming and herding communities.

Whereas late Paleolithic economies are based on low species diversity with marginal dietary alternatives, clear evidence exists for greater Mesolithic resource breadth and dependability. Though large ungulates are still a major resource, there is a shift to more solitary forms and use of a broader range per site (number of mammal species per site: $\overline{X} = 7.0$, $SD = 3.92$, $N = 139$; data from R. R. Newell, personal communication, 1981). Heavy use of fish and shellfish is apparent (Newell and Anderson 1982), and there is evidence for considerable use of plant food resources. Food resources were also more evenly spread throughout the annual cycle. The result is a population less subject to economic base disruption. The evidence suggests a broadly adapted population, showing dynamic responses to the better opportunities of the Holocene environment.

The Mesolithic economy sees the appearance of semipermanent settlements, increased density of more evenly spaced sites, stability of regional occupation (see also Meiklejohn 1978), and evidence for increased regional cultural identification over time (Newell et al. 1982). Net growth is apparent in a number of regions. Closest control has been achieved for sites in the North German Plain (Newell 1973). Before circa 5700 B.C. there is an increase in site number, different site sizes reflecting different structural poses, but all remaining below an area of circa 1000 m^2. Between 5700 and 3500 B.C., site sizes increase by up to fourfold and there is evidence for longer periods of site occupation. The total data set suggests a steady-state growth rate of circa 0.1%/annum, an order of magnitude greater than suggested for the Upper Paleolithic and comparable to the rate suggested for Middle Eastern Neolithic populations (Carneiro and Hilse 1966). Applying the derived rates yields a density for the terminal Mesolithic of the order of 1 person/km^2, a figure close to that of primitive farming populations (Carneiro and Hilse 1966). Calculated growth rates are compatible with modern hunter-gatherer societies with extended birth-spacing mechanisms. Early Neolithic farming communities are thus found in the context of societies already exhibiting comparable growth rates and densities.

Farming communities appear first in the southern and southeastern portions of the region under discussion, in the Mediterranean and Danube-Rhine basins beginning about 6200 B.C. (Guilane 1979). From here they spread north and west, appearing at dates ranging from 5700 B.C. in the southeast to 4400 B.C. in the southern part of the Netherlands, 3500 B.C. in the central part of the Netherlands and England, 3700 B.C. in Ireland, 4000 B.C. in Brittany, and 3500 B.C. in central Portugal (see Ammerman and Cavalli-Sforza 1973; Guilane 1979; Milisauskas 1978). The dynamics of the spread of farming are complex and currently available evidence does not always clearly separate models of intrusive agriculturalists from diffusion and/or the regional adaptation of local indigenes (Lewthwaite 1981).

DATA BASE AND ANALYSIS

Introduction

Data have been recorded for pathology and trauma in both dental and skeletal materials, as has material relevant to trends in skeletal dimorphism and stature. A major portion of the Mesolithic series has been examined by the senior author.

For the Neolithic period, except for material from the early Neolithic Swifterbant sites (Constandse-Westermann and Meiklejohn 1979; Meiklejohn and Constandse-Westermann 1978), all data are from the available literature. The distribution of sites by country is given in Table 4.1.

Representative Nature of the Data Base

In collecting data for this report it became clear that there were gaps in the reporting of information. In addition, the very nature of many of the series raised questions about their representative nature. These points must be examined if the collected data are to be placed in context. In many cases it is difficult to determine from the literature whether pathology has been sought in a given sample. In preparing the Mesolithic provenience catalog (Newell et al. 1979), we were forced to conclude that no study of pathology had occurred when no specific statement was made. At this stage, then, it is unclear whether this is a biasing factor. It is equally difficult to discover whether further pathology exists on some samples for which pathology is reported. For example, we suspect some underreporting or nonreporting of whole classes of pathology and/or trauma. Thus we do not claim universal coverage of pathology for the series under consideration.

The approach taken to the reporting of pathology and trauma must also be broached. The focus of this study is on demography and anthropology, with population as the essential unit of study. This is a central difference between anthropological and clinical medical approaches to disease process. However, much of the data reported here are clearly presented within the clinical paradigm. Pathology is well described but is not placed into the context of the sample. It is sometimes difficult to discover whether cases of pathology in a particular series are or are not from a single individual, and it may not be possible to calculate the frequency of a pathology.

Finally, it must be asked whether the sample is representative of the population from which it is drawn. We do not have sufficient control of the Neolithic sample to test the problem adequately. However, one of use has tested the potential for bias in the Mesolithic sample (Schentag 1982). Multiple regression analysis was performed on the sample using several independent

TABLE 4.1. Distribution of Sites by Country

Country	*Sites*	
	Mesolithic	*Neolithic*
Norway	*3*	--
Sweden	*10*	--
Denmark	*27*	--
Federal Republic of Germany	*7*	--
German Democratic Republic	*2*	--
Great Britain	*5*	--
The Netherlands	*1*	*6*
Luxembourg	*1*	--
Belgium	--	*5*
Switzerland	*1*	--
France	*14*	*31*
Italy	*3*	--
Spain	*3*	--
Portugal	*3*	*9*
	80	*51*

variables. Primary results are as follows. The more complete a specimen, the greater its chance of being reported as pathological. State of preservation was found to be significant when polynomial regression was performed. Thus completeness of the skeleton has a linear relationship to reporting of pathology, whereas the effect of preservation is curvilinear. The latter finding suggests that while reporting of pathology is greater for a relatively complete specimen, there appear to be systematic occurrences of reported pathology in relatively fragmentary materials. Results related to age of the specimen, location, context, and date of publication were less clear. It can be concluded, however, that significant biasing effects are involved in the reporting of both frequency and distribution of pathology in the Mesolithic sample.

We would also point out that certain classes of data considered elsewhere in this volume have not been reported for European series of the time frame under consideration, including Harris lines and trace element analysis for such bone constituents as strontium. In Mesolithic samples, measurement of the latter is complicated by the ubiquitous presence of marine resources (T. D. Price, personal communication, 1982).

Cranial Pathology

There are only three classes of cranial pathology from the Mesolithic sample. None appear to be of major importance, and no meaningful frequency data can be generated. Only one case of arthritis is reported; slight arthritis of the mandibular condyles (Melby, Denmark). The individual also has postcranial arthritis. Cranial infection is also reported in a single case (Mannlefelsen, France), an occipital depression apparently not the result of a fracture.

For the Neolithic, cranial arthritis appears to be of the same order of magnitude as in the Mesolithic. However, the frequency of cranial infections appears to be higher, though apparently of a broad range of etiologies, making quantification difficult to interpret. Four French sites (Fontenay-le-Marmion, L'Homme-Mort, Laris Goguet, and Vigneau) report arthritis. These are partitioned into temperomandibular arthritis (five cases in two sites [*N* = ca. 126], glenoid cavity arthritis (one case), and occipital condyle arthritis (three cases in one site [*N* = 17]). No site reports more than one type of arthritis. Since *N* represents the number of individuals in the samples, not the number of cases with the area intact for inspection, frequency data cannot be calculated. We cannot comment at this time on whether arthritis is correlated with the age of affected individuals in the respective samples.

Evidence for generalized cranial pathology, including infection, suggests considerably higher levels in the Neolithic than in the Mesolithic. However, the nature of the reporting hampers generalization. Data in this category were recorded from 17 sites listed within the following categories: tumefaction (one case), osteophytoses (one), benign osteoma (one), osteomyelitis (one), bony exostoses (three), eroded bone surfaces and/or thinning-rarefaction (six), circular lesions (two), hematoma (two), mandibular cyst (one), and general bony depressions (three). These categories are not necessarily mutually exclusive. Materials of very different etiology appear to be present. This is, however, a category that appears to be more frequent in later samples. It can be tentatively hypothesized that increased levels of generalized infection can be expected in more sedentary populations of greater density, which have greater potential for acting as reservoirs of infection.

The final category of cranial pathology noted in the Mesolithic, osteoporosis, is reported in only 2 cases of 46 sites with cranial pathology studied (Cuzoul de Gramat, France, and Falkensteinhöhle, BRD). Such a low frequency suggests that dietary insufficiency is rare. The same conclusion also extends to the Neolithic, with only one reported case (Hastières, *N* = ca. 50). This trait shows no clear trend.

Similarly, cribra orbitalia is not a major factor in either period. There are no reported cases in the Mesolithic, and only four cases from one site in the Neolithic (Laris Goguet, *N* = 60). Hengen (1971) also makes no mention of early cases. Cribra orbitalia, like osteoporosis, provides no evidence for a shift in general health status between the Mesolithic and the Neolithic. Major dietary strain, the suggested etiology for those traits in other geographic areas, cannot be supported for either period.

Postcranial Pathology

Postcranial pathology in the Mesolithic period suggests the primacy of bony changes resulting from heavy use and concomitant degeneration, primarily noted as osteochondrosis and arthritis. Possibly related are cases of scoliosis-kyphosis.

There are only two other reported pathologies, one only reported from a single site. Periostotic hypertrophy is reported from Teviec 5 and with a nutritional etiology. There is no equivalent from the Neolithic sample. More generally reported is the category of infection. These include reports of ulnar osteitis (Trou Violet A), inflammatory reactions of the lower limbs (Cuzoul de Gramat and Bonifacio), and a bone abscess of the right ulna (Höedic 5), all from France, plus a draining sore in the humerus (Ageröd I, Sweden). Postcranial infection is also present in the Neolithic sample, but in low amounts. There is a possible infection in a deltoid tuberosity (Swifterbant S2), generalized swelling and periostotic reaction on a tibia (Fontenay-le-Marmion), and bone rarefaction of a scapula (Abri Pendimoun). Bony exostoses are reported from Baumes-Chaudes, Grotte de Route and Laris Goguet. At Grotte de Route this may be secondary to trauma. There are also generalized descriptions of "pronounced excavation" of a fibula (Grotte de Route), and of bony depressions and exposure of spongy tissue (Laris Goguet) that may fit here. It can be suggested that postcranial infection was a problem in both time periods. No clear trends are visible in the available data.

Arthritis and related features are reported from 13 of 46 Mesolithic sites with reported pathology studies (28.3%). In 3 sites with multiple individuals, frequencies were 13% in 2 cases (Bøgebakken, Denmark--3 of 23, Teviec--3 of 23) and 21% in the third (Höedic--3 of 14). The spinal column and pelvic region show highest frequencies (11 of 21 individuals = 52%), broken down into: cervical vertebrae (4), thoracic vertebrae (2), lumbar vertebrae (3), sacrum and pelvis (3), nonspecific (4). To these figures can be added osteochondrosis of the thoracic and lumbar vertebrae from Bonifacio, the presence of thoracic vertebral displacement in Teviec 3 and 6, and lumbar deviation in Loschbour, Luxembourg.

In the limbs, 9 of 21 individuals (43%) showed arthritis of the shoulder girdle and/or upper limb and 6 of 21 (29%) showed arthritis of the lower limb, primarily the foot. These figures suggest that stress is greater in the vertebral column and upper limb than in the lower limb during the Mesolithic.

When the Neolithic series is examined, there is an immediate impression that vertebral arthritis is less frequent than in the

Mesolithic. Only three sites report degenerative changes. Hyperostosis is reported from l'Abri Pendimoun (N = 1) (atlas and lumbar region). Fontenay-le-Marmion (N = 66) has reported osteophytes, enlargement of articular facets, cartilage destruction, patterns of fusion, and general alteration. Laris Goguet (N = ca. 60) has reported arthroses and general deformation, and the only reporting of frequencies with 36-40% of thoracic vertebrae affected (N = 73-81), 31% of lumbar vertebrae I-IV (N = 70) and 71% of lumbar vertebra V (N = 34). However, though fewer Neolithic sites have reported evidence of vertebral arthritis, sites such as Laris Goguet have higher within-series frequencies than those seen in the Mesolithic. Whether this represents inconsistent reporting for the Neolithic, major differences in stress patterns between sites, or both, is unclear. The data from Fontenay-le-Marmion do, however, point to intersite differences.

Eight sites have reported arthritis of the limbs or girdles. At Swifterbant S2, arthritis was quite limited, restricted to two cases of arthritis in the foot and one case in the sacroiliac joint. This sample clearly was not prone to arthritic changes. The 7 other sites (all French) have 21 cases of arthritis of the upper limb and girdle (36 total cases of arthritis), 15 cases of arthritis of the lower limb and girdle, and 2 cases of arthritis of the ribs. Within-site frequencies cannot be calculated. Of the 36 individuals reported with arthritis, 58% showed arthritis of the upper limbs, 42% showed arthritis of the lower limbs. These figures are not equivalent to those noted for the Mesolithic. For the Neolithic it is not possible to link postcranial and vertebral cases of arthritis.

The above figures provide a prima facie case for slightly higher overall incidences of arthritis in the Mesolithic as compared to the Neolithic. This can be derived both from slightly higher involvement rates within individuals with reported arthritis, and (since the total number of cases for the Neolithic is lower than would be expected) from examination of the sample sizes of the respective populations. We suggest that the arthritis data support a model of heavier biomechanical stress in the Mesolithic than in the Neolithic.

Finally, two suggested cases from the Neolithic are of types not recorded in the Mesolithic. A possible case of Paget's disease is noted at Fontenay-le-Marmion, and a case of advanced osteomyelitis at Laris Goguet. The latter may reflect population size in relation to disease reservoirs, as noted in the section on cranial pathology. Six cases of hip subluxation and one case of knee subluxation at Fontenay-le-Marmion may be further markers for different biomechanical stress patterns in the Mesolithic and the Neolithic.

TABLE 4.2. Reporting of Caries in Mesolithic Samples

Site	*Number of teeth*	*Number of caries*	*Number of individuals*	*Number of individuals with caries*
Backaskog	*31*	*0*	*1*	*0*
Stora Bjers	*32*	*0*	*1*	*0*
Stora Mosse	*11*	*0*	*1*	*0*
Bergmansdal	*9*	*0*	*1*	*0*
Bøgebakken	*357*	*0*	*14*	*0*
Brovst	*4*	*1*	*4(?--Loose)*	*1*
Korsør Nor	*32*	*0*	*1*	*0*
Melby	*20*	*0*	*1*	*0*
Mullerup	*4*	*0*	*1*	*0*
Nivaagaard	*2*	*0*	*2(?--Loose)*	*0*
Sølager	*2*	*0*	*1*	*0*
Svaerdborg 1921	*18*	*0*	*1*	*0*
Swaerdborg 1943	*2*	*0*	*2(?--Loose)*	*0*
Tybrind Vig	*6*	*0*	*1*	*0*
Vedbaek	*29*	*0*	*1*	*0*
Villingbaek Øst	*1*	*0*	*1*	*0*
Durrenberg	*32*	*0*	*1*	*0*
Falkensteinhöhle	*3*	*0*	*1*	*0*
Cnoc Coig	*4*	*0*	*4(?--Loose)*	*0*
Gough's Cave	*24*	*0*	*2*	*0*
Loschbour	*23*	*0*	*1*	*0*
Birsmatten	*21*	*5*	*1*	*1*
Bonifacio	*32*	*0*	*1*	*0*
Culoz	*33*	*0*	*2*	*0*
Cuzoul de Gramat	*29*	*0*	*1*	*0*
Höedic	*133*	*7*	*8*	*3*
Mannlefelsen	*12*	*0*	*1*	*0*
Rastel	*29*	*1*	*1*	*1*
Teviec	*352*	*8*	*13*	*4*
Trou Violet	*7*	*0*	*1*	*0*
Vatte di Zambana	*28*	*0*	*1*	*0*
Colombres	*32(?)*	*1*	*1*	*1*
Moita do Sebastião	*428*	*10*	*16(?)*	*?*
	1780	*33 (1.9%)*	*90*	*11 (14.9%)*

Dental Pathology

Dental pathology has been approached more systematically than any other pathology under discussion. However, even here there are differential levels of reporting.

The best reported dental pathology is caries. Mesolithic data are reported for 33 sites (Table 4.2), 7 (21.2%) with reported caries. In terms of numbers of individuals, 11 of 74 individuals (14.9%) have caries (not including Moita do Sebastião, for which no figures by individual are available). When individual teeth are considered, 33 of 1780 permanent teeth are carious (1.9%). No caries were reported in Mesolithic deciduous teeth. Of 33 reported carious teeth, 22 can be identified by position. No carious involvement is seen in either the incisors or the canines, and there is only one case of premolar caries. The frequencies of caries of the molars increase as one proceeds from M1 to M3. We do not believe that there is any significance to frequency differences between upper and lower dentitions. An open area for investigation lies in the relationship between percentage of teeth carious and percentage of individuals with carious teeth. Some individuals have more caries than expected from frequency data alone. Of 11 individuals with caries, 1 has 5 caries (Birsmatten), 2 have 3 caries each (Höedic 1, Teviec 1), and 4 have 2 caries each (Höedic 7, 9; Teviec 4, 13). It seems unlikely that caries is evenly distributed through the sample. Similarly, Bøgebakken shows clear underrepresentation. Using the individual figures from Table 4.2 (removing Bøgebakken from consideration), we would expect 18.3% of any sample to show carious teeth. For Bøgebakken this would be 2.5 (N = 14). In similar fashion, we would expect 2.3% of teeth to be carious. For Bøgebakken this would be 8.2 teeth (N = 357).

From the Neolithic series some comparisons can be made (Table 4.3). Sixteen sites have reported caries. No sites are reported as showing no caries, a condition noted in 26 of 33 (78.8%) Mesolithic sites. While the latter figures in part reflect small individual samples, this clearly is not the only factor. There is no systematic reporting of figures for numbers of Neolithic individuals with caries. Sixty-nine of 1654 individual teeth are carious (4.2%), over twice the Mesolithic number. The difference between the two samples is highly significant ($\chi^2 = 15.98$ with 1 *df*, $p < .005$). Caries of deciduous teeth is also reported in one sample (Rouffignac). Caries location is not systematically reported. It does appear, however, that premolar and molar caries predominate, representing all cases at Strépy, Baumes-Chaudes, Dolmen des Bretons, and l'Homme-Mort. At Fontenay-le-Marmion involvement of M1 is reported as most frequent, while at Matelles premolars and molars are primarily affected.

Dental wear may be a major factor in caries development. Heavy wear impedes caries development by scouring the surface of microorganisms, thereby impeding the initial stages of the pathologic process. As a clear example, samples from Bøgebakken, with no reported caries, show considerable dental wear. Similarly, wear is reported as heavy in several Neolithic series. Full analysis of differences in caries frequency must await a study of the covariation of these two variables. Despite this, dental

TABLE 4.3. Reporting of Caries in Neolithic Samples

Site	Number of teeth	Number of caries (%)	Number of individuals	Number with caries (%)	
Belgium					
Hastières	86	2 (2.3)	~50	--	--
Strépy	7	2 (28.6)	1	1	(100)
France					
Baumes-Chaudes	--	2 --	--	--	--
Bec des Deux Eaux	163	7 (4.5)	~12	--	--
Dolmen de la Roche (Mand.)	47	1 (2.1)	22	--	(4.5)
Dolmen de la Roche (Max.)	--	0 --	22	0	(0)
Dolmen des Bretons	116	9 (7.8)	14	--	--
Eteauville (Mand.)	204	5 (2.4)	~90	1	(1.1)
Eteauville (Max.)	20	1 (5.0)	~90	1	(1.1)
Fontenay-le-Marmion[b]	--	-- (11.7)	64	--	--
L'Homme Mort	--	3 --	~17	--	--
Laris Goguet	728[a]	31 (4.3)	20[a]	6	(30)
Matelles[b]	--	-- (2.5)	~150	--	--
Rouffignac	152	4 (2.6)	--	--	--
Terrevaine II	--	5 --	25	--	--
Vigneau	18	1 (5.6)	~9	--	(5.5)
Portugal					
Bugelheira en Almonda	113	3 (2.6)	--	--	--
Carvalhal	--	7 --	--	--	--
	1654[c]	69[c] (4.2)[d]	ca. 198[c]	--	--

[a]Total teeth are reported as are numbers of individuals with caries. Numbers of individuals with teeth are not reported.

[b]Actual counts are not presented, although percentages are.

[c]Total where numbers are reported.

[d]Figure in cases where raw data are presented. When percentage figures only are averaged, the figure is 6.3%.

caries rates suggest marked dietary differences between the Mesolithic and Neolithic periods.

Other Mesolithic dental variables are suggestive of heavy stress. There is considerable alveolar degeneration, reported as alveolar abscessing, periapical infection, general alveolar bone loss, and antemortem loss of teeth. Though these are not systematically reported, they are present in high amounts where studied. Alveolar bone loss, bone infection, and periapical abscessing are noted in various combinations in eight individuals each from Höedic and Teviec in the best individual study of this region. Associated with this is the loss of 14 elements in 4 individuals from Teviec. In the Neolithic sample antemortem tooth loss is noted in nine cases, although without frequency data. Dental abscesses are noted in four sites, periapical infections in four cases. Related are reports from several sites of alveolar resorption or atrophy, and reference to "pyorrhea," "periodontitis," and "gingivitis." One basic anomaly often interpreted as a stress marker, enamel hypoplasia, is essentially unreported. It is noted only at the Mesolithic site of Melby and in individual I of the Neolithic site S22 at Swifterbant. It is unclear whether this represents effective absence of this marker in earlier European samples or systematic nonreporting.[2]

Trauma

Trauma may reflect both social conditions of a population and demographic stress. For the Mesolithic the available data are presented by Constandse-Westermann and Newell (1984). Of interest was the determination of whether clear cases of trauma reflecting conflict as opposed to accident would increase in frequency during the course of the Mesolithic. The logic behind this suggestion lies in the indication that later Mesolithic populations showed increasing density and complexity. It has been suggested that within such a continuum, aggression is positively correlated with density. For the Mesolithic, trauma was apportioned differently between male and female samples, suggestive of different patterns of labor. Trauma also increased in older individuals, with no reported trauma in individuals less than 15 years of age ($N = 9$) and with all individuals over 55 years of age showing trauma ($N = 3$). Finally, incidence of trauma was tested against chronological age of the specimens. The results were nonsignificant. Apart from five clear cases of interpersonal violence involving embedded projectiles (all male), Constandse-Westermann and Newell

[2] *Enamel hypoplasia is reported by Brothwell (1963) in a combined European and North African Mesolithic series (total $N = 42$). However, without further partitioning of the series into its component parts, the European frequencies cannot be computed.*

conclude that reported trauma in Mesolithic samples primarily represents accidental injury rather than group conflict.

Trauma appears to be less frequent in the Neolithic sample. Cases are relatively rare (seven sites, three with individual cases). Only two involve embedded projectiles (Caïres, Terrevaine II). It may tentatively be argued that a reduction in overall accidental trauma reflects a more sedentary existence. There is also no evidence for increase in interpersonal conflict.

Dimorphism

Dimorphism from the Upper Paleolithic to the Neolithic has been discussed most specifically by Frayer (1978, 1980, 1981). Using dental, cranial, and body size data he argues for a decrease in dimorphism for this period. He suggests that the decrease relates to progressive gracilization in the male sample, related to a decrease in robusticity required for Mesolithic as opposed to Upper Paleolithic hunting activity, and to increased sharing of economic chores as one proceeds towards the Neolithic (Frayer 1980). He further suggests a selection for reduced metabolic demands (Frayer 1981). Though Frayer (1981) rejects a nutritional model for the change, it must remain as an alternative model.

Dental dimensions from our Mesolithic sample, which differs from Frayer's sample, show the same decrease in dimorphism suggested by Frayer (1978) (Blachford 1982). Results for individual teeth do, however, differ slightly. Full results will be presented elsewhere. We have not yet analyzed our craniometric sample for congruity with Frayer's results. When we compare our stature data with those of Frayer (1981), we find the same overall trends but the scale is reduced. When dimorphism is considered separately from stature, the trend is less clear than indicated by Frayer. He indicates a change from 11.3% in the Upper Paleolithic to 7.1% in the Mesolithic (Table 4.4), a decrease of 37.2%. Our data indicate a change from only 8.7 to 7.8%, a decrease of only 10.3%. Furthermore, in our results there is a succeeding increase to a dimorphism of 8.6% in the Neolithic, back to the late Upper Paleolithic figures.

Stature

Analysis of stature rests on a stronger base than does analysis of dimorphism. A considerable data base on stature, however, is derived from several methodologies of varying accuracy and comparability.

An initial analysis of statural trends (Key 1980) suggested a model of stature decline from the Upper Paleolithic through the Mesolithic, followed by stature increase from the Neolithic onward. Somewhat similar results are suggested by Frayer (1980) in tabular format with small sample sizes.

TABLE 4.4. Stature Estimations

	Frayer		Current authors	
	$\overline{X}$	*N*	$\overline{X}$	*N*
Early Upper Paleolithic				
Male	174.2	10		
Female	161.3	5		
Late Upper Paleolithic				
Male	174.4	10	170.4	19
Female	156.7	4	156.7	10
Mesolithic				
Male	164.8	26	167.7	46
Female	153.9	15	155.6	36
Neolithic				
Male			167.3	102
Female			154.1	88
Resulting Dimorphism				
Early Upper Paleolithic	8.0%			
Late Upper Paleolithic	11.3%		8.7%	
Mesolithic	7.1%		7.8%	
Neolithic			8.6%	

We have expanded the results obtained by Key in order to have firmer figures. Whereas Key used raw limb lengths in his analysis, we have used stature estimations based on the method of Trotter and Gleser (1952). This permits us to compare all individuals for whom any long bone lengths are reported and to compare individuals with reported long bone lengths to individuals for whom only Trotter-Gleser statures are reported in the literature. (We restrict ourselves to samples for which either raw limb lengths or Trotter-Gleser estimates are reported.)

In order to account for variability in relative long bone lengths within individuals, we averaged the various stature estimations in those cases where we had several bones or bone combinations. We then used regression of individual statures against estimated absolute ages for each site, using linear and quadratic approaches. For linear regression our independent variable was stature; our dependent variable was age. For quadratic regression our independent variable was stature; our dependent variables, date and date^2 (Table 4.5).

The results at this stage are clearer for the linear regression than for the quadratic regression: the relation appears to be linear. The overall linear regression was significant at the $p = .05$ level for combined male-female, male, and female samples, indicating a significant decrease in average stature from the

TABLE 4.5. Statural Change[a]

Cultural period	*Sex*	*N*	$\overline{X}$ *Stature*	*Linear regression*	*Quadratic regression*
Upper Paleolithic-	*M-F*	*301*	*161.93*	$p > .0012$[b]	$p > .0049$[c]
Mesolithic-	*M*	*167*	*167.76*	$p > .0471$[b]	$p > .1352$
Neolithic	*F*	*134*	*154.69*	$p > .0096$[b]	$p > .0347$[c]
Upper Paleolithic-	*M*	*65*	*168.49*	$p > .1331$	$p > .3190$
Mesolithic	*F*	*46*	*155.80*	$p > .1131$	$p > .2591$
Mesolithic-	*M-F*	*272*	*161.54*	$p > .0500$[b]	$p > .1296$
Neolithic	*M*	*148*	*167.41*	$p > .9271$	$p > .9629$
	F	*124*	*154.42*	$p > .0377$[b]	$p > .1136$
Upper Paleolithic	*M*	*19*	*170.43*	$p > .9145$	$p > .8148$
	F	*10*	*156.73*	$p > .0189$[b]	$p > .0058$[b]
Mesolithic	*M*	*46*	*167.68*	$p > .8263$	$p > .8736$
	F	*36*	*155.55*	$p > .2102$	$p > .3897$
Neolithic	*M*	*102*	*167.29*	$p > .6391$	$p > .0636$[d]
	F	*88*	*154.11*	$p > .3167$	$p > .5701$

[a]*Due to space limitations we have presented only tests of significance. Full regression tables will be published with our expanded analysis.*

[b]*Significant.*

[c]*The quadratic regression equation is significant but the quadratic term (i.e., $[date]^2$) is not.*

[d]*The quadratic term is significant (i.e., $[date]^2$, $p > .0218$).*

Upper Paleolithic through the Neolithic. The trend appears to be more strongly manifest in the female sample than in the male sample. However, none of the subsamples show a significant decrease from the Upper Paleolithic to the Mesolithic. There is a significant decrease from the Mesolithic to the Neolithic in the overall and female samples. The female subsample is defining the trend. Within individual time periods the only significant result is the decrease in female stature during the Upper Paleolithic.

For the Neolithic we suspect a manifest curvilinear pattern, a trend toward decreasing stature from the Upper Paleolithic to the Neolithic being replaced by increasing stature within the Neolithic. This can be tested only by adding to our sample for Neolithic and post-Neolithic time periods. At this point we conclude that there is significant stature decline from the Upper Paleolithic through the Neolithic, with possible reversal from that point onwards, in agreement with Frayer (1980) and Key (1980).

TABLE 4.6. Analysis of Variance for the Region Effect--Inland-Coastal Dichotomy

Sex	*Region*	*N*	*ANOVA[a] for region effect*	*Mean*
Male-Female	*Coastal-inland*	*111*	*p > .1167*	*163.23*
	Coastal	*84*		*162.55*
	Inland	*27*		*165.36*
Male	*Coastal-inland*	*65*	*p > .3549*	*168.48*
	Coastal	*48*		*168.11*
	Inland	*17*		*169.55*
Female	*Coastal-inland*	*46*	*p > .0603*	*155.81*
	Coastal	*36*		*155.13*
	Inland	*10*		*158.24*

[a]*ANOVA, analysis of variance.*

At this time, we cannot identify the point at which the change in direction of the trend occurs.

We also examined our Mesolithic sample for a coastal-inland dichotomy, based on suggestions made that there might be statural stunting in samples with high usage of marine resources due to trace element imbalance (Table 4.6). Though the results were not significant, all inland samples were taller for age than coastal samples in all groups. Further analysis is required in which percentage of marine resources is included as a variable.

CONCLUSION

This survey attempts to provide a base for further examination of trends in paleopathology in western and west-central Europe during the Mesolithic and the Neolithic. The data base for the Mesolithic is fully inclusive, the problem of sample provenience being the subject of intensive study. For the Neolithic the sample base is, at best, representative, derived from a published sample emphasizing recent work and larger sample sizes.

In general terms, the number of obvious trends from the Mesolithic to the Neolithic is low. For most characters there are no clear differences between the two broad groups. In addition, where there are potential trends, there may be several possible interpretations.

For cranial and postcranial pathology much that is reported is idiosyncratic, of low frequency, and without clear interpretive mode for the site and/or period in question. In most cases the nature of the data does not permit recognition of trends over time. With reference to population pressure and concomitant evidence of stress, the incidence of both cribra orbitalia and porotic hyperostosis is very low in both agricultural and preagricultural samples. Differences in arthritis patterns probably reflect differences in the economic base rather than indicate stressors responsible for the change.

Significant difference is noted in caries frequency between the Mesolithic and the Neolithic, not a new finding in itself. This is, in all probability, correlated with both dental wear and condition of the alveolar processes. However, our data base on the latter two areas is insufficient to define the nature of the correlation. In all three cases we may be looking at either items resulting from economic change or items correlated with the cause of the change. Tauber (1981) indicates a major dietary shift at the Mesolithic-Neolithic boundary using ^{13}C content.

In similar fashion, the data on group trauma are insufficient to distinguish directly between trauma related to economic activity and trauma resulting from violence in a population subject to density stress. Though we might predict increased violence from density data, we are unable to confirm it.

Our most suggestive evidence relates to statural change. Stature decreases from the Upper Paleolithic through the Mesolithic. Increase is suggested once the Neolithic is underway. One mode of interpretation would view the decline as related to increasing stress, alleviated by the introduction of food producing. However, this view is complicated by the evidence of different trends in males and females. Thus we have models based either on dietary stress or, per Frayer, on alterations in activity pattern.

The limits of our data sample notwithstanding, the results reported here do appear to confirm previously reported patterns of skeletal pathology for the region (Dastugue 1979; Dastugue and de Lumley 1976a,b) and to confirm the results of more specialized studies such as those of teeth by Brabant (1965, 1968, 1969).

Thus we feel that the data presented in this chapter are reflective of the current work in Europe as displayed in the literature. We caution against the use of these data either to support or to deny particular models of cause and effect of the socioeconomic changes from the late Upper Paleolithic to the Neolithic. Though we are confident of our coverage of the Mesolithic, sample size is a limitation at present. For the Neolithic it is clear that samples exist that can provide critical evidence for the questions asked in this volume. However, few are published in a manner permitting answers to demographic, as opposed to clinical, questions.

APPENDIX . Neolithic Materials in the Study

Country/Site	Number of individuals	References
Netherlands		
Molenaarsgraaf	3	Knip (1974)
Swifterbant S21	10	Meiklejohn and Constandse-Westermann (1978); Constandse-Westermann and Meiklejohn (1979)
Swifterbant S22	7	Meiklejohn and Constandse-Westermann (1978); Constandse-Westermann and Meiklejohn (1979)
Swifterbant S23	1	Meiklejohn and Constandse-Westermann (1978); Constandse-Westermann and Meiklejohn (1979)
Swifterbant S11	2+	Meiklejohn and Constandse-Westermann (1978); Constandse-Westermann and Meiklejohn (1979)
Swifterbant S2	9+	Meiklejohn and Constandse-Westermann (1978); Constandse-Westermann and Meiklejohn (1979)
Belgium		
Avennes	3	Janssens (1960); Verdin (1959)
Hastière	19	Riquet (1963a)
Obourg et Strépy	2	Riquet (1963b)
Porte-Aïve	∿25	Riquet (1963b)
Spiennes	6	Riquet (1963b)
France		
Abri Pendimoun	1	de Lumley (1962)
Argenleuil	9(?)	Larroque and Riquet (1966)
Barbonne-Fayol	2	Larroque and Riquet (1966)
Baumes-Chaudes	23	Toureille (1962)
Bec-des-Deux-Eaux	12+	Riquet and Cordier (1957)
Caïres	3	Charles (1959)
Conflans-Sainte-Honorine	3	Larroque and Riquet (1966)
Dolmen de la Roche	22+	Riquet and Cordier (1958)
Dolmen des Bretons	14+	Fusté (1952)
Dolmen de Villaine	12	Riquet (1972a)
L'Elang-la-Ville	∿150	Larroque and Riquet (1966)
Eteauville	90	Nouel et al. (1965)
Feigneux	18	Larroque and Riquet (1966); Patte (1976)

Appendix (Continued)

Country/Site	Number of individuals	References
France continued		
Fontenay-le-Marmion	*66+*	*Dastugue et al. (1973); Torre and Dastugue (1976); Brabant and Lecacheux (1973)*
Grotte de la Route	*9+*	*Arnal and Riquet (1956)*
L'Homme-Mort	*17*	*Toureille (1962)*
Laris Goguet	*55+*	*Patte (1971)*
Marly-le-Roi	*3*	*Larroque and Riquet (1966)*
Matelles	*150+*	*Brabant et al. (1961)*
Meudon	*∿200*	*Larroque and Riquet (1966)*
Nogent-les-Vierges	*2*	*Larroque and Riquet (1966)*
Pas-Estret	*9*	*Ampoulange (1953)*
Rouffignac	*15+*	*Sahly et al. (1962)*
Rouvignoux	*22(?)*	*Charles (1970)*
Tancoigné	*1*	*Patte (1953)*
Terrevaine (2 sites)	*29*	*Charles (1952)*
Vauréal	*∿40*	*Larroque and Riquet (1966)*
Vernou	*1*	*Riquet and Cordier (1953)*
Vichel-Manleuil	*10*	*Larroque and Riquet (1966)*
Vigneau	*9+*	*Riquet and Cordier (1958)*
Portugal		
Bugalheira en Almonda	*7+*	*Riquet (1972b)*
Carvalhal de Aljubarrota	*18+*	*Riquet (1972b)*
Casa de Moura	*3*	*Riquet (1972b)*
Casal Pardo	*3*	*Riquet (1972b)*
Cascais (Poço Velho)	*10*	*Riquet (1972b)*
Fontainhas	*5*	*Riquet (1972b)*
Logares	*1(?)*	*Riquet (1972b)*
Monte Pedroço Vimioso	*2*	*Riquet (1972b)*
Zambujal	*9(?)*	*Riquet (1972b)*

BIBLIOGRAPHY

Ampoulange, A.
1953 Sépulture néolithique dans un gisement du paléolithique supérieur. *Bulletin de la Société Préhistorique Française* *50*:613-624.

Arnal, J., and R. Riquet
1956 La Grotte de la Route, Saint-Martin-de-Londres (l'Herault). *Bulletin de la Société Préhistorique Française* *53*:64-79.

Brabant, H., and B. Lecacheux
1973 Etude de la denture des restes humaines d'âge Néolithique trouvés dans le tumulus de la Hoguette à Fontenay-le-Marmion (Normandie). *Bulletin du Groupement International pour la Recherche Scientifique en Stomatologie* *16*:131-162.

Appendix (Continued)

Brabant, H., A. Sahly, and M. Bouyssou
1961 Etude des dents préhistoriques de la station archéologique des Matelles (département de l'Herault, France). *Bulletin du Groupement International pour la Recherche Scientifique en Stomatologie 4*:382-448.
Charles, R. P.
1952 Les Sépultures préhistoriques de Terrevaine près de la Ciotat (B. du Rh.). *Cahiers Ligures 1*:29-61.
1959 Observations sur les restes humaines du Dolmen des Caïres, commune de Laissac (Aveyron). *Bulletin de la Société Préhistorique Française 56*:118-120.
1970 Les Sujets néolithiques de la grotte I du Ravin de Rouvignoux. *Cahiers Ligures 19*:119-148.
Constandse-Westermann, T. S., and C. Meiklejohn
1979 The human remains from Swifterbant. *Helinium 19*:237-266.
Dastugue, J., S. Torre, and L. Buchet
1973 Neolithiques de Basse-Normandie. Le deuxième tumulus de Fontenay-le-Marmion (étude anthropologique). *L'Anthropologie 77*:579-619.
de Lumley, M. A.
1962 Lésions osseuses de l'homme de Castellar (A.M.). *Bulletin du Musée d'Anthropologie Préhistorique de Monaco 9*:191-205.
Fusté, M.
1952 Les ossements humaines du dolmen des Bretons, Marne. *Bulletins et Mémoires de la Société d'Anthropologie de Paris Ser. 10 3*:118-155.
Janssens, P.
1960 Le squelette Néolithique d'Avennes: Sa perforation sternale. *Bulletin de la Société Royale Belge d'Anthropologie et de Préhistoire 71*:43-46.
Knip, A. S.
1974 Late Neolithic skeleton finds from Molenaarsgraaf (Z.H.). *Analecta Praehistorica Leidensia 7*:379-395.
Larroque, J. M., and R. Riquet
1966 Documents anthropologiques inédits sur la civilization de la Seine-Oise-Marne. *Bulletins et Mémoires de la Société d'Anthropologie de Paris Ser 11 9*:29-43.
Meiklejohn, C., and T. S. Constandse-Westermann
1978 The human skeletal remains from Swifterbant, Earlier Neolithic of the Northern Netherlands. I. *Palaeohistoria 20*:39-89.
Nouel, A., M. Dauvois, G. Bailloud, R. Riquet, T. Poulain-Josien, N. Planchais, and P. Horemans
1965 L'ossuaire néolithique d'Eteauville, Commune de Lutz-en-Dunois (Eure-et-Loir). *Bulletin de la Société Prehistorique Française 62*:576-648.

Appendix (Continued)

Patte, E.
1953 Sépulture néolithique de Tancoigné (Maine-et-Loire). *Gallia 11*:273-282.
1971 Les restes humaines de la grotte Sépulcrale du Laris Goguet à Feigneux (Oise). *Bulletins et Mémoires de la Société d'Anthropologie de Paris Ser 12 7*:381-452.
1976 Os pathologique ou anormaux de la grotte de Feigneux (Oise). *L'Anthropologie 80*:655-668.
Riquet, R.
1963a Les Néolithiques d'Hastière. *Bulletin de la Société Royale Belge d'Anthropologie et de Préhistoire 73*:57-116.
1963b Quelques crânes Néolithiques Belges. *Bulletin de la Société Royale Belge d'Anthropologie et de Préhistoire 73*:117-137.
1972a Le site archéologique du Dolmen de Villaine à Sublaines (Indre-et-Loire). *Gallia Préhistoire 15*:93-110.
1972b Anthropologie de quelques Néolithiques Portugais. *Homo 23*:154-187.
Riquet, R., and G. Cordier
1953 Une Sépulture Néolithique à Vernou (Indre-et-Loire). *Bulletin de la Société Préhistorique Française 50*:518-527.
1957 L'ossuaire Néolithique du Bec-des-Deux-Eaux, Commune de Ports (Indre-et-Loire). *L'Anthropologie 61*:28-44.
1958 L'ossuaire du Vigneau et le Dolmen de la Roche, commune de Manthelan (Indre-et-Loire). *L'Anthropologie 62*:1-29.
Sahly, A., H. Brabant, and M. Bouyssou
1962 Observations sur les dents et les maxillaires du Mésolithique et de l'âge du fer, trouvés dans la grotte de Rouffignac, département de la Dordogne, France. *Bulletin du Groupement International pour la Recherche Scientifique en Stomatologie 5*:252-285.
Torre, S., and J. Dastugue
1976 Néolithiques de Basse-Normandie. Le deuxième tumulus de Fontenay-le-Marmion (Pathologie). *L'Anthropologie 80*:625-653.
Toureille, M.
1962 Les squelettes préhistoriques des Baumes-Chaudes et de l'Homme-Mort. *L'Anthropologie 66*:44-68.
Verdin, G.
1959 Le néolithique de la Vallée de la Méhaigne (Hesbaye Liègoise). Etude Morphologique et anthropologique des ossements préhistoriques d'Avennes. *Bulletin de la Société Royale Belge d'Anthropologie et de Préhistoire 70*:46-54.

ACKNOWLEDGMENTS

The authors acknowledge the numerous colleagues who have graciously permitted collection of Mesolithic data within their control. Funds for various stages of data collection and preparation have been received by the senior author from the Canada Council, Social Science and Humanities Research Council of Canada, and the University of Winnipeg.

The senior author thanks Dr. T. S. Constandse-Westermann, University of Utrecht, and Dr. Raymond R. Newell, University of Groningen, for assistance in the original collection of the Mesolithic data base and in analysis of its provenience. The Mesolithic data base used is the result of cooperative work between 1976 and 1981.

REFERENCES

Ammerman, A. L., and L. L. Cavalli-Sforza
1973 A population model for the diffusion of early farming in Europe. In *The explanation of culture change: Models in prehistory*, edited by C. Renfrew, pp. 343-357. Duckworth, London.

Binford, L. R.
1973 Interassemblage variability--the Mousterian and the "functional" argument. In *The explanation of culture change: Models in prehistory*, edited by C. Renfrew, pp. 227-254. Duckworth, London.

Blachford, L.
1982 Dental trends in Palaeolithic and Mesolithic Europe. Unpublished ms. on file, University of Winnipeg.

Bouville, C., T. S. Constandse-Westermann, and R. R. Newell
1983 Les restes humains Mésolithiques de l'Abri Cornille, Istres (B. de R.). *Bulletins et Mémoires de la Société d'Anthropologie de Paris* Ser. 13, Vol. 10, pp. 89-110.

Brabant, H.
1965 Observations sur l'évolution de la denture temporaire humaine en Europe occidentale. *Bulletin du Groupement International de la Récherche Scientifique en Stomatologie 8*:235-302.
1968 La denture humaine à l'époque Néolithique. *Bulletin de la Société Royale Belge d'Anthropologie et de Préhistoire 79*:105-141.
1969 Observations sur les dents des populations megalithiques d'Europe occidentale. *Bulletin du Groupement International de la Récherche Scientifique en Stomatologie 12*:429-460.

Brothwell, D. R.
1963 The macroscopic dental pathology of some earlier human populations. In *Dental anthropology*, edited by D. R. Brothwell, pp. 271-288. Macmillan, New York.

Burch, E. S., Jr.
1972 The caribou/wild reindeer as a human resource. *American Antiquity 37*:339-368.

Campbell, J. B., Jr.
1977 *The Upper Palaeolithic of Britain: A study of man and nature in the late ice age.* Oxford University Press (Clarendon), London and New York.

Carneiro, R. L., and D. F. Hilse
1966 On determining the probable rate of population growth during the Neolithic. *American Anthropologist 68*:177-181.

Constandse-Westermann, T. S., and C. Meiklejohn
1979 The human remains from Swifterbant. *Helinium 19*:237-266.

Constandse-Westermann, T. S., and R. R. Newell
1984 Mesolithic trauma: Demographical and chronological trends in Western Europe. *Proceedings of the 4th European Palaeopathology Conference*, Middelburg/Antwerpen, 1982, in press.

Constandse-Westermann, T. S., C. Meiklejohn, and R. R. Newell
1984 A reconsideration of the Mesolithic skeleton from Rastel, Commune de Peillon, Alpes - Maritimes, France. *Bulletin du Musée d'Anthropologie Préhistorique du Monaco 26*:75-89.

Dastugue, J.
1979 Pathologie des Mésolithiques de France. *L'Anthropologie 83*:602-625.

Dastugue, J., and M. A. de Lumley
1976a Les maladies des hommes préhistoriques du Paléolithique et du Mésolithique. In *La préhistoire française* (Vol. I), edited by H. de Lumley, pp. 612-622. Centre Nationale Recherche Scientifique, Paris.
1976b Les maladies des hommes préhistoriques. In *La préhistoire française* (Vol. II), edited by J. Guilane, pp. 153-164. Centre Nationale Recherche Scientifique, Paris.

de Lumley, H. (editor)
1976 *La préhistoire française* (Vol. I). Centre Nationale Recherche Scientifique, Paris.

Frayer, D. W.
1978 The evolution of the dentition in Upper Paleolithic and Mesolithic Europe. *University of Kansas Publications in Anthropology* No. 10.
1980 Sexual dimorphism and cultural evolution in the Late Pleistocene and Holocene of Europe. *Journal of Human Evolution 9*:399-415.
1981 Body size, weapon use and natural selection in the European Upper Paleolithic and Mesolithic. *American Anthropologist 83*:57-73.

Gramsch, B. (editor)
1981 Mesolithikum in Europa. *Veröffentlichungen des Museums für Ur-und Frühgeschichte Potsdam* No. 14-15.
Guilane, J.
1979 The earliest Neolithic in the West Mediterranean: A new appraisal. *Antiquity 53*:22-30.
Hengen, O. P.
1971 Cribra orbitalia: Pathogenesis and probable etiology. *Homo 22*:57-76.
Key, P.
1980 Evolutionary trends in femoral sexual dimorphism from the Mesolithic to the late Middle Ages in Europe. *American Journal of Physical Anthropology 52*:244.
Kozlowski, S. K. (editor)
1973 *The Mesolithic in Europe*. Warsaw University Press, Warsaw.
Larsson, L.
1980 Stenalders jägarnas boplats och gravar vid Skateholm. *Limhamniana 1980*:13-39.
1981 En 7,000 - årig Sydkustboplats. Nytt om gammalt Från Skateholm. *Limhamniana 1981*:17-46.
1982 Skateholmsprojektet. Nys gravar och ett nytt gravfält Från Jägarstenåldern. *Limhamniana 1982*:11-41.
Larsson, L., C. Meiklejohn, and R. R. Newell
1981 Human skeletal material from the Mesolithic site of Ageröd I: HC, Scania, Southern Sweden. *Fornvännen 76*: 161-168.
Laville, H., J. P. Rigaud, and J. Sackett
1980 *Rock shelters of the Perigord*. Academic Press, New York.
Lewthwaite, J.
1981 Ambiguous first impressions: A survey of recent work on the early Neolithic of the West Mediterranean. *Journal of Mediterranean Archaeology and Anthropology 1*:292-307.
Meiklejohn, C.
1977 Genetic differentiation and deme structure: Considerations for an understanding of the Athapaskan/Algonkian continuum. In *Problems in the prehistory of the North American Subarctic: The Athapaskan question*, edited by J. Helmer, F. J. Kense, and J. Van Dyke, pp. 106-110. University of Calgary, Calgary.
1978 Ecological aspects of population size and growth in Late Glacial and Early Postglacial Northwestern Europe. In *The Early Postglacial settlement of Northern Europe*, edited by P. Mellars, pp. 65-79. Duckworth, London.
Meiklejohn, C., and T. S. Constandse-Westermann
1978 The human skeletal material from Swifterbant, Earlier Neolithic of the Northern Netherlands. I. Inventory and demography. *Palaeohistoria 20*:39-89.
Mellars, P. (editor)
1978 *The Early Postglacial settlement of Northern Europe*. Duckworth, London.

Milisauskas, S.
1978 *European prehistory.* Academic Press, New York.
Newell, R. R.
1973 The postglacial adaptations of the indigenous population of the Northwest European plain. In *The Mesolithic in Europe*, edited by S. K. Kozlowski, pp. 399-440. Warsaw University Press, Warsaw.
Newell, R. R., and S. H. Anderson
1982 The distribution of Mesolithic bone tools. Unpublished M.S. on file, State University of Groningen, Groningen, the Netherlands.
Newell, R. R., T. S. Constandse-Westermann, and C. Meiklejohn
1979 The skeletal remains of Mesolithic man in Western Europe: An evaluative catalogue. *Journal of Human Evolution 8*: 1-228.
Newell, R. R., A. L. van Gijn, D. Kielman, and W. van der Sanden
1982 An enquiry into the ethnic resolution of Mesolithic regional groups: A study of their decorative ornaments in space and time. Unpublished M.S. on file, State University of Groningen, Groningen, the Netherlands.
Rozoy, J. G.
1978 *Les derniers chasseurs: L'Epipaléolithique en France et en Belgique.* Société Archéologique Champenoise, Charleville-Mezières.
Schentag, C.
1982 The bias inherent in the reporting of pathology on skeletal remains: A statistical analysis. Unpublished M.S. on file, University of Winnipeg.
Slobodkin, L. B., and H. L. Sanders
1968 On the contribution of environmental predictability to species diversity. *Brookhaven Symposia in Biology 22*: 82-95.
Spiess, A.
1979 *Reindeer and caribou hunters: An archaeological study.* Academic Press, New York.
Tauber, H.
1981 ^{13}C evidence for dietary habits of prehistoric man in Denmark. *Nature (London) 292*:332-333.
Trotter, M., and G. C. Gleser
1952 Estimation of stature from long bones of American whites and Negroes. *American Journal of Physical Anthropology 10*:463-514.
Wobst, H. M.
1976 Locational relationships in Paleolithic society. *Journal of Human Evolution 5*:49-58.

CHAPTER 5

ARCHAEOLOGICAL AND SKELETAL EVIDENCE FOR DIETARY CHANGE DURING THE LATE PLEISTOCENE/EARLY HOLOCENE IN THE LEVANT

Patricia Smith

Department of Anatomy
Hebrew University-Hadassah School of Dental Medicine

Ofer Bar-Yosef

Institute of Archaeology
Hebrew University, Mt. Scopus Campus

Andrew Sillen

National Museum of Natural History
Smithsonian Institution

INTRODUCTION

In the Levant the period between the Upper Paleolithic and Neolithic, dating from approximately 17,000 B.C., is generally referred to as the "Epipaleolithic."[1] Several overviews of the Epipaleolithic and Neolithic sequence in the Levant have been published in recent years (Bar-Yosef 1980, 1981a,b, 1978; Cauvin 1978; Redman 1978). These reviews necessarily have emphasized a geographical approach to archaeological questions, since the region encompassed by the term "Levant" is so ecologically diverse (Fig. 5.1). For example, in this small area of the Eastern Mediterranean, one can define at least three topographic belts (the coastal plain, the eastern mountains and central highlands, and the rift valley) as well as three major vegeta-

[1]*The term "Mesolithic" was abandoned for the Near East 15 years ago; most archaeologists prefer to limit its use to northwestern Europe during the early Holocene (Kozlowski 1973).*

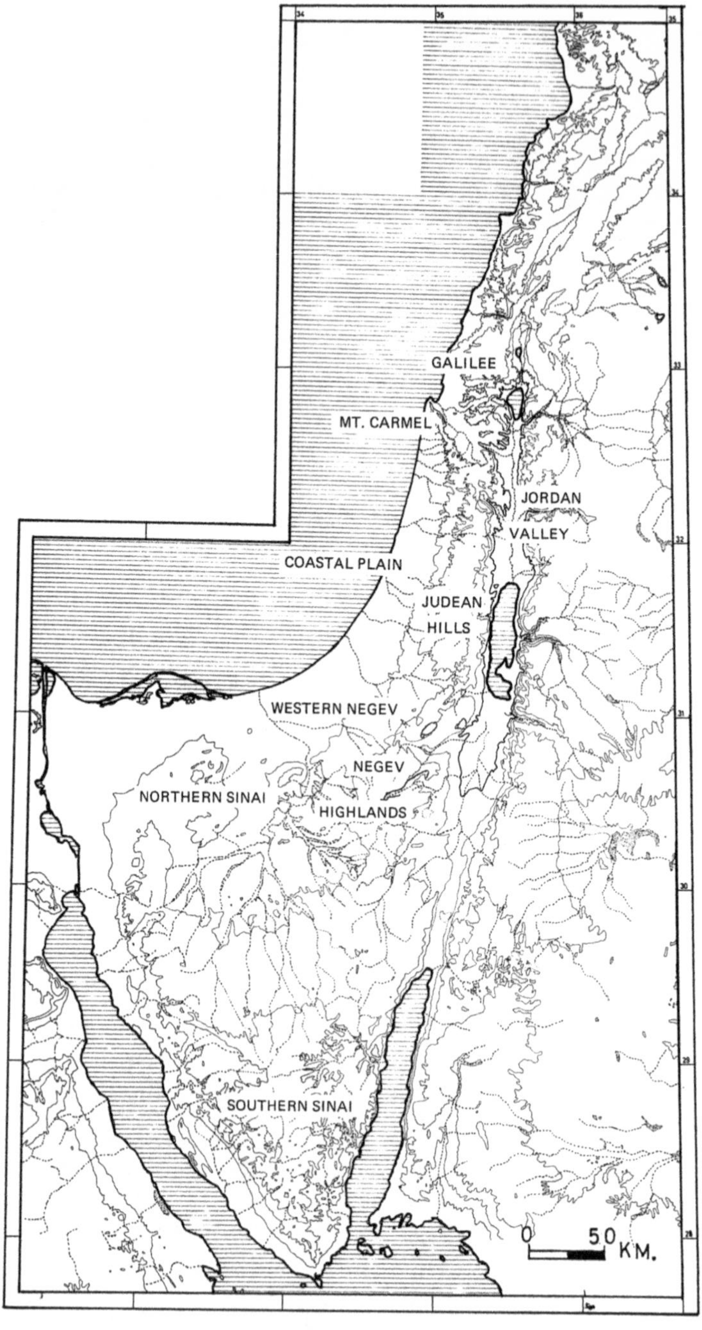

FIGURE 5.1. Map of Southern Levant indicating major geographic subdivisions.

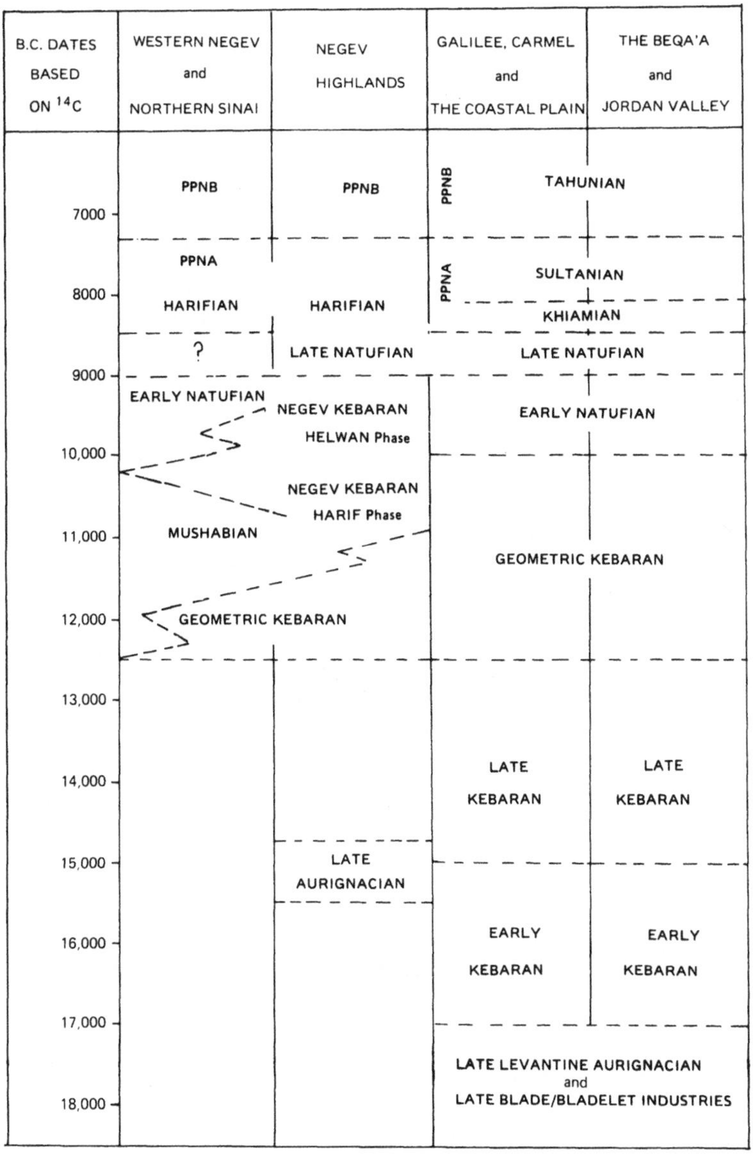

FIGURE 5.2. Archaeological sequence in major geographical regions of the southern Levant (taken from Bar-Yosef 1980).

tional regions (the Mediterranean Forest belt, Irano-Turanian steppe, and Saharo-Sindian desert).

Regional studies of small areas within the Levant nevertheless have been successful, and as ^{14}C dates have become available, the sequence for each subzone has been compared to that of its neighbors (see Bar-Yosef 1981a,b for appendices of ^{14}C dates). This regional approach has enabled us to build archaeological sequences (Figure 5.2) and to formulate hypotheses concerning seasonal exploitation strategies, long-range diffusions, patterns of exchange, etc.

In this chapter, we will summarize the archaeological and skeletal evidence for diet and dietary change over the course of the Epipaleolithic and Neolithic in the region. It should be recognized at the outset that the available data are of unequal quantity and quality. For example, the paleobotanical finds are scarce and sometimes of doubtful nature, while the faunal collections are relatively abundant but in many cases have been studied only partially (i.e., mammals alone). Even the archaeological remains per se (structural relicts, stone tools, etc.) have not always been adequately published.

Fortunately, the last decade has seen a considerable increase in archaeological and biological information. For one thing, the number of archaeological sites available for study is on the increase. Also, the data are complementary in nature, being derived from disparate sources. For example, it is difficult to determine the proportionate amount of meat versus vegetable foods by reference to the archaeological sequence alone. However, the archaeological record does provide a good indication of the specific foods likely to have been utilized. The skeletal evidence complements this information by providing quantitative evidence for classes of foods exploited (e.g., strontium analyses) and nutrition (e.g., dental, paleopathological data). An interdisciplinary approach should then provide a reasonably complete picture of social, technological, and dietary change. We offer this chapter as an interim report in this ongoing cooperative effort.

ARCHAEOLOGICAL EVIDENCE FOR DIETARY CHANGE

Direct archaeological evidence for dietary change can be derived from three sources: (1) shifts in the vegetal diet as exhibited in the plant and seed remains; (2) shifts in the faunal spectra as compiled from bone collections of hunted and/or domesticated animals; and (3) changes in tools used for food collection, storage, preparation, etc. Population density can also be addressed by reference to the number and size of archaeological sites. The available information on each of these points for the Levant is outlined below.

Site Size as an Expression for Population Increase/Decrease

Site size during the Kebaran and Geometric Kebaran (circa 17,000-10,500 B.C.) ranged from 25 to 400 m^2 (and is similar to that of the preceding Upper Paleolithic period). It shifted into larger units (up to 3000 m^2 as a cautious estimate) in the Natufian (10,500-8500 B.C.) with evidence for architectural remains (rounded structures, terrace walls, etc.). A considerable increase took place in the Pre-Pottery Neolithic A period, when the largest sites were 2-4 ha. in area (Netiv Hagdud, Gilgal I, Jericho). The maximal size maintained itself during the "Pre-Pottery Neolithic B" period (until 6000 B.C.) but dropped later in the southern Levant. In the northern Levant (northern Syria and southern Anatolia), the size increase that took place in the seventh millennium B.C. (up to 12 ha.) maintained its steady growth.

Population estimates derived from site size were recently given detailed attention (Hassan 1981). However, in view of the fragmentary data, we prefer even more cautious estimates. They are as follows: (1) Kebaran and Geometric Kebaran: 5-15 persons/site (or perhaps one to three nuclear families); (2) an increase to 30-50 persons/site during the Natufian; and (3) another increase (ca. 8500-8000 B.C.) to 300-2000 persons/site (Bar-Yosef 1981a; Hassan 1981).

Functional Aspects of the Lithic Industries

The main technological changes over the course of time were in the production of blanks. While the earlier complexes were characterized by bladelet manufacture (for shaping microliths), a small increase in blades is noted in the Natufian and a higher one in the Khiamian (when microlithic tools decreased to about 25% of the total assemblage). Around 8000 B.C. blade production is dominant (along with the appearance of numerous axes-adzes, flake tools, etc.). Blades were shaped into arrowheads, sickle blades, saw blades, etc. Sickle blades are designated by the clear luster on one or two edges and they became a constant component of each assemblage (up to 7% of the total "tools") from the Natufian onwards (until the Iron Age, i.e., 600 B.C.). Experimental work as well as microwear analysis has indicated that the contention of Garrod and Neuville was probably correct and the specific sheen resulted from cutting cereals (Anderson 1980). Therefore, one may still infer from these data that the intensive use of cereals as a staple food was commenced by the Natufians even though there are clear indications that this resource was utilized earlier.

Grinding stones occur archaeologically at least since the early millennia of the Upper Paleolithic in the Levant. Pounding stones are known already from Kebaran and Geometric Kebaran sites (Figure 5.2). Their purpose is unclear; they could have been used for processing acorns and wild cereal grains (probably after roasting), as well as for pounding ochre. The possibility of pounding cereals seems to fit the model that interprets these scarce mortars and pestles as preadaptation preceding the Natufian. Indeed, the Natufian base camps provide large collections of pounding tools and sickle blades as mentioned earlier in this section (see Bar-Yosef 1981a).

A discernible shift occurred with the Pre-Pottery Neolithic A when the number of cup holes and grinding tools (querns and hand-stones) increased considerably. This phenomenon correlates well with the clear evidence for domesticated wheat and barley (Cauvin 1978; Hopf 1969). From circa 7500 B.C. the grinding stones became almost the sole type of processing device and this was maintained through the following millennia in the Levant. The diffusion of grinding stones into the desertic region took place during the seventh millennium or slightly earlier (by a few centuries). If this observation is correct, there is a short lapse of time (several hundred years) before the groups who exploited the semiarid zones adopt the new tools. It is not yet possible to determine whether they grew the cereals or obtained them from the farmers of the Mediterranean zone. The paleoclimatic evidence points to a wetter period (the seventh millennium B.C.), and the possibility of cultivating barley during a seasonal migratory pattern (like that of Bedouin groups) should not be ruled out.

The Botanical Remains

The scarcity of paleobotanical remains is partly, but not solely, due to the use of inappropriate recovery techniques in the past. The main reasons for the disappearance of plant remains are the physical nature of the deposits and the seasonal climatic variations typical of the Mediterranean zone. The annual wetting and drying of the clayey *terra rossa* soils and of the loamy clay *hamra* soils (in the coastal plain) destroyed most of the organic substances in the sites under discussion. Moreover, the summer cracking of these soils enabled minute specimens to penetrate earlier layers. As a result, even the availability of charcoal samples for dating is limited. Fortunately, the fairly good preservation of bones compensates for this. The situation in the semiarid regions is the reverse; charcoal is well preserved but the bones have mostly decayed. The better preservation of plant remains occurred in siltic deposits on the margin of the deserts as in Jericho and Salibiya IX (in the Lower Jordan Valley).

The scant available grains from the southern Levant (including those analyzed in unpublished data) indicate that Emmer wheat, and possibly a form of domesticated barley can be found from the Pre-Pottery Neolithic A (8300-7500 B.C.) onwards (Hopf 1969). Except for a rare occurrence of *Triticum dicoccum* in Kebaran layers at Nahal Oren (Noy et al. 1973), isolated grains indicate the use of wild cereals until the beginning of the Pre-Pottery Neolithic A and even later.

Cultivation of wheat and wild barley was recently confirmed for early eight millennium sites in the Damascus Basin (Van Zeist and Bakker-Heeres 1979). Similar situations are known already from Jericho, Tell Mureybit, and Abu Hureira in the Euphrates valley and the later site of Beidha (Helbaek 1966; Hopf 1969; Moore 1978; Van Zeist 1970).

Collection of wild fruits and nuts (almonds, pistachio) continued in the following millennia. The gathering of wild pulses slowly gave way during the eighth millennium to their systematic cultivation (Van Zeist and Bakker-Heeres 1979; Zohary and Hopf 1973). One may therefore conclude that the exploitation of wild cereals, pulses, fruits, and nuts shifted in the same order into systematic cultivation, which led through its ongoing annual procedures to the domestication of various species. Farming of grains and seeds preceded the gardening of fruit trees by about three millennia.

This fragmentary evidence is not really amenable to the testing of any hypotheses concerning the relative proportions of vegetable and meat foodstuffs during the periods under discussion within each of the various archaeological entities. For this reason we have undertaken a comprehensive program of strontium analyses of faunal and human bones, discussed below.

Shifts in the Faunal Spectra

Keeping in mind the preliminary nature of some of the reports, we have summarized the faunal data published by various investigators in Figure 5.3. The histograms represent the frequencies of bone counts (and not the minimum number of individuals). The overall pattern exhibits a clear shift from available game to dominance of caprovines during the Pre-Pottery Neolithic B (ca. 7500-6000 B.C.). (The presence of ibex in sites such as Rosh Horesha and Abu Salem in the Negev Highlands illustrates the local environment and not an early domestication. The scarcity of Capra in the earlier period should be noted.)

From comparison of the changes in the faunal spectra with the shifts in vegetal resources, one may conclude that animal domestication followed cereal cultivation by several centuries.

Site Locations, Site Contents, and Patterns of Exploitation

Figure 5.4 is a tentative reconstruction of the major economic activities and interregional pattern of annual movement or mere expeditional exploitation, supplemented with rough estimates of site size (Bar-Yosef, in preparation). The prime area in which the transition to cultivation and herding domesticated animals originally took place is the "Pistachio-Quercetum zone"

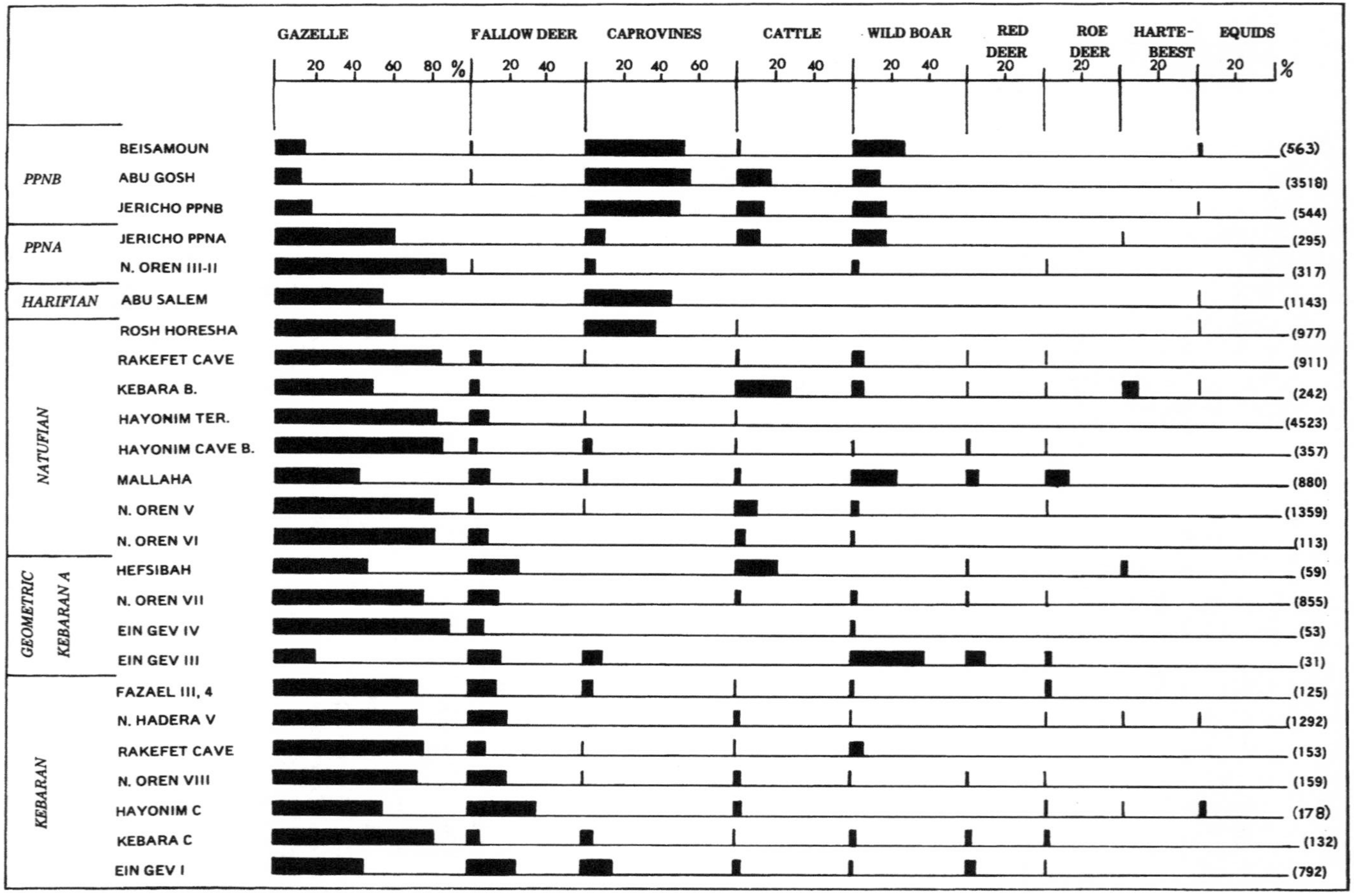

GAZELLE
FALLOW DEER
CAPROVINES
CATTLE
WILD BOAR
RED DEER
ROE DEER
HARTE-BEEST
EQUIDS
20 40 60 80 %
%
PPNB
PPNA
HARIFIAN
NATUFIAN
GEOMETRIC KEBARAN A
KEBARAN
BEISAMOUN (563)
ABU GOSH (3518)
JERICHO PPNB (544)
JERICHO PPNA (295)
N. OREN III-II (317)
ABU SALEM (1143)
ROSH HORESHA (977)
RAKEFET CAVE (911)
KEBARA B. (242)
HAYONIM TER. (4523)
HAYONIM CAVE B. (357)
MALLAHA (880)
N. OREN V (1359)
N. OREN VI (113)
HEFSIBAH (59)
N. OREN VII (855)
EIN GEV IV (53)
EIN GEV III (31)
FAZAEL III, 4 (125)
N. HADERA V (1292)
RAKEFET CAVE (153)
N. OREN VIII (159)
HAYONIM C (178)
KEBARA C (132)
EIN GEV I (792)

^{14}C YEARS B.C.	GALILEE MT. CARMEL JUDEAN HILLS COASTAL PLAIN	JORDAN VALLEY	NEGEV HIGHLANDS	WESTERN NEGEV NORTHERN SINAI	SOUTHERN SINAI
5000	FARMING HERDING (HUNTING) GARDENING	FARMING HERDING GARDENING	HERDING	FARMING HERDING (GARDENING & HUNTING)	METAL WORK HERDING ("FARMING" & HUNTING)
6000	FARMING HERDING HUNTING	FARMING HERDING HUNTING		FARMING HERDING HUNTING	?
7500	FARMING HERDING & HUNTING LARGE & SMALL SITES	FARMING HERDING & HUNTING	HERDING & HUNTING (FARMING ?)	?	HUNTING & FISHING GATHERING
	SULTANIAN FARMING & HUNTING & GATHERING LARGE & SMALL SITES		?	HUNTING (GATHERING ?)	?
8700	KHIAMIAN GATHERING & HUNTING LARGE & SMALL SITES		HARIFIAN HUNTING & GATHERING LARGE SITES	SMALL SITES	HUNTING & FISHING GATHERING
	NATUFIAN LARGE & SMALL SITES HUNTING & GATHERING FISHING		LATE NATUFIAN GATHERING & HUNTING LARGE SITES	SMALL SITES	?
10,500			HUNTING & GATHERING SMALL SITES		
12,500	GEOMETRIC KEBARAN HUNTING & GATHERING FISHING SMALL SITES		NEGEV KEBARAN MUSHABIAN GEOMETRIC KEBARAN		?
	KEBARAN HUNTING & GATHERING SMALL SITES		=	=	=

FIGURE 5.4. Tentative summary of major economic activities in the prehistoric sequence of the southern Levant.

(de Contenson and Van Liere 1964). In terms of vegetational zones at the end of the Pleistocene and early Holocene, it includes the Mediterranean and Irano-Turanian regions on both sides of the Jordan Valley, stretching into inland Syria to the Euphrates Valley. In the marginal, semiarid, and arid areas (wetter during the seventh millennium B.C.), local adaptations enabled the emergence of pastoral societies.

FIGURE 5.3. Summary of ungulate faunal spectra from major sites in the archaeological sequence of the southern Levant (taken from Bar-Yosef 1980).

SKELETAL EVIDENCE FOR CHANGE IN DIET AND HEALTH STATUS

Specimens Available for Study

The period preceding the Natufian is poorly represented, with only two fairly complete skeletons, both female, from Ein Gev. One, from Ein Gev I, is dated to circa 13,750 B.P.; the other from Nahal Ein Gev, is dated to circa 1700 B.P. (Arensburg 1977; Arensburg and Bar-Yosef 1973). In addition, there are fragmentary remains, mainly teeth and jaws, from the Aurignacian deposits at El Wad and Kebara, as well as one intact humerus from Kebara (McCown and Keith 1939). There are no precise dates for these specimens, which McCown and Keith considered indistinguishable from the Natufian remains at the site, although Henry and Servello (1974) have proposed an approximate date of 13,000 B.C.E.

The Natufian is much better represented, with over 200 skeletal remains from different sites. Most of these are in the northern and central regions of Israel: Shukbah (Garrod 1942b), El Wad (Garrod and Bate 1937), Kebara (Turville-Petrie 1932), Nahal Oren (Noy et al. 1973; Stekelis and Yizraeli 1963), Eynan (Perrot 1966; Valla 1981), Hayonim (Bar-Yosef and Goren 1973), and Rakefet.

In most cases the Natufian burials were dug into the living floors of earlier levels of occupation. At El Wad, specimens have been resorted and relabeled several times, and it is difficult to determine the original associations of most of the specimens described in Garrod and Bate (1937). At Eynan, the best-preserved skeletons are those from the earliest phase, although teeth and jaws from all phases are well represented (Valla 1981). At Hayonim, most of the burials date to the Early Natufian phase (Bar-Yosef and Goren 1973). At Nahal Oren, most of the burials date to the Late Natufian. At Erq el Ahmar and Kebara, most burials date to the Early Natufian (Neuville 1951; Turville-Petrie 1932).

For the Neolithic, the skeletal record is less complete. At Jericho, the largest site excavated, with both Pre-Pottery Neolithic A and Pre-Pottery Neolithic B remains, there is as yet no final report available. Most of the published data are drawn from field notes (Kurth and Röhrer-Ertl 1981). Most of the other sites have yielded much smaller samples, mainly from the Pre-Pottery Neolithic B levels. These include Beisamoun and Abu Ghosh (Lechevallier 1978), Sheikh Ali (Ferembach 1974), Abu Madi, Wadi Tbeik, and Ugrat el Mahed from southern Sinai (Bar-Yosef 1980; Herschkowitz, 1982).

Physical Characteristics and Microevolutionary Trends

Early *Homo sapiens* in the Levant, represented by skeletal remains from Skhul and Qafzeh, were tall and gracile in comparison with Neandertals from Europe. The specimens available, except for Skhul 5, are dolicocephalic, with large and prominent faces and teeth (McCown and Keith 1939; Smith, in preparation); Vandermeersch 1981). The best-preserved of the Upper Paleolithic remains, which are from Ein Gev, are separated from these early specimens by more than 20,000 years. They differ from them in stature, craniofacial morphology, and tooth size, and bear a close resemblance to the later Natufians in these features (Arensburg and Bar-Yosef 1973; Arensburg 1977; Smith 1977). The more fragmentary remains from El Wad and Kebara described by McCown and Keith (1939) also resemble the Natufians. Although there are few specimens from the Upper Paleolithic, it seems that by the latter half of this period, those physical characteristics typical of the Natufians were already established in the region.

The physical characteristics of the Natufians have been described in some detail (Arensburg 1973; Bar-Yosef et al. 1971-1972; Crognier and Dupouy-Madre 1974; Ferembach 1959, 1961, 1977; Keith 1931, 1934; McCown 1939; Smith 1970, 1979; Soliveres 1976; Vallois 1936). The Natufians were of short to medium stature, with males averaging 165 cm and females 152 cm in height (Table 5.1). Their skulls were also dolicocephalic, with large cranial capacity; broad, short faces; prominent zygoma; and a tendency to alveolar prognathism (Table 5.2). The mandibles are characterized by low, broad rami with short body length and deep symphyses (Table 5.3). The teeth are narrow mesiodistally but broad buccolingually, with large lingual tubercles on the mexillary incisors and canines and large Carabelli cusps on the maxillary first molars. The premolars and third molars in both jaws are especially small and agenesis of third molars is frequent (Smith 1970, 1973).

While all those who have studied the Natufians agree their essential homogeneity, Ferembach (1961, 1977), Soliveres (1976), and Crognier and Dupouy-Madre (1974) found some statistically significant differences between samples from Eynan and Nahal Oren in head form, facial breadth, and mandibular and postcranial robusticity. The Nahal Oren specimens tend to have shorter, rounder crania, with reduced bizygomatic and ramal width. Samples from the other Natufian sites fall between these extremes, with Eynan among the most robust and Nahal Oren the most gracile. When these two samples are compared with those found at other Natufian sites, Nahal Oren appears to be the most divergent (tables 5.2 and 5.3), and resembles the later Neolithic samples. For example, ramus width in males at Nahal Oren is significantly smaller than at any other site ($p < .05$). Eynan, as Ferembach (1977) pointed out, diverges in the opposite direction toward extreme robusticity, and in this feature is matched only by a few specimens from other Natufian sites.

It has been postulated that dietary differences may account for the observed differences in robusticity between specimens from Nahal Oren and Eynan (Ferembach 1977). However, the specimens from Eynan described by Ferembach (1961) are attributed to the earliest phase of the Natufian (Valla 1981), whereas those from Nahal Oren belong to the terminal Natufian. The morpholocical

TABLE 5.1 Stature and Dimorphism in Different Periods[a]

Period	Male No.	Male $\overline{X}$	Female No.	Female $\overline{X}$	Total range	Dimorphism[b] %
Mousterian						
Skhul, Qafzeh	3	180	2	166	162-185	11.2
Natufian (total)	10	167	3	158	145-169	10.6
El Wad	1	168				
Shukbah (43)[c]		(160)		(152)		
Eynan	2	168				
Nahal Oren	4	167	2	160		
Hayonim	3	165	1	154		
Neolithic						
Jericho PPNA[d]	29	167	28	157	157-176	10.6
Jericho PPNB[e]	23	171	11	158	153-181	10.8
Abu Gosh[f]	1	(174)	1	(155)	155-174	
Beisamun[f]	1	170	1	(168)	168-170	
South Sinai[f]	1	160				
Chalcolithic						
Jericho	4	170	6	159	154-175	10.6
Byblos	5	167	4	152	147-172	11.0
Bronze Age						
Jebel Qaaqiir	6	164	4	154	150-180	10.6
Sasa	2	169	3	156	152-180	10.8
Jericho	10	171	6	154	153-179	11.1
Hellenistic						
Jericho	12	166	12	152	145-180	10.9
Arab						
Dor	17	169	13	156	150-180	10.8

[a]All data based on femur length, except where stated otherwise.
[b]Percentage dimorphism calculated as $\frac{\text{male}}{\text{female}} \times \underline{100}$.
[c]Based on estimates from Keith (1934).
[d]Pre-Pottery Neolithic A.
[e]Pre-Pottery Neolithic B.
[f]Calculated from long bones other than femur.

differences between these two sites, then, may also be considered to reflect a chronological difference rather than a regional one. The intermediate status of the other Natufian sites is also compatible with their chronologically mixed composition of samples from both early and late phases of the Natufian. Unfortunately, the sample size is too small to permit proper testing for morphological change over time at Eynan. However, a strontium-calcium study (see below) along these lines is feasible, and may be used to investigate the extent of dietary change over this period.

In the Neolithic, the few Pre-Pottery Neolithic A specimens that have been described from Jericho resemble the Nahal Oren Natufians. The Pre-Pottery Neolithic B samples show that a clear division exists between northern and central groups, which were adopting agriculture, and the southern Sinai group, which continued to depend on hunting and gathering. The southern Sinai specimens show a close resemblance to the Natufians in stature, cranial length, bizygomatic width, and mandibular size. The main difference between them is found in cranial breadth, which is exceptionally narrow in the southern Sinai sample.

In the more northerly sites, a marked increase in stature is found in all Pre-Pottery Neolithic B samples. At Jericho, the increase in male stature between Pre-Pottery Neolithic A and Pre-Pottery Neolithic B was statistically significant with a mean increase in height of 4 cm. Female stature showed no significant increase over the same period of time, with mean stature of 157 cm for Pre-Pottery Neolithic A and 158 cm for Pre-Pottery Neolithic B. As Table 5.1 shows, there was no significant increase in stature between Natufian and Pre-Pottery Neolithic A populations; moreover, the increased male stature found in the Pre-Pottery Neolithic B was not maintained in later periods.

Cranial morphology, but not tooth size, also shows significant changes from the Natufian to the Neolithic. In the northern and central Neolithic groups, the crania are shorter and the bizygomatic breadth is reduced. In keeping with the longer faces, the mandibles are longer than those of the Natufians, with increased maximum length and corpus length as well as ramus height but reduced ramus width. These Neolithic populations, then, resemble the Nahal Oren Natufians. In the southern Sinai Neolithic sample, neither stature nor craniofacial morphology departs from the Natufian norm to the extent found in the northern sites. This may be related to the dichotomy in life-styles suggested by the archaeological findings. The complex of changes found in the craniofacial complex of populations associated with agriculture, including more globular skulls with longer, narrower faces and mandibles, is maintained by later populations in this region. The only statistically significant change is a unidirectional reduction in tooth size between Pre-Pottery Neolithic B and Bronze Age populations.

Similar changes have been described elsewhere in populations adopting agriculture (Carlson and Van Gerven 1973). They have been interpreted as being associated with a reduction in the selective pressures maintaining large teeth and powerful masticatory activity in tall, large-muscled hunters. As Tables 5.3 and 5.4 (A and B) indicate, the sequence of changes in Israel and

TABLE 5.2 Craniofacial Measurements[a]

	Maximum length		Maximum breadth		Minimum frontal breadth		Nasion-prosthion height		Nasal height		Nasal breadth		Bizygomatic breadth	
	No.	$\bar{X}$	No.	$\bar{X}$	No.	$\bar{X}$	No.	$\bar{X}$	No.	$\bar{X}$	No.	$\bar{X}$	No.	$\bar{X}$
Natufian														
El Wad	11	188.6	11	138.3	11	96.7	2	88.2	5	47.6	2	25.5		
Shukbah	1	189.0	1	128.0									1	126.0
Eynan	3	197.0	3	131.0	2	97.0	1	97.0	1	61.0			2	141.0
Nahal Oren	3	190.3	2	135.0	4	96.2	1	68.0	2	47.0	1	22.0	1	125.0
Hayonim	5	191.2	5	138.6	3	102.0	3	64.7	3	55.3	4	29.5	3	137.0
Neolithic														
Jericho PPNA[b]	1	198.0	1	126.0	1	103.0	1	67.0	1	49.0	1	27.0		
Jericho PPNB[c]	4	190.5	3	131.6	3	93.0	4	63.5	4	48.0	4	26.2		
Abu Ghosh	1	170.0	3	143.0	1	90.0	1	61.0	1	43.0	1	24.0		
South Sinai	2	190.0	1	120.0	2	93.0	3	64.0	4	48.0	2	22.0	1	126.0

Chalcolithic														
Megiddo	6	190.5	6	135.2	4	97.3							1	132.0
Sinai	9	190.0	9	125.0	9	95.0	9	62.0	9	51.0	9	24.0	7	125.0
Azor	7	188.0	7	136.6	5	97.2								
Jericho	8	189.9	8	133.2	4	94.5	6	67.2	6	51.0	5	25.4	6	124.2
Byblos	12	186.0		135.9	11	92.4	6	68.7	6	52.5	6	26.1	2	121.5
Bronze Age														
MBI	12	186.4	11	135.5	12	94.6	10	69.0	9	53.4	9	22.8	7	128.1
MBII	9	182.2	8	140.1	7	97.9	5	59.4	6	48.8	6	23.7	2	124.0
Byzantine														
Roman	99	181.4	95	142.9	79	96.4	32	67.3	35	52.2	36	24.0	22	131.5
Arab														
Dor	20	182.5	19	140.2	19	97.6	18	69.1	22	53.1	20	24.0	15	131.4

[a]Measurements based on males only except for El Wad and Shakbah.
[b]Pre-Pottery Neolithic A.
[c]Pre-Pottery Neolithic B.

TABLE 5.3 Mandibular Measurements in Different Groups[a]

	Maximum length		Body length		Symphyseal height		M1–M2 height		Ramus height		Ramus breadth		Mandibular angle	
	No.	$\overline{X}$	No.	$\overline{X}$	No.	$\overline{X}$	No.	$\overline{X}$	No.	$\overline{X}$	No.	$\overline{X}$	No.	$\overline{X}$
Natufian														
El Wad[a]	9	101.8	9	77.3	9	34.3	9	34.0	9	53.6	9	37.0	9	117.4
Kebara	1	110.0	1	90.0	1	38.0	1	34.0	1	49.0	1	38.0		--
Eynan[a]	4	116.0	5	94.2	4	39.0	4	32.0	3	61.3	3	36.3	3	125.0
Nahal Oren	4	106.5	4	76.7	5	30.8	8	28.1	4	61.5	6	33.0	5	127.0
Hayonim	4	104.5	4	80.5	4	33.5	4	30.0	4	63.5	4	39.5	4	115.5
Neolithic														
Abu Ghosh[a]	1	113.0	1	85.0	4	32.0	8	29.0	1	56.0	7	33.0	1	122.0
South Sinai	2	110.0	2	84.0	3	35.0	4	28.8	3	56.3	4	37.0	3	123.7
Chalcolithic														
Megiddo		--		--	1	32.0		--		--	1	37.0		--
Bronze Age														
MBI	8	103.1	8	75.0	8	33.9	12	30.0	9	63.5	9	34.1	8	121.7
MBII	7	90.4	4	74.2	8	31.9	10	30.1	6	56.9	9	34.0	7	126.6
Roman-Byzantine														
Jerusalem, Ein Gedi	27	101.5	25	74.3	30	28.7	28	27.0	15	59.6	29	33.1	31	119.8
Arab														
Dor	18	107.5	22	77.9	18	32.3	19	27.8	21	61.1	23	32.3	22	124.1

[a]Measurements based on males only, except for El Wad, Eynan, and Abu Ghosh.

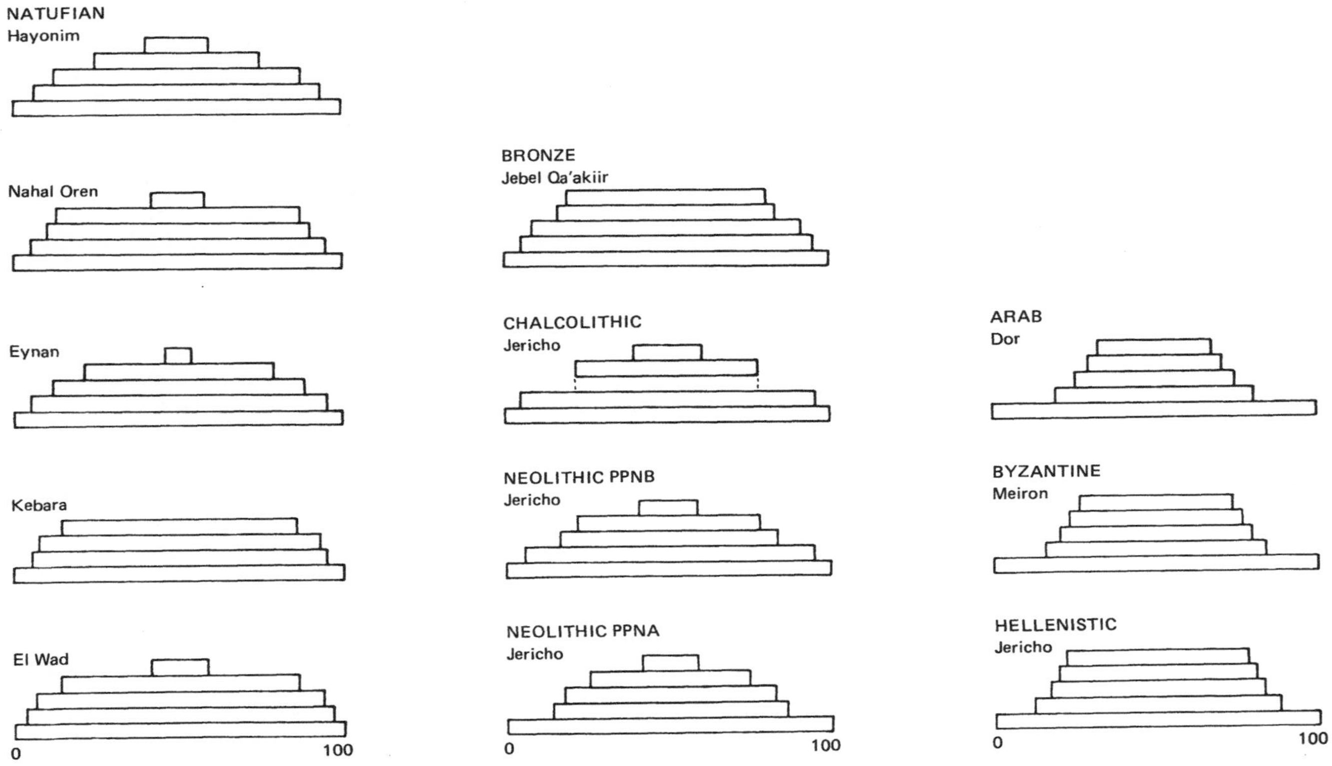

FIGURE 5.5. Frequency distribution of different age groups based on skeletal remains.

TABLE 5.4A Mesiodistal Measurements of Teeth in Different Periods

	Epipaleolithic			*Neolithic*			*Bronze*		
Tooth	*No.*	$\overline{X}$	*SD*	*No.*	$\overline{X}$	*SD*	*No.*	$\overline{X}$	*SD*
				Maxilla					
I1	*31*	*9.1*	*0.7*	*7*	*8.7*	*0.4*	*3*	*8.6*	*0.5*
I2	*47*	*6.8*	*0.7*	*12*	*6.6*	*0.7*	*6*	*6.6*	*0.2*
C	*57*	*7.7*	*0.6*	*10*	*7.8*	*0.5*	*7*	*7.5*	*0.4*
P1	*69*	*7.1*	*0.5*	*8*	*7.3*	*0.5*	*4*	*6.6*	*0.4*
P2	*74*	*7.0*	*1.0*	*8*	*7.3*	*0.3*	*6*	*7.0*	*1.2*
M1	*75*	*10.4*	*0.8*	*10*	*10.6*	*0.5*	*10*	*10.1*	*0.7*
M2	*66*	*9.7*	*0.5*	*9*	*10.0*	*0.4*	*7*	*9.1*	*0.8*
M3	*49*	*8.9*	*0.7*	*6*	*9.1*	*0.7*	*2*	*8.6*	*0.2*
				Mandible					
I1	*46*	*5.3*	*0.4*	*3*	*5.3*	*0.2*	*3*	*5.3*	*0.2*
I2	*56*	*6.0*	*0.6*	*11*	*6.0*	*0.3*	*6*	*5.8*	*0.7*
C	*63*	*6.9*	*0.5*	*10*	*7.0*	*0.4*	*9*	*6.7*	*0.3*
P1	*82*	*7.2*	*0.7*	*7*	*7.1*	*0.4*	*13*	*6.9*	*0.4*
P2	*90*	*7.7*	*1.3*	*9*	*7.1*	*0.3*	*10*	*7.0*	*0.3*
M1	*96*	*11.4*	*0.6*	*16*	*11.2*	*0.6*	*21*	*10.9*	*0.6*
M2	*97*	*10.8*	*0.6*	*13*	*10.9*	*0.5*	*19*	*10.9*	*0.7*
M3	*73*	*10.5*	*0.6*	*9*	*10.7*	*0.2*	*7*	*10.5*	*0.6*

Jordan appears to consist of reduced robusticity followed by dental reduction. These findings are not inconsistent with the conclusions of Carlson and Van Gerven.

Paleodemography

The Upper Paleolithic Ein Gev females were found as primary burials beneath living floors. At El Wad and Kebara, the Aurignacian remains were fragmentary and probably represent disturbed secondary burials. Taken together, they provide little information on paleodemography but do indicate differences in burial practices that are repeated in the Natufian.

At the Natufian and Neolithic sites, both primary and secondary single and multiple burials were found. This pattern is repeated in later periods. The dissociation of bones in secondary burials compounds the difficulty of identification and age determination and is also associated with poor recovery of infants and children because of either poor preservation or their disposal elsewhere.

TABLE 5.4B Buccolingual Measurements of Teeth in Different Periods

	Natufian			Neolithic			Bronze		
Tooth	No.	$\bar{X}$	SD	No.	$\bar{X}$	SD	No.	$\bar{X}$	SD
				Maxilla					
I1	28	7.3	0.4	7	7.3	0.6	7	7.1	0.5
I2	45	6.6	0.5	10	6.5	0.6	3	6.3	0.3
C	56	8.7	0.5	7	8.6	0.8	7	8.2	0.5
P1	68	9.7	0.7	8	9.6	0.6	4	9.0	0.6
P2	70	9.8	0.6	12	9.3	0.6	8	9.1	0.6
M1	72	12.2	0.7	15	11.9	0.7	12	11.2	0.5
M2	65	12.2	0.7	9	12.8	0.8	8	11.1	0.8
M3	46	11.2	1.0	5	11.0	1.0	3	10.0	0.6
				Mandible					
I1	43	6.1	0.4	5	6.2	0.2	8	5.8	0.5
I2	52	6.5	0.4	12	6.4	0.2	11	6.1	0.3
C	51	7.8	0.7	13	8.2	0.9	16	7.4	0.5
P1	77	8.1	0.5	10	8.2	0.4	17	7.3	0.5
P2	90	7.7	1.3	14	8.3	1.3	12	8.0	0.4
M1	96	11.4	0.6	16	10.8	0.3	25	10.4	0.8
M2	97	10.8	0.6	12	10.6	0.3	24	10.0	0.5
M3	73	10.5	0.6	9	10.3	0.1	9	9.6	0.2

This last point can be demonstrated by examining the deviations from mortality profiles of populations for which reliable data are available (Grinblat 1982). Mortality is normally highest in the first year of life, falls slightly in early childhood, and is lowest in late childhood and adolescence. In populations with low life expectancy, the percentage of infant deaths may exceed 40%. This is associated with a high frequency of young adult deaths with only a few individuals surviving to middle or old age.

Increased longevity is associated with both a lower frequency of infant deaths and a higher ratio of older to younger individuals. Figure 5.5 gives the distribution of age at death for Natufian and later groups. Included are three samples from sites where primary burial was practiced and recovery was good. Hellenistic Jericho represents a population in relatively good health with good life expectancy (Hachlili et al. 1981). Byzantine Meiron is representative of a population with poorer life expectancy (Smith et al. 1981) and the early Arab population from Dor represents a group in poor health with low life expectancy (Smith and Berkowitz, in preparation). In each group there is an inverse correlation between the percentage of infant deaths and that of older adults.

However, the Natufian sites show no such patterning. At Shukbah and at El Wad, Keith reported 38 and 26% subadults, respectively. At Nahal Oren 14%, at Eynan 27%, and at Hayonim 59% of those found were identified as subadults. However, very few of the Natufian adults were found in the older adult category. Similar distortions of the expected pattern are found in the Neolithic samples and in secondary burial sites from later periods. The inference is that some other means must be adopted to estimate longevity in these populations.

Analysis of the ratio of young to old adults can provide this information. Using this approach, it seems that longevity increased in the Neolithic period and showed a second but temporary increase in the late Hellenistic and Roman period. Arensburg (1973) estimated an average life span of 30 years for the Epipaleolithic, increasing to 34 in the Neolithic, 39 in the Hellenistic and Roman periods, and dropping slightly thereafter to 32 years in early Arabs. Female life expectancy over the same periods averaged some 4 years less in each group.

Skeletal Pathology

Skeletal pathology has not yet been analyzed in detail for either the Epipaleolithic or the Neolithic. At least four adults from Nahal Oren and three from Eynan have mild cribra orbitalia and parietal pitting. Cranial thickness in all Natufian skulls is greater than that of later groups (Ani 1983), but this may represent genetic rather than pathological variation, especially since the cortical thickness of their long bones is also greater than that of later populations. There is no mention of cribra orbitalia in analyses of Neolithic specimens, but thickening of the diploe in two crania from Jericho was reported by Kurth and Röhrer-Ertl (1981). In all subsequent periods the incidence of cribra and parietal pitting is high, with some 40% of adults and 60% of children affected (Table 5.5). Since the condition seems to have affected males and females similarly (Nathan and Haas 1966; Smith and Berkowitz, in preparation), the condition here may be attributable to infectious disease rather than to diet.

The thickness of cortical bone in the humerus of Middle Paleolithic Natufian and more recent groups has recently been measured by Smith et al. (1984a,b). According to Bloom and Laws (1970), a value of 7.0 or less for combined cortical thickness (CCT) of humerus is diagnostic of osteoporosis. This condition was diagnosed in one female from El Wad, in 20-30% of Bronze Age and Roman samples, and in 53% of females from the early Arab site of Dor. With CCT values corrected for age and size, CCT in the Natufians and Middle Paleolithic specimens is similar and significantly larger than in later populations (Table 5.6). This may reflect functional differences in use of the arms as well as better nutritional status in the earlier populations.

TABLE 5.5 Cribra Orbitalia[a]

Group	Children		Adults	
	Number examined	Frequency (%)	Number examined	Frequency (%)
Natufian	2	50	11	40
Chalcolithic	4	100	2	100
M. Bronze	5	100	35	63
Roman-Byzantine	21	62	36	65
Early Arab	33	84	42	47

[a]Only mild category--porosities--present in Natufians. In all other groups the condition varies from mild to very severe, after the classification employed in Nathan and Haas (1966).

While no Neolithic bones were included in this study, some descriptions of bone pathology have been provided by Kurth and Röhrer-Ertl (1981). They found that long bones of 28 individuals showed signs of cortical hypertrophy, which was tentatively attributed to calcium deficiency. They also described one two-year-old infant with bony deformities possibly due to hereditary vitamin D-resistant rickets. The Chalcolithic remains are too scant to provide much information. However, juvenile skeletons from Ghassul show exceptionally thin cortical bone for size in relation to length and an average of six growth arrest lines in the tibia. All have enamel hypoplasia and cribra orbitalia.

Few signs of trauma or fracture have been reported, with only three cases described for Neolithic Jericho in the abovementioned report. However, few cases of trauma or deformities have been reported from any site in this region regardless of period. There is, therefore, little evidence to suggest injury during hunting or as a result of inter- or intragroup aggression.

Dental Pathology

In the discussion of dental pathology, a distinction must be made between enamel hypoplasia and other pathological lesions. Enamel hypoplasia reflects developmental disturbances during tooth formation, and so relates to specific events in prenatal life and early infancy, when tooth crown development takes place. Attrition, caries, and periodontal disease are, in contrast, cumulative diseases that reflect in adults the sum of past dietary habits.

TABLE 5.6 Measurements in the Humerus of Females (Left Side Only)

	CCT[a]			CCT/Length			Maximum Length		
	No.	$\overline{X}$		No.	$\overline{X}$		No.	$\overline{X}$	
Paleolithic	1	10.0	10.0	1	3.4	3.4	1	330	--
Natufian	12	8.8	10.5-6.0	4	3.2	3.4-2.8	6	282	288-277
M. Bronze	10	7.7	10.1-4.1	8	2.4	3.2-1.4	8	306	321-293
Roman	19	8.0	9.7-5.7	11	2.7	3.3-2.0	11	287	302-265
Arab	14	7.3	10.1-4.3	11	2.4	3.2-1.5	11	301	332-281

[a]Combined cortical thickness.

TABLE 5.7 Distribution of Dental Pathology by Period and Age Group[a]

	Total number examined	Aged ≥ 6 years	Aged ≥ 20 years	Frequency (%)		
				Hypoplasia	Caries	Tooth loss
Natufian						
El Wad	58	54	42	15	2.1	22.5
Kebara				23	0.5	4.0
Shukbah						
Eynan	42	37	25	27	2.8	26
Nahal Oren	19	18	15	61	5.3	25
Hayonim	16	5	10	10	0	22
Neolithic						
Jericho PPNB	25	17	9	38	11	30
Abu Ghosh	12	10	9	47	14.2	28
Chalcolithic						
Azor	120	80	40	80		
Arad	6	4	4	(100)	(66)	(50)
Beersheba	6	5	5	(100)	(17)	
Bronze Age						
Jebel Qa'akiir	30	28	28	59	3	28
Sasa	28	28	28	91	7	42
Jericho	29	28	25	53	20	44
Roman Jerusalem and Ein Gedi	63	63	63	50	20	49

[a]*Hypoplasia calculated as percentage of individuals with permanent teeth with hypoplasia (i.e., aged six or more). Caries and tooth loss calculated as percentage of adults (i.e., aged 20 or more) with either condition.*

[b]*Numbers in parentheses reflect frequencies derived from small samples.*

Enamel Hypoplasia

In the Natufians, enamel hypoplasia was found in less than 1% of primary teeth, but in 20-30% of individuals with permanent teeth from all sites except Nahal Oren. At Nahal Oren, the prevalence of enamel hypoplasia was higher, with 54% affected (Table 5.7). Hypoplasia was most commonly found on the cervical third to half of canines, representing that portion of the tooth formed between the ages of three and four years (Scott and Symons 1980). A similar pattern of enamel hypoplasia was found at the North African Epipaleolithic site of Taforalt, but in higher frequencies (Poitrat-Targola 1962). It presumably represents dietary disturbances associated with weaning. It has recently been suggested that it is associated with episodes of lowered levels of serum calcium values of the order associated with tetany; that is, 8.0 mg (Nikiforuk and Fraser 1981).

As Table 5.7 shows, the prevalence of hypoplasia at the Natufian sites is similar to that found in Middle Paleolithic hominids. Enamel hypoplasia is slightly more prevalent in the Neolithic samples, and increases again in later populations. At these later sites, hypoplasia is found with some regularity in primary teeth. It is also found on the first permanent molars and incisors, which develop at an earlier age than the canines. This suggests that children were weaned at an earlier age in later periods, a finding compatible with the presumably decreased interval between childbirths.

A method for examining the pattern of dietary supplementation and weaning on the basis of strontium-calcium ratios in juvenile bones has recently been demonstrated for the Arab population at Dor. In this population a mean age of 2.5 years for weaning was estimated (Sillen and Smith 1984). We hope to apply this method to the Natufian and Pre-Pottery Neolithic sample to examine further the relationship between weaning age and economic change in the Levantine archaeological sequence.

The higher frequency of hypoplasia in the later periods presumably reflects a higher incidence of childhood disturbances in the later groups. It may also mean that a similar percentage was affected in the earlier populations but that fewer survived such episodes. However, the condition has been found in extremely high frequencies in Australian pre-contact hunters and gatherers. In different samples ranging from 6000 B.P. to 1800 A.D., the incidence of hypoplasia varied between 70 and 80%. It affected mainly canines, as in the Natufians. There was no evidence to suggest that this was associated with reduced life expectancy.

Other Dental Evidence

Inter-site differences in age of individuals are to some extent reflected in frequency of antemortem tooth loss. This is most pronounced at El Wad (where two completely dentureless individuals were found), followed by Eynan, Nahal Oren, Hayonim, and Kebara in decreasing order of frequency (Table 5.8). Mean values for attrition vary. Attrition was most severe at El Wad and Eynan, and least severe at Kebara and Hayonim. These differences were maintained using age-corrected scores (Smith 1970). Given the homogeneity of tooth size, these differences can be considered evidence of differences in the abrasive quality of the foods ingested.

TABLE 5.8 Frequency Distribution of Dental Disease in Natufian Adults[a]

Site	*Number of teeth*	*Percentage caries*	*Percentage antemortem loss*
El Wad	*601*	*2.8*	*15.0*
Kebara	*306*	*0.3*	*0.9*
Hayonim	*70*	*(0.5)*	*2.8*
Eynan	*327*	*3.7*	*2.7*
Nahal Oren	*264*	*7.6*	*2.6*

[a]*Taken from Smith (1970).*

Further grounds for assuming differences in the rate of attrition are provided by the differences between levels of attrition in first and second permanent molars. Since eruption times of these two teeth differ by 6 years, differences in attrition values between these two teeth reflect this 6 year period. When pronounced, these differences indicate severe attrition rates. In a comparison of attrition scores in first and second molars, significantly lower rates of attrition were demonstrated for Kebara as compared to El Wad, Eynan, and Nahal Oren (Smith 1970, 1972). Carious lesions were found in less than 1.5% of teeth from Hayonim and Kebara and in 2-3% of teeth from El Wad and Eynan, but in 6.8% of teeth from Nahal Oren. Periodontal disease, measured by the extent of alveolar recession, was also more pronounced at Nahal Oren (Table 5.3). Nahal Oren, then, shows evidence of dental disease patterns usually found in association with a sticky carbohydrate diet (periodontal disease and caries) as well as a higher incidence of hypoplasia than that found at other Natufian sites. This evidence for dietary change agrees with the observed changes in craniofacial morphology discussed in the section on skeletal pathology.

Dental disease patterns at the Neolithic sites resemble those found at Nahal Oren, with slightly more caries, periodontal disease, antemortem tooth loss, and hypoplasia than that characteristic of the Natufians in general. Dental health status at this time, however, is still significantly superior to that of later agriculturalists. Here possible differences in food preparation following the introduction of pottery, as well as differences in food selection, may be responsible. The main differences found are in the increased frequency of hypoplasia, periodontal disease, and antemortem tooth loss in the later populations.

Strontium-Calcium Ratios

Research into the environmental chemistry of strontium and calcium has delivered an unanticipated benefit: a method for the determination of the proportionate amounts of meat and vegetable foods in prehistoric diets by reference to the relative concentration of these elements in skeletons. Since vegetable foods contain higher strontium-calcium (Sr/Ca) ratios than do meat foods, diets heavily dependent on vegetable foods result in relatively high Sr/Ca ratios in bone. In contrast, diets heavily dependent on meat foods result in relatively low Sr/Ca ratios in bone. Detailed background information on the technique has been presented elsewhere (Sillen and Kavanagh 1982).

At least two Sr/Ca studies have been directed specifically at the Levantine sequence. Schoeninger (1981, 1982) explicitly set out to determine whether the development of agriculture in the Near East was primarily an economic or a subsistence change. She examined the Levantine sequence represented by specimens from levels G-B (Mousterian-Natufian) at El Wad, and a similar sequence at Kebara. On the basis of comparisons of human specimens to herbivore specimens, she concluded that "within the Levant the non-agricultural populations at Kebara B and El Wad B (Natufians) were including large proportion of plant material in their "diets" (Schoeninger 1981, p. 87). This conclusion was independently established by data we have gathered for the Natufian at Hayonim Cave (Sillen 1981a,b). In our study, it was found that Natufian human Sr/Ca levels fell midway between the Sr/Ca levels of Natufian carnivores and those of herbivores, reflecting a clearly omnivorous dietary pattern.

A more controversial conclusion reached by Schoeninger derives from her comparison of the Natufian results to those from Kebara C (Kebaran). Based on a comparison of human to herbivore bone, she concludes that the Natufian "represents (an) increased use in plant material when compared with the earlier human population of Kebara C (Schoeninger 1981, p. 87). In turn, this conclusion is used to support the "broad-spectrum" hypothesis of Flannery that the major subsistence change in the region occurred well before the development of cultivation, and that cultivation developed as a means to perpetuate this subsistence pattern.

However, the investigation of pre-Natufian Epipaleolithic diets with Sr/Ca analyses is complicated by the paucity of skeletal samples from this period, and the probability of chemical change during interment. For example, no difference in Sr/Ca ratios between herbivore and carnivore fauna is detectable for the Kebaran at Ein Gev (A. Sillen, unpublished). Also, the charred nature of the human sample from Kebara C (Kebaran) raises the question of whether it is comparable to uncharred bone from later periods.

Strontium-calcium analyses can nevertheless provide useful information regarding dietary change before and/or concomitant with the beginning of food production if reasonable sample sizes, appropriate sites, and faunal and other controls are employed. To this end, in 1980, we designed an in-depth study of the relevant faunal and human material from some 10 sites, including Nahal Oren, Hayonim Cave and Terrace, Eynan, Kebara, El Wad and Mureybet, Jericho, Abu Gosh, and Beisamoun. The study, which is still underway, incorporates well over 500 specimens, including carnivores, herbivores, and humans of known age and sex.

For the purpose of this chapter, we have conducted a preliminary analysis of the data gathered from the Pre-Pottery Neolithic B of Jericho, and have compared these data to data already published for the Natufian at Hayonim Cave. It should be emphasized that the data presented in Table 5.9 represent an interim finding and should not be taken as a conclusive result of the study.

In the Pre-Pottery Neolithic B it is clear that human diets have shifted to a greater dependence on meat products as compared to the Natufian. This phenomenon is easily seen when the data for humans are compared to the midpoint between the average Sr/Ca values of herbivores and carnivores. At Hayonim, the average Sr/Ca value for the humans is indistinguishable from the midpoint for fauna at that site. However, at Jericho (Pre-Pottery Neolithic B), the mean human value is considerably lower than the corresponding faunal midpoint. It is of interest that this finding coincides with both the faunal evidence for dependence on animal husbandry in the Pre-Pottery Neolithic B and the skeletal evidence for increased stature during the same period.

DISCUSSION

From the presently available data, it is difficult to establish the severity of environmental factors operating on Upper Paleolithic populations in the Levant. The differences found in stature and general skeletal morphology between Middle Paleolithic and Upper Paleolithic populations are, however, sufficiently large to indicate a significant change in the interaction of humans with their environment. Synchronous changes occur in Europe at this time (Frayer 1980), but not in North Africa (Ferembach 1962) or the Nile Valley (Anderson 1968; Greene and Armelagos 1972; Smith 1979). In these instances, Epipaleolithic populations maintained large stature, robusticity, and large tooth size.

Since there is no evidence to suggest large-scale population replacement in any region at this time, the morphological changes observed may be interpreted as long-term microevolutionary trends. An association between stature reduction and changes in hunting strategies has been proposed for European Upper Paleolithic populations (Brace 1973; Frayer 1980). These investigators have suggested that improved technology (specifically, the use of missile points), as well as increased emphasis on hunting smaller, less dangerous mammals, removed earlier selective pressures that had

TABLE 5.9 Sr/Ca Values from the Hayonim Natufian and Jericho Pre-Pottery Neolithic B[a]

Sample	*N*	*Sr/Ca*	*SD*
Hayonim Natufian B			
Carnivores (Felis sp. only)	5	.60	.07
Herbivores (Gazella sp. only)	12	.98	.20
Midpoint between herbivores and carnivores		.79	
Humans			
All adult humans	14	.77	.10
Males	8	.74	.10
Females	4	.84	--
Jericho Pre-Pottery Neolithic B			
Carnivores (Felis sp. only)	3	3.12	.19
Herbivores (Gazella sp. only)	24	4.73	.95
Midpoint between herbivores and carnivores		3.93	
Humans			
All adult humans	12	3.36	.21
Males	6	3.35	.14
Females	6	3.37	.28

[a]*Hayonim Natufian humans are indistinguishable from the midpoint between herbivore and carnivore fauna. On the other hand, Jericho Pre-Pottery Neolithic B humans are shifted considerably in the direction of carnivores.*

maintained the large size and marked dimorphism of earlier human populations.

In the Levant there is little evidence to support this view. Few changes in patterns of animal exploitation are evident before the Pre-Pottery Neolithic B; moreover, dimorphism in stature shows no significant difference from the Middle Paleolithic until recent times. Many mammalian species as well as human populations in the Levant and Northern Europe do, however, show a reduction in size towards the end of the Pleistocene, with predators especially affected (Davis 1977, 1981). There are, however, few precedents for relating the observed changes in human stature to size change in carnivores.

Ethnographic studies have demonstrated that a common response to stress in hunter-gatherer societies is population restriction. The archaeological findings for the Levant indicate that by the end of the Upper Paleolithic, the population of this region had, in fact, considerably *increased* in size as shown by the increase in number, size, and density of settlements. This suggests that, if anything, a more positive balance had been achieved, presumably due to altered modes of production.

The archaeological findings discussed, in this chapter, as well as studies of dental pathology and skeletal strontium, demonstrate that by the Natufian there was considerable inter-site diversity in resource utilization, with intensive cereal consumption at some sites (Sillen 1984). The early claim for domesticated dogs in the Natufian (Garrod and Bate 1937) has now been vindicated (Davis and Valla 1978), although no other domesticated plants or animals have been definitely associated with the Natufian. Ethnographic reports have demonstrated that many hunter-gatherer societies have domesticated dogs without other domesticates. Therefore, the Natufian dogs cannot be taken as evidence for the domestication of herd animals.

The well-built structures from the Natufian, together with storage pits, indicate at least some degree of permanent settlement as well as the use of stored foods. At Hayonim, the continued use of the same site by members of the same lineage is further suggested by the presence in successive layers of burials of individuals with congenital absence of third molars in far higher frequencies than at other Natufian sites (Smith 1973).

The greatly increased size of settlements in the Neolithic is indicative of improved reliability of resources. The association of Pre-Pottery Neolithic B culture with increased stature may reflect secular trends associated with improved food supplies: the Sr/Ca data collected from Jericho so far indicate a proportional increase of meat and/or dairy protein in diets. The sudden abandonment of Pre-Pottery Neolithic B sites suggests, however, that this period of plenty was short lived. This has been attributed to various factors including increasing competition for declining resources associated with aridification, and mounting population pressure.

Given the present deficiencies of the skeletal record, we cannot state the implications of these changes for longevity, but the data presented here do demonstrate that the health status of the Natufian and pre-pottery Neolithic populations was superior to that of later agriculturalists in this region.

We may thus conclude that, at least in this region, the initial steps in plant and animal domestication were not associated with environmental stress or deteriorating health status. Rather, health status in the Epipaleolithic Natufians was comparable to that of Middle Paleolithic hunter-gatherers and probably was superior to that of North American hunter-gatherers of the same period. Good health status was maintained in pre-pottery Neolithic populations, and it is only in the later periods, when intensive agriculture and husbandry were fully established, that health standards declined markedly. This deterioration and systemic health seems to be related to chronic disease rather than to periodic bouts of food shortages, as indicated by the distribution of developmental lesions in the teeth and bones and the poor condition of all individuals examined. If, then, we should consider the implications of increased population density and permanent settlements for the presence of endemic disease, it is only in these later periods that their presence is manifest in skeletal pathology.

ACKNOWLEDGMENTS

Different aspects of this research were supported by a number of organizations, including the Israel Academy of Sciences, the Wenner-Gren Foundation for Anthropological Research, the National Science Foundation, and the Smithsonian Institution. Human skeletons from Jericho were sampled from the Kurth collection at the Zoologische Staatssammlung (Munich).

We thank Denise Ferembach (Maître de Recherche, CNRS), Monique Lechevallier (Universite de Paris VI), Olav Röhrer-Ertl (Zoologische Staatssammlung, Munich), Gottfried Kurth (Carolina-Wilhelmina Technical University), Juliet Clutton-Brock (British Museum [Natural History]), Baruch Arensburg (University of Tel Aviv), and Aviv Eytan (Israel Department of Antiquities) for providing access to the collections in their care.

We would further like to express our appreciation to these individuals for the valuable discussions that took place during the course of this research.

REFERENCES

Acreche, N.
1982 *Cranial variation between EBIV and MBII: A discriminant analysis.* M.Sc. thesis, Hebrew University, Jerusalem.

Anderson, J. E.
1968 Late Paleolithic skeletal remains from Nubia. In *Prehistory in Nubia* (Vol. II), edited by F. Wendorf, pp. 996-1017. S.M.U. Press, Dallas.

Anderson, P. C.
1980 A testimony of prehistoric tasks: Diagnostic residues and stone tool working edges. *World Archaeology 12*:181-194.

Ani, S.
1983 *The relation of cranial thickness to size and shape of the skull: A radiographic study.* DMD thesis, Hebrew University, Jerusalem.

Arensburg, B.
1973 *The people in the land of Israel from the Epi-Paleolithic to present times.* Ph.D. thesis, Tel Aviv University, Israel.

1977 New Upper Paleolithic remains from Israel. In *Eretz-Israel* (Vol. XIII), edited by B. Arensburg and O. Bar-Yosef, pp. 208-215. Israel Exploration Society, Jerusalem.

Arensburg, B., and O. Bar-Yosef

1973 Human remains from Ein Gev I, Jordan Valley, Israel. *Paleoorient 1*:2201-2206.

Arensburg, B., P. Smith, and R. Yaker

1978 The human remains from Abou Gosh. In Abou Gosh and Beisamoun, edited by M. Lechevallier. Memoires et travaux du centre de recherches prehistoriques de Jerusalem, No. 2, pp. 95-105.

Bar-Yosef, O.

1978 The Levantine Epi-Paleolithic as the background for the "Neolithic Revolution." Paper presented at conference on The Origins of Agriculture and Technology: East or West Asia? [Proceedings volume of the same title, edited by P. Mortensen and P. Sorensen, in press, 1984.] In press.

1980 Prehistory of the Levant. *Annual Review of Anthropology 9*:101-133.

1981a The "Pre-Pottery Neolithic" period in the Southern Levant. In *Prehistoire du Levant, Colloques Internationaux*, edited by J. Cauvin and P. Sanlaville, pp. 555-569. Editions, CNRS, Paris.

1981b The Epi-Paleolithic complexes in the Southern Levant. In *Prehistoire du Levant, Colloques Internationaux*, edited by J. Cauvin and P. Sanlaville. Editions CNRS, Paris.

In preparation. The Prehistory of Israel.

Bar-Yosef and N. Goren

1973 Natufian remains from Hayonim Cave. *Paleorient 1*:49-68.

Bar-Yosef, O., B. Arensburg and P. Smith

1971-1972 Algunas Notas Acerca de la cultura Natufience. *Ampurias 33*:1-42.

Bloom, R. A., and J. W. Laws

1970 Humeral cortical thickness as an index of osteoporosis in women. *British Journal of Radiology 43*:522-527.

Brace, C. L.

1973 Sexual dimorphism in human evolution. *Yearbook of Physical Anthropology 16*:31-49.

Carlson, D. S., and D. P. Van Gerven

1973 Masticatory function and post-Pleistocene evolution in Nubia. *American Journal of Physical Anthropology 46*:495-506.

Cauvin, J.

1978 Les premiers villages de Syrie-Palestine de IXe au VIIe millenaire avant J. C. Collections de la Maison de l'Orient Ancien No. 4.

Chamla, M. C.

1980 The settlement of non-Saharan Algeria from the Epipaleolithic to modern times. In *The physical anthropology of European populations*, edited by I. Schwidetsky, B. Chiarelli and O. Necrasov, pp. 257-270. Mouton, The Hague.

Clutton-Brock, J.
1979 The mammalian remains from Jericho Tell. *Proceedings of the Prehistoric Society 45*:135-157.
Crognier, E., and M. Dupouy-Madre
1974 Les Natoufiens du Nahal Oren. *Paleorient 2*:103-121.
Davis, S. J.
1977 Size variation in the fox, Vulpes vulpes in the Palalarctic today and in Israel during the late Quaternary. *Journal of Zoology 182*:343-351.
1978 Etude de la faune. In Abou Gosh et Beisamoun, edited by M. Lechevallier. Memoires et travaux du centre de recherches prehistoriques de Jerusalem, No. 2, pp. 195-197.
1981 The effects of temperature change and domestication on the body size of Late Pleistocene to Holocene mammals of Israel. *Paleobiology 7*:101-114.
Davis, S. J., and F. Valla
1978 Evidence of domestication of the dog 10,000 years ago in the Natufian of Israel. *Nature (London) 276*:608-610.
de Contenson, H., and W. J. Van Liere
1964 Sondages a Tell Ramad en 1963, rapport preliminaire. *Annales Archeologiques de Syrie 14*:109-124.
Ferembach, D.
1958 Note preliminaire sur les ossements humaines decouvertes a Safadi Israel. Laboratorie d'Anthropologie Physique de l'ecole des hauts Etudes. Paris. Physique de l'ecole des hauts Etudes. Paris.
1959 Note sur un crane brachycephale et deux mandibules du Mesolithique d'Israel. *Israel Exploration Journal 9*:65-73.
1961 Squelettes du Natoufien d'Israel, étude anthropologique. *L'Anthropologie 65*:46-66.
1962 La necropole Epipaleolithique de Taforalt (Maroc Oriental). Rabat, CNRS.
1974 Note sur le squelette d'enfant neolithic de Sheikh Aly (Israel). *Tekufat Ha-even 12*:47-49.
1977 Les Natoufiens de Palestine. In *Eretz-Yisrael* (Vol. XIII), edited by B. Arensburg and O. Bar-Yosef. Israel Exploration Society, Jerusalem.
1978 Les Natoufiens et l'homme de Combe Capelle. *Bulletin et Memoire de la Société Anthropologiques de Paris 5*:131-136.
Ferembach, D., and M. Lechavallier.
1973 Decouverte des cranes surmodeles dans une habitation du VIIienne millenaire a Beisamoun, Israel. *Paleorient 1*:223-230.
Field, H.
1952 *The Faiyum, Sinai, Sudan, Kenya E.* Cambridge University Press, Cambridge.
Frayer, D. W.
1980 Sexual dimorphism and cultural evolution in the Late Pleistocene and Holocene of Europe. *Journal of Human Evolution 9*:399-415.

Garrod, D. A. E.
1942a Excavations in the caves of Wadi el-Mughara, 1929-1930. *Bulletin of the American School of Prehistoric Research* *7*:5-11.
1942b Excavations at the cave of Shukbah, Palestine, 1928. *Proceedings of the Prehistoric Society N.S.* *8*:1-20.
1957 The Natufian culture: The life and economy of a Mesolithic people in the Near East. *Proceedings of the British Academy* *43*:211-227.
Garrod, D. A. E., and D. M. A. Bate
1937 *The Stone Age of Mount Carmel: Excavations at the Wadi el-Mughara* (Vol. 1). Oxford University Press (Clarendon), London and New York.
Greene, D. L., and G. J. Armelagos
1972 The Wadi Halfa Mesolithic population. *Department of Anthropology University of Massachusetts Amherst Research Report* No. 11.
Grinblat, J.
1982 Aging in the world: Demographic determinants, past trends and long term perspectives to 2075. *World Health Statistics* *35*:124-132.
Hachlili, R., B. Arensburg, and A. Killebrew
1981 The Jewish necropolis at Jericho. *Current Anthropology* *22*:701-702.
Hassan, F.
1981 Demographic archaeology. Academic Press, New York.
Helbaek, H.
1966 Pre-Pottery Neolithic farming at Beidha. *Palestine Exploration Quarterly* *98*:61-66.
Henry, D. O., and A. F. Servello
1974 Compendium of C14 determinations derived from Near Eastern prehistoric deposits. *Paleorient* *2*:19-44.
Hershkowitz, I.
1982 The Neolithic population of the South Sinai and its relation to other Mediterranean groups: An anthropological study. M.Sc. thesis, Tel-Aviv University, Israel.
Hopf, M.
1969 Plant remains and early farming in Jericho. In *The domestication and exploitation of plants and animals*, edited by P. J. Ucko and G. W. Dimbleby, pp. 355-359. Duckworth, London.
Hughes, D. R.
1965 Appendix II: Human bones. In *Jericho II*, edited by K. M. Kenyon, pp. 664-685. Oxford University Press, London.
Keith, A.
1931 *New discoveries relating to the antiquity of man*. Norton, New York.
1934 The late Paleolithic inhabitants of Palestine. *Proceedings of the International Conference of Prehistory and Protohistory Sciences 1st*, pp. 46-47.

Kozlowski, S. K.
1973 *The Mesolithic in Europe*. Warsaw University Press, Warsaw.
Kurth, G., and O. Rohrer-Ertl
1981 On the anthropology of the Mesolithic to Chalcolithic human remains from the Tell es-Sultan in Jericho, Jordan. In *Excavations at Jericho* (Vol. III), edited by K. M. Kenyon, pp. 407-499. British School of Archaeology, Jerusalem.
Lechevallier, M. (editor)
1978 Abou Gosh et Beisamoun. Deux gisements du VIIe millenaire avant l'ère chretienne en Israel. Memoires et travaux du centre de recherches prehistoriques de Jerusalem, No. 2.
Mastin, B. A.
1964 The extended burials at Magharet el Wad. *Journal of the Royal Anthropological Institute 94*:44-50.
McCown, T. D.
1939 *The Natufian crania from Mount Carmel*. Ph.D. dissertation, University of California, Berkeley.
McCown, T. D., and A. Keith
1939 The Stone Age of Mount Carmel (Vol. II). Oxford University Press, Oxford.
Moore, A. M. T.
1978 *The Neolithic of the Levant*. Ph.D. thesis, Oxford University.
Nathan, H., and N. Haas
1966 Cribra orbitalia. A bone condition of the orbit of unknown nature. *Israel Journal of Medical Sciences 2*:171-191.
Neuville, R.
1951 Le Paleolithique et le Mesolithique du Desert de Judee. *Archives de l'Institute de Paleontologie humaine Memoire* No. 24.
Nikiforuk, G., and D. Fraser
1981 Etiology of enamel hypoplasia: A unifying concept. *Journal of Pediatrics 98*:888-893.
Noy, T., A. J. Legge, and E. S. Higgs
1973 Recent excavations at Nahal Oren, Israel. *Proceedings of the Prehistoric Society 39*:75-99.
Ozbek, M.
1974 Etude de la deformation cranielle artificielle chez les Chalcolithiques de Byblos. *Bulletins et Memoires de la Société d'Anthropologie de Paris 13*:155-481.
1975 *Hommes de Byblos. Etude comparative des squelettes des âges de metaux au Proche-Orient*. Ph.D. dissertation, University of Paris, France.
Peretz, B.
1980 Dental morphology and pathology of Middle Bronze Age populations in Israel. DMD thesis, Hebrew University, Jerusalem.
Perrot, J.
1966 Le gisement Natoufien de Mallaha (Eynan) Israel. *L'Anthropologie 70*:437-454.

Poitrat-Targola, M.
1962 Pathologie dentaire et maxillaire. In *La Necropole epipaleolithique de Taforalt*, edited by D. Ferembach, pp. 161-171. Centre Nationale Recherches Scientifique, Paris.

Redman, C. L.
1978 *The rise of civilization*. Freeman, San Francisco.

Schoeninger, M.
1981 The agricultural "revolution:" Its effect on human diet in prehistoric Iran and Israel. *Paleorient* 7:73-92.

Scott, J. H., and N. B. Symons
1980 *Introduction to dental anatomy*. Livingstone, London.
1982 Diet and the evolution of modern human form in the Middle East. *American Journal of Physical Anthropology* 58:37-52.

Sillen, A.
1981a Strontium and diet at Hayonim Cave. *American Journal of Physical Anthropology* 56:131-137.
1981b Postdepositional changes in Natufian and Aurignacian bones from Hayonim Cave. *Paleorient* 7:81-85.

Sillen, A.
1984 Dietary variability in the Epipaleolithic of the Levant. *Paleorient*, in press.

Sillen, A., and M. Kavanagh
1982 Strontium and paleodietary research: A review. *Yearbook of Physical Anthropology* 25:67-90.

Sillen, A., and P. Smith
1984 Strontium/calcium ratios reveal weaning-age in a skeletal population. *Journal of Archaeological Science*, in press.

Smith, P.
1970 *Dental morphology and pathology in the Natufians: The dental evidence for dietary specialization*. Ph.D. thesis, University of Chicago, Chicago.
1972 Diet and attrition in the Natufians. *American Journal of Physical Anthropology* 37:233-238.
1973 Family burials at Hayonim. *Paleorient* 1:69-71.
1977 Regional variation in tooth size and pathology in fossil hominids. *American Journal of Physical Anthropology* 47:459-466.
1979 Regional diversity in Epipaleolithic populations. *International Journal of Skeletal Research* 6:243-250.
In Preparation. Craniofacial variation in the Upper Pleistocene.

Smith, P., and J. Berkowitz. In preparation. An anthropological approach to the past: Dor, a case study.

Smith, P., R. A. Bloom, and J. Berkowitz
1983 Bone morphology and biomechanical efficiency in fossil hominids. *Current Anthropology* 24:662-663.

Smith, P., R. A. Bloom, and J. Berkowitz
1984 Diachronic trends in humeral cortical thickness of Near Eastern Populations. *Journal of Human Evolution*, in press.

Smith, P., E. Bournemann, and J. Zias
1981 The skeletal remains in the Meiron excavations. In *Excavations at Ancient Meiron, Meiron Excavation Project, Vol. III*, pp. 100-118. American School of Oriental Research, Chapel Hill, North Carolina.

Smith, P., and S. Tau
1978 Dental pathology in the period of the Roman Empire: A comparison of two populations. *International Journal of Skeletal Research* 5:35-41.

Soliveres, O.
1976 *Les Natoufiens de Mallaha (Israel)*. Ph.D. thesis, University of Paris, France.
1978 Les restes post-cephaliques. In Abou Gosh et Beisamoun, edited by M. Lechavallier. *Memoires et Travailles de CNRS*, pp. 181-194.

Stekelis, M. and T. Yizraeli
1963 Excavations at Nahal Oren. *Israel Exploration Journal 13*: 1-12.

Turville-Petrie, F.
1932 Excavations in the Mugharet el-Kebarah. *Journal of the Royal Anthropological Institute 62*:271-276.

Valla, F.
1981 Les etablissements natoufiens dans le nord d'Israel. Colloques Internationaux du CNRS No. 598, pp. 409-419.

Vallois, H. V.
1936 Les ossements Natoufiens d'Erq el-Ahmar (Palestine). *L'Anthropologie 46*:529-539.

Vandermeersch, B.
1981 Les hommes fossiles de Qafzeh (Israel). *Cahiers de Paleontologie (Paleoanthropologie) du CNRS.*

Van Zeist, W.
1970 The Oriental Institute excavations at Mureybet, Syria: Preliminary report on the 1965 campaign. III. The paleobotany. *Journal of Near Eastern Studies 29*:167-176.

Van Zeist, W., and J. A. H. Bakker-Heeres
1979 Some economic and ecological aspects of the plant husbandry of Tell Aswad. *Paleorient 5*:161-169.

Zohary, D., and M. Hopf
1973 Domestication of pulses in the Old World. *Science 182*: (4115):887-894.

CHAPTER 6

SKELETAL PATHOLOGY FROM THE PALEOLITHIC THROUGH THE METAL AGES IN IRAN AND IRAQ

Ted A. Rathbun

Department of Anthropology
University of South Carolina

INTRODUCTION

It is somewhat ironic that in this area that has received extensive archaeological investigation into the domestication and urbanization processes, so little is known about the physical aspects of the groups in general and their pathology in particular. When viewed in historical perspective, the early excavation process with minimal attention given to human remains can, perhaps, be understood; however, the vagaries of excavation, preservation, and less than proper analysis and reportage of osteological data preclude systematic comparisons required to understand temporal change. The neglect of these potentially significant data in reports and research designs is illustrated by the summary comments in an archaeological synthesis of the Middle East Neolithic (Mellaart 1974): "It is only in the last few decades that scholars have learned to pay proper attention to plant and animal remains, but how many have realized the potential of anthropological studies, demography, and the pathology of the human skeletal remains? [p. 274]"

The areas of Southwest Asia considered in this chapter have been characterized as an ecological and cultural mosaic. The range of environmental zones in close proximity include plateaus, intermontane valleys, piedmont steppe, alluvial desert, and river valleys. The local ecological mosaic has also produced chronologies in cultural development that are regionally specific within the general Old World categories of cultural stages.

Few human remains have been reported or analyzed from the preagricultural periods before 900 B.C. Some burials have been noted, but too frequently the poor preservation prompted excavators to discard the material in the field or fail to submit the remains for osteological analysis.

The emergence of Neolithic society in Southwest Asia between 9000 and 5000 B.C. has been treated from a number of theoretical perspectives. Wright (1971) summarized many of the models and ideas. Mellaart (1974) and Singh (1974) provide systematic coverage of the major sites and regional developments. Oates (1973) surveys the communities in the Zagros region and Mesopotamia. Voight (1977) presents a particularly good and detailed account of the subsistence economy of one of the Iranian intermontane valleys. Changes in population density and aggregation were investigated in the Deh Luran plain by Hole et al. (1969) and Hole (1977). Mixed farming with domestication of both plants and animals provides a unique combination of factors in this important subsistence change. Local variants of the process produced divergent adaptations congruent with general environmental conditions. Although more burials are reported from this period, extensive data sets are not available. Pathology is sometimes mentioned, but fragmentation and small sample sizes at particular sites limit generalized statements.

The urban cultures of the metal ages apparently shared common features of intensified agricultural economies, larger population centers, extensive trade networks, and migration of various sorts. Although more skeletal material is available from this period, less than adequate reportage again makes comprehensive comparisons tenuous. Much of the early physical anthropological research attempted to trace migrations and there has been a strong concern with racial history in the area. Synthesis of earlier reports suggests a basic morphological stability of populations in the general area (Cappieri 1969, 1970; Finkel 1974; Rathbun 1972, 1975, 1979). Demographic factors have been suggested as important for the maintenance of the regional stability (Rathbun 1982). Pathology specifically has yet to be considered adequately, but disease and migration have been suggested as important features in regional developments (McNeill 1976, 1979).

Table 6.1 lists sites that produced human remains during excavation. As can be seen, the types of osteological information vary greatly, as do the specific times within the larger cultural stages. The multicomponent nature of many of the later sites and some ambiguity of the provenience of burials complicate specific period designations.

MORTUARY PRACTICES

As might be expected with the range of local cultural adaptations, the mortuary practices vary considerably over time and space. Primary as well as secondary inhumations are recorded. The general impression given by archaeological reports is that the earlier periods include more frequent secondary burials as indicated by bin ossuaries with multiple skeletons associated with houses and serendipitous recovery of body parts. Single inhumations beneath house floors and occasional cremations have been found. Separate cemetery areas with primary burials are reported with some of the Neolithic sites. The metal ages also reflect variety in disposal of the dead. These periods appear to include many more separate burying grounds and differential treatment of the dead by social categories. This range of burial practice has contributed to our less than complete and systematic coverage of the human populations.

DEMOGRAPHY

The subsidiary recovery of human remains during traditional excavation in this area provides little assurance that the materials recovered are adequate samples of the populations. The regional increase of population size and density appears general, but specific developments have been only estimated by site size and distribution, number of houses, and ethnographic analogy. Settled villages rather than individual homesteads mark the Neolithic, and the metal ages include urban centers with satellite peasant villages. This pattern of land use still is observable with contemporary groups. Total population estimates and growth rates in the area have been suggested by Carneiro and Hilse (1966) and Hassan (1973, 1979).

Although considerable interest exists in anthropology for demographic analysis of past populations, the data base in Southwest Asia is insufficient for a viable temporal comparison of survivorship and life expectancy. Empirical and model life tables have been generated from skeletal collections (see Table 6.2 for a metal age example). Problems of sampling, underrepresentation of preadults, unsystematic excavation, and sporadic osteological analysis make demographic specifics tenuous.

The lack of preadult skeletons in the collection samples appears to be due to the friability of the younger bone and the frequent discarding of the material in the field than to rarity of interment. Archaeological reports commonly state this unfortunate course of events. Childhood mortality, however, is usually suggested to be high in reports for the Neolithic, the later metal ages, and extant groups (Rathbun and Bass 1977). Unfortunately, the lack of precision in aging and insufficient data for specific age categories preclude systematic comparisons of the demographic features of survivorship and mortality. The representativeness of collections of adult skeletons has also been seriously questioned (Nowell 1980). Problems of interobserver differences in criteria of aging on frequently fragmentary skeletons must also be considered.

TABLE 6.1 Human Remains in Iran and Iraq

Cultural Stage	*Dates B.C.*	*Individuals reported*	*Demography*	*Pathology reported*	*Cranial metrics*
Preagricultural					
Shanidar					
Neanderthals	58,000-43,000	9	Yes	Yes	Yes
Hotu		3	Yes	Yes	Yes
Belt Cave	8500-6000	6	No	No	1
Period totals		18	12	12	13
Neolithic					
Zawi Chemi	8920	46	Yes	Yes	Yes
Ganj Dareh	8500-7000	49	Yes	Yes	Yes
Jarmo	6750	7	No	No	No
Deh Luran	8000-4000	45	No	No	No
Choga Sefid	6300-5900	8	No	No	No
Tepe Guran	6500-6000	4	No	No	No
Belt Cave	6500	3	No	No	No
Hassuna	6000-4000	5	Yes	Yes	Yes
Hajii Firuz	5400-5000	30	Yes	Yes	No
Tell as-Sawwan	5500-4858	130	No	No	No
Sialk 1,2,3	5000	16	Yes	No	Yes
Period totals		343	146	130	116
Chalcolithic					
Tepe Gawra	4500-4000	24	1	No	1
Sialk 4	4000	3	Yes[a]	No	Yes
Seh Gabi	4100-3700	30	Yes	Yes	No
Hissar I	4000-3000	5	Yes	Yes	Yes
Period totals		62	9	35	9
Bronze					
Hasanlu VII-IX	5000-3000	7	Yes	Yes	Yes
Hissar II	3500-3000	16	Yes	Yes	Yes
Hissar III	3000-2000	138	Yes	Yes	Yes
Geoy	3000-2000	7[b]	Yes	Yes	Yes
Sharh-i-Sokhta	2900-2000	58 45[c]	Yes	No	Yes
Kish 1-5	2900-2000	116	Yes	Yes	Yes
Dinkha IV	1900-1600	13	Yes	Yes	Yes
Period totals		355	355	297	355

Infra-cranial metrics	*Stature*	*Dentition*	*Source*
Yes	Yes	Yes	Trinkaus (1978, 1980); Stewart (1977)
Yes	Yes	Yes	Angel (1952); Angel and Coon (1952); Coon and Angel (1953)
No	No	1	Coon (1951); Angel (1952)
12	12	13	
Yes	Yes	Yes	Ferembach (1970)
Yes	Yes	Yes	Lambert (1979, 1980); Meikeljohn et al. (1980)
No	No	Yes	Braidwood and Braidwood (1950); Dahlberg (1960)
No	No	No	Hole et al. (1969, 1967)
No	No	No	Hole (1977)
No	No	No	Mortensen (1964)
No	No	Yes	Coon (1951)
No	No	Yes	Coon (1950); Abdul Aziz and Slipka (1966)
No	Yes	Yes	Voight (1983); Turnquist (1976)
No	No	No	El-Wailly (1964)
No	1	Yes	Vallois (1938)
95	126	156	
No	No	Yes	Krogman (1950)
No	No	Yes	Vallois (1938)
No	No	No	Skinner (1980); Hamlin (1973)
1	1	Yes	Krogman (1940a, 1940b, 1940c)
1	1	32	
Yes	Yes	Yes	Rathbun (1972)
No	Yes	Yes	Krogman (1940a, 1940b, 1940c)
Yes	Yes	No	Krogman (1940a, 1940b)
No	No	Yes	Cave and Centeno (1951)
Yes	Yes	No	Pardini (1977)
			Pardini and Sarvari-Negahban (1977)
Yes	Yes	Yes	Rathbun (1975)
Yes	Yes	Yes	Rathbun (1983)
332	348	159	

(Continued)

(Table 6.1 continued)

Cultural Stage	*Dates B.C.*	*Individuals reported*	*Demography*	*Pathology reported*	*Cranial metrics*
Iron					
Shah Tepe	2000	32	No	No	Yes
Giyan	2000	5	Yes	Yes	Yes
Dinkha II-III	1350-800	34	Yes	Yes	Yes
Hasanlu III-V	1350-800	141	Yes	Yes	Yes
Sialk 5,6	1200-1000	20	Yes	No	Yes
Dailaman	1000	78	Yes	No	Yes
Nippur	900-500	73	Yes	Yes	Yes
Kish, 6, 7, U	530	429	Yes	Yes	Yes
Takht-i-Suleiman	450	29	Yes	Yes	Yes
Yorgan	300 A.D.	27	Yes	Yes	Yes
Period totals		868	836	738	868

[a] *Infants only.*
[b] *Crania.*
[c] *Postcrania.*

Table 6.3 presents mortality information on individuals by sites and periods as reported in the literature. Incomparable sample sizes between the preagricultural and later groups do not allow valid statistical treatment. Analysis for significant differences between later periods for both sexes pooled, as well as individual comparisons, revealed no statistically significant differences between adjacent periods. Although there is a consistent sexually dimorphic trend in mortality, with males dying at a greater age, none of the major cultural periods revealed a significant difference at the p = .05 level. Within the Neolithic, Chalcolithic, and Iron ages, however, differential by sex in age at death approaches statistically significant levels. This differential in the metal ages has been suggested as a contributing factor to population variation by gender and differential migration in the area (Rathbun 1982).

Infra-cranial metrics	*Stature*	*Dentition*	*Source*
Yes	Yes	No	Furst (1939)
No	No	No	Vallois (1935)
Yes	Yes	Yes	Rathbun (1983)
Yes	Yes	Yes	Rathbun (1972)
No	Yes	Yes	Vallois (1938)
Yes	Yes	No	Ikeda (1968)
Yes	Yes	Yes	Swindler (1956); Rathbun and Mallin (1978)
Yes	Yes	Yes	Rathbun (1975); Carbonell (1958, 1966)
Yes	Yes	No	Storm (1976)
No	No	Yes	Starr (1939)
816	836	724	

GROWTH AND DEVELOPMENT

Growth curves of long bone development have been used as good indicators of nutritional stress related to subsistence. To date, no series from Southwest Asia has sufficient subadult data for this type of analysis.

Table 6.4 presents adult stature and the male-female ratios of sexual dimorphism. Adult stature is considered a fairly poor indicator of nutritional status since growth is controlled and influenced by a multitude of factors. The slight changes over time should not be considered definitive since the sample sizes in some periods are tiny and the range of environmental contexts during each period varies considerably. The slight decrease in the Neolithic from the preagricultural stage may be suggestive and would be consistent with adjustments to a different economic base.

It is interesting to note as well that the female mean height stays very steady from the Neolithic through the Iron Age while the male means are more irregular. Individual comparisons of mean height from contiguous periods for each sex did not reach significant levels for either gender. The sexual dimorphism index also varies irregularly with time and again no significant levels are seen across cultural periods. Within-period comparisons by

TABLE 6.2 *Life Table, Pooled Populations, Dinkha Tepe, Iran*

Age (x)	d_x	d'_x	l_x	q_x	L_x	T_x	e_x
0	2	4.35	100	.0435	489.12	2839.04	28.39
5	1	2.17	95.65	.0230	472.82	2349.92	24.57
10	2	4.35	93.48	.0465	456.52	1877.10	20.08
15	4	8.70	89.13	.0976	448.90	1420.58	15.94
20	8	17.39	80.43	.2162	358.68	971.68	12.08
25	9	19.57	63.04	.3104	341.28	631.00	9.72
30	9	19.56	43.47	.4500	168.45	271.72	6.25
35	7	15.22	23.91	.6366	81.52	103.27	4.32
40	4	8.70	8.70	1	21.75	21.75	2.50

TABLE 6.3 *Mean Age at Death After Age 15 Years*

Site	Males		Females		Pooled	
	Age	N	Age	N	Age	N
Preagricultural						
Shanidar Neandertal	40	5	28	1	38	6
Hotu	40	1	32	2	35	3
Neolithic						
Zawi-Chemi	28	1	33	2	28	4
Ganj Dareh						
All levels	27	10	24	8	25	19
Level 4	28	5	26	3	27	8
Level 6	23	2	23	3	22	6
Hassuna	40	2	20	1	33	3
Hajii Firuz	34	5	21	4	28	9
Sialk I,II,III						
All levels	35	6	33	6	34	12
Period I	32	3	34	3	33	6
Period II	40	2	34	2	37	4
Period III	35	1	28	1	32	2
Period totals	33	SD 5.39	26	SD 6.40	30	SD 3.74
Chalcolithic						
Gawra			25	1	25	1
Sialk IV	35	1	33	1	34	2
Hissar I	35	2	30	2	33	4
Period totals	35	SD 0	29	SD 4.00	31	SD 4.89
Bronze Age						
Hasanlu VII-IX	33	1	25	4	27	5
Hissar II	30	9	26	7	28	16
Hissar III	31	105	28	33	29	138

(Table 6.3 continued)

Site	*Males*		*Females*		*Pooled*	
	Age	*N*	*Age*	*N*	*Age*	*N*
Geoy	42	3	46	2	44	5
Shahr-i Sokhta						
All levels	31	32	28	26	30	58
Period I	31	5	26	4	29	9
Period II	30	14	28	20	29	34
Period III	30	9	33	1	31	10
Kish I-V						
All levels	30	24	30	13	30	37
Period II	26	3	31	3	29	6
Period III	30	20	30	9	30	29
Dinkha IV	25	5	28	5	26	10
Period totals	32	SD 5.19	30	SD 7.14	31	SD 6.08
Iron Age						
Giyan	37	3	24	2	32	5
Dinkha II,III						
All levels	32	15	35	12	33	27
Period II	34	8	39	4	36	12
Period III	30	7	33	8	32	15
Hasanlu III-V						
All levels	29	63	27	34	28	101
Period III	29	7	29	3	29	10
Period IV	29	50	26	24	28	77
Period V	33	6	29	7	30	14
Sialk V,VI						
All levels	39	11	35	9	37	20
Period VI	40	10	35	8	38	18
Dailaman						
1000 B.C.	32	?	30	?		
300-500 B.C.	29	?	26	?		
Nippur	30	37	29	20	30	57
Kish VI,VII, unknown						
All levels	29	84	27	62	28	167
Period VI	28	11	27	7	28	19
Unknown	29	73	27	55	28	148
Takht-i Suleiman	41	10	39	6	40	16
Yorgan	32	15	29	10	31	25
Period totals	33	SD 4.47	30	SD 4.69	32	SD 4.12

Table 6.4 Stature

Site	Males Stature (cm)	Males N	Females Stature (cm)	Females N	Female-male ratio
Preagricultural					
Shanidar					
Neandertals	166	4	149	1	.90
Hotu	176	1	162	2	.92
Neolithic					
Zawi Chemi	164	2	152	1	.93
Ganj Dareh	177	1	164	4	.93
Tepe Sialk					
I-IV	174	1			
Period totals	172	SD 6.78	158	SD 8.48	.93
Bronze Age					
Hasanlu VII-IX	--		163	3	
Hissar II	164	2	158	2	.96
Hissar III	168	43	157	9	.93
Shahr-i Sokhta	175	16	159	14	.91
Kish E.D. III	180	3	159	3	.88
Dinkha IV	181	2	156	4	.86
Period totals	174	SD 7.41	159	SD 2.43	.91
Iron Age					
Shah Tepe	165	12	157	2	.95
Dinkha II,III	173	13	154	10	.89
Hasanlu III-V	168	36	158	19	.94
Sialk V, VI	170	4	157	1	.92
Dailaman I	165	7	156	8	.95
Dailaman II	165	6	158	3	.96
Nippur	166	29	156	22	.94
Kish VI,VII,U	171	9	161	14	.94
Period totals	168	SD 3.16	157	SD 2.00	.94

gender indicated significant differences in all cases except the Neolithic. Even with the decrease in size of the males in the Iron ages, sexual dimorphism did not exhibit a significant decline. It is not known if the convergence in mean male and mean female height is due to dietary differences or changes in childhood influences such as activity levels or economic roles. It has been suggested (Gray and Wolfe 1980) that greater male height is associated with polygynous marriage but not with the degree of sexual dimorphism, which is influenced by dietary factors and genetics. The stability of the female stature means over time and the variability of the male means may suggest greater activity change for the males. Intraregional migration during the metal ages must also be recognized as a possible feature of the differences as well as temporal trends.

Sexual dimorphic cranial dimensions of metal age samples have shown no clear tendency to vary by either geographical subregion or time (Finkel 1982). Similarities in the percentages of sexual dimorphism of the skull for Neolithic and Bronze age samples were attributed to the continuation of earlier commonality of activity. Increases in the percentage of sexual dimorphism were noted with proto-urban and urban populations that presumably have developed marked differences in economic activity by gender. Sexual dimorphism in urban centers was also found to be greater in samples of upper-class individuals with good nutrition and health. The elite and non-elite groups were markedly different in percentage of sexual dimorphism. These findings support the contention that health, nutrition, settlement type, and form of economic subsistence are associated.

Growth disturbance and recovery during development is suggested by the occurrence of Harris lines among some of the populations. The three preagricultural individuals from Hotu appear to lack the lines. They occur in the skeletons from a few sites in the Neolithic and succeeding periods. Not all samples have been examined radiographically, but the trend appears to be one of increase over time. The Neolithic population from Ganj Dareh had a 10% frequency (Meiklejohn et al. 1980); 69% of the infants from the Chalcolithic site Seh Gabi (Skinner 1980) and 92% of the Bronze and Iron age adults at Dinkha Tepe (Rathbun 1981) exhibited lines. At the latter site, the frequencies of lines decreased slightly through time. Although the sample sizes are small, the Bronze Age group had significantly more lines than the Iron Age ones, especially for males. The age of formation was also significantly different, with Bronze Age children experiencing growth disturbance more in the later childhood years and the late Iron Age sample showing disturbance more in earlier childhood.

A combined study of Harris lines and linear enamel hypoplasias at this metal age site indicated general conditions. Table 6.5 presents the composite picture of age of developmental disturbance with regular periodic stress between ages 2 and 11. The frequency of Harris line formation peaked between 7 and 11 years, but periodic stresses are indicated throughout the developmental years. Seasonal food inadequacies, rather than chronic malnutrition, are suggested by the etiology of the line formation, which requires a recovery phase. The relatively low level of Harris lines in earlier Neolithic groups may be due to the death of stressed individuals at a younger age and hence their exclusion from the adult sample. It is interesting to note, however, that 71% of the postnatal infant sample at the transitional site, Seh Gabi, evidenced skeletal stunting (Skinner 1980). No definitive comparative statements are possible without sufficient subadult samples and comparable collections with similar age structure, completeness, and preservation.

TABLE 6.5 Age Distribution of Stress Occurrences at Dinkha Tepe, Iran

	B	*1*	*2*	*3*	*4*	*5*	*6*	*7*	*8*	*9*	*10*	*11*	*12*	*13*	*14*	*15*	*16*	*17*	*18*	*19*
Harris Lines																				
Period II																				
Males (2)													1		1					
Females (4)	1	1	1	1		1	2	2	2	1			1							
Period III																				
Males (8)			1	1		2	1	3	3	1	1	1	1	2		1	3	1		
Females (6)		1				1	1	2	5	3	2		1							
Period IV																				
Males (2)										1	2		1			1	1	2	1	
Females (3)					1		1	1		1	3	1	1							
Total (%)	4	8	8	8	4	16	20	32	40	28	32	8	24	8	4	8	16	12	4	
Hypoplasias																				
Period II																				
Males (8)			3	4	2	4														
Females (4)			1	1	1		1													
Subadults (3)	1	1	3	2	2	2	1													
Period III																				
Males (8)		2	5	5	6	5	2													
Females (5)			3	4	1	2														
Subadults (3)		2	2	2	3	2														
Period IV																				
Males (5)		1	4	4	2	1	1													
Females (4)					1	1														
Total adults (%)		9	47	53	38	38	21													

NUTRITIONAL DEFICIENCIES

Porotic hyperostosis in Southwest Asian populations is reported from the Neolithic onward. Some descriptions, however, do not make clear whether only orbital lesions are present or other cranial changes were observed. No mention is made of direct observation or radiographic analysis of an expanded diploe. No firm suggestion of a genetic anemia is indicated; rather, the lesions are presumed to indicate nutritionally derived iron-deficiency anemia.

No cases of cribra orbitalia were noted at Ganj Dareh but 42% of the Zawi Chemi sample showed strong indications of anemia. The average of these two sites, then, gives a Neolithic average of 21%. The somewhat later Seh Gabi infants expressed a 28% rate of orbital lesions, but there is some question concerning the differential diagnosis and significance of the lesions. In the metal age groups of the Iranian plateau and the Mesopotamian valley an average of 23% of the individuals had orbital lesions (Rathbun 1980). No regional differences were detectable in the pooled data for these urban groups even though the association of malaria with irrigation agriculture in Mesopotamia would suggest a probable higher rate. Subadults there exhibited a higher rate of occurrence of the condition than did subadults in Iran, but in both areas males were least affected. The higher rate for females and children may suggest the effects of differential food access, pregnancy, lactation, and parasitism.

No clear distinction is made in many of the reports among cranial osteoporosis, pitting in general, and porotic hyperostosis with expanded diploe. If the cranial pitting reflects nutritional factors, then a temporal trend emerges. One of three pre-Neolithic individuals at Hotu exhibited slight occipital pitting and 33% of the Neolithic Hajji Firuz and Ganj Dareh, Iran, samples had such lesions, but only 1 of 18 (6%) of the postnatal infants at Seh Gabi and 3% of the metal age samples exhibited cranial lesions. Age differences were not noted among the metal age Iranian groups, but Mesopotamian subadults had a significantly higher frequency than adults. The lower rate of occurrence during the later periods may reflect a decreased severity of anemic conditions, but this rationale is hard to justify with the relative stability of the orbital lesions through time.

DENTAL PATHOLOGY

The expression of dental pathology is conditioned by the genetic component of the dentition, metabolic events, the consistency and nutritive nature of the diet itself, food processing techniques, and oral hygiene. Dental attrition probably reflects the combination of factors in the most striking way. The degree and rate of attrition is usually given in the literature of Southwest Asia in relative terms. Reports from the Neolithic describe the degree as marked and strong. At Hajji Firuz the rate of attrition was slow enough for secondary dentine to form, and a "silty" diet is suggested at Jarmo. No mention is made of attrition for the pre-Neolithic Hotu group, but the Shanidar Neandertals exhibited marked attrition. The degree of attrition generally is associated with age in all the groups. The metal age populations also exhibit attrition, especially of the molars, and it is described as medium to marked in severity. Food preparation techniques with inclusion of grit are usually suggested as the major contributing factor to the condition.

Carious lesions are common in Southwest Asia. In those reports sufficiently complete to enable one to derive a frequency rate, 33% of the Neolithic individuals exhibited carious lesions, but the frequencies range from 3 to 43% (Table 6.6). At Hajji Firuz the condition is described as common. The Bronze and Iron age samples from Iran and Mesopotamia expressed a 36% rate. The general impression is that interproximal lesions at the crown-root juncture are more common than lesions on the crown. It is likely that in both the earlier and later groups attrition has obscured the crown caries. The caries rate varies considerably by individual site during the metal ages with a range of 8-54%. The Mesopotamian valley sites of Kish and Nippur had significantly lower rates than the contemporary groups on the Iranian Plateau. Males had the highest rates for both caries and alveolar abscessing in both regions.

Alveolar abscesses are frequently found in conjunction with carious lesions, periodontoclasia, and attrition. All three of the pre-Neolithic individuals exhibited periapical abscesses; 20% of the Neolithic samples and 37% of the metal age groups exhibited abscesses. This erratic temporal trend, and the regional and sex distribution with male Iranians having the highest rate, remains unexplained.

The frequency of periodontoclasia appears to have remained fairly stable. Half of the Shanidar Neandertals, 60% of the Neolithic individuals, and 52% of the metal age sample at Kish, Mesopotamia, exhibited resorption. Although no precise figures are given, other reports frequently note periodontoclasia and calculus deposits around the posterior teeth. This pattern would suggest oral hygiene as well as diet as contributing factors in resorption.

The frequency and timing of linear enamel hypoplasia formation only recently have been investigated in these skeletal samples. Careful reading of earlier reports suggests that interobserver differences in scoring the presence and severity of the hypoplasias is a serious problem in developing comparisons. Individual site variation is also notable. The general temporal change is an increase in frequency and severity of these dental defects. It is unclear whether any of the pre-Neolithic samples exhibited the condition. Only Ganj Dareh in the Neolithic has been examined specifically for the trait, with 6% of the individuals exhibiting

TABLE 6.6 Dental Pathology

	Paleolithic		*Pre-Neolithic*		*Neolithic*		*Chalcolithic*		*Bronze and Iron Age*	
	Percentage	*N*	*Percentage*	*N*	*Percentage*	*N*	*Percentage*	*N*	*Percentage*	*N*
Caries	?		0		33	91	?		36	512
Abscesses	0		100	3	20	21	?		37	516
Periodontal	50	6	0		60	70	0		52	56
Hypoplasia	?		?		6	49	45	30	14	297
Attrition	marked		?		strong-marked		?		medium-marked	

lines. Forty-five percent of the postnatal infants at Seh Gabi of the late Neolithic-Chalcolithic reflected this type of stress indicator. The average rate of occurrence for the metal age groups was 14%. Regional comparisons indicate a significantly higher frequency in the Iranian samples. Males and subadults in Iran had a significantly higher rate than their counterparts in Mesopotamia, but the rates in females were similar.

A more detailed study of stress indicators that included both Harris lines and linear enamel hypoplasias of the Bronze and Iron age samples from Dinkha Tepe, Iran (Rathbun 1981) revealed a very high rate of hypoplasias (77%) with both temporal and sexual differences. When only hypoplasias of moderate to severe expression were examined, statistically significant differences appeared. The earlier Iron Age group had a higher rate than the later Iron Age sample. Within-period variation was also significant in a few instances: Bronze Age males had a higher rate than females and late Iron Age subadults expressed a higher rate than adults. The greater frequency and generally more severe expression of the hypoplasias in subadults suggest that their earlier death was linked to the amount and frequency of stress. The generally higher rate for adult males, although not at the $p = .05$ level of significance, supports the contention that growing males are more vulnerable to stress.

Although the frequencies of stress episodes as indicated by Harris lines and linear enamel hypoplasias indicate general conditions, the composite age patterns of formation revealed periodic stress between the ages of 2 and 11. The onset of the majority of hypoplasias occurs in the age range in which weaning and stress from diarrheas and fevers with gastrointestinal infections are highly probable. Although contemporary populations reflect hypoplasia formation most frequently in the first 2 years of life, the Dinkha Tepe sample appears to have been more prone to stress somewhat later, which suggests a delayed weaning period (see Table 6.5).

Although Buikstra and Cook (1980) caution against combining these stress indicators as evidence for single disruptions due to their different etiologies, the composite picture of timing of the indicators extends the range of information. The continued periodic stress into later childhood, as indicated by the Harris lines, supports the contention of a periodic nutritional deprivation. In fact, the process of Harris line formation with the necessary recovery phase would support the hypothesis of seasonal food inadequacies rather than chronic malnutrition. The relative infrequency of Harris lines during early childhood may be due to the nature of the stress, the etiology of the indicators, or quite probably the remodeling of the earlier lines.

The slight temporal reduction of Harris line frequency among males from the Bronze through the Iron ages may indicate a slight improvement in the subsistence base, but there was no significant difference in timing or frequency for the females. The Iron Age populations apparently suffered growth disruptions earlier than the Bronze Age ones, but the sample sizes are too small for a definitive statement.

Periodic nutritional inadequacy cannot be considered the only stressor, however, since other pathologies and diseases have been documented that could, in serial combination, produce recurrent developmental disruptions. Although it is dangerous to extrapolate present conditions to the past since pathogens as well as populations and cultural systems change, West Azerbaijan has been host to a number of endemic diseases: visceral leishmaniasis, malaria, Ornithodoros tholozani, endemic relapsing fever, anthrax, leprosy, brucellosis, shigellosis, typhoid fever, and schistosomiasis (Hekmat 1970). Intestinal parasite infestation and the organisms' yearly cycles may be critical because utilization of nutrients depends not only on what goes in, but on what stays in.

CHEMICAL ANALYSIS

Investigations into the amount of plant and animal materials in the diet through the analysis of the relative amounts of strontium and calcium in human bone have been conducted on two Neolithic sites in Iran. Schoeninger (1981, 1982) found that the Sr/Ca ratio was 5.03 at Ganj Dareh and 6.70 at Hajji Firuz. She concluded that these Iranian Neolithic populations had a diet with relatively high amounts of meat in addition to cultivated plants and that there was a variety in diet between individuals at these sites. She also documented that the Iranian agriculturalists did not rely significantly more on plants than did a hunter-gatherer group in the Levant. She concluded that domesticated sheep and goats were far more important in the Zagros than in the Levant. To date, no trace element analysis of this kind has been conducted on other samples in the area.

The human remains from the metal age site, Dinkha Tepe, have been analyzed for skeletal lead burden (Aufderheide et al. 1982). Since lead ingestion can contribute to pathology levels, the material was analyzed to determine whether food storage and preparation technology was a contaminating source. Only 4 of the 45 samples had concentrations of lead above the 2 ppm/g bone ash level. Most of the values were at or near zero. The samples with elevated levels were probably contaminated after excavation. Even though metal technology was developed and some lead glazes were used, lead ingestion was not a contributing factor to the health and disease conditions in this Iranian sample.

TABLE 6.7 Common Pathologies in Iran and Iraq

	Paleolithic		*Pre-Neolithic*		*Neolithic*		*Chalcolithic*		*Bronze and Iron Age*	
	Percentage	*N*	*Percentage*	*N*	*Percentage*	*N*	*Percentage*	*N*	*Percentage*	*N*
Harris lines	?		0		10	49	81	16	92	25
Cribra orbitalia	0		0		21	56	28	18	23	461
Cranial osteoporisis	0		33	3	33	56	6	18	3	467
Infection	17	6	0		30	56	26	30	3	540
Trauma	67	6	0		57	7	26	30	15	474
Arthritis	50	6	100	3	63	8	--		35	333

INFECTION

Even though it is commonly argued that infectious disease usually increases with population density and settlement aggregation, evidence of chronic infection in the skeleton is relatively rare in Southwest Asian samples. The synergistic interaction of infective processes and diet have been well documented. As can be seen in Table 6.7, the documented rate of infection declines through time in the area. A number of the infections are localized and may be the result of trauma. The decline from approximately 30% of the individuals in the Neandertal and Neolithic samples through 26% of the transitional Seh Gabi infants to a general rate of 3% among metal age populations, however, may be due to increases in acute and epidemic infections that caused death before skeletal reaction could occur. Very few specific infection patterns have been diagnosed.

Radiographic examination of 15 metal age skulls from Dinkha Tepe documented osseous change in the middle ear from acute and chronic inflammation originating from the nasopharynx (Rathbun and Mallin 1977). Three of seven individuals from the Iron Age and three of four Bronze Age individuals exhibited these changes. Five of six males, one of six females, and none of the three subadults were affected. Age at death for the afflicted adults was under 35 years. Since 40% of this small sample were affected with otitis media, it can be suggested that cold-related infections or possibly measles and the possible resultant hearing impairment would lower the productivity of the afflicted individuals. The incidence suggests that middle ear disease was an important illness in this society.

TRAUMA

Analysis of trauma as a pathology is complicated by the difficulty of discerning whether the trauma is the result of accident or hostility and whether it is related to habitat and terrain or to types of physical activity. The temporal trend appears to be one of decline. Two-thirds of the Shanidar Neandertals (four of six) exhibited evidence of trauma (Trinkaus and Zimmerman 1982). The reports of the Neolithic samples range from nonreporting of trauma to 57% of the adults afflicted at Hajji Firuz. Twenty-six percent of the transitional Seh Gabi infants (5 of 19) reflected localized infection and trauma. The metal age survey (Rathbun 1980) indicated a trauma rate of approximately 15%. In this study some of the traumas were obviously the result of hostility, from sword and mace blows. Some of the postcranial fractures were equally dramatic. It is difficult to determine whether these traumas were from falls or, perhaps, from kicks by animals. The areal analysis revealed a much higher rate of head wounds for Iranian males than females, but no such sex difference was significant in Mesopotamia. The Iranians, however, had a higher rate than that found in the Mesopotamian samples. No significant difference by either area or sex was noted in the postcranial material. Age, however, was important since children exhibited fewer postcranial traumas in both areas.

Although artificial breaching of the skull cannot be associated directly with trauma, it is interesting to postulate that the instances of trephination noted at Zawi Chemi (Ferembach 1970) and at Dinkha Tepe (Mallin and Rathbun 1976) may have been attempts to relieve depressed fractures and other trauma (Rathbun and Mallin 1979).

OSTEOARTHRITIS

Even though degenerative joint disease and specific nutritional factors of past populations have not been linked directly, the pattern and frequency of such changes with types of physical activity may suggest activity patterns. Edynak (1976) attempted to establish life-styles from skeletal material using this approach. Similar types of analysis have not been attempted in Soutwest Asia with any precision.

The reported frequency of osteoarthritic changes varies considerably by time period and by area. Half of the Shanidar Neandertals exhibited arthritic changes and all of the pre-Neolithic individuals at Hotu reflected stress, especially of the lower back and hands (Angel 1952). At the Neolithic site of Hajji Firuz, osteoarthritis was the most common pathology present and afflicted 63% of the adults. At other sites during this time, no degenerative joint disease was present at Ganj Dareh and none was mentioned for the Zawi Chemi sample. In the latter case, however, it is not clear whether the condition was not present or simply not reported. In the metal age samples arthritic changes were common. The frequency ranges from 6 to 35% with the most common locations in descending frequency as follows: vertebrae--35%, knee--27%, elbow--21%, shoulder--13%, hip--11%, mandible--6% (Rathbun 1980).

It should be remembered that the average age at death for all of these samples was low. The relatively high frequency and severity of degenerative change can be attributed to physical stress and not to age alone. The trend for decreasing frequency through time probably can be related to changes in economic activities associated with urban life. Type of terrain appears to play a role in the expression of the pathology since the Iranian samples typically revealed a higher frequency than the Mesopotamian ones.

NONPATTERNED PATHOLOGY

The final notation of idiosyncratic and nonpatterned disease states and pathologies is included to complement the preceding surveys of possible indicators of changing economic conditions.

During the Neolithic one case of cranial hypervascularis that was attributed to tuberculosis, syphilis, or metastatic cancer was reported by Ferembach (1970) for the Zawi Chemi sample. She also indicated a possible case of Hand-Schüller-Christian disease, one instance of osteolysis of the atlas left posterior arc, one case of spina bifida occulta (also observed in the metal age groups), and all observable temporal bones with auditory tori. One case of osteolytic skull lesions, one instance of a child with generalized metabolic disease, perhaps from multiple vitamin deficiency, and hypercementosis in 37% of the dental elements were reported from Ganj Dareh (Meiklejohn et al. 1980). Possible stillborn and co-joined twins were reported at Hassuna (Abdul Aziz and Slipka 1966). The Hajji Firuz Neolithic sample also included a congenital hip deformity or aseptic necrosis, a possible metastatic tumor that occurred along the superior sagittal venous sinus, and thick vaults in all adult crania (Turnquist 1976).

The considerable stressing before and after birth of the Seh Gabi Chalcolithic infant sample was supported by the frequency of bone rarefaction: 14 of 16 or 88% of the postnatal specimens. The mean age at death for the 30 recovered infants was approximately 6 months, with 10 of the 30 deaths occurring around parturition (Skinner 1980).

The later metal age samples include a variety of individual pathologies. Krogman (1940a,b) reported a variety of pathological conditions at Tepe Hissar, and Rathbun (1972, 1975) reviews individual skeletons for pathological states. Differential diagnosis for a number of abnormal bones is not definitive.

TEMPORAL TRENDS

The picture of the health and disease conditions of these past populations in Southwest Asia is indeed hazy. No single period has been analyzed adequately from this perspective and when a time dimension is added, the effect is much like that of looking through an extremely shadowy kaleidoscope.

In attempting to summarize the different periods under consideration, one can make only a few tenuous generalizations about each period. The Paleolithic samples appear to be characterized by high rates of trauma, degenerative joint disease, dentition with attrition but few caries, frequent tooth loss, and periodontal disease. Sexual dimorphism appears to be similar to that of recent humans.

The preagricultural sample also had frequent degenerative joint disease (especially of the vertebrae), periapical abscesses, and traces of osteoporosis but no Harris lines that would indicate recovery from metabolic insult.

The composite from the Neolithic samples also includes high rates of degenerative joint disease, frequent trauma, marked attrition, and frequent carious lesions. Infection was relatively common.

The metal age groups were subject to a range of pathology-producing conditions. Age at death is not markedly different from earlier samples. Although there is a decrease in male stature, the reasons for this are not at all clear.

The detection and firm articulation of temporal trends in the qualitative and quantitative expression of pathology in the skeleton and their association with socioeconomic change in Southwest Asia are currently next to impossible. The skeletal sample sizes are extremely erratic and small in critical periods, the published literature is inadequate in both extent and comparability, and reported methods of diagnosis and criteria traditionally have been vague. Many of the inadequacies of the data base stem from the historical lack of concern for the skeleton as an archaeological resource.

In this review of the published literature, and with the previously stated caveats, it appears that demographic stability, rather than a marked improvement in longevity, is indicated with the major changes from preagriculture to village farming to the urban state. Males consistently lived longer than females, but the data are inadequate for life table construction with subadult segments of the populations. Population aggregation in the later periods appears more important than a proposed demographic transition linked to food availability.

Evaluations of estimates of stature of the populations and temporal trends are complicated by the differences in adaptation to different ecological niches and by migration. No single environmental zone has sufficient skeletal samples to document the changes over time. Migrations within the area are archaeologically and historically documented. Sexual dimorphism in adult stature does not change temporally at a statistically significant level. Within each period except the Neolithic, males were significantly taller than females. The only temporal trend appears to be stability in female stature and a reduction in average male stature during the urban metal ages. A number of explanations are possible, but the existence of fewer differences in the gender-related socioeconomic roles appears to be the most likely explanation.

Recovery from metabolic insult from disease or dietary inadequacy does appear as a trend. The increase in the rate of the observable Harris lines is time progressive. It should be noted, however, that there is great variation by individual site and that many of the samples have not been radiographically analyzed. The higher rate associated with the metal age groups may reflect a higher rate of recovery from insult or a higher pathogen exposure from the combination of urban living, hygiene, parasite loads, and periods of relative dietary inadequacy. It also should be noted that there appears to be a reduction in the evidence of infection from the Neolithic to the later metal ages.

Expression of trauma in the skeleton appears to decrease through time. However, I hasten to mention that much of the trauma seen in the later cultural phases appears to be from human violence. It is impossible to differentiate at other times among human violence, trauma through accident in rugged terrains, and possible injury from work with animals.

No great differences in dietary iron quality between preagricultural and intensified agricultural samples are noted by the frequency of cribra orbitalia. The lower incidence among males may be due to differential access to iron resources or to the metabolic demands of pregnancy and lactation in females and of development in children.

The analysis of the relative amounts of calcium and strontium preserved in the bone at Neolithic sites did not indicate a significant difference from hunter-gatherers in the general area. Marked individual variation within samples was noted. The role of animal husbandry in the agricultural groups is a significant element of Southwest Asian cultural history. Comparison with urban populations possibly would be enlightening.

Dental conditions associated with cultural practices of food preparation and hygiene also appear relatively stable. There is a very slight reduction in the degree and onset of attrition of the tooth crowns, but carious lesions, abscesses, and periodontal disease were common features throughout time.

Physical stress, as indicated by degenerative changes in various joints, decreases with urban life. No simple pattern or explanation should be invoked since osteoarthritic changes occur early in life compared to modern standards. The distribution of the stress at particular joints varies greatly by site and within each period.

CONCLUSIONS AND RESEARCH RECOMMENDATIONS

The sad picture of the paucity of specific information on health, disease, and socioeconomic change in Southwest Asia at present can be improved. Although there are significant gaps in the temporal sequence of available skeletal series, systematic restudy of the available materials in museums and other collections with a focus on pathology would provide a priority basis for further research. The restudy project not only should include diagnosis through gross observation, but should employ radiographic, chemical, and microscopic methods. Since a multidisciplinary approach appears most profitable, some consideration must be given to the use of comparable criteria and methods of data collection. Problems of archaeological information and representativeness of the samples will remain for this material excavated in the past. Restudy with new techniques of extant collections, no matter how limited, could provide significant new information (Buikstra and Gordon 1981; Peebles et al. 1981). The most serious limitations of the present collections are small sample size for some periods, fragmentation of individual skeletons, lack of subadult series, and lack of proper curation.

Research strategies involving new materials probably will require a regional approach. Although multicomponent sites are present in the area, individual site analysis, although extremely important, should be approached with the realization that the area is characterized by ecological diversity. Resources as well as reciprocity among the articulated populations in their diverse ecozones must be considered. The identification and excavation of human remains from sites in the Upper Paleolithic with a hunter-gatherer resource base, the transitional Mesolithic samples, and a range of Neolithic adaptations in the mountain valleys and the adjacent plains would be the ideal situation. Some strides have been made in the analysis of floral remains and the faunal materials have received intensive attention at specific sites and in some regions with sophisticated methodologies (Meadow and Zeder 1978). Considerations of the domestication process and the cultural dynamics involved are important, but somewhat less attention has been given to the dietary utilization of these resources. Especially lacking is the consideration of the synergistic effects of the presence of pathogens in animals and human susceptibility to disease. Mixed farming and pastoral adaptations have been characteristic of this area for significant periods of time. Since pathogens and human populations have adapted to each other through time, the epidemiological perspective should be productive in this regard.

Ethno-osteology and comparative analysis of extant grain farmers, mixed farmers, pastoralists, and urban groups generate directions for model extensions into the past. Although such models are important heuristic devices, empirical data from skeletal series are essential for a full understanding of past cultural dynamics and the effects of socioeconomic change on the health of the populations.

Specific attention must be given to the collection of sufficient skeletal material to allow valid statistical manipulation for demographic and comparative studies. Especially critical is a representative sample of subadult materials, which traditionally have not been collected. Local and regional variation in resources, population distribution, environmental factors affecting health, nutritional adequacy of food resources, and the nature of the pathogens still must be considered in detail. The importance of gender roles, age and sex social relations, and class distinctions in stratified cultural systems are other significant factors to be considered in a comprehensive analysis of the effects of socioeconomic change on health.

This review of skeletal indicators of health status of groups from the Middle Paleolithic through the metal ages in Iran and Iraq highlighted how little attention has been given to this important data resource. Even though many important data have been lost due to inattention to skeletal remains in the area, extant collections may yet yield insights into biological adaptation associated with changes in cultural systems. Previous archaeological research in the area has not provided the information needed to attempt to address the many interrelated questions of health and socioeconomic change. Future cooperation among archaeologists, physical anthropologists, and other specialists will be necessary to document the health-related factors of particular groups and temporal trends. In our attempts to address the problems of health change over time, we must also come to terms with the meaning of these possible trends: are they causes or consequences of socioeconomic change?

ACKNOWLEDGMENTS

Appreciation is extended to Professors Cohen and Armelagos for the invitation to participate in the Wenner Gren-sponsored symposium. A number of colleagues shared references and unpublished data during the preparation stage. I am especially grateful for the contributions of Babette Rathbun. Her unflagging support and, more important, her library research and the tedious work involved in table preparation and calculation of probability tests for the demography and stature sections, made the completion of this project possible.

REFERENCES

Abdul Aziz, M. H., and J. Slipka
1966 Twins from Tell Hassuna. *Sumer* *22*(1-2):45-50.
1977 Human skeletons from Tell Aswad. *Sumer* *27*:59-61.

Angel, J. L.
1952 The Human skeletal remains from Hotu Cave, Iran. *Proceedings of the American Philosophical Society* *96*(3):258-269.

Angel, J. L., and C. S. Coon
1952 Axial skeleton of an Upper Palaeolithic woman from Hotu. *American Journal of Physical Anthropology* *10*(3):252.

Aufderheide, A. C., G. Rapp, and W. Lorentz
1982 Skeletal lead analysis, Dinkha Tepe, Iran. Ms. on File, Archaeometry Laboratory and Department of Pathology, University of Minnesota, Duluth.

Braidwood, R. J., and L. Braidwood
1950 Jarmo: A village of early farmers in Iraq. *Antiquity 24:* 189-195.

Buikstra, J. E., and D. C. Cook
1980 Palaeopathology: An American account. *Annual Review of Anthropology 9*:433-470.

Buikstra, J. E., and C. C. Gordon
1981 The study and restudy of human skeletal series: The importance of long term curation. *Annals of the New York Academy of Sciences 376*:449-465.

Cappieri, M.
1969 The Mediterranean race in Asia before the Iron Age. *Occasional Paper* No. 8. Field Research Projects, Miami.
1970 The Mesopotamians of the Chalcolithic and Bronze Ages. *Occasional Paper* No. 12. Field Research Projects, Miami.

Carbonell, V. M.
1958 *The dentition of the Kish population, 3,000 B.C.* Master's thesis, University of Chicago.
1966 The paleodental pathology of ancient Mesopotamians. *Journal of Dental Research 45*:413.

Carneiro, R. L., and D. F. Hilse
1966 On determining the probable rate of population growth during the Neolithic. *American Anthropologist 68*:177-180.

Cave, A. J. E., and E. H. A. Centeno
1951 The human crania. In *Excavations in Azerbaijan in 1948*, edited by Burton Brown, pp. 206-225. Murray, London.

Coon, C. S.
1950 Three skulls from Tell Hassuna. *Sumer 6*:93-96.
1951 *Cave explorations in Iran.* University Museum, University of Pennsylvania, Philadelphia.

Coon, C. S., and J. L. Angel
1953 Interpretations of the Hotu Skeletons. *American Journal of Physical Anthropology 11*:256.

Dahlberg, A. A.
1960 The dentition of the first agriculturalists (Jarmo, Iraq). *American Journal of Physical Anthropology 18*:243-256.

Edynak, G. J.
1976 Life-styles from skeletal material: A medieval Yugoslav example. In *The measures of man*, edited by E. Giles and J. S. Friedlaender, pp. 408-432. Peabody Museum Press, Cambridge.

El-Wailly, F.
1964 Foreword. *Sumer 20*:1-3.

El-Wailly, F., and B. A. es-Soof
1965 The excavations at Tell Es-Sawwan: First preliminary report. *Sumer 21*:17-32.

Ferembach, D.
1970 Etude anthropologique des ossements humains proto-Neolithique de Zawi-Chemi Shanidar (Iraq). *Sumer 26*:21-64.
Finkel, D. J.
1974 *The dynamics of Middle Eastern skeletal populations.* Ph.D. dissertation, University of Oregon.
1982 Sexual dimorphism and settlement pattern in Middle Eastern skeletal populations. In *Sexual dimorphism in Homo Sapiens; A question of size,* edited by R. L. Hall, pp. 165-185. Praeger, New York.
Furst, C. M.
1939 The skeletal material collected during the excavations of Dr. T. J. Arne in Shah Tepe at Astrabad-Gorgan in Iran. Reports from the scientific expedition to the North-western provinces of China under the leadership of Dr. Svan Hedin. *The Sino-Swedish Expedition* Publication No. 9 (Archaeology 4). Bokforlogs Aktiebolaget Thule, Stockholm.
Gray, J. P., and L. D. Wolfe
1980 Height and sexual dimorphism of stature among human societies. *American Journal of Physical Anthropology 53*(3): 441-456.
Hamlin, C.
1973 The 1971 excavations of Seh Gabi, Iran. *Archaeology 26*: 224-247.
Hassan, F. A.
1973 On mechanisms of population growth during the neolithic. *Current Anthropology 14*:535-543.
1979 Demography and archaeology. *Annual Review of Anthropology 8*:137-160.
Hekmat, M.
1970 Geographical distribution guide to endemic diseases of Iran. Study No. 40. Field Research Projects, Coconut Grove, Miami.
Hole, F.
1977 Studies in the archeological history of the Deh Luran Plain. *Memoirs of the Museum of Anthropology University of Michigan Ann Arbor* No. 9.
Hole, F., and K. V. Flannery
1967 The Pre-history of South-Western Iran: A preliminary report. *Proceedings of the Prehistoric Society 33*:147-206.
Hole, F., K. V. Flannery, and J. A. Neely
1969 Prehistory and human ecology of the Deh Luran Plain. *Memoirs of the Museum of Anthropology University of Michigan Ann Arbor* No. 1.
Ikeda, J.
1968 Anthropological studies of West Asia. II. Human remains from the tombs in Dailaman Northern Iran. *Tokyo University Iraq-Iran Archaeological Expedition* No. 9.

Krogman, W. M.
1940a Racial types from Tepe Hissar, Iran, from the late fifth to the early second millenium B.C. A chapter in the protohistory of Asia Minor and the Middle East. *Verhandelingen der Koninklijke Nederlandsche Akademie van Wetenschappen Afdeeling Natuurkunde Tweede Sectie* Deel 39, No. 2.
1940b The skeletal and dental pathology of an early Iranian site. *Bulletin of the History of Medicine 8*:28-48.
1940c The peoples of early Iran and their ethnic affiliations. *American Journal of Physical Anthropology 26*:269-308.
1950 Report on a skull from the Well in Area A. In Excavations at Tepe Gawra (Vol. II) edited by A. Tobler, pp. 216-220. *University of Pennsylvania Museum Monographs* No. 2.
Lambert, P. J.
1979 Early Neolithic cranial deformation at Ganj Dareh Tepe, Iran. *Canadian Review of Physical Anthropology 1*(2):51-54.
1980 *An osteological analysis of the Neolithic skeletal population from Danj Dareh Tepe, Iran.* Master's thesis, University of Manitoba.
Mallin, R., and T. A. Rathbun.
1976 A trephined skull from Iran. *Bulletin of the New York Academy of Medicine 52*(7):782-787.
McNeill, W. H.
1976 *Plagues and peoples.* Doubleday, New York.
1979 Historical patterns of migration. *Current Anthropology 20*(1):95-102.
Meadow, R. W., and M. A. Zeder
1978 Approaches to faunal analysis in the Middle East. *Peabody Museum of Archaeology and Ethnology Bulletin* No. 2.
Meiklejohn, C., P. Lambert, and C. Byrne
1980 Demography and pathology of the Ganj Dareh population: Early Neolithic Iran. *American Journal of Physical Anthropology 52*(2):255.
Mellaart, J.
1974 *The Neolithic of the Near East.* Scribner's, New York.
Mortensen, P.
1964 II. Early village farming occupation. *Acta Archaeologica 34*:110-121.
Nowell, G. W.
1980 Miles method of aging dentitions of Tepe Hissar: A good method, a bad sample, but yielding tools of possible use for other samples. *American Journal of Physical Anthropology 52*(2):263.
Oates, J.
1973 The background and development of early farming communities in Mesopotamia and the Zagros. *Proceedings of the Prehistoric Society 39*:147-181.

Pardini, E.
1977 Gli inumati di Shahr-i-Sokhta (Sistan, Iran). Studio Osteologico Preliminare--II Parte. *Archivio per l-Anthropologia e la Etnologia CVII*:159-235.

Pardini, E., and A. A. Sarvari-Negahban
1977 Craniologia degli inumati di Shahr-i-Sokhta (Sistan, Iran). Studio preliminare. *Archivio per l-Antropologia e la Etnologia CVI*:1-49.

Peebles, C. S., M. J. Schoeninger, V. P. Steponatis, and C. M. Scarry
1981 A precious bequest: Contemporary research with the WPA-CCC collections from Moundville Alabama. *Annals of the New York Academy of Sciences 376*:433-447.

Rathbun, T. A.
1972 *A study of the physical characteristics of the ancient inhabitants of Hasanlu, Iran.* Study No. 68. Field Research Projects, Coconut Grove, Miami.
1975 *A study of the physical characteristics of the ancient inhabitants of Kish, Iraq.* Study No. 87. Field Research Projects, Coconut Grove, Miami.
1979 Metric and discrete trait variation among Metal Age Iranian and Mesopotamian populations. *American Journal of Physical Anthropology 50*(3):473.
1980 Patterns of pathology among Metal Age Iranian and Mesopotamian populations. *American Journal of Physical Anthropology 52*:269.
1981 Harris lines and dentition as indirect evidence of nutritional states in early Iron Age Iran. *American Journal of Physical Anthropology 54*(3):266.
1982 Morphological affinities and demography of Metal Age Southwest Asian Populations. *American Journal of Physical Anthropology 59*:47-60.
1983 Skeletal material from Dinkha Tepe, Iran. Ms. on File, Department of Anthropology, University of South Carolina.

Rathbun, T. A., and W. M. Bass
1977 Physical and demographic features of two groups in Northwestern Iran. *Anthropologie XV*/1:55-61.

Rathbun, T. A., and E. F. Mallin
1978 Skeletal remains. In Excavations at Nippur Twelfth Season, M. Gibson, J. A. Franke, M. Civil, M. L. Bates, J. Boessneck, K. W. Butzer, T. A. Rathbun, and E. F. Mallin. *Oriental Institute Communications 23*:139-152.

Rathbun, T. A., and R. Mallin
1977 Middle ear disease in a prehistoric Iranian population. *Bulletin of the New York Academy of Medicine 53*(10):901-905.
1979 A probable trephination: Not an enlarged parietal foramen. *Bulletin of the New York Academy of Medicine 55*(7):717-723.

Schoeninger, M. J.
1981 The agricultural "revolution"; Its effect on human diet in prehistoric Iran and Israel. *Paleorient* 7:73-92.
1982 Diet and the evolution of modern human form in the Middle East. *American Journal of Physical Anthropology* 58(1):37-52.
Singh, P.
1974 *Neolithic cultures of Western Asia.* Seminar Press, New York.
Skinner, M. F.
1980 Pathologies among infants from Seh Gabi, Iran. *American Journal of Physical Anthropology* 52(2):280.
Starr, R. F. S.
1939 *Nuzi, report on the excavations of Yorgan Tepa near Kirkuk, Iraq, 1927-1931* (Vol. I). Harvard University Press, Cambridge.
Stewart, T. D.
1977 The Neanderthal skeletal remains from Shanidar Cave, Iraq: A summary of findings to date. *Proceedings of the American Philosophical Society* 121(2):121-165.
Storm, S.
1976 *Die Skelete vom Takht-i-Suleiman (Nord-West Iran).* Ph.D. thesis, Freie Universität, Berlin.
Swindler, D. R.
1956 *A study of the cranial and skeletal material excavated at Nippur.* University Museum Monograph, University of Pennsylvania, Philadelphia.
Trinkaus, E.
1978 Dental remains from the Shanidar adult Neanderthals. *Journal of Human Evolution* 7:369-382.
1980 Sexual differences in the Neanderthal limb bones. *Journal of Human Evolution* 9:377-397.
Trinkaus, E., and M. R. Zimmerman
1982 Trauma among the Shanidar Neanderthals. *American Journal of Physical Anthropology* 57(1):61-76.
Turnquist, J.
1976 The Neolithic skeletal population from Hajji Firuz Tepe. Appendix In Voight, M., Hajji Firuz Tepe: An Economic Reconstruction of a Sixth Millenium Community in Western Iran. Ph.D. Thesis. Philadelphia: University of Pennsylvania. Appendix C: pp. 823-846.
Vallois, H. V.
1935 Notes sur les tetes osseuses. In Fouilles de Tepe Giyan, Iran, edited by G. Contenau and R. Ghrishman. *Musée du Louvre Paris Serie Archeologique* 3:119-134.
1938 Les ossements humains de Sialk, contribution a l'etude de l'histoire raciale de l'Iran ancien. In *Fouilles de Sialk pres de Kashan 1933, 1934, 1937* (Vol. II), edited by R. Ghirshman, pp. 113-171. Geuthner, Paris.

Voigt, M. M.
1977 The subsistence economy of a sixth millenium village in the Ushnu Solduz Valley. *Bibliotheca Mesopotamica, Undena, Malidu,* pp. 307-346.
1983 Hajji Firuz Tepe: The Neolithic settlement. In *Hasanlu excavation reports* (Vol. I). pp. 70-94. University Museum Monographs, No. 50, University of Pennsylvania, Philadelphia.

Wright, G. A.
1971 Origins of food production in Southwestern Asia: A survey of ideas. *Current Anthropology 12*:447-475.

CHAPTER 7

GROWTH, NUTRITION, AND PATHOLOGY IN CHANGING PALEODEMOGRAPHIC SETTINGS IN SOUTH ASIA

Kenneth A. R. Kennedy

Ecology and Systematics
Division of Biological Sciences
Department of Anthropology
Cornell University

This chapter summarizes recent investigations of the skeletal biology of human populations marking the socioeconomic transition from hunting and gathering to intensive food production strategies in South Asia. This region is defined as including India, Burma, Pakistan, Bangladesh, Afghanistan, and the Himalayan countries of Nepal, Sikhim, and Buthan, as well as Sri Lanka and other islands of the Indian Ocean and Bay of Bengal. Both field and laboratory research into the skeletal biology of ancient mortuary samples and the published archival record are discussed against the background of the archaeological record. Particular reference is made to changing patterns of individual growth and development, paleodemography, skeletal and dental pathology, and nutrition. It is concluded that the adoption of intensified utilization and processing of vegetable food sources by Neolithic and later populations permitted increasing population density but led to lower quality nutrition and an increase in certain pathologies. There are indications of a highly successful economic homeostasis for many preagricultural Mesolithic populations, but it is suggested that population growth may have placed stress on these groups and encouraged their greater exploitation of the food resource base through incipient pastoralism and plant cultivation.

THE ARCHAEOLOGICAL AND SKELETAL RECORD

Recent summaries of the archaeology of South Asia (Agrawal 1982; Allchin and Allchin 1982; Deraniyagala 1981; Fairservis 1975; Jacobson 1979; Khan 1968; Sankalia 1974, 1977), although employing varying terminologies and classifications, recognize a sequence of technological stages roughly analogous to the Paleolithic-Iron Age sequence of Europe. However, there continues to be uncertainty over the correct usage of terms such as "Neolithic," "Chalcolithic," and "Megalithic" when they are applied to specific sites in the region. And, although there is a general succession of cultural traditions from Paleolithic-Mesolithic hunting and gathering groups to Neolithic, Chalcolithic, and Iron Age lifeways, the times of the emergence of new economies vary considerably in different parts of the subcontinent and not all of the cultural traditions are represented in every region. Local "survivals" of more ancient lifeways may form symbiotic relationships with "more advanced" cultures in a given area such that a chronology of uniform culture periods does not readily apply. A somewhat broader set of economic categories will therefore be employed here (Table 7.1). There exists today a human skeletal record of over 1700 individual specimens from 63 burial sites covering a temporal span of 30,000 years for which some description of skeletal biology and archaeological context are published. This chapter, building on a recent catalogue of the 63 sites (Kennedy and Caldwell 1984), organizes these data into categories of specimens of Pleistocene or uncertain antiquity, early Holocene and recent hunting and gathering communities, early farming-herding communities, mature farming communities, early (Harappan, Bronze Age) civilizations, and Iron Age populations. The larger skeletal series are derived from early and mature farming sites of central and south India and from sites of the Harappan civilization of the northwestern sector (Table 7.2). Not included in this catalog are recently described skeletons from three sites for which published data were not yet available at the time the catalog was prepared: the early "Neolithic" sites of Burzahom and Kashmir (Basu and Pal 1980) and Mehrgarh in Baluchistan and the later farming site of Inamgaon in Maharashtra (J. R. Lukacs, personal communication). In addition to the above-mentioned sites, there are more than 108 sites reported, yielding more than 1000 skeletal specimens that are as yet undescribed but of which many are known to be both complete and relatively well preserved.

Summary sources of South Asian skeletal data are authored by Büchi (1968), P. Gupta (1975, 1976), S. P. Gupta (1972), Jain (1979), Kennedy (1975b), Murty (1974), Sahni (1956), and Sarkar (1964, 1972). Problem-oriented studies are fewer (Kennedy 1973a,b, 1975a,c, 1980a; Lukacs 1983a, 1984; Lukacs et al. 1984; Sen 1964). Studies of South Asian burial practices in which some attention is given to skeletal anatomy or mortuary disposition have focused on

TABLE 7.1 Chronology of South Asia Prehistoric Cultures[a]

Culture	Geographical Region								
	Baluchistan[b]	Greater Indus Valley[b]	Rajasthan	Gandhara[b]	Kashmir[b]	Indo-Gangetic Plain	Deccan Plateau	South India	Sri Lanka[c]
Iron Age	900–800 Cairn burials	1000–500 Pirak	1000 Painted Gray Ware	1000	1000	1000	1300–600	1100 BC–AD 100	300?
						1300		MEGALITHS	
	Kulli/Mehi	INDUS CIVILIZATION							
Mature food producing communities	III			1500	1500	Hunting communities / Farming communities	Hunting communities / 1800 / Farming communities	Hunting communities / Farming communities	
	II Damb Sadaat I								
Early food-producing communities			2300 Banas Early villages	2500	2400			2400	
				4000 Sarai Khola		4500			4500
	4500 Kili Ghul Mohammad								
		6000 Mehrgarh	6000 Early herding communities				5500		
Early Holocene hunters and gatherers	////	////	8000	////	////	10,000			
Upper Paleolithic	30,000–10,000		18,000–8000	30,000–10,000		>22,000		>23,000 / >36,000	? / ?
Middle Paleolithic	38,000–30,000								?
Lower Paleolithic	1,000,000–38,000								

[a] BC dates are given unless indicated otherwise.
[b] //// = little or no evidence of a specific culture present.
[c] ? = possible existence of a culture of a specific period of time in a region.

TABLE 7.2 South Asian Archaeological Sites and Human Skeletal Specimens for Which There Are Published Descriptions: Breakdown by Cultural Context[a]

Cultural Context	*Number of sites*[b]	*Number of specimens*	*Percentage of total for all cultural contexts*
Paleolithic	*6*	*7*	*0.4*
Hunter-gatherer communities	*11*	*> 98*	*6.3*
Early farming-herding communities in central and South India	*11*	*> 603*	*38.6*
Harappan	*10*	*> 368*	*23.6*
Gandharan	*3*	*> 309*	*19.8*
Iron Age (Megalithic)	*14*	*> 161*	*10.3*
Uncertain temporal and/or cultural context	*8*	*> 16*	*1.0*
	63	*>1562*	*100.0*
Reported sites with undescribed human skeletal specimens	*108*	*? (over 1000)*	

[a]*Sites not included: Burzahom (10 specimens), Mehrgarh (17 specimens), and Inamgaon (176 specimens).*

Iron Age (Krishnaswami 1949), Harappan (Hasan 1975; Sarkar 1937, 1964), and Gandharan (Stacul 1973) practices, although more general reviews exist as well (Gupta 1972; Kennedy and Caldwell 1984; Singh 1970). Current repositories of human skeletal remains are described by Kennedy (1980b) and Kennedy and Caldwell (1984). Interpretations of the sociological significance of mortuary data are available (Durrani 1978; Leshnik 1967). Collections of osteological specimens from historic or from nonarchaeological sources (tribal cemeteries, hospitals, biological supply houses, comparative anatomy collections) constitute another important research base (Annandale 1909; Kennedy 1972b).

PALEODEMOGRAPHY

Paleodemographic research has emerged in South Asia since the 1960s as the result of the work of both Indian scholars (Datta 1959, 1962; Sharma 1969-1970, 1972, 1982) and Western scholars (Bernhard 1967; Kennedy 1969, 1974, 1975a, 1976, 1982a; Lukacs 1978, 1980b, 1983b; Lukacs and Badam 1981). However, comprehensive studies of paleodemographic factors of population size, density, mortality, survivorship, and life expectancy based on skeletal data are few at the present time.

Fairservis (1975) has suggested that the period of the post-Pleistocene hunting-gathering lifeway brought with it a dramatic population expansion following the longer and more stable Paleolithic period. Certainly more permanent settlements and a hunting-gathering lifeway that was combined in some areas with incipient pastoralism, exploitation of new habitation sites in a variety of ecological settings, and more efficient methods of hunting and gathering with the acquisition of the dog, bow and arrow, and precision microlithic tools argue for increasing regionalization and a higher population density of localized communal bands. The apparent stability of the food resource base for many hunting-gathering communities may be reflected in the relatively high ages at time of death for skeletalized individuals from these sites compared to lower ages at time of death for representatives of later farming-herding communities. At the terminal Pleistocene site of Mahadaha in the Gangetic Plain some human remains have been recovered that are assessed as having died in the fifth and sixth decades of life (Kennedy 1984b,c). These paleodemographic investigations are tempered by the biases inherent in all studies of mortuary populations (see Datta 1962). However, the high incidence of dental pathology and attrition in certain terminal and post-Pleistocene hunting-gathering series is attributable, in part, to the greater number of older individuals found in these series when comparisons are made with mortuary populations of prehistoric farming communities (Lukacs 1978).

GROWTH AND DEVELOPMENT

Stature

Estimation of stature during life based on regression statistics utilizing length measurements of long bones of the upper and lower extremities provides one measure of skeletal growth and development. Although most investigators have used the Trotter (1970) correlations based on standards for American white males, Athawale (1964) has established standards of stature from lengths of forearm bones based on a study of 100 Maharashtrian male adults between ages 25 and 30 years. Earlier methods for determining stature have been used as well, with the result that stature estimations published for prehistoric skeletal remains from South Asia do not follow a uniform standard of reconstructed body height. When long bone length measurements have been remeasured by a single investigator and the Trotter formulas applicable for adult white males used, the values reveal a number of features that reflect trends in growth and development of prehistoric South Asians over the course of 12 to 14 millennia.

One trend is reduction of stature for both males and females that occurs with the socioeconomic transition from the hunting-gathering lifeway to food-producing economic strategies. Paleolithic data are not available, but the Gangetic sites of Sarai Nahar Rai and Mahadaha, which may have an antiquity of from 14,000 to 12,000 years B.P., constitute a combined series of some 65 skeletal specimens of which many are sufficiently well preserved to provide mensural data of long bone lengths. These were people of tall stature, the range of estimated statures for Sarai Nahar Rai males being from 174 to 192 cm; for Mahadaha males the range is from 168 to 190 cm. Female statures overlap this range and for Mahadahans the range is from 162 to 176 cm. Accompanying this striking feature is another indicator of skeletal growth and development--degree of skeletal-muscular robusticity. The early Gangetic hominids are exceptionally robust in cranial and post-cranial anatomy, their large heads supporting well-developed supraorbital tori, sharp nuchal lines, large mastoid processes with prominent supramastoid crests, and well-marked temporal lines. Mandibles are massive and have well-formed mental eminences and everted gonia. These features of tall stature and skeletal robusticity lead to the conclusion that these people of terminal Pleistocene times realized the full potential of their ontogenetic development.

Comparative analysis of these Gangetic specimens with skeletons from other preagricultural sites in South Asia spans a temporal hiatus of over five millennia, i.e., from *circa* 12,000 years B.P. to 6500 years B.P. In this period considerable modifications of body size and cranial robusticity took place. Examination of Indian hunting-gathering series from sites in Uttar Pradesh, Madhya Pradesh, Gujarat, and Rajasthan reveals a trend toward reduced stature and skeletal strength. The decrease in stature that occurs in prehistoric South Asia with the onset of food production is coincident with a reduction in sexual dimorphism. More gracile body form characterizes skeletons of individuals of both sexes.

Studies of geographic distribution of stature among modern South Asian populations show that there is a gradient from northwest to east and south (Büchi 1968). Inhabitants of Rajasthan, Panjab, Kashmir, and Baluchistan are generally taller than people of other regions, especially among the higher castes. Takahashi (1971) correlates South Asian stature variables with climatic zones, noting that taller statures are found in arid zones of the northern and northwestern portions of the subcontinent and shorter statures in hot, rainy, and humid regions of the southern and eastern belt. Diet is another factor in stature, according to Takahashi; the shorter peoples of the southlands subsist on a basic diet of rice whereas the taller people of the north take much more dairy food. Only in a very general way does this present picture of stature distribution in South Asia correlate with prehistoric stature distribution, and this remains an area for future research.

Tooth Size

Paralleling the temporal stature trends is tooth size reduction, which is obvious when comparisons are made between early and late skeletal series in South Asia. This phenomenon has been documented for European Paleolithic and Mesolithic series by Frayer (1978) and for Australasian and Far Eastern ancient series by Brace and Mahler (1971). Brace and Montagu (1977) have observed that in South Asia the smallest teeth appear today in populations in the northern and northwestern sectors of the subcontinent. Teeth become larger in the peoples of western and central Deccan, and the largest teeth occur in populations in south India and Sri Lanka. Their survey is correlated with the archaeological data, which reveal that higher technologies, including those relating to food production and preparation, are of greater antiquity in north India than in the Peninsula, as attested by the emergence of the Harappan civilization in the Indus Valley before 3000 B.C. Brace (1978) argues that there has been a trend toward tooth size reduction in different parts of the world where more advanced technologies have developed to relax selection pressures, whereas in earlier and precivilized contexts large teeth were highly adaptive for maximization of masticatory stress. Hence the longer period of time a population has practiced advanced technologies, particularly in the area of food preparation, the smaller are its teeth. Dutta (1983) has examined teeth from the site of Harappa and concludes that molar size is reduced when comparisons are made with pre-Bronze Age dentitions from Europe and western Asia.

The question of cultural variation and dental reduction in South Asia was addressed in a paper by Lukacs (1982a; see also Lukacs 1977, 1981b) presenting the first detailed study of prehistoric South Asian dentitions and focusing on the question of tooth size reduction. Lukacs (1982a) concluded that:

> Mode of subsistence, dietary preference and food preparation methods are closely related to the pattern of tooth size variation in South Asia. Mesolithic hunters and gatherers exhibit large tooth size while full-time agriculturalists have very small teeth. Samples drawn from mixed economic systems display an intermediate range of tooth sizes. The pattern of dental reduction in South Asia is

consistent with trends described for Eastern Mediterranean and southeast Asian populations, though the evolutionary mechanisms remain in dispute. (p. i)

In the body of his paper, Lukacs notes that parallel reduction of dental dimensions from "Mesolithic" to "Neolithic" times in South and Southwest Asia implies that natural selection rather than random mutation is the evolutionary mechanism of dental reduction. This same author has also noted (Lukacs 1983a) that, in samples of prehistoric farming populations, the smallest teeth were found in those populations with the longest history of agricultural practices and in those for whom hunting and gathering played the smallest role. To these observations may be added the point that dental reduction is one aspect of facial reduction, and continued decrease in the use of the mouth as a tool came about as a consequence of technological innovations as well as socioeconomic changes.

Growth Arrest

Recording of Harris lines and related markers of interrupted growth patterns is a recent practice in South Asian paleodemographic investigations (Kennedy 1981). Somewhat greater attention has been given to the observation of presence, frequency, or absence of hypoplastic lines and pits in dental enamel. One study of Harappan skeletal series from the sites of Harappa, Mohenjodaro, and Lothal notes the low incidences of Harris lines and enamel hypoplasia, and offers the interpretation that fluctuations of the food resource base may have been infrequent in these Bronze Age urban centers. No obvious distinction between social groups at these sites could be made on the basis of these indicators of interrupted growth and development (Kennedy 1978, 1982c). (These data may accord with the apparent absence of royal tombs and other evidence of preferential treatment of the dead in Harappan mortuaries.)

Enamel hypoplasias occur in low frequency in other prehistoric populations, occasionally in association with the lateral bowing of the diaphyses of long bones. Hypoplasias occur with greatest frequency in farming or herding communities and with lowest frequencies in hunting and gathering groups.

Paleopathology

Data available for the comparative analysis of pathology come from a variety of sources (Begley et al. 1981; Branfill 1881; Gupta et al. 1962; Kennedy 1965, 1972a, 1982b, 1984b,c; Kennedy and Malhotra 1966; Kennedy et al. 1984; Lukacs 1976, 1977, 1978, 1980a, 1981a,b, 1982b, 1983b; Lukacs et al. 1982; Rao 1970, 1973; Sarkar 1960, 1972). Most of the reports relate to dental pathology (Table 7.3). Comparative analysis of these data suggests results paralleling those of other regions. Relatively low rates of various dental pathologies appear in skeletal series from hunting and gathering groups. Dentitions in South Asian hunters and gatherers show the lowest levels of dental pathology in the form of caries, malocclusion, agenesis of teeth, and crowding. However, severe occlusal attrition is relatively common in the dentitions of these same series. Alveolar resorption (periodontal disease) with antemortem tooth loss is also a feature common to the South Asian hunter-gatherers.

Lukacs (1981a) has noted a dramatic rise in caries frequency with increasing dependence on agricultural subsistence. However, later populations show relatively few signs of heavy masticatory stress, antemortem tooth loss, dental abscesses, and alveolar resorption. Dental calculus (tartar) is reported sporadically among hunting and gathering and early food-producing populations. Its apparent absence in Harappan and Iron Age series may be due to the failure of earlier investigators to record it.

Other pathological features of South Asian prehistoric skeletons are of sporadic occurrence and distribution. Aside from a summary study published by D. N. Banerjee (1941) over 40 years ago, most references to pathological markers on prehistoric human bones from South Asia appear in connection with reports of specific skeletal series (Table 7.3). Many of the reports of bone pathologies are based on inaccurate assessments of postmortem damage to specimens that have undergone fracturing and distortion of bone from pressure and temperature changes. So-called wound marks on skeletons from the preagricultural site of Langhnaj in Gujarat (Ehrhardt 1960) and the fabled "massacre victims" from Mohenjodaro (Sewell and Guha 1931; Wheeler 1968) are examples of these kinds of misinterpretation of data (Kennedy 1982c, 1984a).

Of the terminal Pleistocene series from the Gangetic Plain, a single adult male from Sarai Nahar Rai exhibits osteocartilaginous exostoses on the right radius and left metatarsals. Dutta and his associates (Dutta et al. 1972) have interpreted the shape of another male skull from this site as being indicative of the effects of a minor birth trauma leading to incomplete infantile hemiparesis, but they note that "this condition might also occur due to congenital aplasia or hypoplasia of (the) right side of the frontal cortex extending to the right parietal region" (pp. 119-120). They concluded that this condition affected normal growth of the left side of the body as determined by differences in measurements of limb bones (those of the left side being shorter than those of the right). Pathological conditions found in the neighboring Mahadaha series include one case of osteosarcoma or chondrosarcoma of the right ilium of an adult individual and one case of pronounced osteophytosis of the lumber vertebrae accompanied by osteoarthritic lipping. A third individual from Mahadaha has a small exostosis spur on the diaphysis of the left humerus. A mandibular lesion that might be attributed to osteomyelitis

TABLE 7.3 *Pathological Conditions Observed in South Asian Prehistoric Skeletal Series*

Culture and site name	Size of series	Pathology: Trauma	Porotic hyperostosis	Osteophytosis	Bowing of diaphysis	Caries	Abscess
Hunting-gathering							
Baghai Khor[a]	1		+				
Bellanbandi Palassa	15				+		
Bagor	1						
Bhimbetka[a]	16			+			
Langhnaj	14					+	
Lekhahia ki Pahari[a]	19					+	
Mahadaha	26			+	+	+	
Sarai Nahar Rai	35					+	
Farming-Herding							
Burzahom	10					+	+
Mehrgarh[a]	16					+	
Piklihal	3			+		+	
Tekkalakota	9						
T. Narasipur	1					+	
Apegaon	1					+	
Bagor	3					+	
Chandoli	24				+	+	
Inamgaon	53	+	+			+	
Nevasa	130				+	+	
Harappan							
Chanhudaro	1		+				
Harappa	265		+	+		+	+
Kalibangan	11	+					
Lothal	21						
Makran (Shahi-tump)	3						
Nal	18	+					
Mohenjodaro	46	+	+	+		+	+
Iron Age (Megalithic)							
Adittanalur	16						
Bhimbetka[a]	1	+					
Brahmagiri	20						
Khapa[a]	5					+	
Mahujhari	28				+	+	
Pomparippu	27					+	
Ruamgarh	2						
Yelleswaram	16						
Gandharan							
Butkara II	50	+					

[a]No published description available as of September 1982.

Pathology *Alveolar border resporption*	*Calculus*	*Enamel Hypoplasia*	*Severe dental attrition*	*Slight dental attrition*	*Other pathological conditions*
+			+		
	+			+	
		+	+	+	
+		+			
+	+				
+		+			*Osteosarcoma*
		+			*Osteocartilaginous exostosis; infantile hemiparesis*
+	+		+		
	+	+			
+					*Lumbar spondylolisthesis*
+	+		+		
+					
			+		
+				+	
+	+	+			*Endocranial lesions, scurvy?*
			+	+	
+					
+			+		
					"Paralytic case"
+				+	
			+		
			+		
+			+		
+					*Bulbous frontal bones (rickets?)*
+					
			+		
+		+			*Hypercementosis*
		+			
				+	
+			+		

appears in a specimen from reputed "Paleolithic" levels at a rock shelter at Bhimbetka, and a published description awaits confirmation of its antiquity from dating analysis now being conducted (Kennedy et al. 1984).

Of early farming community skeletons, reports of pathological features include a description of a spondylolisthesis condition in a lumbar vertebra from Piklihal. J. R. Lukacs (personal communication) has noted an endocranial lesion on the frontal bone of an infant from Inamgaon. Periosteal lesions in Inamgaon infants may be attributed to a variety of causes, including infantile cortical hyperostosis, physiologic periostitis of the newborn, scurvy (vitamin C deficiency), hypervitaminosis A, and infection. Diagnoses of these pathologic specimens from Inamgaon were undertaken by F. P. Saul and R. T. Steinbock for the describer of the Inamgaon skeletal series. In a forthcoming paper (Sankalia and Lukacs 1984) Lukacs observes that a pathologic condition observed in an Inamgaon specimen that suggests cranial yaws could also be a partially healed depressed fracture. A. K. Sharma (1982) refers to "a paralytic case" among Harappan skeletons from Kalibangan, a male about 30 years of age with pronounced deformities of limb and hand bones.

Osteophytosis of vertebrae appears in high frequency in skeletal series from all cultural periods. It is associated with osteoarthritic remodeling of bone, more severe degenerative changes occurring in individuals who have survived into the fourth decade of life. These changes are of particular interest with respect to the early series from the Gangetic Plain since the onset of arthritic bone modification appears to occur at a somewhat younger age than is the case with other series, as early as the beginning years of the third decade of life for certain individuals of these populations.

Traumatic lesions are frequently reported as pathological conditions in the literature (Alciati and Fedeli 1965). The best authenticated cases of trauma occur at the following sites:

1. Kalibangan (Harappan)--a deep vertical cut on the left knee caused by a sharp instrument and with no sign of healing
2. Nal (Harappan)--compression of right temporal-sphenoidal region with no sign of healing
3. Inamgaon (mature farming)--a completely healed humeral fracture
4. Butkara II--traumatic lesions on two skulls and one clavicle and
5. A reputed "Iron Age" deposit at Bhimbetka--healed lesions on the left parietal bone

These marks of traumatic interference are associated with other kinds of biological or archaeological evidence of massacres. Although trauma is apparent in one or two specimens from Mohenjodaro, the "massacre hypothesis" does not seem to find support any longer with respect to this Harappan site (Kennedy 1982c). It is interesting that these certain cases of traumatized individuals occur in the cultural contexts of urban or village settings.

NUTRITION

Much of what has been discussed in this chapter with respect to differences of attainment of ontogenetic potentials of growth, as manifest in stature and skeletal robusticity, also pertain to nutrition. The food resource base is itself a complex concept, involving food quantity and quality, constant supply or periodic fluctuation of food availability, individual metabolic responses to specific nutrients, food preferences of individuals and social groups, and seasonal factors of food selection and availability in different ecological settings. Hence it is often difficult to isolate nutritional stress from other kinds of stresses of the cultural or noncultural environment that affect ontogenetic growth and development.

One index of the nutritional base is the effect of relative carbohydrate and protein levels. Stini (1975) has noted that small body size is an adaptive response to circumstances of chronic protein deprivation. This observation seems relevant to nutritional studies of living South Asian populations that exist, for the most part, under chronic nutritional stresses, especially with respect to protein deficiency and high carbohydrate intake. This nutritional pattern may be of considerable antiquity in the subcontinent, beginning over 8000 years ago in areas where the earliest transition from food gathering to food producing took place.

Because skeletal changes are partially developmental and responsive to different nutritional adaptations, there is an expected diversity of body size and form in socioeconomic groups within the Indian subcontinent today. Tall stature and skeletal robusticity appear sporadically, however, and there are no contemporary human groups in South Asia that possess the total morphological pattern of the terminal Pleistocene populations of the Gangetic Plain. Even surviving tribal populations that retain a certain number of cultural features of the hunting-gathering lifeway obtain a high proportion of their nutrients in the form of grain and luxury foods from neighboring settled agriculturalists according to ancient customs of barter. Such tribal enclaves have long been incorporated as symbiotic subcultures within the economic patterns of sedentary macropopulations surrounding them, and gene flow has served for centuries to tie the forest dwellers to the food producers of the fertile valleys and plains.

In an important paper Dutta (1969) discussed the pathological significance of bilateral thinning in a Harappan skull he had examined. This condition, when thinning of the bones of the cranial vault is restricted to the outer table of compact osseous tissue and is combined with porosity and extensive remodeling of postcranial bones, is diagnostic of a chronic state of anemia for the individual. Investigation of skeletons from Mohenjodaro and Harappa reveals that varying degrees of porotic hyperostosis modification appear in the skeletal series (Kennedy 1981, 1984d).

This condition was not reported by Sewell and Guha (1931), who first examined the Mohenjodaro material, nor was it mentioned by subsequent students of Harappan series. The incidence of porotic hyperostosis is as high as 25% of the total Harappan samples investigated by the author in 1964, 1977, and 1980. Its presence is documented for individuals of both sexes and ages from infancy to adulthood. Krogman and Sassman (1943) describe the adult female skull from Chanhudaro (Harappan) as exhibiting vascular pitting of the ectocranial plates of both parietal bones, and ascribe this to "evidence of a slight nutritional disturbance in childhood, too slight, however, to result in any aberrancy in the cranio-facial pattern" (p. 254).

In the sample of Harappan skeletons, porotic hyperostosis appears consistently on the parietal bones and frontal bones and there are 3 cases in every 10 in which the maxilla exhibits this condition. In no case do we encounter porotic hyperostosis of the occipital bone by itself. In a single case where the occipital bone does exhibit porosity, the same modification occurs on the frontal and parietal bones as well. The hair-on-end condition appears in very low frequency in our sample, i.e., in only 3% of the cases. From these data, which were observed on specimens of both sexes who ranged in age at time of death from about 12 years to middle age, it is suggested that either thalassemia or sicklemia, or both, were present in the Harappan population. (In India today the sickle cell gene attains a frequency of 5-10% in the central part of the Deccan plateau, rises to 15-20% in the southernmost part of the peninsula, and drops to less than 5% in Assam and Burma. In the northwestern sector of the subcontinent the sickling gene ranges from 5-20% in local areas. This distribution coincides well with the broad distribution of falciparum malaria in India before 1930.)

Porotic hyperostosis has been found in the farming population of Inamgaon (Lukacs and Badam 1981). However, with the single exception of a specimen from Baghai Khor, preagricultural human skeletal remains in India and Sri Lanka do not exhibit porotic hyperostosis.

The diagnostic cranial features of rickets are found in 5 of the 16 crania recovered from the Iron Age site of Adittanalur, but no adequate description of postcranial bones from this series has been published. Better evidence of rickets is present in the Iron Age skeletons from Mahujhari, in which the limb bones are bowed and diaphyseal ends are moderately flared. Specimens of ancient hunting-gathering communities from Bellanbandi Palassa in Sri Lanka and Mahadaha in the Gangetic Plain, and Maharashtrian farming community specimens from Chandoli and Nevasa, exhibit moderate bowing of femora and tibiae. Features associated with rickets are not found in skeletons from the Harappan sites.

CONCLUSIONS

In South Asia, cultural associations with respect to technology, subsistence patterns, and food preparation are more significant than chronological contexts because socioeconomic transitions have been initiated at different times in different regions, and certain cultural horizons are entirely absent in some areas. The most appropriate model for South Asian cultural change is that of a histogram with vertical plots representing regional populations attaining various economic strategies at differing rates in time and space. Nevertheless, biological trends marking the socioeconomic transitions from food collecting to food producing lifeways are discernible in the prehistoric skeletal record from South Asia when it is viewed within its archaeological and ecological contexts.

Three paleodemographic conclusions are derived from this study:

1. The adoption of intensified utilization and processing of vegetable food sources that allowed for greater food stability led to lower quality nutrition and increase in certain pathologies with the onset of agricultural economic patterns in South Asia, although population density increased in village and urban centers because of a heightened capacity to feed more people. These pathological variables are represented in skeletal remains by higher incidences of porotic hyperostosis, caries, abscess, and a broad spectrum of specific diseases identified in individual specimens as lumbar spondylolisthesis, endocranial lesions, long bone deformations attributed by certain authors to paralytic conditions, rickets, and scurvy. However, osteophytosis and alveolar border resorption do not appear to increase in frequency when mature food producing economic systems are attained. Evidences of trauma are highest in farming communities, and although they are present in the Harappan center of Mohenjodaro, earlier reports of "massacre victims" from this site have been seriously questioned in the course of recent study of the entire series. The relatively high incidence of porotic hyperostosis in Harappan series raises the issue of the presence of malaria in the Indus Valley some four millennia ago, as may have been the case in the Aegean world of Neolithic and Bronze Age times. Dental attrition occurs to some degree in all South Asian prehistoric skulls, but it is most severe among hunters and gatherers. Moderate to slight dental attrition characterizes the ancient farming communities and this variable continues into the Iron Age and historic periods.
2. While there are indications of a highly successful economic homeostasis for many preagricultural populations, increasing population growth may have placed stress on these groups and encouraged greater exploitation of the food

resource base by practices of incipient pastoralism and plant cultivation. Certainly full-scale agricultural communities tended to limit the range of foodstuff of their inhabitants, wheat becoming the staple grain in northern India whereas rice was the chief food of the common citizen of southern India and Sri Lanka during periods of mature food production. Farming communities throughout the subcontinent where their remains are found appear to have combined a high proportion of flesh foods with their cultigens, but this practice was substituted for the one of barter with forest dwelling "tribal" populations as alluvial valleys and terraced hillside areas led to a reduction in game. Nomadic herding populations have been a potential source of flesh foods to sedentary communities, but domesticated animals had their chief value as beasts of burden and producers of wool and hair or milk. Caste regulations involving dietary practices had had a considerable effect on protein intake in India for several millennia, although it is probable that the chicken was first demesticated in this part of the world from wild jungle fowl. Thus, with greater exploitation of the food resource base came dietary taboos with respect to consuming meat, a custom widely if not universally practiced among Hindus today. The origins of these taboos are uncertain, as they are not sanctioned by the Vedic texts, but they appear to have been influential in many social enclaves of Indian society by the time of the establishment of classical Hindu culture in the Gangetic plain in the sixth century B.C.

3. During the transitional phase between mixed hunting-gathering and full farming-herding systems, food shortages occurred, a situation that became more frequent with intensification of agricultural practices. A symbiotic relationship of village cultivators with forest hunters and gatherers mitigated to some degree the extremes of food shortages and nutritional deficiencies, a practice that continues in some South Asian communities to the present day. Evidence for nutritional fluctuations appears in the higher incidences of dental enamel hypoplasia, Harris lines, and bowing of diaphyses of long bones in individuals from food producing populations. These expressions of arrested growth are present in hunting-gathering communities, including those of terminal Pleistocene times in the Gangetic plain, but examples are fewer. Stature and body size decrease in many local areas with the abandonment of a full-time hunting-gathering economy, and it is interesting that specimens whose ages at time of death are estimated to be in the fifth and later decades of life are seldom observed in sedentary and agricultural communities. Aged individuals appear in the terminal Pleistocene site of Mahadaha.

Paleodemographic research has a history of only two decades in South Asia and at present the laborers in the harvest are few. Many areas of investigation are unexplored--chemical analysis for introduced trace elements and stable isotopes, estimates of degrees of sexual dimorphism, observation of Harris lines and cortical bone areas as indicators of nutritional stress and periods of arrested growth, more sophisticated estimates of size and density of prehistoric populations, and intelligent use and interpretation of multivariate analysis and other statistical measures that may be applied to questions of biological distances between different prehistoric series and with respect to the living peoples of the Indian subcontinent. These exciting areas of research deserve the attention of paleodemographers seeking a rich, diversified, and rewarding area for future work.

ACKNOWLEDGMENTS

The results of this study come from a long-term research program conducted in India, Pakistan, and Sri Lanka over the course of two decades. Those institutions that have been most generous in providing financial support for both field and laboratory research are the National Science Foundation, the American Institute of Indian Studies, the American Institute of Pakistan Studies, the Howard Foundation, the Smithsonian Institution, and Cornell University.

REFERENCES

Agrawal, D. P.
1982 *The archaeology of India.* Curzon Press, London and Malmo.

Alciati, G., and M. Fedeli
1965 On some traumatic lesions in human bone remains of the necropolis of But-Kara II (Swat, Pakistan). *East and West 15*:168-173.

Allchin, B., and R. Allchin
1982 *The rise of civilization in India and Pakistan.* Cambridge University Press, Cambridge.

Annandale, N.
1909 Preface. In *Craniological data from the Indian Museum, Calcutta,* edited by B. A. Gupta, p. i. Ethnographic Survey of India, Calcutta.

Athawale, M. C.
1964 Estimation of height from lengths of forearm bones: A study of one hundred Maharashtrian male adults of ages

between twenty-five and thirty years. *American Journal of Physical Anthropology 21*:105-112.

Banerjee, D. N.
1941 Studies in palaeopathology. *Journal of the Indian Medical Association 10*:263-267.

Basu, A., and A. Pal
1980 *Human remains from Burzahom*. Anthropological Survey of India, Calcutta.

Begley, V., J. R. Lukacs, and K. A. R. Kennedy
1981 Excavations of Iron Age burials at Pomparippu. *Ancient Ceylon 4*:49-132.

Bernhard, W.
1967 Human skeletal remains from the cemetery of Timargarha. *Ancient Pakistan 3*:291-407.

Brace, C. L.
1978 Tooth reduction in the Orient. *Asian Perspectives 19*:203-252.

Brace, C. L., and P. E. Mahler
1971 Post-Pleistocene changes in the human dentition. *American Journal of Physical Anthropology 34*:191-203.

Brace, C. L., and A. Montagu
1977 *Human evolution: An introduction to biological anthropology* (second ed.). Macmillan, New York.

Branfill, B. R.
1881 On the savandurga Rude Stone cemetery, Central Maisur. *The Indian Antiquary 10*:1-12.

Büchi, E. C.
1968 Rassengeschichte des indopakistanischen Subkontinents. In *Rassengeschichte der Menschheit* (Vol. I), edited by K. Saller, pp. 109-184. Oldenbourg, Munich.

Datta, J. M.
1959 Demography of prehistoric man. *Man in India 39*:257-270.
1962 Demographic notes on Harappa skeletons. In *Human skeletal remains from Harappa*, edited by P. Gupta, P. C. Dutta, and A. Basu, pp. 6-12. Anthropological Survey of India, Calcutta.

Deraniyagala, S. U.
1981 Prehistoric Research in Sri Lanka 1885-1980. In *P. E. P. Deraniyagala commemorative volume*, edited by P. L. Prematilleke, W. T. P. Gunawardana, and R. Silva, pp. 152-207. Lake House Investments, Colombo.

Durrani, F. A.
1978 Ethnographical facts and archaeological theory through ancient burials. *Journal of Social Science 1*:22-38.

Dutta, P. C.
1969 Bilateral parietal thinning in Bronze Age skull. *British Medical Journal 1*:53-55.
1972 The Bronze Age Harappans: A re-examination of the skulls in the context of the population concept. *American Journal of Physical Anthropology 36*:391-396.

1983 Molar crown characters of the Bronze Age Harappans and natural selection. In *Symposium on three decades of development in palaeontology and stratigraphy in India,* Geological Survey of India, Hyberabad.

Dutta, P. C., A. Pal, and J. N. Biswas
1972 Late Stone Age human remains from Sarai Nahar Rai: The earliest skeletal evidence of man in India. *Bulletin of the Anthropological Survey of India 21*:114-138.

Ehrhardt, S.
1960 Schlagspuren, Brüche und Sprünge an den Skeletten von Langhnaj im nördlichen Gujarat, Vorderindien. *Anthropologische Anzeiger 24*:178-183.

Fairservis, W. A.
1975 *The roots of ancient India: The archaeology of early Indian civilization* (second ed.). University of Chicago Press, Chicago.

Frayer, D. W.
1978 The evolution of the dentition in Upper Palaeolithic and Mesolithic Europe. *University of Kansas Publications in Anthropology* No. 10.

Gupta, P.
1975 Human remains in the Indian subcontinent during Pre- and Protohistoric periods. In *Bio-anthropological research in India,* edited by H. K. Rakshit, pp. 9-19. Anthropological Survey of India, Calcutta.
1976 Antiquity of man in India. In *Anthropology in India: Physical anthropology,* edited by H. K. Rakshit, pp. 96-106. Anthropological Survey of India, Calcutta.

Gupta, P., P. C. Dutta, and A. Basu
1962 *Human skeletal remains from Harappa.* Anthropological Survey of India, Calcutta.

Gupta, S. P.
1972 *Disposal of the dead and physical types of ancient India.* Oriental Publishers, Delhi.

Hasan, K.
1975 The burial practices among the people of the Indus Velley civilization. In *Proceedings of the International Symposium on Moenjodaro, 1973,* pp. 94-99.

Jacobson, J.
1979 Recent developments in South Asian prehistory and protohistory. *Annual Review of Anthropology 8*:467-502.

Jain, K. C.
1979 *Prehistory and protohistory of India.* Kala Prakashan, New Delhi.

Kennedy, K. A. R.
1965 Human skeletal material from Ceylon, with an analysis of the island's prehistoric and contemporary populations. *Bulletin of the British Museum (Natural History) 11*:135-213.

1969 Palaeodemography of India and Ceylon since 3000 B.C. *American Journal of Physical Anthropology 31*:315-320.

1972a Anatomical description of two crania from Ruamgarh: An ancient site in Dhalbhum, Bihar. *Journal of the Indian Anthropological Society 7*:129-141.

1972b The concept of the Vedda phenotypic pattern: A critical analysis of research on the osteological collections of a remnant population. *Spolia Zeylanica 32*:25-60.

1973a Biological anthropology of prehistoric South Asians. *The Anthropologist 17*;1-13.

1973b The search for fossil man in India. In *Physical Anthropology and its expanding horizons*, edited by A. Basu, pp. 25-44. Orient Longman, Bombay.

1974 The palaeodemography of Ceylon: A study of the biological continuum of a population from prehistoric to historic times. In *Perspectives in palaeoanthropology*, edited by A. K. Ghosh, pp. 93-112. Firma Mukhopadhyay, Calcutta.

1975a Biological adaptations of prehistoric South Asian populations to different and changing ecological settings. In *Biosocial interrelations in population adaptation*, edited by E. Watts, F. E. Johnston, and G. W. Lasker, pp. 65-90. Mouton, The Hague.

1975b India, Pakistan, Sri Lanka. In *Catalogue of fossil hominids* (Part III), edited by K. P. Oakley, B. G. Campbell, and T. I. Morreson, pp. 89-101, 171-175, 179-187. British Museum (Natural History), London.

1975c *The physical anthropology of the Megalith-builders of South India and Sri Lanka.* Australian National Museum, Canberra.

1976 Biological anthropology of prehistoric populations in South Asia: A summary of current research efforts. In Ecological backgrounds of South Asian prehistory, edited by K. A. R. Kennedy and G. L. Possehl, No. 4, pp. 166-178. *Occasional Papers and Theses of the Cornell University South Asia Program.*

1978 Measures of biological stress of prehistoric man in India: A palaeodemographic analysis. *Abstracts of the 10th International Congress of Anthropological and Ethnological Sciences, New Delhi* Abstract 0194:94-95.

1980a Integration of Western and Indian patterns of biological anthropology: An historical study. *South Asian Anthropologist 1*:1-9.

1980b Prehistoric skeletal record of man in South Asia. *Annual Review of Anthropology 9*:391-432.

1981 *Skeletal biology: When bones tell tales. Archaeology 34*: 17-24, 51.

1982a Palaeodemographic perspectives of social structural change in Harappan society. In Anthropology in Pakistan: Recent socio-cultural and archaeological perspectives, edited by S. Pastner and L. Flam, pp. 211-218. *Occasional Papers and Theses of the Cornell University South Asia Program.*

1982b Recently discovered Late Pleistocene hominid remains from India: Morphological evolution and technological change. *American Journal of Physical Anthropology* Abstract 57:201-202.

1982c Skulls, Aryans and flowing drains: The interface of archaeology and skeletal biology in the study of the Harappan civilization. In *Harappan civilization: A contemporary perspective*, edited by G. L. Possehl, pp. 289-295. Oxford and IBH, New Delhi.

1984a A reassessment of the theories of racial origins of the people of the Indus Valley civilization from recent anthropological data. In *Studies in the Archaeology and palaeoanthropology of South Asia*, edited by K. A. R. Kennedy and G. L. Possehl, in press. Oxford and IBH, New Delhi.

1984b Biological adaptations and affinities of Mesolithic South Asians. In *The people of South Asia*, edited by J. R. Lukacs, in press. Plenum, New York.

1984c Preliminary report on the Mesolithic human remains from Sarai Nahar Rai, India: Their skeletal biology and evolutionary significance. In *History and archaeology* (Vol. II), edited by G. R. Sharma, in press. Allahabad University Centre of Advanced Study, Allahabad.

1984d Trauma and disease in the ancient Harappans: Recent re-assessments of the skeletal record. In *Aspects of Harappan culture. Sir Mortimer Wheeler commemorative volume*, edited by S. P. Gupta, in press.

Kennedy, K. A. R., and P. C. Caldwell

1984 South Asian prehistoric human skeletal remains and burial practices. In *The people of South Asia*, edited by J. R. Lukacs, in press. Plenum, New York.

Kennedy, K. A. R., and K. C. Malhotra

1966 Human skeletal remains from Chalcolithic and Indo-Roman levels from Nevasa: An anthropometric and comparative analysis. *Deccan College Building Centenary and Silver Jubilee Series* No. 55.

Kennedy, K. A. R., J. R. Lukacs, V. N. Misra, S. C. Tiwari, V. S. Wakankar, and C. B. Burrow

1984 *Skeletal biology of the human remains from the Mesolithic and Palaeolithic levels of the Bhombetka Rockshelters of Madhya Pradesh, India.* Deccan College, Poona.

Khan, A. R.

1968 Ancient settlements in Karachi Region. *Dawn Sunday Magazine Section*, July 21, 28.

Krishnaswami, V. D.

1949 Megalithic types in South India. *Ancient India* 5:35-45.

Krogman, W. M., and W. H. Sassman

1943 Skull found at Chanhu-Daro. In *Chanhu-Daro excavations 1935-1936*, edited by J. H. Mackay, pp. 252-264. American Oriental Society, New Haven.

Leshnik, L. S.
1967 Archaeological interpretation of burials in the light of Central Indian ethnography. *Zeitschrift für Ethnologie 92*:23-32.

Lukacs, J. R.
1976 Dental anthropology and the biological affinities of an Iron Age population from Pomparippu, Sri Lanka. In Ecological backgrounds of South Asian prehistory, edited by K. A. R. Kennedy and G. L. Possehl, No. 4, pp. 197-215. *Occasional Papers and Theses of the Cornell University South Asia Program.*
1977 *Morphological aspects of dental variation in North India: A morphometric analysis.* Unpublished Ph.D. thesis, Department of Anthropology, Cornell University, Ithaca.
1978 Bio-cultural interaction in prehistoric India: Culture, ecology and the pattern of dental disease in Neolithic-Chalcolithic populations. In *American studies in the anthropology of India*, edited by S. Vatuk, pp. 425-444. Manohar, New Delhi.
1980a The Apegaon mandible: Morphology and pathology. *Deccan College Bulletin 39*:88-95.
1980b Palaeodemography in prehistoric India: Mortality and morbidity at Post-Harappan Inamgaon. *American Journal of Physical Anthropology*, Abstracts, p. 250 (Abstr.).
1981a Dental pathology and nutritional patterns of South Asian Megalith-builders: The evidence from Iron Age Mahujhari. *Proceedings of the American Philosophical Society 125*:220-237.
1981b Crown dimensions of deciduous teeth from prehistoric India. *American Journal of Physical Anthropology 55*:261-266.
1982a *Cultural variation and dental reduction: Evolutionary mechanisms and evidence from South Asia.* Paper presented at the Indian Statistical Institute Conference on Human Genetics and Adaptation, Calcutta.
1982b Dental disease, dietary patterns and subsistence at Harappa and Mohenjodero. In *Harappan civilization: A contemporary perspective*, edited by G. L. Possehl, pp. 301-307. Oxford and IBH, New Delhi.
1983a Dental reduction in South Asia: An odontometric analysis of prehistoric and modern dental variation in India. Unpublished manuscript.
1983b Human dental remains from early Neolithic levels at Mehrgarh, Baluchistan. *Current Anthropology 24*:390-392.
1984 *The people of South Asia: The biological anthropology of India, Nepal and Pakistan.* Plenum, New York.

Lukacs, J. R., and G. L. Badam
1981 Palaeodemography of post-Harappan Inamgaon: A preliminary report. *Journal of the Indian Anthropological Society 16*:59-74

Lukacs, J. R., V. N. Misra, and K. A. R. Kennedy
1982 *Bagor and Tilwara: Late Mesolithic cultures of Northwest*

India, the human skeletal remains. Deccan College, Poona.

Lukacs, J. R., K. A. R. Kennedy, and C. B. Burrow
1984 *The human remains from Mahujhari, an Iron Age site in Madhya Pradesh.* Deccan College, Poona.

Murty, M. L. K.
1974 Twenty-five years of research on human osteological remains from prehistoric sites in India. *Deccan College Bulletin 34*:116-133.

Rao, V. V.
1970 Skeletal remains from Takalghat and Khapa excavation. In *Excavations at Takalghat and Khapa (1968-1969)*, edited by S. B. Deo, pp. 60-61. Nagpur University Press, Nagpur.
1973 Skeletal remains from Mahujhari. In *Mahujhari excavations*, edited by S. B. Deo, pp. 63-76. Nagpur University Press, Nagpur.

Sahni, M. R.
1956 A century of palaeontology, palaeobotany and prehistory in India and adjacent countries. *Journal of the Palaeontological Society of India 1*:7-51.

Sankalia, H. D.
1974 *Prehistory and Protohistory of India and Pakistan.* Deccan College, Poona.
1977 *Prehistory of India.* Munshiram Manoharlal, New Delhi.

Sankalia, H. D., and J. R. Lukacs
1984 Post-Harappan populations of the Deccan Plateau: A demographic analysis. In *People of South Asia: The biological anthropology of India, Nepal and Pakistan*, edited by J. R. Lukacs, in press. Plenum, New York.

Sarkar, S. S.
1937 Disposal of the dead at Harappa. *Science and Culture 2*:632-634.
1960 Human skeletal remains from Brahmagiri. *Bulletin of the Department of Anthropology Calcutta University 9*:5-26.
1964 *Ancient races of Baluchistan, Panjab and Sind.* Bookland, Calcutta.
1972 *Ancient races of the Deccan.* Munshiram Manoharlal, New Delhi.

Sen, D. K.
1964 Ancient races of India and Pakistan: A study of methods. *Ancient India 20*:178-205.

Sewell, R. B. S., and B. S. Guha
1931 Human remains. In *Mohenjo-daro and the Indus civilization, being an official account of archaeological excavations carried out by the government of India between the years 1922 to 1927*, edited by J. Marshall, pp. 599-648. Arthur Probsthain, London.

Sharma, A. K.
1969-1970 Kalibangan human skeletal remains: An osteoarchaeological approach. *Journal of the Oriental Institute 19*:109-113.

1972 Harappan cemetery at Kalibangan: A demographic survey. *Proceedings of the Indian Archaeological Congress, 4th*, pp. 113-116.
1980 Some palaeo-pathological observations in skeletal remains from Mahadaha and Sarai Nahar Rai. In *Beginnings of agriculture*, edited by G. R. Sharma, V. O. Misra, D. Mandal, B. B. Misra, and J. Pal, pp. 231-232. Abinash Prakashan, Allahabad.
1982 The Harappan cemetery at Kalibangan: A study. In *Harappan civilization*, edited by G. L. Possehl, pp. 297-299. Oxford and IBH, New Delhi.

Singh, P.
1970 *Burial practices in ancient India.* Prithivi Prakashan, Varanasi.

Stacul, G.
1973 Inhumation and cremation in North-West Pakistan at the end of the second millenium B.C. In *South Asian archaeology*, edited by N. Hammond, pp. 197-201. Noyes, Park Ridge, New Jersey.

Stini, W. A.
1975 Adaptive strategies of human populations under nutritional stress. In *Biosocial interrelations in population adaptation*, edited by E. S. Watts, F. E. Johnston, and G. W. Lasker, pp. 19-41. Mouton, The Hague.

Takahashi, E.
1971 Geographic distribution of human stature and environmental factors: An ecologic study. *Journal of the Anthropological Society of Nippon 79*:259-286.

Trotter, M.
1970 Estimation of stature from intact limb bones. In *Personal identification in mass disasters*, edited by T. D. Stewart, pp. 71-83. National Museum of Natural History, Washington, D.C.

Wheeler, M.
1968 *The Indus civilization* (third ed.). Cambridge University Press, Cambridge.

CHAPTER 8

THE EFFECTS OF SOCIOECONOMIC CHANGE IN PREHISTORIC AFRICA: SUDANESE NUBIA AS A CASE STUDY

Debra L. Martin

School of Natural Science
Hampshire College

George J. Armelagos
Alan H. Goodman[1]

Department of Anthropology
University of Massachusetts-Amherst

Dennis P. Van Gerven

Department of Anthropology
University of Colorado, Boulder

INTRODUCTION

This chapter examines the effects of the transition to agriculture and the subsequent intensification of agricultural production on the biology of ancient populations from Lower Nubia. The analysis was derived from the human remains, and from an understanding of the geographical setting and the cultural adaptation of populations living in the area during the last 12,000 years. Specifically, we have examined the pattern of population growth, changes in morphology, alterations in growth and development, the impact of mortality and morbidity on life expectancy, and the impact of disease stress.

The selection of Lower Nubian remains is based on the excellent archaeological and skeletal remains recovered from the area. The Nubian material represents one of the most intensively studied archaeological populations in the world with 36 major

[1]*Present address: Department of Orthodontics, University of Connecticut Health Center, Farmington, Connecticut 06032.*

excavations completed in the last 75 years and more than 1000 sites excavated (Adams 1977). These sites span a period from the hunting-gathering stage to agricultural intensification in the area.

Although Nubia provides an excellent opportunity for examining the impact of agricultural development on the biology of earlier populations, there are a number of problems that complicate attempts to measure the magnitude of that impact. The most important problem is that we do not have large samples of material from the critical periods during which the transformation to agriculture occurred. The best evidence comes from the phases in Nubian prehistory during which there is an intensification of agricultural production.

Lower Nubia is the portion of the Nile River Valley extending from the First Cataract at Aswan to the Second Cataract at Wadi Halfa (Figure 8.1). The region represented a main line of communication connecting sub Saharan Africa and the Meditteranean (Trigger 1965). The study will focus on the skeletal materials excavated near Wadi Halfa, and also on materials (from the Kulubnarti site) in an adjacent portion of Upper Nubia known as the Batn el Hajar.

CULTURE HISTORY

Populations used in this study include materials from the Mesolithic (ca. 12,000 B.C.), Neolithic (5000-3600 B.C.), A-Group (3400-2400 B.C.), C-Group (2400-100 B.C.), Meroitic (350 B.C.-A.D. 350), X-Group or Ballana (A.D. 350-550), and Christian (A.D. 550-1350) periods (Table 8.1). The skeletal material in this study was excavated during the course of the first University of Colorado Nubian Expedition, 1963-1964 season (of which Armelagos was a member), and the Colorado-Kentucky Expedition (in which Van Gerven was Principal Investigator).

The seven periods of Nubian prehistory can be placed into three broader phases of cultural development that are relevant to the interpretation of the impact of agriculture on biology. The first phase represents a period of transition from gathering and hunting to agriculture and includes the mesolithic and Neolithic periods. In Lower Nubia, the Neolithic development never resulted in the intensive exploitation of plants and animals that occurred in other areas. The next phase represents a nonintensive agricultural period in which the A-Group and C-Group utilized an annual cycle of produce. During the third phase, intensive utilization of the Nile Valley became possible because of the use of the waterwheel. The Meroitic, X-Group, and Christian periods display varying degrees of intensive agriculture. Summarized briefly in the next section are the cultural changes that have occurred during the major time periods.

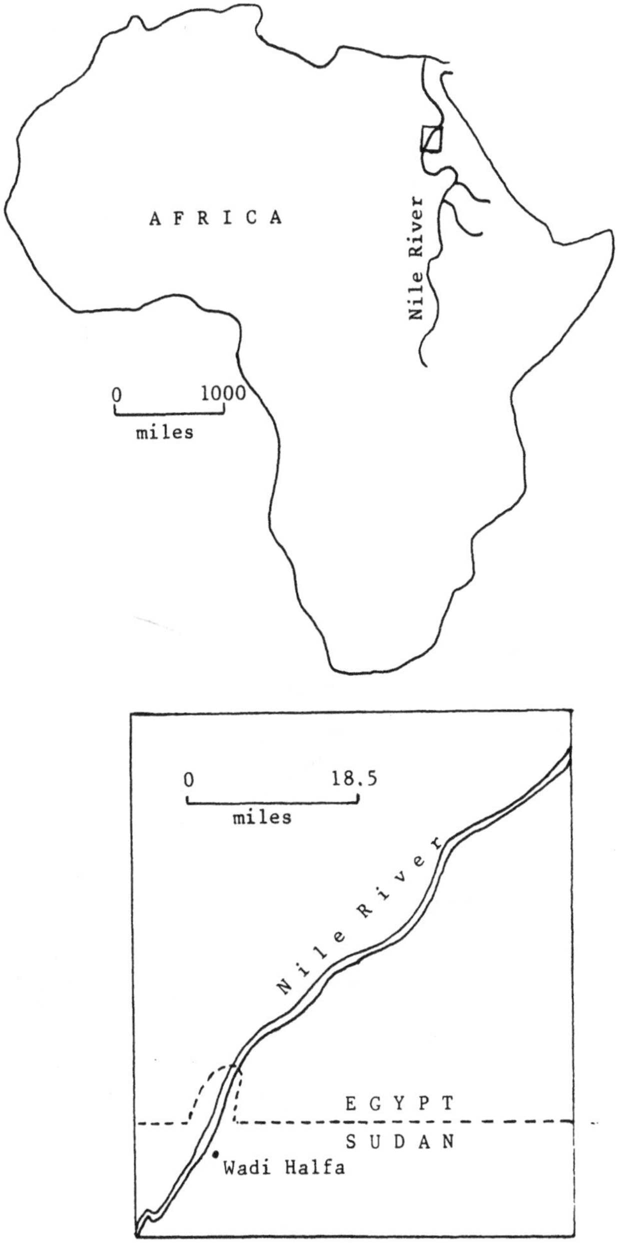

FIGURE 8.1. Map of Africa with enlarged section showing location of Wadi Halfa (reproduced from Martin 1983).

TABLE 8.1 Chronology and Sample Size of Remains Used in This Study[a]

Phase	Time	Scandanavian	Colorado	Kentucky-Colorado
Mesolithic	11,950-6400 B.C.		39	
A-Group	3400-2400 B.C.	105		
C-Group	2400-1200 B.C.	653	21	
Meroitic	350 B.C.-A.D. 350	135	129	
X-Group	A.D. 350-550	156	218	
Christian	A.D. 550-13	57	403	188

[a]The Scandanavian sample is used by Vagn Nielson (1970), the Colorado sample is from the Wadi Halfa area, and the Kentucky-Colorado sample is from the Batn el Hajar region of Kulubnarti.

Transitional Phase

Mesolithic (11,950-6400 B.C.)

The archaeological evidence indicates that the Mesolithic populations in Lower Nubia relied on the exploitation of large game, fish, and seed collecting (Greene and Armelagos 1972). Saxe (1966) cites evidence of large game hunting; the occurrence of bones of large bovine species in sites suggest semisedentary occupations. Fishing and shellfish gathering were substantiated by numerous fish vertebrae and shellfish remains found with the burials and throughout the sites. Many small and large grinding stones suggested the importance of gathering and utilization of wild grass seeds.

Neolithic (6000-3600 B.C.)

The development of agriculture appears late in Lower Nubia and is not pronounced in the archaeological record. The late occurrence of domesticated plants and animals may reflect geographic factors that impeded the spread from northern Africa into the southern portion, or may indicate that seed-collecting and fishing were extremely successful. In the Wadi Halfa Neolithic sites there is an indication of heavy reliance on fishing and hunting; some cultigens are found, however, implying at least incipient agriculture.

Nonintensive Agricultural Phase

A-Group (3400-2400 B.C.)

A-Group represents a transition from the Neolithic period in terms of both technology and subsistence. Economic behavior was specialized for Nile ecology and involved a mixed strategy. The archaeological record shows that domesticated grains, hunted animals, fish, and gathered seed constituted the dietary base. The farming strategy was not an intensive one; single annual crops were harvested and the success was dependent on the annual overflow of the Nile during the flood season (August-November) (Trigger 1965). The major crop, which was used as both a food source and fodder, was millet. Millet was less efficient in terms of productivity and nutritional content than other potential crops (such as barley and wheat), but could more predictably be harvested prior to the flood season.

The continuity of the A-Group population from Neolithic populations is substantiated in consistent settlement patterning, pottery styles, and burial practices (Adams 1977). Therefore, an indigenous development of transitional economy grew from existing conditions and local populations.

C-Group (2400-100 B.C.)

Similar to the A-Group in adaptive strategies, C-Group populations exhibited a mixed economy with reliance on domesticated grains (primary millet), fish, and hunted animals. There was an increase in trade items from the North (Egypt). The relative prosperity of the region was high.

The C-Group populations are directly descended from the A-Group, although they occur following a brief abandonment of Lower Nubia brought on by political and economic factors (Trigger 1965). Political pressure from the Old Kingdom had pushed indigenous Nubians from Lower to Upper Nubia during the A-Group to C-Group transition. The biological homogeneity of the two groups emphasizes the role of exogenous political and economic factors in the brief abandonment after the A-Group time period (ca. 2400 B.C.) (Adams 1977).

Following the C-Group period there was another exodus of Nubians southward. A slow but continual decrease in population size resulted from continued political pressure from Egypt (Trigger 1965). For 1000 years following the C-Group period, the region of Lower Nubia remained unoccupied because a decrease in the Nile water level created an effective barrier to exploitation of the area.

TABLE 8.2 Estimates of Population Growth Based on Settlement Patterns of Excavated Archaeological Sites in Lower Nubia[a]

Phase	*Population Estimate*
Nonintensive	
A-Group	*13,000*
C-Group	*17,500*
Intensive	
Meroitic	*60,000*
X-Group	*44,000*
Christian	*50,000*

[a]*Trigger 1965:160.*

Intensive Agricultural Phase

Meroitic (350 B.C.-A.D. 350)

The reoccupation of Lower Nubia occurred simultaneously with the development of the waterwheel (*saqia*) in Upper Nubia (Adams 1970). The waterwheel increased the productive potential of the region, permitting support of a larger population than before (Table 8.2). Farmers could now grow several crops a year, and the level areas farther back from the Nile (as well as the high banks) could be watered and used (Trigger 1965). However, crops grown on these lands required a much greater investment acre-by-acre than did single annual crops grown on the alluvial flood plains. The new system therefore required increased inputs of both time and energy.

The Meroitic culture flourished at this time and Lower Nubia was important for trade and communication between the Mediterranean and sub Saharan Africa. However, most of the settlements were small and relatively poor. The inhabitants of Lower Nubia were being ruled from Upper Nubia and may have been supporting the area with agricultural products (Adams 1977). Even with the waterwheel, agricultural potential was relatively low, and trade accounted for much of the growth (Trigger 1965).

The archaeological record shows a farming strategy that now involved three growing seasons. Crops harvested included millet, wheat, barley, beans, tobacco, lentils, peas, and watermelon (Trigger 1965). Dates, mangoes, and citrus trees could also be kept watered during dry seasons to produce more fruit. Cattle, sheep, and goats probably were herded and animal husbandry may have been only slightly less important than agriculture (Adams 1977). Cattle were used to run the waterwheel, and were not eaten. Trigger (1965) suggests that milk and butter may have been important sources of food for trade.

The Meroitic people had a strong incentive for development of the full agricultural potential of their region. Immediately to the north lay the wealthy Roman province of Dodekashoenos, a terminus for the caravan trade with sub Saharan Africa. The Lower Nubians, subjects of the Upper Nubian Kingdom of Meroë, traded their surplus agricultural produce to this "industrialized" Roman province (Adams 1970). In return they received a bountiful range of the trade goods of Mediterranean civilization. Toward the later stage of the Meroitic period, the Lower Nubians had achieved a more sophisticated level of cultural development than the area had ever seen before. Settlement patterns indicate that the population size increased and clustered into dense pockets around the irrigated fields (Trigger 1965).

By A.D. 350, the decline of the Kingdom of Kush and the Kingdom of Meroë brought an end to prosperity in Lower Nubia. The Roman Empire was beset with governmental instability, famine, plagues, and wars (Adams 1977).

X-Group (Ballana Culture) (A.D. 350-550)

During the X-Group period, the large population centers fissioned into smaller villages concomitant with a decentralization of power and an increase in local village autonomy (Trigger 1965). Several researchers have emphasized qualitative differences in artifacts between Meroitic and X-Group populations and have suggested a cultural decline due to an invasion of new population into Lower Nubia (e.g., Batrawi 1946; Morant 1925). However, an analysis of artifacts suggests that there are no striking differences (Adams 1977). Burial patterns, pottery types, iron spears, arrowheads, and tools were common to both periods (Trigger 1965). While the quality of X-Group pottery may not have been equal in fabric or decoration to that previously produced in Meroitic times, it was very similar and all differences could be traced to a Mediterranean origin (Adams 1970). It would appear, therefore, that indigenous Nubian influences remained strong into the X-Group period. Similarities in technological and ideological realms suggest continuity (Trigger 1965; Vagn Nielson 1970). Genetic and biological continuity has also been documented using discrete dental traits (Greene 1966) and cranial traits (Berry and Berry 1973; Berry et al. 1967).

X-Group subsistence activities were similar to the Meroitic strategy of intensive agriculture with moderate animal husbandry (Vagn Nielson 1970). Due to local autonomy of Nubian villages, trade networks and trade items were not very pronounced. This lack of luxury and exotic artifacts in the archaeological record has been interpreted as a "decline" in the cultural achievements previously reported for the Meroitic (Adams 1977). Whether the shift in percentage of trade items is due to a decline in artistic ambitions or to a decline in necessity of reciprocal trading of agricultural goods for "hard" goods is debatable. While there is no evidence supporting a change in the underlying subsistence pattern, X-Group people were more independent, and were not obliged to trade agricultural products. It is not clear from the archaeological record to what degree the X-Group may have been practicing intensive agriculture, but there appears to have been a reduced demand for food from neighboring cities.

Christian (A.D. 550-1300)

The Christian period shows much cultural growth and religious reunification. Initially controlled by Egypt, the church rose to become the focus of Nubian independence. Urbanization and stratification are evident in the housing styles, architecture, and settlement patterns (Adams 1977). Populations began to cluster in large centers and monastic communities toward the end of the time period, but there was not an increase in population size on a large scale (Table 8.2).

Subsistence strategies were a continuation of the previous two time periods. Agricultural practices did seem to intensify, however. In environmentally poor regions, artificial terraces were built as high as the waterwheel could reach (Trigger 1965). Trade networks were once again very strong. Trigger (1965:145) states that Nubians were trading several hundred slaves to Egypt each year in return for wheat, barley, lentils, cloth, and horses. In addition, dates, figs, grapes, and other fruits were imported from Egypt. Intensification of agricultural activities, with no evidence for large increases in the population size, suggests a greater demand for goods in the cities.

Summary

The archaeological reconstruction of the culture history shows the impact of environmental variables and political and religious change. There are periods of environmental instability (decline in the level of the Nile) in which Nubia was not habitable, such as the 1000-year hiatus following the C-Group occupation. In other periods during which environmental factors were constant, political and religious factors were primary features of cultural change. The transitions from Meroitic to X-Group to Christian phases were due to such sociopolitical factors.

The major shift in the food base in Nubia occurred during the Mesolithic-Neolithic transition (3600 B.C.). During this time, the subsistence activities changed from a reliance on hunted and gathered food to a food base that included a single annual crop of millet during the following nonintensive phase (A- and C-Group phase, 3400-100 B.C.). While cultigens appear to be part of the diet, the ecological uncertainty of the Nile precluded total reliance on them. With the adoption of the waterwheel, agricultural potential increased and the cultigens became very important in the diet as well as in trade. The Meroitic (350 B.C.-A.D. 350) shows an intensive use of the land to produce three annual cycles of harvesting, which promoted a dependence on a broad variety of cultigens. The Christian group (A.D. 550-1350) shows a similar pattern of intensive agriculture. The time period between the Meroitic and the Christian phase, the X-Group (A.D. 350-550), does show a decrease in intensive farming, reflecting sociopolitical changes.

During the Meroitic and Christian periods, large power centers outside the local villages linked the area into pronounced trade networks. This influenced the flow of goods and access to goods. Because of reciprocal trade ties, the Meroitic and Christian groups showed an intensified pattern of production that was not related to an internal increase in population size (refer to Table 8.2). This pattern suggests a flow of the cultigens to the neighboring cities. The X-Group resembles the earlier A- and C-Groups, with little political interaction, loosely structured autonomous villages, and little or no trade with neighboring cities. The X-Group villages were more evenly spaced along the Nile.

Ecologically, the area was marginal with respect to agriculture. The amount of arable land was limited and even slight declines in available land could have had significant effects on the agricultural potential. While the waterwheel allowed some independence from random fluctuations in the water table and allowed for irrigation when necessary, agricultural potential remained limited. The exploitation of farming villages during periods of outside political control, therefore, could have a dramatic impact on the food available for the local peasantry.

POPULATION GROWTH

There are at present no published reports estimating the populations size during the Mesolithic-Neolithic transitional phase. Trigger (1965:160) estimates that the population size for the A-Group was 13,000 and that it rose to 17,500 in the C-Group period in Lower Nubia. During the Meroitic, the population rose to 60,000, but there was a 26% decrease in the X-Group period (to 44,000). There was a slight increase during the Christian phase to 50,000 (Table 8.2). These estimates are based on the size and relative numbers of settlement components in the archaeological samples, and not on absolute numbers.

During the period of nonintensive agriculture (A- and C-Group), population size averaged 15,000. Reliance on annual flooding for produce severely limited population growth. Moreover, the decline in the Nile water level made the area inhospitable for 1000 years. Then, with the rise in the Nile and the use of the waterwheel, the intensification of agriculture became a major factor in population growth. In addition, the unification of Nubia under Meroitic political influence also stimulated intensification of agricultural

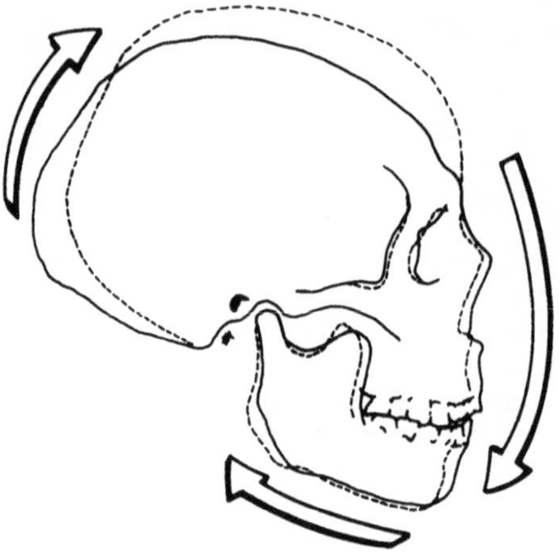

FIGURE 8.2. Changes in cranial morphology from the Mesolithic (——) to the MXCH (Meroitic, X-Group, and Christian, combined) (----). These changes involved a reduction in the size of the masticatory muscles, a reduction in the size of the lower face, a reduction in cranial length, and an increase in cranial height.

production and population growth. Following the breakup of the Meroitic empire, there was a loss of one-quarter of the population. This decline during the X-Group period likely represents a lack of demand for intensified agricultural activity, and a decrease in the amount of overall activity in Lower Nubia related to trade and communication between the Mediterranean and sub Saharan Africa. The slight growth during the following period reflects the impact of religious re-unification.

MORPHOLOGICAL CHANGES RELATED TO THE DEVELOPMENT AND INTENSIFICATION OF AGRICULTURE

Cranial-Facial Changes

Nubian Mesolithic populations are characterized by robust crania, typically with large brow ridges, large flattened faces, and bun-shaped occiputs (Greene and Armelagos 1972). Changes in later Nubian populations involve a progressive decrease in the robusticity of the entire craniofacial complex, a rotation of the mid-face and lower face to a position more inferior to the cranial vault, and a relative increase in cranial height with a decrease in length (Carlson and Van Gerven 1977; Van Gerven et al. 1979) (Figure 8.2).

Earlier interpretations of the change in craniofacial morphology relied on racial admixture hypotheses which explains all changes in cranial morphology in terms of replacement of one population by another (Batrawi 1946). More recent biocultural models have proposed that a dietary change involving a reduction in attrition rate and an increase in cariogenic foods could have precipitated selection for smaller and morphologically less complex teeth. This then could have led to a reduction in facial architecture with a compensatory change in the cranial vault and base to meet the stresses acting on them (Carlson and Van Gerven 1977; Greene and Armelagos 1972).

The most dramatic change in facial morphology occurs from the Mesolithic phase to the nonintensive agricultural phase of A- and C-Group. Unfortunately, Neolithic material is not available to document the period of most rapid change. The morphological changes described continue from the nonintensive phase to the intensive phase. Given the archaeological reconstruction of dietary changes, the impact of a shift from foods obtained by gathering and hunting to a staple consisting of millet may have provided the impetus for natural selection and the changes in craniofacial morphology.

Stature

Stature has been assessed for all the major groups except for the Neolithic. Based on the maximum length of the femur, the greatest difference between mean values (for both males and females) is found between the A-Group and the X-Group. This difference is significant at the 5% level (Vagn Nielson 1970). Although the reduction in stature is similar for both males and females, only the males show a statistically significant decline. For males, the greatest average length of femur occurs for the A-Group, with 47.6 cm, and it decreases to 45.5 and 45.0 cm in the C-Group and Meroitic, respectively. However, the X-Group males show a significant decrease to 44.5 cm, and femoral length increases to 45.0 cm in the Christians. Females show less variation in femur length, with the A-Group having a mean of 42.5 and the C-Group a mean of 42.1 cm. The Meroitic, X-Group, and Christian females all show femur lengths of approximately 41 cm (Table 8.3).

INTENSIFICATION OF AGRICULTURE AND CHANGES IN THE PATTERN OF DISEASE

The lack of extensive skeletal material from the Mesolithic-Neolithic phase makes it difficult to directly assess the impact of the transition from gathering and hunting to agriculture. In our sample, there is even difficulty in analyzing material from

TABLE 8.3 Maximum Femoral Lengths for the Combined Excavated Sites from Lower Nubia[a]

	Males		Females		
Phase	*Maximum femoral length (cm)*	*N*	*Maximum femoral length (cm)*	*N*	*Dimorphism (%)*
Mesolithic	*46.05*	*4*	*43.76*	*6*	*105.23*
A-Group	*47.6*	*3*	*42.5*	*7*	*111.92*
C-Group	*45.5*	*55*	*42.1*	*47*	*107.94*
Meroitic	*45.0*	*28*	*41.9*	*35*	*107.61*
X-Group	*44.5*	*36*	*41.8*	*27*	*106.55*
Christian	*45.0*	*10*	*41.4*	*12*	*108.55*

[a]*Data as summarized by Vagn Nielson (1970:86).*

the nonintensive agricultural period. What we have been able to demonstrate is that during the period of intensive agriculture (Mroitic, X-Group, and Christian), there is a pattern of nutritional deficiency that is related to the intensification of agriculture. We do not know whether this pattern existed in periods of less intense agricultural activity, but the few indications that we do have suggest that the earlier dietary base was sufficient.

Long Bone Growth and Development

The pattern of long bone growth and development in the juvenile portion of the prehistoric Nubian remains (representing the Meroitic, X-Group, and Christian phases) was studied in order to identify periods of probable stress (Armelagos et al. 1971). Unfortunately, no such data from the earlier Nubian groups are available for comparison.) This analysis provides a measure of the amount of developmental stress experienced by the subadult portions of the agricultural phase. While no intergroup comparisons are available, the data for the combined intensive agricultural phases suggest that the subadults were experiencing developmental stress.

A comparison of the Nubian data with the data for a sample of present-day American boys highlights the effects of this stress. Among Americans, growth is accelerated for the first several years of life, and decelerates rapidly thereafter. The second period of acceleration begins in mid-childhood and reaches a peak during the adolescent growth spurt. By contrast, Nubian growth apparently declined steadily from the first through the seventh years of life, reaching a point of little or no increase between the ages of five and seven. The two periods of "catch-up" growth are visible as episodes of sharply accelerated increase in bone length.

Although the patterns of Nubian long bone lengths do not appear grossly abnormal, both the rapid deceleration of growth in early childhood and the cessation of growth around age six suggest the presence of stress at these periods. Since the process of growth requires high inputs of energy and protein, any factor that interferes with these requirements can affect growth. Growth retardation could be a result of either decreased nutrient intake or increased nutrient requirements, as in the case of trauma or infection.

Porotic Hyperostosis

Vagn Nielson (1970) has analyzed all adult skeletons with crania present for the presence of cribra orbitalia and porotic hyperostosis. Unfortunately, there are no published accounts for the Mesolithic-Neolithic rates of porotic hyperostosis, but there are reports for the A-Group through the Christian phases. Cribra orbitalia significantly decreases in adult males in the C-Group relative to those in the A-group. Frequencies of cribra orbitalia then increase slightly in the Meroitic, X-Group, and Christian groups. The females show a very different pattern of involvement. The highest frequency of cribra orbitalia for females is in the X-group and the lowest frequency is in the Christian group. The A-Group, C-Group, and Meroitic show relatively higher frequencies for females than for males (Table 8.4).

The Christian site of Kulubnarti has even higher frequencies of porotic hyperostosis. The two Christian cemeteries have frequencies of 94.4 and 82.0, with most cases showing slight or moderate pitting. Plotting the probability of individuals dying with and without porotic hyperostosis shows that those with the affliction had a much higher probability of dying in all age groups (Van Gerven et al. 1981).

Dental Caries and Enamel Microdefects

Armelagos (1969) analyzed the frequency of carious lesions for the Nubian series from Wadi Halfa. The percentage of carious lesions on the dentition was recorded by total number of teeth observed. The frequency was very low (1.0%) in the Mesolithic sample and increased to 18.0% in the Christian phase.

Rudney (1981) analyzed enamel microdefects for the Meroitic and X-Group populations from Wadi Halfa. Pathological band scores were derived from the frequency of bands per tooth and enamel hypoplasias were added to the score when they appear independent of a microdefect. For both the mesiobuccal and distolingual cusps, the pathological band scores are greater for subadults and

TABLE 8.4 Frequency of Cribra Orbitalia in Males and Females during the A-Group through the Christian Phases in Nubia[a]

	Males		Females	
Phase	Frequency (%)	N	Frequency (%)	N
A-Group	14.3	21	18.2	22
C-Group	2.9	140	11.2	18
Meroitic	5.2	77	14.6	89
X-Group	9.8	92	26.6	79
Christian	11.1	27	2.8	36

[a]*Data reported in Vagn Nielson (1970).*

adults in the Meroitic, and less in the X-Group subadults and adults. Two-way analysis of variance showed that the difference between the mean scores was significant ($p \leq .001$). There are no other data to make even gross comparisons to other phases. This two-phase study is important, however, because it points to different patterns of stress between two groups that are agriculturalists. Because the X-Group shows less developmental stress, it suggests that this period characterized by local autonomy and dispersed settlement patterns may have been less stressful.

Premature Osteoporosis

Huss-Ashmore (1978) analyzed microradiographs of femoral cross sections of 75 Wadi Halfa Nubian juveniles aged from birth to 14 years. Cortical thickness was measured and compared with the total midshaft diameter (Figure 8.3). Cortical thickness not only fails to increase with age, but shows evidence of an actual decrease after the age of 10. The mean percentage of cortical area was also plotted for the combined sample; it increased during the first two years and then declined sharply (Armelagos et al. 1982). A comparison with a modern well-nourished population illustrated important differences. Whereas the modern population (Garn 1970) showed a steady increase in percentage of cortical area from birth, the Nubian sample showed a decrease after the age of two. This information suggests that long bone growth was maintained at the expense of cortical bone growth. Since this study included only the subadults from the intensified agricultural periods (Meroitic, X-Group, and Christian), no comparison can be made with the transitional or non-intensive phases.

Evidence also exists that young adult females in the intensive agricultural phases were experiencing nutritional problems. There was a definite and continual loss of cortical bone (as measured by

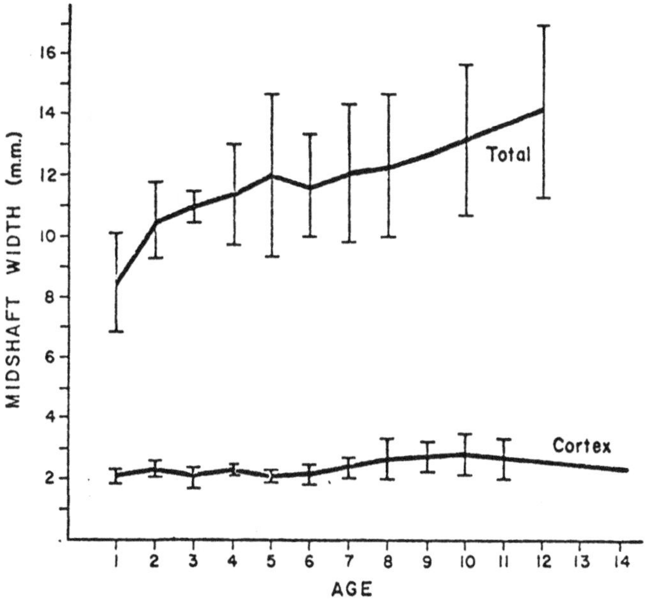

FIGURE 8.3. Femoral cortical thickness and midshaft width (means and standard deviations) plotted for subadult age. While total midshaft width increases with age, the actual thickness of the cortex does not, indicating the maintenance of growth at the expense of thickness. This is in response to protein-calorie malnutrition.

the percentage of cortical bone) in females following the twentieth year and continuing throughout life (Martin and Armelagos 1979). The early age of onset and the distinctive pattern of bone loss suggest that the female segment of the population was apparently characterized by premature bone loss not normally related to the aging process.

A microscopic study was undertaken to investigate the underlying processes that influenced the occurrence of premature osteoporosis (Martin 1983). Two separate processes at the histological level appear to be the determinants of the total amount of bone present. First, young females exhibit bones that are extremely porous due to the increase in resorption activity, and second, the bone that is present is not well mineralized, suggesting a slower rate of formation than normal.

Taken together, the trends in premature osteoporosis for subadults and young adult females suggest that the intensive agricultural phase produced nutritional inadequacies. While there is no comparison with the nonintensive and transitional phases, the presence of poorly mineralized bone and active resorption suggests that intensive agricultural strategies may produce subgroups at risk. These subgroups, because of increased nutrient demands, do not have access to necessary resources. In terms of skeletal growth, development, and mineralization, the nutritional problems could be general protein-calorie malnutrition, imbalances in the calcium/phosphorus ratio, or malabsorption of nutrients because of infections or trauma. These results are important, even without direct comparison to earlier groups, because the problems in mineralization and the resultant premature osteoporosis provide indisputable evidence of nutritional problems that can result from reliance on a single staple crop (in this case, millet).

Infectious Disease

The frequency of infectious lesions is extremely low in the Nubian Wadi Halfa populations. Unfortunately, there are no available data on the frequency of infectious lesions in the transitional or nonintensive agricultural phases. Among the Meroitic samples, only 6.6% of the individuals show evidence of infectious lesions. In the X-Group, 12.0% show evidence of infections, and the combined Christian sample shows 15.0% (Armelagos 1968). These comparatively low rates may be explained by evidence that prehistoric Nubians were ingesting tetracycline, a broad-spectrum antibiotic (Basset et al. 1981). Storage of grain in mud bins may have provided the environmental conditions for the growth of *Streptomyces*, a mold-like bacterium that produces tetracyclines. The amount of tetracycline ingested has not been determined, but a preliminary analysis of femoral cortical bone suggests at least "therapeutic" levels.

Fluorescent microscopy on the skeletal remains from Kulubnarti also show evidence of tetracycline ingestion, but at a lower rate (3.6%) (Hummert and Van Gerven 1982). The differences between the Wadi Halfa group (which shows extreme amounts of fluorescence) and the Kulubnarti sample may be the result of environmental and economic differences. Kulubnarti was an extremely isolated region, with small-scale flood plain agriculture on family-owned plots. These plots probably provided direct familial use and little in the way of long-term storage, which would minimize grain spoilage.

Because even low-level ingestion of naturally occurring antibiotics can have an impact on infectious disease rates, it should be investigated via fluorescent microscopy on all prehistoric skeletal samples that come from cultures that may have stored grain.

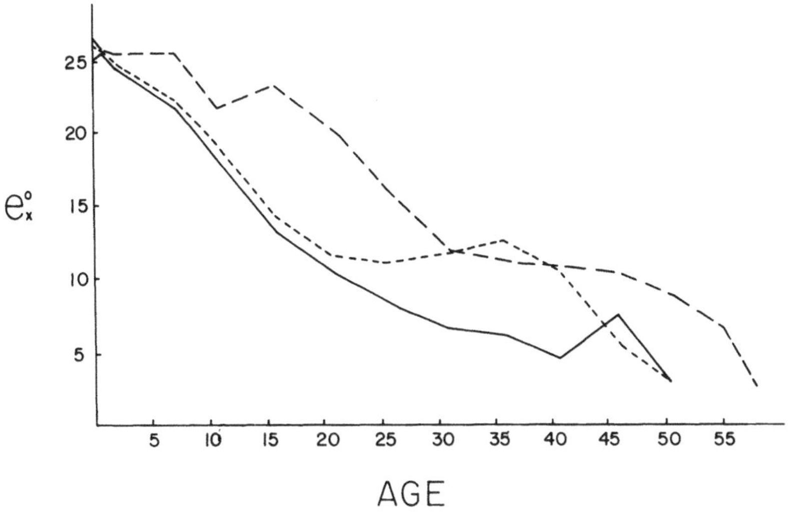

FIGURE 8.4. Life expectancy for each age group based on the mean age at death for the Meroitic (——), X-Group (----), and Christian (—–) phases.

MORTALITY

The analysis of mortality profiles of the samples from the Meroitic, X-Group, and Christian cemeteries show that age-specific life expectancies of the Meroitic and X-Group populations were very similar, whereas life expectancy in the Christian sample was greater (Figure 8.4). The X-Group population experienced some improvements in life expectancy in early childhood, but the Christians show a greater life expectancy at every age. In general, mortality is high among infants, levels off slightly among young adults, and increases sharply among older adults (Armelagos 1969). Figure 8.4 presents the life expectancy at various ages for the three intensive agriculture phases. While mean ages at death for the Meroitic and X-Group are similar (24.48 and 25.17 years, respectively), after the age of 20 the X-Group show a distinct trend toward greater life expectancy.

Mortality data suggest that in the Wadi Halfa area, the breakup of the Kingdom of Meroë did not result in a decline in life expectancy. The re-unification of Nubia under Christianity, however, did result in considerable improvement in life expectancy.

SUMMARY

The shift from gathering and hunting in Nubia is difficult to identify in the archaeological record. While we can distinguish the transition from Mesolithic to Neolithic, the changes in adaptation are not as marked as one would expect. The Neolithic populations continued to supplement their diet with gathered seeds and hunted game. Even during the nonintensive phase (A- and C-Group), gathering and hunting continued to supplement agricultural products. The intensification only occurred during the Meroitic, X-Group and Christian periods when the waterwheel was used for irrigation.

The following observations have been made:

1. Significant population growth occurred with the transition to agriculture. The intensification of agriculture led to further increases. The intensification can be attributed to changes in the environment (the level of the Nile), technological factors (use of the waterwheel), and political influence such as the unification of the area into a wider political sphere. Specifically, there was a fourfold population increase during the earlier phase of intensification (Meroitic phase). The decline of Meroitic control of the area is reflected in a 21% decline in population size and is represented by the X-Group. With the re-unification under Christianity there was a 12% increase in population size.

2. The shift to agriculture and subsequent intensification had a significant impact on craniofacial morphology. There was a reduction in robusticity of the face, an increase in cranial height, and a decrease in cranial length. The trend in facial reduction continued from the Mesolithic to the Christian period with the exception of a slight increase in prognathism during the X-Group period.

3. There is a reduction in the size and complexity of the teeth from the transitional phase (Mesolithic) to the intensive agricultural phase (Meroitic). Information is not available from the nonintensive phase (A- and C-Group).

4. The frequency of dental caries increases from 1% in the transitional Mesolithic phase to 18% in the intensive agriculture phase. The attrition of dental enamel may have been a factor in the low frequency of caries in the Mesolithic population. Lower intake of carbohydrates and sugar is obviously another factor. During the intensive agriculture phase, the trend was to increased periodontal disease, with a peak in the Christian period.

5. There is evidence of iron deficiency anemia in populations from both nonintensive and intensive phases of Nubian agricultural development.

6. During the intensive phase of agricultural development, there are a number of indicators that suggest serious nutritional deficiencies in the subadults. Combined with incidences of porotic hyperostosis, there is evidence also of premature osteoporosis and

retardation. These findings suggest that long bone growth is being maintained at the expense of cortical thickness.

7. During the intensive phase of agricultural development there are indications that there were nutritional problems in the adult portions of the populations. Although both males and females show evidence of iron deficiency anemia and premature osteoporosis, there is a higher frequency of these pathologies among young females. In the 20-29-year age range there is evidence that bone is being resorbed and formation of new bone is being curbed. The loss of nutrients and minerals during repeated pregnancies and long lactation periods may be the cause of the problem. Problems with mineralization may also be due to protein deficiency.

8. The low frequency of infectious disease during the intensive agriculture phase was probably related to the ingestion of tetracyclines that contaminated the grain.

9. Variations in mortality during the intensive phase of agriculture may be related to changes in political structure. The lower life expectancy in the Meroitic population may reflect their marginal location to the center of the Kingdom of Meroë. The improvement during the X-Group period indicates that localized control may have some advantages, especially with respect to access to resources. Further improvement occurs during the Christian period (under reunification with the Wadi Halfa area as the political power center).

In sum, the bulk of the skeletal remains from Lower Nubia have been used to show a differential pattern of biological response related to agricultural *intensification*, and not to agricultural origins. While the agricultural food base changes little during the latter phases, the political and economic activities that defined the level of intensity of the agricultural strategy do change. Health indicators reflect the degree to which human groups have access to the actual cultigens that they grow. If cultigens are used as trade items to support the cities, the health of the group will decline as cultigens are traded for "hard goods." This is precisely what is seen in the Meroitic and Christian phases.

The data from Lower Nubia suggest that the larger core areas such as the Kingdom of Meroë and Egypt were supported in part by imported goods and slaves from the outer local peasantries. Lower Nubia near Wadi Halfa provided a corridor connecting Egypt with sub Saharan Africa. Lower Nubia, as a case study of the impact of socioeconomic change, shows that while dependence on a single staple crop may be deleterious to health, the level of political and economic interactions is just as significant for health. The health data on the X-Group and the data from Kulubnarti suggest that agricultural groups fare better in terms of health when left to their own devices. Local autonomy and lessened trade interactions assure that the cultigens being grown will circulate throughout the villages, and that health and longevity will improve.

ACKNOWLEDGMENTS

This research has been supported in part by a University of Massachusetts Biomedical Research Support Grant NIH-RR07048. We would like to thank Mark Cohen and Lynn Miller for their helpful comments on earlier drafts of this paper.

REFERENCES

Adams, W. Y.
1970 A re-appraisal of Nubian culture history. *Orientalia 39*:269-279.
1977 *Nubia: Corridor to Africa*. Princeton University Press, Princeton.

Armelagos, George J.
1968 *Paleopathology of three archaeological populations from Sudanese Nubia*. Ph.D. Dissertation, Department of Anthropology, University of Colorado, Boulder.
1969 Disease in ancient Nubia. *Science 163*:255-259.

Armelagos, George J., James H. Mielke, Kipling H. Owen, Dennis P. Van Gerven, J. R. Dewey, and Paul E. Mahler
1972 Bone growth and development in prehistoric populations from Sudanese Nubia. *Journal of Human Evolution 1*:89-119.

Armelagos, George J., Rebecca Huss-Ashmore, and Debra L. Martin
1982 Morphometrics as indicators of dietary stress in prehistoric Nubia. *Museum Applied Science Center for Archaeology Journal 2*:22-26.

Bassett, E., Margaret Kieth, George J. Armelagos, Debra L. Martin, and A. Villanueva
1981 Tetracycline-labeled human bone from prehistoric Sudanese Nubia (A.D. 350). *Science 209*:1532-1534.

Batrawi, A. M.
1946 The racial history of Egypt and Nubia, Part II. *Journal of the Royal Anthropological Institute 76*:132-156.

Berry, A. C., and R. J. Berry
1973 Origins and relations of the ancient Egyptians. In *Population Biology of Ancient Egyptians*, edited by D. R. Brothwell and B. A. Chiarelli, pp. 200-208. Academic Press, New York.

Berry, A. C., R. J. Berry, and P. J. Ucko
1967 Genetical change in ancient Egypt. *Man 2*:551-506.

Carlson, David S., and Dennis P. Van Gerven
1977 Masticatory function and post-Pleistocene evolution in Nubia. *American Journal of Physical Anthropology 46*:495-506.

Garn, Stanley M.
1970 *The earlier gain and later loss of cortical bone in nutritional perspective.* Thomas, Springfield.

Greene, D. L.
1966 Dentition and the biological relationship of some Meroitic, X-Group and Christian populations from Wadi Halfa, Sudan. *Kush 14*:285-288.

Greene, D. L., and George J. Armelagos
1972 The Wadi Halfa Mesolithic population. *Department of Anthropology, University of Massachusetts, Amherst Research Report* No. 11.

Hummert, J. R., and Dennis P. Van Gerven
1982 Tetracycline-labeled human bone from a Medieval population in Nubia's Batn el Hajar (550-1400 A.D.). *Human Biology 54*:355-364.

Huss-Ashmore, Rebecca
1978 Nutritional determination in a Nubian skeletal population. *American Journal of Physical Anthropology 48*:407 (Abstr.).

Martin, Debra L.
1983 *Paleophysiological aspects of skeletal remodeling in the Meroitic, X-Group and Christian populations from Sudanese Nubia.* Ph.D. dissertation, Department of Anthropology, University of Massachusetts, Amherst.

Martin, Debra L., and George J. Armelagos
1979 Morphometrics of compact bone: An example from Sudanese Nubia. *American Journal of Physical Anthropology 51*:571-578.

Morant, G. M.
1925 A study of Egyptian craniology from prehistoric to Roman times. *Biometrika 17*:1-52.

Rudney, J. D.
1981 *The paleoepidemiology of early childhood stress in two ancient populations from Nubia.* Ph.D. dissertation, Department of Anthropology, University of Colorado, Boulder.

Saxe, A. A.
1966 *Social dimensions of mortuary practices in a Mesolithic population from Wadi Halfa, Sudan.* Paper presented at the American Anthropological Association meetings, Pittsburg.

Trigger, Bruce G.
1965 *History and settlement in Lower Nubia.* Yale University Press, Cambridge.

Vagn Nielson, O.
1970 *The Nubian skeleton through 4000 Years.* Andelsbogtrykkeriet i Odense, Copenhagen.

Van Gerven, Dennis P., David S. Carlson, and George J. Armelagos
1979 Racial history and biocultural adaptation of Nubian archaeological populations. *Journal of African History 14*:555-564.

Van Gerven, Dennis P., M. K. Sanford, and J. R. Hummert
1981 Mortality and culture change in Nubia's Batn el Hajar. *Journal of Human Evolution 10*:395-408.

CHAPTER 9

THE LOWER ILLINOIS RIVER REGION: A PREHISTORIC CONTEXT FOR THE STUDY OF ANCIENT DIET AND HEALTH

Jane E. Buikstra

Department of Anthropology
Northwestern University

The prehistory of west central Illinois is an ideal context for investigating the long-term impact of dietary change on the human condition. Archaeological research in the area has been intensive, documenting a rich prehistoric record for more than 8 millennia of human occupation. During this time, we find evidence of a relatively stable and abundant resource base that human groups have chosen to collect selectively, to manipulate, and ultimately to supplement through the addition of cultivated plant resources.

Importantly, the period of transition from hunting and gathering to agriculture is nearly as old as man himself in this region, for we find the beginnings of a shift toward the manipulation of locally available plants many millennia prior to the domestication *sensu strictu* of these resources. This initial manipulation of weedy plants occurs centuries before the appearance of significant quantities of maize, an introduced tropical cultigen, in the archaeological record. The detailed documentation of such significant subsistence changes, coupled with the availability of large and well-preserved samples of human skeletal remains, makes the region an appropriate "natural laboratory" for the study of diet and health in evolutionary perspective.

Successful investigation of the relationships among diet, nutrition, and health requires careful and critical analysis of archaeological and biological data. As with all studies of this type, accurate paleodietary reconstruction--emphasizing both composition and nutritive value--is a key consideration. Careful evaluation of climatic and environmental data is required to determine resource availability. The excavation and analysis of midden and features from archaeological sites that fully represent the annual cycle of food procurement for temporally sequential populations is also necessary to define patterns of dietary change, against which health parameters can be evaluated. The impact of food preparation strategies and storage on nutritive value are additional factors that should not be ignored.

In the study of human remains, either in estimating diet or in evaluating health status, it is crucial that researchers consider the various biases that may affect their data base. Selective burial customs, differential skeletal preservation, and incomplete archaeological recovery all can lead to inappropriate interpretations of prehistoric skeletal attributes. It is also important to evaluate the way in which genetic diversity and demographic patterning might limit and/or enhance the interpretation of health in prehistoric peoples. Inherited characteristics of the skeletons provide indirect evidence concerning group interaction and structure, and they are also important as we generate paleoepidemiological models. Thus, the appearance of a new group with a new subsistence strategy and a new disease load reflects a process quite different from the development of a distinctively different disease profile in local groups initiating a new subsistence strategy. Paleodemographic projections--drawing on both habitation and mortuary site data--are particularly important in paleodietary study as they are so often cited as prime movers or as dependent variables in models of changing subsistence strategies. As we shall see, it will be hard to resist invoking altered demographic patterns as factors of major significance in this analysis.

The structure of this chapter will be as follows: First, I will provide an introduction to west central Illinois prehistory, including a discussion of the advantages and disadvantages of addressing the symposium theme in this region. Then I will briefly summarize cultural chronology and subsistence, in parallel to the development of social organizational complexity. (The consideration of social complexity is important in any discussion of diet and health statuses, for it is probable that social as well as environmental variables have limited access to food resources, particularly in groups with well-developed status differences.) Finally, I will describe human demographic patterns, focusing on regional population estimates and aggregate size, along with discussion of genetic diversity and social organizational complexity. In Chapter 10 Della Cook will summarize the actual skeletal evidence for changing health patterns that correlate with these documented changes in diet, social complexity, and demography.

CLIMATIC AND ENVIRONMENTAL RECONSTRUCTION

The region spanned by our data sets includes the lower 100 km of the Illinois River region and adjacent uplands. The core area of this region is indicated in Figure 9.1, although we are now utilizing additional comparative data sets from farther north along the Illinois River valley and to the west, including the eastern valley of the Mississippi River.

Following Asch et al. (1979), it is appropriate to define the region in terms of three distinctive ecological zones: (1) the upland prairie, (2) the forests, and (3) the river floodplains. The first, the prairie, has the lowest resource potential, except at forest margins. Mobile hunting groups ventured onto the prairies, but these were not the site of significant prehistoric settlement. The other two zones were exceptionally rich sites of resource availability. Deer, turkey, and small mammals are found in the forests that line the river valleys and in the river valleys themselves. Deer are the single most important animal resource during much of prehistory. Nut crops, somewhat less mobile but still unevenly distributed, form the other major forest food resource. The river floodplains and the river itself provide remarkable resource potential. Fish and mussels from the river, as well as backwater lakes and sloughs, are cited as being "perhaps the most abundant and secure prehistoric wild food resource in Illinois [Asch et al. 1979:80]." Migratory waterfowl were also significant. Tubers, roots, and seed crops are other potential foods of the floodplain.

I should emphasize that these resource zones have been presented in inverse order to their carrying capacity. During most seasons, the floodplains could support a much larger human population than other adjacent areas. In addition, it should be noted that many of these animal resources do not easily--if ever--suffer permanent degradation due to intensive exploitation. This is particularly true of fish and mussels, and perhaps of deer to a lesser extent (Asch et al. 1979; Styles 1981; Styles et al. 1982).

There is a well-documented Holocene record of climatic variation within eastern North America that had significant ecological effects in many areas. Frequently cited is the Hypsithermal, a period of drier and possibly warmer temperatures that lasted from circa 8500 to 5100 B.C. (Brown and Vierra 1983). Geomorphological study of the Lower Illinois Valley (Hajic 1981; Hajic and Styles 1982) indicates that the Illinois River had become entrenched by the early portion of the Hypsithermal, with associated seasonal development of floodplain backwater lakes. The latter are important in explaining the sedentism and intensive utilization of floodplain resources that are characteristic of Middle Archaic and later occupations of the valley (Brown and Vierra 1983; Carlson 1979). This timing for entrenchment and the development of backwater lakes is not unequivocally accepted (see Butzer

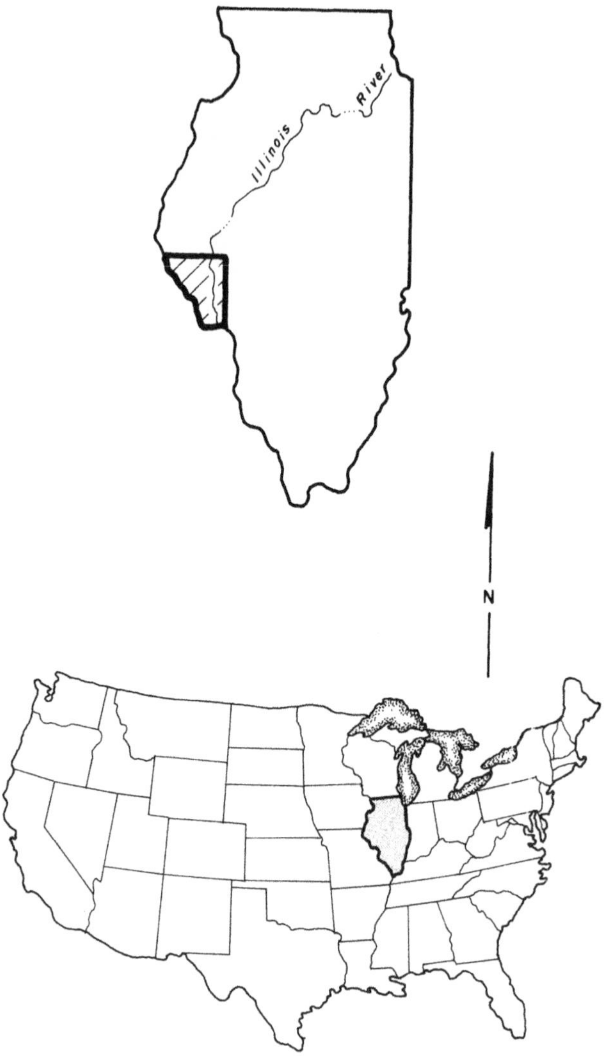

FIGURE 9.1. Map showing location of the research area.

1977, 1978); however, it is consistent with significant geomorphological (Hajic 1981; Hajic and Styles 1982) and paleofaunal evidence (Hill 1975; Neusius 1982; Styles et al. 1982). Also important for this period is the fact that forest margin ecozones may have become increasingly capable of supporting foragers such as deer, squirrels, and other nut consumers (Brown and Vierra 1983; Hewitt 1983; Styles et al. 1982).

After the Hypsithermal, there are minor climatic fluctuations that probably did not significantly affect resource availability in the lower Illinois Valley region. There is evidence that natural environmental zones may have shifted location slightly in parallel to the main river trench, but there is no evidence for replacement or significant depletion of resources due to environmental causes during the post-Hypsithermal period (Asch et al. 1972). The one exception may be the so-called Neoglacial period, which signaled cooler times and began circa A.D. 900. However, this period has not been extensively investigated by geomorphologists and paleoenvironmentalists in the study region. Thus, we can assume that, in general, explanations for shifting subsistence strategies that postdated the Hypsithermal should emphasize human choice, somewhat tempered by necessity in the face of altered human ecological relationships. There is no compelling reason to believe that significant climatic change should be an important component of any such models in this region.

REGIONAL PREHISTORY AND THE ARCHAEOLOGICAL RECORD

The lower Illinois Valley has been the site of fairly continuous human occupation during the Holocene, especially since circa 8000 B.C. Archaeologists such as Stuart Struever (1962, 1964, 1965, 1968; Struever and Houart 1972; Brown and Struever 1973) have created a significant research tradition, focusing substantially on the reconstruction of subsistence-settlement systems. Given the nearly 25 years of such work, these reconstructions provide a detailed accounting of changing human diets, settlement size and density, and artifact production.

In addition, the mortuary record itself for the Illinois Valley is relatively complete (Buikstra 1981a). Through much of the most recent periods of prehistory, mound burial (Figure 9.2) formed the primary, if not exclusive, form of mortuary behavior. Thus, the mounds provide an easily recognizable set of sites that can be systematically counted and subsampled. Our ability to estimate temporal association and numbers of burials for unexcavated sites facilitates the investigation of regional paleodemographic patterning in ways not possible using data from habitation sites alone.

In general, skeletal preservation in most mortuary sites is quite good. Not only adult bones, but even fragile juvenile elements are well preserved. In addition, the internal structure of the complex mounded cemeteries is preserved in observable soil differences. Such distinctions facilitate the determination of status-related differential treatment within prehistoric burial programs.

Although skeletal preservation is quite good and the cemeteries inclusive, two factors limit certain forms of bioarchaeo-

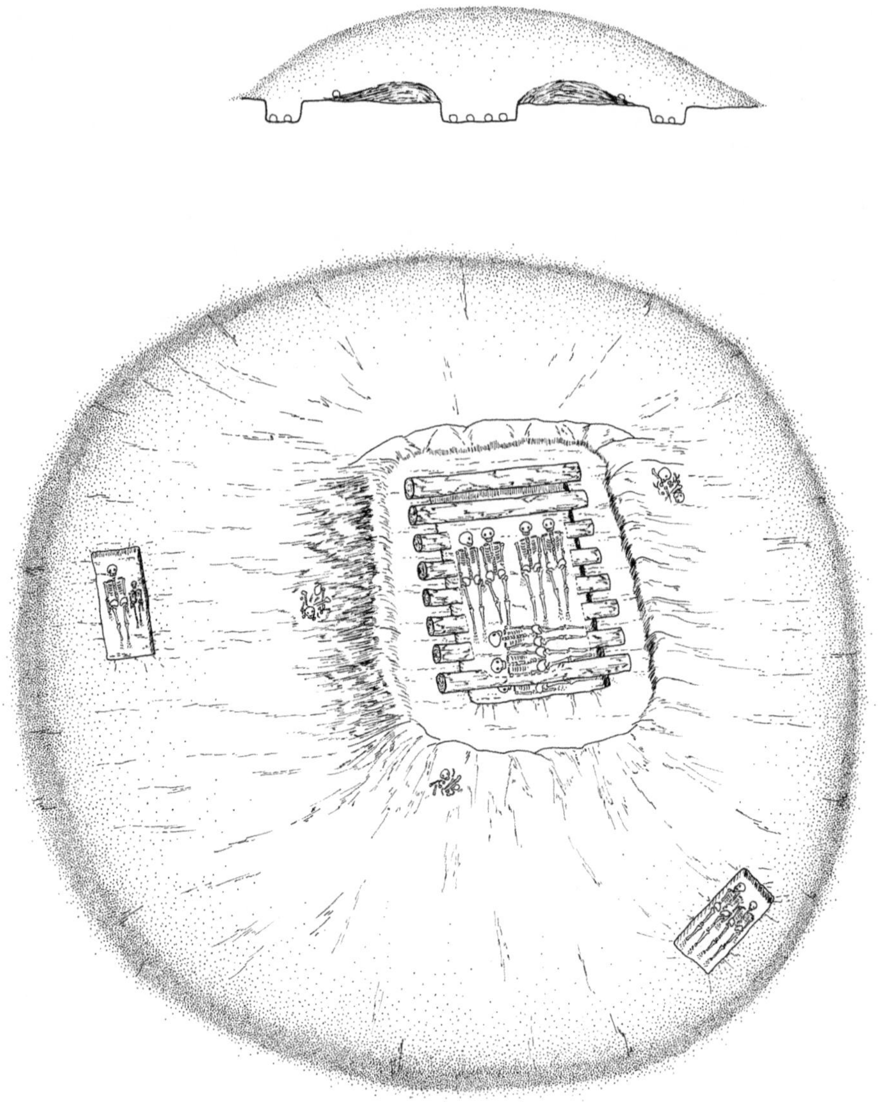

FIGURE 9.2. Middle Woodland mortuary structure, including plan view (below) and profile (above).

logical study. First, chronological control is sometimes a problem. When charcoal is available, we are able to estimate temporal associations for sites within less than two centuries. However, many mortuary sites lack charcoal, and we have been less than satisfied with collagen dates thus far. Second, the location of the cemeteries--spatially removed from habitation sites--is somewhat of a mixed blessing. It is an advantage to have bluff-crest cemeteries in situations in which soil conditions are ideal for bone preservation, and it is also pleasant to be able to design excavation strategy without the complications presented by nonmortuary structures. But these bluff-crest mounds may also be difficult to associate with specific floodplain village sites, thus making it difficult to link skeletons conclusively to the areas they inhabited in life. We can infer by association that a given mound group on a bluff-crest adjacent to a floodplain habitation site contains the dead of that village. But this association may be less explicit than one might like, especially when both the cemeteries and the village site cover a considerable time span.

Initial entry of human groups into west central Illinois dates to approximately 8000 B.C., commonly cited as the paleoindian-Early Archaic interface. Fluted points occur as surface remains on a few earlier sites, but there has been little systematic study of these most ancient contexts. Geomorphological study suggests that impoundment of the Illinois Valley, due to Pleistocene outflow of the Mississippi River, would have significantly limited human occupation and/or site recognition before 8000 B.C. (Hajic 1981; Hajic and Styles 1982). The Early Archaic period extends from 8000 B.C. until approximately 6000 B.C. From these Early Archaic sites we have recovered a very few human remains from seasonally occupied village sites (Brown and Vierra 1983).

The practice of interring the dead within villages continues into the Middle Archaic, but there is now also evidence of spatial segmentation of cemeteries: certain individuals are interred within floodplain habitation sites; others are interred in mounds on the bluff-crests. I have argued elsewhere (Buikstra 1981b) that this spatial division is dependent to some extent on achieved status; that those who either by age or by infirmity could not perform the full range of adult activities were relegated to burial near the village. Those adults not so defined were accorded mound interment. Such relatively simple status distinctions are not unexpected in what is generally accepted as a hunting and gathering community. That these groups also may have been experimenting with the cultivation of local seeds will be discussed later.

With the appearance of large projectile points, probably associated with more intensive hunting of deer, in sites that date between circa 3000 B.C. and circa 1000 B.C., we recognize the Late Archaic period. Human groups at this time continue to maintain significant settlements in the main valley while extending their range significantly into upland forest zones. The only known Late Archaic cemeteries from which skeletal remains have been recovered are mounded, some including cremations (Charles et al. 1983; Perino 1968).

After the Late Archaic, we find the crude ceramics that are horizon markers for the earliest part of the Woodland period. A few Early Woodland human remains have been recovered from village site midden in the floodplain, but in general this period is very poorly known archaeologically. As with most circumstances of sparse data bases, much controversy has ensued. Some argue that the paucity of archaeological remains reflects a depopulation; others suggest that sites are buried or have been eroded by the river during subsequent active periods of re-entrenchment. Charles et al. (1983) have recently argued that there is evidence in the structure of Early Woodland mortuary sites for the complex pattern later characteristic of the Middle Woodland period. According to this model, social change predated the notable population increases of the later Woodland times.

Following the currently enigmatic Early Woodland period is the richest part of the archaeological record, both for habitation and for mortuary sites. The Middle Woodland period, during which large monumental burial mounds were constructed both in the floodplain and on the bluff-crests that line the major and tributary valleys, dates from circa 150 B.C. to circa A.D. 400. Here there is for the first time clear evidence of social status distinctions, as preferential and extended treatment is accorded certain individuals within the central log tombs of the Middle Woodland burial mounds. Within these tombs the high-status dead are buried along with elaborate, aesthetically pleasing grave goods termed "Hopewell items" after an Ohio site, made of raw materials that are not locally available.

This control of wealth may also have ramifications for studies of nutrition and health status. After an analysis of estimates of stature (Buikstra 1976), compared by burial location, it was discovered that males who received disproportionately expensive burial treatment were also significantly taller than the remainder of the males in the skeletal sample. Various explanatory hypotheses can be offered, including the possibility that status was achieved by persons of special abilities that were related to body build (see Brues 1959). Opponents of this perspective point out that it implies achievement of status during the Middle Woodland period, which is inconsistent with the special treatment afforded juveniles in mortuary contexts (Tainter 1975a,b; 1977a,b). A second possibility, given that linear dimensions (including stature) are inherited, is that our high-status individuals may represent a genetic background distinctively different from that of the shorter persons. An extreme model would derive them from immigrant populations, perhaps from Ohio. In that selective exogamy has produced similar stature differentials in ethnographically documented societies, status-based marriage rules also could have produced this pattern. However, these genetic explanations are weakened by the fact that other inherited characteristics of the skeleton do not differ between groups.

At this time, a dietary model seems most reasonable. This explanation recognizes that those individuals who have special access to scarce and expensive resources at death, e.g., burial in central log tombs accompanied by Hopewell artifacts, also may have had increased access to rare items during life, particularly foods during the growing years. Such special availability of food during youth would have allowed privileged individuals to attain more of their genetically determined growth potential and thus to appear as taller adults in burial context. Rather than supporting the notion of achieved status, the dietary hypothesis is compatible with status acquired through birth, i.e., inherited status.

Although our test of the dietary hypothesis is in its preliminary stage, information from Della Cook's (1981) study of dental developments, the microscopically visible striae or lines of Retzius, lends support to the dietary model. Significantly more developmental stress occurred in individuals buried in inferred low status positions than in high status burials. A second argument in favor of the dietary hypothesis comes from the presence of differential distributions of trace elements across status groups in Middle Woodland (Lambert et al. 1977). Given that these trace element distributions apparently reflect different diets, they lend further support to the dietary hypothesis as the most efficient explanation for the observed stature differentials in Middle Woodland mortuary sites.

During the A.D. 400-500 period, the elaborate Hopewell grave goods that conspicuously characterize Middle Woodland cease to be found in mortuary context. Pottery styles generally become much less elaborate and small projectile points are added to the artifact repertoire. These are typical characteristics that archaeologists use to define the Middle to Late Woodland transition. Mounded cemeteries continue into Late Woodland, in many instances structured similarly to Middle Woodland sites although elaborate grave goods are absent. Thus, certain rules for organizing a cemetery persist, but there are new social definitions concerning access. In addition, cremation--absent during Middle Woodland--reappears as a minor aspect of the Late Woodland burial program.

Late within the Late Woodland period, circa A.D. 800, the structure of mortuary sites is further altered. Burial areas are still located on bluff-crests, but these are no longer conical earthworks positioned at the apex of the bluff. Rather, these are mounded cemeteries, organized as if to follow a superannual cycle of mortuary activities. Central charnel structures occur in these contexts. It has been argued that increased status distinctions are to be found in these sites, based on the diversity of burial customs (Tainter 1975a,b, 1977a,b), although this interpretation has been disputed (Braun 1977, 1979). Stylistic analyses of artifactual materials, however, in concert with site structure, suggest that Late Woodland mortuary sites are symbolic of an increasingly regionally integrated local polity and that direct comparisons in terms of heirarchically ordered social complexity between Middle and Late Woodland are inappropriate (Kerber 1983).

The most recent significant, well-documented prehistoric culture change in west central Illinois is the appearance of the Mississippian culture, circa A.D. 1000-1100. Maize agriculture, introduced in major proportions during the Late Woodland period, now becomes a more central focus of the subsistence strategy.

Artifacts show new attributes; some archaeologists would argue that Mesoamerican styles are conspicuous. The lower Illinois region at this time is best described as a series of farmstead communities, satellites within the influence of the major center at Cahokia, near present-day St. Louis (Goldstein 1980). Mississippian peoples do not construct burial mounds in the lower Illinois region, although their cemeteries may be located adjacent to Late Woodland earthworks. Status distinctions are evident in these Mississippian cemeteries, both in terms of spatial location and in reference to burial associations. Just as in the Woodland period, there is evidence for the unequal apportionment of wealth.

SUBSISTENCE

The earliest evidence of plant harvesting occurs circa 5500 B.C., during the Middle Archaic period. Before this there are very low levels of nut and/or seed remains to be found in archaeological context. At this point, however, nutshells assume major prominence, becoming as common as wood charcoal in sites such as Koster. Hickory nutshells are in highest frequency: as reported by Asch et al. (1972), they appear in all samples and constitute over 90% of total nutshells, as measured by weight. Nutshells (and by inference, nut meats) continue in high relative volume through the Middle Woodland into the earlier part of the Late Woodland period. The focal dominance of hickory changes in Middle Woodland to include a significant frequency of hazelnut. Other nut resources--walnut, pecan, and acorn--are used as well. However, the preference first for hickory and then for hazelnut is clear.

Nutritionally, hickory and hazelnuts can be considered of equivalent value as excellent sources of protein and fat. Black walnuts and pecans show a similar pattern, with acorns providing a contrastive emphasis on carbohydrates and relatively less fat and protein. In that nut protein is of high quality and to some extent parallels the meat of large mammals, Asch et al. (1972) suggest that the nut protein and fat may have been a suitable or perhaps necessary complement to an Archaic diet that emphasized fish, such as that of Middle Archaic peoples at the Koster site.

Although the nutritive value of nuts is high, it must be remembered that the distribution of nut trees tends to be patchy and that productivity varies from year to year. Botantists (Asch et al. 1972) record a mast cycle for the hickories of at least 2 to 3 years, with great variability in productivity. Variability in hazelnut production is less well documented, though it is important to note that they ripen in August, contrasting with the September-October harvest season for the other nut trees mentioned here.

In sum, nuts provide a high-quality food resource that was utilized by Archaic and Middle Woodland peoples. Although nuts are highly storable (once wrested away from the aggressive squirrels that inhabit Illinois forests), to be a dependable food source for large human groups they must be harvested over an extensive and discontinuous distribution. This last-mentioned factor may have influenced the decreased utilization of nuts during the Late Woodland and presumably during Mississippian times.

Although less prominent in the Middle Archaic archaeological record, seeds become increasingly frequent during later Middle Archaic times. By Middle Woodland, seed resources are heavily utilized, with one Middle Woodland site showing 38 times the ratio of seeds to nuts, as compared to Middle Archaic Koster. Given our current focus on diet and nutritive value, it is important to differentiate between two classes of seed resources: those Asch and Asch (1977, 1978, 1982) term the "oily seeds" and those that are contrastingly starchy.

Marsh elder, or *Iva annua*, was a significant food for both Archaic and Woodland peoples. Seeds from this plant are termed "oily," and they are a very nutritious food resource. Attractive because of the high fat and low moisture content of the kernel, this concentrated source of food energy provides more calories per 100 g than starchy seeds or roots, approximately the same as sunflower and less than nuts. Protein content is also high, although the protein quality is poor. Asch and Asch (1978) report that given the high ratio of protein to food energy, if an individual is meeting his caloric requirement, the poor quality of the protein of *Iva* would be satisfactory. In addition, *Iva annua* seeds are an excellent source of vitamins and minerals.

Although it may have been cultivated as early as the Middle Archaic, there is clear evidence that *Iva* was domesticated during the Woodland period. Significant size increase marks *Iva* from Woodland sites as a domesticate. Cultivation, perhaps in a forest-swidden context, probably encouraged the domestication of this highly storable and fairly dependable food crop (Asch and Asch 1978).

Just as with nut resources, *Iva* ceases to be conspicuous in the archaeological record during the earlier part of the Late Woodland period. There is some speculation that it had been replaced by the sunflower, *Helianthus annuus*, which it resembles nutritionally. Improved sunflower varieties may have developed at this time, which would have been more compatible with the field cultivation of maize (Asch and Asch 1982).

In addition to marsh elder three starchy seeds, knotweed (*Polygonum erectum*), maygrass (*Phalaris caroliniana*), and goosefoot (*Chenopodium bushianum*), are conspicuous in the Middle and Late Woodland archaeological record. It appears that these starchy seeds were cultivated, but not domesticated, with the possible exception of one type of chenopodium. Starchy seeds obviously were harvested and presumably were utilized in great quantity, providing an apparently dependable and highly storable resource (Asch and Asch 1982).

These starchy seeds are vastly inferior to *Iva*, *Helianthus*, and hickory nutmeat in terms of protein and fat, although carbohydrate content is much higher. Thus, they more closely resemble maize as a nutritive resource (Asch and Asch 1978).

The three members of the so-called Mesoamerican triad have somewhat different histories in west central Illinois. Squash (*Cucurbita pepo*) occurs by 5000 B.C. in several Middle Archaic sites, making this its earliest occurrence in eastern North America. By the Middle Woodland period, both the squash and the bottle gourd (*Lagenaria siceraria*) are ubiquitous in pit features (Asch and Asch 1982).

By contrast, maize is not conspicuous in the archaeological record until the Late Woodland period. The earliest dates for significant quantities of corn come from the Deer Track site and date to circa A.D. 530. Following this, increasing amounts of maize are recovered from sites that postdate A.D. 800. (Asch and Asch 1982).

The relatively recent nutritional dependence on maize as suggested by village refuse is confirmed by independent evidence: biochemical studies of human bones from Archaic, Middle Woodland, Late Woodland, and Mississippian sites. After analyzing stable carbon isotope ratios for samples from five sites, van der Merwe and Vogel (1978) found evidence of significant presence of a C_4 plant, probably maize in this context, only in samples postdating the latter part of the Late Woodland period. These earliest C_4 samples are characterized by a great deal of variability in maize dependence, which is to be expected in groups experimenting with a new resource. van der Merwe and Vogel (1978) estimate the proportion of carbon entering the diet from maize as varying between 0 and 55% in terminal Late Woodland sites. Predictably, Mississippian remains indicate a more uniform degree of dependence: approximately 40-55% of the dietary carbon came from maize, according to van der Merwe.

Beans, as the third member of the triad, are conspicuously absent from the west central Illinois archaeological record. Farther south, in the American Bottoms region, *Phaseolus vulgaris* has been recovered in strata dated to A.D. 1000. However, to conclude that beans also were present in west central Illinois at this point requires an inference based on little evidence (Asch and Asch 1982).

As noted earlier, faunal resources within the lower Illinois region are abundant. Deer is the dominant large mammal, although there is a variety of small mammal resources as well as waterfowl, fish, and freshwater mussels. In general, a broad-spectrum faunal assemblage was present at most sites from Middle Archaic through Middle Woodland. Deer is clearly the most significant mammal, having assumed prominence relative to smaller mammals at the end of the Early Archaic period. Dependence on deer is emphasized during the Late Archaic, and there seems to be a significant decrease only at the beginning of the Late Woodland period. For instance, Styles (1981) reports that the early Late Woodland components of the Apple Creek site show a decrease in white tailed deer by nearly half (minimum number of individuals equals 30.4 and 17.9% of the fauna, respectively). Locally available aquatic resources such as fish and mussels are much more intensively harvested at this time, and there is appreciable variability among sites in species counts. In general, it appears that collector territories for faunal resources are significantly localized during the early Late Woodland. Styles (1981) attributes this to increased population densities and competition between human groups in the main valley of the Illinois River, although the archaeological documentation of this phenomenon is somewhat equivocal (Asch et al. 1979).

In sum, it appears that cultivation and occasional domestication of plants has considerable time depth in the lower Illinois valley. There is a clear trend, especially evident in the Woodland period, for increased dependence on high-carbohydrate, storable, reliable plant resources such as starchy seeds. Resources that are available in either smaller or less dependable quantities, such as hickory nuts and marsh elder, are first supplemented by North American starchy seeds during Middle Woodland, and then are largely supplanted when maize joins the cultigen complex. The study of faunal assemblages, while not demonstrating observable indications of nutritional inadequacy, does bespeak increased competition for resources during the earlier part of the Late Woodland period. Mammal protein probably was less important at this time than before, with aquatic resources assuming prominence. In general, these fish and mussels are higher in carbohydrates (especially mussels) and contain proportionately less fat than do mammals.

GENETIC AND DEMOGRAPHIC FACTORS

The remainder of this chapter will concentrate on two additional dimensions of variability that are significant to our interpretation of health status: (1) evidence for genetic continuity through the period under investigation, and (2) demographic patterning for the Woodland period.

There is no evidence from inherited skeletal morphological traits to suggest significant movement of persons into the research area during the Woodland period. Obviously, given the degree of sensitivity of skeletal markers, this does not necessarily document a total absence of individual movement or interaction. However, all our data sets are consistent with the hypothesized presence of localized and somewhat isolated communities during Middle Woodland, a pattern that continues into the Late Woodland and even the early Mississippian. Skeletal nonmetric traits show significant differences in frequency between Middle Woodland sites separated by as little as 50 km (Buikstra 1976). If these Middle Woodland sites are compared with Late Woodland, it is clear that the frequencies of shared traits are higher in sites that are spatially close than in those that are contemporary but spatially distant (Buikstra 1975). The single exception to this pattern occurs in the more recent component of the Mississippian Schild cemetery, the southernmost knoll (Knoll B), where both metric and nonmetric analysis document distinctive morphological differences in males (Buikstra 1975; Droessler 1981). Apparently, the process of Mississippianization has effected a significant breakdown in the localization that so prominently characterizes the Woodland period.

In evaluating demographic patterns, it is important to consider both the degree to which given populations should be characterized as sedentary and the relative numbers of people on the landscape. Looking first at the data from habitation sites, it is clear that base camps--probably inhabited year-round--existed during the Middle Archaic, circa 4000 B.C. These impressive, deep, thick and organically stained middens document well an intensity of living that long predates maize agriculture. It is difficult to estimate population size for these Archaic base camps, but it is generally accepted that there was no significant population increase during the Early Woodland (Charles et al. 1983). Early Woodland surface scatters of habitation debris never exceed 1 ha in area and contrast sharply with the subsequent Woodland period sites, which may cover 2-4 ha and occasionally are over 15 ha in area (Asch et al. 1979). It is difficult to estimate absolute population numbers from either habitation or mortuary sites, although in this region the latter appear to be more reliable. Using burial mounds as a basis for inference, Asch has estimated human density in the Illinois drainage as being circa 40 persons/km^2 during Middle Woodland times (Asch 1976). Significantly, if the population is concentrated in the main valley, as we have every reason to believe, we would infer a population approximately 25 persons/km of Illinois River frontage during Middle Woodland (Asch et al. 1979). Working with mortuary site survey data, DeRousseau (1973) documents an increase in population density throughout the Late Woodland period. Unfortunately, our temporal control at this point is not sufficient to indicate just when, and in association with what subsistence strategy, this increase began. An intuitively pleasing argument would specify steadily increasing population numbers beginning in Middle Woodland. Styles's (1981) site distribution data would support this notion.

An interesting speculation concerning demographic patterning emerges from trace element studies. In Middle Woodland sites there is no significant male-female difference in bone strontium content. The strontium levels are, however, significantly different between the sexes in the terminal Late Woodland agriculturalists, the females showing more strontium (Lambert et al. 1977). Perhaps, as Sillen suggests elsewhere in this volume (Chapter 5), the pattern reflects the elevated reproduction of this rapidly expanding population. On the other hand, this may indicate differential consumption of animal protein between the sexes. It would not be unexpected for males in an agricultural society to have greater access to animal protein, perhaps as a result of opportunistic snacking when hunting.

There is no clear evidence of continued population increase into the Mississippian--perhaps the contrary. With the later part of the Late Woodland, groups begin to disperse into the uplands, apparently lowering population density in the main river valley. This is important in our evaluation of health status, particularly the conditions necessary for epidemic disease. Apparently, the pool of susceptibles may have been more dispersed during Mississippian times than during Woodland times. However true this may be for our research area, we must remember that our region is now a participant in a larger sphere of direct influence, effectively serving as the breadbasket for much larger populations a few kilometers to the south. Estimates of population size, perhaps only seasonally during market and/or ceremonial periods, reach 30,000-40,000 (Gregg 1975). With increased communication and continued sedentism, it is hardly surprising that we find the presence of a new chronic infectious pathology--probably tuberculosis--within our Mississippian peoples (Buikstra 1977; Buikstra and Cook 1978, 1981).

This, then, is the context and the subsistence change. Increasingly larger human groups in west central Illinois first cultivated local seed crops and then turned to maize as a high-carbohydrate plant resource. Sedentism is not tied to maize cultivation, however, because we have evidence of settled, long-term habitation of base camps during the Middle Archaic period. It appears that the immensely rich Illinois River floodplain served for millennia as a magnet attracting peoples to the rich variety of its resources. As human groups existed here in growing numbers, emphasis was placed on resources that were dependable, easily stored, and available nearby. Thus, local villages developed subsistence strategies that emphasized resources proximal to habitation areas, intensively harvesting riverine bounty rather than extending their collector territories to distant nut crops or searching for the elusive and highly mobile deer. In association with this close packing of the main trench of the Illinois, increasingly complex social organization and regional integration developed. From our Western perspective, we would tend to view this population increase as desirable, or at least inevitable. And a dependable resource base, even one high in carbohydrates, has certain advantages when compared to the possibility of seasonal "hunger" times. Thus, these attributes are positive: greater population size and increased predictability of food resources. It is likely, however, that certain health-related compromises were made: a deterioration in dental health and the introduction of a new and virulent epidemic disease. The degree to which these should be viewed as "causes" or "consequences" of shifting subsistence strategies is now at question. This is the topic of the companion analysis by Della Cook (Chapter 10), which will directly address the health status of Woodland and Mississippian populations from west central Illinois

REFERENCES

Asch, D. L.
1976 The Middle Woodland population of the lower Illinois Valley: A study in palaeodemographic methods. *Northwestern University Archeological Program Scientific Papers* No. 1.

Asch, D. L., and N. B. Asch
1977 Chenopod as cultigen: A re-evaluation of some prehistoric collections from eastern North America. *Midcontinental Journal of Archaeology 2*:3-45.
1978 The economic potential of *Iva annua* and its prehistoric importance in the lower Illinois Valley. In The nature and status of ethnobotany, edited by Richard I. Ford. *University of Michigan Museum of Anthropology Anthropological Papers* 67:300-341.
1982 A chronology for the development of prehistoric horticulture in west-central Illinois. Paper presented at the 47th Annual Meeting of the Society for American Archaeology, Minneapolis.

Asch, D. L., K. B. Farnsworth, and N. B. Asch
1979 Woodland subsistence and settlement in west-central Illinois. In *Hopewell archaeology: The Chillicothe Conference*, edited by D. S. Brose and N. Greber, pp. 80-85. Kent State University Press, Kent, Ohio.

Asch, N. B., R. I. Ford, and D. L. Asch
1972 Paleoethnobotany of the Koster site: The Archaic horizons. *Illinois State Museum Reports of Investigations* No. 24.

Braun, D. P.
1977 *Middle Woodland--Early Late Woodland social change in the prehistoric central midwestern U.S.* Ph.D. dissertation, Department of Anthropology, University of Michigan, Ann Arbor.
1979 Illinois Hopewell burial practices and social organization: A re-examination of the Klunk-Gibson mound group. In *Hopewell archaeology: The Chillicothe Conference*, edited by D. Brose and N. Greber, pp. 66-79. Kent State University Press, Kent, Ohio.

Brown, J. A., and S. Struever
1973 The organization of archaeological research: An Illinois example. In *Research and theory in current archaeology*, edited by C. Redman, pp. 261-280. Wiley, New York.

Brown, J. A., and R. K. Vierra
1983 What happened in the Middle Archaic? Introduction to an ecological approach to Koster site archaeology. In *Archaic hunters and gatherers in the American Midwest*, edited by J. Phillips and J. Brown, pp. 165-195. Academic Press, New York.

Brues, A.
1959 The spearman and the archer. *American Anthropologist 61*: 458-469.

Buikstra, J. E.
1975 *Cultural and biological variability: A comparison of models.* Paper presented at the annual meeting of the American Association of Physical Anthropologists, Denver.
1976 Hopewell in the lower Illinois Valley: A regional study of human biological variability and prehistoric mortuary behavior. *Northwestern University Archaeological Program Scientific Papers* No. 2.
1977 Differential diagnosis: An epidemiological model. *Yearbook of Physical Anthropology* 1976:316-328.
1981a The Northwestern archeological program. In Prehistoric tuberculosis in the Americas, edited by J. E. Buikstra. *Northwestern University Archeological Program, Scientific Papers*, No. 5, pp. v-vi.
1981b Mortuary practices, paleodemography and palaeopathology: A case study from the Koster site (Illinois). In *The archaeology of death*, edited by R. Chapman, I. Kinnes, and K. Randsborg, pp. 123-132. Cambridge University Press, London and New York.

Buikstra, J. E., and D. C. Cook
1978 Pre-Columbian tuberculosis: An epidemiological approach. *Medical College of Virginia Quarterly 14*;32-44.
1981 Pre-Columbian tuberculosis in west-central Illinois: Prehistoric disease in biocultural perspective. In Prehistoric tuberculosis in the Americas, edited by J. E. Buikstra. *Archeological Program Scientific Papers*, No. 5, pp. 115-139.

Butzer, K. W.
1977 Geomorphology of the lower Illinois valley as a spatial-temporal context for the Koster Archaic site. *Illinois State Museum Reports of Investigations* No. 34.
1978 Changing Holocene environments at the Koster site: A geoarchaeological perspective. *American Antiquity 43*:408-413.

Carlson, D. L.
1979 *Hunter-gatherer mobility strategies: An example from the Koster site in the lower Illinois valley.* Ph.D. dissertation, Department of Anthropology, Northwestern University, Evanston, Illinois.

Charles, D., J. E. Buikstra, and L. Konigsberg
1983 Terminal Archaic and Early Woodland mortuary practices in the lower Illinois River Valley: The behavioral implica-

tions. *Northwestern University Archeological Program Scientific Papers*, in press.

Cook, D. C.
1981 Mortality, age-structure and status in the interpretation of stress indicators in prehistoric skeletons: A dental example from the lower Illinois Valley. In *The archaeology of death*, edited by R. Chapman, I. Kinnes, and K. Randsborg, pp. 123-132. Cambridge University Press, London and New York.

DeRousseau, C. J.
1973 *Mortuary site survey and paleodemography in the lower Illinois Valley*. Paper presented at the 72nd annual meeting of the American Anthropological Association, New Orleans.

Droessler, J.
1981 Craniometry and biological distance: Biocultural continuity and change at the Late Woodland--Mississippian interface. *Center for American Archeology at Northwestern University Research Series* No. 1.

Goldstein, L. G.
1980 Mississippian mortuary practices: A case study of two cemeteries in the lower Illinois valley. *Northwestern University Archeological Program Scientific Papers* No. 5.

Gregg, M. L.
1975 A population estimate for Cahokia. In Perspectives in Cahokia archaeology. *Illinois Archaeological Survey Bulletin 10*:126-136.

Hajic, E. R.
1981 *Geology and paleopedology of the Koster archeological site, Greene County, Illinois*. Master's thesis, Department of Geology, University of Iowa.

Hajic, E., and T. Styles
1982 *Dynamic surficial geology of the lower Illinois Valley region and the impact on the archaeological record.* Paper presented at the 47th annual meeting of the Society for American Archaeology, Minneapolis.

Hewitt, J.
1983 *Optimal foraging models for the lower Illinois Valley.* Ph.D. dissertation, Department of Anthropology, Northwestern University, Evanston, Illinois.

Hill, F.
1975 *Effects of the environment on animal exploitation by Archaic inhabitants of the Koster site, Illinois.* Ph.D. dissertation, Department of Zoology, University of Louisville, Kentucky.

Kerber, R.
1983 *Late Woodland mortuary sites in west-central Illinois: Some Sociological Interpretations*. Ph.D. candidacy paper, Department of Anthropology, Northwestern University, Evanston, Illinois.

Lambert, J. B., C. B. Szpunar, and J. E. Buikstra
1977 Chemical analysis of excavated human bone from Middle and Late Woodland sites. *Archaeometry 21*:115-129.
Neusius, S. W.
1982 *Early-Middle Archaic subsistence strategies: Changes in faunal exploitation at the Koster site*. Ph.D. dissertation, Department of Anthropology, Northwestern University, Evanston, Illinois.
Perino, G.
1968 The Pete Klunk mound group, Calhoun County, Illinois: The Archaic and Hopewell occupations (with an appendix on the Gibson Mound Group). In Hopewell and Woodland site archaeology in Illinois, edited by J. A. Brown. *Illinois Archaeological Survey Bulletin* No. 6, pp. 9-124.
Struever, S.
1962 Implications of vegetal remains from an Illinois Hopewell site. *American Antiquity 27*:584-587.
1964 The Hopewell interaction sphere in Riverine-western Great Lakes culture history. In Hopewellian studies, edited by J. R. Caldwell and R. L. Hall. *Illinois State Museum Scientific Papers 12*:85-106.
1965 Middle Woodland culture history in the Great Lakes-Riverine area. *American Antiquity 31*:211-233.
1968 Woodland subsistence-settlement systems in the lower Illinois Valley. In *New perspectives in archeology*, edited by L. R. Binford and S. R. Binford, pp. 285-312. Aldine, Chicago.
Struever, S., and G. Houart
1972 An analysis of the Hopewell Interaction Sphere. In Social exchange and interaction, edited by E. N. Wilmsen. *Anthropological Papers of the Museum of Anthropology University of Michigan 46*:47-79.
Styles, B. W.
1981 Faunal exploitation and resource selection: Early Late Woodland subsistence in the lower Illinois Valley. *Northwestern University Archeological Program Scientific Papers* No. 3.
Styles, B. W., S. W. Neusius, and J. R. Purdue
1982 *The evolution of faunal exploitation strategies: A case study in the lower Illinois valley.* Paper presented at the 47th annual meeting of the Society for American Archaeology, Minneapolis.
Tainter, J. A.
1975a *The archaeological study of social change: Woodland systems in west-central Illinois.* Ph.D. dissertation, Northwestern University, Evanston, Illinois.
1975b Social inference and mortuary practices: An experiment in numerical classification. *World Archaeology 7*:1-15.
1977a Woodland social change in west-central Illinois. *Midcontinental Journal of Archaeology 2*:67-98.

1977b Modeling change in prehistoric social systems. In *For theory building in archaeology*, edited by L. R. Binford, pp. 327-351. Academic Press, New York.

van der Merwe, N. J., and J. C. Vogel
1978 ^{13}C content of human collagen as a measure of prehistoric diet in Woodland North America. *Nature (London) 276*:815-816.

CHAPTER 10

SUBSISTENCE AND HEALTH IN THE LOWER ILLINOIS VALLEY: OSTEOLOGICAL EVIDENCE

Della Collins Cook

Department of Anthropology
Indiana University

In west central Illinois the archaeological record presents a picture of gradual intensification of food production. The dominant element in this picture is a mixed hunting and gathering economy that stresses deer and other terrestrial game, nut harvesting, and riverine resources. Evidence of collection and cultivation of oily and starchy seeds, squash, and gourds appears in the record as early as we have human skeletal remains with which to test inferences about the biological effects of subsistence base change. From Middle Archaic through Woodland times these plants play an increasingly important role in subsistence. After A.D. 800, in late Late Woodland times, maize appears in the record, and during the Mississippian period it becomes perhaps the most important element in the food economy (Asch and Asch 1977; Asch et al. 1972; Asch et al. 1979; Ford 1977). These changes are accompanied by changes in community size, social complexity, regional integration, and extraregional trade, reaching their zenith in two periods of what Caldwell has called cultural florescence or climax: Middle Woodland and Mississippian (Caldwell 1962). The intervening Late Woodland period is one of rapid change in subsistence accompanied by intensification of exploitation of local resources and by relative social insularity (Styles 1981). Jane Buikstra's contribution to this volume (Chapter 9) provides a detailed review of the rich and varied information that is available on these aspects of the prehistory of the region.

This paper presents evidence for the effects of intensification of food production on health in west central Illinois. In reviewing these data I would like to focus on three issues. The first is the comparative costs and benefits of intensification as reflected in skeletal biology. The second concerns the comparability of the various kinds of data that can be marshalled in assessing health. The third regards the contrary effects of variables linked to subsistence--for example, population size, settlement pattern, social stratification, and the epidemiology of infectious diseases--on the interpretation of data from skeletal remains.

However sophisticated the models we wish to test in prehistory, we inevitably confront limitations imposed by the vagaries of preservation and recovery. West central Illinois has produced large and well-preserved series of skeletal remains. However, these series are not equally representative of the periods of time that are of interest in studying subsistence change.[1] The Middle Archaic period is represented by 25 individuals from the Koster site (6000-3000 B.C.) and by 36 individuals from the Gibson Mound group. The Late Archaic component from the Pete Klunk Mound group is the only analyzed series representing this period (Buikstra 1981; Charles and Buikstra 1983). Early Woodland materials are fragmentary and of questionable provenience (Charles et al., n.d.). In contrast, the Middle Woodland, early Late Woodland, late Late Woodland, and early Mississippian periods are represented by several series each, and series of 200 or more are the rule. After A.D. 1200 there is little evidence for substantial population in the region, and there are no skeletal remains suitable for analysis. For a picture of health in later Mississippian times we must turn to the central Illinois Valley to the north (Goodman et al., Chapter 11, this volume), or to the Cahokia region to the south (Milner 1982).

[1]*Assignment of all individuals in a given skeletal series to a time period may be problematic, especially where Late Woodland materials are concerned. Most researchers in the region have assigned specimens that cannot be associated with minor components on stratigraphic or artifactual grounds to the dominant component at a given mortuary site, and there is likely to be some chronological heterogeneity in most of the series discussed below. For a discussion of dating of Middle Woodland mortuary components, see Buikstra (1976). Conner has recently undertaken a revision of the dating of Late Woodland mortuary components that incorporates collagen dates and many dates from larger series. See Conner (1983, n.d.); Tainter (1975) for fuller discussions.*

SKELETAL GROWTH AND DEVELOPMENT

Bone growth and development is mirrored in juvenile height for age, stature, bone proportions, and sexual dimorphism in adults, cortical bone maintenance, and growth arrest indicators. All of these sources of data may be used to study nutritional status in the living, and they provide the first line of evidence in past populations. Interpretation of these sources of information is a complicated issue, however, for all reflect influences apart from nutrition. For example, population-specific genetic factors, heterosis, and disease load affect both skeletal growth and final adult stature, even though nutrition plays an important role in both. Similarly, disease load and mortality levels are reflected in stress indicator frequencies and bone maintenance. These interactions complicate the interpretation of data on growth and development derived from prehistoric skeletons, but the interactions themselves provide a useful perspective on health and adaptation.

Juvenile Height for Age

Perhaps the most common tool that anthropologists use in assessing nutrition in living groups is growth in children. However, the interpretation of bone length for age in skeletal remains presents problems. Children in cemetery samples are there as children because they failed to survive the stresses of childhood. Differences in apparent growth among cemetery samples are thus biased toward finding evidence for nutritional stress, and may overstate the differences that one might have seen in the living communities. On the other hand, these data do provide a way of looking at nutritional status as it relates to natural selection, and hence may provide a better view of the biological meaning of subsistence than would measurements of surviving children.

In evaluating growth I have chosen a strategy that differs somewhat from those employed by other contributors to this volume. In Illinois Valley series--as we expect in natural mortality samples--the distribution of age at death in juveniles is strongly biased toward younger ages. By considering only the age range birth to 6 years, one can minimize sample size problems, permitting statistical testing of differences in apparent growth. In this age range sex differences in height are small; hence the lack of reliable sex indicators is less important than in older children. Moreover, children under 6 years of age are more sensitive to nutritional insult than are older children.

Figure 10.1 presents a study of the relationship of femur diaphysis length to dental age in children under six from eight lower Illinois Valley series (Cook 1979; n.d.a.). Regression equations of the form

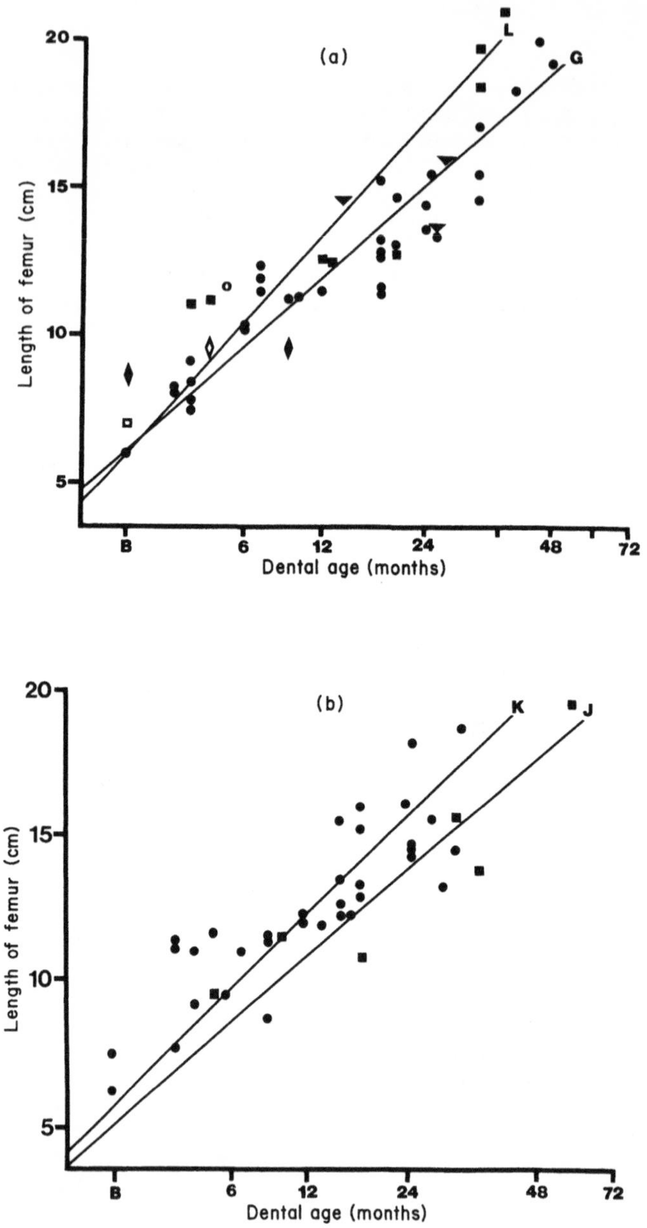

FIGURE 10.1. Long bone length for age in children under 6 years of age from four temporal components: (a) Middle Woodland series from Gibson (○), L'Orient (□), Bedford (▽), and Joe Gay (◊). (b) Early Late Woodland series from Koster Mounds (●)

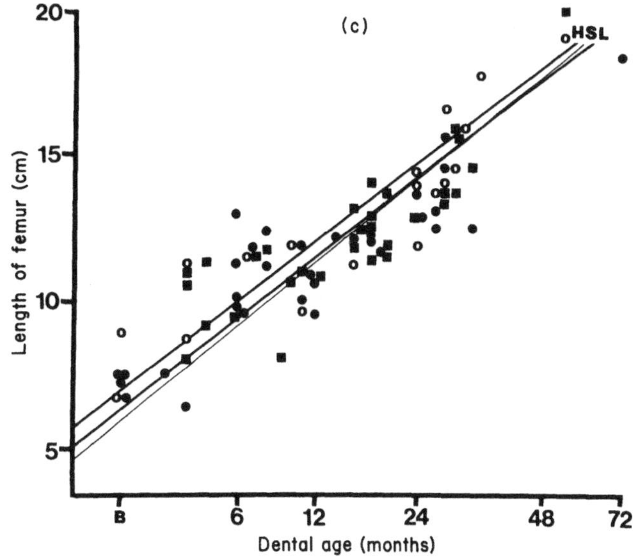

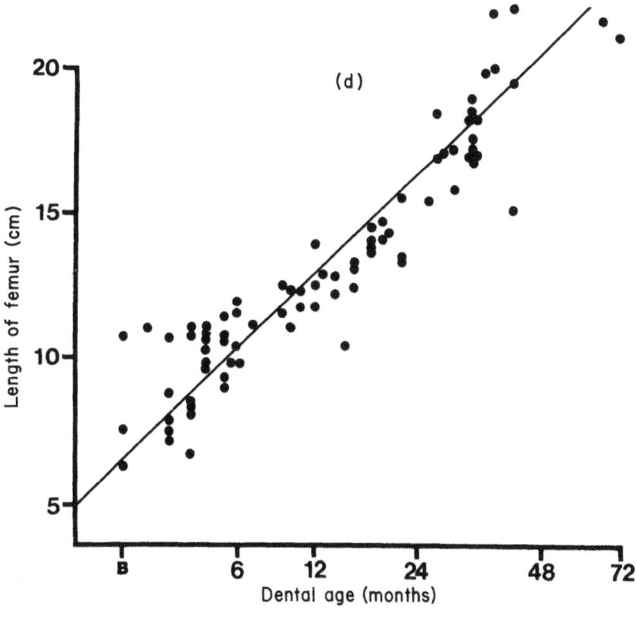

and Joe Gay (◘). (c) Late Late Woodland series from Ledders (●), Schild (■), and Helton (o). (d) Mississippian series from Schild (●). Femur length (vertical scale) was calculated from other long bone lengths as necessary.

$$\ell n(\text{dental age in months} + 9) = A + B(\text{femur diaphysis length})$$

give a linear fit to the data. *T* tests for difference in slope show that the late Late Woodland series differ from both earlier and later groups in having shorter femurs for age, or apparent growth retardation. Individuals in all samples who are short for age have higher frequencies of cribra orbitalia and circular caries than do those with long femurs for dental age, a result that supports the inference that nutritional deficiencies are responsible for the apparent growth retardation. However, Middle Woodland children who were afforded elaborate burial treatment do not differ in femur length for age from children of apparently lower status, despite other evidence for the nutritional significance of Middle Woodland status distinctions (Cook 1981, 1983), suggesting that the disadvantage experienced by late Late Woodland children under 6 years of age may have been relatively great when compared with distinctions due to social stratification. Archaic samples are too small to be evaluated.

Stature

Body size in adults is an obvious source of information on change in nutritional status in a region in which there is little evidence for geographical or chronological genetic differentiation (Buikstra 1976, 1977; Conner 1983; Droessler 1981). However, equally obvious are the many influences apart from nutrition that may contribute to differences in adult stature in closely related populations. Heterosis, work load in childhood, and disease load are perhaps the most important such factors that emerge from studies of living populations, and they are largely inaccessible to us in studies of the dead.

Stature data for adults in 10 skeletal series are shown in Figure 10.2. Samples are grouped by time period. There are no obvious time trends in the data for males, although our Late Archaic males and most of the later series are taller than earlier Archaic series from the Midwest whose subsistence was focused more fully on hunting and gathering (Newman 1962; Neumann 1952; Stewart 1973:174).[2] The two shortest male series--from the Late Woodland

[2] *There are risks in comparing stature estimates from studies that differ in technique or that do not state the methods used. Newman (1962) reports Indian Knoll stature as 165.2 cm in males, and Stewart (1973) considers this, rather than earlier, smaller estimates, essentially correct for this wide-ranging Middle Archaic series. Newman, like Neumann in his typological studies (Neumann 1952, 1960) reports a trend toward increasing stature when Indian Knoll and other Middle Archaic series are compared with later materials. Our Late Archaic males and all later series except the problematic Ledders and Joe Gay series are at least 2 cm taller on average than are any of the eastern North American Middle Archaic series that appear in the literature.*

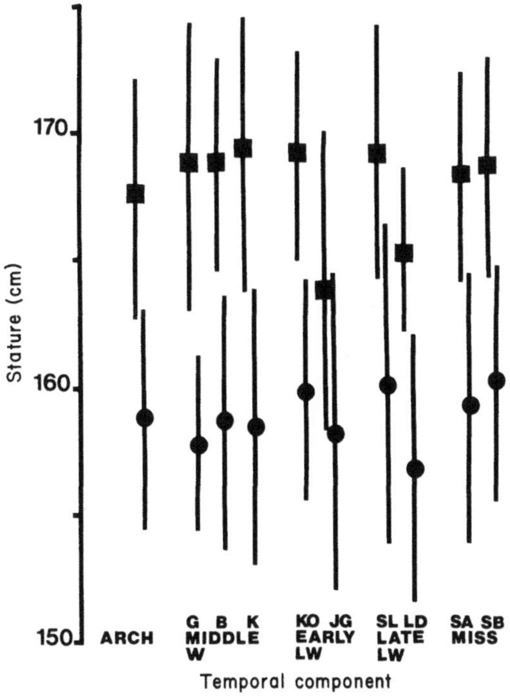

FIGURE 10.2. Adult stature in 10 temporal components arranged in chronological order. Male mean (■), female mean (●) and standard deviations are plotted using the Genovés standards. Sites and sample sizes are as follows: Klunk Archaic (ARCH 8M, 9F), Gibson (G 24M, 26F), Bedford (B 14M, 15F), Klunk Middle Woodland (K 74M, 78F), Koster (KO 47M, 41F), Joe Gay (JG 14M, 11F), Schild Late Woodland (SL 32M, 35F), Ledders (LD 19M, 19F), Schild Knoll A (SA 31M, 38F), and Schild Knoll B (SB 44M, 36F). Data for Gibson and Bedford are from Buikstra (1972), for the Mississippian components at Schild from Protos (1982), and for Klunk from Young (1982). I thank C. J. DeRousseau for her unpublished data on Ledders.

Ledders and Joe Gay sites--are significantly shorter than all the remaining series except the Archaic. For females there is a weak time trend toward taller stature in later samples, but the only significant differences are between the two shortest and the three tallest samples. Intersite correlations between male and female samples are high. While our search for time trends related to subsistence change is disappointing, there is some evidence for geographical heterogeneity. Samples from the eastern bluffs of the Illinois River--Koster and the various components at Schild--are relatively tall, whereas Mississippi Valley series--Ledders and Joe Gay--are relatively short. Further inquiry into adult stature differences is clearly needed, but it is useful to note that adult stature differences *do not* explain the subsistence-related trends in juvenile height for age seen in the previous section.[3]

A perspective on the meaning of adult stature differences is provided by the differential access to grave goods and elaborate mortuary treatment that characterizes the Middle Woodland period in our region. Males who were afforded access to limited portions of the mortuary program were taller than those of apparently lower status, both in the Gibson series (Buikstra 1976) and in the Klunk series; high-status and low-status females, on the other hand, did not differ in stature (Young 1983). Facile interpretations of this result--for example, patrilineal ruling groups--are not warranted, because studies of other sorts of biological indicators fail to confirm this apparent sex difference. Both male and female status groups differ in trace element content (Szpunar 1977) and in the frequency of stress-related dental defects (Cook 1981). Low-status females are more platypellic than high-status females, whereas male pelvic form does not differ with status (Brinker, n.d.). Angel (1975, 1978, 1982) has shown that increased flattening of the pelvic inlet is consonant with other indicators of nutritional stress. These findings, taken together, suggest that status groups in Middle Woodland society differed in health, both among males and among females. The 3.3-cm difference in stature in high-status and low-status males in the collections studied by Young and Buikstra reflects only a portion of this difference (Young 1983). The absence of stature differences in females who differ in other biological attributes may reflect sex differences in the timing of growth events, in susceptibility to stress, or in underlying environmental factors not recoverable from the archaeological record. That status differences in stature within a sample are of the same order as the between-sample differences in Figure 10.2 suggests that adult stature may provide an ambiguous picture of changing biological success over time.

[3]Droessler (1981) has presented an interesting perspective on this issue. She suggests that smaller crania in late Late Woodland samples as compared with both early Late Woodland and Mississippian materials reflect nutritional stress. Since the ages of attainment of adult stature and adult cranial dimensions are similar, this seems unlikely in the face of the lack of patterned stature differences. However, the issue she raises suggests that further attention to environmental effects on total morphological pattern may be rewarding. Since adult brain size is attained by 10 years of age, final cranial dimensions may be particularly responsive to nutritional deficits in childhood (Baer and Harris 1969).

Sexual Dimorphism

While sexual dimorphism has been proposed in some modern contexts as a relatively simple index of nutritional status, it would appear to present equally complicated problems in interpretation. There is clearly a genetic component to population differences in sexual dimorphism (Eveleth 1975), and age, activity, and survivorship differences can be demonstrated as well (Hamilton 1982). Hamilton has presented a very careful analysis of dimorphism in most of the series included in the study of stature just presented here. These are the Middle Woodland Gibson-Klunk series, considered a single population in her analysis; the Koster early Late Woodland series; the Schild late Late Woodland series; and the combined Schild Mississippian series. Her materials are selected for completeness of size-independent pelvic sex indicators and for sample size. She finds that her early Late Woodland sample shows decreased dimorphism as a result of increased female size with respect to stable male size when compared with Middle Woodland materials. Females also become more robust, the most salient difference being in the development of the deltoid tuberosity. In late Late Woodland times dimorphism increases because relative female size decreases. In Mississippian times dimorphism is again reduced because female size increases, both with respect to the immediately antecedent Late Woodland population and with respect to the remaining earlier series in her study. Dimorphism in deltoid tuberosity development is also reduced, again because females are more robust, both when compared with late Late Woodland and with Middle Woodland, and female deltoid development increases smoothly throughout.

Hamilton finds these results somewhat paradoxical in their relationship to the nutritional stress model, because under this model one would expect reduced dimorphism in conjunction with decrease in both male and female size and robusticity. She suggests a more intricate scenario, in which early Late Woodland and Mississippian are characterized by more favorable resource distribution within communities, resulting in equitable distribution of nutrients and larger female stature. This argument is buttressed in her view by significant dimorphism in trace element composition in the Ledders series, where males appear to enjoy a higher meat intake than females (Lambert et al. 1979, 1982). However, Ledders is not one of the sites included in Hamilton's study, and the less carefully selected data presented in Figure 10.2 suggest that Ledders may be characterized by reduced sexual dimorphism. Heterogeneity within time periods and between geographical areas may again be a problem, and since only Hamilton's four series have been subjected to rigorous analysis of dimorphism, and only two series have produced trace element data, resolution of this problem must await further research.

Hamilton's finding of progressive increase in development of the deltoid tuberosity in females from Middle Woodland through

Mississippian times is interesting in the light of the concurrent intensification of food production that the botanical record documents. Bridges (1982, 1983) has reported similar increases in robusticity in females in a study comparing Alabama Archaic and Mississippian materials. She suggests that activities related to cultivation may account for this increase because females had primary responsibility for most horticultural tasks in eastern North American Indian societies. A similar model may account for a portion of the differences that Hamilton documents.

Cortical Bone Maintenance

Bone maintenance can be related more directly to aspects of nutritional status than can the gross morphological features reviewed above. Perzigian (1971) evaluated cortical and trabecular density in the distal radius using photon absorptiometry, comparing the Middle Archaic Indian Knoll series with the Klunk Middle Woodland series. He demonstrated greater osteoporotic bone loss in the Illinois Middle Woodland series than in the Kentucky hunter-gatherer material with more pronounced sex differences in Indian Knoll than in the Klunk series. O'Connor (1977) has reevaluated Perzigian's data, showing that his statistical procedure evaluates the rate of loss rather than the absolute amount of loss. Klunk Middle Woodland males and females lose bone at a faster rate with increasing age than do their Kentucky Archaic counterparts, but they do not become as osteoporotic because their initial bone density at age 15 is higher. Stout (1978) has pointed out that diagenesis may be a factor in producing the relatively flat bone density data Perzigian obtained from Indian Knoll, suggesting histological study as a prerequisite for direct bone density measurement. No comprehensive study of bone density for the collections discussed in this paper is as yet available, but the increased rate of bone loss that Perzigian observes when comparing his Middle Woodland data with modern clinical standards suggests that this may be a fruitful avenue of research.

Histological analysis of bone maintenance is similarly promising, but incomplete. Stout (1978) compared rib cortex remodeling rates in the Gibson Middle Woodland and Ledders terminal Late Woodland series. He attributes the higher remodeling rates in the latter series to secondary hyperparathyroidism resulting from low tryptophan levels provided by a high maize diet. However, other plausible explanatory models might include relative protein-calorie malnutrition, low dietary calcium, low phosphorus-calcium (P-Ca) ratio, high iron intake, and high disease load, among others (Bernstein et al. 1966; Garn et al. 1969; Lynch et al. 1967; Mazess and Jones 1974; Mazess and Mather 1975; Pfeiffer and King 1983). Studies that may resolve some of these issues in west central Illinois materials are underway. Bradtmiller (n.d.) has demonstrated that sample sites within the individual show important differences in remodeling rates, drawing his sample from a single terminal Late Woodland and Mississippian site. Hansen has begun a study of femur midshaft histology that will compare samples from the various Woodland and Mississippian components discussed here.

The only comprehensive data on bone maintenance available for west central Illinois is the least technically sophisticated. In the study of juvenile height for age presented earlier I evaluated femoral Nordin's index[4] in the Gibson Middle Woodland and Ledders terminal Late Woodland samples. Children 2-3 years of age--in Ledders weaned to a diet high in maize--showed significantly lower bone maintenance than did the children of earlier intensive collectors in the Gibson sample (Cook 1979). I interpreted this result to indicate relative protein-calorie malnutrition in the Late Woodland sample. However, the same criticisms apply to this extrapolation from two samples as to Stout's interpretation of his rib remodeling data above. More recently, I have seen similar low cortical bone diameter in Mississippian samples that show high juvenile height for age (Cook n.d.a,d). This would support maize-related hyperparathyroidism, calcium levels and the like as more parsimonious explanations.

Radiographic data on cortical bone diameters are available for adult series representative of the full range of time components in west central Illinois (Figure 10.3). Again Nordin's index for the femur is presented. This choice of technique has an advantage in applications of this sort in that measurements of cortical thickness taken on antero-posterior radiographs of the femur are relatively insensitive to age-related involution in the femoral cortex, which is first seen in the anterior cortex and the pilaster. Nevertheless, Illinois Valley samples from all time periods I have examined show early and profound bone loss as evidenced by emphasis on vertical trabeculation and a so-called ground-glass appearance in long bone areas that normally show trabeculation. Some individuals in all age groups show these changes, and at their most extreme they are associated with very low values of Nordin's index. Because these markers of cortical bone loss appear as early as the third decade of life in west central Illinois samples, I have chosen to limit comparisons to samples 20-34 years of age in an effort to minimize the effects of age-progressive bone loss. In Figure 10.3 the observed ranges of Nordin's index are very wide, and distributions are skewed toward higher values. However, means are essentially similar from Late Archaic through Mississippian times, and no differences are statistically significant. We can see no chronological trend in adult cortical bone maintenance associated with either the gradual

[4]Nordin's index is cortical diameter/total diameter read on a radiographic image in standard position. All data reported here are for midshaft of femur, A-P view.

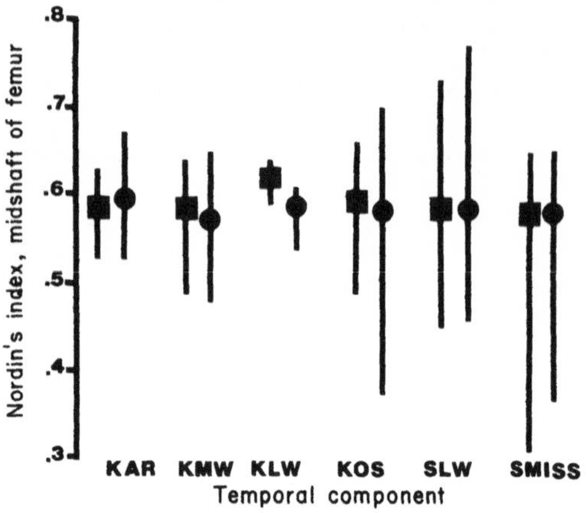

FIGURE 10.3. Means and ranges of Nordin's index for the midshaft of femur in six temporally sequential components. Note that means are highly skewed in the Mississippian sample (SMISS). Male (■) and female (●) values are virtually identical in these 20- to 34-year-old samples. Sample sizes are as follows: Klunk Archaic (KAR 4M, 6F), Klunk Middle Woodland (KMW 22M, 35F), Klunk early Late Woodland (KLW 3M, 7F), Koster early Late Woodland (KOS 21M, 17F), Schild late Late Woodland (SLW 13M, 14F), and Schild Mississippian (SMISS 24M, 24F).

intensification of food production that occurred during this sequence or the emphasis on maize in late Late Woodland times.

It is tempting to speculate that the relatively early onset of cortical involution and the lack of change through time reflect the stable dietary features of Caldwell's "primary forest efficiency" in the Midwest. For example, Mazess has associated high P-Ca ratios in living Eskimos. A similar circumstance may have applied in our populations, who made heavy use of both nuts and fish so small that substantial quantities of bone must have been ingested. P-Ca ratios provided by the various starchy and oily seed plants used throughout our sequence deserve attention as well, and it is interesting that such modern analogues as sunflower seed and buckwheat, as well as maize, have high P-Ca ratios (Ensminger 1970). Ericksen (1982) has pointed out that most prehistoric populations for which there are data appear to show accelerated bone loss with respect to clinical norms. She suggests that inadequacies in the aging of skeletal samples are responsible for this consistent difference, but dietary factors deserve attention as well, particularly in contexts where bone loss is prominent in young adults.

The extremely low range for Nordin's index in our Mississippian sample is noteworthy. The lowest values are found in individuals who show evidence for skeletal tuberculosis or some very similar agent (Buikstra and Cook 1981). This profound loss of bone density in young adults supports the diagnosis of tuberculosis, but it complicates inferences about nutritional change or change in general health that employ this indicator.

Sex differences in cortical bone maintenance are absent in these young adults (Figure 10.3). This is surprising, given that one would expect greater demand on calcium reserves in pregnant and lactating women in this age range. It is possible that the differential demands imposed by reproduction may have been less heavy in lower Illinois River valley populations than in other prehistoric populations in which early and pronounced sex differences in bone maintenance have been found (Carlson et al. 1976; Dewey et al. 1969). On the other hand, the relative insensitivity of radiographic measures of cortical involution may be a factor (van Gerven et al. 1969). We look forward to the completion of more technically sophisticated work on this topic.

Growth Arrest: Harris Lines

Harris lines in the long bones and the partially analogous microscopic and macroscopic disturbances of enamel development provide a record of stress experienced during childhood that is useful in relating subsistence and health. Most recent work on the biology of these indicators emphasizes that they reflect developmental stability rather than the quality of diet and health per se. In them we see the effects of acute episodes of stress, be they nutritional, disease related, or from some other source. This is particularly true for Harris lines, which reflect resumed growth and may be absent in poorly nourished populations because growth is not sufficient to allow lines to form (Dreizen et al. 1964; Garn 1966; Murchison et al., n.d.).

Temporal comparisons of Harris line frequencies are available for children under six and for young adults. Figure 10.4 shows means and ranges for Harris line counts in children from three series: Gibson Middle Woodland, Ledders terminal Late Woodland, and Schild Mississippian. These last two samples allow us to contrast early and late maize-using populations with the antecedent intensive harvest collectors of Middle Woodland times. In Figure 10.4, the maximum Harris line count is presented for the distal radius, proximal and distal tibia, and distal femur. Thus an individual may be represented by between one and four sites. While aggregation procedures such as this one can be criticized (see Buikstra and Cook 1980 for review), vagaries of preservation in these samples make statistical testing difficult if sites are analyzed separately because many of the sample sizes are quite small. The picture of frequency differences obtained with maximum line count data is consistent with patterns present in the four sites analyzed separately; hence I do not feel that the procedure misrepresents the underlying biology.

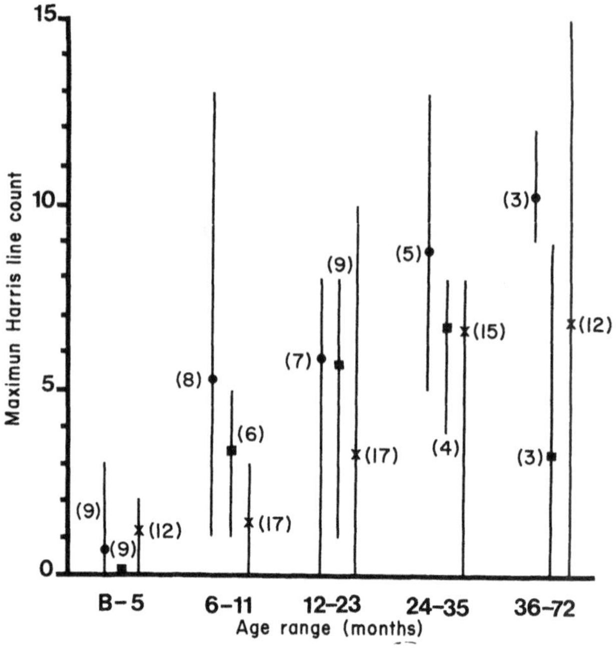

FIGURE 10.4. Means and ranges of Harris line counts for children under 6 years of age. Samples are as follows: Gibson Middle Woodland (●), Ledders terminal Late Woodland (■), and Schild Mississippian (x). Sample sizes given in parentheses.

For all three samples, Harris line count rises with age in children under six, lines being virtually absent in children aged 5 months or less. After 6 months, line counts become quite variable; ranges are large, and distribution of scores is irregular. Average line counts remain low in the Mississippian sample at all ages relative to the two earlier groups, the differences being statistically significant in children 2 years of age and above when Schild is compared with Gibson. The Ledders terminal Late Woodland sample resembles the Middle Woodland one through the second year of life. After 2 years of age Harris line counts approximate those in the Mississippian sample. Again, in this age group, differences between Ledders and the Middle Woodland Gibson sample are statistically significant.

The introduction of maize thus would seem to be reflected in lower Harris line counts in children who failed to survive childhood. In Ledders, the earlier and less maize dependent of the two, evidence for lower levels of acute stress begins at 2 years of age. I have argued that this difference in Middle Woodland and terminal Late Woodland children reflects weaning to a high-carbohydrate maize diet and resulting growth failure, using the evidence for lesser height for age in the Ledders children to buttress this interpretation (Cook 1979). The same interpretation cannot apply to the Mississippian sample, because there is no evidence for growth failure. Either Mississippian children experienced less acute stress than did Middle Woodland children, or other factors are responsible for this difference.

Some appreciation for the magnitude of the possible complicating factors can be gained from a look at possible causes of endosteal resorption which might result in loss of Harris lines through remodeling. Garn has reported that children with protein-calorie malnutrition lose endosteal bone (Garn et al. 1969), an explanation consistent with the interpretation of low Harris line frequencies in the Ledders children presented here. This factor can be present at birth if maternal protein intake is sufficiently poor (Krishnamachari and Iyengar 1975). Conversely, obese subjects have increased cortical thickness (Garn and Solomon 1981) and might be expected to retain Harris lines longer than lighter subjects might. Since body composition is not presently reconstructible from skeletal remains, the effects of this source of variation are unknown, although data on living populations lead one to expect higher obesity rates in sedentary populations dependent on carbohydrate-rich food sources. Bone remodeling differences due to such factors as P/Ca ratio, secondary hypoparathyroidism, activity levels, and the like may also be implicated. These considerations lead us to accept our evidence for lesser levels of acute stress in childhood among maize users with considerable caution.

Harris line frequencies in adults are available for a wider range of samples. Figure 10.5 presents Harris line counts for the distal femur in adults 20-34 years of age in six samples ranging from Late Archaic through Mississippian times. This truncated age range is chosen because previous study has shown decreased line frequencies in adults over age 35 in samples from the region (Cook 1976), and the stability of Nordin's index in these samples (Figure 10.3) supports the choice. Distributions of line counts are highly skewed and bimodal, there being many individuals with no lines present. For this reason the data are presented in three forms: percentage of individuals without lines, average line count including these zero values, and average line count in individuals with Harris lines present. Percentage without lines varies widely, and all samples but one show substantial sex differences. While data on modern populations indicate that females may form lines more readily than males (Marshall 1968), as is the case in four of the five dimorphic samples here, the size of these differences is unexpected, and it is difficult to suggest a scenario that would account for the observed pattern. One might argue that acute stress experience increased for males through time, ameliorating in the Mississippian period, whereas acute stress decreased for females from Archaic through Woodland times,

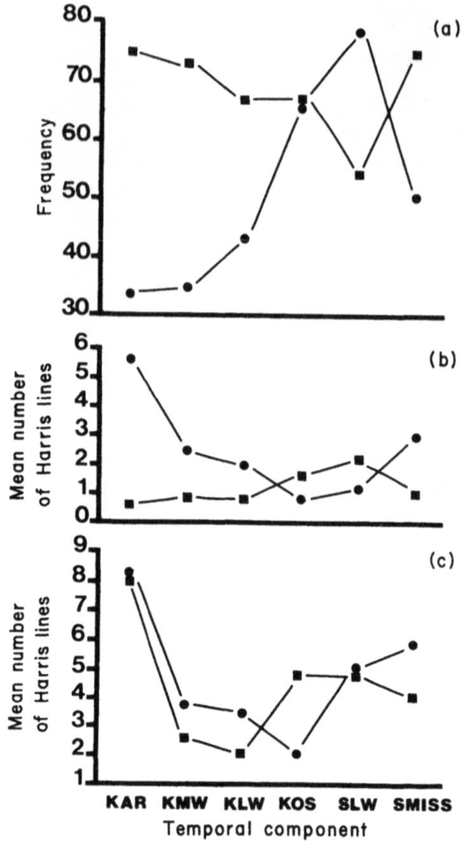

FIGURE 10.5. Harris line counts in young adult males (■) and females (●). Values presented are frequency of individuals with no lines visible at the distal femur (A), mean line count including these zero values (B), and mean line count in those with Harris lines present (C). Sample data correspond to those for Figure 10.3.

only to worsen in the Mississippian period. However, the other available evidence fails to support this improbable scenario.

Average line counts including zero values are more or less similar through time, and it is difficult to justify the use of means in these data on statistical grounds. When only those individuals with lines are considered, temporally distinct patterns emerge. Line counts are high in the few Late Archaic specimens included in this study; thereafter, frequencies are markedly lower. Within the Woodland sequence there is a tendency toward increasing line counts through time, the late Late Woodland and Mississippian maize-using samples showing highest values.

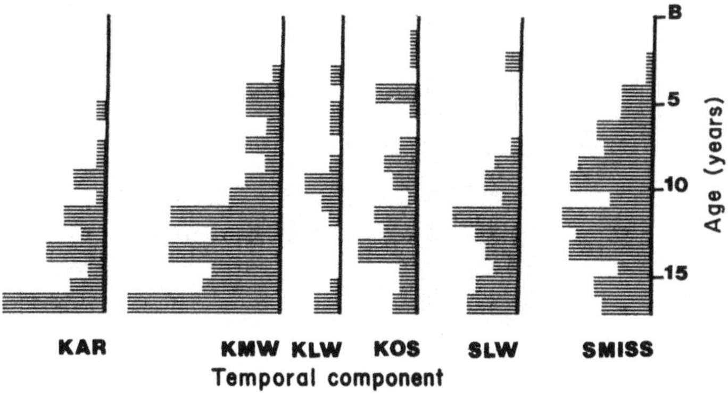

FIGURE 10.6. Age of formation of Harris lines at the distal femur in young adults, sexes combined. Number of lines observed for each annual growth increment is plotted from birth through age 17. Sample data are given in legend to Figure 10.3.

However, only the difference between the Koster female mean and the Schild female mean is statistically significant. We may cautiously argue that food production brings an initial decrease in acute stress experience followed by a modest increase in stress associated with maize-centered intensification.

Some additional perspective on this indicator can be gained for the Archaic period from a study of Harris lines comparing the Klunk Late Archaic sample used here with two small Middle Archaic components (Buikstra 1981). No significant temporal trends were found, supporting the archaeological picture of relative stability of Archaic adaptations.

Harris lines also provide useful information on the timing of stress episodes during development. Figure 10.6 shows the distribution of age of formation determined using the method of Hunt and Hatch (1981). The Klunk Archaic and Klunk Middle Woodland samples are alike in showing a trend toward increased rates of line formation--or lesser opportunity for resorption--in later adolescence. The later samples show a more even distribution of age of formation. No sample shows many lines assignable to the first 6 years of life. The high frequency of Harris lines in children 2-6 years of age suggests that resorption of early lines may be a substantial problem in these data, as does the frequency with which evidence for trabecular involution can be seen.

Age of formation data can also be analyzed for evidence of annual or seasonal stress. All of the Archaic individuals who had Harris lines showed evidence for annual periodicity. Buikstra (1981) in a study of a wider age sample from this collection found periodicity in the Klunk Archaic remains to be high, but significantly less than in two small Middle Archaic samples. However, this comparison does not adjust for zero line counts. In contrast, only 1 of the 180 Woodland and Mississippian femora included in this study showed annual periodicity in Harris lines. Likewise, there is little evidence for seasonal stress in the juvenile Harris line data (Cook 1976). We infer that one benefit of the transition to food production in the lower Illinois Valley was buffering against seasonal periods of scarcity.

Growth Arrest: Dental Markers

Dental indicators of stress experience offer advantages in that they are not subject to remodeling and they are less dependent on rate of growth. As with the Harris line studies, data are available for both juvenile and adult samples for various developmental ranges.

Circular caries is a developmental lesion of the deciduous teeth in which enamel formed in the antenatal or perinatal period shows chronologic hypoplasia. The resultant transverse bands are prone to caries attack after the teeth erupt. In modern disadvantaged populations, children with this marker of early stress are more likely to develop protein-calorie malnutrition during the weaning period than are their peers without this history of stress. In a comparison of Middle and Late Woodland materials, Buikstra and I have argued that differences in the distribution of age at death in children with and without these hypoplastic lesions provide evidence for nutritional stress during the weaning period (Cook and Buikstra 1979). In Figure 10.7 our 1979 data are analyzed separating the two Late Woodland components it included and adding a Mississippian sample. The percentage of children with antenatal or perinatal hypoplasia is similar in all four samples. A parallel study of widely separated skeletal collections from other parts of North America shows that the frequency of this class of hypoplasia varies geographically rather than with subsistence (Cook n.d.c). The frequency of caries is, not surprisingly, related to diet; it increases as a function of maize use, as measured in ^{13}C content of collagen (van der Merwe and Vogel 1978).[5] Distributions of age at

[5]*Some caution is needed in interpreting ^{13}C studies. A particular level of ^{13}C in bone indicates the amount of ^{13}C in the food chain, or the percentage of dietary carbon, not the proportion of the diet contributed by maize or other tropical cultigens. Secondary and much higher quality ^{13}C consumption could result if deer, raccoon, and turkeys were taken when they were attracted to corn fields. Meat from such animals would contribute to human ^{13}C consumption. Meat from domestic dogs fed on maize or wastes would also make a contribution, as ^{13}C levels in Amerindian dogs show (Burleigh and Brothwell 1978). Thus it is not likely to be the case that maize constituted 24% of the diet in late Late Woodland times or 52% of the diet for Mississippians in our region (van der Merwe and Vogel 1978).*

A. Circular Caries Frequency

Sites	Component	N	Percentage Hypoplastic	Percentage Carious	Percentage C_4 Plants[a]
Gibson[b]	MW	98	60	16	0
Klunk					
Joe Gay[b]	LW[c]	32	50	22	0
Ledders[b]	LLW	38	53	24	24
Schild	MISS	56	59	42	52

[a]van der Merwe and Vogel, 1978
[b]Cook and Buikstra, 1979
[c]This sample dates to approximately the point of transition to maize use (Tainter 1975). The C_4 value for LLW may be appropriate.

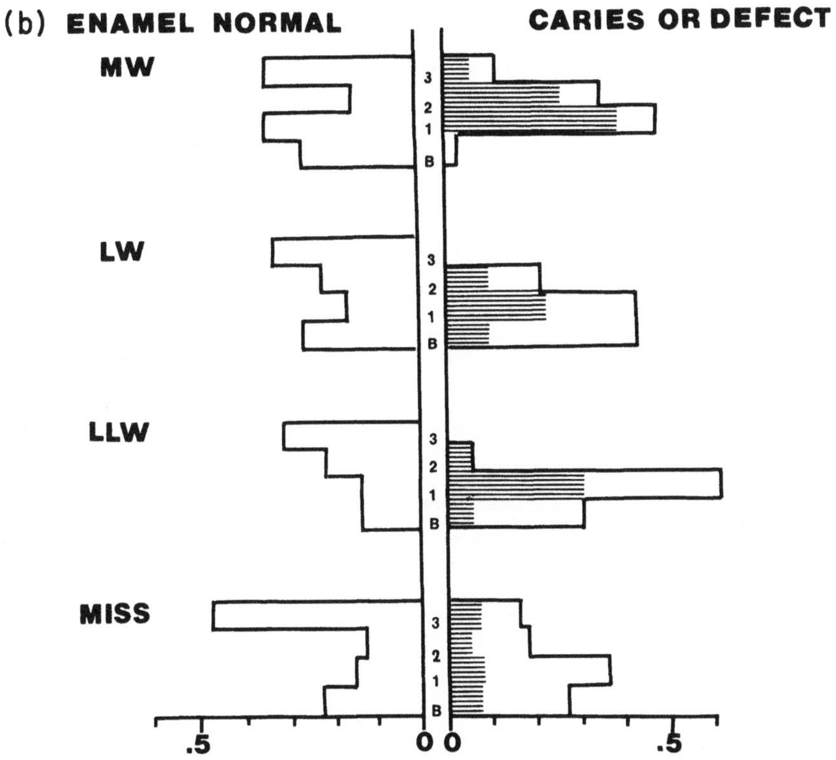

FIGURE 10.7. B. Distribution of normal deciduous enamel and defective deciduous enamel by age at death. Defective enamel that exhibits circular caries is indicated by shaded bars. Age at death in years is indicated between the two sets of histograms.

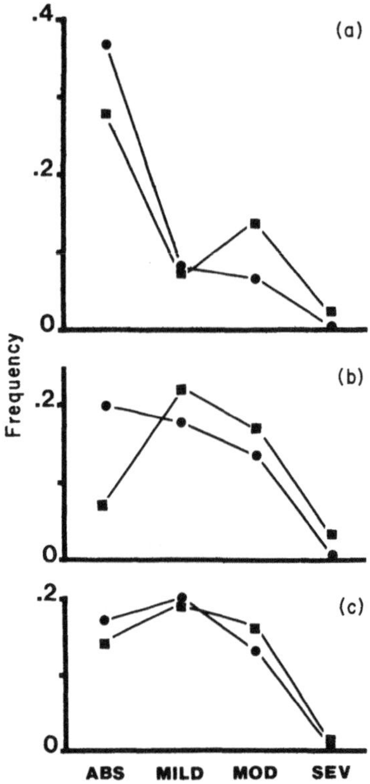

FIGURE 10.8. Linear enamel hypoplasia in the permanent canine of young adults from the Klunk Middle Woodland (●) and Schild Mississippian (■) samples (Clifton 1982). Maximum severity score for the occlusal (a), middle (b), and cervical (c) thirds of the crown are analyzed separately. Scores are absent, mild, moderate, and severe.

death are unlike in all four samples, but the differences are more marked in our two Late Woodland samples, in which no hypoplasia cases appear to survive to 3 years of age. Again we have evidence for greater childhood stress during the Late Woodland period when it is compared with earlier and later groups. The available samples do not permit an extension of this study to the Archaic.

Studies of linear enamel hypoplasia (LEH) in the permanent dentition are still preliminary. Clifton has compared LEH frequencies in the canines of adults 20-34 years of age from the Klunk Middle Woodland and Schild Mississippian samples (1983). She finds a modest but significant increase in lesion frequency in the later sample (Figure 10.8). Knick (1981) has shown that a major portion of this increase can be attributed to the presence of tuberculosis or a similar condition in the Schild population. Individuals with skeletal lesions account for the majority of the

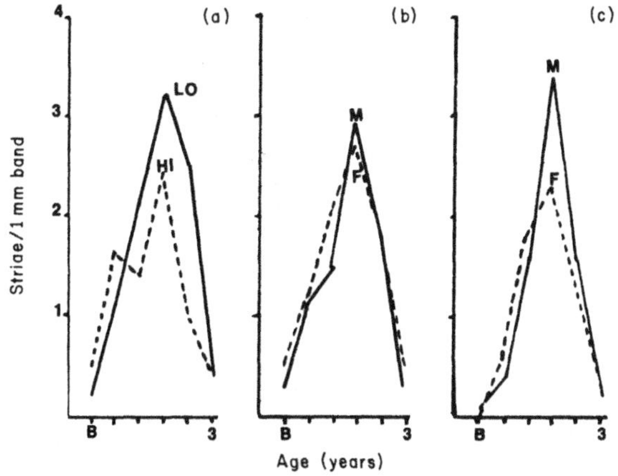

FIGURE 10.9. Frequency of pronounced striae of Retzius. Vertical axis is striae/1 mm band defined on the dentinoenamel junction. Horizontal axis is 1 mm bands arranged from cusp (birth) to cementoenamel junction (3 years of age at formation). Data are for the first permanent molar. From the left, graphs compare high and low status categories in the Klunk Middle Woodland sample (a), sexes in the Klunk Middle Woodland sample (b), and sexes in the Schild Mississippian sample (c).

moderate and severe LEH lesions of the incisors and canines. From this he infers childhood onset of the disease, again supporting the diagnosis of tuberculosis. Enamel forming after 7 years of age was similar in individuals with and without tuberculosis-like lesions. Comparable study of Archaic and Late Woodland materials remains to be done.

Histological defects in the enamel have been studied in Middle Woodland and Mississippian materials as well. Rose (1977) compared a canine sample from the Middle Woodland Gibson site with Late Woodland and Mississippian materials from the central Illinois Valley. He found very low frequencies of striae of Retzius and of pathological bands in the Gibson sample, whereas the Mississippian samples showed many defects. I have evaluated both striae of Retzius and pathological bands in first permanent molars from the Klunk Middle Woodland and Schild Mississippian collections. I find no evidence for temporal differences in combined-sex samples of young adults (Figure 10.9). However, both samples are heterogeneous in interesting ways. High- and low-status components in the Klunk mortuary program differ significantly in the frequency of striae of Retzius (Cook 1981), whereas there is no apparent sexual dimorphism. In contrast, the Schild sample shows little differentiation by burial type, but significant sexual dimorphism of the same order as the status differences in the earlier sample. A possible complicating factor is the issue of sampling bias at the Schild cemetery. Schild is demographically incomplete, a large proportion of adult males being absent from the recovered collection. The unusual dimorphism in stature and in stress indicators we have seen in this sample may reflect a systematic bias against the inclusion of large, favored males (Cook n.d.b). The ultimate significance of this problem remains to be assessed. If the Schild sample is representative of Mississippian population biology, it provides us with little evidence for stress associated with maize use in the lower Illinois Valley. The relatively high levels of enamel defects that Rose notes in his central Illinois Valley samples may reflect environmental, temporal, or cultural differences outside the scope of a regional study.

A final source of information on stress that can be assessed from studies of teeth is fluctuating asymmetry. O'Connell has produced an exhaustive study of asymmetry in both cranial discrete traits and odontometrics for 16 temporally distinct samples from lower Illinois Valley sites (1983). She views asymmetry as an indicator of developmental stability rather than of environmental quality. She finds greatest asymmetry in late Middle Woodland and late Late Woodland samples. Her early Middle Woodland, early Late Woodland, and especially Mississippian samples are developmentally stable in comparison. Her interpretation of these results focuses on change per se as the stressor to which fluctuating asymmetry corresponds.

PATHOLOGY

Several aspects of pathological change in the skeleton offer useful information about the health consequences of subsistence change. Sampling bias is a preliminary issue that can be shown to be important in our region in at least two periods. Buikstra has shown that the high frequencies of severe pathological conditions observed in remains from Middle Archaic habitation sites is the result of bias introduced by aboriginal mortuary practices. Middle Archaic peoples in the region produced two complementary types of mortuary site: mounded cemeteries containing adults in the prime of life and habitation site interments for the young, the old, and the disabled. Neither component is demographically complete, and inferences about the extreme rigors of Archaic life based on disease frequencies in the latter type (Neumann 1967) are fallacious (Buikstra 1981). Access to portions of the Middle Woodland mortuary system are biased by age and sex (Buikstra 1976) as well as by prior history of stress episodes (Cook 1981). But there is no evidence for biases related to other pathological conditions (Cook 1976), and we have no reason to believe that the larger Woodland cemeteries of the region misrepresent disease frequencies. The largest Mississippian sample we have available shows significant demographic bias, and several anomalies in the age and sex distribution of stress indicators that suggest that it

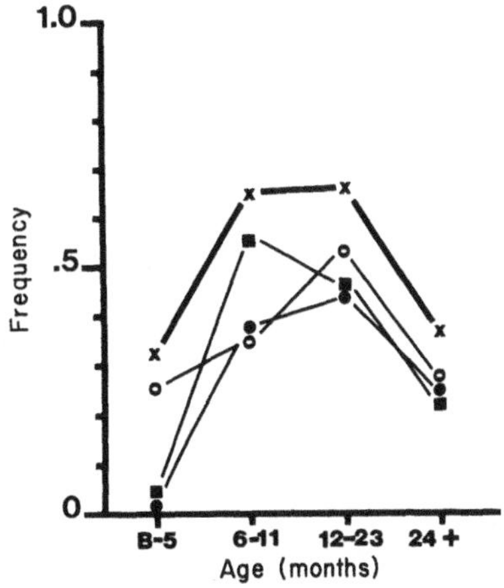

FIGURE 10.10. Frequencies of cribra orbitalia in children under 6 years of age in aggregate samples from the Middle Woodland (●), early Late Woodland (■), late Late Woodland (o), and Mississippian (x). Samples and sample sizes correspond to those in Figure 10.1.

may misrepresent the frequency of pathological conditions as well (Cook n.d.b). However, analysis of the distribution of disabling injuries and severe chronic conditions across burial types within the site fails to produce any evidence of cultural distinctions based on pathology (Goldstein 1980).

Cribra Orbitalia

As nonspecific indicators of anemia, cribra orbitalia, as well as the related vault and endosteal changes, provide a useful marker in assessing nutrition and health in the past when they are present in frequencies higher than what one might expect from rare causes--for example, leukemias (see Cook 1976, 1979 for reviews). Cribra orbitalia is common only among juveniles in our region. Frequency data for juveniles are available for components from the Middle Woodland through the Mississippian. Samples from Archaic sites are too small to permit age class analysis, but no lesions were seen in the 12 juveniles from the Klunk Late Archaic component in whom the orbits or vault could be evaluated. We may safely infer that Archaic levels of anemia in childhood were lower than in any subsequent period. The three Woodland components are relatively similar (Figure 10.10), and differences among the three Woodland components are not significant. Frequencies are higher in the Mississippian sample in all age groups, and significantly so in children under 6 months of age (Cook n.d.a). It is unlikely that this change is nutritional in nature, because nutritional anemia is rare in this age group. Anemia in this age group may be related to the presence of a tuberculosis-like pathology in this sample (Buikstra and Cook 1981), or such otherwise inaccessible features of prehistoric culture as stripping of cord blood may provide a plausible scenario (Anonymous 1976). In children older than 6 months in these samples, cribra orbitalia is significantly correlated with other markers of nutritional stress including the presence of circular caries and small stature for age (Cook n.d.a). This supports an interpretation of weaning age protein-calorie malnutrition that is most pronounced in the late Late Woodland series.

Dental Pathology

It is hardly surprising that the introduction of maize is accompanied by changes in oral health. Not only is maize higher in carbohydrate content than most other foods used in the prehistoric Midwest; both archeological and ethnographic evidence suggest that its use was associated with a shift toward porridges and other boiled foods that one would expect to be more sticky and hence more cariogenic than those eaten by earlier peoples (Braun 1984; Rusch-Behrend n.d.).

In addition to the data on caries formation in hypoplastic lesions of the deciduous teeth presented in Figure 10.7, two temporal comparisons of oral health are available. Modest differences in the age distribution of caries and tooth loss are noted in a comparison of the Gibson Middle Woodland and Ledders late Late Woodland series (Cook 1979). Mean number of decayed or lost teeth is higher for the terminal Late Woodland juveniles and middle adults, reflecting pit-and-fissure caries. Among adults 50 years of age and above, this difference is reversed, reflecting severe attrition and resulting tooth loss in the Middle Woodland series.

Rusch-Behrend has compared the Klunk Middle Woodland series with the Schild Mississippian series, the latter the most extensive users of maize available for our region. Permanent dentition caries rates are similar in subadults, but after age 20 relative frequencies of caries in the Mississippian series are roughly twice those in the Middle Woodland series, particularly for the mandibular teeth. ANOVA results show site and age as significant, and sex as not significant. Antemortem loss is more common in the Mississippian sample. Periodontal disease is related to attrition and hence is correlated with age in both, but this effect is more pronounced in the Woodland sample, which shows greater attrition at all ages (Rusch-Behrend n.d.).

Chronic Inflammations of Bone

Periostitis and osteitis are very common in skeletal collections from the Midwest, and our lower Illinois Valley materials are no exception. Age distribution of lesions, distributions by body part, and lesion types in Middle Woodland and Late Woodland series point to endemic treponematosis as the modern clinical entity that most closely corresponds to the observed epidemiologic pattern. Overall prevalence is slightly more than 50%, with closer resemblances to endemic syphilis in the Middle Woodland sample and to yaws in the Late Woodland one (Cook 1976).

A similar pattern of lesion distribution and frequency is present in the Klunk Late Archaic series, but the overall prevalence is 31 cases in 123 scorable individuals, or 25%. This suggests that a treponematosis was present, but at substantially lower levels than in Woodland times.

In the Schild Mississippian series both the prevalence and the epidemiological pattern of periosteal lesions are similar to values for Middle and Late Woodland series. Extensive proliferative lesions in adults are somewhat more common than in the two earlier series. The resemblance to yaws that characterizes our late Late Woodland samples is thus somewhat more pronounced, and as with the Woodland groups, disability due to this disease must have been a significant burden for the Schild population (Cook n.d.b).

A second significant disease burden appears in Mississippian times in the lower Illinois Valley region. Destructive bone lesions, appearing most commonly in adolescents and young adults, conform in most details to bone tuberculosis, although blastomycosis may be an appropriate diagnosis as well. If the disease is, as we suspect, tuberculosis, the frequency of bone lesions is such that pulmonary disease of some degree must have been present in most of the population. Its appearance coincides with a major change of epidemiologic importance: the appearance of a large population aggregate at Cahokia, a Mississippian center to which the Mississippian settlements of the lower Illinois Valley were satellites. At its height Cahokia may have included 25,000-43,000 people (Gregg 1975). Tuberculosis is a density-dependent disease and may have become established in human populations as the result of the appearance of such aggregates (Buikstra and Cook 1981).[6]

[6] *Milner has shown that much of the difference in bone lesion frequency, ignoring diagnosis, that is reported for Mississippian sites in the American Bottoms, lower Illinois Valley, and central Illinois Valley can be explained by site aggregation and size (1982; 1983). The relative contribution of the various diseases that can be identified in skeletal remains and the degree to which temporal change is a factor in these results remain to be explored.*

Arthritis

Temporal change in arthritis patterning has been evaluated in a recent study by Pickering (1984). For Woodland and Mississippian samples several features of arthritis patterning are constant. Relative joint size is correlated with body size but uncorrelated with joint disease. Age at onset is earlier in females than in males, but females at a given age do not show more severe arthritis than do males. There are no symmetry differences in males and females.

Temporal change in arthritis patterning occurs in association with the beginnings of maize cultivation in both males and females. Late Late Woodland and Mississippian females present more arthritis of the left arm and spine than do Middle Woodland and early Late Woodland females. In males arthritis in the arms becomes more symmetrical in late Late Woodland and Mississippian samples, a change Pickering associates with the change from use of the atlatl to use of the bow. Males show no severity changes, while females show no pattern changes.

Warfare

Perino has suggested that the incidence of projectile points and point fragments imbedded in bone or within body cavities in Late Woodland mortuary sites is evidence for warfare (Perino 1973a,b,c). A survey of such injuries in the Joe Gay and Homer Adams mound groups, both multicomponent sites, found evidence for wounds in 2% of the combined Middle Woodland components and 4% of the combined Late Woodland components (Cook 1976), suggesting that warfare may have been a feature of both societies. Styles presents evidence for limitation of village catchments in Late Woodland times (1981) that may reflect conflict as well. Both Late Woodland and Mississippian collections contain some individuals with skull fractures compatible with celt wounds (Perino 1971). Thus we have evidence for conflict throughout the sequence, with perhaps some increase in frequency in Late Woodland times.

PALEODEMOGRAPHY

I share with a number of others who have contributed to this topic a considerable skepticism about the usefulness of paleodemography (Bocquet-Appel and Masset 1982; Howell 1982; Petersen 1975). Nevertheless, demographic studies offer some useful perspectives on health changes in the region. Buikstra (1981) applies a simulation technique to Middle Archaic data in order to correct the mortuary practice biases discussed previously. She finds no evidence for changes in population structure during the Archaic period, despite hypotheses others have derived from material culture for increasing adaptive efficiency from Middle to Late Archaic times. Comparisons of Late Archaic materials with Middle Woodland remains suggest that life span increased somewhat in Middle Woodland times (Blakely 1971; Masset 1976). Several analytical procedures suggest that late Late Woodland samples show an increase in age-specific mortality compared with both earlier and later materials (Cook 1976; Cottom n.d.).

DISCUSSION

What are the effects of the intensification of food production on health? The picture is a complicated one, and the more kinds of data we marshall the more complicated the picture becomes. Woodland food production seems to have allowed an increase in longevity and some buffering against seasonal stress. The introduction of maize in late Late Woodland times is attended by a variety of evidence for worsening health in childhood, and this transitional population appears to be at a relative disadvantage when compared with both earlier and later populations. I have argued that these findings support a Boserupian model of population pressure on scarce resources as the force behind the transition from seed-horticulture and collecting economies to systems including maize cultivation (Cook 1979; n.d.a). It is conceivable that other causes, for example decreased birth spacing, might produce the apparent childhood health problems, but data on settlement systems and faunal resource exploitation offer independent support for the Boserupian model. Late Late Woodland people made increasing use of maize after A.D. 800 in the lower Illinois Valley, and many of the indicators discussed above link our maize-using populations. Because Mississippian peoples made more extensive use of maize than did their antecedents, and because we have very little evidence for nutritional disease or stress among Mississippian peoples, this low-protein staple food does not in itself account for the apparent ill health of late Late Woodland peoples. The incorporation of maize into the continuing collecting and seed-horticulture economy seems ultimately to have been of biological benefit. The only negative aspect of this change appears to be a secondary consequence of the increases in population size and aggregation that food production permitted: Mississippians suffered from density-dependent infectious disease that was previously absent.

No single source of information examined here is definitive in what it tells us about this temporal sequence, and the various kinds of data give different, complementary information about the past. In several instances a given source of data is misleading if analyzed without regard to other variables. A unilinear model of the relationship between subsistence and health is clearly inappropriate. The complicated array of variables--both cultural and ecological--that are linked to subsistence must be understood before we have an adequate context in which to evaluate health changes.

ACKNOWLEDGMENTS

Collection of new data presented in this paper was supported by the National Science Foundation, BNS 77-25310. I wish to thank the many colleagues who shared manuscript materials with me.

REFERENCES

Angel, J. L.
1975 Paleoecology, paleodemography, and health. In *Population ecology and social evolution*, edited by S. Polgar, pp. 167-190. The Hague.
1978 Pelvic inlet form: A neglected index of nutritional status. *American Journal of Physical Anthropology 48*:378.
1982 A new measure of growth efficiency: Skull base height. *American Journal of Physical Anthropology 58*:297-305.

Anonymous
1976 Cultural practices and anemia in Nigeria. *Nutrition Review 34*(9):269-270.

Asch, D. L., and N. B. Asch
1977 Chenopod as cultigen: A re-evaluation of some prehistoric collections from Eastern North America. *Midcontinental Journal of Archaeology 2*:3-45.

Asch, D. L., K. B. Farnsworth, and N. B. Asch
1979 Woodland subsistence and settlement in west central Illinois. In *Hopewell archaeology: The Chillicothe Conference*, edited by D. S. Brose and N. Greber, pp. 80-85. Kent State University Press, Kent, Ohio.

Asch, N. B., R. I. Ford, and D. L. Asch
1972 Paleoethnobotany of the Koster site: The Archaic horizon. *Illinois State Museum Report of Investigations* No. 24.

Baer, M., and J. E. Harris
1969 A commentary on the growth of the human brain and skull. *American Journal of Physical Anthropology 30*:39-44.

Bernstein, D. S., N. Sadowski, D. M. Hegsted, C. D. Guri, and F. J. Starf
1966 Prevalence of osteoporosis in high- and low-fluoride areas in North Dakota. *Journal of the American Medical Association 198*:499-504.

Blakely, R. L.
1971 Mortality curves of prehistoric Indians. *American Journal of Physical Anthropology 34*:43-54.

Bocquet-Appel, J.-P., and C. Masset
1982 Farewell to paleodemography. *Journal of Human Evolution 11*:321-333.

Bradtmiller, B.
n.d. Intra-individual variability in human bone remodelling. Ph.D. dissertation, Department of Anthropology, Northwestern University, Evanston, Illinois, in preparation.

Braun, D. P.
1984 Absolute seriation: A time series approach. In *The Analysis of archaeological data structures*, edited by C. Carr, in press. Academic Press, Orlando.

Bridges, P. S.
1982 Postcranial dimensions in the Archaic and Mississippian cultures of Northern Alabama: Implications for prehistoric nutrition and behavior. *American Journal of Physical Anthropology 57*:172-173.
1983 Subsistence activities and biomechanical properties of long bones in two American populations. *American Journal of Physical Anthropology 60*:177.

Brinker, R. A.
n.d. Pelvic index in Illinois Hopewell. Unpublished manuscript.

Buikstra, J. E.
1976 Hopewell in the Lower Illinois Valley: A regional approach to the study of human biological variability and prehistoric behavior. Northwestern University Archeological Program Scientific Papers No. 2.
1977 Biocultural dimensions of archeological study: A regional perspective. *Southern Anthropological Society Proceedings 11*:67-84.
1981 Mortuary practices, paleodemography and paleopathology: A case study from the Koster site (Illinois). In *The archaeology of death*, edited by R. Chapman, I. Kinnes, and K. Randsborg, pp. 123-132. Cambridge University Press, London and New York.

Buikstra, J. E., and D. C. Cook
1980 Paleopathology: An American account. *Annual Review of Anthropology 9*:433-470.
1981 Pre-Columbian tuberculosis in west-central Illinois: Prehistoric disease in biocultural perspective. In *Prehistoric tuberculosis in the americas*, edited by J. E. Buikstra, pp. 115-139. Northwestern University Archeological Program Scientific Papers, No. 5.

Burleigh, R., and D. Brothwell
1978 Studies on Amerindian dogs, 1: Carbon isotopes in relation to maize in the diet of domestic dogs from early Peru and Ecuador. *Journal of Archaeological Science 5*:355-362.

Caldwell, J. R.
1962 Eastern North America. In *Courses toward urban life*, edited by R. J. Braidwood and G. R. Willey, pp. 288-308. Aldine, Chicago.
Carlson, D. S., G. J. Armelagos, and D. P. van Gerven
1976 Patterns of age-related cortical bone loss (osteoporosis) within the femoral diaphysis. *Human Biology 48*:295-314.
Charles, D. R., and J. E. Buikstra
1983 Archaic mortuary sites in the Central Mississippi drainage: Distribution, structure, and behavioral implications. In *Archaic hunters and gatherers in the American Midwest*, edited by J. L. Phillips and J. A. Brown, pp. 117-145. Academic Press, New York.
Charles, D. R., J. E. Buikstra, and L. Konigsberg
n.d. Terminal Archaic and Early Woodland mortuary practices in the lower Illinois River Valley: The behavioral implications. Northwestern University Archeological Program, Scientific Papers, in press.
Clifton, K. M.
1983 A review of enamel hypoplasia and its presence in a prehistoric Illinois population. Ms. on file, Department of Anthropology, Indiana University.
Conner, M. D.
1983 Late Woodland biological variation and prehistoric population structure. *American Journal of Physical Anthropology 60*:184.
n.d. Doctoral dissertation, Department of Anthropology, University of Chicago. Manuscript in preparation.
Cook, D. C.
1976 Pathologic states and disease process in Illinois Woodland populations: An epidemiologic approach. Ph.D. dissertation, Department of Anthropology, University of Chicago.
1979 Subsistence base and health in prehistoric Illinois Valley: evidence from the human skeleton. *Medical Anthropology 3*: 109-124.
1981 Mortality, age structure, and status in the interpretation of stress indicators in prehistoric skeletons: A dental example from the Lower Illinois Valley. In *The archaeology of death*, edited by R. Chapman, I. Kinnes, and K. Randsborg. Cambridge University Press, London and New York.
1983 Social status and health: A comparison of Middle Woodland and Mississippian populations from westcentral Illinois. *American Journal of Physical Anthropology 60*:184.
n.d.a Human growth: a perspective on subsistence base change. Northwestern University Archeological Program Scientific Papers, in press.
n.d.b Paleoepidemiology of the Schild cemetery: Health consequences of regional integration. In *Cahokia and the Hinterlands: Mississippian cultural variation in the American Midwest*, edited by T. E. Emerson and R . B. Lewis. Unpublished manuscript.

n.d.c Epidemiology of circular caries: A perspective from prehistoric skeletons. Unpublished manuscript

n.d.d Manuscript in preparation.

Cook, D. C., and J. E. Buikstra

1979 Health and differential survival in prehistoric populations: Prenatal dental defects. *American Journal of Physical Anthropology 51*:649-664.

Cottom, C.

n.d. Paleodemographic analysis of Illinois River Valley populations. Northwestern University Archeological Program Scientific Papers, in press.

Dewey, J. R., G. J. Armelagos, and M. H. Bartley

1969 Femoral cortical involution in three Nubian archaeological populations. *Human Biology 41*:13-28.

Dreizen, S., C. N. Spirakis, and R. E. Stone

1964 The influence of age and nutritional status on "bone scar" formation in the distal end of the growing radius. *American Journal of Physical Anthropology 22*:295-306.

Droessler, J.

1981 Craniometry and biological distance: Biocultural continuity and change at the Late-Woodland-Mississippian interface. Center for American Archeology at Northwestern University, Evanston.

Ensminger, M. E.

1970 Swine science. Interstate Printers and Publishers, Danville.

Ericksen, M. F.

1982 Aging changes in thickness of the proximal femoral cortex. *American Journal of Physical Anthropology 59*:121-130.

Eveleth, P. B.

1975 Differences between ethnic groups in sex dimorphism of adult height. *Annals of Human Biology 2*:35-39.

Ford, R. I.

1977 Evolutionary ecology and the evolution of human ecosystems: A case study from the midwestern USA. In *Explanation of prehistoric change*, edited by J. Hill, pp. 153-184. University of New Mexico Press, Albuquerque.

Garn, S. M.

1966 Malnutrition and skeletal development in the pre-school child. In *Pre-school child malnutrition*. National Academy of Science-National Research Council, Washington.

Garn, S. M., M. A. Guzmán, and B. Wagner

1969 Subperiosteal gain and endosteal loss in protein calorie malnutrition. *American Journal of Physical Anthropology 30*:153-156.

Garn, S. M., and M. A. Solomon

1981 Do the obese have better bones? *Ecology of Food and Nutrition 10*:195-197.

Goldstein, L. G.
1980 Mississippian mortuary practices: A case study of two cemeteries in the Lower Illinois Valley. Northwestern University Archeological Program Scientific Papers, No. 4.

Gregg, M. L.
1975 A population estimate for Cahokia. *Illinois Archaeological Survey Bulletin 10*:126-136.

Hamilton, M. E.
1982 Sexual dimorphism in skeletal samples. In *Sexual dimorphism in Homo sapiens*, edited by R. L. Hall, pp. 107-163. Praeger, New York.

Howell, N.
1982 Village composition implied by paleodemographic life table: The Libben site. *American Journal of Physical Anthropology 59*:263-269.

Hunt, E. E., and J. W. Hatch
1981 The estimation of age at death and ages of formation of transverse lines from measurements of human long bones. *American Journal of Physical Anthropology 54*:461-470.

Knick, S. G.
1981 Linear enamel hypoplasia and tuberculosis in pre-Columbian North America. *Ossa 8*:131-138.

Krishnamachari, K. A. V. R., and L. Iyengar
1975 Effect of maternal malnutrition on the bone density of the neonates. *American Journal of Clinical Nutrition 28*:482-486.

Lambert, J. B., C. B. Szpunar, and J. E. Buikstra
1979 Chemical analysis of excavated human bone from Middle and Late Woodland sites. *Archaeometry 21*:115-129.

Lambert, J. B., S. M. Vlasak, A. C. Thometz, and J. E. Buikstra
1982 A comparative study of the chemical analysis of ribs and femurs in Woodland populations. *American Journal of Physical Anthropology 59*:289-294.

Lynch, S. R., I. Berelowitz, H. C. Seftel, G. B. Miller, P. Krawitz, R. W. Charlton, and T. H. Bothwell
1967 Osteoporosis in the Johannesburg Bantu. *South African Journal of Medical Science 32*:59.

Marshall, W. A.
1968 Problems in relating the frequency of transverse lines in the radius to the occurrence of disease. In *The skeletal biology of earlier human populations*, edited by D. R. Brothwell, pp. 245-262. Pergamon, New York.

Masset, C.
1976 Sur la mortalité chez les anciens Indiens de Illinois. *Current Anthropology 17*:128-132.

Mazess, R. B., and R. Jones
1974 Weight and density of Sadlermiut Eskimo long bones. *Human Biology 44*:537-548.

Mazess, R. B., and W. B. Mather
1975 Bone mineral content in Canadian Eskimos. *Human Biology 47*:45-63.

Milner, G. R.
1982 Measuring prehistoric levels of health: A study of Mississippian period skeletal remains from the American Bottom, Illinois. Ph.D. dissertation, Department of Anthropology, Northwestern University.
1983 The cultural determinants of Mississippian community health: An examination of populations from two areas of western Illinois. *American Journal of Physical Anthropology 60*:227-228.

Murchison, M. A., D. W. Owsley, and A. J. Riopelle
n.d. Transverse line formation in protein deprived rhesus monkeys. Unpublished manuscript.

Neumann, G. K.
1952 Archeology and race in the American Indian. In *Archeology of the Eastern United States*, edited by J. B. Griffin, pp. 13-34. University of Chicago Press, Chicago.
1960 Origins of the Indians of the Middle Mississippi area. *Proceedings of the Indiana Academy of Sciences 60*: 66-68.

Neumann, H. W.
1967 The paleopathology of the Archaic Modoc Rock Shelter inhabitants. *Illinois State Museum Reports of Investigations* 11.

Newman, M. T.
1962 Evolutionary change in body size and head form in American Indians. *American Anthropologist 64*:237-257.

O'Connell, B. L. H.
1983 Fluctuating asymmetry as a measure of developmental stability in Illinois Woodland populations. Ph.D. dissertation, Department of Anthropology, Northwestern University.

O'Connor, N. J.
1977 A methodological study of the paleodemography of various Late Archaic populations of Eastern North America. Master's thesis, Department of Anthropology, Indiana University.

Perino, G.
1971 The Mississippian component at the Schild site (No. 4), Greene County, Illinois. *Illinois Archaeological Survey Bulletin 8*:1-148.
1973a The Late Woodland component at the Schild sites, Greene County, Illinois. *Illinois Archaeological Survey Bulletin 9*:90-140.
1973b The Late Woodland component at the Pete Klunk site, Calhoun County, Illinois. *Illinois Archaeological Survey Bulletin 9*:58-89.

1973c The Koster Mounds, Greene County, Illinois. *Illinois Archaeological Survey Bulletin* 9:141-210.
Perzigian, A.
1971 Gerontal osteoporotic bone loss in two prehistoric Indian populations. Ph.D. dissertation, Department of Anthropology, Indiana University.
Petersen, W.
1975 A demographer's view of prehistoric demography. *Current Anthropology* 16:227-245.
Pfeiffer, S., and P. King
1983 Cortical bone formation and diet among protohistoric Iroquoians. *American Journal of Physical Anthropology* 60:23-28.
Pickering, R. B.
1984 An examination of patterns of arthritis in Middle Woodland, Late Woodland, and Mississippian skeletal series from the Lower Illinois Valley. Ph.D. dissertation, Department of Anthropology, Northwestern University.
Protos, M.
1982 A biological test of Goldstein's hypothesis that outlying mortuary sites will be egalitarian in social structure. Paper presented at the annual meeting of the Indiana Academy of Sciences, Notre Dame, Indiana.
Rose, J. C.
1977 Defective enamel histology of prehistoric teeth from Illinois. *American Journal of Physical Anthropology* 46:439-446.
Rusch-Behrend, G. D.
n.d. Culture change and dental health in prehistoric Illinois. Ph.D. dissertation, Department of Anthropology, Indiana University.
Stewart, T. D.
1973 *The people of America*. Scribner's, New York.
Stout, S. D.
1978 Histological structure and its preservation in ancient bone. *Current Anthropology* 19:600-604.
Styles, B. W.
1981 Faunal exploitation and resource selection: Early Late Woodland subsistence in the Lower Illinois Valley. Northwestern University Archeological Program Scientific Papers, No. 3.
Szpunar, C. B.
1977 Atomic absorption analysis of archeological remains: Human ribs from Woodland mortuary sites. Ph.D. dissertation, Department of Chemistry, Northwestern University.
Tainter, J. A.
1975 The archaeological study of social change: Woodland systems in west-central Illinois. Ph.D. dissertation, Department of Anthropology, Northwestern University.
van der Merwe, N. J., and J. C. Vogel
1978 ^{13}C content of human collagen as a measure of prehistoric

diet in Woodland North America. *Nature 276*:815-816.

van Gerven, D. P., G. J. Armelagos, and M. H. Bartley
1969 Roentgenographic and direct measurement of femoral cortical involution in a prehistoric Mississippian population. *American Journal of Physical Anthropology 31*:23-38.

Young, S. G.
1983 Sexual dimorphism and stress at Klunk mounds. Bachelor's Honors Paper on file, Department of Anthropology, Indiana University.

CHAPTER 11

HEALTH CHANGES AT DICKSON MOUNDS, ILLINOIS (A.D. 950-1300)

Alan H. Goodman[1]

Department of Anthropology
University of Massachusetts-Amherst

John Lallo

Department of Anthropology
Cleveland State University

George J. Armelagos

Department of Anthropology
University of Massachusetts-Amherst

Jerome C. Rose

Department of Anthropology
University of Arkansas-Fayetteville

INTRODUCTION AND BACKGROUND

Purpose and Overview

Economic and cultural changes are powerful determinants of the patterns of morbidity, mortality, and stress (see Cassel, 1976; Dubos 1965; Hinkle 1974). This chapter presents a case study of the health effects of economic and cultural change for prehistoric populations from Dickson Mounds, Illinois (ca. A.D. 950-1300). The purposes of this chapter are twofold. The first is to document changing patterns of stress. Stress, or physiological disruption, is used as a general term for any indication of decreased

[1] *Present address: Department of Orthodontics, University of Connecticut Health Center, Farmington, Connecticut 06032.*

ability to adapt biologically. Changing patterns for ten indicators of stress are presented. Indicators include measures of growth disruption, growth retardation, disease, and mortality. Patterns include mean frequency, severity, and distribution of stress by age and sex. The second purpose of this chapter is to make inferences about the role of particular cultural and economic changes as causes of the observed patterns of stress.

Eight of ten indicators of stress increase in severity and/or frequency through time at Dickson. The traditional interpretation of this increase is that it is due to local, ecological changes such as increased population density and intensification of agriculture (see Goodman et al. 1980; Lallo 1973; Lallo et al. 1977, 1978, 1980). We argue that the broad pattern of increasing stress evidenced at Dickson may be equally due to Dickson's increasing involvement in Mississippian-based exchange systems (Harn 1978, 1980).

The Middle Mississippian represents the culmination of three trends at Dickson: (1) increased population density and sedentism, (2) intensification of maize agriculture, and (3) extension and intensification of trade. Increased population density and sedentism and intensification of maize agriculture are essentially local ecological processes, while the extension and intensification of trade represents an extension of local processes into regional systems. In this system, Dickson populations may have become increasingly involved with more powerful Mississippian sociopolitical systems to the south. As Dickson was brought into social and economic spheres controlled by these more powerful Mississippian centers (such as Cahokia), it is likely that Dickson populations would have lost control over their means of production. As Cahokia and other core Mississippian areas expanded their influence, Dickson and other peripheral sites are likely to have become more involved with and dependent on participation in a regional trade-exchange system. The interaction of internal, local processes (i.e., increased population size and density) and regional processes seems to have had a profoundly negative effect on health.

Archaeological Reconstruction

Dickson Mounds is a multicomponent habitation-burial complex. It is located near Lewistown, Illinois, at the confluence of the Illinois and Spoon rivers in the Central Illinois Valley (Figure 11.1). Three cultural horizons have been delimited at the site. These are defined as Late Woodland, Mississippian Acculturated Late Woodland, and Middle Mississippian.

The Late Woodland (LW) occupation (circa A.D. 950-1100) is characterized by a generalized hunting and gathering economy with seasonal camp sites utilized by a relatively small (75-125) group of people. At this time Mississippian culture was developing 180 km to the south at Cahokia in the American Bottoms (see Fowler 1978). At the end of this horizon the LW had come under the

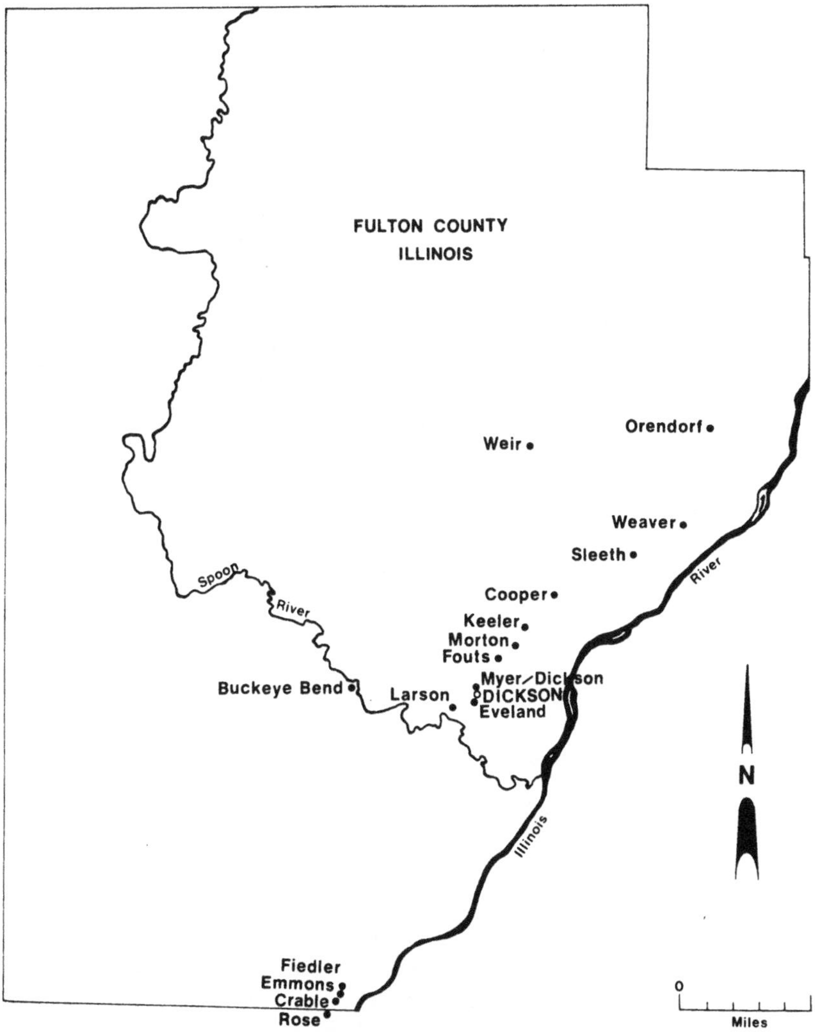

FIGURE 11.1. Area map of Dickson and selected Spoon River Tradition sites (after Harn 1980:x).

influence of the Middle Mississippian (MM) culture sufficiently to be redefined as Mississippian Acculturated Late Woodland (MALW) (approximately A.D. 1100-1200).

The MALW presents a mixed hunting-gathering and agricultural economy. The Eveland site, 230 m to the southwest of the burial complex, covered less than 1.5 ha and is estimated to have been permanently occupied by approximately 50-75 individuals (Harn, personal communication). By the end of this period evidence for long-distance trade is seen in the form of village refuse and grave offerings (Conrad and Harn 1972).

The MM at Dickson (ca. A.D. 1200-1300) represents the culmination of the Mississippian influence begun at the end of the LW. The settlement pattern is characterized as one of hamlets with surrounding support camps, extractive sites, and work stations tied to a local ceremonial center (Harn 1978). The Myer-Dickson site is such a hamlet. Its houses are arranged in rows with an open plaza. It is approximately 8 ha in area and was occupied by as many as 440 individuals (Harn n.d., Table 1). Myer-Dickson is one of 7 hamlets and 31 camps assumed to be associated with the Larson ceremonial center 11 km to the southwest. Larson is fully Mississippian. The site includes 32 ha of dispersed occupation debris and 8 ha of concentrated occupation. A palisade enclosed the mound, plaza, and at least 6 ha of settlement. Large quantities of foreign-made items are found in debris and cemeteries. Harn (1978:251) suggests a population of between 600 and 1170 individuals based on an estimated maximum of 234 habitation structures.

Skeletal Materials

The skeletal materials utilized in the studies cited in this chapter were loaned for study by the staff of the Dickson Mounds Museum, a branch of the Illinois State Museum. These materials include the remains from all 595 burials that were excavated during the 1966 and 1967 field seasons at Dickson. Cultural affiliations were made based on burial clusters and grave furniture by archaeologists at Dickson (Alan Harn, personal communication with John Lallo; Lallo 1973:27).

Age and sex determinations were based on the agreement of multiple methods. Methods utilized in aging subadults (0-15 years) included the following: (1) the pattern of dental eruption (after Schour and Massler 1944), (2) epiphyseal closure (after Krogman 1962), (3) fusion of the vertebrae (after Anderson 1962), and (4) the appearance of centers of ossification (after Krogman 1962). Methods utilized to age adults (15-65 years) included the following: (1) the pattern of dental eruption (after Schour and Massler 1944), (2) epiphyseal closure (after Krogman 1962), (3) changes in the public symphysis (Todd-Lyon [after Todd 1937] and McKern-Stewart [1957]), and (4) the dental attrition pattern for Dickson Mounds (see Harn 1971 and 1980).

Based on these methods, age was determined to yearly intervals for subadults (e.g., 0-1, 1-2, 3-4, ..., 14-15) and to 5-year intervals for adults (e.g., 15-20, 20-25, 25-30, ..., 60-65). For purposes of analysis these age classes have been collapsed, as is evidenced in the life tables (see Tables 11.1 and 11.2) (Lallo et al., 1978).

TABLE 11.1 Life Table for the Late Woodland and the Mississippian Acculturated Late Woodland for the Ages 0-60 Years

x	d'_x	d_x	l_x	q_x	L_x	E_x
0	45	128	1000	128	936	26
1	28	80	872	92	832	29
2	18	51	792	64	2299.5	30
5	21	60	741	81	3555.0	29
10	13	37	681	54	3312.5	27
15	26	74	644	115	3035.0	23
20	49	140	570	246	5000	21
30	33	94	430	219	3830	16
40	70	199	336	592	2365	10
50	48	137	137	1000	685	5
	351	1000	0			

TABLE 11.2 Life Table for the Middle Mississippian for the Ages 0-60 Years

x	d'_x	d_x	l_x	q_x	L_x	E_x
0	48	217	1000	217	891.5	19
1	19	86	783	110	740	23
2	16	72	697	103	1983	24
5	17	77	625	123	2932.5	24
10	10	45	548	82	2627.5	22
15	23	104	503	207	2255	18
20	24	109	399	273	3445	18
30	27	122	290	421	2290	13
40	25	114	168	678	1110	8
50	12	54	54	1000	270	5
	221	1000	0			

Sex determination for adults commenced after completion of age determinations. The following methods were utilized in determination of sex (after Lallo 1973:36): (1) dental metrics for Dickson Mounds (see Ditch and Rose 1972); (2) discriminant function analysis based on Dickson Mounds pelvic measures (see Gustav 1972), complemented by observation of the sciatic notch and preauricular sulcus; (3) discriminant function analysis based on Dickson Mounds femoral measures (Van Gerven 1972), and (4) cranial morphology (after Ascadi and Nemeskeri 1971): supra-orbital ridge, nuchal crest, mastoid process, eye orbits, and general robusticity.

State of preservation was generally good to excellent. Periosteal bone generally suffered little from interment. Most individuals were represented by near-complete or complete skeletons. Therefore, all but a handful of individuals (*N* = 38) could be aged, sexed, *and* assigned to a cultural horizon. The following studies are based on the sample that could be given an age, sex, and cultural assignment (*N* = 557). While analysis of mortality includes this entire sample, other analyses, dependent on the availability of specific bone or teeth, are based on sub-samples of these individuals. Although representativeness cannot be measured for archaeological populations, it is reasonable to assume that the sample is a fair representation of the base populations based on archaeological evidence for exclusive use of the burial mounds (see Harn 1980).

An additional strength of these materials for an analysis of health changes through time is a high degree of genetic homogeneity through time. Cohen (1974) assessed the relative degree of genetic distance between the three Dickson populations and Mound 72 from Cahokia, a Mississippian group (Fowler 1969). In her analysis, Cohen compares distances based on dental traits considered to be of either high or low heritability. As well, relative distance measures such as Mahalanobis *D*-square were computed based on a variety of measures. Analysis of the Dickson series revealed no significant differences between cultural phases in traits of high heritability. However, comparison of Dickson with the Cahokia series yielded significant differences in incisor and canine shoveling, median ridges, gingival borders, Carabelli's cusp, and molar groove patterns. All of these traits are considered to be under strong genetic control. Mahalanobis *D*-square values corroborate these findings. The *D*-square for comparison of Dickson with Cahokia is nearly ten times greater than the *D*-square for internal comparison (4.01 versus 0.41). These results strongly suggest that the Dickson series is genetically continuous and they strongly suggest against rapid *in situ* evolution or migration-population replacement senarios.

In summary, Dickson affords an excellent opportunity for studying the health effects of cultural change. The skeletal material provides an excellent data base for a paleoepidemiological analysis. Extensive archaeological reconstruction has pointed toward the wholesale nature of cultural and ecological change. In other words, Dickson represents a well-preserved skeletal sample of a population that underwent rapid cultural and economic change.

INDICATORS OF STRESS

Model for Studying Stress in Skeletal Populations

Our paleoepidemiological study is organized with reference to a model of the causes of physiological disruptions and indicators of disruption available for study in skeletal populations (Figure 11.2) (Armelagos et al. 1980; Huss-Ashmore et al. 1982). The biophysical environment imposes constraints (resource limitations and stressors) on human populations (box 1 in Figure 11.2). Although cultural systems may function to buffer or modify the effects of biophysical constraints, often cultural features may act to impose new stressors or to limit access to critical resources (box 2). For example, while agricultural intensification may lead to a greater net extraction of energy, it may come at a cost of decreased availability and use of other essential resources and increased exposure to critical stressors such as novel pathogens.

The impact of constraints on an individual is also mediated by host resistance factors (box 3). The general health of an individual, age, sex, genetic makeup, and many other factors may influence the magnitude of physiological disruption (stress) caused by a given constraint (box 4). While physiological disruption is not directly measurable in the dead, it may be inferred from a variety of its effects (box 5). If stress is severe and long lasting, then it will be evidenced in growth disruption, in mortality, and ultimately in death (Selye 1976). Death may be the ultimate measure of the biological organism's inability to suffer the consequences of poorly buffered stressors and resource limitations (Huss-Ashmore et al. 1982).

The model is operationalized as follows. Impacts of stress are measurable in a skeletal series. Variations in the resulting indicators of stress are assumed to be due to variations in the experience of physiological disruptions. These, in turn, are assumed to be a function of the amount of cultural buffering and

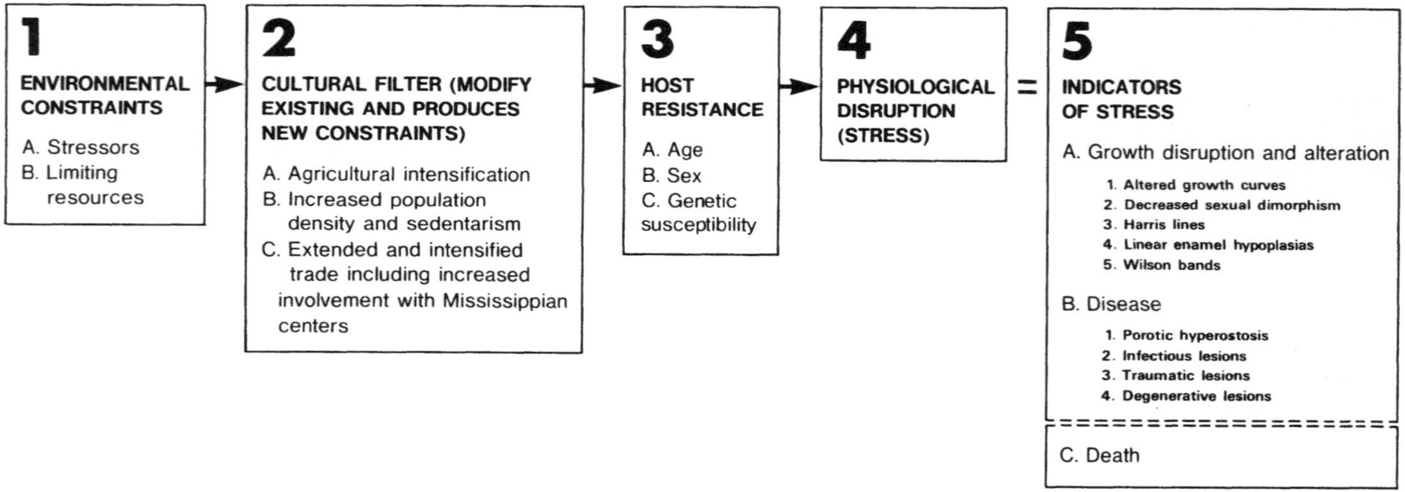

FIGURE 11.2 Model of the causes of physiological disruptions and indicators of disruption.

host resistance subtracted from the severity of culturally and ecologically produced constraints.

For the Dickson case study, one can assume that environmental constraints have remained roughly constant through time (Harn 1980). As well, since the population shows a high degree of genetic continuity through time (Cohen 1974), it is likely that genetically based host resistance factors have remained constant (save for changes that are a function of cultural constraints). Thus, we are left to assume that changes in stress levels may be due to changes in cultural factors. These changes are evaluated with reference to multiple indicators of disruption.

Long Bone Growth

Attained Length and Circumference. Lallo (1973) has presented an analysis of length and circumference data for tibiae, humeri, and femora. Data are presented as incremental increase, relative percentage increase, and attained distance. Below we present data from Lallo (1973) in the form of distance curves. Five hundred fifty-seven burials are included in the following analysis. This represents the entire sample that could be aged, sexed, and assigned to a cultural horizon.

Figures 11.3 and 11.4 are distance curves for total length and circumference of the tibia. On average, the Middle Mississippian tibia are longer at birth (Figure 11.3). However, there is a slowing of growth in the Mississippian relative to the Late Woodland and Mississippian Acculturated Late Woodland samples. This relative slowing is most evident from 2 to 5 years of age. It is at this time that the attained length for the MM falls below that for the MALW and the LW. Once the greater attained growth of the LW and MALW samples are achieved, they remain relatively constant until maturity.

Figure 11.4 demonstrates that the pattern observed for attained circumference is similar to the pattern presented for attained length. The main similarities are the greater size at birth of the Middle Mississippians and the slowing of growth of the Mississippian relative to the other populations, resulting in a lesser attained growth by the age of five. The circumference curves differ from the length curves in the following ways: (1) the age at which the differences between growth curves is greatest, (2) the amount of "catch-up" growth evidenced from ages 15 to 25, and (3) the relative differences in actual attained growth at different ages between cultural horizons. The greatest distance between growth curves is found between ages 10 and 15 with subsequently the greatest catch-up by age 25.

A series of analyses of variance (ANOVAs) were performed in order to ascertain whether or not differences in attained growth were statistically significant for any of the age groups (Table 11.4). Significant results ($p \leq .05$) were obtained for both tibial length and circumference for the 5- 10-year age group. However, no significant differences are found for either measure in any of

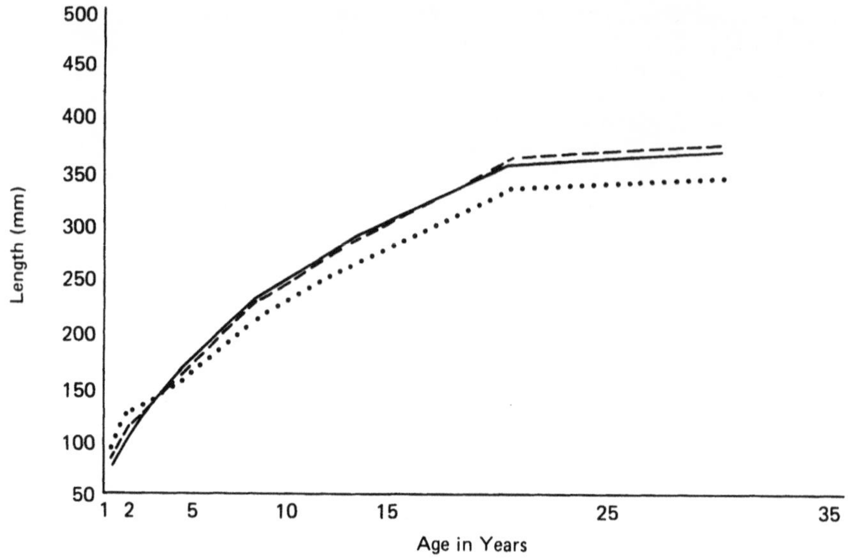

FIGURE 11.3. Distance curves of tibial length for the Late Woodland (——), Mississippian Acculturated Late Woodland (----), and Mississippian (•••••) cultural horizons (ages 0-35 years). Values for ages 15, 25, and 35 years include the epiphysis (from Lallo 1973:84).

the other age classes. While most results are not statistically significant, all measures from the 2-5-year class to older age classes are in the expected direction.

Evidence for an unusual decrease in growth velocity around the age of two also comes from an attempt to fit tibial length against dentally aged individuals (birth to 7 years, data from Bickerton 1979). A third-degree polynomial gave a significantly better fit to the data than the standard second-degree function (Goodman 1980). The additional degree utilized for curve fitting seems to be a result of the decrease in observed length over that "predicted" by the second-degree fit for individuals between the ages of 1.5 and 3 years. In summary, tibial growth data suggest increased stress in the Middle Mississippian. Furthermore, these data highlight the 2-5 year period as one in which stress may be most severe.

Sexual Dimorphism

While Lallo (1973) was able to ascertain that long bone length and circumference growth velocities and achieved growth are generally dampened in the Middle Mississippian relative to the prior cultural horizons, it remained to be seen whether this slow-

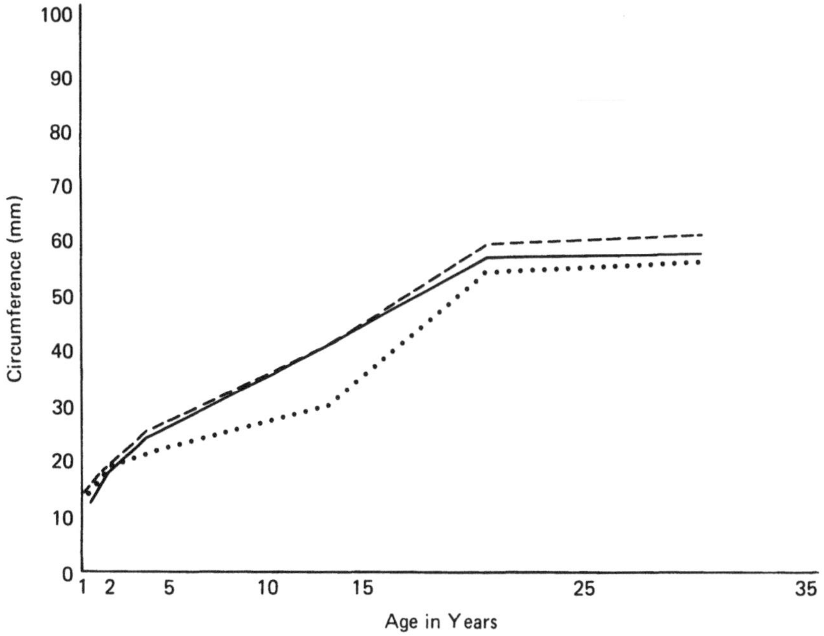

FIGURE 11.4. Distance curves for tibial circumference for the Late Woodland (———), Mississippian Acculturated Late Woodland (-----), and Mississippian (•••••) cultural horizons (ages 0-35 years) (Lallo 1973:87).

ing of growth differentially affected males, thus decreasing the amount of sexual dimorphism.

Lallo utilized an extensive set of osteometric measures of the pelvis and femur in his analysis of sexual dimorphism. These measures and data were obtained from Gustav (1972) for the pelvis and Van Gerven (1972) for the femur. Both of these studies include stepwise discriminant analyses of sex based on the respective femoral or pelvic measures. Lallo, therefore, had the advantage of utilizing two sets of measures that had previously been isolated as discriminators of sex in the Dickson collection.

A series of two-way ANOVAs (sex and culture as main effects) were run with data from 14 femoral and 21 pelvic measures (Lallo, 1973:112-113). If sexual dimorphism decreases through time, then we would expect a significant interaction between sex and culture (the two main effects). However, significant interactions were not found.

While the sexual dimorphism results are not significant, they require discussion. The hypothesis that stress would differentially affect males derives from Stini (1969), who theorizes that the female endocrinological system is better able to buffer nutritional insults. However, he is referring to a differentiation

TABLE 11.3 Summary Statistics of Long Bone Measurements for Late Woodland, Mississippian Acculturated Late Woodland, and Mississippian Individuals Ages 5-10 Years (Sexes Combined)

Measurement	N	Mean	SD	f-value[a]	df
Tibia length				3.56	2/23
LW	16	228.6	6.3		
MALW	31	229.2	10.6		
M	20	209.0	8.4		
Tibia circumference				3.96	2/23
LW	16	33.3	2.6		
MALW	31	32.8	2.4		
M	20	25.2	1.9		

[a]Denotes significant f-value at .05.

that occurs beginning with sexual maturation. This hypothesis may not be relevant to the Dickson situation, as it appears that maximum stress is evidenced much *before* sexual maturation. Finally, the Stini hypothesis does not account for the possibility that males were able to "keep up" relative to females because they were given greater access to resources and were more buffered from stress.

There are also a series of methodological reasons why the Stini hypothesis may not be evidenced in the Dickson data. First and foremost is the confounding problem of both sexing and analyzing for stress using the same set of measures. Second, the sample sizes utilized in this study are small (84 in the pelvic measures and 97 for the femoral measures) for a two-way ANOVA with six cells. And third, the study of Gustav (1972) and Van Gerven (1972) purposely excluded pathological specimens. While this is sensible in an analysis of measures that discriminate for sex, it may greatly reduce the possibility for discovering differences in the degree of sexual dimorphism based on the amount of stress.

We conclude that the amount of sexual dimorphism is relatively invariable among the three Dickson cultural horizons. While these data may be evidence that stress did not increase through time at Dickson, they may also be insignificant to this hypothesis.

Harris Lines

Frequencies. Goodman and Clark (1981) have presented an analysis of changing stress through time at Dickson as evidenced in the frequency and time of occurrence of Harris lines on distal and proximal tibia. Means and standard deviations for the frequency of Harris lines are presented in Table 11.5. Results are given per individual and are given for the entire sample (N = 130), and are broken down by age class (younger and older adults), sex, and cultural horizon.

TABLE 11.4 Harris Lines in the Dickson Mounds Populations: Means and Standard Deviations for the Number of Lines on Distal and Proximal Tibias

Sample (N)	Distal tibia		Proximal tibia	
	Mean	Standard deviation	Mean	Standard deviation
By Culture:				
LW (10)	1.30	1.49	0.70	1.88
MALW (47)	1.19	1.33	0.49	1.00
MM (51)	1.06	1.22	0.57	1.03
By Age:				
15-39 years (40)	1.38	1.30	0.75	1.43
40-60 years (30)	1.23	1.19	0.57	0.73
By Sex:				
Females (43)	1.21	1.23	0.53	0.98
Males (65)	1.46	1.30	0.74	1.33
Total Sample (130)	1.13	1.27	0.55	1.12

The mean number of lines/tibia is 1.68 (1.13 distally and 0.55 proximally). This frequency is within the range given by Wells (1967) for his Anglo-Saxon populations (0.8-5.1 lines/tibia). The figure is less than that found by Nichens (1975) for a Mesa Verde sample and by Woodall (1968) for a sample from Casas Grandes. On the other hand, McHenry (1968) reports a mean of 8.01 lines/*femur* for a prehistoric series from the San Joaquin Valley, California.

There are more Harris lines found on the distal than on the proximal end (mean of 1.13 versus 0.55). This confirms the finding of other researchers (Garn et al. 1968; Park 1964).

Cultural differences in the percentage of individuals with and without one or more Harris lines on the proximal or distal tibia were tested for statistical significance. No cultural comparison yielded a significant chi-square value (based on Siegel 1956). Furthermore, the slight trend of decreased frequency of Harris lines through time runs counter to the hypothesis.

Although the differences were not found to be statistically significant, males have a higher frequency of lines than do females. This trend may support the view that the growing male is more susceptible to stress than the growing female. However, somewhat contrary to the Stini hypothesis, females have a greater frequency of Harris lines during the adolescent growth spurt while males have a higher frequency during the first 7 years of life.

Distribution by Age at Occurrence. The distribution of Harris lines by the time of their development for the distal tibia is presented in Figure 11.5. Chronologies are presented for the MALW

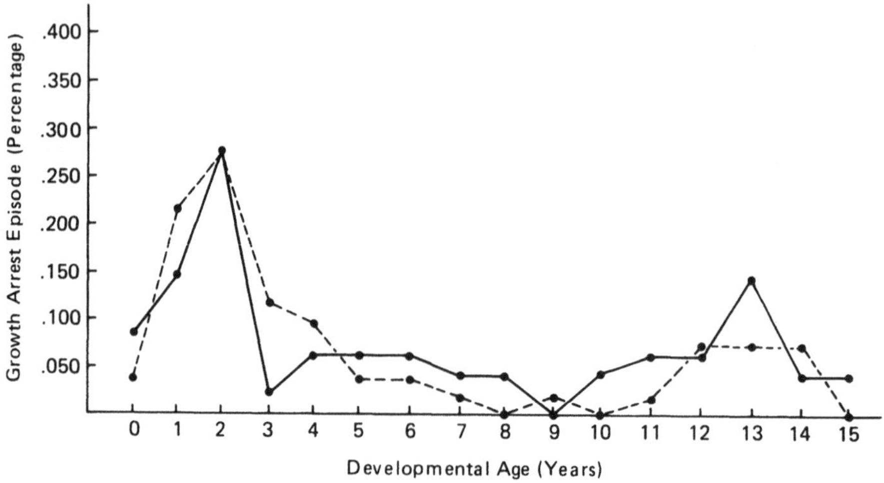

FIGURE 11.5. Percentage of growth arrest lines in combined male and female distal tibias for Mississippian Acculturated Late Woodland (——) (N = 47) and Middle Mississippian (-----) (N = 51) populations (Goodman and Clark 1981:45).

and MM samples. Both chronologies show two peaks. A major peak is found between the ages of birth and 3 years, and a minor peak around the ages of 12-14 years. The chronologies do not differ significantly from each other (Kolmogorov-Smirnov test) and, indeed, are remarkably similar in shape.

The Harris line frequency data do not support the view that health decreased through time at Dickson. Indeed, there is a trend of increased frequency of lines in the earlier groups. These data are equivocal. Recent reviews (Buikstra and Cook 1980; Huss-Ashmore et al. 1982) suggest that the frequency of Harris lines may not be a valid indicator of the degree of physiological disruption (stress). This reasoning lies mainly with the poor association of Harris line frequencies with other measures of stress in archaeological populations and the poor associations of Harris lines with known stressors in both animal and human clinical studies. If one questions whether or not Harris lines themselves are valid stress indicators, then chronologies of Harris lines as reflections of the degree of physiological stress through periods of skeletal maturation also must be questioned. Our data show a peak frequency of Harris lines precisely when growth velocity is greatest and when the growing individuals might be expected to be more susceptible to growth disruption. Thus, the Harris line chronologies may reflect host susceptibility to stress more than exposure to and strength of stressors.

TABLE 11.5 Mean Number of Growth Disruptions (Hypoplasias) per Individual in the Dickson Populations

	Growth disruptions/individual							
	All individuals				Individuals with complete measurements[a,b]			
Population	*M*	*F*	*A*	*Total*	*M*	*F*	*A*	*Total*
LW	*.17*	*1.42*	*.00*	*.90*	*.00*	*1.29*	*.00*	*.90*
MALW	*1.26*	*.82*	*2.00*	*1.18*	*1.25*	*1.29*	*2.00*	*1.45*
MM	*1.43*	*1.47*	*3.25*	*1.61*	*1.43*	*1.64*	*3.25*	*1.86*
	1.20	*1.24*	*2.09*	*1.31*	*1.25*	*1.44*	*2.09*	*1.52*

[a]*M, males; F, females; A, adolescents.*
[b]*Birth to 7 years.*

Linear Enamel Hypoplasia

Frequencies. Enamel hypoplasias are deficiencies in enamel thickness resulting from systemic physiological disruptions (Goodman et al. 1980). The pattern of hypoplasias on dental enamel can be read as a kymographic record of physiological disruption (stress) during the time of the enamel's development (Kreshover 1960; Sarnat and Schour 1941). And, because mature enamel is unalterable by internal biological events, hypoplasias may provide a permanent "memory" of physiological disruptions during the time of the enamel's development (Goodman et al. 1980).

Goodman and co-workers (1980) have presented an analysis of the frequency of enamel hypoplasias for the Dickson Mound individuals with permanent dentitions. The sample consisted of all adolescents and adults with relatively complete dentition ($N = 111$). Ages of individuals and available enamel (a potential source of error due to tooth loss and attrition) did not vary significantly by sex or cultural horizon.

The mean number of hypoplasias per individual in the Dickson population is presented in Table 11.6. The means are presented both for all individuals in the sample and for individuals with complete enamel allowing measurements from birth to 7 years of age. This second set of means helps to control for differential availability of enamel for study caused mainly by dental attrition.

A clear trend of increased growth disruption is evident through time at Dickson. Mean frequencies by cultural horizon increase from 0.90 in the LW to 1.18 in the MALW to 1.61 in the MM. This trend is also evident in individuals with complete measurements from birth to 7 years (Table 11.6) and is evidenced that the trend is not due to a differential availability of enamel for study. In fact, when controlling for enamel availability, the

TABLE 11.6 Number of Individuals without Growth Disruptions (Hypoplasias) and the Number of Individuals with One or More Growth Disruptions by Cultural Horizon

	Hypoplasias		One or more hypoplasias		Total	
	No.	%	No.	%	No.	%
Late Woodland (LW)	11	55	9	45	20	100
Mississippian Acculturated Late Woodland (MALW)	18	40	27	60	45	100
Middle Mississippian (MM)	9	20	37	80	46	100
	38	34	73	66	111	100

Summary of Chi-Square Tests Where the Frequency of Individuals with One or More Growth Arrest Episodes Were Compared to Those without a Growth Arrest Episode (see Table 3). Yates' Correction Is Used When df Equals 1

	Chi-square value (df)
LW versus MALW	.7 (1)
LW versus MM	6.8 (1)[a]
MALW versus MM	3.8 (1)[b]
LW versus MALW versus MM	11.0 (2)[a]

[a] $p \leq .01$.
[b] $p \leq .05$.

trend toward increased frequencies of hypoplasias becomes more pronounced.

Chi-square analyses are performed in order to determine whether these cultural differences are of statistical significance. The sample was dichotomized into those with one or more growth disruptions and those without growth disruptions (see Table 11.7). The LW and MALW did not differ significantly from each other. However, the MM differed significantly from both the LW and the MALW ($p \leq .01$ and $p \leq .05$, respectively). In sum, the hypoplasia data support the hypothesis that physiological disruption was more frequent and severe in the Middle Mississippian.

Annual Cycles of Stress (Seasonality). Frequencies of occurrence of two growth disruptions separated by 12 and 6 months are presented in Table 11.8. The number of growth disruptions separated by a year is greater than the number of disruptions separated by 6 months in all horizons. Results for the MALW approach significance, and overall results are significant ($p = .0336$).

TABLE 11.7 Number of Cases in Which Two Growth Disruptions (Hypoplasias) Are Separated by a Half Year and Number of Cases in Which Two Growth Disruptions Are Separated by a Year

	.5 Years	1.0 Years	Binomial one-tailed probability[a]
Late Woodland	1	3	--
Mississippian Acculturated Late Woodland	5	12	.072
Middle Mississippian	10	14	.271
	16	29	.0336

[a]Siegel 1956.

The occurrence of growth disruptions over time within an individual is not random. The occurrence of growth disruption separated by yearly intervals is greater than that predicted by chance. This phenomena is likely to be due to an annual cycle of stress (Goodman et al. 1980) such as might occur if a given season were regularly more stressful than the others. Since agriculture may provide a resource base to buffer these seasonal deprivations, these data may help to explain why agriculture became intensified in the Middle Mississippian.

Wilson Bands

Frequencies. Rose et al. (1978) have presented a thorough analysis of Wilson bands in a Middle Woodland sample from Gibson Mound and the MALW and Middle Mississippian from Dickson. Data are presented on the frequency of occurrence of Wilson bands (see Table 11.9), the chronology and peak period of their development, and their association with age at death (see Table 11.10). The sample was randomly selected from individuals 15 years old or older and includes 87 mandibular canines.

A nearly fourfold increase in percentage of individuals with Wilson bands is seen if one compares the MW at Gibson (10.3%) to the MALW at Dickson (21.4%) and the Mississippian at Dickson (40.0%). These researchers also calculated the percentage of half-year enamel units with Wilson bands (a method used to control for differential availability of enamel). This method of calculation reduces the difference between the two Dickson samples. The percentage of enamel units with Wilson bands is 4.4 in the MALW and 7.7 in the MM. Only the difference between the MW and MM was found to be statistically significant (chi-square test corrected for continuity; Siegel 1956).

TABLE 11.8 Prevalence and Percentages per Individual and One-half Year Enamel Unit of Wilson Bands

	Wilson bands	Indi-viduals	Enamel units	Percentage indi-vidual	Percentage enamel unit
Middle Woodland (Gibson)	3	29	157	10.3	1.9
MALW (Dickson)	6	28	136	21.4	4.4
Mississippian (Dickson)	12	30	163	40.0	7.4
	21	87	456	24.1	4.6

TABLE 11.9 A Comparison of the Mean Ages at Death (in years) of Individuals with At Least One Wilson Band and Those without Wilson Bands

	With Wilson bands	With no Wilson bands	Difference
Middle Woodland (Gibson)	20.0	45.0	25.0
MALW (Dickson)	28.4	40.2	11.8
Mississippian (Dickson)	27.6	40.4	12.8

Distribution by Age at Occurrence. The mean age of occurrence and the chronology of occurrence of Wilson bands were also calculated. The mean age of occurrence is 2.25 years for the MW, 2.92 years for the MALW, and 2.40 years for the MM. The chronological distributions of bands are also slightly different. The MW curve has a broad and flat peak from 0.5 to 4.0 years. The MALW has a broad peak from 2.0 to 4.5 with a high point at 2.25 years. The MW has a plateau from 1.0 to 3.5 with high peaks at 1.75 and 3.25 years.

Association with Age at Death. Rose et al. (1978) examined the relationship between Wilson bands and age at death in adulthood (see Table 11.7). This analysis yielded two noteworthy results. First, the mean age at death for individuals with Wilson bands is lower than that for individuals without Wilson bands in all cultures--from 11.8 to 25.0 years earlier. Furthermore, this difference is greater in the Dickson series than in the less stressed

Gibson Mound series. Statistical analysis of the relationship between age at death and childhood stress (Wilson band frequencies) is not presented.

The analysis of Wilson bands helps to refine the picture of increased stress at Dickson. First, Wilson band frequency data are strong evidence for increased stress through time. Second, the chronologies, with peak periods of stress around the ages of 2-3 years, corroborate the timing of maximum stress evidenced in the Harris line and long bone growth data. Finally, the Wilson band data demonstrate that childhood stress, as measured by Wilson band frequencies, is "predictive" of age at death. Therefore, childhood stress (or a covariate of it) is highly significant to survival. Furthermore, this relationship increases in importance through time.

Porotic Hyperostosis

Frequencies. Porotic hyperostosis is a general term used to identify bony lesions that are localized on the superior border of the orbits and the external surface of the crania and are characterized by a thinning of the subperiosteal cortical bone and corresponding expansion of the dipole (Armelagos 1967; Carlson et al. 1974; Lallo et al. 1977). Lallo and co-workers (1977) provide a detailed study of the presence of porotic lesions in subadult crania from Dickson. This sample consists of 238 individuals, of which 87 (36.5%) show evidence for porotic hyperostosis (Table 11.11). The frequency of porotic hyperostosis increases from 13.6% in the LW to 32.2% in the MALW and 51.5% in the MM. Differences between cultural horizons in the frequency of porotic hyperostosis are statistically significant by chi-square analysis ($p \leq .05$; Lallo et al. 1977).

Degree of Involvement (Severity) of Porotic Hyperostosis. The frequency of occurrence of porotic hyperostosis by site and type of involvement is presented in Table 11.8. The orbits are the primary site of occurrence of porotic hyperostosis. In the LW, porotic hyperostosis is limited to the orbitas (cribra orbitalia). However, in the MALW and MM, individuals with cribra orbitalia tend increasingly to have porotic involvement at other sites in the form of spongy hyperostosis and/or osteoporotic pitting. The involvement of porotic hyperostosis at sites other than the orbits suggests a more inclusive and a more severe manifestation. Not only does porotic hyperostosis show a four-fold increase in frequency, but it also increases in percentage of "severe" cases from 0.0% in the LW to 6.5% in the MALW to 17.8% in the MM. As these authors hypothesized, the frequency and degree of involvement of porotic hyperostosis increases with increased utilization of maize agriculture.

TABLE 11.10 The Age-Specific Frequency of Porotic Hyperostosis[a]

Age	N	Porotic Hyperostosis	Cribra Orbitalia	Osteoporotic Pitting	Spongy Hyperostosis	O.P.[b] and S.H.
Late Woodland, Dickson Mounds						
0-.9	11	0	0	0	0	0
1-1.9	7	0	0	0	0	0
2-4.9	9	2 (22.2)	2 (100.0)	0	0	0
5-9.9	10	3 (30.0)	3 (100.0)	0	0	0
10-14.9	7	1 (14.3)	1 (100.0)	0	0	0
	44	6 (13.6)	6 (100.0)	0	0	0
Mississippian Acculturated Late Woodland, Dickson Mounds						
0-.9	29	3 (10.3)	3 (100.0)	0	0	0
1-1.9	19	4 (21.1)	4 (100.0)	1 (25.0)	1 (25.0)	0
2-4.9	18	7 (39.0)	7 (100.0)	1 (14.3)	1 (14.3)	2 (28.6)
5-9.9	18	12 (66.7)	12 (100.0)	2 (16.7)	1 (8.3)	3 (25.0)
10-14.9	9	3 (33.3)	3 (100.0)	1 (33.3)	1 (33.3)	1 (33.3)
	93	29 (31.2)	29 (100.0)	5 (17.2)	4 (13.8)	6 (20.7)
Middle Mississippian, Dickson Mounds						
0-.9	39	13 (33.3)	13 (100.0)	2 (15.4)	3 (23.1)	1 (7.7)
1-1.9	19	9 (47.4)	9 (100.0)	2 (22.2)	3 (33.3)	2 (22.2)
2-4.9	16	11 (68.8)	11 (100.0)	4 (36.4)	2 (18.2)	5 (45.5)
5-9.9	17	13 (76.5)	13 (100.0)	4 (30.8)	2 (15.4)	7 (53.8)
10-14.9	10	6 (60.0)	6 (100.0)	2 (33.3)	1 (16.7)	3 (50.0)
	101	52	52 (100.0)	14 (26.9)	11 (21.2)	18 (34.6)

[a]Percentages in parentheses.
[b]O.P. and S.H. = osteoporotic pitting and spongy hyperostosis.

Infectious Lesions

Frequencies. Lallo and co-workers (1978) have summarized the evidence for changing frequencies of infectious lesions through time at Dickson. The analysis is based on both adults and subadults. The LW and the MALW are combined into a low-intensity agriculture population and this combined sample is compared to a MM sample. Infectious lesions include periostitis and osteomyelitis. Although these two types of infection were recorded separately, this analysis considers them together. Frequencies are for the combination of either or both types of infectious lesions.

The percentage of individuals with infectious lesions doubles from the low-intensity agriculture LW-MALW horizons to the more intensified MM period (31 to 67%) (Table 11.12). This overall pattern is evidenced in both the adult and subadult segments of the population and in females and males. In summary, the increased rate of infection through time is a general phenomenon, characteristic of all age and sex classes.

Severity and Association with Age at Death

Severity of infection was determined by analysis of the degree of infectious involvement for the tibia. The selection of the tibia was based on the following: (1) its high rate of preservation among long bones, (2) its broad periosteal surface, which facilitates observation, and (3) the fact that it is the bone with the highest rate of infection in this sample (Lallo et al. 1978). Severity was determined on the basis of the following criteria: (1) extent of involvement of the periosteal surface, (2) characterization of the tissue destruction (pitted, ridged, scarred, or sinus tracked), and (3) the amount of bone tissue destructions. Nine stages of severity (from Lallo 1973) were combined into three severity levels (Lallo et al. 1978).

The percentage of tibiae with evidence for infection increases from 26% in LW-MALW sample to 84% in the MM sample (Table 11.13). Thus, the pattern of infection through time for the tibia is similar to the pattern of infection through time for all skeletal remains, save for an even more pronounced rate of increase in the MM sample. For individuals aged 15-25 years, the frequency of tibial infections increases from 25% in the low agricultural intensity sample to 77% in the agriculturally more intensified MM (Table 11.14). Furthermore, of individuals with infections in this age class, those in the MM are much more likely to have either moderate or severe involvement (Table 11.4). Finally, these researchers have also noted that the mean age at death for adults with tibial infections is less than the mean age at death for adults without tibial infections and that this relationship holds for both samples in this study. As an example, the mean age at death for adults (over 20 years) in the MALW is 39.5 years. However, the mean age at death for individuals with slight tibial infections is 37 years and 35.1 years for individuals with severe infections.

TABLE 11.11 Summary Figures for the Frequency of Occurrence of Infectious Disease

Age	N	Number with infection	%[a]
0–59.9 years[b]			
LW + MALW	351	108	31
MM	221	149	67
0–14.9 years[b]			
LW + MALW	125	34	27
MM	110	74	67
15–59.9 years[b]			
LW + MALW	226	74	33
MM	111	75	68
15–15.9 years			
Females			
LW + MALW	110	35	32
MM	61	43	71
Males			
LW + MALW	116	39	34
MM	50	32	64

[a]All percentages have been rounded off to the nearest whole number.
[b]These frequencies include the combined male and female totals.

TABLE 11.12 Frequency of Infectious Lesions of the Tibia

	N	Number infected	%[a]
LW + MALW	353	90	26
MM	194	163	84

Severity of Tibial Involvement

	N	Slight	Moderate	Severe
LW + MALW	90	56 (62%)	27 (30%)	7 (8%)
MM	163	45 (28%)	80 (49%)	38 (23%)

[a]All percentages have been rounded off to the nearest whole number.

These data are evidence that infection and its variates are significant health events for all populations.

TABLE 11.13 Frequency of Infectious Lesions of the Tibia, Young Adults (15-25 Years)

	N	Number infected	%[a]
LW + MALW	114	28	25
MM	43	33	77

Severity of Tibial Involvement

	N	Slight	Moderate	Severe
LW + MALW	28	21 (75%)	5 (18%)	2 (7%)
MM	33	10 (30%)	16 (49%)	7 (21%)

[a]*All percentages have been rounded off to the nearest whole number.*

Traumatic Lesions

Lallo (1973) has presented an analysis of both cranial and postcranial traumatic pathologies. Data presented below are for postcranial fractures (Table 11.15). The most common sites of fractures are the humerus, clavicle, ulna, and radius. Since the distribution of pathologies within individual skeletons is not significantly different among cultural horizons, all postcranial freactures are combined. For the entire sample (ages 0-65 years), the Mississippian has a slightly higher frequency of fractures than the MALW and the LW (19.5, 16.4, and 13.4%, respectively). However, this pattern is not consistent among age and sex classes. For subadults the overall trend is reversed. LW subadults have a higher frequency of fractures than those in the MALW and the MM (10.2, 9.8, and 6.4%, respectively). Adults (males and females combined) in the Mississippian have nearly twice the frequency of traumatic pathologies as adults in the MALW and LW groups (32.4 to 16.4 and 20.5%). Finally, when data for the sexes are analyzed separately, it becomes clear that adult males, especially in the Mississippian, are most frequently affected by traumatic conditions. The frequency of traumatic lesions increases from 23.5% in LW females and 16.4% in MALW females to 31.1% in MM females. The frequency of traumatic lesions increases from 17.9% in LW males and 16.4% in MALW males to 38.0% in MM males. In summary, postcranial traumatic pathologies follow the trend of increased incidence through time. Furthermore, this trend is most pronounced for males.

TABLE 11.14 Summary of the Analysis of Variance and Duncan's New Multiple Range Test for Trauma for the Late Woodland, Mississippian Acculturated Late Woodland, and the Mississippian (Ages 0-65)

Age (years)	Mean frequency of trauma	Duncan's New Multiple Range Test
0-65		
LW	16.4	
MALW	13.4	
M	19.4	
0-15		
LW	10.2	
MALW	9.8	
M	6.4	
15-65		
LW	20.5	
MALW	16.4	
M	32.4	
15-65 (Females)		MALW LW M
LW	23.5	16.4 17.9 38.0
MALW	16.4	
M	31.1	
15-65 (Males)		
LW	17.9	
MALW	16.4	
M	38.0[a]	

[a]Denotes significant f-value at $p \leq .05$.

Degenerative Pathologies

Lallo (1973) has presented an analysis of osteoarthritis, osteophytosis, and degeneration of the vertebral centrum in the Dickson populations (Table 11.16). For all adults there is a significant increase in the frequency of degenerative pathologies (of all sites combined) from 39.7% in the LW to 41.8% in the MALW and 65.8% in the MW. All cultural frequencies are significantly different from each other (Duncan's multiple ranges test; see Lallo 1973:222). This trend is similar and is evidenced in both males and females.

Data are also presented for stages of severity of degeneration of the centrum and osteophytosis (see Lallo 1973:223-248). Data are for individual vertebrae and not for individual persons. For both centrum degeneration and osteophytosis there is a clear trend of increased frequency of affected vertebrae by cultural horizons,

TABLE 11.15 Summary of the Analysis of Variance and Duncan's New Multiple Range Test for Degenerative Pathology Frequencies among Cultural Horizons

	Mean frequency of degenerative pathology	Duncan's multiple range test results		
		LW	MALW	M
Females aged 15-65				
LW	41.2	41.2	41.0	67.4
MALW	41.0			
M	67.4[a]			
Males aged 15-65				
LW	38.5[a]	38.5	42.6	76.0
MALW	42.6[a]			
M	76.0[a]			

[a]Denotes significant f-value at $p \leq .05$.

increased frequency of severe cases by cultural horizons, and more serious affliction of males than females.

In sum, the pattern of degenerative pathologies is similar to that of traumatic pathologies. Degenerative pathologies significantly increase through time and affect males more frequently than females.

Mortality

Mortality or age-at-death information has been presented using a wide variety of methods for prehistoric populations. These methods include composite life tables, probability-of-dying curves, age-specific mortality curves, and mean age at death-life expectancy figures. Lallo and colleagues (Lallo et al. 1978; 1980) have presented an analysis of mortality changes at Dickson. While they utilize a variety of methods in their analysis, they started by constructing life tables. They argue that life tables, once constructed, provide the maximum amount of information about the mortality of a population.

Life tables for the three cultural horizons are presented in Tables 11.1-11.2. The d_x values (age-specific mortality) and q_x values (age-specific probability of dying) consistently increase through the horizons at Dickson while the l_x (survivorship) and e_x^o (age-specific life expectancy) consistently decrease through the cultural horizons. In all age classes there appears to be a general trend toward increased chance of dying in the MM relative to the LW. The statistical significance of this trend was determined using the Kolmogorov-Smirnov two-tailed test (see Siegel 1956:117-138). Kolmogorov-Smirnov is a test of differences in distribution

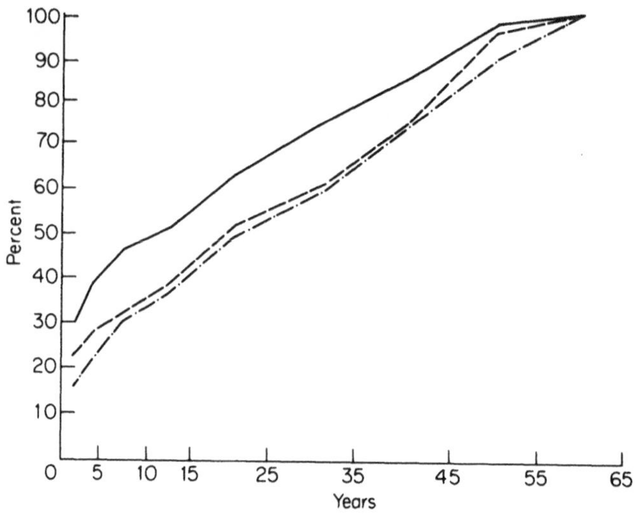

FIGURE 11.6. Cumulative percentages of mortality by age for the Late Woodland (—•—), Mississippian Acculturated Late Woodland (-----), and Middle Mississippian (———) populations (ages 0-65) (from Lallo et al. 1980:220).

and is utilized to test whether or not two distributions are sufficiently similar to have been drawn from the same population. Kolmogorov-Smirnov was applied to the cumulative distributions of mortality (Figure 11.6). The maximum difference between the LW and the MALW was not significant. However, the maximum differences between the LW and the MM, and between the MALW and the MM, were significant ($p \leq .05$) (Lallo et al. 1980:219-220).

In summary, the LW and MALW demonstrate similar patterns of distribution of mortality, while the difference between those patterns and that of the MM is significant. The maximum differences occur during childhood. In comparison of the LW and the MM, the maximum difference is 16.1% and occurs in the 2-5-year age class (21.8-37.9% dead). In comparison of the MALW and MM, the maximum difference is 14.5% and occurs in the 10-15-year age class (38.8-50.3%). Since the distribution by age class of mortality in prehistoric populations is generally considered to be relatively homogeneous (see Weiss 1973), evidence for statistically significant differences in temporally different populations from the same site is notable.

DISCUSSION AND CONCLUSIONS

Changing Patterns of Stress

We have presented evidence for an increased level of general stress through time at Dickson. This pattern is evidenced in 8 of 10 indicators of stress (Table 11.17). Increases in stress are indicated by (1) decreased age-specific attained long bone length and circumference, (2) increased frequency of enamel hypoplasias, (3) increased frequency of Wilson bands, (4) increased frequency of porotic hyperostosis, (5) increased frequency of infectious lesions, (6) increased frequency of degenerative lesions, (7) increased frequency of traumatic lesions, and (8) increased cumulative mortality. No differences are found for the frequency of Harris lines and the degree of sexual dimorphism. Independent observations consider Harris lines and sexual dimorphism to be weak and/or low-validity indicators of stress (Buikstra and Cook, 1980; Huss-Ashmore et al. 1982). Therefore, these results are considered to be multiple confirmations of the general hypothesis that stress increased through time at Dickson.

There seems to be more than one critical stressor or cultural dimension leading to increased stress. Growth indicators (long bone length and circumference, enamel hypoplasias, and Wilson bands) are consistent in demonstrating a decrease in growth velocity and an increase in growth disruption around the ages of 2-4 years. Based on ethnographic observations on weanling time and practice among Amerindians (Cook 1971), these data may implicate the diet of the weanling and, specifically, the increased use of maize in this diet. These data, in consort with an increase in the frequency and severity of porotic hyperostosis, point to the increased adoption of a maize diet, especially among weanlings, as a cause of poor nutrition and an increase in nutrition-related stress indicators.

Other stress indicators may implicate other cultural changes. The increased frequency of infection may be bound synergically to nutritional problems resulting from ubiquitous pathogens that were becoming increasingly virulent under the influence of decreased host resistance due to under-nutrition (Dubos 1965; Scrimshaw 1964). Decreased host resistance is therefore likely to have been one cause of the increase in infectious lesions, as there is evidence for association of infectious and nutritional (porotic hyperostosis) lesions in prehistoric populations (see Mensforth et al. 1978). However, it is unlikely that decreased quality of diet is the only cause of the increasing frequency and severity of infection. Changing settlement practices with increased population density and sedentism, combined with the use of virgin agricultural soils, a less complex ecosystem, and increased trade, affords ample chance for the introduction of novel pathogens and their maintenance within the population. In sum, increases in infectious disease may be due to a variety of causes that perhaps worked together in synergetic fashion.

TABLE 11.17 Summary of Stress Indicators

Indicator	Patterns of stress[a]	Subgroup affected (age in years)	Differences observed	General comment
Long bone growth	+	1-7	Attained growth is less for tibia and femur in the 5-10-yr. group[b]	Decreased growth velocity at 2-5 yr.: chronic (nutrition-related) stress in infancy and childhood. Some catch-up occurs.
Sexual dimorphism	0		None (pelvic and femoral measures)	Weak indicator-test of stress for methodological and theoretical reasons.
Harris lines	0		None (distal and proximal tibia)	Weak indicator based on experimental evidence
Enamel hypoplasia	+	2-4	Frequency and lines in MM is twice that of LW. MALW is intermediate[b]	Good seasonal (nutrition-related) stress indicator.
Wilson bands	+	2-4	Approximately 70% increase from MALW to MM.	Nutritionrelated. Strong predictor of age at death.

Porotic hyperostosis	++	0-15	Fourfold increase from LW to MM with increase in severity and involvement[b]	Nutrition stress (iron). Modeled and unremodeled not distinguished.
Infectious lesions	++	All ages	Threefold increase from LW-MALW to MM. Also, increase in severity[b]	Chronic infection. Endemic in MM. Synergistic with porotic hyperostosis. Good predictor of age at death.
Trauma	+	15-65	Twofold increase from LW-MALW to MM for appendicular fractures	Strongest difference noted in males. Suggests interpersonal strife.
Degenerative lesions	+	15-65	65% increase from LW to MM. Increase in severity (centrum and osteophytosis)[b]	Chronic wear and tear (physical stress) is greatest in males.
Mortality	++	0-10	$d_x + g_x$ increase while l_x and e_x^o decrease. Cumulative differences are significant.[b]	Best indicator of stress and inability to adapt. Most severe in subadults.

[a] –, decrease through time; 0, no change through time; +, increase through time; ++, strong increase through time.

[b] Observed differences were statistically significant.

The frequency of degenerative and traumatic pathologies increased over time in adults and especially adult males. Degenerative pathology is inferred to be due to increased physical-work stress. Traumatic pathology may be interpreted as the result of physical-work stress or interpersonal strife. The latter explanation is not unlikely given the evidence for fortification at the Larson site. These data point to an increased degree of competition.

Toward a Regional Model of Prehistoric Health

The Dickson Mounds case is one in which increased population density and sedentism occur roughly contemporaneously with intensified agriculture and increased evidence for physiological disruption. However, it is difficult to explain the extreme degree to which stress increases based only on these or other local ecological factors. Harn (1980:1,7-8) documents the unusually well-balanced natural environment of the Dickson area (Fulton County) and believes that the natural productivity of the area is great enough throughout Dickson's prehistory to sustain even the larger MM population (also see Caldwell 1958). Furthermore, there is abundant evidence from artifact analyses that hunting and gathering are major activities throughout the MM (Harn 1980:81-82). Local archaeological and ecological reconstruction leads one to believe that this is an excellent environment for a prehistoric population and that abundant use was made of the local resources throughout the period of occupation. One would predict that nutrition would be adequate. Left to its own, as a closed cultural-ecological system, Dickson would seem to be able to do well. However, it is not a closed system and the evidence is that it does not do well.

The model we propose for Dickson is one of increased stress through time resulting primarily from its occupying exploitable position in a regional system of ideological and economic exchange. Increases in population density and sedentism and increased use of agriculture may be of secondary importance to the possession of an exploitable position within a larger system. Increased population density and sedentism and increased use of agriculture may become important only when local ecological conditions are poor and/or are related to a regional system of exploitation. At Dickson it appears that the stresses of agriculture are absorbed locally but the benefits are enjoyed at a place outside of the local ecosystem. The biocultural systems of the Dickson populations may have been able to adjust to the constraints of local changes such as an increase in populations and intensification of maize agriculture. However, participation in regional Mississippian systems in the Illinois Valley placed additional constraints on the local populations. The interaction of local and regional changes, especially those revolving around a possibly unbalanced flow of economic resources, may have imposed a stress load that could no longer be buffered by the subordinate populations such as Dickson.

In conclusion, we have presented Dickson as a case study of health change at a single site. Our data have provided multiple confirmations that stress increased through time. This is evidenced in measures of growth disruption and retardation, disease, and mortality. Our conclusions about the causes of increased stress are based on an examination of both local and larger regional processes. Just as it would be ill advised to explain patterns of disease in contemporary societies without reference to their involvement in the modern world system, so also would it be ill advised to explain health at this prehistoric site without reference to the precapitalist systems of which the Mississippian culture is an example. The bones and teeth from Dickson tell a tale of increased stress which may be due to the exploitable position of the Dickson population within a regional system. Testing this model is possible by comparison of the health effects of agricultural intensification, increased population density, and increased sedentism on populations that vary in their involvement in larger systems and in their position within these systems. Information for a preliminary testing of this model may be provided within this volume.

ACKNOWLEDGMENTS

We wish to acknowledge the work of Mark Cohen, State University of New York College at Plattsburgh, in providing the opportunity for summarizing the paleoepidemiological data. Greatest appreciation is accorded to Alan Harn, Dickson Mound Museum, Lewistown, Illinois, for his patience and kind spirit in clarifying archaeological data and interpretations. The final writing of this chapter was supported in part by NIDR Grant No. DE07047-07.

REFERENCES

Anderson, J. L.
1962 *The human skeleton: A manual for archeologists.* National Museum of Canada, Toronto.

Armelagos, G. J.
1967 Future work in paleopathology. In Miscellaneous papers in paleopathology, edited by W. D. Wade, pp. 1-8. *Museum of Northern Arizona Technical Series* No. 7.

Armelagos, G. J., A. H. Goodman, and S. Bickerton
1980 Determining nutritional and infectious disease stress in prehistoric populations (Abstract). *American Journal of Physical Anthropology* *52*:201.

Ascadi, G., and J. Nemeskeri
1971 *History of human life span and mortality.* Akademia, Budapest.
Bickerton, S.
1979 Porotic hyperostosis in a prehistoric Amerindian population from Dickson Mound. Paper presented at the Northeastern Anthropological Association, Henniker, New Hampshire.
Buikstra, J., and D. Cook
1980 Paleopathology: An American account. *Annual Review of Anthropology 9*:433-470.
Caldwell, J. R.
1958 Trend and tradition in the prehistory of the eastern United States. *Illinois State Museum Scientific Papers 10.*
Carlson, D. S., G. J. Armelagos, and D. P. Van Gerven
1974 Factors influencing the etiology of cribra orbitalia in prehistoric Nubia. *Journal of Human Evolution 3*:405-410.
Cassel, J.
1976 The contribution of the social environment to host resistance. *American Journal of Epidemiology 104(2)*:107-123.
Cohen, J.
1974 *Population differences in dental morphology viewed in terms of high and low heritability.* Paper presented at the annual meetings of the American Association of Physical Anthropologists, Amherst.
Conrad, L., and Alan Harn
1972 The Spoon River culture in the central Illinois Valley. Ms. on file, Dickson Mounds State Museum, Lewistown, Illinois.
Ditch, L., and J. Rose
1972 A mutivariate dental sexing technique. *American Journal Physical Anthropology 37(1)*:61-64.
Dubos, R.
1965 *Mankind adapting.* Yale University Press, New Haven.
Fowler, M. L.
1969 The Cahokia site. In Investigations in Cahokia archeology, edited by M. Fowler. *Illinois Archeology Survey Bulletin* No. 7.
1978 Cahokia in the American Bottom: Settlement archeology. In *Mississippian settlement patterns*, edited by B. Smith, pp. 455-477. Academic Press, New York.
Garn, S. M., F. N. Silverman, K. P. Hertzog, and C. G. Rohman
1968 Lines and bands of increased density: Their implication to growth and development. *Medical Radiography and Photography 44*:58-89.
Goodman, A.
1980 Polynomial regressions of dental age with long bone length for Dickson Mounds subadults. Ms. on file, Department of Anthropology, University of Massachusetts, Amherst.
Goodman, A. H., and G. R. Clark
1981 Harris lines as indicators of stress in prehistoric Illinois

populations. In Biocultural adaptation: Comprehensive approaches to skeletal analysis, edited by D. L. Martin and M. P. Bumstead, pp. 35-46. *Department of Anthropology University of Massachusetts Amherst Research Reports* No. 20.

Gustav, B.
1972 *Sexual dimorphism in the adult bony pelivis of a prehistoric human population from Illinois.* Ph.D. dissertation, Department of Anthropology, University of Massachusetts, Amherst.

Harn, A.
1971 *The prehistory of Dickson Mounds: A preliminary report.* Illinois State Museum, Springfield.
1978 Mississippian settlement patterns in the central Illinois River Valley. In *Mississippian settlement patterns*, edited by B. Smith, pp. 233-268. Academic Press, New York.
1980 The prehistory of Dickson Mounds: The Dickson excavation. *Illinois State Museum Report* No. 36.
n.d. The archeology of Dickson Mounds. Ms. on file, Dickson Mounds Museum, Lewistown, Illinois.

Hinkle, L. E.
1974 The effect of exposure to cultural change, social change and changes in interpersonal relationships on health. In *Stressful life events: Their nature and effects*, edited by B. S. Dohrenwend and B. P. Dohrenwend, pp. 9-44. Wiley, New York.

Huss-Ashmore, R., A. H. Goodman, and G. J. Armelagos
1982 Nutritional inference from paleopathology. In *Advances in archeological method and theory*, Vol. 5, edited by M. Schiffer, pp. 395-474. Academic Press, New York.

Kreshover, S.
1960 Metabolic disturbances in tooth formation. *Annals of the New York Academy of Science 85*:161-167.

Krogman, W.
1962 *The human skeleton in forensic medicine.* Thomas, Springfield.

Lallo, J.
1973 *The skeletal biology of three prehistoric American Indian societies from Dickson Mounds.* Ph.D. dissertation, Department of Anthropology, University of Massachusetts, Amherst.

Lallo, J., G. J. Armelagos, and R. P. Mensforth
1977 The role of diet, disease and physiology in the origin of porotic hyperostosis. *Human biology 49*(3):471-483.

Lallo, J., G. J. Armelagos, and J. C. Rose
1978 Paleoepidemiology of infectious disease in the Dickson Mounds population. *Medical College of Virginia Quarterly 14(1)*:17-23.

Lallo, J., J. C. Rose, and G. J. Armelagos
1980 An ecological interpretation of variation in mortality within three prehistoric American Indian populations from

Dickson Mounds. In Prehistoric North Americans, edited by D. Bowman, pp. 203-238. Moulton, The Hague.

McHenry, H.
1968 Transverse lines in long bones in prehistoric California Indians. *American Journal of Physical Anthropology 29:* 1-17.

McKern, T. W., and T. D. Stewart
1957 Skeletal age changes in young American males. The technical report. The Quartermaster Research and Development Command, Natick, Massachusetts.

Mensforth, R. P., C. O. Lovejoy, J. W. Lallo, and G. J. Armelagos
1978 The role of constitutional factors, diet, and infectious disease in the etiology of porotic hyperostosis and periosteal reactions in prehistoric infants and children. *Medical Anthropology 2*:1-59.

Nichens, P.
1975 Paleoepidemiology of Mesa Verde Anasazi populations: Lines of increased density. Ms. on file, Department of Anthropology, University of Colorado, Boulder.

Park, E. A.
1964 The imprinting of nutritional disturbances on the growing bone. *Pediatrics 33* (Suppl.):815-862.

Rose, J. C., G. J. Armelagos, and J. W. Lallo
1978 Histological enamel indicators of childhood stress in prehistoric skeletal samples. *American Journal of Physical Anthropology 49*:511-516.

Sarnat, B. G., and I. Schour
1941 Enamel hypoplasia (chronic enamel aplasia) in relationship to systemic diseases: A chronological, morphologic and etiologic classification. *Journal of the American Dental Association 28*:1989-2000.

Schour, I., and M. Massler
1944 Development of the human dentition. The American Dental Association, Chicago.
1945 The effects of dietary deficiencies upon oral structures. *Journal of the American Dental Association 32*:871-879.

Scrimshaw, N.
1964 Ecological factors in nutritional disease. *American Journal of Clinical Nutrition 14*:112-122.

Selye, H.
1976 *Stress in health and disease.* Buttersworth, Boston.

Siegel, S.
1956 *Nonparametric statistics for the behavioral sciences.* McGraw-Hill, New York.

Stini, W. A.
1969 Nutritional stress and growth: Sex differences in adaptive response. *American Journal of Physical Anthropology 31*: 417-426.

Todd, T. W.
1937 *Atlas of skeletal maturation.* Mosby, St. Louis.

Van Gerven, D.
1972 *Skeletal dimorphism in the adult femur*. Ph.D. dissertation, University of Massachusetts, Amherst.

Weiss, K.
1973 Demographic models for anthropology. *Society for American Archeology Memoirs* No. 27.

Wells, C.
1967 A new approach to paleopathology: Harris lines. In *Disease in antiquity*, edited by D. R. Brothwell and A. T. Sandison, pp. 390-404. Thomas, Springfield.

Woodall, J.
1968 Growth arrest lines in long bones of the Cases Grandes population. *Plains Anthropology 13*:152-160.

CHAPTER 12

SKELETAL EVIDENCE FOR PREHISTORIC SUBSISTENCE ADAPTATION IN THE CENTRAL OHIO RIVER VALLEY

Claire Monod Cassidy

Division of Behavioral and Social Sciences
Department of Anthropology
University of Maryland

The central Ohio River Valley is important for the analysis of the relationship between prehistoric subsistence and health because the area is ecologically rich and was steadily utilized in prehistoric times, because it seems to have been the point of origin for the earliest practice of agriculture in eastern North America, and because a large number of sites have been dug and at least partially analyzed.[1]

In this chapter I consider skeletal and dietary evidence from three archaeological culture periods: the *Archaic* (about 7500-2250 B.P.); *Adena* (early to middle Woodland, about 3000-1750 B.P.); and *Fort Ancient* (Mississippian, about 1250-275 B.P.). Geographically the analysis is limited to selected sites in Kentucky and contiguous or culturally related areas of western Tennessee and southeastern Ohio (Figure 12.1).

Because the developmental questions we pose cannot be analyzed *in situ* at any one site in the region, conclusions are drawn from cross-comparisons among sites. This procedure is reliable because the region is environmentally homogeneous and because populations are genetically also quite homogeneous. Thus observed health changes can appropriately be explained primarily in terms of changing cultural-subsistence variables. Existing data permit this analysis to cover nearly 6000 years.

[1] *Many Kentucky sites were excavated before 1950; the site reports often lack quantitative and population perspectives or analytic interest in skeletal pathology or subsistence mode, limiting their utility for the present analysis. Brose (1973) and Schwartz (1967) discuss the historical development of archaeological method relevant to the central Ohio River Valley.*

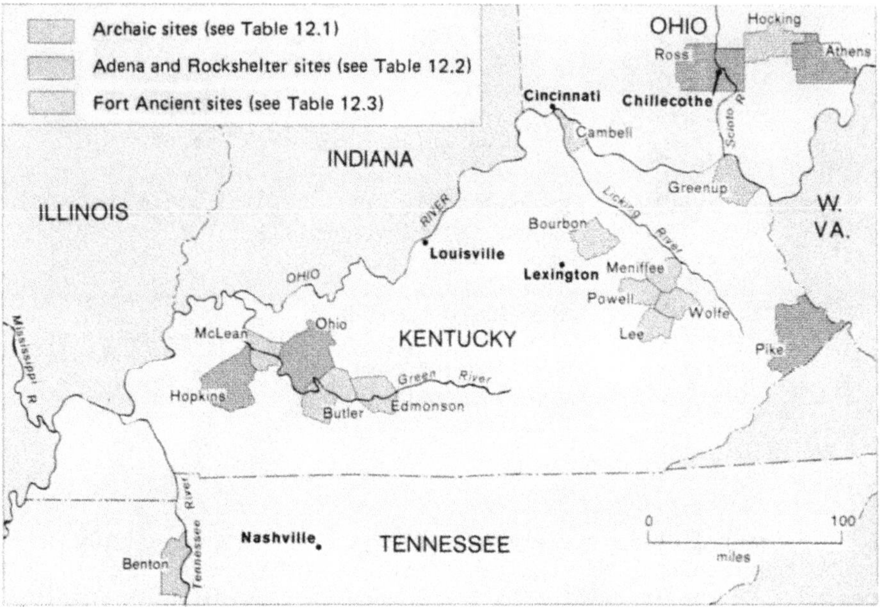

FIGURE 12.1. Selected central Ohio River Valley archaeological sites by county.

OVERVIEW OF ARCHAEOLOGICAL CULTURES, FOOD, AND DIET

The physical environment of the Kentucky region changed little from about 11,000 B.C. to the eighteenth century A.D., although slightly warmer and drier conditions existed during the Altithermal (5000-2500 B.C.; Rolingson 1964). Now-extinct large food mammals ("megafauna") disappeared between about 7500 and 4000 B.C. (Rolingson 1964). Afterward, food animals included deer, elk, and black bear, many smaller mammals, birds, turtles, fish, insects, snails, and mussels. Common wild plant foods included a large variety of fruits, berries, nuts, and seeds. Mesoamerican domesticates appeared individually over a long period, with gourd and pumpkin-squash being earliest, followed by corn and, only late, by beans. Indigenous domesticates such as sunflower and marsh elder appeared as early as 2000 B.C., but may have had a limited distribution.

The *Paleoindian* period (about 13,000-?6000 B.P.; Rolingson 1964) is primarily known through surface collections of projectile points. Paleoindians inhabited the northern and western areas of the state, near the major rivers. They hunted and gathered, depending on the megafauna for food.

The *Archaic* period (ca. 8000-2500 B.P., overlapping the Early Woodland, but ceasing by 4000-3000 B.P. in some areas) begins with the extinction of the megafauna and ends, by definition, with the advent of pottery. Archaic people were efficient gatherer-hunters, and by the late Archaic they had a food base sufficient to support considerable leisure and sedentism, increasing populations, and increasing ceremonialism (Brown 1977; Caldwell 1958, 1962; Jennings 1974; Winters 1968). They stored large amounts of food, and they may have begun the process of domestication by gathering and storing wild grains for winter use, or by protecting the reproductive capacities of wild foods.

The best-known expression of the Archaic in Kentucky is the mid- to late date Green River complex, typified by deep shell-filled mounds along river banks in the western part of Kentucky (Table 12.1). Winters (1969) argued convincingly for a settlement pattern consisting of repeatedly used large winter "settlements" and summer "basecamps" and briefly used special purpose camps.

It is difficult to estimate population densities for Archaic groups either regionally or within sites, although site frequencies increase over time and there are large numbers of flexed pit burials in middens. Winters' (1969) settlement analysis yields an estimate of 100 persons in winter settlements. Based on exhaustive analysis of trade and local artifacts in burials, Winters (1968) argues for an egalitarian society.

The quantities of mussel shell at larger sites indicate that bivalves were an important food. Specialists are divided as to whether mussels were a valued and high-quality food pivotal for supporting sedentism (Webb 1946; Webb and Haag 1940; Winters 1969), or a food used mainly in times of hunger (Lewis and Kneberg-Lewis 1961; Perzigian 1977). Another possibility is that mussels were used when available but that changes in river levels periodically drowned the beds, forcing reliance on other resources (Lewis and Kneberg-Lewis 1961). Shell Mound people also utilized deer and wild plant foods; cup mortars and pestles for grinding nuts and perhaps wild grains are abundant at the sites.

At the related Eva site in western Tennessee, subsistence emphases appear to have shifted from deer in the early phase to mussels in the second phase, and to nuts and other vegetable foods in the third phase. Lewis and Kneberg-Lewis view the late shift as a response to the loss of mussels due to bed flooding, and of deer due to over-hunting. However, this phase verges on or overlaps the early Woodland period, which seems everywhere characterized by reliance on plant foods. At other Archaic sites such as those at Fishtrap Reservoir, deer were preferred and mussels were unimportant (Dunnell 1966).

The *Woodland* period followed directly out of the Archaic (Brown 1977; Dragoo 1976; Jennings 1974; Morgan 1952), with early sites closely resembling Archaic sites but for the presence of pottery. Archaic tendencies towards sedentism, population increase, and specialized burial practices continued in this period. Subsistence practices appear to become increasingly focal

TABLE 12.1 Central Ohio River Valley Archaic Sites Discussed in This Chapter

Archaeological culture period	Site name	Location	Radiocarbon dates[a] B.P.	Food remains[b]	Human remains[c]
Archaic					
Green River Complex	Chiggerville[d] (Newton Brown)	Ohio County, Ky.		(+)	114 skeletons; npa
	Cypress Creek[e]	McLean County, Ky.		+	Ward: 433 skeletons; npa Kirkland: 73 skeletons; npa
	Indian Knoll[f]	Ohio County, Ky.	5302 ± 300[m] 4112 ± 300[m]	+	1234 skeletons; pa (Table 12.5)
	Barrett[g] and Butterfield	McLean County, Ky.		(+)	Barrett: 412 skeletons; npa Butterfield: 153 skeletons; npa
	Carlson Annis[h]	Butler County, Ky.	4250 ± 80[n] 4040 ± 180[n] 5149 ± 300[m] 2336 ± 250[m] 7374 ± 500[m] 4900 ± 250[m] 4311 ± 300[m]	(+)	390 skeletons, not preserved, npa
	Read[i]	Butler County Ky.		(+)	247 skeletons; npa
	Parrish[j]	Hopkins County, Ky.		(+)	133 skeletons; npa

Eva, Three Mile, Big Sandy Phases	Eva[k]	Benton County, Tenn.	7150 ± 500[o]	+	180 skeletons; pl
Sloane, Thacker, Sims Creek Phases	Fishtrap Reservoir[l]	Pike County, Ky.	3840 ± 120[l] 1530 ± 105[l]	(+)	28 skeletons; npa

[a]Footnotes to site dates refer to publication source for date, wherein find discussions of validity-interpretation.

[b]Key: +: Quantified food data for site. (+): Descriptive (listing) food data for site.

[c]Key: pa: pathological analysis (population perspective) of skeletons; pl: pathology listing for skeletons; npa: no pathological analysis (metric analyses exist for some sites).

[d]Moore 1916; Webb and Haag 1939 (physical anthropology by Ivar Skarland).

[e]Webb and Haag 1940 (physical anthropology by C. Snow).

[f]Moore 1916; Leigh 1925; Rabkin 1943; Webb 1946 (animal bone analysis by Opal Skaggs); Snow 1948; Johnston and Snow 1961; Sarnas 1964; Winters 1968, 1969; Cook 1971; Cassidy 1972, 1980a; Perzigian 1973, 1977; Sciulli 1977, 1978.

[g]Webb and Haag 1947a (physical anthropology by C. Snow).

[h]Webb 1950a (physical anthropology by C. Snow); Marquardt and Watson 1974. Other spellings include Carlton Annis, Carlston Annis, Annis.

[i]Webb 1950b (physical anthropology by C. Snow).

[j]Webb 1951 (physical anthropology by C. Snow).

[k]Lewis and Kneberg 1959; Lewis and Kneberg-Lewis 1961; Winters 1969.

[l]Dunnell 1966.

[m]Webb and Baby 1957.

[n]Marquardt and Watson 1974.

[o]Lewis and Kneberg 1959.

TABLE 12.2 Central Ohio River Valley Woodland Sites Discussed in This Chapter

Archaeological culture period	Site name	Location	Radiocarbon dates[a] B.P.	Food remains[b]	Human remains[c]
Adena (Early Woodland)	Pooled data, many sites[d]	Ohio, Kentucky, some W. Va. and Pa.		+	several hundred skeletons and cremations; pl
	Caldwells's Little Bluff[e]	Ross County, Ohio		(+)	2 skeletons; pl
	Daines Mounds[f]	Athens County, Ohio	2230 ± 140[o]	+	7 skeletons; npa
	Rock Riffle Run Mound[g]	Athens County, Ohio		(+)	8 skeletons, 2 cremations; pl
Rockshelter sites, attributed to Adena	Red Eye Hollow, etc.[h]	Lee County, Ky.		(+)	16 skeletons, not preserved; npa
	Multiple sites[i]	Wolfe and Powell counties, Ky.		+	'some'; npa
	Newt Kash Hollow, etc.[j]	Menifee County, Ky.	2600 ± 300[p]	+	'some'; npa
	Mammoth Cave, Salts Cave, etc.[k]	Edmonson County, Ky.	2250 ± 65[k]	+	2 mummies, 41 fragmentary skeletons, feces; pa
	Dameron[l]	Johnson County, Ky.	2070 ± 80[l] 1070 ± 90[l] 2355 ± 65[l]	+	1 skeleton; pl

Middle Woodland	Haystack[m]	Powell County, Ky.	1470 ± 65[m]	+	None
			1415 ± 60[m]		
			1485 ± 55[m]		
			1345 ± 60[m]		
			1245 ± 60[m]		
Late Woodland	Chesser Cave[n]	Athens County, Ohio	880 ± 140[n]	+	None

[a]Footnotes to site dates refer to publication source for date, wherein find discussions of validity-interpretation.

[b]Key: +: Quantified food data for site. (+): Descriptive (listing) food data for site.

[c]Key: pa: pathological analysis (population perspective) of skeletons; pl: pathology listing for skeletons. npa: no pathological analysis (metric analyses exist for some sites).

[d]Webb and Snow 1945; Webb and Baby 1957; Dragoo 1963; Murphy 1975. For specific Kentucky sites see Funkhouser and Webb 1935; Webb and Funkhouser 1940; Webb 1940, 1941a,b, 1942, 1943a,b; Webb and Elliott 1942; Webb & Haag 1947b.

[e]Prufer and McKenzie 1975.

[f]Murphy 1975.

[g]Murphy 1975.

[h]Funkhouser and Webb 1929.

[i]Funkhouser and Webb 1930.

[j]Webb and Funkhouser 1936; Jones 1936. For plant remains also see Goslin 1957; Yarnell 1964, 1965; Streuver and Vickery 1973; Asch and Asch 1977.

[k]Nelson 1917; Watson 1974 (physical anthropology by Robbins, Molnar and Ward; parasites by Dusseau and Porter, Fry; food remains by Stewart, Yarnell). For plant remains also see Yarnell 1964, 1965; Streuver and Vickery 1973; Asch and Asch 1977.

[l]Vento et al. 1980 (physical anthropology by D. Dirkmaat).

[m]Cowan 1979.

[n]Prufer and McKenzie 1975.

[o]Streuver and Vickery 1973; Murphy 1975.

[p]Webb and Baby 1957.

(Streuver and Vickery 1973). In the central Ohio River Valley this period demonstrates two regional cultural climaxes, the *Adena*, focused within a 150-mile radius of Chillecothe, Ohio, and the *Hopewell* (see Perzigian et al., Chapter 13 this volume). These existed from perhaps 1000 B.C. to A.D. 600, with Adena slightly predating and predeceasing Hopewell. Alongside these climaxes a simpler, much less known, Woodland culture persisted (Cowan 1979; Jennings 1974; Prufer and McKenzie 1975).

The Adena culture (Dragoo 1963; Webb and Baby 1957; Webb and Snow 1945) is distinguished by the production of large earthworks, and conical burial mounds containing both cremations, and extended burials in log, bark, or clay tombs. No complete Adena village has been excavated. Rockshelters and cave sites in Kentucky, considered Adenan by Webb and Snow (1945) and Webb and Baby (1957), provide the best evidence on Adena dietary patterns. The frequency of Adena sites, both mounds and rockshelters (Table 12.2), attests to population growth in this period, but population estimates must await the excavation of undoubted Adena village sites.

Adena burial mounds yield few or no food remains. Burial artifacts suggest various animals, mussels, and nuts were consumed. The occasional presence of hoes and spades early led Webb and Funkhouser to argue that Adenans practiced a simple agriculture. Subsequently gourd, pumpkin-squash, chenopodium, and a single corncob have been found at Adena sites in Ohio (Murphy 1975; Streuver and Vickery 1973; Yarnell 1964).

The rockshelter and cave sites in Kentucky contain well-preserved vegetable food remains that provide evidence for an independent eastern North American development of agriculture based on indigenous cultigens (Asch and Asch 1977; Goslin 1957; Jones 1936; Streuver and Vickery 1973; Yarnell 1964, 1965, 1974). Sometimes called the "Eastern Agricultural Complex," this independent development dates to as early as 700 B.C. and includes as definite cultigens two Mesoamerican plants, gourd and squash-pumpkin, and two "weedy" North American plants, sunflower and marsh elder. Less certainly cultivated but part of the complex are chenopodium, amaranth, canary grass, smartweed, and giant ragweed.

The use of these plants for food is confirmed by the finding of their seeds in feces, as at Mammoth and Salts caves. Many wild plants were also in use, particularly nuts. At Salts Cave 65-80% of fecal bulk was plant food remains, especially marsh elder, sunflower, and hickory nut (Stewart 1974). Approximately 77% of the total was cultivated. Animals made only a small contribution to diet. Watson (1974) concludes that the Salts Cave people were primarily vegetarians, and that cultivated seeds of the Eastern Agricultural Complex, with hickory nuts, made up most of their diet. The seeds were evidently gathered in fall and stored over the winter, for feces containing both fall seeds and remains of perishable spring fruits were found at Salts Cave.

Not all Adena sites contain cultigens, nor are all sites containing indigenous domesticates culturally Adena. For example, Adena components at the Dameron and Sparks rockshelters (Vento et al. 1980), contain *no* cultigens. However, the Middle Woodland (non-Adena) Haystack rockshelters (Cowan 1979) contain both wild plants and indigenous cultigens, showing that the latter continued to be used after the Adena period. Corn was not an important cultigen in Adena and Middle Woodland times despite its occasional appearance in sites (Streuver and Vickery 1973). However, by the Late Woodland the better adapted northern flint variety of corn (Galinat 1965) was becoming widespread.

The next cultural climax in the central Ohio River Valley region is the *Mississippian*, represented by the regional variant *Fort Ancient* (about A.D. 950-1675), (Griffin 1943, 1967; Prufer and Shane 1970). Fort Ancient people lived in permanent villages, often fortified, with central plazas and platform mounds. Burial was in mounds and beside houses. Fort Ancient disappears as a distinct culture at the beginning of the historic period, apparently without the people having experienced direct contact with Europeans (Hanson 1968; Prufer and Shane 1970).

Growing population densities characterize the Fort Ancient period. Blain Village, a small early site, may have contained 100-400 people (Prufer and Shane 1970); Cassidy (1980a) estimates that Hardin Village, a late site, initially contained just over 100 people and by abandonment 150 years later contained over 350. Sites are numerous along the rivers, so populations in the range of tens of thousands may have existed.

Scholars question whether Fort Ancient represents an influx of people carrying Mesoamerican ideas, or is a local development influenced by the diffusion of ideas, not people, from outside (Murphy 1975; Prufer and Shane 1970; Robbins and Neumann 1972). The weight of evidence[2] seems to favor genetic continuity and an indigenous development for Fort Ancient.

There is no strict dividing line between Fort Ancient and earlier periods in terms of foods, because dependence on corn agriculture apparently occurs in the late Woodland. However, Fort Ancient people (Table 12.3) seem to have intensified a bottomland agriculture (Dunnell 1966) focusing heavily on corn, beans, and

[2]*Prufer and Shane (1970) argue on archaeological grounds that some human influx may have occurred early in Fort Ancient times in the Scioto Valley. Robbins and Neumann (1972) measured skeletons and found, in contrast, that indigenes of the "Ilinid" type were in Ohio and most of Kentucky during most of the Fort Ancient period, and only late did southern "Muskogid" peoples enter northern Kentucky and nearby Ohio. Murphy (1975), also favoring indigenous development, noted that corn arrived well before the Mississippian period and that Late Woodland villages show many typical Fort Ancient characteristics.*

TABLE 12.3 Central Ohio River Valley Fort Ancient Sites Discussed in This Chapter

Archaeological culture period	Site name	Location	Radiocarbon dates[a] B.P.	Food Remains[b]	Human remains[c]
Fort Ancient (Mississippian)	Pooled data, many sites[d]	Ohio, Ky.		(+)	many skeletons, npa or pl
	Blain Village[e]	Ross County, Ohio	(AD 970–1225)[e]	+	8 skeletons, pl
	Graham Village[f]	Hocking County, Ohio	770 ± 145[f] (AD 1180)	+	1 skeleton; npa
	Gabriel[g]	Athens County, Ohio	550 ± 155[g] (AD 1450)	+	none
	McCune[g]	Athens County, Ohio	630 ± 100[g] (AD 1320)	+	2 skeletons, pl
	Fishtrap Reservoir, Woodside Phase[h]	Pike County, Ky.	479 ± 125[h] (AD 1471)	(+)	none
	Bintz[i]	Campbell County, Ky.		(+)	none
	Buckner[j]	Bourbon County, Ky.		-	78 skeletons, pl

Hardin Village[k]	Greenup County, Ky.	(AD 1550-1675)[l]	(+)	296 skeletons; pa

[a]Footnotes to site dates refer to publication source for date, wherein find discussions of validity-interpretation.

[b]Key: +: Quantified food data for site; (+): Descriptive (listing) food data for site.

[c]Key: pa: pathological analysis (population perspective) of skeletons; pl: pathology listing for skeletons; npa: no pathological analysis (metric analyses exist for some sites).

[d]Mills 1906; Smith 1910; Hooton and Willoughby 1920; Beckner 1926; Webb and Funkhouser 1928; Griffin 1943; Robbins and Neumann 1972.

[e]Prufer and Shane 1970; see their discussion of radiocarbon date interpretation. Also see Schambach 1971.

[f]Prufer and McKenzie 1975.

[g]Murphy 1975.

[h]Dunnell 1966.

[i]MacCord 1953.

[j]Robbins 1971; archaeology unpublished.

[k]Hanson 1968; Cassidy 1972, 1980a.

[l]Hanson 1968.

TABLE 12.4 *Changes in Dietary Emphasis Traceable in the Central Ohio River Valley*

	Population Size			
	Low	Rising	Rising	Highest
Selected Foodstuffs				
Deer	Heavy	Medium	Medium	Light
Mussels	Light	Heavy	Present	Light
Nuts and Other Wild Plant Foods	Medium	Medium	Heavy	Light
Sunflower, Marshelder and Other Indigenous Cultigens	Absent	Absent	Heavy	Absent?
Gourd and Squash	Absent	Absent	Light	Medium
Corn and Beans	Absent	Absent	Present	Heavy

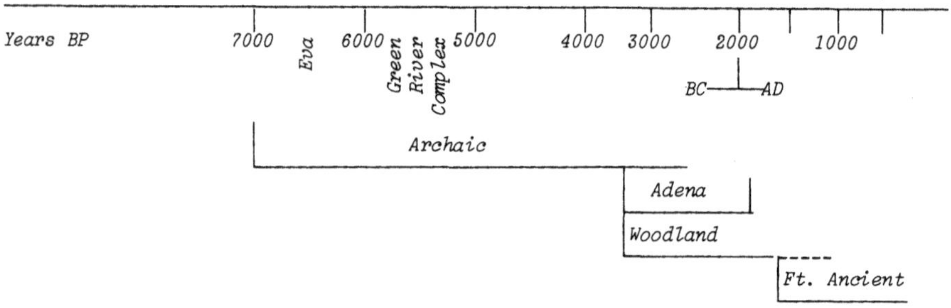

squash. A seasonal hunting pattern continued but was apparently inefficient and was based quite narrowly on deer and perhaps elk. Wild plant foods and mussels continued to be used.

Much of the evidence for intensive corn agriculture is indirect, for few actual cobs have been found. Thus although archaeologists are united in their belief that Fort Ancient people depended on corn, excavations have not actually demonstrated the proportions in which Fort Ancient people used their various foods.

Diet

Although the record is clouded by problems of preservation, recovery, and quantification of food remains, several trends can be distinguished (Table 14.4):

1. Although wild foods were used throughout the prehistoric period, as time passed there was conversion from a broad to narrow subsistence focus. This shift correlated with increasing population densities, sedentism, and cultural elaboration, but the causative relationships are obscure.

2. The Indians seem to have altered econiches to increase the extent or frequency of desired ones, as to favor weedy plants (Brown 1977; Dunnell 1966; Streuver and Vickery 1973) or deer ("semidomestication," Hudson 1976).

3. Hunting was practiced throughout the period; deer was the preferred animal. The dietary importance of animals apparently declined as earlier efficient broad-spectrum seasonal exploitation slowly transformed to a narrow ecozone focus using inefficient hunting techniques. By late prehistoric times, deer (and other animals) were merely supplementary to a cultivated grain-legume diet.

4. A wide variety of wild plant foods was utilized throughout the period; they made an important contribution to diet at least until Fort Ancient times.

5. Two climaxes occurred with regard to the use of cultivated foods, with an early, largely indigenous set of cultigens appearing in Late Archaic-Early Woodland times and being heavily utilized into the Middle Woodland; and with a well-adapted northern flint corn arriving in Middle Woodland times, followed by beans, so that from the Late Woodland and clearly during Fort Ancient times, subsistence depended on Mesoamerican cultigens.[3]

The lack of plant food evidence from the Archaic may result as much from the fact that sites were excavated before flotation technique was known as to actual low use of plant foods by these people. Whatever the case, their diets traditionally have been visualized as high in animal protein. After the Archaic, diets were increasingly vegetarian, first based in wild foods and indigenous cultigens, and later in Mesoamerican cultigens.

[3]*The dietary and subsistence trends, including the use of cultigens, seem to have been utilized by* ***all*** *of the people in the region, and not just by those who participated in climax cultures. Although archaeological materials are adequate to analyze the relationship of subsistence and health diachronically (as herein), a "best test" of the problem would include a synchronic analysis, that is, comparison of health parameters between climax and non-climax sites (= peoples) of the same date. Such an analysis would help clarify the specific relationship of cultural complexity to health. More non-climax regional sites must be excavated before such an analysis can be performed.*

TABLE 12.5 *Health Indicators for Indian Knoll and Hardin Village Sites*[a]

Health Indicators	Indian Knoll N = 295	Hardin Village N = 296	Statistical Significance of Site Differences
Demographics			
Percentage of all deaths			
0–48 months	32.6[b]	33.1	ns
0–12 months	22.8[c]	13.2	not calc
13–48 months	9.8[d]	19.9	
Percentage of deaths in childhood (≤ 17)	44.6[e]	53.7	$p \leq .05$
Percentage of childhood deaths			
0–48 months	65.8	73.2	ns
0–12 months	70.0	40.0	
13–48 months	30.0	60.0	$p \leq .001$
Percentage of deaths 40+ years	16.2[f]	5.7	not calc
Life expectancy			
Birth, years	m 21.84; f 17.92	m 16.10; f 17.15	
Year 4.5	m 26.44; f 23.48	m 19.32; f 20.72	
Year 15	m 20.27; f 18.08	m 14.10; f 15.94	
Year 35	m 13.05; f 12.10	m 7.38; f 9.55	
Dental Health—Adult			
Mean number caries/mouth	m 0.73; f 0.91; ns	m 6.74; f 8.51; S[h]	S[i]
Percentage of mouths w/apical abscesses	m 28.7; f 33.3; ns	m 25.0; f 18.3; ns	ns
Mean number apical abscesses/mouth	m 2.02; f 1.52; ns	m 1.52; f 0.60; ns	S[j]
Percentage of mouths w/inflammations	m 6.9; f 7.2; ns	m 11.5; f 13.3; ns	ns
Mean number inflammations/mouth	m 0.75; f 0.52; ns	m 0.75; f 1.08; ns	ns
Mean number pulp exposures/mouth	m 2.16; f 1.34; ns	m 0.49; f 1.14; ns	S[k]

Dental Health--Child ($\leq$17)			
Mean number caries/mouth	*0.0*	*ad 3.74; mid 5.6; early 2.34*	*
Percentage of mouths w/apical abscesses	*0.0*	*0.0*	
Percentage of mouths w/inflammations	*0.0*	*ad 0.0; mid 5.6; early 0.0*	*
Percentage of mouths w/pulp exposures	*0.0*	*ad 4.3; mid 0.0; early 5.1*	*
Diseases[g]			
Percentage w/osteoporosis symmetrica or cribra orbitalia (anemia)	*(see text)*	*8.2*	
Percentage of adults w/vertebral arthritis	*58.5*	*44.3*	*ns*
Percentage of adults w/severe vertebral arthritis	*13.9*	*9.5*	*ns*
Percentage w/vertebral arthritis, years			
17–29	*m 34.6; f 28.6*	*m 18.5; f 30.8*	
30–39	*m 47.4; f 40.0*	*m 36.8; f 42.9* } $p \leq .05$	*ns*
40+	*m 84.8; f 80.0*	*m 52.4; f 75.8*	
Percentage w/joint arthritis, years			
17–29	*m 7.7; f 0.0*	*m 0.0; f 11.5*	
30–39	*m 0.0; f 0.0*	*m 15.8; f 14.3* } *ns*	*ns*
40+	*m 23.9; f 33.3*	*m 19.1; f 33.3*	
Percentage w/bone infections, all ages	*24.1*	*23.9*	*ns*
Percentage of children w/bone infections	*2.4*	*10.5*	$p \leq .02$
Percentage w/disseminated periosteal reactions syndrome, all ages	*2.4*[k]	*31.4*[k]	$p \leq .001$
Percentage w/long bone fractures, all ages	*9.4*	*5.7*	*ns*

(Continued)

Table 15.5 (Continued)

Health Indicators	Indian Knoll N = 295	Hardin Village N = 296	Statistical Significance of Site Differences
Other Health Indicators			
Mean number growth arrest lines/tibia	11.3 (R = 2 - 25)	4.1 (R = 0 - 18)	
Percentage w/lineal enamel hypoplasia, adult C, all ages and degrees	m 86.5; f 86.0; ns; ad 93.8	m 91.9; f 73.0; ns; ad 91.3	ns
Percentage with severe LEH only	m 2.1; f 2.3; ns; ad 18.8	m 13.5; f 8.1; ns; ad 4.3	$p \leq .05$
Percentage w/LEH, M3, all degrees	m 11.5; f 7.0; ns	m 13.5; f 16.2; ns	ns
Percentage LEH deciduous incisors	0.0	9.1	*
Percentage LEH deciduous canines and molars	0.0	12.1	*
Mean value cortical index, 17-29	m 51; f 51	m 37; f 37	m: $p \leq .01$; f: $p \leq .01$
Mean value cortical index, 30-49	m 47: f 36	m 37; f 33	m: $p \leq .01$; f: ns

[a]Source: Cassidy 1972; random sample of University of Kentucky Indian Knoll collections, entire Hardin Village sample. Key: m = male; f = female; ad = adolescent 12-16 years; mid = mid-childhood 6-11 years; early = early childhood 0-5 years; S* = Statistically significant, see indicated footnote; ns = not statistically significant; not calc = not calculated; * = indicator value zero at one site so statistical tests cannot be performed.

[b]Snow (1948) in the total sample of 1234 skeletons found 27.1% died in the first 48 months.

[c]Snow (1948) divided the skeletons into 'newborn and a few months' = 6.2% and 'infants to 3' = 21.0%. Johnston and Snow (1961) found 19.5% died in the first 12 months.

[d]Johnston and Snow (1961) found 9.6% of deaths in months 12-60; Cassidy (1972) found 10.9% in the same interval.

[e]Snow (1948) found 49.4% died under 17. Johnston and Snow (1961) found 41.4% died by age 14 and 48.1% by age 19.

[f] Johnston and Snow (1961) found 3.3% died over age 40; Snow (1948) found 4.9% died over age 36. Differences among authors are due mainly to differences in aging techniques used.

[g] In addition to diseases listed in table, Snow (1948) found rickets in one 8 months infant, 3 cases of kidney/bladder stones and many external auditory exostoses. Cassidy found 6.7% of adult males had exostoses so large as to nearly occlude the meatus.

[h] Hardin Village females had significantly more caries than Indian Knoll females for upper M3, all other upper teeth and lower molars; remaining lower teeth had no caries at Indian Knoll. Hardin Village males had significantly more caries than Indian Knoll males for all molars, C and P2; remaining teeth had no caries at Indian Knoll.

[i] Indian Knoll males and females had significantly more molar abscesses than Hardin Village males and females. At other tooth positions site differences are not statistically significant.

[j] Indian Knoll males had significantly more pulp exposures than Hardin Village males in upper M1, P12; Hardin Village males had no pulp exposures of upper M2, C, I1 and lower P1, I12; there were no significant differences in remainder. Hardin Village females had significantly more pulp exposures than Indian Knoll females at upper M3, lower P12, C, and no pulp exposures at upper and lower I1, and Indian Knoll females none at lower I12; remaining teeth were not significantly different in frequency of pulp exposures. Antemortem tooth loss is not age related at Hardin Village, but occurs mainly in the elderly at Indian Knoll. Indian Knoll males lost significantly more teeth antemortem than Indian Knoll females. Males at Indian Knoll and Hardin Village lost similar numbers of teeth antemortem; Hartin Village females lost significantly more teeth antemortem than Indian Knoll females. Relative tooth wear at Indian Knoll is "heavy"; at Hardin Village "moderate."

[k] "Possible" cases accounted for an additional 3.1% at Indian Knoll and 6.1% at Hardin Village.

SKELETAL PATHOLOGY

Only four sites in the Kentucky region have been well analyzed for pathology. Our knowledge of the Archaic is too dependent on Indian Knoll, whereas numerous skeletons from other sites, including Eva, have not been adequately analyzed. Hundreds of Fort Ancient skeletons exist, and though measured (Robbins and Neumann 1972) are not yet analyzed. The exception is Hardin Village (Cassidy 1972). A similar situation exists for Adena, which is additionally handicapped by the complexity of burial modes and their interpretation.

Archaic: Indian Knoll Site

Because little is known of the stratigraphy, all Indian Knoll skeletons must be treated as one Archaic population despite artifactual evidence of brief Early Woodland site use. Social stratification does not seem to have affected burial patterns, so subsamples can reflect the whole population.

Demographics of Health

Cassidy (1972; Table 12.5) found 13.3% of children died as newborns, 9.5% in the following 11+ months, and 9.7% in demographic years 2-4 (months 12-48). Only 1.8% died in the fifth year. Thus, the Indian Knoll population demonstrates a higher mortality rate in infants than in toddlers, a pattern like that of modern urban populations but unlike that of many modern peasant populations. The relatively high mortality rate in newborns may indicate some social mortality (infanticide). About 5% of the population survived past the age of 50 years. Life expectancies were lower for females than males at all ages.

Dental Health

Leigh (1925), Rabkin (1943), Snow (1948), Sarnas (1964) and Cassidy (1972), although working with different degrees of precision, found similar patterns of dental health. Briefly, caries were rare to absent in children and adolescents, and although they were widespread in the adult population, they were infrequent on a per-mouth basis (Table 12.5). Tooth wear occurred rapidly and was the main cause of pulp exposures, apical abscessing, and antemortem tooth loss, all of which primarily affected the older adults. Males and females demonstrated similar patterns of change, although males showed slightly higher rates of wear-related stress. Calculus was largely lacking; periodontitis infrequent. Sarnas attributed the high wear rates, coupled with lack of tooth cracks or enamel chips, to the presence of *finely ground* abrasives in the diet. This suggests much food was ground (in the nut-grain mortars?) rather than consumed unprocessed.

Bone Pathologies

Snow (1948) identified lumbar arthritis in 60% of adults and "collapsed" centra (L1-2) in 4.5%. Cassidy (1972) found increased frequency and severity of arthritis with age, three cases of healed compression fractures, and no significant difference in arthritis rates between the sexes. Snow believed both dental abscessing and arthritis to be infectious diseases, causatively linked. Inglemark et al. (1959) found an epidemiological correlation between vertebral arthritis and dental abscesses, but declined to make a causal link. Cassidy (1972) concluded that the main cause of arthritis at Indian Knoll was degeneration, not infection.

Osteoporosis symmetrica and cribra orbitalia, expressed respectively as rarefaction and other changes of the skull vault and as porous plaque formation in the orbits, are now considered expressions of long-standing iron deficiency (or other) anemia. In 1948 Snow identified pitting of vaults as "probably osteoporosis symmetrica," (p. 498) and said it was frequent and "evidence of some kind of dietary deficiency" (p. 498). Cassidy (1972) found mild pitting of the vault or (less often) porotic changes in the orbits in 31.7% of her sample. She concluded these changes were *not* classical osteoporosis symmetrica, and not pathological, and that anemia was not prevalent at Indian Knoll. Significantly, children under five, the group most likely to suffer iron deficiency anemia, had the lowest frequencies of change.

Cassidy classified localized inflammatory changes of bones which were not the result of trauma, congenital malformation, or degenerative disease as "infections." One-fourth of Indian Knollers showed evidence of such infections; only children under age six had none.

A syndrome of disseminated periosteal reactions, familiar to all students of Amerindian bones, affected 2.4% of skeletons, most ages, and both sexes (Cassidy 1972). This syndrome is probably a treponemal infection, possibly potentiated by malnutrition, but almost certainly is not venereal syphilis (although frequently and too casually given this designation. Snow, for example, identified four cases of "probably syphilis" at Indian Knoll). A comparison of the Indian Knoll rate to that at Hardin Village shows the former rate was quite low.

Other Evidence of Health Status

The mean number of growth arrest lines/tibia was 11.3, suggesting growth arrest in childhood was somewhat frequent (Cassidy 1972). Lines were distributed periodically, suggesting that their cause was a regularly recurring stress such as an annual hunger period.

Enamel hypoplasia of the adult canine (indicating growth arrest from about 4-5 months to 6-7 years) was frequent but usually mild. Third molars (growth arrest in mid-childhood) were less often affected. *No* deciduous teeth showed hypoplasia. These data suggest that growth arrest episodes *in utero* or in the first few months of life were unusual, growth arrest in the later months and early childhood was frequent but short-lived, and growth arrest in mid-childhood was infrequent and mild.

Cortical index values were similar to those found in modern urban populations for both younger and older individuals; females lost significantly more cortical bone with age than did males (Cassidy 1972). Perzigian (1973) found that bone demineralization rates were higher in Hopewell populations than at Indian Knoll. He believed that the Hopewell diet was superior to the Archaic diet, and concluded that bone demineralization rates are genetically controlled rather than environmentally responsive. In this opinion he differs from most students of the subject.

Perzigian (1977) found that Indian Knoll had more fluctuating asymmetry than several unrelated agricultural populations. Arguing that Indian Knoll also demonstrated other signs of poor nutritional status (quoting data from Cassidy 1972; Cook 1971), Perzigian concluded that Indian Knollers were less healthy because their diets were inferior to those of technologically more advanced people. Snow, citing high rates of infection (arthritis and dental abscesses) and nutritional deficiency (osteoporosis symmetrica), also concluded that Indian Knollers were not particularly healthy.

In contrast, other workers (cited above) have tended to find Indian Knollers quite healthy, both by within-site assessment and by between-site assessment. Their higher rates of wear-related stress beginning at earlier ages, suggest that males may have been more physically active than females. Similarities of disease experience for males and females provide supporting evidence for the archaeological proposal of an egalitarian society.

Other Archaic Sites

The partially analyzed teeth and skeletons from other Green River complex sites (Table 12.1) show many similarities to Indian Knoll. Among these sites, Eva perhaps most of all deserves reanalysis, for although 180 skeletons are reported, no full analysis was performed (Lewis and Kneberg-Lewis 1961). However, the authors did argue that the frequency of infant-toddler deaths in stratum II was significantly increased over frequencies in strata I and III. They speculated that increased dependence on mussels in stratum II may have caused lactation failure, lowered the age of weaning, and increased the "infant" (actually weanling) mortality rate.

Early Woodland: Adena

The pathological interpretation of skeletal material from Adena sites is complicated because (1) mound and rockshelter sites are only assumed to contain the same physical group, (2) Adenans used a wide range of burial practices and the social and health implications of these are uncertain, (3) most early skeletal analysis used techniques that probably yielded inaccurate sex and age distribution patterns, and (4) fragmentary skeletons were discarded (this includes most cave material), making reanalysis impossible.

Snow (Webb and Snow 1945) found that Adena mounds contained more males than females and more adults than children, while cave sites yielded only women and children (Funkhouser and Webb 1929, 1930; Webb and Funkhouser 1936).[4] Webb and his colleagues proposed that the rockshelters were the domain of women, while mound tombs housed the remains of upper class people, notably males. They proposed that Adenans had developed a stratified society; cremations within the mounds were those of commoners, and only the upper class practiced head deformation. They argued that since knowledge of pathology was limited to the upper classes, whatever was observed necessarily erred toward the healthy. Some have tended to utilize these arguments,[5] but I am inclined to believe that Adenan burial practices deserve thorough reexamination. It should be noted that, although the construction of a log tomb is expensive, the cost of cremation is even greater, for the number of *dried* logs necessary to reduce a fresh body to a lense of ashes (described in the various Adena sources) is much greater than the number of green (cheaper) logs needed to build a log tomb. In much of modern Asia only the most wealthy can afford the honor of cremation. Additionally, upper classes are not necessarily healthier than lower classes. For these several reasons, I herein treat the Adena mound "upper class" as *representative* of all Adenan people.

To summarize pathological data on mound materials (pooled data from H. T. E. Hertzberg or C. S. Snow reported in Webb and Snow 1945; also Funkhouser and Webb 1935; Webb 1940, 1941a,b, 1942, 1943a,b; Webb and Elliott 1942; Funkhouser 1940): Mild arthritis was reported at some *but not all* sites and was referred to as "common" (my calculations yield high values of 19 and 20%).

[4]*Male skeletons have been found at recently excavated rockshelter sites including Dameron (Vento et al. 1980) and Salts Cave (Watson 1974).*

[5]*For example, Lovejoy (1975) argues that two pit burials at Caldwell's Little Bluff, with undeformed heads, were therefore commoners. Sciulli (1978) worries that his finding of comparatively lower rates of linear enamel hypoplasia among Adenans may be an artifact of a population sample skewed toward the wealthy.*

Osteoporosis symmetrica was identified at most sites; it occurred at all ages but was most common in young adult males. The description and unusual age distribution could mean that these changes were not pathological. "Periostitis-osteitis" was absent at several sites and displayed frequencies of 2, 12.5, and 20% (my calculations) on small samples at other sites. Frequency on the pooled data was 3%; that is, the inflammatory changes were uncommon, although some sites showed elevated frequencies. (These changes, hesitantly ascribed to "syphilis" in the 1940s are presumably the same syndrome of disseminated periosteal reactions discussed above.) A possible case of tuberculosis was recorded at Ricketts Mound. Dental caries were absent or uncommon at most sites; Snow's pooled data record caries as occurring only in young adults (5.3%). Dental abscesses were uncommon in youth but the pooled data show 18.8% of adults up to age 35, and 11.1% of older adults, were affected.

No pathological data are available from rockshelters excavated prior to 1950. Skeletons from Caldwell's Little Bluff (*N* = 2 "commoners," Lovejoy 1975) and Dameron Rockshelter (*N* = 1, Vento et al. 1980) have no significant pathologies. Thirteen non-Adenan Woodland skeletons intrusive into the Hartman Mound (Webb 1943a) are pathologically indistinguishable from Adenans, possibly implying a lack of health differentials between Adenans and non-climax Woodland peoples.[3]

Sciulli compared linear enamel hypoplasia in Indian Knoll, Adena, and later samples, in deciduous (1977) and adult (1978) teeth. He found that "severe linear enamel hypoplasia...is found in every Amerindian group and is present at a significantly higher frequency in focal [=late] agricultural groups" (1978:193). A possible slight decline in frequency occurred in the Adena compared to both the preceding and succeeding periods. Adena males may have been more severely affected than females.

The Mammoth Cave Area

Salts Cave yielded 2 mummies and remnants of 41 skeletons (Robbins 1974). One male mummy, about 45, was unanalyzed. The other, a boy aged nine, may have died of an aortic rupture; he

[3]*The dietary and subsistence trends, including the use of cultigens, seem to have been utilized by all of the people in the region, and not just by those who participated in climax cultures. Although archaeological materials are adequate to analyze the relationship of subsistence and health diachronically (as herein), a "best test" of the problem would include a synchronic analysis, that is, comparison of health parameters between climax and non-climax sites (= peoples) of the same date. Such an analysis would help clarify the specific relationship of cultural complexity to health. More non-climax regional sites must be excavated before such an analysis can be performed.*

had no growth arrest lines and no signs of bone pathology. The 41 skeletons, represented by splintered and crushed bones, were too fragmentary for pathological analysis. Robbins suggested that the Salts people may have practiced culinary cannibalism. Molnar and Ward (1974) studied dental remains from 14 children and adolescents and concluded that the population was "rather healthy." Teeth displayed few enamel or dentine imperfections and none had caries. Dusseau and Porter (1974) found no parasites except one uncertain nonpathogenic nematode in 13 feces, while Fry (1974) found possible evidence of *Ascaris* infection in one case.

In summary, available data suggest that Adenans were relatively healthy, with low caries rates, low infection and arthritis rates, and moderate reported levels of possible osteoporosis symmetrica. There was some tendency for males to experience more pathologies than females, which may be an artifact of sample size or which may deserve a second look since the same pattern seems to characterize the later Hardin Village population.

Mississippian: Fort Ancient--Hardin Village Site

The late Fort Ancient site of Hardin Village existed for about 150 years and was abandoned about A.D. 1675 without contact with Europeans (Hanson 1966).

Demographics of Health

Among infants, 8.4% died as newborns and another 4.7% in the next 11+ months (Cassidy 1972; Table 12.5). From ages 2-4 years (12-48 months) almost one-fifth of the entire population died. Thus more children died in the weaning years than in infancy, a pattern resembling that of some modern peasant populations and arguing for nutritional deficiency (possibly associated with infections) during the weaning period. Only 1% of the population (3 females) survived more than 50 years. Life expectancies were higher for females than males at all ages, a reversal of the usual preindustrial pattern.

Dental Health

Caries were common to rampant at all ages after infancy (Table 12.5; for tooth by tooth analysis see Cassidy 1972). Caries were the main cause of pulp exposures and abscessing, which occurred even in children, and of antemortem tooth loss, which began in adolescence. Periodontitis was common in adults. Tooth wear was moderate; calculus deposition was often heavy. The pattern of wear and disease is very similar to that seen today in populations that consume highly processed carbohydrate diets and do not practice effective oral hygiene.

Bone Pathology

Vertebral arthritis, although increasing in frequency with age, also affected youth including adolescents aged 12-16 years (3 cases). These adolescents showed severe arthritic changes, also present in young adults aged 17-29 years. The distribution suggests that infection was a frequent cause of arthritic change in youth, and degeneration was an added cause with age.

Osteoporosis symmetrica and cribra orbitalia of classical character affected individuals of all ages but was commonest in children under six and women aged 30-39 years, age groups commonly affected by iron deficiency anemia, which was judged present at Hardin Village.

Bone infections affected one-fourth of the population, with males having insignificantly more; just over 10% of children were affected.

Disseminated periosteal reactions affected 31.4% of all skeletons. Eight persons had severe manifestations with large swellings, sinuses, and massive long-bone malformations; two were under age six. All postnatal ages were affected, and one possible case occurred among 13 fetuses. There were no sex differences in occurrence. This syndrome was so common at Hardin Village as to indicate the presence of a serious health stressor, most likely a treponemal infection, *not* identical with venereal syphilis, and probably potentiated by malnutrition (for metabolic cause argument see Robbins 1971).

Other Evidence of Health Status

The mean number of growth arrest lines was 4.1, and the lines were deposited at unequal intervals, suggesting their source in an unpredictable health stressor, such as infection.

Linear enamel hypoplasia occurred in both the permanent and deciduous dentitions. It was common in the adult dentitions and severe in 9.3% of adult canines. Six children had hypoplasia of the milk incisors, indicating growth arrest *in utero* or possibly premature birth. Eight children had hypoplasia of the milk canine and molars, indicating growth arrest within 6 months of birth. A conservative interpretation of these data suggest that mothers were seriously undernourished during and soon after birth, due to dietary malnutrition, infections, or both, and were unable to sustain steady growth in their infants.

Cortical thickness at Hardin Village was relatively low in young adults for both sexes; bone loss with age was slow for females and not apparent for males.

In summary, Hardin Villagers suffered from high rates of dental disease and numerous infections, and showed signs of malnutrition in the elevated toddler death rates, the presence of enamel hypoplasia in deciduous teeth, the low values of the cortical index, the presence of anemia, and the low life expectancies.

The overall picture at Hardin Village closely parallels that common in modern peasant villages in developing countries, particularly those dependent on a corn-beans diet (Cassidy 1972, 1980a). Sciulli (1977, 1978) made a similar argument for post-Hopewell groups in Ohio.

Limited pathological information on other Fort Ancient sites (Beckner 1926; Hooton and Willoughby 1920; Mills 1906; Prufer and Shane 1970; Robbins 1971; Smith 1910; Webb and Funkhouser 1928) closely matches the data on Hardin Village: high frequencies of caries, infection, trauma, disseminated periosteal reactions, and other disease.[6]

Comparison of Hardin Village and Indian Knoll

That Hardin Villagers were not particularly healthy is even more strongly demonstrated by their comparison to the relatively healthier Indian Knoll population (Table 12.5).

Dental caries, infectious arthritis, severe enamel hypoplasia, and the syndrome of disseminated periosteal reactions occurred significantly more often at Hardin Village. Anemia was positively identified only at Hardin Village. Hypoplasia of the deciduous dentition was seen only at Hardin Village. Hypoplasia of the permanent dentition was more often severe at Hardin Village. More children experienced bone infections at Hardin Village. Cortical bone thickness was significantly lower in young adults of both sexes at Hardin Village. Life expectancy was lower at all ages for both sexes, and mortality in the toddler years was significantly higher at Hardin Village, suggesting weaning stress.

Only one health indicator, the frequency of growth arrest lines, was higher at Indian Knoll than at Hardin Village.[7] Growth

[6]Four non-Fort Ancient Mississippian sites in Western Kentucky resembles Fort Ancient in apparently displaying high frequencies of pathology, although skeletons from these sites have been incompletely analyzed (Page-Glover site, Webb and Funkhouser 1930, Vietzen 1956; Tolu site, Webb and Funkhouser 1931; Duncan site, Funkhouser and Webb 1931; Chilton site, Funkhouser and Webb 1937).

[7]If it proves common for growth arrest lines to occur more frequently in hunter-gatherer populations than in agricultural populations (also see McHenry 1968), and it is also found common for cortical thickness to be reduced in agricultural populations compared to hunter-gatherer populations, then it will be well to reconsider the meaning of high frequencies of growth arrest lines. As higher rates of bone remodeling may destroy growth arrest lines, the lower rates in agricultural populations may be artifactual, and not indicative of actually lower rates of growth arrest in the populations. Although Cassidy (1972) attempted to control for this problem in her analysis, enamel hypoplasia nevertheless is probably the better measure of the actual incidence of growth arrest.

TABLE 12.6 Changes in Some Important Health Indicators from Late Archaic to Fort Ancient Times in the Central Ohio River Valley

Indicator	Pattern of Change	Significance
Life expectancy	Falls, both sexes, but possibly more for males.	Overall health distress rose over time.
Infant death rate	Falls somewhat	Since other indicators indicate an increase in causes of illness, this decrease suggests that the social practice of infanticide decreased.
Toddler death rate	Rises sharply	Increased weaning stress, probably of complex etiology, occurred.
Vertebral arthritis	Overall rate steady, but disease occurs at younger ages in late group.	Suggests a change in primary etiology from degeneration concomitant with aging to infection (possibly related to high bone infection and dental decay rates).
Bone infections	Overall rate steady, but more childhood infections in late group.	Greater exposure to infections and/or less resistance to infections in later group.
Syndrome of disseminated periosteal reactions	Rises sharply.	Causative factor(s) more prevalent; probably an infectious organism acting synergistically with malnutrition in persons with low resistance.

Osteoporosis symmetrica and cribra orbitalia	Character changes toward classic picture, and frequency rises; highest incidence in toddlers and young women in late group.	Anemia (iron deficiency?) becomes more common, and is concentrated in the two most stressed age groups.
Cortical thickness	Decreases, both sexes.	Nutritional deficiencies, especially for calcium and phosphorus rise over time.
Growth arrest lines	Frequency falls; periodicity disappears.	Growth arrests which are mild and short-term, possibly due to recurrent brief periods of hunger, are replaced by more severe, longer-term episodes of growth arrest associated with infections or possibly crop failure and starvation.
Enamel hypoplasia, adult dentition	Total rate steady, but frequency of severe cases rises in late group.	
Enamel hypoplasia, deciduous dentition	Absent to rare early; moderate rate in late group.	Indicates severe reproductive stress in mothers, and possibly lactation insufficiency, probably associated with poor diet and high rates of infections.
Caries rate	Rises sharply.	Shows change to soft, sticky, highly processed diet from a coarse more abrasive diet.
Abscess rate	Falls slightly, occurs at younger ages in late group.	In earlier populations abscesses are a result of extreme tooth wear; in later group of extensive dental decay.

arrest lines at Indian Knoll occurred periodically, suggesting recurrent undernutrition episodes such as an annual hunger period, while those at Hardin Village were irregular in occurrence, suggesting infectious episodes as the source. Combining these data with those on enamel hypoplasia, we see that while the total numbers of episodes of growth arrest at the two sites were not significantly different, episodes of mild (short-term) growth arrest were significantly more frequent at Indian Knoll. Episodes of severe growth arrest were more frequent at Hardin Village. Thus growth arrest, while frequent at Indian Knoll, probably permitted complete recovery. At Hardin Village, however, growth arrest reflected stressors that may have contributed to the low life expectancies.

The age patterns of stress at the two sites are also different. At Indian Knoll, health is reasonably good into "old age" (over age 30), when degeneration of teeth and bones becomes frequent. At Hardin Village stress was life long, and affected everyone from the fetal period onwards, with the reproductive years for females and the weaning years for all being particularly stressful.

DISCUSSION AND SPECULATION: DIET AND ADAPTATION IN THE CENTRAL OHIO RIVER VALLEY

The diachronic health trends detailed above and summarized in Table 12.6 indicate that late agricultural populations were less healthy than earlier groups, whether hunter-gatherer *or* agricultural. Archaic and Adena populations are not (on current evidence) readily distinguishable from one another with regard to health even though their subsistence practices and diets were different. In contrast, Adena and Fort Ancient populations are distinguishable by health indicators, despite the fact that both groups' diets were largely vegetarian and cultivated. Early and late agricultural diets differed in quality; the late diet based on Mesoamerican cultigens was inferior, and only in late populations are there signs of dietary malnutrition.[8] Thus, *in the central Ohio River Valley there is an apparent lack of change in health during a transition from a wholly wild to a largely cultivated diet, followed by a striking drop in health during or after the adoption of a* different kind *of cultivated diet.*

[8] *Malnutrition is formally an encompassing term for all situations in which nutrient and energy intake are imbalanced. In common usage, and in this paper, hunger (absolute lack of food, or relative excess of nutrients to energy) is distinguished from (protein-energy) malnutrition (relative excess of energy to nutrient intake). Malnutrition results from a nutritionally imbalanced diet, while hunger is caused by food insufficiency.*

The occurrence of two succeeding agricultural "revolutions" in the central Ohio River Valley makes this region somewhat unusual and a good location to examine whether subsistence system per se is pivotal in explaining change in dietary quality and physical health. My data suggest that it is not. Alternatively, one can focus on population growth as an explanatory factor, as Cohen does. Cohen has elsewhere (1977, 1980, Chapter 1 this volume) summarized worldwide evidence that shows that primitive agricultural diets are typically of lower quality than hunter-gatherer diets, that they are often composed of foods of low desirability (such as small seeds) requiring considerable labor input, and that even when people know of agriculture they are often reluctant to practice it. Why do they? Cohen argues that population pressure (i.e., the absolute need for more food) was the main force that drove people to become cultivators, for agriculture "had no economic advantage over hunting and gathering except that it provided a greater total number of calories for each unit of space" (1977:279).

An increase of food energy per unit of space is not necessarily accompanied by an equivalent increase in nutrient value. Additionally, agriculturalists tend to specialize in a few plants, decreasing dietary variety and the buffering effect it provides. In terms of health, the virtue of producing "more food" may be illusory if the quality of that food is reduced.

Modern nonscientific peoples recognize population increase as a threat to their precarious subsistence stability, and most attempt to control population growth, even while strongly desiring children (Cassidy 1980b). Common overt ways include infanticide and restrictive marriage or intercourse rules. Other social practices have the *indirect* effect of decreasing population but often it is not known whether practitioners are aware of these effects. Such social practices include those that decrease the quantity or quality of foods available ("appropriate") to reproducing women and weanlings, the two most nutritionally sensitive groups. These rules effectively, if not consciously, potentiate protein-energy malnutrition in weanlings and relatively inefficient reproduction in women. Such practices are commonplace and have observable effects today among many peasant agriculturalists. Hunger short of starvation is reversible and has few sequelae besides decreased stature, but protein-energy malnutrition (relative excess of energy over nutrient intake) is more serious, often fatal, and has sequelae including poor growth, small stature, and lowered resistance.

With these data it is possible to propose a simple feedback model to illuminate the prehistoric relationships between diet and health in the central Ohio River Valley.

The General Model

Because humans are inefficient at population control, a positive feedback loop exists between population increase (increasing food needs) and increasingly intense environmental exploitation. Population, dietary quality, and dietary quantity all can increase up to some pivotal point at which needed energy yield per unit of space outstrips the nutrient yield necessary to maintain good health. At this point malnutrition appears. It is not necessary that this pivot point be associated with any particular subsistence system, but it is more *likely* to be associated with farming because farming is a destabilized system that permits people to raise their production above the natural capacity of the land, and the most desirable cultigens (i.e., high energy yielders) typically have relatively low nutrient densities. High-carbohydrate diets are correlated with decreased birth intervals, which causes an increase in the potential rate of population growth (i.e., an acceleration of rate of flow through the feedback loop), and may result in a population surge.

With the increasing need for cultivated food comes an increased need for cultivators, for farming is more labor intensive than hunting-gathering. A conflict is exacerbated between the partly recognized need for population control and the fully recognized desire for people (fieldhands), and I suggest that this exacerbation results in a shift in the timing of population control from birth (control by infanticide, a frankly numerical practice) to pre-birth (reproducing women) and weaning, which permits some "choice" to be expressed as to which individuals thrive (control by proscriptive feeding rules). Reproduction failures and weaning deaths represent losses both of those physically less resistant to diet and infection stresses, and of those less socially desirable. Children who survive weanling malnutrition are smaller in size, grow more slowly, and require less food for maintenance. They may even be hunger resistant (Cassidy 1980b, 1983; Stini 1975), and all of these are advantages in an unstable economy such as one based on few cultigens of low nutritional value. Such a cultural mechanism in effect simultaneously decreases the rate of population growth *and* the food needs of the remaining population (i.e., *decelerates* the rate of flow through the positive feedback loop). In the eyes of Western industrialized peoples this mechanism may appear costly; its commonness and persistence among peasant agriculturalists suggests that they find it adaptive. That is, the deaths of some toddlers and decreases in health appear to be acceptable tradeoffs for the achievement of desired cultural goals.

The Model Applied to the Central Ohio River Valley

In this region we know from evidence given that: (1) population increase was continuous over the prehistoric period and by late times high densities prevailed, (2) as time passed exploitive patterns focused more narrowly and intensely on limited ecozones and food resources, and (3) health and dietary quality fell by the late period. There were three transitions in the region; from hunter to broad-spectrum forest-efficient gatherer-hunter (late Archaic), from the latter to the farmer-gatherers of the Adena, and finally to the farmers of the Late Woodland-Fort Ancient periods.

Archaic-Adena Transition

Brown (1977) has suggested that the use of small seeds in the Adena represented an effort to increase the food (energy) base by using foods of low desirability, and that the innovation of cultivating indigenous plants was driven by hunger need. However, since the skeletal evidence shows that the Adena people were quite healthy, we must propose either that Adenans used "new" foodstuffs and became farmers for reasons other than need (e.g., curiosity, accident; see Smith 1975), *or* that their nutritional needs were *met* by the use of the new foods. If the latter, we may say that they successfully negotiated a new relative equilibrium of food income with population, and in the Archaic Adena transition serious health stresses did not develop. Additionally, the Adenan cultivator-gatherer adaptation seems to have supported, for some centuries, much cultural elaboration; thus it was both biologically and culturally successful. Finally, however, Adenans disappear as a cultural entity, and their disappearance may (although the archaeological evidence is lacking) represent the pivot point at which the advantage supplied by their new subsistence pattern was canceled by the pressure of continually increasing population.

Fort Ancient Transition

After Adena comes a gap in the regional archaeological record, and then Fort Ancient, where stress associated with the transition to Mesoamerican cultigens apparently was not well controlled, and ill health was common. Population probably surged when Mesoamerican cultigens became dietary staples, presumably in Late Woodland times; possibly such a population surge supported the cultural elaboration we recognize as Fort Ancient. At the same time, it perhaps also promoted the development of cultural mechanisms to focus malnutrition stress among the most vulnerable groups. Thus we see the demographic pattern of deaths shifted such that highest mortality was among weanlings, and women seem to have been unusually unhealthy/ill-fed during pregnancy and after. It will be recalled that this pattern has the effect of simultaneously functioning as a mechanism to control population size and to control population food needs. Thus, the Fort Ancient adaptation, while biologically comparatively less successful than its regional predecessors, was culturally successful because it represents a means to modify stress from population pressure while achieving other cultural goals. In this pattern of compromised health, toddler malnutrition, low-quality diet, and high population density (= high reproduction rates) Fort Ancient closely resembles modern peasant populations.

In summary, the data discussed in this chapter are congruent with a model that accepts subsistence change as motivated by population pressure, but relates health to the balance struck between dietary quantity and quality, and population size. The mere practice of farming does not "cause" poor health, and cultivated diets are not necessarily inferior diets. In the region, because population continuously increased, all peoples constantly were living in an unstable (positive feedback loop) situation with regard to food adequacy. Subsistence-cultural transitions represent points at which the unstable balance shifted rapidly from relatively excess population toward relative excess of a new diet, a result of innovations that permitted the production of more food. The biologically successful transition was that in which the dietary shift still yielded an adequate amount of energy and nutrients (Archaic to Adena), while the biologically less successful transition was that characterized by the use of a high energy-low nutrient diet (Fort Ancient). Simultaneous cultural adaptations presumably served to buffer the subsistence transition; the Fort Ancient demographic shift is a reconstructable example.

REFERENCES

Asch, D. L., and N. B. Asch
1977 Chenopod as Cultigen: A re-evaluation of some prehistoric collections from Eastern North America. *Midcontinental Journal of Archaeology 2*:3-45.

Beckner, L.
1926 Indian burial ground, Fullerton, Kentucky. *Kentucky Geological Survey (6th series) 26*:263-272.

Brose, D.
1973 The northeastern United States. In *The development of North American archaeology, essays in the history of regional tradition,* edited by J. E. Fitting, pp. 84-115. Pennsylvania State University Press, University Park.

Brown, J. A.
1977 Current directions in Midwestern archaeology. *Annual Reviews in Anthropology 6*:161-179.

Caldwell, J.
1958 Trend and tradition in the prehistory of the eastern United States. *American Anthropologist Memoirs* No. 88.
1962 (Reprinted 1971) Eastern North America. In *Prehistoric agriculture*, edited by S. Streuver, pp. 361-382. Natural History Press, Garden City, New York.

Cassidy, C. M.

1972 *A comparison of nutrition and health in pre-agricultural and agricultural Amerindian skeletal populations.* Ph.D. dissertation, Department of Anthropology, University of Wisconsin. University Microfilms, Ann Arbor (1973).

1980a Nutrition and health in agriculturalists and hunter-gatherers: A case study of two prehistoric populations. In *Nutritional anthropology, contemporary approaches to diet and culture*, edited by N. W. Jerome, R. F. Kandel, and G. H. Pelto, pp. 117-145. Redgrave, Pleasantville, New York.

1980b Benign neglect and toddler malnutrition. In *Social and biological predictors of nutritional status, physical growth, and neurological development*, edited by L. S. Greene and F. Johnston, pp. 109-139. Academic Press, New York.

1983 Commentary on 'Food: Past present and future,' by N. S. Scrimshaw. In *How humans adapt: A biocultural odyssey*, edited by D. J. Ortner, pp. 253-257. Smithsonian Press, Washington, D.C.

Cohen, M.

1977 *The food crisis in prehistory, overpopulation and the origins of agriculture.* Yale University Press, New Haven.

1980 *Population growth and parallel trends in socio-cultural evolution.* Paper presented at the 79th annual meeting of the American Anthropological Association, Washington, D.C.

Cook, D. S.

1971 *Patterns of nutritional stress in some Illinois Woodland populations.* Masters Thesis, Department of Anthropology, University of Chicago.

Cowan, C. W.

1979 Excavations at the Haystack Rockshelters, Powell County, Kentucky. *Midcontinental Journal of Archaeology 4*:3-33.

Dragoo, D. W.

1963 Mounds for the dead: An analysis of the Adena culture. *Annals of the Carnegie Museum* No. 37.

1976 Some aspects of eastern North American prehistory: A review. *American Antiquity 41*:3-27.

Dunnell, R. C.

1966 Archaeological reconnaissances in Fishtrap Reservoir, Kentucky. Mimeo on file, Department of Anthropology, Yale University.

Dusseau, E. M., and R. J. Porter

1974 The search for animal parasites in paleofeces from Upper Salts Cave. In *Archeology of the Mammoth Cave area*, edited by P. J. Watson, p. 59. Academic Press, New York.

Fry, G. F.

1974 Ovum and parasite examination of Salts Cave human paleofeces. In *Archeology of the Mammoth Cave area*, edited by P. J. Watson, p. 61. Academic Press, New York.

Funkhouser, W. D., and W. S. Webb
1929 The so-called 'Ash Caves' in Lee County, Kentucky. *University of Kentucky Publications in Anthropology and Archaeology 1*(2).
1930 Rock shelters of Wolfe and Powell Counties, Kentucky. *University of Kentucky Publications in Anthropology and Archaeology 1*(4).
1931 The Duncan site on the Kentucky-Tennessee Line. *University of Kentucky Publications in Anthropology and Archaeology 1*(6).
1935 The Ricketts site, in Montgomery County, Kentucky. *University of Kentucky Publications in Anthropology and Archaeology 3*(3).
1937 The Chilton site, in Henry County, Kentucky. *University of Kentucky Reports in Archaeology and Anthropology 3*(5).

Galinat, W. C.
1965 The evolution of corn and culture in North America. *Economic Botany 19*:350-357.

Goslin, R. M.
1957 Food of the Adena people. In *The Adena people* (Part II), edited by W. S. Webb and R. S. Baby, pp. 41-46. Ohio State University Press, Columbus.

Griffin, J. B.
1943 *The Fort Ancient aspect.* University of Michigan Press, Ann Arbor (reissued 1966).
1967 Eastern North American archaeology: A summary. *Science 156*:175-191.

Hanson, L. H., Jr.
1968 The Hardin Village site. *University of Kentucky Studies in Anthropology* No. 4.

Hooton, E. A., and C. C. Willoughby
1920 Indian Village site and cemetery near Madisonville, Ohio. *Papers of the Peabody Museum of American Archaeology and Ethnology 8*(1).

Hudson, C. M.
1976 *The Southeastern Indians.* University of Tennessee Press, Knoxville.

Inglemark, B. E., V. Moller-Christiansen, and O. Brinch
1959 Spinal joint change and dental infection. *Acta Anatomica* Suppl. 36.

Jennings, J. D.
1974 *Prehistory of North America* (second ed.). McGraw-Hill, New York.

Johnston, F., and C. E. Snow
1961 The reassessment of the age and sex of the Indian Knoll skeletal population: Demography and methodological aspects. *American Journal of Physical Anthropology 19*: 237-244.

Jones, V.
1936 The vegetal remains of Newt Kash Hollow Shelter. In

Rockshelters in Menifee County, Kentucky, edited by W. S. Webb and W. D. Funkhouser. *University of Kentucky Reports in Anthropology and Archaeology* 3(4):147-165.

Leigh, R. W.
1925 Dental pathologies of Indian tribes of varied environmental and food conditions. *American Journal of Physical Anthropology* 8:179-199.

Lewis, T. M. N., and M. Kneberg
1959 The Archaic culture in the Middle South. *American Antiquity* 25:161-183.

Lewis, T. M. N., and M. Kneberg-Lewis
1961 *Eva, an archaic site.* University of Tennessee Press, Knoxville.

Lovejoy, C. O.
1975 Caldwell's Little Bluff, an unusual Adena burial site. In *Studies in Ohio archaeology*, revised edition, edited by O. H. Prufer and D. H. McKenzie, pp. 252-266. Kent State University Press, Kent, Ohio.

MacCord, H. A.
1953 The Bintz site. *American Antiquity* 18(3):239-244.

Marquardt, W. H., and P. J. Watson
1974 *The Green River, Kentucky, Shellmound archaeological project.* Paper presented at the 73rd annual meeting of the American Anthropological Association, Mexico City.

McHenry, H.
1968 Transverse lines in longbones of prehistoric Californian Indians. *American Journal of Physical Anthropology* 29: 1-18.

Mills, W. C.
1906 Baum prehistoric village. *Ohio Archaeological and Historical Quarterly* 15(1):44-136.

Molnar, S., and S. Ward
1974 Dental remains from Salts Cave vestibule. In *Archeology of the Mammoth Cave area*, edited by P. J. Watson, pp. 163-166. Academic Press, New York.

Moore, C. B.
1961 Some aboriginal sites on Green River, Kentucky. *Journal of the Academy of Natural Sciences (2nd series)* 16(3).

Morgan, R. G.
1952 Outline of cultures in the Ohio region. In *Archaeology of the Eastern United States*, edited by J. B. Griffin, pp. 83-98. University of Chicago Press, Chicago.

Murphy, J. L.
1975 *An archaeological history of the Hocking Valley.* Ohio University Press, Columbus.

Nelson, N. C.
1917 Contribution to the archaeology of Mammoth Cave and vicinity, Kentucky. *American Museum of Natural History Anthropological Papers Vol.* 22(1):1-73.

Perzigian, A. J.
1973 Osteoporotic bone loss in two prehistoric Indian populations. *American Journal of Physical Anthropology 39*:81-83.
1977 Fluctuating dental asymmetry: Variation among skeletal populations. *American Journal of Physical Anthropology 47*:81-83.
Prufer, O. H., and D. H. McKenzie (editors)
1975 *Studies in Ohio archaeology* (revised ed.). Kent State University Press, Kent, Ohio.
Prufer, O. H., and O. C. Shane III
1970 *Blain Village and the Fort Ancient tradition in Ohio.* Kent State University Press, Kent, Ohio.
Rabkin, S.
1943 Dental conditions among prehistoric Indians of Kentucky. *Journal of Dental Research 22*:355-366.
Robbins, L. M.
1971 *The high incidence of bone pathologies in Fort Ancient peoples of Kentucky.* Paper presented at the 40th annual meeting of the American Association of Physical Anthropologists, Boston.
1974 Prehistoric people of the Mammoth Cave area. In *Archeology of the Mammoth Cave area*, edited by P. J. Watson, pp. 137-162. Academic Press, New York.
Robbins, L. M., and G. K. Neumann
1972 The prehistoric people of the Fort Ancient culture of the central Ohio Valley. *University of Michigan Museum of Anthropology Anthropological Papers* No. 47.
Rolingson, M. S.
1964 Paleo-Indian culture in Kentucky, a study based on projectile points. *University of Kentucky Studies in Anthropology* No. 2.
Sarnas, K. V.
1964 The dentition of Indian Knoll man. Dental decay. *Odontologisk Revy 15*:424-444.
Schambach, F. F.
1971 Blain Village and the Fort Ancient tradition in Ohio (review). *American Anthropologist 73*:1402-1404.
Schwartz, D. W.
1967 Conceptions of Kentucky prehistory: A case study in the history of archaeology. *University of Kentucky Studies in Anthropology* No. 6.
Sciulli, P. W.
1977 A descriptive and comparative study of the deciduous dentition of prehistoric Ohio Valley Amerindians. *American Journal of Physical Anthropology 48*:193-198.
1978 Developmental abnormalities of the permanent dentition in

prehistoric Ohio Valley Amerindians. *American Journal of Physical Anthropology* *48*:193-198.

Smith, C. S.
1975 Aesthetic curiosity, the root of invention. *New York Times*, August 24:Section II, page 1, column 1.

Smith, H. I.
1910 The prehistoric ethnology of a Kentucky site. *Anthropological Papers of the American Museum of Natural History* *6*(2):173-241.

Snow, C. E.
1948 Indian Knoll, Site Oh 2, Ohio County, Kentucky, Part II. *University of Kentucky Publications in Anthropology and Archaeology* *4*(3).

Stewart, R. B.
1974 Identification and quantification of components in Salts Cave paleofeces, 1970-1972. In *Archeology of the Mammoth Cave area*, edited by P. J. Watson, pp. 41-48. Academic Press, New York.

Stini, W.
1975 Adaptive strategies of human populations under nutritional stress. In *Biosocial interrelations in population adaptation*, edited by E. S. Watts, pp. 19-41. Mouton, The Hague.

Streuver, S., and K. D. Vickery
1973 The beginnings of cultivation in the Midwest Riverine area of the United States. *American Anthropologist* *75*:1197-1220.

Vento, F., J. M. Adovasio, and J. Donahue
1980 Excavations at Dameron Rockshelter (15JO23A), Johnson County, Kentucky. *Department of Anthropology University of Pittsburgh Ethnology Monographs* No. 4.

Vietzen, R. C.
1956 *The saga of Glover's Cave*. Leidi, Wahoo, Nebraska.

Watson, P. J. (editor)
1974 *Archeology of the Mammoth Cave area*. Academic Press, New York.

Webb, W. S.
1940 The Wright Mounds, sites 6 & 7, Montgomery County, Kentucky. *University of Kentucky Publications in Anthropology and Archaeology* *5*(1).

1941a Mount Horeb Earthworks site 7 and the Drake Mound site 11, Fayette County, Kentucky. *University of Kentucky Publications in Anthropology and Archaeology* *5*(2).

1941b The Morgan Stone Mound, site 15, Bath County, Kentucky. *University of Kentucky Publications in Anthropology and Archaeology* *5*(3).

1942 The C&O Mounds at Paintsville, sites Jo2 and Jo9, Johnson County, Kentucky. *University of Kentucky Publications in Anthropology and Archaeology* *5*(4).

1943a The Crigler Mounds, sites Be20 and Be27, and the Hartman Mound site Be32, Boone County, Kentucky. *University of Kentucky Publications in Anthropology and Archaeology* *5*(6).
1943b The Riley Mound, site Be15 and the Landing Mound, site Be17, Boone County, Kentucky. *University of Kentucky Publications in Anthropology and Archaeology* *5*(7).
1946 Indian Knoll, site Oh2, Ohio County, Kentucky. *University of Kentucky Publications in Anthropology and Archaeology* *4*(3), Part I.
1950a Carlson Annis Mound, site 5, Butler County, Kentucky. *University of Publications in Anthropology and Archaeology* *7*(4).
1950b The Read Shell Midden, site 10, Butler County, Kentucky. *University of Kentucky Publications in Anthropology and Archaeology* *7*(5).
1951 The Parrish Village site, site 45, Hopkins County, Kentucky. *University of Kentucky Publications in Anthropology and Archaeology* *7*(6).

Webb, W. S., and R. S. Baby
1957 *The Adena people* (Part II). Ohio State University Press, Columbus.

Webb, W. S., and J. B. Elliott
1942 The Robbins Mound, sites Be3 and Be14, Boone County, Kentucky. *University of Kentucky Publications in Anthropology and Archaeology* *5*(5).

Webb, W. S., and W. D. Funkhouser
1928 Ancient life in Kentucky. *The Kentucky Geological Survey* Series 6.
1930 The Page site, in Logan County, Kentucky. *University of Kentucky Publications in Anthropology and Archaeology* *1*(3).
1931 The Tolu site in Crittenden County, Kentucky. *University of Kentucky Publications in Anthropology and Archaeology* *1*(5).
1936 Rockshelters in Menifee County, Kentucky. *University of Kentucky Publications in Anthropology and Archaeology* *1*(5).
1940 Ricketts site revisited, site 3, Montgomery County, Kentucky. *University of Kentucky Publications in Anthropology and Archaeology* *3*(6).

Webb, W. S., and W. G. Haag
1939 The Chiggerville site. *University of Kentucky Publications in Anthropology and Archaeology* *4*(1).
1940 Cypress Creek villages, sites 11 & 12, McLean County, Kentucky. *University of Kentucky Publications in Anthropology and Archaeology* *4*(2).
1947a Archaic sites in McLean County, Kentucky. *University of Kentucky Publications in Anthropology and Archaeology* *7*(1).
1947b The Fisher site, Fayette County, Kentucky. *University of Kentucky Publications in Anthropology and Archaeology* *7*(2).

Webb, W. S., and C. E. Snow
1945 The Adena people. *University of Kentucky Publications in Anthropology and Archaeology* No. 6.

Winters, H. D.
1968 Value systems and trade cycles of the Late Archaic in the Midwest. In *New Perspectives in archaeology*, edited by S. R. Binford and L. R. Binford, pp. 175-221. Aldine, Chicago.
1969 The Riverton culture, a second Millenium occupation in the central Wabash Valley. *Illinois State Museum Reports of Investigations* No. 13.

Yarnell, R. A.
1964 Aboriginal relationships between culture and plant life in the Upper Great Lakes Region. *University of Michigan Department of Anthropology Anthropological Papers* No. 23.
1965 Early Woodland plant remains and the question of cultivation. *Florida Anthropologist 18*:78-81.
1974a Intestinal contents of the Salts Cave mummy and analysis of the initial Satls Cave flotation series. In *Archeology of the Mammoth Cave area*, edited by P. J. Watson, pp. 109-112. Academic Press, New York.
1974b Plant food and cultivation of the Salts Caves. In *Archeology of the Mammoth Cave area*, edited by P. J. Watson, pp. 113-122. Academic Press, New York.

CHAPTER 13

PREHISTORIC HEALTH IN THE OHIO RIVER VALLEY

Anthony J. Perzigian
Patricia A. Tench[1]
Donna J. Braun[2]

Departments of Anthropology and Anatomy
University of Cincinnati

INTRODUCTION: THE ARCHAEOLOGICAL BACKGROUND

The prehistory of eastern North America is becoming increasingly better understood. Papers by Griffin (1967), Brown (1977), Ford (1974, 1977), Stoltman (1978), Cleland (1976), and Essenpreis (1978) review the progress, issues, and current directions surrounding the study of this area. The archaeological literature details the successive Paleoindian, Archaic, Woodland, and Mississippian cultural systems that range from the earliest hunter-gatherer groups to the much later maize horticulturalists. This archaeological continuum portrays the experiences of a species that was not ecologically dominant until relatively late, when horticulturalists became dependent on Mesoamerican cultigens.

Populations will be described that represent the major cultural evolutionary changes in Ohio River Valley prehistory that culminated in labor-intensive maize horticulture. This study will focus, for the most part, on the dental and skeletal biology of four groups from southwest Ohio. Other groups within the general Ohio region will be utilized whenever available to provide a more comprehensive picture. The guiding concern throughout will be an

[1]*Present address: Department of Anthropology, Indiana University, Bloomington, Indiana 47405.*
[2]*Present address: Department of Anthropology, University of Pennsylvania, Philadelphia, Pennsylvania 19104.*

appraisal of the health and well being of those aboriginal groups as they underwent socioeconomic changes over the millennia.

The earliest skeletal sample comes from the DuPont site (33Ha11), which is located between the confluence of the Great Miami and Ohio rivers in southwestern Hamilton County. Excavated by the University of Cincinnati, the DuPont site yielded radiocarbon dates ranging from 2535 ± 75 to 2150 ± 65 years B.C. (Dalbey 1977). Hence, occupation of the site was in the Late Archaic, a preceramic, preagricultural period. According to Caldwell (1958), aboriginals become increasingly more efficient in their exploitation of deciduous forest environments over the span of the Archaic period (8000-1000 B.C.). Deer was the primary resource throughout the Archaic although the food base gradually expanded to include nuts, aquatic resources, and, by Late Archaic times, small seeds. Cleland (1976) characterizes Late Archaic economies as diffuse adaptations wherein the seasonal exploitation of a great variety of different resources permitted the maintenance of many subsistence alternatives. Archaic campsites were typically occupied seasonally in phase with ripening nuts, berries, and other wild plant foods. The DuPont site may be regarded as a base camp with activities concentrated from late summer to late fall. Analyses of carbon isotope ratios in bone samples substantiate the basically hunting-gathering diet of the DuPont people (van der Merwe and Vogel 1978).

The introduction of pottery serves as a convenient demarcation between the Late Archaic and Early Woodland (1000-100 B.C.) periods. The subsequent Middle Woodland period (100 B.C. to A.D. 400) is typically associated with the Hopewellian florescence. As in the preceding Late Archaic, hunting, gathering, and fishing remained economically important for both Early and Middle Woodland populations. Moreover, evidence for utilization of small seeds does increase through time and signals a gradual shift in economic activity. This exploitation of seeds contributed to an already complex food web established by the Late Archaic. Of note, carbon isotope studies (Bender et al. 1981) strongly suggest that Hopewellian people in Wisconsin, Illinois, and Ohio did not make use of corn as an important item in the diet.

A Middle Woodland skeletal sample from the Todd's Mound site (33Bu205) was available for study. Excavated in 1977 by the members of the Central Ohio Valley Archaeological Society, the site is located in southeastern Butler County on a small tributary of the Great Miami River. No habitation debris was present; rather, the site is essentially a mortuary-ceremonial complex. Artifacts and radiocarbon dates of A.D. 40 to 215 ± 60 clearly indicate a Hopewell mound. Although only 15 individuals were recovered from the mound, their preservation was excellent; therefore, they are included, especially since information on Ohio Middle Woodland skeletal samples is extremely limited.

By Mississippian-Ft. Ancient times (A.D. 700-1600) many aboriginal groups became committed in Cleland's terms (1976) to focal agricultural economies oriented around Mesoamerican cultigens. Year-round, self-sufficient sedentary villages developed by the Ft. Ancient period as populations became concentrated for labor-intensive agricultural activity; fortified villages approaching 1000 individuals arose. Ft. Ancient populations deliberately promoted simplified ecosystems as cultivated crops, e.g., maize and beans, became the predominant sources of food, with maize constituting up to 70% of the diet (van der Merwe and Vogel 1978); indeed, the food base itself became more simplified compared to that of earlier groups (Ford 1974). Moreover, a high degree of selectivity also characterized Ft. Ancient hunting, as animal exploitation focused on a few major species (Essenpreis 1982).

Two Ft. Ancient samples were available for study. The Turpin site (33HA19), excavated by the Cincinnati Museum of Natural History (Oehler 1973), is located on the east bank of the Little Miami River about 3 miles north of its confluence with the Ohio River. A radiocarbon date of A.D. 1175 ± 150 places the Turpin occupation in a period of increased horticultural dependence and sedentism. Carbon isotope studies on samples from Turpin confirm the ingestion of tropical (C_4) cultigens, e.g., maize (van der Merwe and Vogel 1978). The other Ft. Ancient group is from the State Line site (33Ha58). Excavated in 1979 in a salvage project, the site is located on the Ohio-Indiana border approximately 2 miles north of the Ohio River. Large quantities of charred maize along with dense habitation debris covering approximately 13.4 ha indicate a sedentary, agricultural population. Radiocarbon dates put the occupation at A.D. 1175 ± 60.

With the four aforementioned groups we have, within a tightly circumscribed area in southwest Ohio, the skeletal remains of populations that represent the major stages of cultural evolution. The model used here accounts for observable archaeological changes as arising from local, *in situ* cultural adaptation with little or no migration from or genetic interchange with other regions (Essenpreis 1982; Reichs 1974). Thus, a valuable opportunity to monitor the biological impact of cultural evolution is readily afforded. The discussion proceeds first with a consideration of various biological parameters that reflect conditions during growth and development and second with a consideration of paleopathology and paleodemography.

GROWTH AND DEVELOPMENT

Osteometry

Osteometric data were collected from the four southwest Ohio populations. In addition, limited comparisons to other groups within the region were made. A battery of 12 measurements was used in order to express fully the magnitude of adult variations both within and between samples. The measurements can be subdivided into two groups: (1) measurements of length, i.e., maximum humerus length, radius length, bicondylar femur length, and maximum tibia length, and (2) measurements of robusticity, i.e., clavicle length, diameters of the humeral and femoral heads, distal articular width of the humerus, anteroposterior and mediolateral diameters of the midshaft of the femur, bicondylar width of the femur, and talus length. The following sample sizes represent the number of individuals on whom at least one measurement was taken: DuPont, N = 21; Todd, N = 8; State Line, N = 26; Turpin, N = 114. The latter two, approximately contemporaneous Ft. Ancient groups were compared for the 12 measurements. No statistically significant differences were observed between females; only two significant differences obtained for the males. Thus, with only two measurements yielding significant differences, the Ft. Ancient groups were essentially phenotypically indistinguishable and therefore were combined into one sample.

A simple ranking procedure was first used to compare the groups for the total battery of 12 measurements. For the males the summed rank for the Middle Wodland sample was the highest, while that of the Late Archaic DuPont sample was the lowest; thus, general body size of the former exceeds that of the latter. Differences in summed ranks were, overall, less among females than males across samples.

The percentage of sexual dimorphism for each measurement was next ranked by group. The Late Archaic sample again had the lowest summed rank, and the Middle Woodland, the highest. The same population differences can be observed in Table 13.1, where the percentage of sexual dimorphism is estimated by averaging the dimorphism for the 12 measurements. Of interest, the Middle Woodland value is not easily equated with either that of the Late Archaic or that of the Ft. Ancient periods; in the same vein, Middle Woodland subsistence is also different from that of the other two periods. The data do indicate that Ft. Ancient people were more sexually dimorphic than Late Archaic people. This observation appears consistent with that of Wolfe and Gray (1982). They report that extant groups with agriculture tend to exhibit greater sexual dimorphism in stature than hunter-gatherer groups.

An analysis of statural variation was also performed. Mean stature of the groups was estimated from measurements of the femur following Genoves's (1967) formulas and is provided in Table 13.2. The Madisonville sample, another Ft. Ancient site from Hamilton County (Hooton 1920), and an additional Ohio Hopewell sample (Webb and Snow 1974) are also included. A similar pattern of statural change through time emerges for both males and females: an apparent increase from Late Archaic to Middle Woodland followed by an apparent decrease to Late Archaic Levels or lower by Ft. Ancient times. For males, the chronologic sequence is 169.5 to 171.3 to 168.7 cm; for females, 159.9 to 161.4 to 157.6 cm. Thus, relatively similar differences among groups are suggested by these data and the abovementioned summed ranks.

TABLE 13.1 Mean Sexual Dimorphism in Postcranial Skeleton[a]

	Dimorphism Total (12)	*Length (4)*	*Robusticity (8)*
	%	%	%
Ft. Ancient	*10.47*	*8.44*	*11.49*
Middle Woodland	*12.16*	*9.15*	*13.66*
Late Archaic	*8.33*	*7.74*	*8.63*

[a]Number of measurements is given in parentheses. Sexual dimorphism equals 1 - $(\bar{\chi}♀ \div \bar{\chi}♂) \times 100$.

TABLE 13.2 Mean Stature (CM) and Percentage of Sexual Dimorphism Estimated from the Femur

		Males		*Females*		*Sexual Dimorphism*
Period	*Group*	*Stature (cm)*	*N*	*Stature (cm)*	*N*	*(%)*
Late Archaic	*DuPont*	*169.5*	*5*	*159.9*	*5*	*5.9*
Middle Woodland	*Ohio Hopewell*	*168.1*	*20*	*160.2*	*13*	*4.7*
	Todd's Mound	*174.5*	*3*	*162.7*	*4*	*6.8*
	Woodland mean	*171.3*		*161.4*		*5.8*
Ft. Ancient	*Madisonville*	*167.6*	*29*	*155.9*	*18*	*7.0*
	Turpin-State Line	*169.8*	*44*	*159.2*	*30*	*6.3*
	Ft. Ancient Mean	*168.7*		*157.6*		*6.7*

One should not overinterpret these osteometric data, especially with limited sample sizes for the Archaic and Woodland groups. Moreover, the relationships between and among adult body size, nutrition, and genetics are neither perfectly clear nor well understood. Nevertheless, if we can take the data prima facie, a modest improvement in nutrition and health appears on the one hand concomitant with the Late Archaic to Woodland continuum. On the other hand, no enhancements of growth are particularly noticeable with the growing commitment to sedentism and maize agriculture along with the correspondingly less diversified diet of Ft. Ancient people. Any actual osteometric changes observable across time in this region can be viewed most parsimoniously as (1) basically secular in nature, (2) occurring *in situ*, and (3) well within a range of variation attributable to differential growth, nutrition, and activity levels. That economic and nutritional changes took place can be safely assumed. That changes in activity level took place can be illustrated by comparisons of the femoral midshaft index (ML/AP × 100). Assuming that greater degrees of mediolateral flattening of the femur, like that of the tibia (Lovejoy and Trinkhaus 1980), reflect greater physical demands, then lower indices should reflect a more biomechanically stressful existence. For males the mean index is 89.8% for the two Ft. Ancient and 83.1% for combined Late Archaic-Woodland samples; similarly, for females the Ft. Ancient mean of 92.6% exceeds the earlier group mean of 90.1%. In short, a somewhat less physically demanding way of life seems to characterize Ft. Ancient people vis-à-vis earlier Archaic and Woodland groups.

Harris Lines of Growth Arrest

Data on Harris lines of growth arrest in the radius are available for the southwest Ohio groups. When observations from an earlier study by Pape (1977) are combined with those of the authors, the following samples result: Late Archaic (N = 15), Middle Woodland (N = 6), Ft. Ancient (N = 44). Although the femur and tibia are more commonly studied, the radius was selected for reasons of better archaeological preservation. Of note, when well-defined scars do form in the femur and tibia, they are usually also present in the distal end of the radial shaft. Dreizen et al. (1964) reported from a longitudinal data set that the frequency of bone scars in the radius is greatest in infancy and early childhood. This heightened period of sensitivity, i.e., the first 4-5 years of life, is coterminous with the periods of greatest rate of increase in the length of the radius and greatest susceptibility to exanthematous diseases. Unfortunately, a dearth of subadults in whom lines are most likely to be present was available for study. Though lines can persist into adulthood, the frequency of scarring is expected to vary inversely with chronologic age due to resorption and remodeling. Nine individuals or 69% of the Late Archaic sample exhibited Harris lines with a range from 0 to 12 and mean of 3 lesions. In contrast, conspicuously lower proportions of individuals with lines were observed in the later groups: 33% of Todd, 29% of Turpin, and 22% of State Line. Lower means and more restricted ranges also notably characterize the later groups: Todd ($\overline{X}$ = 1.3, 0-7); Turpin ($\overline{X}$ = 1, 0-5); State Line ($\overline{X}$ = 0.5, 0-3). Of note, the greater predeliction for Harris lines in the Late Archaic sample cannot be attributable to a greater proportion of subadults when compared to the samples from the later populations. Indeed, just under one-sixth of the Late Archaic sample and just over one-fifth of the Ft. Ancient samples were comprised of subadults. Hence, the likelihood of observing lines might be considered, if anything, greater in the later groups when compared to the earlier Late Archaic sample. These results are quite reminiscent of Cassidy's (1980); she compared similar groups from

Kentucky and noted the relative infrequency of lines in a late farming group when compared to an earlier hunting group.

Although differences between groups are quite striking, no simple explanations are possible. The prevalence and frequency of lines in the Late Archaic sample could suggest episodic bouts of food shortage exacerbated by or synergistic with infectious diseases. Ammerman (1975) has shown that extreme stochastic fluctuations in the size of hunting populations are not unlikely; thereby, groups might occasionally exceed the carrying capacities of their environments. Regular or seasonal shortages in food supply may contribute as well to the etiology of Harris lines. All of this conjecture, however, is markedly tempered by observations such as those of Mensforth (1981) who, in a critical analysis of growth arrest lines in the Libben skeletal population, demonstrated their very limited reliability as demographically sensitive indicators.

Nevertheless, the conspicuously lower mean and range in the Ft. Ancient groups could suggest a more consistent supply of food vis-à-vis that of the Late Archaic people. Or, one could just as reasonably argue that the lower frequency of the Ft. Ancient samples reflects more chronic, less acute experiences with nutritional insufficiencies when compared to the Late Archaic. Thus, a chronically deprived population would produce fewer lines than one with seasonal periods of want. If, on the other hand, one views the lines as reflecting a restoration of normal growth, then the Ft. Ancient people display far fewer lines of recovery following bouts of undernutrition and illness. Indeed, the severity and duration of growth disruptions may actually have been greater for Ft. Ancient people as indicated by their overall lower frequency of lines. This view must be qualified because of (1) an unfortunately low proportion of subadults in the two samples, (2) the lack of control of age in the samples, and (3) the seeming demographic insensitivity of Harris lines as illustrated by Mensforth (1981).

Linear Enamel Hypoplasia

Data on linear enamel hypoplasia (LEH) are reported in Table 13.3 for the permanent dentition of the southwest Ohio groups. Only cases judged as moderate to severe are tabulated. The moderate to severe category was reserved for prominent, relatively deep horizontal grooves, depressed lines, or series of pits on the buccal surface. LEH was recorded for three different tooth classes: incisors, canines, and molars. Thus, a record of development from birth to about 5 years of age is available. Extreme dental attrition compromised significant proportions of the Late Archaic and Middle Woodland samples; consequently, only 57 and 40 teeth, respectively, were scorable. From Table 13.3, it would appear that risk of exposure to pathogenic factors associated with LEH was three times greater for Ft. Ancient children

TABLE 13.3 Percentage of Teeth with Moderate/Severe Linear Enamel Hypoplasia

	Late Archaic		Middle Woodland		Ft. Ancient[b]	
	N[a]	%	N	%	N	%
Maxilla						
RI1	6	33.3	2	0	50	54.0
LI1	7	28.6	3	0	37	51.4
RC	7	28.6	5	20.0	57	57.9
LC	6	16.6	5	20.0	45	62.2
RM1	6	16.6	4	25.0	49	57.1
LM1	6	16.6	5	20.0	46	63.0
Mandible						
RC	5	20.0	5	20.0	58	79.3
LC	5	20.0	4	25.0	49	57.1
RM1	4	25.0	4	25.0	48	54.2
LM1	5	0	3	33.3	49	46.6
	57	21.0	40	20.0	494	60.3

[a]N = Number of teeth examined.
[b]Represents Turpin site.

when compared to either the Middle Woodland or the Late Archaic. Heterogeneity among the samples was highly significant ($\chi^2 = 71.8$, $p < .005$). About 60% of the Fort Ancient teeth displayed at least one lesion. A rate of only one-third of that seems to characterize the two earlier groups.

The group comparisons are quite similar to those reported by Sciulli (1978) for other Ohio Valley groups. He reports a 52% incidence of severe, general hypoplasia of the permanent teeth for late focal agricultural groups, whereas that of earlier groups with diffuse economies was only 30%. In an earlier study (1977) Sciulli reported on the deciduous dentition of the same groups. When considering the developmental timing of the lesions he concluded that the post-Middle Woodland focal agricultural groups were affected prenatally at a significantly greater frequency than the earlier groups. Results, then, of these separate investigations prompt one to conclude that environmental perturbations (e.g., nutritional stresses, iron deficiencies, and infections) spanning the prenatal and postnatal periods were far more common to later prehistoric farming groups than to either hunting-gathering or earlier Woodland groups. Finally, the frequency along with the severity of the lesions among the later groups such as Ft. Ancient suggests a nutritional status comparable to that of underprivileged and undernourished modern agricultural populations (Nikiforuk and Fraser 1981). At least a modest decline in general health and nutrition appears to attend the increasing commitment to agriculture among Ohio groups. This view, however, must be qualified by the possibility that those samples derived from Early and Middle Woodland burial cult groups (e.g., Adena and Hopewell) represent only the highest status groups and thereby the least deprived segments of those societies.

PALEOPATHOLOGY AND PALEODEMOGRAPHY

Caries

The focus of this chapter so far has been on generalized indicators of disturbance during growth and development. Concern now shifts to dental and skeletal features of a more pathological nature. This section commences with a discussion of dental caries. Indeed, a relatively extensive literature now exists and supports the general observation of increased cariogenicity as a consequence of the transition and increasing commitment to agriculture. The greater frequency of caries among farming populations when compared to hunter-gatherer groups is typically attributed to the greater levels of dietary carbohydrate of the former. Table 13.4 clearly reveals the dichotomy between subsistence groups. Of 159 unworn permanent teeth from the Late Archaic samples, only 4 teeth or 2.5% of the total exhibited one or more caries. For the Middle Woodland, when consumption of starchy seed resources increased, the percentage of carious teeth is more than five times that of the Late Archaic. Finally, for Ft. Ancient 24.8% of the teeth, or almost twice that of the Middle Woodland, were carious. Heterogeneity across samples is statistically significant ($\chi^2 = 49.47$, $p < .005$).

With the availability of the large Fort Ancient sample, a more thorough analysis was permitted. Though the difference is not statistically significant, females had a greater percentage of carious teeth (27.1%) than did males (22.9%). Based on observations of one-half of the dentition, the average individual had four cavities. The mean number of cavities per tooth for the entire sample was 0.33. The molars in all samples were the most commonly implicated tooth group. Of note, the relatively poor enamel formation suggested by the LEH data (Table 13.3) may have predisposed Ft. Ancient teeth to caries.

The results given in Table 13.4 fully corroborate the observations of Addington (1973) on other Ohio Valley groups. He reports the following percentages of individuals with caries: Late Archaic (0%), Early Woodland (33.3%), Middle Woodland (13.3%), Ft. Ancient (100%). These data likewise document a trend of increasing carious involvement. Correspondingly, Sciulli et al. (1982) report a caries frequency of 3.1% for the Late Archaic

TABLE 13.4 Percentage of Carious Teeth by Group

	Late Archaic		Middle Woodland		Ft. Ancient[b]	
	N[a]	%	N	%	N	%
Maxilla						
I1	9	0	3	0	56	12.5
I2	8	0	5	0	56	16.1
C	9	0	6	0	67	10.4
P1	6	0	6	0	60	16.7
P2	7	0	6	0	59	15.3
M1	8	0	6	0	61	32.8
M2	11	18.2	5	20.0	61	47.5
M3	8	0	4	25.0	43	46.5
Mandible						
I1	9	0	5	0	56	1.8
I2	11	0	6	0	62	1.6
C	13	0	6	0	71	7.5
P1	13	0	7	14.3	70	11.4
P2	13	0	7	0	67	11.9
M1	11	0	7	28.6	61	57.4
M2	12	0	7	71.4	54	70.4
M3	11	18.2	6	33.3	49	57.1
	159	2.5	92	13.0	953	24.8

[a]N = Number of teeth examined.
[b]Represents Turpin site.

Williams site sample; they observed 1597 teeth. Finally, Sciulli and Carlisle (1977) reported a frequency of 27.7% for three Late Woodland samples from western Pennsylvania, a value substantially higher than that of typical preagricultural groups.

In sum, the cultural and economic changes that resulted in the shift away from a primary dependence on hunting and gathering in favor of a reliance on agriculture had an unmistakably pathologic influence on dental health and oral biology. The evidence is unequivocal that caries became a prominent feature and characteristic burden of the late groups who relied more heavily on maize agriculture.

Nonspecific Skeletal Lesions

Paleopathological studies typically consider nonspecific inflammatory lesions of the long bones, e.g., osteomyelitis and periostitis. References to such lesions appear in the earliest

TABLE 13.5 Percentage of Long Bones with Periosteal Inflammatory Reactions

	Late Archaic		Middle Woodland		Ft. Ancient	
	N[a]	%	*N*	%	*N*	%
Humerus	17	17.7	9	11.1	131	7.6
Radius	19	10.5	9	11.1	133	7.5
Ulna	20	0	7	28.6	147	6.1
Femur	20	5.0	8	37.5	160	10.6
Tibia	16	18.8	8	50.0	136	24.3
Fibula	19	15.8	8	37.5	85	28.2
	111	10.8	49	28.6	792	13.0

[a]*N* = *Number of bones examined.*

literature (Hooton 1920; Langdon 1881) on Ohio Valley groups. Table 13.5 provides a preliminary assessment of adult lesions for the southwest Ohio groups. No effort was made either to distinguish among the possible pathologies or to record the degree of severity; rather, pathological involvement was recorded if any inflammatory response was expressed on the periosteal surface. The frequency of lesions per sample may be influenced here by demographic considerations. Indeed, more frequent lesions may be anticipated in a sample of older individuals than in a sample of younger individuals. In addition, an individual with multiple lesions may inflate the total frequency in a small sample. The Middle Woodland sample is quite small; only 49 bones were examined. More than twice that was available for the Late Archaic, and just under 800 bones were evaluated from the two Ft. Ancient samples. Variation in the frequency of lesions was significant ($\chi^2 = 10.35$, $p < .01$). Whatever the etiologic factors were that contributed to long bone lesions, especially in the lower extremity, they appear to be more influential in the Middle Woodland and Ft. Ancient periods than in the Late Archaic. Tibial lesions, especially, seem to characterize archaeological collections of both adults and subadults (Mensforth et al. 1978).

The data given in Table 13.5 can preliminarily suggest that at least a modest decline in skeletal health followed the abandonment of hunting and gathering and consequent adoption of labor-intensive agricultural economies. These results and conclusions are in accord with those published by Lallo (1979) on a neighboring Ft. Ancient group from the Anderson Village site. Working with a sample of 44 individuals ranging in age from birth to 60 years, he observed osseous infections in 36, or 81.8%, of the individuals. He argued that infections contributed significantly to both subadult and adult mortality. To him, the interaction between disease, malnutrition, and mortality was epidemiologically and demographically significant. A later group, the Eiden population (A.D. 1490 ± 55 years) from northern Ohio, has also been described. Lallo and Blank (1977) recorded the frequency of both periostitis and osteomyelitis in this maize agriculture group; of 122 individuals from ages 0 to 59.9 years, 84, or 70% exhibited some form of infectious manifestation. In sum, the data available so far suggest the presence of endemic infections (e.g. *S. aureus*) that are more than coincidentally associated with the increasing commitment to maize agriculture. Whatever the interplay was among nutrition, population density, occupational activity, and microbial agents, it resulted in 1) chronic infections of the lower extremity with debilitating consequences for many adults, and 2) possible death in the first years of life as suggested by data from the Libben collection (Mensforth et al. 1978).

Skeletal Tuberculosis

The senior author and others (Hooton 1920; Katzenberg 1976; Means 1925; Perzigian and Widmer 1979; Widmer and Perzigian 1981) have suggested the presence of a crowd infection, i.e. tuberculosis, in the Fort Ancient people from Hamilton County. In a roentgenologic study of five individuals from the Turpin site, vertebral fusions, kyphoses, and destruction are well depicted (Perzigian and Widmer 1979). The location, expression, and pattern of the spinal lesions are strongly persuasive of the presence of tuberculosis. Klepinger (1982) has recently supported this hypothesis and considered the possible origins of a New World mycobacterial infection in humans.

Buikstra (1976) has noted that purported cases of prehistoric tuberculosis are reported more frequently for later agriculturally based groups than for earlier hunting and gathering groups. By implication, then, infectious diseases can become endemic at certain levels of population density and size such as those reached by Ft. Ancient people. The probability of endemicity of tuberculosis is, thus, conventionally viewed as proportional to the opportunity for transmission. Previous papers by the senior author adopt such a view concerning the primacy of density in understanding the distribution and maintenance of crowd infections.

The thrust of this chapter, however, may suggest yet other important factors in addition to density and transmission in the maintenance of crowd infections. The data so far marshalled suggest (1) some reduction in general nutrition and dietary diversity, and (2) some overall increase in stress among the later farming groups. It is well known that malnutrition due to deficiencies of protein, calories, vitamins, or trace elements can forestall immunological defense mechanisms; moreover, intrauterine growth retardation due to maternal malnutrition produces profound adverse effects on postnatal immunocompetence. For example, impaired antibody response was seen in the F_1 and F_2 offspring of starved female rats even though the litters in both generations had free access to food (Chandra 1975); in addition, reduced immunocompetence persisted for three generations after pregnant mice were fed a zinc-deficient diet (Beach et al. 1982). Perhaps then, depressed levels of immunocompetence associated with poor nutrition can account for epidemiologic patterns.

Youmans (1979) and Huels (1981) address the significance of resistance in explaining distributions of tuberculosis in human groups. Resistance to tuberculosis (Youmans 1979) specifically results from an acquired cellular immunity; T lymphocytes and macrophages are the primary agents of defense. As long as acquired cellular immunity is maintained, the infection is controlled in the individual despite frequent exposure. With a breakdown in immunity, the disease progresses to a tissue-destructive phase as seen, for example, in the Ft. Ancient vertebrae. It is only at this phase that persons with adequate immunity will not participate as agents of transmission. As noted above, defenses can be disturbed or suppressed by nutritional imbalances. Hence, resistance to tuberculosis might be reduced via the dietary and consequent immunological changes that accompanied the intensification of agriculture. Concerning the paleoepidemiology of tuberculosis, factors of transmission may be viewed as secondary to factors of resistance. A picture emerges of Ohio Valley aboriginals confronted with microparasitic infections, their defenses to which were increasingly eroded as the commitment to sedentary maize agriculture intensified.

Porotic Hyperostosis and Cribra Orbitalia

Although no good comparative data are currently available that span Ohio Valley prehistory, some data on porotic hyperostosis and cribra orbitalia are available. These lesions of the vault and orbit are believed to result from dietary iron deficiencies (Von Endt and Ortner 1982) and various disease states. Mensforth et al. (1978) report a statistically significant association between porotic hyperostosis and periosteal lesions in the 6-24-month age range for the Late Woodland Libben population from northern Ohio. Lallo (1979) reports on the Ft. Ancient people recovered from the Anderson Village site. Twenty-nine of 44 individuals (65.9%) exhibited porotic hyperostosis. He concluded that the interaction between malnutrition and infection contributed to the mortality of this group. Lallo et al. (1977) report very similar data for the Eiden population; cribra orbitalia and porotic hyperostosis appeared together in 51.7% of a subadult sample of 31 individuals. Seventy-five percent of the subadults displayed some postorbital involvement, e.g., osteoporotic pitting, porotic hyperostosis. These results are (1) quite similar to those reported for the Middle Mississippian population from Dickson Mound in Illinois (Lallo et al. 1977), and (2) contribute to the notion that later farming groups were exposed to more malnutrition and disease than their forebearers. Indeed, the Late Woodland Libben people who lived 500 years before the Eiden people have been portrayed in a thorough paleodemographic analysis by Lovejoy et al. (1977) as a basically healthy population. More specifically, Mensforth et al. (1978) claim that chronic malnutrition that might be due to poor diet, weaning practices, or parasitic infestations was "basically absent at Libben." Thus, data published on porotic hyperostosis and cribra orbitalia reinforce the claim that dietary insufficiencies and microparasitic infections combined to complicate and compromise the lives of late prehistoric farming people from Ohio to degrees not readily noticeable among their predecessors in Archaic and Woodland times. Finally, this view is not contradicted by a preliminary survey of the Ft. Ancient material from the State Line site, where both cribra orbitalia and porotic hyperostosis were observed (Schmidt 1981).

Paleodemography

Paleodemographic analyses have been performed on Ohio groups, the most thorough of which was conducted by Lovejoy et al. (1977). A sample of 1327 Late Woodland individuals was studied. They report a class 2 survivorship pattern that is typical of prehistoric skeletal populations. Infant mortality was considered low, which suggests a healthy, successful population; life expectancy at birth was 20 years. Demographic data on the Ft. Ancient group from the Anderson Village site have also been published by Lallo (1979). He cautiously notes that his sample of 44 individuals is quite small and therefore possibly biased; under-representation of both infants and general subadult mortality is exceedingly likely. For example, only 18.18% of the Ft. Ancient sample died by 15 years of age, as compared to 61.36% at Libben. Correspondingly, life expectancies at birth contrasted markedly between Anderson Village and Libben, i.e., 33 versus 20 years, respectively. Thus, demographic comparisons of the two groups are severely limited. Nonetheless, both studies report survivorship well into the fifth and sixth decades. Individuals were certainly living long enough at Libben to experience age-progressive cortical involution of the femur (Mensforth 1978) in amounts quite similar to what Perzigian (1973) observed in an earlier study of osteoporosis in a Late Archaic population.

Archaeologists agree that profound demographic changes occurred with the growing commitment to maize agriculture; indeed, villages arose and increased in size and number; population densities reached unprecedented levels. In association with these demographic changes, the authors observe a seeming increase in hostility and violent death by post-Woodland times. While Lovejoy and Heiple (1981) contend that there is no strong evidence for Late Woodland warfare in the Libben sample, appreciable evidence of arrow wounds is reported for Ft. Ancient groups. Hooton (1920) claimed that 22% of the adult males at Madisonville suffered cranial and postcranial wounds. Violent encounters are also reported for Blain Village (Lovejoy and Heiple 1970), State Line (Schmidt 1981), and Anderson Village (Morgan 1946).

CONCLUSIONS

Some tentative generalizations are now in order for southwest Ohio prehistory. Evidence reviewed and compiled in this chapter does not support a view that eventual improvements in health and nutrition resulted from (1) the abandonment of hunting and gathering as exclusive economic pursuits, and (2) the subsequent development of focal agricultural economies by Ft. Ancient times. The limited osteometric data may be interpreted to show some gains in nutrition and health for the Middle Woodland people over that of the Late Archaic; nevertheless, further advances cannot be demonstrated for the Ft. Ancient groups. Dental and skeletal health appear to decline noticeably as evidenced by trends in caries, enamel hypoplasia, and skeletal lesions. All such trends mutually reinforce each other and probably reflect a growing synergism among diet, population density, and disease. With a dramatically increased commitment to maize agriculture and a commensurately decreased dependence on hunting and gathering as observed by Ft. Ancient times, fertility probably approached that of contemporary noncontraceptive, preindustrialized societies and resulted in population densities higher than ever before. A growing population, concentrated for labor-intensive focal agriculture, may have not uncommonly taxed its ecological and cultural support systems or suffered an occasionally disastrous crop failure. The maize, itself, may have depleted the soil. In such a general context, lessened dietary variation, nutritional imbalances, and deficiencies were likely and would have led to reduced levels of immunocompetence and altered states of pathogenicity. For now, the conclusion that sociocultural change is pre-eminent in explaining epidemiological changes in prehistoric Ohio is warranted.

ACKNOWLEDGMENTS

The Cincinnati Museum of Natural History kindly provided the authors with access to the Turpin site skeletal collection. The authors wish to express their sincerest appreciation to the Museum for its cooperation. Members of the Central Ohio Valley Archaeological Society worked indefatigably and conscientiously during the excavation, processing, and analysis of much of the skeletal material. Special and warm thanks go to Arlene Basham, Jerry

Alford, and Donna Neu for their unswerving dedication and spirit. Facilities for radiography were graciously provided by Dr. Paul Jolly of the Hamilton County Coroner's Office. Procedures for collecting dental hypoplasia data were recommended by Dr. Della Cook. Completion of this study would have been impossible without generous support from the Department of Orthopaedic Surgery of the University of Cincinnati and its former chairman, Dr. Edward H. Miller. Mrs. Kay Klein provided expert assistance in preparation of the manuscript. Dr. Joseph F. Foster, chairman of the Department of Anthropology, provided excellent administrative assistance.

REFERENCES

Addington, J. E.
1973 *Collectors or farmers: Dental attrition and pathology as related to subsistence in the Ohio Valley.* Paper Presented to the annual meeting of the American Anthropological Association, New Orleans.

Ammerman, A. J.
1975 Late Pleistocene population dynamics: An alternate view. *Human Ecology 3*:219-233.

Beach, R. S., M. E. Gershwin, and L. S. Hurley
1982 Gestational zinc deprivation in mice: Persistence of immunodeficiency for three generations. *Science 218*:469-471.

Bender, M. M., D. A. Baerreis, and R. L. Steventon
1981 Further light on carbon isotopes and Hopewell agriculture. *American Antiquity 46*:346-353.

Brown, J. A.
1977 Current directions in Midwestern archaeology. *Annual Review of Anthropology 6*:161-179.

Buikstra, J. E.
1976 Differential diagnosis: An epidemiologic model. *Yearbook of Physical Anthropology 20*:316-328.

Caldwell, J. R.
1958 Trend and tradition in the prehistory of the eastern United States. *American Anthropological Association Memoir* No. 88.

Cassidy, C. M.
1980 Nutrition and health in agriculturalists and hunter-gatherers. *Nutritional anthropology*, edited by N. W. Jerome, R. F. Kandel, and G. H. Pelto, pp. 117-145. Redgrave, New York.

Chandra, R. K.
1975 Antibody formation in first and second generation offspring of nutritionally deprived rats. *Science 190*:289-290.

Cleland, C. E.
1976 The focal-diffuse model: An evolutionary perspective on the prehistoric cultural adaptations of the eastern United States. *Midcontinental Journal of Archaeology 1*:59-76.

Dalbey, T. S.
1977 *Molluscan (Naiads) utilization and exploitation at the DuPont Site (33Ha11) in southwestern Ohio.* Paper presented at the annual meeting of the Central States Anthropological Society, Cincinnati.

Dreizen, S., C. N. Spirakis, and R. E. Stone
1964 The influence of age and nutritional status on 'bone scar' formation in the distal end of the growing radius. *American Journal of Physical Anthropology 27*:375-378.

Essenpreis, P. S.
1978 Fort Ancient settlement: Differential response at Mississippian--Late Woodland interface. In *Mississippian settlement patterns*, edited by B. D. Smith, pp. 141-167. Academic Press, New York.
1982 *The Anderson Village site: Redefining the Anderson phase of the Fort Ancient tradition of the middle Ohio Valley.* Unpublished Ph.D. dissertation, Department of Anthropology, Harvard University.

Ford, R. I.
1974 Northeastern archaeology: Past and future directions. *Annual Review of Anthropology 3*:385-413.
1977 Evolutionary ecology and the evolution of human ecosystems: A case study from the Midwestern U.S.A. In *Explanation of prehistoric change*, edited by J. N. Hill, pp. 153-184. University of New Mexico Press, Albuquerque.

Genoves, S.
1967 Proportionality of the long bones and their relation to stature among Mesoamericans. *American Journal of Physical Anthropology 26*:67-78.

Griffin, J. B.
1967 Eastern North American archaeology: A summary. *Science 156*:175-191.

Hooton, E. A.
1920 Indian village site and cemetery near Madisonville, Ohio. *Papers of the Peabody Museum of American Archaeology and Ethnology 8(1)*:83-134.

Huels, B. R.
1981 *An ecological model of tuberculosis.* Paper presented to the annual meeting of the Central States Anthropological Society, Cincinnati.

Katzenberg, M. A.
1976 An investigation of spinal disease in a Midwest aboriginal population. *Yearbook of Physical Anthropology 20*:349-355.

Klepinger, L. L.
1982 Tuberculosis in the New World: More possibilities, probabilities and predictions. *American Journal of Physical Anthropology 57*:203 (Abstr.).

Lallo, J. W.
1979 Disease and mortality at the Anderson Village site. *Ohio Journal of Science 79*:256-261.

Lallo, J. W., and J. E. Blank
1977 Ancient disease in Ohio: The Eiden population. *Ohio Journal of Science 77*:55-62.

Lallo, J. W., G. J. Armelagos, and R. P. Mensforth
1977 The role of diet, disease, and physiology in the origin of porotic hyperostosis. *Human Biology 49*:471-483.

Langdon, F. W.
1881 The Madisonville prehistoric cemetery: Anthropological notes. *Journal of the Cincinnati Society of Natural History 4*:237-257.

Lovejoy, C. O., and K. G. Heiple
1970 The Blain Mound. In *Blain Village and the Fort Ancient tradition in Ohio*, edited by O. H. Prufer and O. C. Shane III, pp. 151-184. Kent State University, Kent, Ohio.
1981 The analysis of fractures in skeletal populations with an example from the Libben Site, Ottawa County, Ohio. *American Journal of Physical Anthropology 55*:529-541.

Lovejoy, C. O., and E. Trinkhaus
1980 Strength and robusticity of Neanderthal tibia. *American Journal of Physical Anthropology 53*:465-470.

Lovejoy, C. O., R. S. Meindl, T. R. Pryzbeck, T. S. Barton, K. G. Heiple, and D. Kotting
1977 Paleodemography of the Libben site, Ottawa County, Ohio. *Science 198*:291-293.

Means, H. J.
1925 A roentgenological study of the skeletal remains of the prehistoric Mound Builder Indians of Ohio. *American Journal of Roentgenology 13*:359-367.

Mensforth, R. P.
1978 Femoral cortical involution in a Late Woodland skeletal population: Epidemiologic and biomechanical observations. *American Journal of Physical Anthroplogy 48*:419 (Abstr.).
1981 *Growth velocity and chondroblastic stability as major factors influencing the pathogenesis and epidemiological distribution of growth arrest lines.* Paper presented to the 50th annual meeting of the American Association of Physical Anthropologists, Detroit.

Mensforth, R. P., C. O. Lovejoy, J. W. Lallo, and G. J. Armelagos
1978 The role of constitutional factors, diet, and infectious disease in the etiology of porotic hyperostosis and periosteal reactions in prehistoric infants and children. *Medical Anthropology 2*:1-59.

Morgan, R. G.
1946 *Fort Ancient.* The Ohio State Archaeological and Historical Society, Columbus.

Nikiforuk, G., and D. Fraser
1981 The etiology of enamel hypoplasia: A unifying concept. *Journal of Pediatrics 98*:888-893.

Oehler, C.
1973 Turpin Indians. *Journal of the Cincinnati Museum of Natural History* *23*(2):1-65.

Pape, W. K.
1977 *A comparison of Harris lines in two prehistoric Ohio Valley populations.* Paper presented to the annual meeting of the Central States Anthropological Society, Cincinnati.

Perzigian, A. J.
1973 Osteoporotic bone loss in two prehistoric Indian populations. *American Journal of Physical Anthropology* *39*:87-96.

Perzigian, A. J., and L. Widmer
1979 Evidence for tuberculosis in a prehistoric population. *Journal of the American Medical Association* *241*:2643-2646.

Reichs, K. J.
1974 *Biological variability and the Hopewell phenomenon: An interregional approach.* Unpublished Ph.D. dissertation, Department of Anthropology, Northwestern University.

Schmidt, M. A.
1981 *Descriptive analysis of the skeletal remains from the Stateline site (33Ha58).* Unpublished Master's thesis, Department of Anthropology, University of Cincinnati, Ohio.

Sciulli, P. W.
1977 A descriptive and comparative study of the deciduous dentition of prehistoric Ohio Valley Amerindians. *American Journal of Physical Anthropology* *47*:71-80.
1978 Developmental abnormalities of the permanent dentition of prehistoric Ohio Valley Amerindians. *American Journal of Physical Anthropology* *48*:193-198.

Sciulli, P. W., and R. Carlisle
1977 Analysis of the dentition from three western Pennsylvania Late Woodland Sites. II. Wear and pathology. *Pennsylvania Archaeologist* *47*:53-59.

Sciulli, P. W., B. W. Aument, and L. R. Piotrowski
1982 The Williams (33WO7a) Red Ocher cemetery: Preliminary descriptive and comparative analysis of acquired dental pathologies. *Pennsylvania Archaeologist* *53(2)*:17-24.

Stoltman, J. B.
1978 Temporal models in prehistory: An explanation from eastern North America. *Current Anthropology* *19*:703-746.

van der Merwe, N. J., and J. C. Vogel
1978 ^{13}C content of human collagen as a measure of prehistoric diet in Woodland North America. *Nature (London)* *276*:815-816.

Von Endt, D. W., and D. J. Ortner
1982 Amino acid analysis of bone from a possible case of prehistoric iron deficiency anemia from the American Southwest. *American Journal of Physical Anthropology* *59*:377-385.

Webb, W. S., and C. E. Snow
1974 *The Adena people.* The University of Tennessee Press, Knoxville.

Widmer, L., and A. J. Perzigian
1981 The ecology and etiology of skeletal lesions in Late Prehistoric populations from eastern North America. In Prehistoric tuberculosis in the Americas, edited by J. E. Buikstra. *Northwestern University Archaeological Program Scientific Papers* No. 5, pp. 99-113.

Wolfe, L. D., and J. P. Gray
1982 Subsistence practices and human sexual dimorphism of stature. *Journal of Human Evolution 11*:575-580.

Youmans, G. P.
1979 *Tuberculosis.* Saunders, Philadelphia.

CHAPTER 14

HEALTH AND DISEASE IN PREHISTORIC GEORGIA: THE TRANSITION TO AGRICULTURE

Clark Spencer Larsen

Department of Anthropology
Northern Illinois University

INTRODUCTION

Prehistoric mortuary activity in Georgia has been well documented through an extensive series of archaeological investigations in both inland and coastal regions. With respect to the former, human skeletal remains representing hundreds of individuals have been recovered, primarily from late prehistoric contexts. Unfortunately, with the exception of preliminary discussion of pathology of human remains from the Etowah site (Blakely 1977, 1980), there are no reported descriptions or analyses of skeletal pathology from this rather large series.

The Georgia coast has also produced an abundance of human skeletal remains. Unlike the interior region of Georgia, a significant portion of these remains has been described in publication and in manuscript (see Larsen 1982; Larsen and Thomas 1979).

Because there is such a paucity of data based on prehistoric populations from the Georgia interior, this chapter will focus on the Georgia coast for an examination of human skeletal and pathological changes (see also Larsen 1980a,b, 1981a, 1982, 1983a,b,c). The following will summarize available data with regard to two types of stress as they are exhibited in the skeleton and dentition: disease-nutritional stress and mechanical stress. The pathological conditions to be considered include periosteal reactions and dental caries (disease-nutritional stress) and degenerative joint disease (mechanical stress). Moreover, the impact of these stresses on human skeletal size and morphology will be discussed. No detailed information is available for either Harris lines or most of the dental pathologies considered in the other contributions to this volume (i.e., enamel hypoplasia, microdefects, attrition, periodontal disease, and abscessing).

Analysis of economic information from the Georgia coast indicates that before circa A.D. 1150, the Georgia coastal subsistence economy was based primarily on hunting, gathering, and fishing; after that date, agricultural food production (maize, in particular) became an important component of the dietary regime. This lifeway reconstruction seems most plausible because (1) maize has been archaeologically recovered in post-A.D. 1150 contexts only, (2) there is a marked increase in habitation site density and distribution after A.D. 1150, and (3) the ethnohistoric record indicates that maize was a major constituent of diet, providing support for large, centrally located, permanent villages (see discussion in Jones 1978; Larsen 1982).

MATERIALS

Since this study represents an analysis of human skeletal remains from populations differing only in mode of subsistence, the cultural periods have been divided into two groups. The earlier pre-A.D. 1150 periods constitute a *preagricultural group* that consists of human skeletal remains from four prehistoric periods; two later prehistoric periods (A.D. 1150-1550) constitute an *agricultural group* (Table 14.1).

The human skeletal remains from 19 preagricultural and 14 agricultural period mortuary sites from the Georgia coast were utilized in this investigation. The preagricultural group includes 272 individuals and the agricultural group includes 344 individuals. A detailed discussion of these sites and their associated skeletal materials has been presented elsewhere (see Larsen 1982).

GEORGIA COASTAL PALEOPATHOLOGY

Because periosteal reactions, dental caries, and degenerative joint disease are age progressive, any differences in their frequency in the preagricultural group as compared to the agricultural group may, in fact, simply reflect age structure differences between the two groups. Therefore, let us examine and compare the population sample profiles of the preagricultural and agricultural groups.

Table 14.2 shows the age distributions for the preagricultural and agricultural groups. Statistical treatment of these profiles reveals that the two groups are significantly different in structure at the $p = .01$ level (Kolmogorov-Smirnov). Careful examination of

TABLE 14.1 Subsistence Modes and Associated Periods from the Georgia Coast[a]

Subsistence modes	*Periods*	*Terminal dates*
Agriculture with hunting, gathering, and fishing[b]	*Irene*	*A.D. 1550*
	Savannah	*A.D. 1300*
Hunting, gathering, and fishing[c]	*St. Catherines*	*A.D. 1150*
	Wilmington	*A.D. 1000*
	Deptford	*A.D. 500*
	Refuge	*400 B.C.*

[a]*After Larsen 1982.*

[b]*Mortuary localities associated: North End Mound, Shell Bluff (Low Mound), Townsend Mound, Deptford Mound, Norman Mound, Kent Mound, Lewis Creek Mounds (A, B, E), Red Knoll, Seven Mile Bend Mound, Oatland Mound, Seaside Mound II (Burial 8), Irene Mound.*

[c]*Mortuary localities associated: South New Gound Mound, Cunningham Mounds (C, D, E), McLeod Mound, Seaside Mounds (I, II), Evelyn Plantation, Airport, Deptford, Walthour, Cannons Point, Cedar Grove Mounds (A, B, C), Sea Island Mound, Johns Mound, Marys Mound, Charlie King Mound.*

TABLE 14.2 Age Distributions of the Georgia Coastal Preagricultural and Agricultural Groups[a]

Age interval (years)	*Preagricultural*		*Agricultural*	
	N	*%*	*N*	*%*
0.0- 2.0	*7*	*4.6*	*12*	*6.8*
2.1-12.0	*19*	*12.5*	*30*	*16.9*
12.1-16.0	*13*	*8.6*	*25*	*14.1*
16.1-20.0	*22*	*14.5*	*33*	*18.6*
20.1-25.0	*27*	*17.8*	*38*	*21.5*
25.1-30.0	*14*	*9.2*	*11*	*6.2*
30.1-35.0	*6*	*3.9*	*8*	*4.5*
35.1-40.0	*14*	*9.2*	*9*	*5.1*
40.1-45.0	*11*	*7.2*	*6*	*3.4*
45.1 plus	*19*	*12.5*	*5*	*2.8*

[a]*Does not include unaged individuals.*

the overall age structure of these two groups shows, of course, that these materials are representative of realistic population survivorship for neither preagricultural nor agricultural groups. That is, the remarkably high survivorship for the preadults in

TABLE 14.3 Frequency (%) of Periosteal Reactions in Preagricultural and Agricultural Groups: Adult (Females, Males, Indeterminate Sex Combined) Comparisons

Skeletal element	Preagricultural %	Preagricultural N^a	Agricultural %	Agricultural N^a	% change[b]
Clavicle	1.9	107	4.7	274	2.8
Humerus	0.5	190	3.2	273	2.7
Ulna	0.7	147	3.7	327	3.0
Radius	0.7	136	4.5	335	3.8
Femur	2.1	193	6.8	410	4.7
Tibia	4.5	156	15.0	374	10.5
Fibula	1.7	116	8.3	289	6.6

[a]Number of bones observed for presence-absence of periosteal reactions.

[b]Computed by the following formula: % Agricultural-% Preagricultural.

both groups is undoubtedly a product of gross underrepresentation of individuals with an age-at-death of 15 years or younger. More importantly, however, the materials at hand indicate that the preagricultural skeletal sample is represented by a decidedly older age-at-death sample of human skeletal remains than the agricultural sample.

Periosteal Reactions

The frequency of periosteal reactions in skeletal elements of adults (females, males, and indeterminate sex combined) in the preagricultural and agricultural groups and the percentage of change in occurrence of these lesions are presented in Table 14.3. In general, the agricultural adults have higher frequencies of bones affected by periosteal reactions than the preagricultural adults. All of the seven skeletal elements examined show increases ranging from 2.7 (humerus) to 10.5% (tibia).

Analysis of these data by sex shows that females have increases for all skeletal elements (Table 14.4). These percentage differences between the preagricultural group and the agricultural group are particularly pronounced for the lower limb. The males (Table 14.5) show increases for all skeletal elements except the clavicle. As in the females, the increases in percentage of bones affected by the pathology are most apparent for the skeletal elements of the lower limb. Moreover, comparisons of the sexes within the preagricultural and agricultural groups (cf. Table 14.4 with Table 14.5) suggest that the increases in periosteal reactions were somewhat

TABLE 14.4 Frequency (Percentage) of Periosteal Reactions in Preagricultural and Agricultural Groups. Female Comparisons

	Preagricultural		*Agricultural*		
Skeletal element	*%*	*N*[a]	*%*	*N*[a]	*% change*[b]
Clavicle	0.0	61	2.9	140	2.9
Humerus	0.0	106	3.7	190	3.7
Ulna	1.2	82	3.6	167	2.4
Radius	0.0	77	4.0	173	4.0
Femur	1.8	110	7.2	207	5.4
Tibia	2.4	84	16.0	187	13.6
Fibula	1.4	74	9.9	152	8.5

[a]Number of bones observed for presence-absence of periosteal reactions.
[b]Computed by the following formula: % Agricultural-% Preagricultural.

TABLE 14.5 Frequency (Percentage) of Periosteal Reactions in Preagricultural and Agricultural Groups: Male Comparisons

	Preagricultural		*Agricultural*		
Skeletal element	*%*	*N*[a]	*%*	*N*[a]	*% change*[b]
Clavicle	5.6	36	5.3	114	-0.3
Humerus	2.0	51	3.6	140	1.6
Ulna	0.0	42	2.3	130	2.3
Radius	0.0	43	2.9	140	2.9
Femur	2.0	49	6.4	156	4.4
Tibia	4.0	50	15.8	146	11.8
Fibula	0.0	37	5.3	114	5.3

[a]Number of bones observed for presence-absence of periosteal reactions.
[b]Computed by the following formula: % Agricultural-% Preagricultural.

greater for the females. That is, the percentage increases are larger in the females than in the males.

Dental Caries

The frequencies of noncarious and carious individuals (dentitions with at least one carious tooth) in the preagricultural and agricultural groups are provided in Table 14.6. The comparisons

TABLE 14.6 Frequency (Percentage) of Dental Caries in Preagricultural and Agricultural Individuals

	Preagricultural (%)	Agricultural (%)
Total sample	(N = 201)[a]	(N = 275)[a]
Noncarious	91.0	41.1
Carious	9.0	58.9
Female	(N = 75)	(N = 108)
Noncarious	89.3	30.6
Carious	10.7	69.4
Male	(N = 49)	(N = 80)
Noncarious	93.9	41.3
Carious	6.1	58.7
Preadult	(N = 36)	(N = 56)
Noncarious	100.0	51.8
Carious	0.0	48.2

[a]Number of individuals observed with at least one tooth present in the maxillary and mandibular dentitions combined.

of these frequencies in the two groups clearly show a marked increase in number of individuals affected by dental caries in the agricultural group. To summarize, for all tooth categories combined (I1 + I2 + C + ... + M3), only 1.3% of the preagricultural group show carious teeth (36/2429). Of the agricultural group, however, 11.6% show carious teeth (486/4189). This represents a 10.3% frequency increase in carious teeth in the agricultural group relative to the preagricultural group.

Comparisons of the preagricultural and agricultural adult females and males show similar patterning in frequency increase of teeth affected by cariogenesis. The females show for all teeth, with the exception of the mandibular first incisor (no change), an increase in frequency of dental caries (Table 14.7).

Table 14.8 presents the frequencies of dental caries in males for the preagricultural and agricultural groups. Although there are increases in frequency of occurrence of carious lesions for all teeth excepting the maxillary central incisor (2.1% decrease), the increases are not as great as those exhibited in either the combined sample or the females.

In sum, dental caries had a minimal impact on the preagricultural hunting and gathering peoples on the prehistoric Georgia coast. There appears to be little or no difference in frequency with regard to age or sex. The agricultural lifeway, on the other hand, clearly represents an entirely different situation; frequency of dental caries increases, but in a very patterned fashion: cariogenesis affects adult females more than males.

TABLE 14.7 Frequency (Percentage) of Dental Caries in Preagricultural and Agricultural Females

	Preagricultural		Agricultural		
Tooth	%	N[a]	%	N[a]	% change[b]
Maxilla					
I1	0.0	48	3.7	82	3.7
I2	0.0	39	6.0	66	6.0
C	0.0	52	17.0	100	17.0
P3	0.0	60	21.0	95	21.0
P4	0.0	61	14.4	111	14.4
M1	0.0	73	16.7	138	16.7
M2	0.0	77	18.3	126	18.3
M3	0.0	73	17.4	109	17.4
Mandible					
I1	0.0	33	0.0	58	0.0
I2	0.0	42	2.4	84	2.4
C	0.0	60	5.1	97	5.1
P3	0.0	65	8.1	123	8.1
P4	0.0	76	13.9	67	13.9
M1	1.3	79	26.8	127	22.5
M2	1.2	86	31.5	127	30.3
M3	1.1	92	26.1	115	25.0
Totals	1.2	1016	15.6	1688	14.4

[a]Number of teeth observed for presence-absence of dental caries.
[b]Computed by the following formula: % Agricultural-% Preagricultural.

Degenerative Joint Disease

Comparisons of each articular joint for adults (females, males, and indeterminate sex combined) in the preagricultural and agricultural groups are presented in Table 14.9. These comparisons show a marked reduction in frequency of alterations of articular joints in the agricultural group relative to the preagricultural group. The reductions in frequency of the pathology are particularly marked for the cervical and lumbar intervertebral joints.

With regard to these comparisons for females only, significantly fewer articular joints in the agricultural group are affected by this condition (Table 14.10). A reduction in frequency of the disease is shown for most articular joints, especially the cervical, lumbar, elbow, and knee joints.

Similarly, males show a reduction in frequency of degenerative joint disease (Table 14.11). The greatest decline in frequency of

TABLE 14.8 Frequency (Percentage) of Dental Caries in Preagricultural and Agricultural Males

	Preagricultural		*Agricultural*		
Tooth	*%*	*N*[a]	*%*	*N*[a]	*% change*[b]
Maxilla					
I1	*2.1*	*37*	*0.0*	*63*	*-2.1*
I2	*0.0*	*31*	*1.7*	*58*	*1.7*
C	*0.0*	*35*	*4.9*	*82*	*4.9*
P3	*0.0*	*39*	*27.6*	*76*	*27.6*
P4	*0.0*	*38*	*13.4*	*82*	*13.4*
M1	*0.0*	*46*	*18.5*	*92*	*18.5*
M2	*0.0*	*47*	*13.5*	*89*	*13.5*
M3	*0.0*	*40*	*16.1*	*81*	*16.1*
Mandible					
I1	*0.0*	*15*	*0.0*	*58*	*0.0*
I2	*0.0*	*24*	*1.4*	*69*	*1.4*
C	*0.0*	*42*	*0.0*	*85*	*0.0*
P3	*0.0*	*43*	*3.2*	*93*	*3.2*
P4	*0.0*	*41*	*8.0*	*88*	*8.0*
M1	*2.1*	*47*	*22.4*	*98*	*20.3*
M2	*2.1*	*47*	*12.9*	*85*	*10.8*
M3	*2.1*	*45*	*22.9*	*96*	*20.8*
Totals	*0.6*	*617*	*11.2*	*1295*	*10.6*

[a]*Number of teeth observed for presence-absence of dental caries.*

[b]*Computed by the following formula: % Agricultural-% Preagricultural.*

joints affected by degenerative changes are the cervical and lumbar intervertebral joints.

In summary, analysis and comparison of articular joints affected by degenerative joint disease show a trend toward reduction in frequency of the condition in the agricultural group. While both females and males appear to show reduction in the disease, frequency changes are more pronounced in the males.

Skeletal Size

As has been shown in other publications, all Georgia coastal skeletal elements examined--clavicle, humerus, radius, ulna, femur, tibia, and fibula--show the same trend in size change in comparison of the preagricultural and agricultural period skeletal series (see Larsen 1981b, 1982). Therefore, for the

TABLE 14.9 Frequency (Percentage) of Degenerative Joint Disease in Articular Joints of Preagricultural and Agricultural Adults (females, males, indeterminate sex combined)

Articular joint	Preagricultural %	Preagricultural N[a]	Agricultural %	Agricultural N[a]	% change[b]
Cervical	26.4	53	5.3	132	-21.1
Thoracic	8.0	50	5.3	131	-2.7
Lumbar	44.4	45	17.8	118	-26.6
Sacral-Lumbar	2.7	40	3.4	87	0.7
Shoulder	4.0	149	1.0	289	-3.0
Elbow	9.1	176	2.3	307	-6.8
Wrist	4.9	142	0.4	266	-4.5
Hand	0.0	82	1.2	245	1.2
Hip	4.1	169	0.3	290	-3.8
Knee	13.7	183	6.5	291	-7.2
Ankle	4.4	158	0.4	285	-4.0
Foot	0.0	81	0.4	232	0.4

[a]Number of articular joints observed for presence-absence of degenerative joint disease.
[b]Computed by the following formula: % Agricultural-% Preagricultural.

TABLE 14.10 Frequency (Percentage) of Degenerative Joint Disease in Articular Joints of Preagricultural and Agricultural Females

Articular joint	Preagricultural %	Preagricultural N[a]	Agricultural %	Agricultural N[a]	% change[b]
Cervical	17.2	29	1.4	73	-15.8
Thoracic	6.7	30	1.4	72	-5.3
Lumbar	32.1	28	12.5	64	-19.6
Sacral-lumbar	4.3	23	6.4	47	2.1
Shoulder	2.4	83	0.7	144	-1.7
Elbow	9.6	94	0.0	167	-9.6
Wrist	2.6	77	0.0	140	-2.6
Hand	0.0	50	0.8	129	0.8
Hip	4.3	93	0.0	148	-4.3
Knee	15.0	94	3.4	147	-11.6
Ankle	4.5	88	0.0	139	-4.5
Foot	0.0	48	0.0	120	0.0

[a]Number of articular joints observed for presence-absence of degenerative joint disease.
[b]Computed by the following formula: % Agricultural-% Preagricultural.

TABLE 14.11 Frequency (Percentage) of Degenerative Joint Disease in Articular Joints of Preagricultural and Agricultural Males

	Preagricultural		Agricultural		
Articular joint	%	N[a]	%	N[a]	% change[b]
Cervical	40.0	20	11.3	53	-28.7
Thoracic	12.5	16	11.8	51	-0.7
Lumbar	69.2	13	27.7	47	-41.5
Sacral-lumbar	0.0	10	0.0	33	0.0
Shoulder	10.5	38	1.7	120	-8.8
Elbow	13.7	51	6.1	114	-7.6
Wrist	2.6	39	0.9	106	-1.7
Hand	0.0	28	2.0	100	2.0
Hip	0.0	51	9.1	110	9.1
Knee	18.6	59	12.6	111	-6.0
Ankle	4.1	49	9.2	109	5.1
Foot	0.0	26	1.1	93	1.1

[a]Number of articular joints observed for presence-absence of degenerative joint disease.

[b]Computed by the following formula: % Agricultural-% Preagricultural.

present discussion, the skeletal size changes will be summarized through presentation of only the results for the femur. A consideration of cranial and dental changes is presented elsewhere (see References).

The summary of the measurements and the preagricultural and agricultural comparisons for the femur is provided in Table 14.12. In a comparison of the preagricultural group with the agricultural group, the size changes show a trend of reduction. For the females, the size reduction ranges from 3.0 (neck horizontal diameter) to 8.3% (subtrochanteric anterior-posterior diameter). For the males, the size reductions range from 0.2 (maximum length) to 5.6% (subtrochanteric transverse diameter). In summary, the average reductions of the femoral dimensions are 5.9 and 3.4% for the females and males, respectively.

Comparisons of femoral indexes imply some degree of reduction in skeletal robusticity in the agricultural group relative to the preagricultural group (Table 14.13). In the females, there is a slight increase in the midshaft index (0.9%), a slight decrease in the platymeric index (0.7%), and a more substantial decrease in the robusticity index (3.2%). In the males, there are increases in both the midshaft and platymeric indexes (2.3 and 4.8%, respectively) and a marked decrease in the robusticity index (3.0%).

Similar comparisons of preagricultural and agricultural stature show size reduction in the agricultural group (Table 14.14).

TABLE 14.12 Comparison of Femoral Dimensions of Preagricultural and Agricultural Females and Males

	Female					Male				
	Preagricultural		Agricultural			Preagricultural		Agricultural		
Dimension	Mean (mm)	N	Mean (mm)	N	% change[a]	Mean (mm)	N	Mean (mm)	N	% change[a]
Head diameter	41.1	31	39.0	61	-4.9	45.5	14	43.8	58	-3.8
Neck vertical diameter	27.2	29	25.8	64	-5.3	30.7	12	29.7	60	-3.4
Neck horizontal diameter	22.7	31	22.0	64	-3.0	25.9	13	25.0	58	-3.3
Maximum length	434	19	416	54	-4.2	449	9	448	47	-0.2
Midshaft a-p diameter	26.7	44	25.2	86	-5.8	31.1	21	29.5	68	-5.0
Midshaft trans. diameter	24.3	44	23.1	86	-5.9	26.4	20	25.7	68	-2.4
Midshaft circumference	80	44	76	86	-5.0	90	21	86	68	-4.4
Subtrochanteric a-p	23.9	47	21.9	91	-8.3	25.4	19	25.1	70	-0.9
Subtrochanteric trans.	31.7	45	29.3	92	-7.4	34.5	19	32.5	69	-5.6

[a]Computed by the following formula: $-(1 - \overline{X}_{Ag}/\overline{X}_{Preag})100$.

TABLE 14.13 Comparison of Femoral Indexes in Preagricultural and Agricultural Females and Males

	Female					Male				
	Preagricultural		Agricultural			Preagricultural		Agricultural		
Index	Mean	N	Mean	N	% change[a]	Mean	N	Mean	N	% change[a]
Midshaft	91.3	44	92.1	86	0.9	85.7	20	87.7	68	2.3
Platymeric	75.6	45	75.1	91	-0.9	73.6	19	77.3	69	4.8
Robusticity	18.8	18	18.2	51	-3.2	20.0	9	19.4	46	-3.0

[a]Negative values computed by the following formula: $-(1 - \overline{X}_{Ag}/\overline{X}_{Preag})100$; positive values computed by the following formula: $+(1 - \overline{X}_{Preag}/\overline{X}_{Ag})100$.

TABLE 14.14 Comparison of Stature of Preagricultural and Agricultural Females and Males[a]

	Female					Male				
	Preagricultural		Agricultural			Preagricultural		Agricultural		
	Mean (cm)	N	Mean (cm)	N	% change[b]	Mean (cm)	N	Mean (cm)	N	% change[b]
Left femur	162.2	19	157.5	54	-2.9	167.9	9	167.5	47	-0.2
Right femur	160.7	21	156.4	52	-2.7	168.9	12	167.1	48	-1.1

[a]Computed from formulas provided by Genovés (1967); measurements are in cm.
[b]Computed by the following formula: $-(1 - \overline{X}_{Ag}/\overline{X}_{Preag})100$.

Estimation of stature, as based on the left and right femora, shows respective reduction of 2.9 and 2.7% for the females and 0.2 and 1.1% for the males.

DISCUSSION

A number of trends can be shown in the comparisons of prehistoric Georgia coastal hunter-gatherers (pre-A.D. 1150) with the successive agriculturalists (A.D. 1150-1550):

1. Increase in frequency of periosteal reactions
2. Increase in frequency of dental caries
3. Decrease in frequency of degenerative joint disease
4. Decrease in bone size
5. Decrease in skeletal robusticity
6. Decrease in stature

Let us examine these trends in some detail.

With regard to the preagricultural-to-agricultural changes observed in frequency of pathology--dental and postcranial--two primary conclusions can be drawn. On the one hand, status of health deteriorates as is indicated by a respective increase in periosteal reactions and dental caries in the postcranium and dentition. On the other hand, there is a reduction in functional demand placed on the postcranial skeleton as is indicated by the decreased frequency of degenerative joint disease. Both trends are a result of the shift in economy and associated lifeway from one that was based on hunting and gathering to one that was based, at least in part, on maize agriculture.

Perhaps the increase in periosteal reactions was a result of the analysis of a skeletal sample that is representative of a longer surviving population in the agricultural group relative to the preagricultural group. Certainly, such an age discrepancy between these skeletal series would tend to show an increase in frequency of the pathology. However, as shown above, it is the *preagricultural* group that is representative of an older skeletal sample. Alternatively, the increase in infectious lesions might be related to the introduction of a new disease after A.D. 1150. However, if a new disease had been introduced to the later agricultural populations occupying the Georgia coast, the evidence of skeletal infections would follow a more systematic pattern in the skeletal sample of post-A.D. 1150 adults. In fact, periosteal reactions occur for the most part on single bones of individuals affected.

The most likely explanation for the increase in frequency of the pathological condition in the agricultural period is probably associated with the change in settlement of human populations after A.D. 1150. Before the shift in subsistence economy, the Georgia coastal hunter-gatherer settlements were small, transient occupations. Concomitant with the change in subsistence, there is an alteration in settlement patterning: villages become large and, in a number of instances, permanently occupied. It appears that this change in settlement and the resultant increase in population size and density was conducive to the increase in infectious disease in general. Thus, the increase in periosteal reactions, a nonspecific infectious pathology, is reflective of a variety of diseases that are associated with dense, immobile populations.

The increase in frequency of dental caries might be related to an increasing survivorship in later populations on the Georgia coast. Yet it is the preagricultural group that consists of an older skeletal series, thus negating this possibility. The most cogent explanation for the marked increase in dental caries is related to the nature of the food source that formed the focus of subsistence after A.D. 1150: maize. Maize has a high sucrose content and unequivocal evidence has shown that increased oral ingestion of sucrose will produce cariogenic-related cavitation of teeth (Rowe 1975; Leverett 1982).

Unlike periosteal reactions and dental caries, the third pathology observed--degenerative joint disease--markedly decreased in frequency in the agricultural group. As with the above pathology changes, age factors should be considered in attempting to explain the marked alteration of the samples that are representative of the two groups. The preagricultural group is in fact comprised of an older skeletal sample than the agricultural group and, as would be expected, has a higher incidence of degenerative joint disease. It is possible, then, that the disparity in frequency of degenerative joint disease between the two groups could account for these differences in pathology affecting articular joint surfaces and margins. However, statistical analysis (Kolmogorov-Smirnov and chi-square) of the age distributions of individuals affected by the disease shows no statistically significant differences between the preagricultural and agricultural groups at the $p = .05$ level. Therefore, the factor of age composition differences between the preagricultural and agricultural groups does not, by itself, explain the differences in relative frequency of degenerative joint disease on the prehistoric Georgia coast.

While degenerative joint disease can result from a variety of factors (see especially discussion by Jurmain 1977), the skeletal changes that are associated with the condition are related in large part to the degree to which the body is subjected to mechanically related functional stress. A number of researchers, for example, have shown that specific behavioral repertoires and the general demand of lifeway in human groups, prehistoric and contemporary, are reflected in the degree and patterning of degenerative joint disease (e.g., Miller 1982; Ortner 1968; Ortner and Putschar 1981; Angel 1966; Haney 1974). I suggest, assuming that the level of mechanical stress is associated with the level of difficulty of lifeway (that is, relative difference in degree of work load), appears that the prehistoric Georgia coastal agriculturalists had a less demanding lifeway than their preagricultural hunter-gatherer predecessors.

The reduction in postcranial size and stature as documented in the analysis of femoral size of pre- and post-A.D. 1150 Georgia coastal Amerindians must be examined in light of the transition to an agricultural-based subsistence economy. Two variables, in particular, stand out for close consideration: level of functional demand (mechanical stress) and undernutrition (disease-nutritional stress).

A postcranial reduction in mechanically related stress is implicated by the changes that are present for the femoral indices: midshaft, platymeric, and robusticity. Both females and males show increases in the midshaft index, and the males show an increase in the platymeric index. The females show virtually no change (slight reduction) in the platymeric index. Moreover, robusticity indexes of both sexes are lower in the agricultural group than in the preagricultural group.

Although low platymeric indexes have been interpreted as representing a change in nutritional quality (e.g., Buxton 1938), this interpretation is not supported by either the morphology associated with low platymeric indexes (i.e., antero-posterior flattening of the femoral shaft distal to the lesser trochanter) or the calculation of area of bone present among groups with differing platymeric indexes (see Buxton 1938; Ruff and Hayes 1983a,b). In general, lower platymeric indexes tend to be associated with the entire range of preagricultural hominids, fossil and extant; higher platymeric indexes appear to be associated with agricultural and urban economies in which the lifeways are presumably less functionally demanding (Buxton 1938; Pearson and Bell 1917-1919; Townsley 1946; Brothwell 1981; Bennett 1973). Thus, we have two independent forms of evidence that suggest a decrease in functional demand on the postcranial skeleton with the adoption of an agricultural lifeway: (1) decrease in degenerative joint disease and (2) change in femoral diaphyseal form (for additional details on the femur as well as on tibial and humeral shaft shape alterations see Larsen 1981b, 1982).

It has been shown in humans and other animals that physical stress is related to bone development. In instances of constant stress, the amount of bone tissue of skeletal elements increases in order to resist efficiently external functional demands. Therefore, it is posited here that in keeping with the general phenomenon that bone is deposited in the presence of functional demand and is resorbed in its absence (Wolff's law), the size reductions as documented in Georgia coastal postcranial skeletal elements reflect a decrease in level of musculoskeletal stress with the change in economic focus.

The second factor to be considered here--disease-nutritional stress--is an equally likely cause of the skeletal size changes on the Georgia coast. That is to say, with the progressive increase in dietary carbohydrates and a decrease in consumption of animal protein, a decrease in skeletal size and stature resulted. Indeed, a decrease in protein consumption is suggested by the data addressed in the foregoing discussion of change in cariogenesis on the Georgia coast. Rowe (1975) and others have shown that the oral environment most suitable for the support of odontolytic organisms in dental plaque is created by a dietary regime low in protein and high in carbohydrates. The marked increase in dental caries on the prehistoric Georgia coast reflects such a dietary reconstruction.

Garn and Frisancho (1971), Garn and Clark (1975), Stini (1969, 1971), Newman (1975), and others have demonstrated that human populations undergoing protein malnutrition have relatively smaller body size and stature than populations with adequate nutrition. The reduced postcranial size and stature in the agricultural group on the Georgia coast would seem to suggest the likelihood of some form of nutritional stress such as protein malnutrition. Compounding the presumed reduction in animal protein consumption is the inadequacy of maize as a protein source. Moreover, if an individual is experiencing an infection, the body's response is to activate the immune system, thereby inhibiting the production of antibodies. This situation results in a reduction of the amount of labile protein that is available for the growth of the skeleton and other tissues (Stini 1969).

Nutritional deficiency in the later Georgia coastal agricultural populations might be examined in light of possible increases in frequency of porotic hyperostosis. For this region, however, only a few preagricultural and agricultural crania exhibit the presence of the pathology (see Zahler 1976; Larsen and Thomas 1982; C. S. Larsen, unpublished). Thus, there is no increase in frequency of the condition. It is suggested, then, that while porotic hyperostosis has been shown to be an important indicator of stress in paleopathological research (see Buikstra and Cook 1980; Huss-Ashmore et al. 1982; Goodman et al., Chapter 11 this volume), its presence or absence within a population certainly should not be considered in isolation from other stress indicators.

In order to distinguish mechanical from nutritional factors, Ruff and co-workers (Ruff et al. 1983) have analyzed cross-sectional geometric properties (bone areas, area moments of inertia) of Georgia coastal femora and have found significant remodeling of this skeletal element that appears to be related to a decrease in mechanical stressing of the lower limb in the agricultural group. The analysis also revealed that parameters that indicate strength (area moments of inertia) decrease relatively more than bone area. These data suggest, then, that although certain features of skeletal change may be related to diet--reduction in overall size--other features can be best interpreted in light of relative reduction in mechanical stress as was implicated by the aforementioned reduction in frequency of osteoarthritis and alterations in bone size and shape.

In summary, although the mechanisms by which the trends in skeletal size and form came about remain imprecise, it is possible

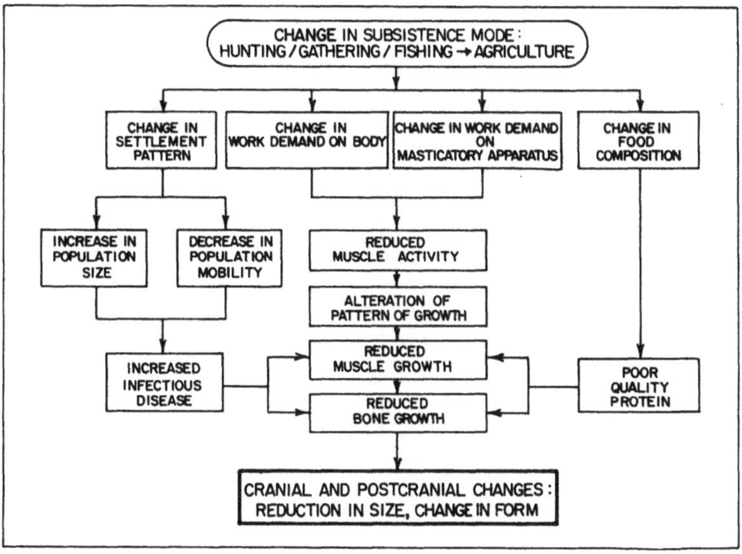

FIGURE 14.1. Processual model of biocultural adaptation on the prehistoric Georgia coast.

at this juncture to provide a preliminary model outlining the processes behind the changes documented in this chapter. In particular, it seems most likely that a combination of changes in health and nutrition and musculoskeletal stress led to progressive alteration in pattern of skeletal growth (see Figure 14.1).

Sexual Dimorphism

One intriguing change with regard to the transition from hunting and gathering to agriculture that will be addressed in the following discussion is that having to do with the differences seen between the female skeletal samples and their male counterparts. Three differences are present and can be summarized as follows:

1. Females show a greater increase in periosteal reactions than males.
2. Females show a greater increase in dental caries than males.
3. Females show a greater decrease in skeletal size and robusticity and stature than males, thus indicating an increase in the percentage of sexual dimorphism in the agricultural group (Table 14.15).

These sex differences represent a pattern and point to an important dichotomy in diet and associated behavior.

TABLE 14.15 Percentage of Sexual Dimorphism in Stature in Preagricultural and Agricultural Groups

Skeletal element	Preagricultural			Agricultural		
	Female mean stature[a]	Male mean stature[a]	% Sexual dimorphism[b]	Female mean stature[a]	Male mean stature[a]	% Sexual dimorphism[b]
Left femur	162.2	167.9	+3.4	157.5	167.5	+6.0
Right femur	163.7	171.4	+4.5	158.1	167.5	+5.6

[a]Computed from formulas provided by Genovés (1967); in cm.
[b]Computed by the following formula: $+(1 - \bar{X}_F/\bar{X}_M)100$.

Ethnographic accounts have demonstrated that there are strict divisions of labor among non-Western populations for the procurement of food, and, although the data are scarce, the impression one gets from a reading of the literature is that these divisions result in inequitable distributions of recovered dietary items. Among hunter-gatherer groups, women perform most of the activities that are associated with plant foods while men do most of the hunting; it is the latter sex, therefore, that has greater differential access to protein (see Bowdler 1976; Hayden 1981; Lee 1968; Meehan 1977a,b).

With regard to the Georgia coast, there are, of course, no data on food sharing and division of labor among the pre-A.D. 1150 hunter-gatherer populations, but there is pertinent information in the ethnohistoric record for the southeastern United States in general. Swanton (1942, 1946) and Hudson (1976) have pointed out that marked sexual division occurred for most activities: males were responsible for hunting; females were responsible for most agricultural activities, particularly those related to care of crops and food preparation. It is suggested here that the sex-difference trends that have been documented in the foregoing can be explained in a large part by role differences in subsistence-related behavior. On the one hand, females may have been exposed more to infectious conditions because they were spending more time in the village environment while males, because they were involved in more activities away from the village, were not exposed as much to pathogens responsible for the onset and maintenance of infection. Moreover, if there had been differential access to animal protein during critical periods of growth and development and adulthood, then the sex receiving relatively less protein--the females--would show a relatively greater reduction in skeletal size. Finally, it is important to keep in mind that female physical activity patterns may be more altered with the shift to sedentism than those of males; that is, in reference to the scenario presented above, women may have had a less mechanically demanding behavioral repertoire than males after A.D. 1150 and, hence, a relatively greater reduction in bone area and skeletal size.

COMPARISONS WITH OTHER STUDIES

The first description of pathology in Georgia prehistoric human skeletal remains is in the work of Clarence Bloomfield Moore (1897). In his skeletal descriptions, he noted instances of ankylosis, healed fracture, "inflammations" of long bones, pseudarthrosis, "diseased" long bones, alveolar abscessing and resorption, and dental caries.

Additional human remains recovered from the Georgia coast were studied by Wallace (1975) and Zahler (1976). These materials, composed of remains from the northern end of St. Simons Island, are from late prehistoric and protohistoric village and mound contexts. Employing a herbivore control (*Odocoileus virginianus*), chemical analysis of these remains revealed that burials from a later component (Taylor Mound) had a lower mean strontium content than burials from an earlier component (Couper Field), which was attributed to subsistence shift "from a marine-oriented, fishing-and-shellfishing economy (with consequently high strontium readings) to one that is pronouncedly horticultural" (Wallace 1975: 233). These findings should be considered preliminary since neither control with the use of another element (calcium, in particular) nor inclusion of carnivores in the control sample were used (see Sillen 1981; Smith et al., Chapter 5, this volume) in the analysis.

In support of the findings presented by Larsen (1982, see above), Zahler (1976) reported a high incidence of dental caries, suggesting a high carbohydrate intake. The investigator also reported the presence of porotic hyperostosis; this was attributed to iron deficiency anemia associated with increasing dependence on maize agriculture. Instances of vertebral degenerative joint disease and periosteal reactions were also noted. While none of these findings are contradictory to other studies utilizing Georgia coastal skeletal remains, the author did not present a clear discussion of frequency (percentage) of individuals affected by the pathologies. Consequently, comparisons with other localities are limited and should be made in only a general sense.

In contrast to the findings of Zahler (1976) and Larsen (see above), Hulse (1941) reported a rarity of dental caries in dentitions from the Irene Mound site, a late prehistoric habitation-ceremonial complex on the north Georgia coast. Hulse (1941:60) suggested that Irene peoples had subsisted more on a diet consisting largely of foods "obtained from hunting, fishing, and gathering, than upon an agricultural diet." This subsistence mode, in combination with abrasive foodstuffs, was thought to have prevented dental decay. My reexamination of the dental remains (Larsen 1982), however, indicates that the Irene Mound materials actually exhibit a rather high frequency of dental caries, and, most certainly, archaeological and ethnohistoric research has shown that the Irene Mound peoples were full-fledged agriculturalists.

Hulse (1941) also noted the presence of extreme tooth wear, a high frequency of alveolar abscesses, third molar impaction, infection (osteomyelitis, periostitis), and several cases of violence-related cranial trauma. These observations were confirmed by my review of these materials.

Only a small fraction of human remains from the interior of Georgia has been described (see Introduction). Of the descriptions of materials, most notable is the work of R. L. Blakely (1977, 1980) on the remains from the Etowah site, a major Mississippian habitation-ceremonial center in northwest Georgia. This investigator reported on frequencies in adults of infectious lesions (periostitis, osteomyelitis), gerontal osteoporosis, vertebral degenerative joint disease, porotic hyperostosis, periodontal disease, fractures, and tumors (Blakely 1980). For the most part, these conditions were low in frequency (reported in percentage of individuals affected), except that over 50% of adults were affected by vertebral degenerative joint disease. It is interesting that as in the Georgia coast populations a very low occurrence of porotic hyperostosis was found at Etowah (four cases). Blakely (1980) also found that lower status individuals (village area) had a greater frequency of periodontal disease than higher status individuals (Mound C). Although no differences in trace elements were found between these subpopulations (see Blakely and Beck 1981), Blakely (1980) attributed the differences in frequency of periodontal disease to a greater proportion of maize in the diet of lower class individuals. This, then, provides preliminary evidence that the transition to agriculture had not only a differential impact by sex (see Sexual Dimorphism), but also by class or status group.

Finally, in an examination and interpretation of Etowah demographic data and possible disease influences, Blakely (1977) noted that (1) there was little evidence of traumatic injury in young adult males; (2) there was no evidence that there were any European-introduced diseases that could have affected mortality; and (3) there was no apparent evidence of porotic hyperostosis in young preadults.

CONCLUSIONS

This chapter has summarized a series of skeletal and dental changes that developed in populations on the prehistoric Georgia coast in response to dietary and related behavioral alterations consequent to the shift from a diet based on hunting, gathering, and fishing to a diet based, at least in part, on maize agriculture. These data provide good evidence for a decline in health and an associated change in skeletal size. In addition, reduction in frequency of degenerative joint disease and shaft shape modifications in the midshaft and subtrochanteric region of the femur suggest a decrease in level of musculoskeletal stress with the change in lifeway. The impact of the shift to agriculture and increased sedentism was probably greater for the females than for the males. Most of the information from the work of Moore (1897), Zahler (1976), and Blakely (1977, 1980) is preliminary and does not provide total corroborative evidence for my studies as summarized in this paper.

More information is needed for a better understanding of human adaptation in prehistoric Georgia. Pathologic trends within the preagricultural hunting-gathering skeletal sample are not known; the data are available for analysis of the changes in health and disease that precede the transition to an agricultural subsistence mode. More important, the greater body of extant collections of human skeletal remains from the interior of Georgia need to be studied in order to provide a broader biocultural picture of this region of the prehistoric southeastern United States.

ACKNOWLEDGMENTS

Field support for the research from the Georgia coast (St. Catherines Island) was provided by the Edward John Noble Foundation and The American Museum of Natural History. I thank Drs. Douglas H. Ubelaker, National Museum of Natural History, Washington, D.C.; David Hurst Thomas, The American Museum of Natural History, New York; and David J. Hally and Marshall G. Hurlich, University of Georgia, Athens, for access to the Georgia coastal human skeletal remains included in the research summarized here. Dr. Ted A. Rathbun, University of South Carolina, Columbia, kindly gave me unpublished skeletal data collected from the Lewis Creek mounds. A number of individuals provided important aid during the research, writing, and presentation of the results: Drs. David Hurst Thomas, Milford H. Wolpoff, David S. Carlson, Christopher S. Peebles, Nathaniel H. Rowe, Douglas H. Ubelaker, C. Loring Brace, David J. Hally, Bruce D. Smith, T. Dale Stewart, J. Lawrence Angel, Donald J. Ortner, Lucile St. Hoyme, Christopher B. Ruff, Chester B. DePratter, Ms. Becky Carnes, and Mr. Fred C. Cook. Ms. Margot Dembo provided editorial assistance in the preparation of the final manuscript. David S. Carlson (1976) has developed a craniofacial-specific flow model similar, in part, to the general model figured in this chapter (Figure 14.1); I have profited enormously from discussions with him. Mr. Alfred J. Feeley, Graphics Services, Southeastern Massachusetts University, prepared the artwork for Figure 14.1.

The bulk of the research based on human remains from the Georgia coast was initiated and completed in 1978-1979 during tenure as a Fellow in Residence in the Department of Anthropology, National Museum of Natural History, Smithsonian Institution; financial support was provided by a Smithsonian Institution Predoctoral Fellowship.

REFERENCES

Angel, J. Lawrence
1966 Early skeletons from tranquillity, California. *Smithsonian Contributions to Anthropology 2(1)*:1-19.

Bennett, Kenneth A.
1973 The Indians of Point of Pines, Arizona: A comparative study of their physical characteristics. *Anthropological Papers of the University of Arizona* No. 23.
Blakely, Robert L.
1977 Sociocultural implications of demographic data from Etowah, Georgia. In *Biocultural adaptations in prehistoric America*, edited by Robert L. Blakely, pp. 45-66. University of Georgia Press, Athens.
1980 Sociocultural implications of pathology between the Village area and Mound C skeletal material from Etowah, Georgia. In The skeletal biology of aboriginal populations in the southeastern United States, edited by P. Willey and Fred H. Smith, pp. 28-38. *Tennessee Anthropological Association Miscellaneous Paper* No. 5.
Blakely, Robert L., and Lane A. Beck
1981 Trace elements, nutritional status, and social stratification at Etowah, Georgia. *Annals of the New York Academy of Sciences 376*:417-431.
Bowdler, S.
1976 Hook, line and dilly bag: An interpretation of an Australian shell midden. *Mankind 10*:248-258.
Brothwell, Don R.
1981 *Digging up bones* (third ed.). Cornell University Press, Ithaca.
Buikstra, Jane E., and D. C. Cook
1980 Palaeopathology: An American account. *Annual Review of Anthropology 9*:433-470.
Buxton, L. H. Dudley
1938 Platymeria and platycnemia. *Journal of Anatomy 73*:31-36.
Carlson, David S.
1976 Patterns of morphological variation in the human midface and upper face. In *Factors affecting the growth of the midface*, edited by J. A. McNamara, pp. 277-299. Center for Human Growth and Development, Ann Arbor.
Garn, S. M., and Diane C. Clark
1975 Nutrition, growth, development, and maturation: findings from the ten-state nutrition survey of 1968-1970. *Pediatrics 56*:306-319.
Garn, S. M., and A. R. Frisancho
1971 Effects of malnutrition on size and skeletal development. In *Proceedings of a workshop on problems of assessment and alleviation of malnutrition in the United States*, edited by R. G. Hansen and H. N. Munro, pp. 84-93. U.S. Government Printing Office, Washington, D.C.
Genovés, Santiago
1967 Proportionality of the long bones and their relation to stature among Mesoamericans. *American Journal of Physical Anthropology 26*:67-77.

Haney, Patricia
1974 Atlatl elbow in central California prehistoric cultures. In Readings in archaeological method and technique, edited by R. Kautz, pp. 31-34. *Center for Archaeological Research at Davis Publication* No. 4.

Hayden, Brian
1981 Subsistence and ecological adaptations of modern hunter/ gatherers. In *Omnivorous primates: Gathering and hunting in human evolution*, edited by R. S. O. Harding and Geza Teleki, pp. 344-421. Columbia University Press, New York.

Hudson, Charles
1976 *The southeastern Indians*. University of Tennessee Press, Knoxville.

Hulse, Frederick S.
1941 The people who lived at Irene: Physical anthropology. In *Irene mound site*, J. R. Caldwell and C. McCann, pp. 57-68. University of Georgia Press, Athens.

Huss-Ashmore, Rebecca, Alan H. Goodman, and George J. Armelagos
1982 Nutritional inference from paleopathology. *Advances in Archaeological Method and Theory* *5*:395-474.

Jones, Grant D.
1978 The ethnohistory of the Guale coast through 1684. In The anthropology of St. Catherines Island. 1. Natural and cultural history, David Hurst Thomas, Grant D. Jones, Roger S. Durham, and Clark Spencer Larsen. *Anthropological Papers of the American Museum of Natural History* *55*:178-210.

Jurmain, Robert D.
1977 Stress and the etiology of osteoarthritis. *American Journal of Physical Anthropology* *46*:353-365.

Larsen, Clark Spencer
1980a Dental caries: Experimental and biocultural evidence. In The skeletal biology of aboriginal populations in the southeastern United States, edited by P. Willey and Fred H. Smith, pp. 75-80. *Tennessee Anthropological Association Miscellaneous Paper* No. 5.

1980b Human skeletal and dental health changes in the prehistoric Georgia coast. In *Excursions in southeastern geology: The archaeology-geology of the Georgia coast*, edited by James D. Howard, Chester B. DePratter, and Robert W. Frey, pp. 192-201. Geological Society of America, Atlanta.

1981a Skeletal and dental adaptations to the shift to agriculture on the Georgia coast. *Current Anthropology* *22*:422-423.

1981b Functional implications of postcranial size reduction on the prehistoric Georgia coast. *Journal of Human Evolution* *10*:489-502.

1982 The anthropology of St. Catherines Island. 3. Prehistoric human biological adaptation. *Anthropological Papers of the American Museum of Natural History* *57*:155-270.

1983a Behavioral implications of temporal change in cariogenesis. *Journal of Archaeological Science 10(1)*:1-8.

1983b Subsistence role behavior and the infectious disease experience on the prehistoric Georgia coast. *American Journal of Physical Anthropology 60(2)*:216.

1983c Deciduous tooth size and subsistence change in prehistoric Georgia coast populations. *Current Anthropology* 22:422-423.

Larsen, Clark Spencer, and David Hurst Thomas

1979 Mortuary archaeology on the Georgia coast. In The anthropology of St. Catherines Island. 2. The Refuge-Deptford mortuary complex. *Anthropological Papers of the American Museum of Natural History 56*:8-12.

1982 The anthropology of St. Catherines Island. 4. The St. Catherines period mortuary complex. *Anthropological Papers of the American Museum of Natural History 57*:271-342.

Lee, Richard Borshay

1968 What hunters do for a living; or, how to make out on scarce resources. In *Man the Hunter*, edited by R. B. Lee and I. DeVore, pp. 30-48. Aldine, Chicago.

Leverett, Dennis H.

1982 Fluorides and the changing prevalence of dental caries. *Science 217*:26-30.

Meehan, B.

1977a Man does not live by calories alone: The role of shellfish in a coastal cuisine. In *Sunda and Sahul, prehistoric studies in S.E. Asia, Melanesia and Australia*, edited by J. Allen, J. Golson, and R. Jones, pp. 493-531. Academic Press, New York and London.

1977b Hunters by the seashore. *Journal of Human Evolution 6*: 363-370.

Miller, R. J.

1982 Manos, metates, and tennis elbow: Degenerative joint disease in the prehistoric Southwest. *American Journal of Physical Anthropology 57*:210.

Moore, Clarence Bloomfield

1897 Certain aboriginal mounds of the Georgia coast. *Journal of the Academy of Natural Sciences of Philadelphia 11*:4-138.

Newman, Marshall T.

1975 Nutritional adaptation in man. In *Physiological Anthropology*, edited by Albert Damon, pp. 210-259. Oxford University Press, New York.

Ortner, Donald J.

1968 Description and classification of degenerative bone changes in the distal joint surfaces of the humerus. *American Journal of Physical Anthropology 28*:139-156.

Ortner, Donald J., and Walter G. J. Putschar

1981 Identification of pathological conditions in human skeletal remains. *Smithsonian Contributions to Anthropology*. No. 28.

Pearson, K., and J. A. Bell
1917-1919 *A study of the long-bones of the English skeleton.* Draper's Co., London.
Rowe, Nathaniel H.
1975 Dental caries. In *Dimensions of Dental Hygiene* (second ed.), edited by Pauline F. Steele, pp. 198-222. Lea & Febiger, Philadelphia.
Ruff, Christopher B., and Wilson C. Hayes
1983a Cross-sectional geometry of Pecos Pueblo femora and Tibiae--A biomechanical investigation. A. Method and general patterns of variation. *American Journal of Physical Anthropology 60*:359-381.
1983b Cross-sectional geometry of Pecos Pueblo femora and tibiae--A biomechanical investigation. B. Sex, age, and side differences. *American Journal of Physical Anthropology 60*:383-400.
Ruff, C. B., W. C. Hayes, and C. S. Larsen
1983 Changes in femoral structure with the transition to agriculture on the Georgia coast. *American Journal of Physical Anthropology 60(2)*:247-248.
Sillen, Andrew
1981 Strontium and diet at Hayonim Cave. *American Journal of Physical Anthropology 56*:131-138.
Stini, William A.
1969 Nutritional stress and growth: Sex difference in adaptive response. *American Journal of Physical Anthropology 31*:417-426.
1971 Evolutionary implications of changing nutritional patterns in human populations. *American Anthropologist 73*:1019-1030.
Swanton, John R.
1942 Source material on the history and ethnology of the Caddo Indians. *Bureau of American Ethnology Bulletin* 132.
1946 Indians of the southeastern United States. *Bureau of American Ethnology Bulletin* 137.
Townsley, W.
1946 Platymeria. *Journal of Pathology and Bacteriology 58*:85-88.
Wallace, Ronald Lynn
1975 *An archaeological, ethnohistoric, and biochemical investigation of the Guale Aborigines of the Georgia coastal strand.* Ph.D. dissertation, Department of Anthropology, University of Florida, Gainesville.
Zahler, James W., Jr.
1976 *A morphological analysis of a protohistoric-historic skeletal population from St. Simons Island, Georgia.* M.A. thesis, Department of Anthropology, University of Florida, Gainesville.

CHAPTER 15

PALEOPATHOLOGY AND THE ORIGINS OF MAIZE AGRICULTURE IN THE LOWER MISSISSIPPI VALLEY AND CADDOAN CULTURE AREAS

Jerome C. Rose
Barbara A. Burnett
Mark W. Blaeuer

Department of Anthropology
University of Arkansas-Fayetteville

Michael S. Nassaney

Department of Anthropology
University of Massachusetts-Amherst

INTRODUCTION

For many years, archeologists have been concerned with the origins of agriculture and the cultural-ecological mechanisms that stimulated this mode of human adaptation. Despite the extensive research effort expended on this problem, there are many unanswered questions, some of which are addressed in this chapter. For example, does the advent of agriculture adversely affect human health? If so, is it the production and consumption of agriculturally derived foods or some other associated phenomenon that has an impact on human health? Is agriculture adopted because it represents a more reliable dietary base, or is it a necessity for a growing population which has expanded beyond its available resources? There are a number of theoretical and methodological approaches that may be employed for deriving answers to these questions from the archaeological and skeletal data. In choosing the particular approach employed in this chapter, we have made three assumptions.

First, the adoption of agriculture is a complex phenomenon that is often associated with other major cultural changes such as increased sedentism, increased population size and density, and the development of complex sociopolitical organization. Thus an understanding of the reasons for the adoption of agriculture and its ultimate impact on culture and biology can be achieved only if all the associated changes are considered during analysis. Second, dependency on agriculture is a local response to regional environmental carrying capacity, population density, and technology. The observed variability between cultural units in ecology, demography, settlement pattern, and technology can be used to evaluate the separate and cumulative effects of each of these factors on the adoption of agriculture. Third, it is assumed that agricultural dependency requires at least one carbohydrate crop, in this case maize. The use of these assumptions does not imply that agriculture cannot be considered a general phenomenon that occurs simultaneously over large geographic culturally diverse areas. On the contrary, this idea in conjunction with the three previously stated assumptions allows the authors to use the adoption of maize agriculture as a constant while evaluating the variability in the other factors. The authors have employed the above principles in choosing three ecological-cultural areas for this analysis: the Central Mississippi Valley, the Lower Mississippi Valley, and the adjacent Caddo area to the west.

An extensive, but by no means exhaustive, search of the archaeological and osteological literature was conducted for the purpose of locating osteological analyses from the three archaeological areas. The bioarchaeological data used in this chapter are derived from a variety of sources that include everything from published site reports and osteological appendices to skeletal series analyzed by the authors for this chapter.

Because the utilized analyses span a period of almost 80 years and were conducted by a diversity of osteologists, a uniform procedure for extracting the pertinent data was devised. All data were collected from the literature as raw scores whenever possible, and each investigator's methodology and criteria for data evaluation were used to transform the data into consistent categories. If there was any evidence that the data from a particular skeletal series were suspect or were not comparable to the other series, then they were eliminated from this analysis. Each skeletal series was placed into its chronological and cultural context using site reports, regional archaeological syntheses, and consultation with area archaeologists. The mention of archaeological sites in the text refers only to those components or occupations associated with burials. We must take full responsibility for all errors and misinterpretations of the archaeological and osteological data.

The determination of when dependency on maize agriculture occurred within these three areas has proved to be a very difficult problem. Many of the sites to which we refer in this study were excavated before the use of flotation and paleobotanical analysis, which makes it difficult to establish the existence of agriculture. Dental caries are the result of a complex interaction between carbohydrate and sugar content of the diet and the physical consistency of the foods. Turner (1979), using a worldwide series of data, has demonstrated that increased caries rates can be used to establish the presence of agriculturally produced carbohydrates in prehistoric diets. A systematic study (unpublished, J. C. Rose,

University of Arkansas) of caries rates and dental attrition in the Arkansas area has confirmed Turner's conclusions. Consequently, caries rates are used in conjunction with archaeological data for dietary reconstruction.

Paleopathologic data were placed into five categories (i.e., infections, porotic hyperostosis, osteoarthritis, osteophytosis, and trauma) before crude prevalence rates were computed separately for subadults and adults. Only major lesions (e.g., infectious lesions or trauma of skulls and long bones) were included in this tabulation because it was noticed that some osteologists did not record minor lesions such as infected sinuses or broken toes. It should be mentioned that the use of crude rates does not make maximum use of the data, prevents statistical analysis, and limits the precision of the interpretation. Another problem is that despite evidence for social ranking within the areas discussed in this chapter and the possibility of differential access to resources, which might influence disease rates, crude rates were computed without regard to these distinctions. These compromises were necessitated by the desire to include as many skeletal series as possible within this analysis. Because of these limitations, these data are used only to establish general trends that can be used as a basis for further research and hypothesis testing.

ARCHAEOLOGY

Caddoan Archaeology

The Caddoan culture area includes large portions of Texas, Oklahoma, Arkansas, and Louisiana (Figure 15.1). The heartland of the Caddoan culture area is the Great Bend Region of southwest Arkansas, northeast Texas, and southeast Oklahoma. The Red River Valley ecozone is characterized by a moderately broad alluvial valley with associated oxbow lakes, natural levees and backwater swamps, and a highly diverse series of microenvironments produced by this very active river. Two additional subareas are discussed within the chapter: the Arkansas River drainage of northeast Oklahoma and the Ouachita River drainage of south central Arkansas. These two subareas are characterized by narrower river valleys and upland terrain. Many important sites from northeast Texas are not discussed because of the lack of analyzed skeletal collections.

The Fourche Maline culture (400 B.C.-A.D. 900) is a natural extension of the Archaic characterized by an increasingly intensive utilization of collected resources (after Schambach 1982). Late Fourche Maline (A.D. 650-900) sites in both the Red River and Arkansas River areas are small to medium sized hamlets or villages (1-4 ha) with associated mounds (Schambach 1982; Wyckoff 1980).

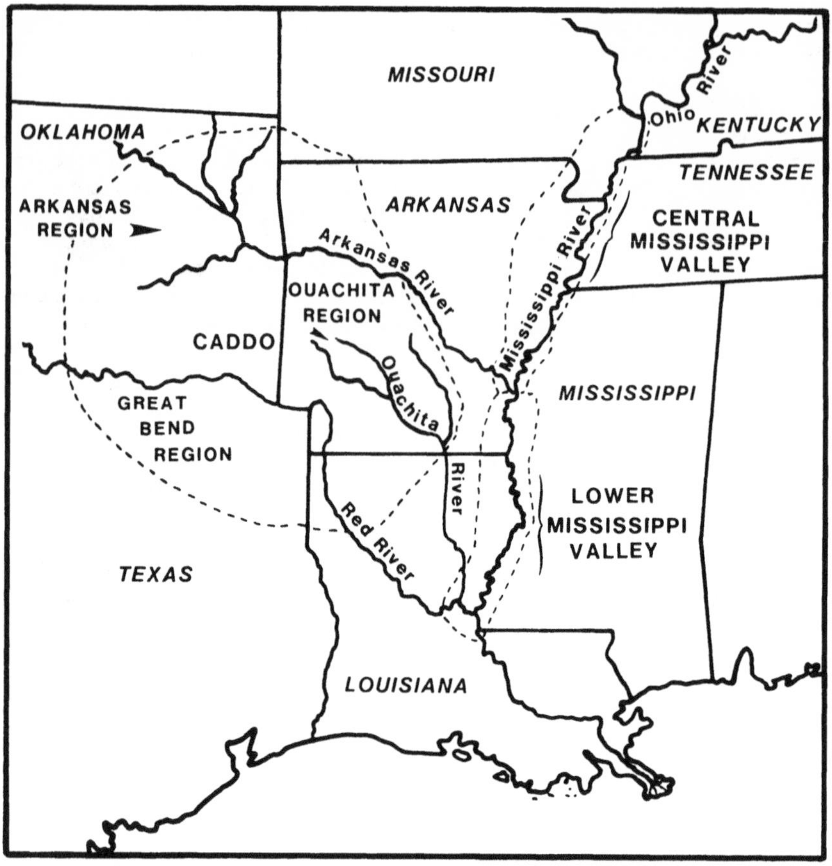

FIGURE 15.1. Map showing geographic limits of the Caddo, Central Mississippi Valley, and Lower Mississippi Valley areas.

There is no evidence of domestication from any of the Fourche Maline sites, although plant domestication is found throughout the neighboring areas during the same time period (Barr 1966; Cutler and Blake 1973; Jones 1949).

Examination of the caries data (Table 15.1) reveals low rates characteristic of nonagricultural groups for most of the Fourche Maline (0.1-1.6 caries/person) and high agricultural rates (4.1-7.6 caries/person) for the Caddo. Examination of the caries rates by site (Table 15.1) shows that the Fourche Maline Oklahoma sites of Mahaffey, Sam, Wann, and McCutchan-McLaughlin have low caries rates. Observation of the molar surfaces with the scanning electron microscope indicates the use of stone grinding implements and the consumption of large quantities of plant fiber at Mahaffey (Rose et al. 1982), but less plant fiber and large quantities of nuts at McCutchan-McLaughlin (Rose et al. 1982).

TABLE 15.1 Proportion of Dental Caries per Person by Specific Site within the Caddoan Cultural Area

Culture and site	Caries/person	N
FOURCHE MALINE		
Mahaffey[a]	0.1	56
Sam and Wann[c]	0.8	45
McCutchan-McLaughlin[b]	1.6	24
Ferguson[a]	4.3	7
Old Martin Place[d]	2.1	8
Caddo I Red River		
Crenshaw[e]	5.6	8
Cooper Lake[f]	6.3	15
Hanna[g]	1.7	6
Caddo II Red River		
Belcher I[h]	8.0	5
Bentsen-Clark[i]	1.7	31
Ferguson[a]	4.4	7
Sam Kaufman[j]	3.0	19
Roden I[k]	2.4	7
Caddo II Arkansas River		
Lundy[l]	1.3	6
Morris[m]	0.9	19
Nagle[n]	0.4	5
Horton[o]	0.6	21
Caddo IV Red River		
Belcher II and III[h]	2.3	15
Kaufman-Williams[p]	3.4	54
Roden II and III[k]	4.0	5
Caddo IV Ouachita River		
Copeland and Hedges[a]	7.6	53
Caddo V Red River		
Cedar Grove[q]	11.7	9

[a]Unpublished data, J. C. Rose, University of Arkansas.
[b]Powell and Rogers 1980.
[c]McWilliams 1970.
[d]Stark 1973.
[e]Powell 1977.
[f]Doehner and Larson 1978.
[g]Thomas et al. 1980.
[h]Webb 1959.
[i]Buikstra and Fowler 1975.
[j]Butler 1969.
[k]Rose et al. 1981.
[l]Buikstra et al. 1973.
[m]Brues 1959.
[n]Brues 1957.
[o]Brues 1958.
[p]Loveland 1980.
[q]Rose 1983.

Although botanical evidence is lacking, Schambach (1982) suggests that agriculture was adopted at some of the larger nucleated Late Fourche Maline sites in the Great Bend region. This contention is supported by an increase in caries at two of these sites: Old Martin Place exhibits a slight increase in caries (2.1 caries/person), and Ferguson with 4.3 caries/person is definitely within the maize consumption range. Further support of this idea must await analysis of additional skeletal series from this area.

The Caddoan cultural sequence is described using the five-period system suggested by Davis (1970), although this system is not used by all Caddo archaeologists. Caddo I (A.D. 900-1200) sites in the Great Bend region are small to possibly medium sized with burial mound complexes and a few richly furnished graves (Hemmings 1980). The evidence for maize cultivation is a single cob from Crenshaw (Schambach 1971). The caries rates (Table 15.1) for Crenshaw and Cooper Lake are high, indicating an agricultural diet. The low caries rate (1.7 caries/person) from Hanna and flotation/paleobotanical work at Spoonbill (Crane 1982) both indicate that some of the Caddo I sites were not dependent on maize agriculture. In the Arkansas drainage to the north, the Caddo I people expanded their territory, grew in population size, and occupied larger settlements (Wyckoff 1980). Evidence for maize consists of three cobs from one site (Wyckoff 1980).

The Caddo II period (A.D. 1200-1400) in the Great Bend region is characterized by dispersed households, vacant ceremonial centers (with small caretaker residential populations), and richly furnished graves (Hemmings 1980). The dispersion of households, each with its own garden plot, appears to have been adopted to take advantage of the small, widely scattered areas of good agricultural land within the valley and to overcome the risks of erratic rainfall (Hemmings 1980). Evidence of maize cultivation consists of 12-, 14-, and 16-row hard flint maize (Cutler and Blake 1973) and 40 cobs from a Caddo II floor at Battle Mound (Hemmings 1980). All but one (Bentsen-Clark) of the Red River Caddo II sites have high caries rates, which are indicative of maize consumption (Table 15.1). These data suggest that the majority of the Red River Caddo II populations are dependent on maize. The Caddo I period in the Great Bend area should be considered a time of transition to an agricultural economy.

In the Arkansas River drainage there are elaborate mound centers such as Spiro that have at best a few caretaker residents and associated large dispersed populations (Wyckoff 1980). There is evidence for both maize and bean agriculture from this period (Wyckoff 1980). The caries rates from these sites, however, are all low (0.4-1.3 caries/person), possibly indicating a nonmaize subsistence base (Table 15.1). These data suggest that agriculture was practiced within the Arkansas drainage, but many of the people were not dependent on an agricultural subsistence base.

The Caddo III period (A.D. 1400-1500) is not well known in Arkansas and the sites are probably indistinguishable from the Caddo IV sites. There is evidence of farmsteads, hamlets, mound centers, and burial clusters throughout the Great Bend region (Hemmings 1980). Unfortunately, there are no skeletal series assignable to this period. In the Arkansas drainage there is a decline in household numbers and a deterioration in regional integration (Wyckoff 1980). Although there is evidence for the cultivation of maize, beans, sunflower, and squash, the agricultural system appears to be breaking down with summer farming and winter bison hunting (Wyckoff 1980).

The Caddo IV period (A.D. 1500-1700) along the Red River is one of population decline and fragmentation of the social organization (Trubowitz 1983). The proposed settlement pattern of vacant ceremonial centers and dispersed farmsteads is corroborated by the Teran Map of 1691-1692 (Trubowitz 1983). There is extensive evidence for maize, beans, and other cultigens incorporated into a diverse subsistence base that includes collected plants and animal protein. The population decline evidenced in the archaeological data is possibly due to the introduction of European diseases into the Red River Valley (Milner 1980).

The caries rates from all Red River sites (Table 15.1) are characteristic of an agricultural subsistence base. It is interesting to note that the individuals interred in one ceremonial center (Belcher Mound) have a lower caries rate (2.3 caries/person) than those (3.4 and 4.0 caries/person) from a dispersed community (Kaufman-Williams and Roden). This suggests that the rural population ate more maize and the high-status individuals interred within the ceremonial centers had access to other sources of food. The enamel microwear patterns from this period show little evidence of plant fiber but do confirm the use of wooden utensils for food preparation (Rose et al. 1981; Rose 1983).

The Caddo IV period along the Arkansas River shows a continuing cultural deterioration and a gradual adoption of a Plains subsistence pattern (Wyckoff 1980). The Ouachita region is not yet well known, but there appears to be a hierarchy of small sites arranged around ceremonial centers located at strategic points along the river system (Early 1982). The caries rate (Table 15.1) for this region is extremely high (7.6 caries/individual) and suggests high maize consumption.

The Caddo V period (A.D. 1700-1800) is well known from historic records, which indicate an extensive array of cultigens utilized by the Caddo: two-crop maize agriculture, several varieties of beans, tobacco, pumpkins, and sunflowers (Hatcher 1927; Swanton 1942; Wyckoff 1980). The Caddoan diet is a complex mixture of domesticated and wild plants supplemented with animal protein. The high Cedar Grove caries rate (11.7 caries/person) supports the archaeological evidence for maize dependency (Table 15.1).

Central Mississippi Valley Archaeology

The Lower Mississippi Valley ecological and archaeological domain is bounded on the north by the Cairo Lowlands (located at the confluence of the Ohio and Mississippi rivers) and extends southward along the alluvial valley to the Gulf of Mexico. This area is divided into two parts at the mouth of the Arkansas River (Figure 15.1) for the purpose of this chapter. The northern division is referred to here as the Central Mississippi Valley, while the southern division is termed the Lower Mississippi Valley.

In the central valley, which has a considerably narrower alluvial valley than the lower valley, the Mississippi River produced a complex topography composed of oxbow lakes, natural levees, clay plugs, and backwater swamps. The lower valley also presents a complex geomorphological pattern with the major stream channel, minor tributaries flowing within old channels, oxbow lakes, natural levees, clay plugs, and backwater swamps. All portions of the valley are rich in resources including hardwood forests, numerous fish and other aquatic life forms, migratory waterfowl, and abundant mammalian species. In short, the entire Mississippi Valley south of the Ohio produced abundant and almost inexhaustible food resources for the prehistoric human inhabitants. The most important feature of this environment is its fine-grained distribution of resources. In other words, the highly diverse microenvironments are distributed fairly evenly throughout the valley and thus prehistoric peoples would not have had to travel far to exploit all available niches (Nassaney 1982).

Our discussion will begin with the Hopewell period (A.D. 0-400), which is labeled Marksville in this area because of its limited participation in the Hopewellian sphere (Toth 1979). The Hopewellian influence appears strongest in the earliest part of this period and is reflected only in the burial customs and not in the differential distribution of Hopewell status items (Toth 1979). The Morses' (1983) reconstruction of the settlement system is one of numerous small autonomous villages dispersed across the valley. There does not appear to be any evidence of maize, but numerous large storage pits are present at most sites (Morse and Morse 1983). We contend that the faunal and floral resources of this area are extremely abundant and that harvesting and storage of these resources made horticulture unnecessary. There are as yet no dietary data derived from the excavated skeletal material from this time period.

The Baytown (A.D. 400-700) settlement pattern is characterized by dispersed single household sites. The increase in site numbers suggests a population increase for the central valley (Morse and Morse 1983). The fact that sites are not located near good agricultural land argues against a dependency on agriculture, as does the absence of maize from flotation samples (Morse and Morse 1980, 1983). The Morses (1983) characterize the subsistence base as incorporating anything edible, while House (1982) documents the extensive use of fish.

The Mississippian period in the Central Mississippi Valley is divided into three parts: Early Mississippian (A.D. 700-1000), Middle Mississippian (A.D. 1000-1350), and Late Mississippian (A.D. 1350-1650). The initial stimulus for the development of Mississippian culture in the central valley arrived from upriver in the American Bottoms (Morse and Morse 1980, 1983). The settlement pattern developed to exploit the rich resources of this meander belt zone consists of civic-ceremonial centers, villages, hamlets, and limited activity sites (Morse and Morse 1980, 1983; Price 1978; Smith 1978). This population dispersal into relatively small habitation units made efficient use of the dispersed wild resources and good agricultural soils. The acquisition of animal proteins, especially waterfowl and fish, is an important ingredient of this adaptive complex (Smith 1978), while maize and other domesticants are important sources of carbohydrates and other nutrients (Morse and Morse 1980, 1983). Trace element analysis supports the hypothesized emphasis on fish and waterfowl rather than on "red meat" (Duncan 1978).

A variety of changes occur over time during the Mississippian, including increased population nucleation, increased defensive structures at ceremonial centers, increased evidence of violence, and an increase in the hierarchical organization of sites (Morse and Morse 1983; Price 1978). All the archaeological and historical data indicate a chiefdom level of social organization (Morse and Morse 1983; Price 1978; Smith 1978). Of all these trends, the most important is the increase in population nucleation and the abandonment in the Late Mississippian of the isolated farmsteads (Morse and Morse 1983).

The caries data for the Central Mississippi Valley indicate an overall reliance on a maize-derived carbohydrate diet (Table 15.2). The Early Mississippian material from Zebree exhibits a marginal maize consuming rate of 2.4 caries/person, and the largest Middle Mississippian sample from Johnny Wilson has a similar rate (2.6 caries/person). The 12 burials from the other Middle Mississippian sites show a much lower, nonagricultural rate, which could be indicative of variation in maize consumption by site. In other words, farmstead residents had greater access to other food resources (e.g., fish, meat, and wild plant foods) and thus consumed less maize. This interpretation is also supported by the high caries rates reported from two Powers Phase nucleated sites (Black 1979). The three large nucleated Late Mississippian sites of Upper Nodena, Middle Nodena, and Hazel all have caries rates indicative of maize dependency (3.6, 3.0, and 2.6 caries/person respectively). In fact, these rates are higher than those found for the earlier Mississippian periods and suggest an increase in maize consumption.

TABLE 15.2 Proportion of Dental Caries per Person by Site within the Mississippi Valley

Culture and site	Caries/person	N
Lower Mississippi Valley		
Baytown		
Gold Mine[a]	1.1	89
Powell Canal[b]	0.5	4
Coles Creek		
Mount Nebo[c]	8.1	86
Mississippian		
Gordon (3AS152)[d]	5.6	14
Central Mississippi Valley		
Early Mississippian		
Zebree[e]	2.4	13
Middle Mississippian		
Zebree[e]	0.0	2
Texas Eastern[d]	1.0	1
Johnny Wilson[d]	2.6	7
Mangrum[d]	1.0	2
Floodway Mounds[d]	0.6	7
Late Mississippian		
Upper Nodena[f]	3.6	129
Middle Nodena[f]	3.0	26
Hazel[d]	2.6	33

[a]Berg 1983; Walker 1980.
[b]Blaeuer and Rose 1982.
[c]Giardino 1977.
[d]Unpublished data, J. C. Rose, University of Arkansas.
[e]Powell 1980.
[f]Powell 1983.

Archaeology of the Lower Mississippi Valley

For the purpose of this chapter, the geographic limits of the Lower Mississippi Valley are the Arkansas River to the north and to a short distance below the confluence of the Red and Mississippi rivers to the south (Figure 15.1). Nassaney (1982) has noted a number of ecological differences between the lower and central valleys. At Helena, Arkansas, the Mississippi alluvial valley widens rapidly to nearly twice the width farther north. The areal extent of the alluvial valley is such that human populations are not subject to the environmental circumscription (i.e., narrow alluvial valley) found in the American Bottoms and to some extent in the central valley. Reduction in valley gradient in the lower valley results in a more dynamic hydrology that created more oxbow lakes, natural levees, and backwater swamps. Additionally, abandoned channels of the Mississippi serve as major tributaries creating an extensive network of waterways. The almost subtropical climate, in conjunction with more than adequate rainfall, created an environment extremely rich in both botanical and faunal resources.

Marksville (A.D. 0-300) is the manifestation of Hopewell in the Lower Mississippi Valley, which consists entirely of Hopewellian type mound burials at the beginning of the period (Toth 1979). Sites consist of burial mounds and small permanent villages located on higher ground adjacent to aquatic resources. These sites appear to be spaced lineally, approximately 3-5 km apart along waterways (Toth 1979). Subsistence emphasized intensive utilization of the abundant plant and animal floodplain resources, although some horticulture must have been practiced (Byrd 1976; Toth 1979). There are at present no skeletal data for dietary reconstruction from this and earlier periods.

The Baytown period (A.D. 300-700) does not appear to be well understood in the archaeological literature. Again, the sites appear to be small, at least semipermanent, and well dispersed across the alluvial valley (House 1982). An apparent increase in number, size, and complexity of archaeological sites led to the inference of population growth and an increasing dependence on agriculture (Phillips et al. 1951). In contrast to this inference of agriculture, paleobiological data suggest a continued exploitation of all available resources with a special emphasis on fish (House 1982). The authors would like to suggest that the socioeconomic development of the Northwest Coast is a possible analogy for the harvesting of fish resources in the Lower Mississippi Valley.

Examination of the Baytown caries rates (Table 15.2) reveals low rates of 1.1/person at Gold Mine and 0.5/person at Powell Canal. These rates clearly are not agricultural. Examination of the Gold Mine and Powell Canal molar surfaces with a scanning electron microscope indicates the mastication of some vegetable fiber, nuts, seeds, and other foods processed with stone implements (Blaeuer and Rose 1982). This microwear pattern is very similar to that observed in some of the hunting and gathering Fourche Maline groups. Both the archaeological and skeletal data indicate that the Baytown subsistence pattern consists of an intensive exploitation of natural resources with a special emphasis on fish and no evidence for maize horticulture, although consumption of some cultigens is possible.

The Coles Creek period (A.D. 700-1200) is an indigenously derived cultural florescence in the Lower Mississippi Valley (Phillips 1970). The settlement pattern consists of dispersed hamlets, small villages, and somewhat larger villages with as many as four small mounds (Brain 1978). Brain (1978:343) described the social organization as "small local centers serving local populations while interacting at the regional level on a relatively equal footing." The populations remain dispersed and even large, elaborate ceremonial centers such as Toltec (near Little Rock, Arkansas) appear to have at best only small caretaker residential populations (Nassaney 1982). Presently, direct subsistence data for this period in the Lower Mississippi Valley suggest continued reliance on nondomesticated faunal and floral resources with perhaps supplementary production of native North American and tropical cultigens. Unambiguous evidence of maize cultivation is conspicuous by its absence (House 1982).

In contrast to the archaeological data, the caries rate of 8.1/person at the Coles Creek site of Mount Nebo indicates a dependency on maize agriculture (Table 15.2). Although not quantifiable, the high caries frequencies reported for the Lake George Site also support maize utilization (Egnatz 1984). The authors would like to suggest two possible scenarios for the Coles Creek subsistence pattern. Since there is no evidence that the Coles Creek population density approached the carrying capacity of the alluvial valleys, it is suggested that maize was cultivated first as a high status or ceremonial food eaten frequently by the elite and on special occasions by the other social groups. A second and more likely alternative is suggested by recent work at the Alexander site, which is located in the Arkansas River Valley west of Little Rock. The high Coles Creek caries rate (6.0/person, $N = 2$) at this site is associated with evidence for extensive utilization of seeds such as Maygrass (*Phalaris caroliniana*), knotweed (*Polygonum erectum*), goosefoot (*Chenopodium* sp.), and wood sorrel (*Oxalis* sp.) (King 1983; Rose and Marks 1983). These data suggest that the high Coles Creek caries rates may be due to reliance on native seeds rather than maize. Additional paleobotanical and skeletal data are needed to test these hypotheses.

In the Mississippi period (A.D. 1200-1680) the indigenous development of the Plaquemine culture from Coles Creek was stimulated by the development of the Mississippian culture in the American Bottoms (Brain 1978). Although the majority of peoples appear to have remained dispersed, certain ceremonial centers located at major river confluences became towns with resident populations by the fifteenth century (Brain 1978). There is no question that a chiefdom level of social organization existed with extensive interaction between regional ceremonial centers.

When considering Plaquemine subsistence, it is important to note that there is no indication that local populations, even at the nucleated centers, ever exhausted the natural resources of the Lower Mississippi Valley, and thus availability of food has never been an important variable in cultural development (Brain 1978). Smith (1978) characterizes the subsistence pattern as selective utilization of a limited number of animal and plant species with fish and waterfowl contributing at least 50% of the total protein. There is archaeological evidence of maize cultivation during this period. The high caries rate (5.6 caries/person) at the Mississippian Gordon site in southeast Arkansas suggests considerable consumption of maize (Table 15.2). Unfortunately, Hrdlicka (1909)

TABLE 15.3 Percentages of Pathologies from the Caddoan Culture Area with Sites Combined by Cultural Period and Geographic Region

	Infections				Porotic hyperostosis				Osteo-arthritis		Osteo-phytosis		Trauma	
	subadult		adult		subadult		adult		adult		adult		adult	
Cultural period	%	N	%	N	%	N	%	N	%	N	%	N	%	N
Fourche Maline (combined)	12.0	57	11.1	169	--	--	1.9	53	8.3	169	15.4	169	6.5	169
Caddo I (Red River)	28.6	7	30.0	20	0.0	7	25.0	20	5.6	18	11.1	18	5.6	18
Caddo II (Red River)	33.3	9	9.8	41	16.7	6	8.3	36	0.0	36	16.7	36	2.8	36
Caddo II (Arkansas River)	8.9	45	23.5	85	8.9	45	7.0	85	7.0	85	4.7	85	4.7	85
Caddo III and IV (Ouachita River)	--	--	18.8	16	--	--	12.5	16	0.0	16	18.8	16	0.0	16
Caddo IV (Ouachita River)	--	--	17.5	40	--	--	5.0	40	2.5	40	7.5	40	5.3	19
Caddo IV (Red River)	15.1	53	11.9	84	14.3	35	19.1	68	16.4	61	33.3	69	6.6	61

did not report caries rates for three large Plaquemine-Mississippian sites (i.e., Boytt's Field, Myatt's Landing, and Ward Place).

PALEOPATHOLOGY AND AGRICULTURE

Caddoan Region

The paleopathology data for the Caddoan area are presented separately by geographic subareas within each period (Table 15.3). The trauma rates are very stable and show only minor fluctuations among subareas and time periods (Table 15.3). These data do not reflect interpersonal violence (i.e., embedded projectile points), but it is interesting to note that embedded projectile points are found only among Fourche Maline groups, where they appear to be quite common (Powell and Rogers 1980). Osteophytosis rates (not age adjusted) do show some minor fluctuations (Table 15.3). The Fourche Maline have a fairly high rate of 15.4%, which declines with the adoption of agriculture (i.e., Caddo I and II) and then increases above the hunting and gathering rate to 33.3% among the mature agriculturalists along the Red River. A similar pattern is observable in the osteoarthritis rates. These patterns suggest that physical stress (i.e., heavy work load) was initially reduced when agriculture was adopted as a supplement to hunting and gathering, but increased among the later Caddo, who were dependent on a mature agricultural system.

The chronological-geographic pattern of infectious disease offers an interesting interpretation of the health consequences of agriculture (Table 15.3). The relatively low subadult (12.0%) and adult (11.1%) infection rates of the Fourche Maline are dramatically increased with the introduction of agriculture during Caddo I (subadult, 28.6%; adult, 30.0%). The increase in porotic hyperostosis from 1.9 to 15.0% indicates that maize was being consumed without access to other dietary iron sources such as red meats. As the Caddoan culture and agriculture developed along the Red River, the infection rates began to drop and almost approached the Fourche Maline level during Caddo IV (subadult, 15.1%; adult, 11.9%). The decline in porotic hyperostosis in conjunction with higher caries rates suggests increased iron consumption (e.g., meat). These data support the contention that stress is greatest during the initial introduction of a new subsistence pattern (Cook and Buikstra 1979) and that it decreases as the culture adapts to the new ecological situation.

In the case of the Caddo there are changes in both subsistence and settlement patterns whose separate influences on health must be evaluated. The Fourche Maline rates do not include any nucleated groups (as postulated by Schambach 1983), while it is possible that the Red River Caddo I (Table 15.3) groups are still

TABLE 15.4 Percent Sexual Dimorphism of Femur Head Diameters by Archaeological Site and Cultural Period within the Caddoan Cultural Area

	Males		Females		
Culture and site	Diameter (cm)	N	Diameter (cm)	N	Sexual dimorphism (%)
Fourche Maline					
McCutchan-McLaughlin[a]	4.5	9	3.8	9	15.5
Old Martin Place[b]	4.6	2	3.9	4	15.2
Caddo I					
Cooper Lake[c]	4.6	7	4.1	6	10.9
Caddo II					
Sam Kaufman[d]	4.6	6	4.1	8	10.9
Bentsen-Clark (mode)[e]	4.6		4.0		13.0
Caddo IV					
Kaufman-Williams[f]	4.6	23	4.0	24	13.0
Roden[g]	4.6	5	4.2	9	8.7
Caddo V					
Cedar Grove[h]	4.6	5	4.1	2	10.9

[a]Powell and Rogers 1980.
[b]Stark 1973.
[c]Doehner and Larson 1978.
[d]Butler 1969.
[e]Buikstra and Fowler 1975.
[f]Loveland 1980.
[g]Rose et al. 1981.
[h]Rose 1983.

nucleated. However, the settlement pattern along the Red River is dispersed by Caddo II and this change is reflected in a lower adult infection rate (9.8%) but no change in the subadult rate (33.3%). Although the sample sizes are small, we offer the hypothesis that the adult infection rate is responsive more to population aggregation, while an increased subadult infection rate is due to the use of maize as a weaning diet. The low subadult rate (8.9%) of the Arkansas River Caddo II is detected in groups whose caries rates indicate that maize was not an important dietary component. The higher adult rates for both the Arkansas and Ouachita River drainages might suggest nucleated settlements, but the settlement pattern data for these subareas are unclear.

The gross paleopathologic data are most productive when complemented by nonspecific stress indicators such as Harris lines and sexual dimorphism. It is unfortunate that so little data have been collected in the Caddoan region. The maximum diameter of the femur head was chosen to examine sexual dimorphism because it is the most frequently reported measurement (Table 15.4). Examination of the percentage of sexual dimorphism shows a consistent reduction in the hunting and gathering Fourche Maline relative to the agricultural Caddo. However, examination of the mean measures show that both males and females become larger with the adoption of agriculture. Both males and females are 0.1 cm more robust at Old Martin Place (possibly a late Fourche Maline transition to agriculture site) than at the nonagricultural McCutchan-McLaughlin site. Interestingly, all means in males from the Caddo sites are 4.6 cm, whereas the means in females range between 4.0 and 4.2 cm. It is the females who increased in size dramatically and variably between the Fourche Maline and Caddo. This increase in femur head diameters probably has two components that include increased protein consumption and increased mechanical stress. Taken in conjunction with both the archaeological and the skeletal data, this pattern of increased size could suggest both greater protein availability for females and increased mechanical stress with the adoption of agriculture.

The Harris line data also support the greater availability of protein during Caddo times. The Fourche Maline McCutchan-McLaughlin site produced the following Harris line means: 3.8 lines/subadult, 1.6 lines/adult, and 2.6 lines/tibia for the entire sample of 20 (Powell and Rogers 1980). In contrast, the Caddo IV site of Kaufman-Williams produced a mean of only 0.35 lines/individual for the 20 subadults examined (Loveland 1980). Thus the Caddo IV children had fewer growth arrest episodes than the Fourche Maline, possibly due to a more even distribution of protein throughout the year and the availability of adequate protein during episodes of childhood illness.

Comparison of the skeletal paleopathology and stress data with our present knowledge of Caddoan archaeology produces the following interpretation of the impact of agriculture. Small sample sizes and incomplete data collection make this interpretation a hypothesis requiring further testing with both archaeological and skeletal data. The Fourche Maline populations were not dependent on agriculture, although future work will undoubtedly demonstrate that they were familiar with the process of domestication.

The paleopathology and stress data suggest that the Fourche Maline lifeway produced a high degree of biological adaptive fitness with a high degree of mechanical stress (i.e., osteophytosis). Late Fourche Maline sites along the Red River are sedentary villages with nearby burial mounds (Hemmings 1980; Schambach 1983; Wyckoff 1980). It appears that over time the Fourche Maline grew in population size and became gradually more sedentary. The high frequency of violent deaths indicates intergroup competition and conflict (Powell and Rogers 1980). The high frequency of Harris lines among the Fourche Maline suggests the possibility of periodic or seasonal food shortages. Caries data from the larger nucleated Fourche Maline sites of the Great Bend region indicate that maize agriculture may have been adopted to supplement the use of native fauna and flora or at least to even out seasonal fluctuations in availability.

During the Caddo I and II periods, maize agriculture spreads sporadically along the Red River. Some Caddo populations consumed large quantities of maize while others utilized small amounts (e.g., Crane 1982). The adoption of maize was probably determined by local population densities and resource availability. This period of transition to an agricultural economy is marked by increases in both subadult and adult infection rates and a reduction in mechanical stress on the spine. It should be noted that porotic hyperostosis rates are initially high and decline as the nutritional system adjusts in order to provide additional iron sources. Since the Fourche Maline data reported here are from nonnucleated groups, the increase in morbidity appears to be associated with both population nucleation and the adoption of agriculture.

The highly dispersed small units of good agricultural land encouraged a settlement pattern of dispersed households and vacant ceremonial centers. With the advent of this dispersed settlement system before the Red River Caddo II, the adult infection rate drops, while the subadult rate remains elevated. We suggest that the drop in the adult rate is a response to dispersion of the population, and the high subadult rate to the use of maize in the weaning diet. A parallel can be observed in the Caddo II Arkansas region, where there is no evidence of maize dependency and thus a low subadult infection rate, while the narrower (i.e., relatively circumscribed) valleys produce higher population densities and a higher adult infection rate than is found in the Fourche Maline.

By Caddo IV the culture has integrated the new subsistence settlement system and provides a high level of adaptive efficiency indicated by morbidity rates similar to those of the Fourche Maline. The low frequency of Harris lines and the increased femur head diameters may indicate that this mature agricultural subsistence system is providing a more reliable nutrition base than that of the Fourche Maline. It should be pointed out that this

TABLE 15.5 *Percentages of Pathologies from the Mississippi Valley by Site and Cultural Period*

Cultural period	Infections				Porotic hyperostosis				Osteo-arthritis		Osteo-phytosis		Trauma	
	Subadult		Adult		Subadult		Adult		Adult		Adult		Adult	
	%	N	%	N	%	N	%	N	%	N	%	N	%	N
Lower Mississippi Valley														
Baytown														
Gold Mine[a]	--	--	25.8	31	--	--	--	--	74.2	31	20.4	49	--	-
Powell Canal[b]	0.0	2	25.0	4	0.0	2	0.0	4	25.0	4	50.0	2	25.0	4
Coles Creek														
Mt. Nebo F[c]	0.0	10	16.7	24	0.0	10	0.0	24	8.3	24	33.3	24	4.2	24
Mt. Nebo A[c]	0.0	13	3.3	30	0.0	13	0.0	30	0.0	30	0.0	30	10.2	30
Lake George[d]	--	--	7.5	80	--	--	--	--	--	--	10.0	80	1.2	80
Plaquemine-Mississippian														
Boytt's Field[e]	--	--	36.0	25	--	--	4.0	25	4.0	25	28.0	25	0.0	25
Myatt's Landing[e]	0.0	1	11.1	18	0.0	1	0.0	18	0.0	18	27.8	18	5.5	18
Ward Place[e]	--	--	25.0	20	--	--	0.0	20	0.0	20	75.0	20	0.0	20
Gordon[f]	0.0	2	18.7	16	0.0	2	31.2	16	18.7	16	26.7	15	12.5	16

Central Mississippi Valley														
Early Mississippian														
Zebree[g]	--	--	50.0	8	--	--	11.1	9	25.0	12	33.3	12	6.2	16
Hyneman[f]	--	--	0.0	1	--	--	--	--	0.0	3	66.7	3	0.0	2
Middle Mississippian														
Zebree[g]	0.0	3	0.0	1	0.0	1	0.0	2	0.0	2	0.0	2	50.0	2
Johnny Wilson[f]	66.7	3	33.3	15	0.0	2	0.0	2	8.3	12	25.0	12	6.6	15
Late Mississippian														
Upper Nodena[h]	--	--	93.1	58	--	--	17.6	142	3.5	86	8.3	12	5.2	58
Middle Nodena[h]	--	--	--	--	--	--	13.3	30	0.0	7	50.0	2	0.0	2
Hazel[f]	--	--	87.5	72	--	--	--	--	--	--	--	--	--	--

[a]Berg 1983; Walker 1980.
[b]Blaeuer and Rose 1982.
[c]Giardino 1977.
[d]Egnatz 1984.
[e]Hrdlicka 1909.
[f]Unpublished data, J. C. Rose, University of Arkansas.
[g]Powell 1980.
[h]Powell 1983.

mature agricultural complex did not develop in the circumscribed Arkansas River area, where the inhabitants adopted a Plains Bison hunting-agricultural system.

Central Mississippi Valley

The paleopathologic data for the Central Mississippi Valley will again be examined both by cultural period and specific sites (Table 15.5). Trauma rates fluctuate between zero and 12.5% and do not indicate any trends. The high Zebree and Powell Canal rates are produced by small sample sizes. Trauma associated with interpersonal violence, such as wounds and projectile points, is not represented in these figures but is quite common only in the Middle to Late Mississippian (Black 1979; unpublished, J. C. Rose, University of Arkansas). Both osteophytosis and osteoarthritis combined rates decline dramatically between the Early (40.0 and 20.0%, respectively) and Late (14.3 and 3.4%) Mississippian. These data suggest a decline in mechanical stress with increased reliance on agriculture.

The pattern of infection rates in the Central Mississippi Valley is quite simple. The Early (44.4%) and Middle (35.3%) Mississippian combined adult infection rates are similar and considerably lower than the 90.0% rate reported for the Late Mississippian. Of significance is the fact that the dramatically high adult infection rate is associated with dramatic nucleation of the population into a few civic-ceremonial centers and abandonment of many dispersed residences in the Late Mississippian.

Table 15.6 shows that there is a slight and variable increase in sexual dimorphism of the femur head between the Early (8.2%) and Late Mississippian (10.9-12.8%). This increase is due to both a slight increase in size among males and a slight decrease in size among females. These differences may be due to changes in both nutrition and mechanical stress, but since the trend is not consistent no interpretation can be offered.

In summary, the impact of the adoption of agriculture in the Central Mississippi Valley cannot be evaluated, as there are no analyzed preagricultural skeletal samples. Both the skeletal and archaeological data suggest that both population nucleation and maize dependency increased during the Mississippian period. Since the adoption of agriculture had occurred during the earliest Mississippian, the only explanation for the high adult infection rate in the Late Mississippian is population nucleation and unknown changes in sociopolitical organization.

Lower Mississippi Valley

Again, the trauma rates in the Lower Mississippi Valley show the same minor fluctuations previously described. There is no evidence from any time period of interpersonal violence. The

TABLE 15.6 Sexual Dimorphism of Femur Head Diameters by Site and Cultural Period within the Mississippi Valley

Culture and site	Males: Diameter (cm)	Males: N	Females: Diameter (cm)	Females: N	Sexual dimorphism (%)
Lower Mississippi Valley					
Baytown					
Powell Canal[a]	4.8	1	4.2	2	12.5
Gold Mine[b]	4.7	19	4.1	24	12.8
Mississippian					
Gordon[c]	4.6	6	3.9	6	15.2
Central Mississippi Valley					
Early Mississippian					
Zebree[d]	4.6	1	4.2	5	8.2
Middle Mississippian					
Johnny Wilson[c]	4.8	2	4.0	6	16.7
Late Mississippian					
Upper Nodena[e]	4.7	21	4.1	15	12.8
Hazel[c]	4.6	21	4.1	23	10.9

[a]Blaeuer and Rose 1982.
[b]Berg 1983; Walker 1980.
[c]Unpublished data, J. C. Rose, University of Arkansas.
[d]Powell 1980.
[e]Powell 1983.

combined osteophytosis rates decline slightly from Baytown (21.6%) to Coles Creek (11.9%), only to rise dramatically to 42.0% in the Plaquemine-Mississippian period. In contrast, combined osteoarthritis rates fall dramatically from a high during the Baytown period (68.6%) to low rates for both Coles Creek (3.7%) and Plaquemine-Mississippian (7.3%). When the osteophytosis rates are examined by site (Table 15.5), the only significant change is the high frequency at Ward Place, which at present cannot be explained. The drop in osteoarthritis rates from Gold Mine (74.2%) to all other sites might represent a real activity change such as the introduction of agriculture during the Coles Creek period.

The pattern of adult infection rates presents an interesting contrast to the two previously described cultural areas. The Baytown combined adult infection rate of 25.7% is much higher than expected, especially when compared to that in the contemporaneous Fourche Maline to the west (Table 15.3). Robbins (1978) notes a high frequency of generalized periostitis that she tentatively diagnoses as a treponemal infection at Morton Shell Mound, a Coles Creek site. These observations could not be quantified and included in Table 15.5 due to the highly fragmented and mixed condition of the burials. Preliminary analysis (Berg 1983) indicates that a similar condition is present at the Gold Mine site. The authors suggest that this condition is ubiquitous in the lush environment of the southernmost portion of the Mississippi Valley. The combined adult Coles Creek infection rate is much lower (8.2%) and suggests that the treponemal disease is not present at these sites. It should be noted that the earlier Stage F skeletal series from Mount Nebo has a higher adult infection rate (16.7%) than the later Stage A material (3.3%) (Table 15.5). It is possible that the earlier high infection rate is a response to the initial introduction of agriculture. The Plaquemine-Mississippian rates fluctuate between 11.1 and 36.0% (Table 15.5). Some of these rates are comparable to those in the Early Caddo, but they are all well below those of the nucleated Late Mississippian. These last rates are derived from fairly large samples from a diversity of sites, which should make them very reliable.

The only nonspecific stress indicator available is sexual dimorphism of the femur head. Examination of the data presented in Table 15.6 shows an increase in sexual dimorphism between Baytown and the Mississippian. This increase, however, is associated with a decrease in size of both males and females. Both Baytown sites show extreme sexual dimorphism with very robust, large-boned males and rather gracile females. In contrast, the Gordon site has relatively gracile males and females. The Gold Mine robusticity appears to be the result of extensive physical activity (i.e., mechanical stress) and possibly better nutrition than at the Gordon site, whose inhabitants were maize consuming.

In summary, assessment of the impact of agriculture in the Lower Mississippi Valley is hindered by a lack of temporal spread in the skeletal data. The Baytown period is characterized by extreme skeletal robusticity, a high incidence of degenerative joint disease, and moderately good health, with the exception of a postulated treponemal infection also reported for the Morton Shell Mound People. The Lower Valley, with its high rainfall, subtropical climate, and swampy topography, can be expected to have harbored many parasites and endemic pathogens. The infection rate differential between Baytown and Fourche Maline is tentatively attributed to environmental differences between the two areas. The decrease in size of both males and females between Baytown and Mississippian is attributed to both a decrease in mechanical stress and a decline in nutritional quality.

Although the caries rates indicate a high maize consumption for Coles Creek, there is no accompanying increase in infections similar to that observed among the Caddo I Red River inhabitants. There are three plausible explanations for this phenomenon. First, maize was consumed as a high status or ceremonial food, not as a dietary staple, and thus any debilitating effects of maize dependency were circumvented. This interpretation is supported by the virtual absence of iron deficiency anemia (i.e., porotic hyperostosis) and the absence of archaeological information suggesting that Lower Mississippi Valley population densities ever approached the carrying capacity of the local environments. The second explanation for the low infection rates is the absence of population nucleation, which appears to be responsible for the elevated adult infection rates among the Red River Caddo I (which are possibly nucleated) and the Late Mississippians of the Central Mississippi Valley (which are nucleated). The third explanation is that the high caries rates are due to increased consumption of native seeds. This would explain the absence of porotic hyperostosis and increased infections. Further discussion must await the analysis of additional Coles Creek skeletal series as well as series from the Marksville period.

CONCLUSIONS

The adoption of maize agriculture in eastern North America appears to be a universal phenomenon that occurs at approximately the same time over large geographic regions and presumably for similar reasons. Two commonly reported ideas are (1) that agriculture was necessary to feed a growing population that had exceeded the carrying capacity of its niche and (2) that, once adopted, agriculture was deleterious to human health. On first examination, these statements appear to be true for the three areas discussed in this chapter, but closer inspection of the paleopathological and archaeological differences among the three areas reveals that the above concepts must be examined in terms of local ecological variation. The four most important ecological variables are the environmental carrying capacity (i.e., biomass), climatic stability (e.g., absence of regular droughts), the absence of environmental circumscription (i.e., geographic extent of the most productive ecological niche), and the distribution of resources within the environment. With the exception of a fine-grained, highly diverse ecology found in all three, the archaeological areas can be ranked in increasing order for the other three ecological variables: Caddoan area (specifically the Red River Valley), Central Mississippi Valley, and Lower Mississippi Valley. These ecological differences are most important for understanding the stimuli for the adoption of agriculture and evaluating its health consequences.

Five important temporal trends are common to the three regions and probably to most of eastern North America.

1. A semisedentary or sedentary settlement pattern developed early in the archaeological sequence (i.e., Late Archaic).
2. The knowledge of agricultural technology, evidenced by the presence of native cultigens, preceded maize agriculture by several centuries.
3. The archaeological data indicate population increases over time.
4. There is evidence of food storage before the adoption of maize, which suggests an attempt to distribute the natural food resources evenly throughout the year.
5. The first evidence of maize agriculture, or at least significant consumption of maize, is found at approximately the same time in each area (probably associated with the appearance of the Northern Flint varieties): terminal Fourche Maline in the Caddo area, Early Mississippian in the Central Mississippi Valley, and Coles Creek in the Lower Mississippi Valley.

Despite these common elements, important differences influenced the adoption of maize agriculture.

The alluvial valleys of the Caddo area, although rich in natural resources that supported a relatively large population, are relatively circumscribed when compared to the Mississippi Valley. In addition, the productivity of this ecozone is limited by a geographically uneven distribution of summer rains and periodic droughts (Hemmings 1980; Wyckoff 1980). The sedentary nucleated late Fourche Maline populations thus were subjected to climatically induced food shortages. At least periodic resource shortages are suggested by the high frequency of Harris lines, small femur head diameters, and intergroup conflict. Both skeletal and archaeological data indicate that some of the Fourche Maline populations adopted maize agriculture as an important storable dietary supplement. The crucial point is that although maize agriculture spread rapidly throughout the region, many groups (even as late as Caddo II) were not dependent on maize as a dietary sample. In other words, dependency on maize was a local response to local circumstances. Although most groups did grow some maize, possibly for ceremonial reasons, only some were dependent on it. One consequence of agriculture that makes the Caddo area fairly unique is the dispersion of population in response to the distribution of adequate agricultural soils.

In contrast, the central Mississippi alluvial valley is much broader, slightly more productive, and not subject to the climatic variation typical of the Caddo Area. Unlike the Fourche Maline, the populations remain dispersed (until the Middle to Late Mississippian) across the alluvial valley in response to the distribution of natural resources. Food storage facilities found early in the archaeological sequence suggest that local groups were "harvesting" the abundant natural food supplies (i.e., nuts and fish) to compensate for summer shortages. There is no evidence to suggest that the growing populations approached the local carrying capacity. The authors hypothesize that maize, introduced from upriver, simply supplemented or replaced the storable natural food resources. Nucleation of the populations did not occur until long after maize adoption, when competition for arable land to the north (i.e., American Bottoms) induced intergroup conflict that resulted in abandonment of the isolated farmsteads and site fortification.

The Lower Mississippi has the largest alluvial valley of the three areas, has the greatest carrying capacity, and is not subject to any major climatic variation (Morse and Morse 1983). Food resource limitation cannot be considered an important factor in any portion of the archaeological sequence (Brain 1978). The authors suggest that the harvesting and storing of natural resources, especially fish, not only provided a reliable food base but also produced a surplus. When evidence of maize consumption does appear during the Coles Creek period, the authors hypothesize that maize is consumed as a status food or for ceremonial reasons by the elite in imitation of their neighbors both to the north and to the west. The low frequencies of porotic hyperostosis in the Lower Valley indicate the availability of adequate dietary iron sources. Additional skeletal data are needed to confirm this hypothesis, as the archaeological data show no evidence of extensive maize agriculture. Maize probably becomes an important dietary staple only after Mississippianization (in response to events upriver) of the Plaquemine culture.

In summary, the adoption of maize agriculture was a response to food shortages among local populations within the Caddo area and a replacement for harvested natural resources in the Central Mississippi Valley. Population nucleation is not a prerequisite for agriculture and does not occur when good agricultural soils are widely dispersed across a noncircumscribed environment.

Just as the reasons for the adoption of maize varied among the three areas, the health consequences of maize consumption differed. In the Caddo area, not only did maize provide a more reliable dietary base (reduction in growth disturbance indicators), but the reduction in degenerative disease indicates a less rigorous life style. In contrast, infection rates increase with the initial adoption of agriculture, only to return to preagricultural levels later in the Caddo sequence. It is not possible to determine whether the decline in morbidity is due to cultural adjustment, to population dispersion, or to a combination of these factors.

A partial answer can be found in the Central Mississippi Valley data, however. The slight decline in adult infection rates between the Early and Middle Mississippian periods might be associated with a cultural adjustment to an agricultural subsistence pattern. Confirmation of this idea must await preagricultural skeletal data. The dramatic Late Mississippian infection rates are definitely associated with population nucleation and not with the introduction of maize agriculture, which occurred much earlier. Comparison of these data to the Caddo indicates that the increases in adult morbidity that are usually thought to be caused by the introduction of agriculture are, in fact, a response to population nucleation (i.e., high local population density). The much higher infection rates in the Late Mississippian than in Caddo I suggest that highly organized sociopolitical structure and widespread trade contribute to the magnitude of infectious disease.

This interpretation is supported in the Lower Mississippi Valley, where the first evidence of maize consumption is associated with a low adult infection rate. Since there is evidence of neither population nucleation nor any reduction in natural resources during the Coles Creek period, it appears that maize agriculture alone does not cause any deleterious health consequences. The adult infection rates from the Plaquemine-Mississippian samples do not significantly exceed those from the preagriculture Baytown samples. Because the Baytown rates are so high, we are forced to assume that the Lower Valley has a high endemic disease rate. Placement of the late sites in approximate chronological order indicates that the infectious disease rates increase slightly with Mississippianization of the Plaquemine culture. Thus culture change in general, not just adoption of agriculture, may be associated with increased stress and disease.

In conclusion, the data presented in this chapter suggest the hypothesis that culture change and population nucleation are the prime stimuli for increased stress and morbidity. The adoption of maize agriculture in itself is not deleterious to health. This hypothesis gains added support when the data presented here are compared to data from the Middle Mississippi Valley (American Bottoms and adjacent river valleys), where natural food resources are not as abundant, agricultural soils are severely circumscribed, and agriculture is associated with population nucleation. The authors acknowledge the inadequacy of the data presented here and offer this material as a multifaceted hypothesis for testing with future data from these archaeologically rich areas.

ACKNOWLEDGMENTS

Funds for original research that made this chapter possible were provided by the Tulsa District U.S. Army Corps of Engineers to New World Research, the New Orleans District U.S. Army Corps of Engineers to the Arkansas Archaeological Survey, and numerous small grants to the senior author by the Arkansas Archaeological Survey. The University of Arkansas awarded to the serior author an off-campus duty assignment that provided the time to write this chapter without distractions. Dr. Jane Treat and the typists from the Office of Research and Sponsored Programs provided editorial and typing services, while Roxann Rackerby of the University Media Center provided the artwork. Many archaeologists generously provided their time and knowledge. To these people we give our thanks without conferring responsibility for our lack of understanding: Ann Early, Marvin Jeter, Fred Limp, Dan Morse, Frank Schambach, and Neal Trubowitz of the Arkansas Archeological Survey; Mike Hoffman of the Anthropology Department, University of Arkansas; and John Belmont, Ian Brown, Jeff Brain, and Steve Williams of the Lower Mississippi Survey Peabody Museum, Harvard University. The senior author would like to thank his wife Cathy for putting up with months of disruption while this chapter was being prepared.

REFERENCES

Barr, T. P.
1966 The Pruitt site: A late Plains Woodland manifestation in Murray County, Oklahoma. *Oklahoma River Basin Survey, Archaeological Site Report* 5. University of Oklahoma Research Institute, Norman.

Berg, R.
1983 *Osteological analysis of selected long bones from the Gold Mine Site, 16RI13, Richland Parish, Louisiana.* Unpublished M.A. thesis, Department of Anthropology, University of Arkansas.

Black, T. K.
1979 The biological and social analysis of a Mississippian cemetery from southeast Missouri: The Turner Site, 23 BU 21A. *Museum of Anthropology, University of Michigan, Anthropology Papers* No. 68.

Blaeuer, M., and J. C. Rose
1982 Powell Canal bioarcheology. In Powell Canal: Baytown period occupation on Bayou Macon in southeast Arkansas, edited by J. H. House, pp. 72-84. *Arkansas Archeological Survey Research Series* No. 19.

Brain, J. P.
1978 Late prehistoric settlement patterning in the Yazoo Basin and Natchez Bluffs regions of the Lower Mississippi Valley. In *Mississippian Settlement Patterns*, edited by B. D. Smith, pp. 331-365. Academic Press, New York.

Brues, A. M.
1957 Skeletal remains from the Nagle site. *Bulletin of the Oklahoma Anthropological Society* 5:101-106.
1958 Skeletal material from the Horton site. *Bulletin of the Oklahoma Anthropological Society* 6:27-32.
1959 Skeletal material from the Morris site (CK-39). *Bulletin of the Oklahoma Anthropological Society* 7:63-70.

Buikstra, J. E., and D. Fowler
1975 An osteological study of the human skeletal material from the Bentsen-Clark site. In *The Bentsen-Clark Site, Red River County, Texas: A Preliminary Report*, edited by L. D. Banks and J. Winters, pp. 79-97. Texas Archeological Society, San Antonio.

Buikstra, J. E., M. Vadeboncouer, and G. Behrend
1973 The Lundy site: Human osteology. *Bulletin of the Oklahoma Anthropological Society* 22:159-170.

Butler, B. H.
1969 Analysis of the human skeletal remains. In Investigations at the Sam Kaufman site, Red River County Texas, edited by S. A. Skinner, R. K. Harris, and K. M. Anderson, pp. 115-136. *Southern Methodist University Contributions in Anthropology* No. 5.

Byrd, K. M.
1976 Tchefuncte subsistence information obtained from the excavation of the Morton Shell Mound Iberia Parish Louisiana. *Southeastern Archaeological Conference Bulletin* 19:170-175.

Cook, D. C., and J. E. Buikstra
1979 Health and differential survival in prehistoric populations: prenatal defects. *American Journal of Physical Anthropology* 51:649-664.

Crane, C. J.
1982 Plant utilization at Spoonbill, an early Caddo site in Northeast Texas. *Midcontinental Journal of Archaeology* 7:81-97.

Cutler, H. C., and L. W. Blake
1973 Plants from archaeological sites east of the Rockies. Ms. on file, Missouri Botanical Garden, St. Louis.

Davis, E. M.
1970 Archaeological and historical assessment of the Red River Basin in Texas. In Archeological and Historical Resources of the Red River Basin, edited by H. Davis, pp. 25-65. *Arkansas Archeological Survey, Research Series* No. 1.

Doehner, K., and R. E. Larson
1978 Archaeological research at the proposed Cooper Lake,

northeast Texas 1974-1975. *Southern Methodist University, Archaeology Research Program.*

Duncan, J. E.
1978 Zebree: An example of trace element analysis in archeology. Ms. on file, Department of Anthropology, University of Arkansas.

Early, A.
1982 Caddoan settlement systems in the Ouachita River Basin. In Arkansas Archeology in Review, edited by N. Trubowitz and M. Jeter, pp. 198-232. *Arkansas Archeological Survey, Research Series* No. 15.

Egnatz, D. G.
1984 Analysis of human skeletal materials from Mound C at the Lake George Site (21-N-1) Yazoo Co., Mississippi. Ms. on file, Peabody Museum, Harvard University.

Giardino, M.
1977 *An osteological analysis of the human population from the Mount Nebo site, Madison Parish, Louisiana.* Unpublished M.A. thesis, Department of Anthropology, Tulane University, New Orleans.

Hatcher, M. A.
1927 Descriptions of the Tejas or Asinai Indians, 1691-1722. *Southwestern Historical Quarterly 31*:150-180.

Hemmings, E. T.
1980 *Spirit Lake (3LA83): Test excavation in a Late Caddo site on the Red River, Southwest Arkansas.* Arkansas Archeological Survey, Fayetteville.

House, J. H.
1982 Powell Canal: Baytown period occupation on Bayou Macan in southeast Arkansas. *Arkansas Archeological Survey Research Series* No. 19.

Hrdlicka, A.
1909 Report on an additional collection of skeletal remains from Arkansas and Louisiana. *Academy of Natural Sciences of Philadelphia Journal 14*:171-249.

Jones, V. H.
1949 Maize from the Davis site: Its nature and interpretation. *Memoirs of the Society for American Archaeology 5*:239-249.

King, Francis B.
1983 Presettlement vegetation and plant remains from the Alexander site (3CN117), Conway County, Arkansas. In *Cultural resources mitigation program Conway water supply relocation project, Alexander site (3CN117), Conway County, Arkansas*, by E. T. Hemmings, J. H. House, F. B. King, B. W. Styles, J. R. Purdue, M. L. Colburn, J. C. Rose, and M. K. Marks, pp. 220-294. Report submitted to the Little Rock District, U.S. Army Corps of Engineers by the Arkansas Archeological Survey.

Loveland, C.
1980 *The skeletal biology of the Caddo Indians of the Kaufman-Williams site, Red River County, Texas.* Unpublished Ph.D.

dissertation, Department of Anthropology, University of Tennessee, Knoxville.

McWilliams, D.
1970 Physical anthropology of Wann and Sam, two Fourche Maline Focus sites in eastern Oklahoma. *Bulletin of the Oklahoma Anthropological Society 19*:101-136.

Milner, G. R.
1980 Epidemic disease in the postcontact Southeast: A reappraisal. *Mid-Continental Journal of Archaeology 5*:39-56.

Morse, D. F., and P. A. Morse
1980 *Zebree Archeological Project.* Report submitted to Memphis District, U.S. Army Corps of Engineers by the Arkansas Archeological Survey.
1983 *Archaeology of the Central Mississippi Valley.* Academic Press, New York.

Nassaney, Michael S.
1982 *Late prehistoric site configuration in the southeast: Designing a sampling strategy for the Toltec Mounds Site.* Unpublished M.A. thesis, Department of Anthropology, University of Arkansas, Fayetteville.

Phillips, Phillip
1970 Archaeological survey in the Lower Yazoo Basin, Mississippi, 1949-1955. *Peabody Museum Papers* No. 60.

Phillips, P., J. Ford, and J. B. Griffin
1951 Archaeological survey in the lower Mississippi Alluvial Valley, 1940-1947. *Peabody Museum Papers* No. 25.

Powell, M. L.
1977 Prehistoric ritual skull burials at the Crenshaw site (3MI6), southwest Arkansas. *Bulletin of the Texas Archaeological Society 48*:111-118.
1980 *Bioarcheology of the Zebree site.* Unpublished M.A. thesis, Department of Anthropology, University of Arkansas, Fayetteville.
1983 The people of Nodena. Ms. on file, Arkansas Archeological Survey, Fayetteville.

Powell, M. L., and J. D. Rogers
1980 *Bioarchaeology of the McCutchan-McLaughlin site.* Oklahoma Archaeological Survey, Norman.

Price, J. E.
1978 The settlement pattern of the Powers Phase. In *Mississippian Settlement Patterns*, edited by B. D. Smith, pp. 220-231. Academic Press, New York.

Robbins, L. M.
1978 Yawslike disease processes in a Louisiana shell mound population. *Medical College of Virginia Quarterly 14*:24-31.

Rose, J. C.
1983 Bioarcheology of the Cedar Grove Site. In *Cedar Grove: An interdisciplinary investigation of a late Caddo farmstead in the Red River Valley*, edited by N. Trubowitz,

pp. 227-256. Arkansas Archeological Survey Research Series, in press.

Rose, J. C., P. M. Clancy, P. M. Moore-Jansen
1981 Bioarchaeology of the Roden site. In *Archeological Investigations at the Roden site, McCurtain County Oklahoma*, edited by G. Perino, pp. 99-129. Museum of the Red River, Idabel, Oklahoma.

Rose, J. C., M. K. Marks, and E. B. Riddick
1982 Bioarcheology of the Bug Hill site. Report submitted to New World Research, Pollock, Louisiana.

Rose, J. C. and M. K. Marks
1983 Bioarcheology of the Alexander site. In *Cultural resources mitigation program Conway water supply relocation project, Alexander site (3CN117), Conway County, Arkansas*, by E. T. Hemmings, J. H. House, F. B. King, B. W. Styles, J. R. Purdue, M. L. Colburn, J. C. Rose, and M. K. Marks, pp. 220-294. Report submitted to the Little Rock District, U.S. Army Corps of Engineers by the Arkansas Archeological Survey.

Schambach, F. F.
1971 Exploratory excavations in the midden areas at the Crenshaw site, Miller County, Arkansas. Ms. on file, Arkansas Archeological Survey, Fayetteville.
1982 An outline of the Fourche Maline culture in southwest Arkansas. In Arkansas Archeology in Review, edited by N. Trubowitz and M. Jeter, pp. 132-197. *Arkansas Archeological Survey, Research Series* No. 15.

Smith, B. D.
1978 Variation in Mississippian settlements patterns. In *Mississippian Settlement Patterns*, edited by B. D. Smith, pp. 499-503. Academic Press, New York.

Stark, M.
1973 *The osteological analysis of the skeletal remains of the Old Martin Place*. Unpublished honors thesis, Department of Anthropology, University of Arkansas.

Swanton, J. R.
1942 Source material on the history and ethnology of the Caddo Indians. *Smithsonian Institution, Bureau of American Ethnology, Bulletin* No. 132.

Thomas, P. M., L. J. Campbell, and S. R. Ahler
1980 The Hanna site: An Alto Village in Red River Parish. *Louisiana Archeology*, No. 5.

Toth, A.
1979 The Marksville connection. In *Hopewell Archaeology*, edited by D. S. Brose and N. Greber, pp. 188-199. Kent State University Press, Kent, Ohio.

Trubowitz, Neal (editor)
1983 Cedar Grove: An interdisciplinary investigation of a late Caddo Farmstead in the Red River Valley. Arkansas Archeological Survey Research Series, in press.

Turner, Christy G.
1979 Dental anthropological indications of agriculture among the Jomon people of Japan. *American Journal of Physical Anthropology 51*:619-636.

Walker, R. A.
1980 *Dental pathologies, wear, and sexual dimorphism of the Gold Mine Site*. Unpublished honors thesis, Department of Anthropology, University of Arkansas, Fayetteville.

Webb, C. H.
1959 The Belcher Mound: A stratified Caddoan site in Caddo Parish, Louisiana. *Memoir of the Society for American Archaeology* No. 16.

Wyckoff, D. G.
1980 *Caddoan adaptive strategies in the Arkansas Basin, Eastern Oklahoma*. Unpublished Ph.D. dissertation, Department of Anthropology, Washington State University, Pullman.

CHAPTER 16

AGRICULTURE, MARGINAL ENVIRONMENTS, AND NUTRITIONAL STRESS IN THE PREHISTORIC SOUTHWEST

Ann M. Palkovich

Anthropology Program
George Mason University

The impact of the adoption of agriculture on human health presumably differed from region to region. The nature of human nutritional and disease response to agriculture must be described in terms of each local ecological base if the dynamics of this transition are to be fully understood. It has been suggested (Euler et al. 1979; Jorde 1977; Wetterstrom 1976) that the adequacy and reliability of subsistence regimes are intimately intertwined with the stability of local environments. Marginal, unstable ecosystems threaten the viability of agriculture as a subsistence strategy. The advent of agriculture in the prehistoric American Southwest is an example of this economic transition in such a marginal environment.

BACKGROUND: THE AMERICAN SOUTHWEST

The earliest archaeologically established occupation of the American Southwest was the Paleoindian-Clovis horizon, which dates to roughly 9500 B.C. (Lipe 1978:332). The term "Paleoindian" usually refers to early Plains-oriented, big-game hunters evident in major portions of Colorado and New Mexico during this period. However, throughout the early Paleoindian-Archaic periods of occupation in the Southwest, hunter-gatherers exhibited diverse subsistence strategies tied to regional variations in resources (Lipe 1978). Unfortunately, lack of human skeletal remains from these early periods precludes skeletal assessment of the nutritional status of these groups.

By approximately 2000 B.C., population growth and the development of regionally distinct manifestations were accompanied by incipient cultivation (Lipe 1978:341). Of the five major regional traditions that developed (Anasazi, Fremont, Hayataya, Hohokam, and Mogollon), the Anasazi of northern Arizona, northern New Mexico, and southwestern Colorado is the best known with respect to human biological dynamics.

The shift to agricultural economies among the Anasazi encompasses two broad cultural phases--Basketmaker and Pueblo. The Basketmaker period (beginning in the first century A.D.) is generally characterized by semipermanent villages and a mixed subsistence economy still dependent largely on hunting and gathering with some incipient food production. A slow shift occurred toward greater dependence on agricultural resources and the construction of more permanent settlements near the end of the period (roughly A.D. 700-750). There is widespread homogeneity in the material culture throughout the Anasazi region during Basketmaker times, but cultural experimentation and local environmental differences are manifest in a great diversity of architectural styles, ceramic types, burial practices, and the like during the following Pueblo phase.

Pueblo occupations reflect larger village settlements (thus also a notable increase in population), regional cultural diversity, and full-fledged dependence on agriculture (Lipe 1978; Martin and Plog 1973).

Environmental Stability and Culture Change

Cyclical environmental conditions in the desert Southwest have been considered a primary cause of shifting prehistoric settlement patterns, particularly during the Basketmaker and Pueblo periods (Euler et al., 1979). The history of occupation in the region can be read as a series of strategies designed to adapt to such conditions, each strategy providing, however, only a temporarily successful, and usually still marginal, existence for human groups.

Throughout the sequence, fluctuations in dietary adequacy appear to have been intimately associated with cyclical short-term and long-term drought conditions (Wetterstrom 1976). The productivity of both natural and cultivated plant species was dependent on, and highly sensitive to, rainfall patterns. Short-term drought conditions reduced the productivity of species already experiencing the limits of marginal growing conditions, and long-term droughts could significantly damage soils and substantially alter the composition of plant communities (Rose et al. 1981; Wetterstrom 1976).

Small hunter-gatherer groups that were primarily dependent on wild food resources could buffer the effects of unpredictable resources by remaining highly mobile, although even the diversified diets of these groups may have been nutritionally marginal in this region. The shift to agriculture seems to have involved the growth and differentiation of populations accompanied by decreasing mobility and the increasingly carefully scheduled use, manipulation, and protection of selected species (Glassow 1972; Irwin-Williams and Haynes 1970; Lipe 1978; Plog 1974). But even altered subsistence strategies such as the use of less desirable foods and the adoption of irrigation agriculture to buffer the diet met with only limited success (Wetterstrom 1976). Large-scale population movements throughout the Basketmaker and Pueblo periods suggest that the instability of the environment frequently upset established subsistence patterns. Apparently, continued population increase and a shift to a primary dependence on produced food served only to heighten the effects of environmental instability and to reduce resource predictability.

The Paleopathological Evidence

The impact of this environmental instability on human biology is complex. Not only should nutritionally related disease patterns be affected, but fertility rates, morbidity rates, and population structure all should show the effects of severe dietary inadequacies on successive cohorts of subadults. Thus, the biological impact on human groups should, ideally, be assessed with adequate, temporally controlled archaeological populations evaluated within the context of relevant local environmental circumstances.

However, a number of constraints limit our ability to interpret the existing skeletal data. First, existing studies have generally emphasized differential diagnosis of pathological manifestations rather than evaluation of the impact of disease on the morbidity and mortality patterns of a poplulation. Second, despite careful attention paid to prehistoric Anasazi mortuary practices, the human skeletal remains themselves often have not been systematically collected or carefully analyzed. Thus, an overriding problem with skeletal studies of Anasazi populations is the paucity of large, well-documented series. Well-controlled and well-documented collections often represent only a handful of individuals; conversely, haphazard recovery of interments (as well as biases in the original mortuary practices) diminish the value of some large collections such as the Pecos series (Hooten 1930; Kidder 1958). As a result, biological characterization of Anasazi groups for most periods is based largely on a handful of available skeletal remains scattered throughout large regions representing broad temporal periods. Analysis of such material tends to focus on the frequency of individual skeletal features characteristic of pathologies rather than on the biological dynamics of archaeologically well-defined groups.

The evidence that does exist shows the presence of skeletal indicators of stress in both Basketmaker and Pueblo periods. El Najjar and his associates (El Najjar 1974, 1977; El Najjar et al. 1975, 1976) have documented the incidence of porotic hyperostosis for several Anazasi groups. (In this region, the condition is

TABLE 16.1 Location, Chronology and Environment of Sites Studied[a]

Site	Location	Cultural period	Date (A.D.)	Environment
Canyon de Chelly	Northeastern Arizona	Basketmaker II-III	400- 700	Canyon site
		Pueblo I, II and III	700-1300	Canyon site
Chaco Canyon	Northwestern New Mexico	Pueblo II-III	900-1156	Canyon site
Inscription House	Northeastern Arizona	Pueblo III	1250-1300	Canyon site
Navajo Reservoir	Northern New Mexico	Pueblo I-II	700-1100	Sage plain
Gran Quivira	Central New Mexico	Pueblo IV-V	1315-1673	Sage plain

[a]Reproduced with permission from El-Najjar et al. 1976:480-481.

TABLE 16.2 Age and Sex Distribution of Porotic Hyperostosis (PH) in the Six Skeletal Series[a]

	Total		Children		Total adults		Adult males		Adult females	
Series	N	% with PH	N	% with PH	N	% with PH	N	% with PH	N	% with PH
Canyon de Chally										
a. Basketmakers	136	49.3	50	72.0	86	36.0	34	26.5	52	42.3
b. Pueblos	78	55.1	17	88.0	61	45.9	39	41.0	22	54.5
Chaco Canyon	32	71.8	12	83.3	20	65.0	7	57.1	13	69.2
Inscription House	24	54.2	11	63.6	13	46.2	4	50.0	9	44.4
Navajo Reservoir	92	13.0	44	15.9	48	10.4	28	10.7	20	10.0
Gran Quivira	177	15.3	66	18.2	111	13.5	47	15.0	64	12.5

[a]Reproduced with permission from El-Najjar et al. 1976:480-481.

TABLE 16.3 Geographic, Age, and Sex Distribution of the Prevalence of Porotic Hyperostosis in the Two Ecological Zones[a]

	%	Number with PH/ total number	%	Number with PH/ total number	χ^2	p
1. Geographic distribution						
	Canyon sites		Sage Plains sites			
Total	54.1	146/270	14.5	39/269	93.5[b]	< 0.0001
Children	76.5	68/ 90	17.3	19/110	68.4[b]	< 0.0001
2. Age distribution						
	Children		Adults			
Canyon sites	75.6	68/ 90	43.3	78/180	25.0[b]	< 0.0001
Sage plains	17.3	19/110	12.6	20/159	1.19	> 0.20
3. Sex distribution						
	Males		Females			
Canyon sites	36.9	31/ 84	49.0	47/ 96	2.65	> 0.10
Sage plains	13.3	10/ 75	11.9	10/ 84	0.08	> 0.90

[a]Reproduced with permission from El-Najjar et al. 1976:480-481.
[b]Statistically significant findings.

considered indicative of iron deficiency anemia. See discussion by Goodman et al., Chapter 11 this volume; Von Endt and Ortner 1982). A high incidence of porotic hyperostosis was noted for both Basketmaker and Pueblo (Tables 16.1 and 16.2) but temporal differences in incidence between the two periods were not statistically significant (El Najjar et al. 1976:482). In six skeletal series, subadults (0-10 years of age at death) consistently showed a higher incidence of porotic hyperostosis than adults (Table 16.2). A striking environmental effect was noted in the contrast between Canyon Bottom groups and Sage Plains groups (Table 16.3). Archaeological evidence shows that Canyon Bottom groups were heavily maize dependent while Sage Plains groups had a varied diet that included beans and squash as well as wild food resources. El Najjar and his associates attributed the significant difference between the rates of porotic hyperostosis in the two groups to the iron-deficient diets of maize-dependent Canyon Bottom populations.

Other skeletal measures of dietary problems (stature and dental disease) did not evidence statistically significant differences between Basketmaker and Pueblo groups (El Najjar 1974).

Brief analyses of the skeletal remains from Pueblo Bonito and Aroyo Hondo are offered below to provide a further assessment of the nature and success of the later agrarian phase of the Anasazi economy.

Pueblo Bonito

The development of cultural buffering systems as adaptive responses to precipitation cycles and environmental shifts is a common theme in the discussion of Pueblo groups. Jorde (1977) suggests, for example, that food storage, irrigation, and settlement aggregation along permanent drainages were cultural means of buffering fluctuations in precipitation in the Chaco Canyon region of New Mexico. He notes that such mechanisms, while apparently effective in damping the effects of short-term (year-to-year) differences in precipitation, yielded only a stopgap adaptive response. Expenditures of time and energy into such measures apparently rendered the system even more susceptible to the effects of long-term fluctuations. Dependence on agricultural productivity achieved through irrigation and similar strategies during good years eventually led to a collapse of the system and disaggregation of the population once rainfall diminished. Thus, large settlements, food storage, and irrigation techniques worked in Chaco Canyon on a year-to-year basis as long as major changes in rainfall patterns did not occur. However, with the onset of the Great Drought dating from A.D. 1276 to 1299, virtually all the major Pueblo sites in the canyon were abandoned. Long-term below average precipitation proved to be an unmanageable stress to the agricultural strategies that had been adopted.

The success of social status as a cultural buffering mechanism among the Chacoan Pueblo can be examined skeletally. Four "burial rooms" in Pueblo Bonito have yielded the largest known single

TABLE 16.4 Pueblo Bonito Composite Life Table, Smoothed[a]

Age class (years)	D_x	Smoothed D_x	d_x	l_x	q_x	L_x	T_x	e_x^0
0- 1	1	1	1.07	100.00	0.0107	99.47	2646.52	26.46
1- 4.9	8	6.67	7.14	98.93	0.0722	381.44	2547.05	25.75
5- 9.9	11	8.67	9.29	91.79	0.1012	435.73	2165.61	23.59
10-14.9	7	8.00	8.57	82.50	0.1039	391.08	1729.88	20.97
15-19.9	6	8.33	8.92	73.93	0.1207	347.35	1338.80	18.11
20-24.9	12	10.67	11.43	65.01	0.1758	296.48	991.45	15.25
25-29.9	14	11.67	12.50	53.58	0.2333	236.65	694.97	12.97
30-34.9	9	11.00	11.78	41.08	0.2868	175.95	458.32	11.16
35-39.9	10	8.00	8.57	29.30	0.2925	125.08	282.37	9.64
40-44.9	5	6.67	7.15	20.73	0.3449	85.78	157.29	7.59
45-49.9	5	5.67	6.07	13.58	0.4470	52.73	71.51	5.27
50-plus	7	7	7.50	7.51	1.0000	18.78	18.78	2.50

[a]*From Palkovich 1980:33.*

cemetery series of interments from the canyon. Architectural, stratigraphic, and ceramic analyses by N. Aikens (personal communication) suggest these rooms were purposefully converted into mortuary facilities, bodies being laid on the hardpacked floor and dirt being brought in to cover the corpses. Some intrusion on earlier interments by later ones is suggested by the numerous disturbed skeletons noted at the time of excavation. It is believed that the majority of skeletal material was retained from these excavations by Judd (1964), but some questions remain about the completeness of the collection.

Ninety-five individuals are represented in the four Pueblo Bonito burial rooms. This skeletal series does not reflect a typical age distribution (Table 16.4). There is a clear paucity of infants; only 20% of the individuals recovered were 10 years of age or younger at death. Despite the generally good to excellent preservation of the observed skeletal remains, infants and children are underrepresented from a demographic standpoint (whether as a result of excavation and recovery bias or mortuary bias). There is also a notable disparity in the sex distribution--females are twice as frequent in the sample as males (42 to 22, respectively).

Based on their assessment of both biological and mortuary evidence, Aikens and Schelberg (1984) suggested that the skeletal remains represented in these four rooms represent one of two separate (social) "lineages" noted among the Pueblo Bonito remains.

Another cluster of burial rooms was excavated by Pepper (1909). Detailed descriptions of the skeletal remains are lacking, but it is clear from Pepper's descriptions of this burial cluster and from the analysis by Aikens and Schelberg that both Pepper's and Judd's "cemeteries" probably represented high-ranking lineages in a stratified Chacoan society. Pepper's cluster evidences a wealth of grave goods befitting a high-ranking lineage; Judd's cluster, though afforded a complex of rooms as a burial facility (and therefore having received a special treatment not found in other instances), has fewer grave goods and therefore possibly represents a lower ranking lineage. Differential treatment within the lineages is also evident by the unequal distribution of goods among individuals within each room cluster. The special status accorded these individuals at death may have been a factor producing the skewed observed age profile noted earlier.

If these were indeed ranking lineages, and these individuals therefore had favored or special status, it seems likely that they would have enjoyed privileged access to food resources. We would therefore expect fewer cases of dietary stress or less severe skeletal involvement for the series from these clusters than is characteristic of other prehistoric Pueblo groups.

From a preliminary analysis (Palkovich 1984), it is immediately apparent that at least the general age profile comparisons argue to the contrary. The Pueblo Bonito series is demographically similar to those populations living nearby in smaller pueblos. Even more persuasive evidence to the contrary is noted among the observed pattern of gross skeletal pathologies. Among the 20 juveniles 0-10 years of age at death in Judd's cluster, 5 cases of porotic hyperostosis, 4 cases of cribra orbitalia and 4 cases of endocranial lesions are evident. In all, 10 individuals (50%) are affected, a high incidence rate of these pathologies. Several studies suggest iron deficiency anemia associated with general dietary inadequacies, nutritional stress, and synergistic infectious insults as the underlying causes of the pathology pattern exhibited in these individuals (El-Najjar 1977; El-Najjar et al. 1975, 1976).

This study suggests that high status may not have been enough to buffer the marked biological effects of dietary inadequacies that affected the prehistoric group interred in the Pueblo Bonito room cluster. Apparently neither subsistence strategies nor the privileges of social status were sufficient buffer against dietary inadequacies in Chaco Canyon.

Arroyo Hondo

It is clear that the Great Drought did not uniformly affect all areas of the American Southwest. Several dendroclimatic analyses (Euler et al. 1979; Rose et al. 1981) show that several regions, the Northern Rio Grande among them, did not experience severe shortages of rainfall coincident with those evidenced at Chaco Canyon.

A long history of population shifts in response to changes in local precipitation patterns is reflected in the regional settlement pattern for the Northern Rio Grande region. Dickson (1975, 1979) noted that the transition to settled agriculture in the Northern Rio Grande began around (A.D. 600). During the period from A.D. 600-900, settlements are located in primary zones of agricultural production where year-round water supplies are available. Indigenous population growth reflected in the number and size of sites also occurred during this period. By A.D. 900-1100 (the Developmental period), agricultural sites had spread into secondary and tertiary zones of production dependent on dry farming techniques; the population doubled approximately every 50 years at this time.

The Coalition period of occupation in the Northern Rio Grande, which began around A.D. 1200, is characterized by drought conditions and aggregation of the population into large sites located in primary and some secondary zones of agricultural production, with tertiary zones being abandoned altogether. There was also an accompanying shift to intensive agricultural practices. As in the case of the Chaco region, this shift in settlement pattern and subsistence strategy led to only short-term stability. The downturn in the long-term precipitation cycle in the 1420s led to the ultimate abandonment of large agricultural communities in the Northern Rio Grande area.

As a major fourteenth-century Pueblo occupation in the Northern Rio Grande, Arroyo Hondo provides a second case study in the relationships among marginal environmental conditions, subsistence strategies, and nutritional adequacy.

Arroyo Hondo, a Coalition period Pueblo occupation, is located on the sloping piedmont immediately west of the foothills of the Sangre de Cristo Mountains in north central New Mexico. Environmental diversity exhibited at the 2150-m elevation of this area and the site's particular location gave its inhabitants ready access to the plant and animal resources of several major ecozones within the immediate area. The site covers approximately 3.2 ha and is composed of over 1000 rooms arranged in 24 roomblocks around 9 plaza acres. One hundred twenty burials, recovered in 5 seasons of excavations, span the entire 125-year occupation of the site.

A detailed dendroclimatic analysis (Rose et al. 1981) reveals an interesting correlation between major building phases at the Pueblo and rainfall conditions. The Pueblo was established in A.D. 1300, at the onset of a period of increasing precipiation. For the first 35 years of occupation, local rainfall remained above average. The agricultural base of corn, beans, and squash was likely highly productive, and ethnobotanical studies show that local wild flora such as leafy plants, seeds, and nuts seasonally supplemented the diet (Wetterstrom 1976). Animal protein was derived from domesticated turkey and over 50 species of locally available wild game. Architectural analysis suggests that maximum settlement size was reached about A.D. 1300.

A shift in the precipitation pattern about A.D. 1335 resulted in a highly variable rainfall. Severe droughts, followed by brief periods of increased rainfall, occurred every few years. Under conditions of such environmental instability, agricultural production was unpredictable. During the same period, a precipitous decline in the resident population at Arroyo Hondo began, and by 1345 the Pueblo was virtually abandoned.

A smaller resettlement of the site began in the early 1370s, which coincides with a temporary return to high local precipitation. Maximum resettlement size was reached in the early 1400s during a 10-year period of continued above-average precipitation. After 1410, a second rapid decline in the site's population began. At this same time, a drop in rainfall occurred. By the time the site was finally abandoned in 1425, the Santa Fe area entered the most severe local drought conditions documented in the tree-ring record.

An ethnobotanical evaluation of the Arroyo Hondo subsistence using standard WHO protein and calorie requirements of children suggests that a young child's diet was likely barely adequate during years of average precipitation (Wetterstrom 1976). Unstable climatic conditions resulting in fluctuating annual agricultural production suggest an uncertain diet and, thus, chronic nutritional inadequacy throughout the occupation of Arroyo Hondo. Clinical and subclinical cases of protein-calorie malnutrition, synergistic infectious diseases, reduced growth rates, general disruption of growth patterns, and deaths attributable to nutritional inadequacy are suggested by Wetterstrom as conditions likely to be exhibited by the Arroyo Hondo children, with a heightened morbidity and mortality response during dry years.

Analysis of the 108 individuals associated with the major phase of occupation at Arroyo Hondo supports the suggestion of chronic biological stress resulting from an inadequate diet. A group of four skeletal pathologies, classified as osteolytic bone responses, stands out in its high incidence within the 0-1 and 1-4.9-year age classes. Forty-nine of the 108 individuals (45%) fall within these two age classes in the Arroyo Hondo skeletal series. Observed incidence of these pathologies is conservative since not all skeletal parts were recovered for each individual, thus rendering an incomplete assessment of pathological involvement for the series.

The pathologies include 10 cases of porotic hyperostosis and eight cases of endocranial lesions. Both pathologies occurred exclusively in children under the age of five. Five cases of cribra orbitalia appear in this age class. The fourth pathology in this group, generalized porosity, consisted of small, clustered points of cortical bone destruction (usually noted at the ends of diaphyses) in the postcranial skeleton. Ten cases of porosity were noted in the 0-1-year age class and two cases in the 1-4.9-year age class. Twenty-three of the 49 individuals (47%) under the age of five exhibited one or more of these pathological conditions (Palkovich 1980:166-167). Other Pueblo occupations in the Northern Rio Grande contemporaneous with Arroyo Hondo also evidence these skeletal pathologies. Hooten noted 28 cases of porotic hyperostosis in subadults and young adults at Pecos, for example (Hooten 1930).

A composite life table (Table 16.5) calculated for these individuals associated with the major phase of occupation at Arroyo

TABLE 16.5 *Arroyo Hondo Composite Life Table, Smoothed*[a]

Age class (years)	D_x	Corrected D_x	Smoothed D_x	d_x	l_x	q_x	L_x	T_x	e_x^0
0- 1	29	29	29	26.35	100.00	0.2635	86.83	1623.17	16.23
1-4.9	20	20	18.00	16.35	73.65	0.2220	261.90	1536.34	20.86
5-9.9	5	5	11.00	9.99	57.30	0.1743	261.53	1274.44	22.24
10-14.9	7	8	6.25	5.68	47.31	0.1201	222.35	1012.91	21.41
15-19.9	4	5.75	6.02	5.47	41.63	0.1314	194.48	790.56	18.99
20-24.9	3	4.31	4.79	4.35	36.16	0.1203	169.93	596.08	16.48
25-29.9	3	4.31	4.79	4.35	31.81	0.1367	148.18	426.15	13.40
30-34.9	4	5.75	8.15	7.41	27.46	0.2698	118.78	277.97	10.12
35-39.9	10	14.38	7.67	6.97	20.05	0.3476	82.83	159.19	7.94
40-44.9	2	2.88	7.67	6.97	13.08	0.5329	47.98	76.36	5.84
45-49.9	4	5.75	3.84	3.49	6.11	0.5712	21.83	28.38	4.64
50-plus	2	2.88	2.88	2.62	2.62	1.0000	6.55	6.55	2.50
?	15								

[a]From Palkovich 1980:33.

Hondo exhibited a mortality pattern with a high infant mortality rate, which is particularly important given the number of cases of osteolytic skeletal pathologies in the youngest age classes. It can be suggested that malnutrition, acting synergistically with infectious diseases, was at least partially responsible for the high level of mortality among infants and young children at Arroyo Hondo.

Apparently, a shift to intensive agricultural practices and population aggregation in large villages located in primary zones of agricultural production were insufficient buffers against the vagaries of rainfall patterns as exhibited at Arroyo Hondo. What were marginal protein-calorie diets in average years were virtually starvation diets in drought years, which heightened the morbidity-mortality stress in the population and led to the ultimate abandonment of the village. Thus, buffering mechanisms of settlement patterns and agricultural strategies could not soften the biological impact of poor diets on the Arroyo Hondo population.

CONCLUSION

The association of dietary shifts with the origins of agriculture should not lead us simply to assume that nutritional inadequacy was experienced for the first time as a serious biological stress for human groups during the Neolithic. For the American Southwest, subsistence--whether based on food collection or food production--was subject to coincident short-term and long-term environmental instabilities, the practical effects of which were unpredictable rainfall patterns and unreliable resource productivity. The Neolithic Revolution, in this case, is not a matter of a change from a healthy diet to an unhealthy one, or a change from a diversified, collected feast to a limited, produced famine. Paleoenvironmental and ethnobotanical studies suggest that the diets of prehistoric Anasazi populations were always marginal--and with the advent of agriculture, the biological impact went from bad to worse. Basketmaker communities were subject to the same vagaries in climatic conditions as were Pueblo groups; thus, similar patterns of biological stress are to be expected. Once mobility to exploit new areas for food resources as a buffering mechanism was no longer possible, heightened susceptibility to food shortage over the long run resulted. However, with diets inherently nutritionally marginal, skeletal patterns of endemic rather than episodic stress were more likely to be exhibited. While less effective cultural buffering mechanisms may have heightened the biological response to marginal diets in the later agricultural groups, overall conditions of endemic nutritional inadequacy for both Basketmaker and Pueblo populations may have resulted in greater levels of biological stress than are found in many other human groups.

REFERENCES

Aikens, Nancy, and John Schelberg
1984 Human burial practices within Chaco Canyon. *The Kiva*, in press.

Dickson, Bruce
1975 Settlement pattern stability and change in the middle northern Rio Grande Region, New Mexico: A test of some hypotheses. *American Antiquity 40*:159-171.
1979 Prehistoric pueblo settlement patterns: The Arroyo Hondo, New Mexico survey. *Arroyo Hondo Archaeological Series* Vol. 2. School of American Research Press, Santa Fe.

El-Najjar, Mahmoud
1974 *People of Canyon de Chelly: A study of their biology and culture.* Ph.D. dissertation, Department of Anthropology, Arizona State University.
1977 Maize, malaria and the anemias in the pre-Columbian New World. *Yearbook of Physical Anthropology, 1976 20*:329-337.

El-Najjar, Mahmoud, B. Lozoff, and D. Ryan
1975 The paleo-epidemiology of porotic hyperostosis in the American Southwest: Radiological and ecological considerations. *American Journal of Roentgenology, Radium Therapy and Nuclear Medicine 25*:918-924.

El-Najjar, Mahmoud, D. Ryan, C. Turner, and B. Lozoff
1976 The etiology of porotic hyperostosis among the prehistoric and historic Anasazi Indians of the southwestern United States. *American Journal of Physical Anthropology 44*:477-488.

Euler, Robert, George Gumerman, Thor Karlstrom, Jeffrey Dean, and Richard Hevly
1979 The Colorado plateaus: Cultural dynamics and paleoenvironment. *Science 205*:1089-1101.

Glassow, Michael
1972 Changes in the adaptations of Southwestern Basketmakers: A systems perspective. In *Contemporary archaeology*, edited by Mark Leone, pp. 289-302. Southern Illinois University Press, Carbondale.

Hooton, Earnest
1930 *The Indians of Pecos Pueblo.* Yale University Press, New Haven.

Irwin-Williams, Cynthia, and Vance Haynes
1970 Climatic change and early population dynamics in the southwestern United States. *Quaternary Research 1*:59-71.

Jorde, L. B.
1977 Precipitation cycles and cultural buffering in the prehistoric Southwest. In *For theory building in archaeology*, edited by Lewis Binford, pp. 385-396. Academic Press, New York.

Judd, Neil
1964 The architecture of Pueblo Bonito. *Smithsonian Miscellaneous Collections* Vol. 147, No. 1.

Kidder, Alfred
1958 Pecos, New Mexico: Archaeological notes. *Robert S. Peabody Foundation for Archaeology Paper* No. 5.

Lipe, William
1978 The Southwest. In *Ancient native Americans*, edited by Jesse Jennings, pp. 327-401. Freeman, San Francisco.

Martin, Paul S., and Fred Plog
1973 *The Archaeology of Arizona.* Doubleday/Natural History Press, Garden City, New York.

Palkovich, Ann M.
1980 Pueblo population and society: The Arroyo Hondo skeletal and mortuary remains. *Arroyo Hondo Archaeological Series* Vol. 3. School of American Research Press, Sante Fe.
1984 Disease and mortality patterns in the burials rooms of Pueblo Bonito: Preliminary considerations. *The Kiva*, in press.

Pepper, George
1909 The exploration of a burial room in Pueblo Bonito, New Mexico. In *Putnam Anniversary Volume: Anthropological Essays*, pp. 196-252. Stechert, New York.

Plog, Fred
1974 *The study of prehistoric change.* Academic Press, New York.

Rose, Martin, Jeffrey Dean, and William Robinson
1981 The past climate of Arroyo Hondo, New Mexico reconstructed from tree rings. *Arroyo Hondo Archaeological Series* Vol. 4. School of American Research Press, Santa Fe.

Von Endt, David, and Donald Ortner
1982 Amino acid analysis of bone from a possible case of prehistoric iron deficiency anemia from the American Southwest. *American Journal of Physical Anthropology* *59*:377-385.

Wetterstrom, Wilma
1976 *The effects of nutrition on population size at Pueblo Arroyo Hondo, New Mexico.* Ph.D. dissertation, Department of Anthropology, University of Michigan.

CHAPTER 17

CENTRAL CALIFORNIA: PREHISTORIC SUBSISTENCE CHANGES AND HEALTH

David N. Dickel
Peter D. Schulz[1]
Henry M. McHenry

Department of Anthropology
University of California, Davis

INTRODUCTION

Although living hunter-gatherers have in common an existence in sparse and scattered environments poorly suited for farming, in some areas of the world dense hunter-gatherer populations once existed in habitats where farming could have been introduced, and within range of potential diffusion of domestic plant species.

Central California is one such region. The major difference between the prehistory of California and that of many areas of North America is that most of California retained an Archaic subsistence pattern. Nevertheless, central California populations were at least semisedentary and dense, and showed cultural elaboration, stratification, and other developments on a level often associated with agricultural societies (Meighan 1959).

Central California prehistory shows a trend toward specialized adaptations to local environments, and later cultures may demonstrate increased efficiency of resource exploitation, especially if efficiency is measured in production per unit space and per unit time as well as in seasonal stabilization of food intake. It has been argued that late prehistoric economies were virtually protoagricultural in many important aspects, especially in what has been termed *natural resource management* (Bean and Blackburn 1976; Bean and Lawton 1973; Heizer and Elsasser 1980; Ziegler 1968). In particular, fire may have been used to maintain subclimatic vegatation communities, to control insect infestation of acorns, and to manipulate other economically important aspects of

[1]*Present address: Resource Protection Division, Department of Parks and Recreation, Sacramento, California 95811.*

the environment; and it is likely that there was inadvertent or purposeful human amplification of local abundance of favored medicinal, recreational, and condiment plants.

The subsistence resources available and utilized by central California Indians covered a very broad spectrum in a manner typical of Archaic cultures, and all major ecological communities were productive sources of harvested food.

Throughout most of the area the single most productive food source was the acorn crop, followed by fish, especially salmon (Baumhoff 1963). While subsistence economies in this region utilized a broad spectrum of resources, they increasingly emphasized a few major staples that shared the attributes of abundance, seasonal concentration in a specific territory, and capability of storage. During the winter months, when hunting and fishing were difficult and fresh vegetal foods unavailable, consumption of stored acorn products may have exceeded that of all other foods. Thus it is hardly an exaggeration to categorize native economies of this area as balanophagous (acorn eating), or, in view of the dense populations associated with them, to consider this adaptation as paralleling in importance the development of agriculture in other areas.

Most of the studies reported in this chapter deal with populations located in the Central Valley of California, especially the lower Sacramento and northernmost San Joaquin valleys. Our concentration on this area was largely due to the existence of adequate samples spanning a considerable temporal range. Reports of pathologies related to health from outside this region are rare, often poorly quantified, and based on fragmentary remains, and they concentrate on individual examples rather than on meaningful population comparisons (see Hoffman and Brunker 1976).

Furthermore, generalizations about all California prehistoric subsistence economies and cultural sequences are difficult. There is a great deal of microenvironmental differentiation and subsequent cultural specialization, and the prehistory of population replacement and movement is complex and unclear. If for no other reason than the historic accident of the Central Valley being the focus of most systematic studies of prehistoric health, we have confined our main discussion to this region.

The prehistoric cultural sequence for much of central California was worked out in the 1930s (Beardsley 1948, 1954; Heizer and Fenenga 1939; Lillard et al. 1939). Three sequential complexes (or horizons, or periods) were recognized, generally designated Early, Middle, and Late, with the Late complex subdivided into prehistoric Phase 1 and protohistoric Phase 2. The term *Windmiller pattern* is used to recognize and distinguish a local Early complex situated within the lower Central Valley. Figure 17.1 summarizes radiocarbon dates associated with the Early, Middle, and Late complexes (see Schulz 1981:58). Details of the Central Valley cultural sequence are available from numerous sources. For the purposes of this chapter it is noted that there is an apparent trend toward increased population size and density,

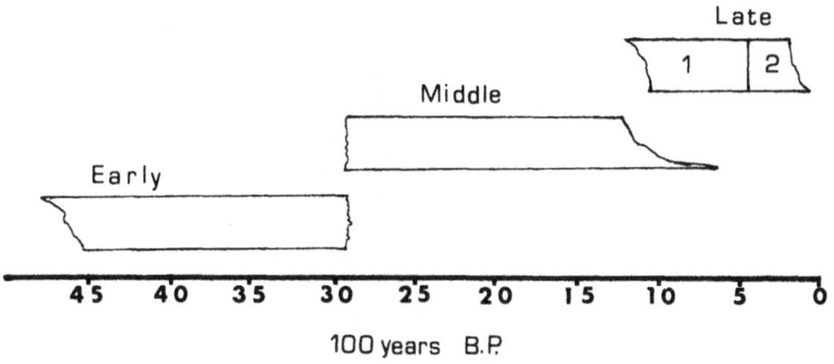

FIGURE 17.1. Temporal distribution of central California cultural complexes (data from Schulz 1981).

sedentism, increased social stratification, and some changes in technology (i.e., changes in relative frequency of stone stools, introduction of small projectile points). Only in Phase 2 of the Late complex do European manufactured goods appear.

Speculation about factors involved with cultural change in interior California have centered on two major and not mutually exclusive themes. One theme suggests partial population replacement, especially in the transition from Early to Middle complexes. The geographical distribution of language families in native California has long been interpreted to indicate past population replacement in the Central Valley. The timing is unclear, but it is suggestive that there is a seemingly dramatic cultural shift between the Early and Middle complexes, as well as increased evidence of warfare in the Middle complex (see Heizer and Elsasser 1980). Skeletal evidence for and against partial population replacement at the Early/Middle transition has appeared (McHenry 1969; Newman 1957; Suchey 1975), but the present chapter does not pursue this point beyond noting that further work would be useful, as no clear consensus has emerged.

The second theme is that the major differences (especially Early *versus* Middle) reflect shifts in subsistence economies. As initially formulated (Heizer 1949), the theme postulated an Early emphasis on hunting relative to fish and vegetal foods, while Middle people adopted (or brought with them) acorn processing, leading to a Late specialization in acorn and a secondary reliance on fish (especially salmon), with Late hunting being least important to caloric intake (Figure 17.2).

Lack of acorn utilization in the Early complex has been a major part of the subsistence shift theme, and was supported both by a logic that expected the Late specialization to have arisen from a more generalized subsistence base, and by archaeological evidence.

Mortars and pestles are considered necessary for acorn processing, and their apparent rarity in Early components seems real. Although Early complex mortars and pestles are known, the

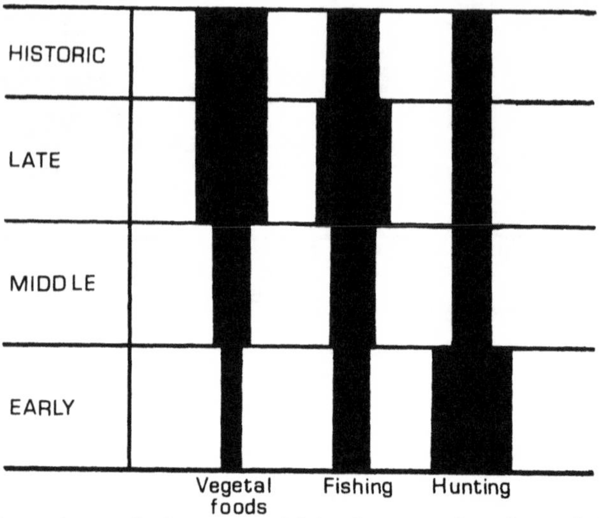

FIGURE 17.2. Subsistence shift from Early through historic times in central California (redrawn from Beardsley 1948:5, figure 2).

Windmiller tradition is distinguished by a low ratio of milling tools of any sort to flaked stone bifaces. Furthermore, five of the seven Windmiller components studied have yielded no mortars or pestles (Schulz 1981). The earliest direct evidence of acorn use in the lower Central Valley dates to the Early-Middle transition (Schulz and Johnson 1980).

Several refinements of the general subsistence shift theme have occurred in recent years. When the Early-Middle-Late sequence was initially proposed, Early sites other than lower Central Valley Windmiller components were either unknown or only tentatively recognized. Since then, analysis of components contemporary with the Windmiller tradition has yielded evidence of Early acorn processing in the San Francisco Bay region (Gerow and Force 1968), and in the North Coast Range north and west of the interior valley (Baumhoff and Orlins 1979; Fredrickson 1974). Thus the scenario is best restricted to the interior valley, as it depends on a central assumption that Early complex was pre-acorn. Reasons for the Windmiller tradition's weak or non-existent utilization of acorn have remained problematic. Lack of appropriate technology does not seem valid in light of the presence of appropriate tools and active trade with possible acorn processing regions. Cultural conservatism may have been a factor in the persistence of a pre-acorn economy, but is difficult to assess archaeologically.

Schulz (1981) has suggested an ecological cause for the lack of acorn utilization in the Windmiller tradition. On the basis of paleoecological data, he concluded that the interior valley was experiencing a series of dry episodes that extended in time through the Early complex to just before the Middle complex transition. Schulz felt that evidence indicated ecological restraints on the range and productivity of the oak woodland in the interior valley (and western Sierra Nevada foothills). This, in turn, inhibited acorn specialization or possibly even utilization.

While the validity and cause of an acornless Windmiller economy has been argued frequently, few studies have addressed the other side of the coin, which is why the acorn was later adopted. The work of Baumhoff (1963) and others suggested that acorn and salmon emphasis developed as a means of decreasing seasonal shortages of food, especially in late winter before spring salmon runs and proliferation of plant foods. The Early subsistence economy was viewed as maintaining only a marginal food surplus. Sedentism, population density, and cultural elaboration followed an initial shift toward stabilization of resources by exploitation of easily stored and productive foods. While this does not explain why the Early complex would endure a pre-acorn regime for so long, it does provide a motivation for the change and specialization that eventually occurred.

At least two testable hypotheses arose from the foregoing investigations. One is termed here the *hunting hypothesis*, although it is actually the idea that Early complex subsustence emphasized meat resources over vegetal food. The other is termed a *seasonal stress hypothesis*, which suggests that Early complex people were more subject to seasonal morbidity and mortality than later peoples, presumably due to periods of winter hardship in food procurement. The two hypotheses are not necessarily independent, as initial formulation of the subsistence theme invoked a hunting economy as a cause of seasonal stress.

The traditional view of California prehistory emphasizing Early complex hunting adaptations was formulated in an era when hunter-gatherers' life-styles were seen as precarious and subject to seasonal hardship. The trend toward acorn specialization was viewed as a progressive move similar to adoption of agriculture elsewhere, and directed toward stabilization of food availability. Although the relationship of subsistence shift and biological health was long postulated, paleopathological investigations in central California were not extensively pursued, and were initially treated as secondary data rather than directly used for hypothesis testing.

PALEOPATHOLOGY

One reason may be that, while spectacular and interesting pathologies have been noted (Bennet 1972; Brooks and Hohenthal 1963; Hoffman 1976a,b,c) general health may have been good (Cook 1955; Heizer and Elsasser 1980). The authors of this chapter have independently noted a general paucity of gross lesions, and

D. Dickel and P. Schulz (unpublished) have independently found that cribra orbitalia and cranial porotic hyperostosis are so rare that meaningful comparisons across age, sex, and temporal samples were not possible. Brues (1966:108), in a specific reference to pathologies in two series of California skeletons (Roney 1966), suggested that they were "so healthy it is somewhat discouraging to work with them." Gerow (Gerow and Force 1968) also notes a lack of pathology in central California skeletal samples. However, some lines of paleopathological research have proved informative.

Harris Lines

McHenry published the results of an investigation of periodic stress in central California based on the occurrence of a fairly common skeletal marker of stress, Harris lines (McHenry 1968). The types of stress associated with Harris line formation are eclectic, but generally the major association has been with Harris lines and illness or malnutrition (for reviews see McHenry and Schulz 1978; Schulz 1981). A basic assumption, based in part on the combined studies of Dreizen et al. (1956, 1964) and Greulich and Pyle (1959), is that Harris lines are poor indicators of chronic stress but good indicators of stress followed by recovery.

In McHenry's (1968) study Harris lines data indicated that more recent publications experienced less periodic stress than the older populations, the strongest reduction being from Early to Middle complexes (Figure 17.3). These results were consistent with a hypothesis of greater Early complex seasonal food shortages, the later decrease being accounted for by the use of stored acorn and salmon.

Schulz (1970, 1981) broadened the evidence of higher seasonal morbidity in the Early complex by looking at the orientation of Windmiller (Early complex) extended burials for evidence of seasonal elevation of mortality. Windmiller burials have long been noted to be consistently oriented westward, and Schulz's study found that 80% of the burials for which data were available occurred in the winter half of the year (Figure 17.4). This supports a hypothesis of Windmiller late winter-early spring seasonal hardship; presumably, increased mortality was due either to direct starvation or, more likely, to the interaction of poor nutrition and poor health. Unfortunately, comparisons with Middle and Late complexes are unavailable with this method as their burials are commonly flexed (if not cremated), and randomly oriented.

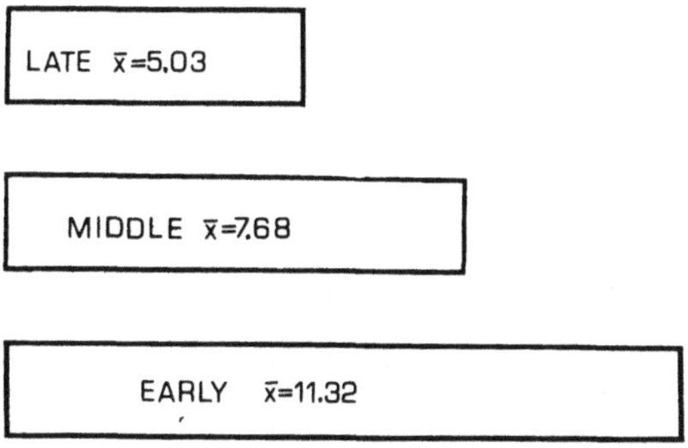

FIGURE 17.3. Average number of Harris lines per femur in Early, Middle, and Late populations in central California (data from McHenry 1968).

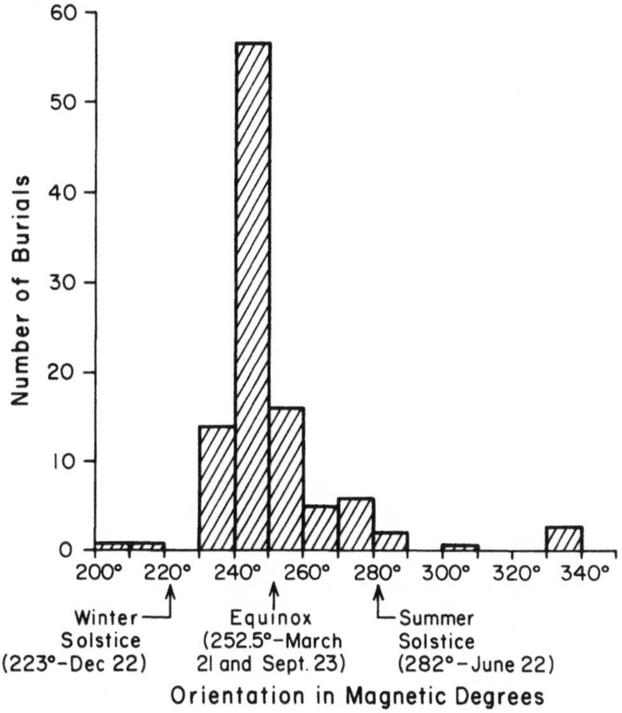

FIGURE 17.4. Orientation of burials from Early complex (Windmiller) in central California (data from Schulz 1970).

Linear Enamel Hypoplasia

McHenry and Schulz (1976) initiated an investigation of linear enamel hypoplasia (LEH) because it was expected to provide support of the seasonal stress hypothesis from a source of paleo-

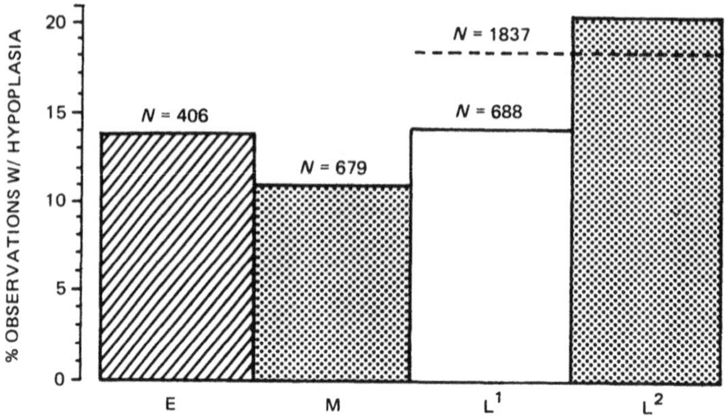

FIGURE 17.5. The frequency of hypoplasia in the Early (E), Middle (M), and Late (Phase 1 [L^1] and Phase 2 [L^2]) populations (redrawn from Schulz 1981:122, Figure 15).

pathological information biologically independent of Harris lines. As with Harris lines, both infectious diseases and malnutrition have been implicated in the development of LEH (for reviews see McHenry and Schulz 1976, 1978; Schulz 1981), and LEH should record periodic stress.

The populations samples for LEH were the same as in McHenry's (1968) study of Harris lines, but the subjects were different and the total sample size larger. The frequency of hypoplastic lines differs among Early, Middle, and Late populations (Figure 17.5). It is apparent that while the decline in frequency of LEH from Early to Middle is in accord with the seasonal stress hypothesis, the Late increase is not. The Late complex spans the transition into historic times, and introduced diseases could be affecting the observed rise in Late LEH incidence. When the Late sample was divided into prehistoric Phase 1 and protohistoric Phase 2, the former group did show a lower incidence. However, the Phase 1 frequency is higher than that of the Middle complex, and LEH data failed to support the seasonal stress hypothesis.

Association of Harris Lines and Linear Enamel Hypoplasia

Of concern was the apparent contradiction of Harris line evidence by what was expected to be corroborating evidence, and an investigation of the association of LEH and Harris lines was initiated. Femora available for 156 subjects used in the LEH study were scored for Harris lines. The new Harris line data indicated two things very clearly. The trend seen by McHenry for a consistent decrease in Harris line frequency through archaeological time was substantiated by samples not used in the previous study. Second, tests of co-occurrence of LEH and Harris lines in specific age categories were totally nonsignificant (McHenry and Schulz, 1976).

Several recent studies have investigated the co-occurrence of these traits with mixed results (see Hunt and Hatch 1981), and they may carry substantially nonredundant information. Certainly the recovery phase necessary for Harris line formation (but not for LEH) emphasizes that the etiologies of these pathologies are only partially overlapping.

It is unclear whether the seasonal stress hypothesis is invalidated by the results of the LEH study, the crux of the matter being whether it is possible to decide if Harris lines or LEH make a better indicator of nutritional stress: the interaction of disease and nutrition may make impossible a general "rule of thumb" about distinguishing the effect of these factors in the development of either. The distinction may lie in that Harris lines record acute stress followed by recovery, and LEH records chronic stress, as suggested by Blumberg and Kerley (1966).

However, it is tempting to speculate about local conditions, even if generalizations are risky. Chronic or short-term famine and nutritional imbalance seem virtually nonexistent in central California at time of contact (see Heizer and Elsasser 1980), although the Late phases show the highest incidences of LEH. This suggests that at least in this study area LEH is not especially due to nutritional stress, but probably records increasing episodes of disease and parasite infestations related to population increase, population density, and sedentism. Disease and parasitism would have become increasingly endemic risks as populations grew, and the relationship of population density and disease has been noted elsewhere (Brothwell 1969; Cohen 1980; Lallo et al. 1978; Larson 1981; Scrimshaw et al. 1968).

Harris lines in central California populations may be good markers of nutritional stress. Ruff (1975) found that an Early San Francisco Bay sample showed about the same rate of Harris line incidence as a Late sample. Presumably, Early bay populations were utilizing acorn crops (Gerow 1974a,b; Gerow and Force 1968), and thus were subject to less seasonal nutritional stress than contemporary interior valley Windmiller people. If Harris lines carry nutritional information relatively unblurred by disease stress, and if LEH records an increase in chronic disease, then the seasonal stress hypothesis is still viable, but with the refinement that it seems probable that subsistence shift toward reliable food sources was accompanied by a change in the nature and source of biological stress rather than a general abatement of all stress.

Stature

Adult stature is possibly an indicator of total health, although genetic and other factors are involved (Buikstra and Cook 1980:449). Average adult femoral length did decrease slightly from Early to Middle times, but there was no appreciable change from Middle to Late. All comparisons across complexes (with or without control for gender) revealed no significant differences in mean femoral lengths. (Sexual dimorphism of femoral lengths also showed no significant changes through time.) Thus there is some indication that total biological stress may have remained approximately equal through time despite changes in the type of stress experienced.

Caries

By the early 1970s there seemed to be tacit agreement that Beardsley's (1948) and Heizer's (1949) model of subsistence in the Early complex was overstated. Nonetheless, summaries of California archaeology emphasized the relative importance of Early hunting, and Willey (1966:369) provides an example of a common "bottom line":

> Slab metates and bowl mortars have been found in the [Early complex Windmiller] sites, but the preponderance of large, stemmed, chipped projectile points; bone fish hooks and gorges: and bone trident fish spears imply that game and fish from the river were more important in the diet than seeds and nuts.

Schulz (1981) directly investigated the question of differential vegetal content of the diet of Early people relative to Middle and Late by examining the incidence of caries in each complex. Because of the importance of carbohydrates as a cariogenic agent, he assumed that the caries experience of populations should be an excellent indicator of the relative carbohydrate content of their diets.

Schulz was not the first to study central California dental pathologies. Leigh (1928) recorded caries frequency, but kept no temporal control of his samples. On the basis of limited sampling, other investigators noticed an increase in the rate of caries in the Late complex, but the significance vis-à-vis the hunting hypothesis was not recognized (Kennedy 1960; Newman 1957). All these studies suffered from shortcomings including small sample sizes, poorly defined age of the individuals, and no control for the effects of postmortem tooth loss.

Schulz (1981) therefore investigated the hunting hypothesis by studying dental pathology in the lower Central Valley, using a very large sample (904 individuals) divided into four relative age classes, stratified by sex and by cultural complex. The most important characteristic of Schulz's results for testing the

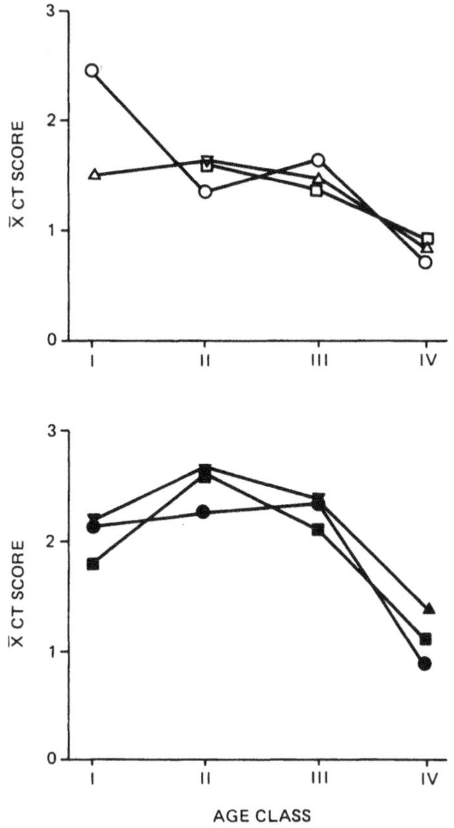

FIGURE 17.6. Mean carious teeth (CT) scores by age group for males and females of Early, Middle, and Late cultural complexes. □, Early males; ■, Early females; o, Middle males; ●, Middle females; Δ, Late males; ▲, Late females. Scored field excludes M3 (redrawn from Schulz 1981:141, Figure 17).

hunting hypothesis is that the frequencies of carious teeth show little tendency to increase through archaeological time (Figure 17.6). In series of tests of differences between values for mean carious teeth in each complex (within relative age and sex classes), only one comparison approached a rather relaxed 90% confidence level. These comparisons failed to show the increases that would be expected to result from a dietary shift from primary reliance on meat to a primary reliance on plant foods high in carbohydrates. Intensification of exploitation of and specialization with a few staple carbohydrates is more likely to mark the Early-Middle-Late transitions than is a shift *to* carbohydrates per se. While the Early complex Windmiller tradition was probably pre-acorn, other carbohydrates may have been utilized to approximately the same extent, indicating the classic hunting hypothesis may be invalid.

PALEODEMOGRAPHY

The seasonal stress hypothesis was initially developed around an assumption of Early reliance on hunting, but it does not depend on this assumption to remain viable. The hypothesis is tentatively supported on the basis of (1) a possibly high concentration of deaths in winter in the Early complex, and (2) Harris line data, especially if Harris lines record periodic nutritional stress. However, the LEH data may indicate that as nutritional stress went into a long-term decline, the transition to specialization in storable food resources was not accompanied by a uniform increase in good health but possibly represented a trade-off of periodic acute stress for chronic stress. The premise that subsistence change was not necessarily a move toward total improvement in health is underscored by paleodemographic studies.

Proponents of the traditional subsistence shift theme suggested a general increase in population through time. This was considered a logical development, as the dense populations known to have existed in protohistoric times must have increased from smaller, earlier populations. Ideas about causes of the population increase were tied into the hunting as well as the seasonal stress hypothesis: it was assumed that smaller populations were maintained due to population mobility and limited carrying capacity of a subsistence strategy directed at k-selected species; eventually, acorn specialization stabilized seasonal fluctuation of food and allowed populations to increase.

Populations in the lower Central Valley were quite dense at contact. Estimates vary from 2.08 (Heizer and Elsasser 1980), to 3.36 (Cook 1976) 4.4 persons/km^2 (Baumhoff 1963). Slaymaker (1982) has indicated that even Baumhoff's figure may be a low estimate.

The exact timing and scale of population increases remain an issue, although the general consensus is that it was most marked in Early to Middle times. Most of the evidence of this postulated increase consists of the number of site components known from each complex, and the trend from a restricted number of Early site components to a large number later appears to have demographic as well as taphonomic implications.

Schulz (1981) summarized the evidence of differential recovery of remains (Figure 17.7). When the quantities of site components recovered are weighed against the temporal duration

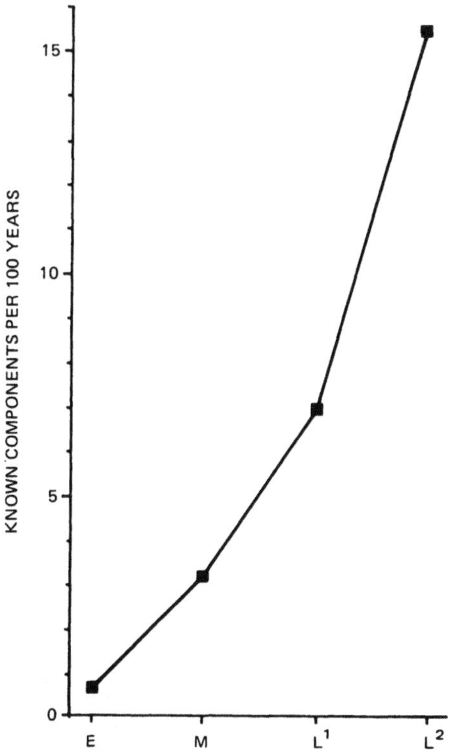

FIGURE 17.7. Chronological distribution of lower Central Valley sites for Early (E), Middle (M), and Late (Phase 1 [L^1] and Phase 2 [L^2]) cultural complexes. Number of known components from each complex is plotted against its duration (redrawn from Schulz 1981:182, Figure 24).

of complexes, a continual increase in the number of sites is apparent and may represent a long-term increase in the number of settlements as well as differential destruction of older sites.

In order to account in part for settlement size, Schulz plotted the distribution of burials against the duration of complexes. Again he found an increase with time, although in contrast to the trend in site distribution there is a visible slowing down of the rate of increase in the Middle to Late periods (Figure 17.8). Schulz also found a general increase in the number of radiocarbon dates from younger *versus* older sites despite a probable bias toward dating material thought to be Early.

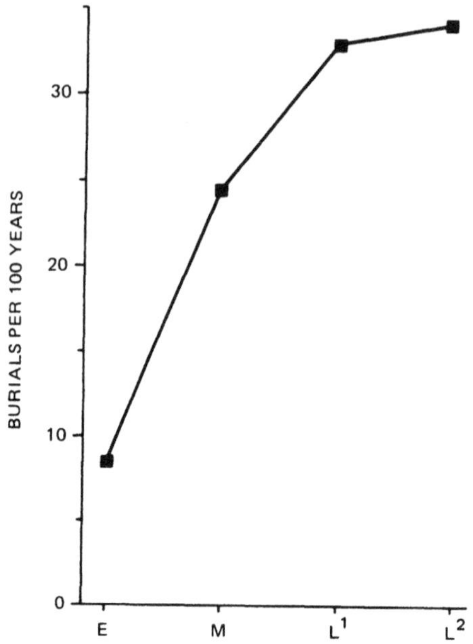

FIGURE 17.8. Chronological distribution of lower Central from Early (E), Middle (M), and Late (Phase 1 [L1] and Phase 2 [L2] cultural complexes. Number of individuals in each complex is plotted against its duration (redrawn from Schulz 1981:183, Figure 25).

Although the distinction between cause and effect is unclear, acorn adaptation presumably played a prominent role in the increase of population densities. In the North Coast Range, balanophagous populations contemporary with the Windmiller tradition seem relatively dense (Baumhoff and Orlins 1979), although evidence from the balanophagous Early San Francisco Bay area is more ambiguous (Ruff 1975). In the western Sierra Nevada foothills few sites occur before Middle times, although balanophagous Late populations were quite large (Johnson 1967; Moratto 1972; Moratto et al. 1978).

Despite uncertainty about Late relative to Middle population growth (Elsasser 1978; Gould 1964) the evidence based on recovery indicates that the major jump is at the Early-Middle transition, with slower increases thereafter.

In the subsistence shift theme it is assumed that decreased morbidity, increased population size, and increased longevity were a single package related to seasonal resource stabilization.

However, a series of studies in central California suggests that longevity may have decreased as acorn specialization increased.

Brabender (1965) compared skeletal samples from the three complexes for relative age based on dental attrition. She found that the Early populations clearly exhibited greater longevity. This was surprising, as increased subsistence reliability is often assumed to be reflected in greater longevity (see Hassan 1973; Nemeskeri 1970). Problems with Brabender's study include small sample size. Most importantly, however, the Early sample is from the interior valley (Windmiller) sites, while the undifferentiated Middle and Late sample is from the San Francisco Bay area. Thus the latter sample does not reflect the Central Valley acorn specialization; it is drawn from population with a heavy reliance on marine resources.

Consequently, a comparison restricted to the lower Sacramento Valley was undertaken by Schulz in an investigation that studied over 900 individuals (for exact methodology see Schulz 1981:98-100). The highest mean dental attrition rates (and presumably greater age) are found among both sexes in the Early sample and among females in the Middle sample. The lowest rate of attrition is found among males in the Late sample, and contrasts between this and all other groups were highly significant. The proportionately greater wear (and greater age) of the Early complex samples supports Brabender's (1965) findings, and longevity may have decreased through archaeological time despite increasing resource stability.

Schulz suggested that cremation practices may bias these results. The observed number of Late males shows a significant drop from the expected number, whereas the male:female ratios for the Early and Middle periods are nearly equal. The practice of cremation increases with archaeological time, and the effort of cremation may have been spent mainly on high-status individuals, especially older males. Thus the appearance of greater longevity of Early samples may be partly an artifact of an increasing diversion of older males from the Late archaeological record. Other demographic work in the lower Sacramento Valley, however, indicates that later populations truly were progressively younger at death.

Doran (1980) studied subadult and adult life tables drawm from a sample of 1254 individuals from all three cultural complexes. Doran's life tables were based on data for males and females combined, which provided a larger sample size but limits testing of some of his concluding hypotheses.

In accordance with what might be expected with a later shift toward acorn subsistence, Doran found overall subadult mortality was generally less for Middle and Late samples than for Early, although mortality for ages 0-2 years actually increased through time (Doran 1980:94). A marked turnaround at age four toward lesser mortality in the later complexes was seen and was attributed to greater reliability of food procurement and decreasing weaning stress. (It is interesting to note that McHenry and Schulz (1978) found peaks at age four for incidence of hypoplastic defects and

Harris lines in all three complexes.) Doran related the greater Middle and Late mortality at ages 0-2 years to trends seen in the adult mortality profile.

As in previous studies, Doran found that adult survivorship at nearly all adult ages was highest for the Early sample. Survivorship progressively worsened with time, especially in the 20-45-year age bracket, which includes the prime reproductive years.

Doran utilized a stationary population distribution to incorporate subadult and adult life table data into a single source of information. He stated that "growing populations are younger populations," and that through time population "growth was occurring, and the rate of growth was lowest in the Early Horizon, intermediate in the Middle Horizon, and highest in the Late Horizon" (Doran 1980:109-110). If this interpretation is correct, then there is no contradiction in the evidence of decreased longevity coincident with increased rate of population growth.

Doran hypothesized that through time (and presumably related to increasingly balanophagous economies), birth spacing decreased as populations grew, and there was increased mortality of young adult females related to increased exposure to the risks of childbirth. Unfortunately, the pooling of sexes in his published life tables precludes a direct examination of this hypothesis. Since Schulz (1981) does not report underrepresentation of younger adult females, the maternal death hypothesis remains an open question. Doran also suggested that the heavier mortality in later complexes for unweaned children aged 0-2 years is related to maternal death, as this age group would be the most adversely affected.

The paleodemographic information from the Central Valley indicates that overall subadult survivorship increased through time while adult survivorship decreased, although cremation may overemphasize the latter trend. All three complexes had a positive and accelerating population growth rate. These paleodemographic changes co-occurred with (1) a major shift from more generalized carbohydrate diet sources to emphasis on a few productive staple foods that could be stored for long periods of time, and (2) major changes in the type of morbidity experienced by populations. It is tempting to speculate on the nature of the interaction of these trends.

Both archaeological interpretations and evidence of dental pathologies indicate that the trend in the Early-Middle-Late complex sequence in the prehistoric interior valley was toward a refinement of an existing pattern of exploitation of plant and animal species, rather than a shift from meat toward vegetal foods. By the time of Western contact and cultural disruption, this trend had culminated in an increased reliance and specialization on a restricted number of staple foods (especially acorn and salmon), and in sedentism, increased population density, and cultural elaboration comparable to that of early food-producing cultures utilizing domesticated staples.

The impetus for this shift is not clear, but several factors may have been involved. One is climatic shift from a relatively prolonged series of dry periods that seems more than coincidentally associated with the Early Windmiller tradition. A general scenario can be visualized: acorn became more productive and reliable enough to warrant increased exploitation, and increased sedentism, population increase, and acorn harvesting became locked into a positive feedback system. The initial step into the feedback system may have been increased sedentism related to harvesting, processing, and especially storage of acorns. Sedentary life may be associated with an increase in population size by leading to a decrease in birth spacing (Bray 1976; Cavalli-Sforza 1973; Fowler 1971; Lee 1972).

Another model explaining subsistence shift involves population pressures (see Cohen 1977). Doran (1980) suggested that all three complexes had a positive growth rate and that populations may have increased "just because" that is what populations tend to do (Cohen 1977, 1981). In addition, it has been suggested that the terminal Early period was marked by migrations into central California. Thus, a scenario along the lines of a population pressure or "bottle theory" (Hayden 1981:521) is possible; external and internal population pressure increased as regional expansion became progressively competitive, and led to exploitation of possibly less desirable and labor-intensive resources that were highly productive and densely located within a restricted area. The rate of population growth increased, again perhaps due to the "locking in" to a feedback system involving sedentism.

A third scenario that can be considered follows Hayden's (1981) resource stress model. The seasonal stress hypothesis in central California can be viewed as a special case of Hayden's more generalized model. The resource stress model suggests that populations attempt to maintain an equilibrium in the frequency with which they experience resource stress. Deviations from this equilibrium result in refinement of existing subsistence patterns within limits of technology, and eventually in subsistence shifts directed toward increasing resource reliability (Hayden 1981:520). Populations are seen as trying to maintain a balance between the costs of morbidity-mortality related to periodic resource stress, and the cost of maintaining population controls. The benefits of retaining this balance include sustaining biological fitness with minimum reproductive waste (Hayden 1981:522). As resource stress decreases, population control relaxes; as population increases, resource stress increases, and cultures again strive either to stabilize resource reliability or to increase population control until a culturally acceptable balance of costs is achieved. This balance is more or less precarious as populations strive to reduce one or the other cost.

What the skeletal data suggest may be somewhat different from a prediction of roughly equal amounts of resource stress within populations utilizing different subsistence strategies. Harris lines indicate that periodic nutritional stress related to resource reliability decreased through time despite population increase. LEH shows a long-term increase from the Early to the Late complex, and total stress (nutrition, disease, etc.), not just resource stress, may be involved in the hypothetical equilibrium. Harris lines and LEH may provide complementary indications of approximately equal total biological stress through time. The results indicate that the nature of the types of stress changed through time, and a balance of the costs of morbidity-mortality and population control may not be related to nutritional stress alone. The data suggest that acute stress decreased while chronic stress increased, and analogous shifts to horticulture may have had much the same effect (Cohen 1981; Lewin 1981).

The types of morbidity and mortality culturally perceived as manipulable by changing subsistence patterns may be a factor in subsistence shifts. While periodic surges in adult mortality may be perceived as being lessened by improved resource stabilization, other forms of mortality may be considered beyond the control of subsistence strategies. An increase in maternal or general mortality related to the complex interaction of decreased birth spacing, population size and density, disease, and subsistence strategy may not be "recognized" as a cost of resource stabilization.

In central California it can be suggested that factors of population growth, seasonal resource stress, and climatic change all contributed to a subsistence shift leading to acorn utilization and subsequent specialization. Population growth and resource stress may have produced a pressure for change in a manner similar to Hayden's proposed "cost of stress-cost of population control" equilibrium, and climatic change may have provided an opportunity to reduce resource stress through elaboration of an existing hunting-gathering strategy without the introduction of horticulture.

REFERENCES

Baumhoff, M.
1963 Ecological determinants of aboriginal California populations. *University of California Publications in American Archaeology and Ethnography 49*:155-236.

Baumhoff, M. A., and R. Orlins
1979 An archaeological assay on Dry Creek, Sonoma County, California. *University of California Archaeological Research Facility Contributions 40*:1-244.

Bean, L., and T. Blackburn
1976 *Native Californians, a theoretical retrospective.* Ballena Press, Socorro, New Mexico.

Bean, L., and H. Lawton
1973 Some explanations for the rise of cultural complexity in

native California with comments on proto-agriculture and agriculture. *Ballena Press Anthropological Papers* *1*:V-XLVII.

Beardsley, R.

1948 Cultural sequences in central California archaeology. *American Antiquity 14*:1-28.

1954 Temporal and areal relationships in central California archaeology, parts I and II. *Reports of the University of California Archaeological Survey, Berkeley*, Nos. 24-25.

Bennet, K. A.

1972 Lumbo-sacral malformations and spina bifida occulata in a group of proto-historic Modoc Indians. *American Journal of Physical Anthropology 36*:435-439.

Blumberg, J., and E. Kerley

1966 Discussion: A critical consideration of roentgenology and microscopy in paleopathology. In *Human Paleopathology*, edited by S. Jarcho, pp. 150-170. Yale University Press, New Haven and London.

Brabender, I.

1965 Beitras zur palaobiologischen Rekonstruktion prahistorischer kalifornischer Populationen. *HOMO 16*:200-230.

Bray, W.

1976 From predation to production: The nature of agricultural evolution in Mexico and Peru. In *Problems in Economic and Social Archaeology*, edited by Gale de G. Sieveking, I. H. Longworth, and K. E. Wilson, pp. 73-95. Ducksworth, London.

Brooks, S., and W. Hohenthal

1963 Archaeological defective palate crania from California. *American Journal of Physical Anthropology 21*:25-32.

Brothwell, D.

1969 Dietary variation and the biology of earlier human populations. In *The Domestication and Exploitation of Plants and Animals*, edited by P. Ucko and C. Dimbleby, pp. 53-545. Aldine-Atherton, Chicago.

Brues, A.

1966 Discussion. In *Human Paleopathology*, edited by S. Jarcho, pp. 107-112. Yale University Press, New Haven and London.

Buikstra, J. E., and D. C. Cook

1980 Paleopathology: An American account. *Annual Review of Anthropology 9*:433-470.

Cavalli-Sforza, L.

1973 Origin and differentiation of human races. *Proceedings Royal Anthropological Institute* 1972:15-25.

Cohen, M.

1977 *The Food Crisis in Prehistory*. Yale University Press, New Haven and London.

1980 Speculations on the evolution of density measurement and population regulation in Homo sapiens. In *Biosocial Mechanisms of Population Regulation*, edited by M. Cohen, R. Malpass, and H. Klein, pp. 275-304. Yale University

Press, New Haven and London.
1981 Comments. *Current Anthropology 22*:532.

Cook, S. F.
1955 The Epidemic of 1830-1833 in California and Oregon. *University of California Publication in American Archaeology and Ethnology 43*(3):303-326.
1976 The conflict between the California Indian and White civilization. University of California Press, Berkeley.

Doran, G.
1980 *Paleodemography of the Plains Miwok ethnolinguistic area, Central California.* Ph.D. dissertation, University of California, Davis.

Dreizen, S., C. Currie, E. Gilley, and T. Spies
1956 Observations on the association between nutritive failure, skeletal maturation rate, and radiopaque transverse lines in the distal end of the radius in children. *American Journal of Roentgenology, Radiological Therapy, and Nuclear Medicine 76*:482-487.

Dreizen, S., C. Spirakis, and R. Stone
1964 The influence of age and nutritional status on bone scar formation in the distal end of the growing radius. *American Journal of Physical Anthropology 22*:295-306.

Elsasser, A.
1978 Development of regional prehistoric cultures. In *Handbook of North American Indians* (Vol. 8), edited by Robert Heizer, pp. 37-57. Smithsonian Institution, Washington, D.C.

Fowler, M.
1971 The origin of plant cultivation in the central Mississippi Valley: A hypothesis. In *Prehistoric Agricultures*, edited by S. Struever, pp. 122-128. Nature History Press, Garden City, New York.

Fredrickson, D.
1974 Cultural diversity in early central California: A view from the North Coast Ranges. *Journal of California Anthropology 1*:41-53.

Gerow, B.
1974a Comments on Fredrickson's cultural diversity. *Journal of California Archaeology 1*:239-246.
1974b Contradictions and convergent trends in prehistoric California. *San Luis Obispo County Archaeological Society Occasional Paper 8*:1-57.

Gerow, B., and R. Force
1968 *An Analysis of the University Village Complex.* Stanford University Press, Palo Alto.

Gould, R.
1964 Exploitative economies and cultural change in central California. *University of California Archaeological Survey Report 62*:123-163.

Greulich, W., and S. Pyle
1959 *Radiographic Atlas of Skeletal Development of the Hand and*

Wrist. Stanford University Press, Palo Alto.

Hassan, F. A.
1973 On mechanisms of population growth during the Neolithic. *Current Anthropology 14*:535-542.

Hayden, B.
1981 Research and development in the Stone Age: Technological transitions among hunter-gatherers. *Current Anthropology 22*:519-531.

Heizer, R.
1939 The archaeology of central California. I: The early horizon. *University of California Anthropological Reports* No. 12.

Heizer, R., and A. Elsasser
1980 *The Natural World of California Indians*. University of California Press, Berkeley and Los Angeles.

Heizer, R., and F. Fenenga
1939 Archaeological horizons in central California. *American Anthropologist 41*:378-399.

Hoffman, J. M.
1976a Studies in California paleopathology: Comminuted fracture of a humerus with pseudo arthrosis formation. *Contributions of the University of California Archaeology Research Facility 30*:25-39.

1976b Studies in California paleopathology: Enlarged parietal foramina. *Contributions of the University of California Archaeology Research Facility 30*:42-61.

1976c Studies in California paleopathology: An anchondroplastic dwarf from the Augustine site. *Contributions of the University of California Archaeology Research Facility 30*:65-105.

Hoffman, J. M., and L. Brunker
1976 Studies in California Paleopathology: California paleopathology bibliography. *Conributions of the University of California Archaeology Research Facility 30*:3-23.

Hunt, E., Jr., and J. W. Hatch
1981 The estimation of age of death and ages of formation of transverse lines from measurements of human long bones. *American Journal of Physical Anthropology 54*:461-469.

Johnson, J.
1967 The archaeology of the Commanche reservoir locality, California. *Sacramento Anthropological Society Papers 6*:1-370.

Kennedy, K.
1960 The dentition of Indian crania of the early and late Archaeological horizons in central California. *Reports of University of California Archaeological Survey* No. 50, 41-50.

Lallo, J., G. Armelagos, and J. Rose
1978 Paleoepidemiology of infectious disease in Dickson Mound populations. *Medical College of Virginia Quarterly 14*:17-23.

Larson, C.
1981 Skeletal and dental adaptations to the shift to agriculture on the Georgia coast. *Current Anthropology* 22:422-423.
Lee, R.
1972 Population growth and the beginnings of sedentary life among the !Kung Bushman. In *Population Growth: Anthropological Implications*, edited by B. Spooner, pp. 329-342. M.I.T. Press, Cambridge.
Leigh, R.
1928 Dental pathology of aboriginal California. *University of California Publications in American Archaeology and Ethnography* 23:399-440.
Lewin, R.
1981 Disease clue to dawn of agriculture. *Science* 211:41.
Lillard, J., R. Heizer, and F. Fenenga
1939 An introduction to the archaeology of central California. *Sacramento Jr. College Bulletin* No. 2.
McHenry, H.
1968 Transverse lines in long bones of prehistoric California Indians. *American Journal of Physical Anthropology* 29:1-18.
1969 Multivariate analysis of California Indian crania. Ms. on file, Department of Anthropology, University of California, Davis.
McHenry, H., and P. Schulz
1976 The association between Harris lines and enamel hypoplasia in prehistoric California Indians. *American Journal of Physical Anthropology* 44:507-512.
1978 Harris lines, enamel hypoplasia, and subsistence change in prehistoric central California. *Ballena Press Publications in Archaeology, Ethnography, and History* 11:35-49.
Meighan, C.
1959 California cultures and the concept of an archaic stage. *American Antiquity* 24:289-318.
Moratto, M.
1972 *A study of prehistory in the southern Nevada foothills, California*. Ph.D. dissertation, University of Oregon, Eugene.
Moratto, M., T. King, and W. Woolfenden
1978 Archaeology and California climate. *Journal of California Anthropology* 5:147-162.
Nemeskeri, J.
1970 Die palaodemosraphoscher Probleme des Mittle-Donau-Beckens in der Bronzezeit. *Homo* 21:80-85.
Newman, R.
1957 A comparative analysis of prehistoric skeletal remains from the lower Sacramento Valley. *University of California Archaeological Survey Reports* No. 39.
Roney, J.
1966 Paleoepidemiology: An example from California. In *Human*

Paleopathology, edited by S. Jarcho, pp. 99-107. Yale University Press, New Haven and London.

Ruff, C.
1975 Transverse lines in the long bones of two prehistoric San Francisco Bay populations. Ms. on file, Department of Anthropology, Stanford University, Palo Alto.

Schulz, P.
1970 Solar orientation and paleodemography in the central California Windmiller tradition. *Center for Archaeological Research at Davis Publication* 2:185-198.
1981 Osteoarchaeology and subsistence change in prehistoric central California. Ph.D. dissertation, University of California, Davis.

Schulz, P., and J. Johnson
1980 An early acorn cache from central California. *Journal of California and Great Basin Anthropology* 2(1):127-128.

Scrimshaw, N., C. Taylor, and J. Gordon
1968 Interactions of nutrition and infection. *World Health Organization Monograph Series* No. 57.

Slaymaker, C.
1982 *A model for the study of Coast Miwok Ethnography*. Ph.D. dissertation, University of California, Davis.

Suchey, J.
1975 *Biological distances of prehistoric central California populations derived from non-metric traits of the cranium*. Ph.D. dissertation, University of California, Riverside.

Willey, G.
1966 *An Introduction to American Archaeology* (Vol. I). Prentice-Hall, Englewood Cliffs.

Ziegler, A.
1968 Quasi-agriculture in north central California and its effect on aboriginal social structure. *Kroeber Anthropological Society Papers 38*:52-67.

CHAPTER 18

PREHISTORIC SUBSISTENCE AND HEALTH STATUS OF COASTAL PEOPLES FROM THE PANAMANIAN ISTHMUS OF LOWER CENTRAL AMERICA

Lynette Norr

Department of Anthropology
University of Illinois at Urbana-Champaign

INTRODUCTION

The relationship between prehistoric subsistence and health is far from simple. It is complicated by numerous factors such as settlement location, population density, resource abundance and seasonal availability, the age structure of the population, and its sanitary habits. In addition, cultural input in the form of food taboos, food preparation techniques, and limited access to resources can alter dietary patterns and availability of nutrients to a population.

Direct relationships between specific nutritional deficiencies and health status are difficult to document in any human population because the biochemical functions and interactions of most nutrients are multiple and complex. Moreover, investigators studying archaeological populations are faced with the task of reconstructing the subsistence base before establishing any relationship it may have with the health status of the population. The chemical analysis of archaeological human and animal bone for either mineral composition or isotopic composition provides a means of dietary reconstruction and corroborates archaeological evidence based on faunal, botanical and artifactual remains. Dietary reconstruction, in conjunction with estimates of health status based on skeletal remains, provides the basis for evaluating the degree to which a population is exploiting and adapting successfully to a particular environmental setting.

The Panamanian Isthmus of lower Central America has a cultural sequence dating from at least 10,000 B.C. Skeletal remains that date from possibly as early as 5000 B.C. span the transition in subsistence from hunting and gathering wild resources to the dependence on seed agriculture. Settlement and subsistence data now available are, for the most part, geographically restricted to the central Pacific coastal plain and parts of western Panama. These areas are rich in natural resources and have supported some of the largest populations of lower Central America. At the time of European contact, large nucleated villages under tribal authority were well established in this region. Firsthand accounts of these populations by Europeans during the sixteenth century aid in our interpretation of the archaeological remains of the early Panamanian cultures.

GEOGRAPHIC SETTING AND SUBSISTENCE RESOURCES

Most of the Isthmus of Panama lies at an elevation of less than 500 m, but it is divided by central mountain ranges averaging 1000-2000 m above sea level. Rainfall varies with elevation and air currents--many parts of the country receive 2000-2500 mm of rainfall annually; some Pacific coastal areas receive less and some Atlantic coastal areas much more. The vegetation covering most of the Pacific slope and coastal plain is a deciduous or semideciduous forest, and easily converted into savanna. The Köppen classification of macroclimates for this region is "tropical wet and dry" (Aw), and provides a diverse pattern of moist and dry subregions within the rainshadow region south of the divide. The area north of the Azuero peninsula and around the Bay of Parita is predominantly a "tropical dry forest" (Myers 1969). In contrast, the Caribbean slopes are covered with continuous, nonseasonal "tropical moist forest" (Af). Evaporation in this area is minimal due to frequent nighttime rainfalls (Bennett 1968; Holdridge and Budowski 1956; Myers 1969; Porter 1973).

Mammals that can be found in Panama today include various species of primates, wild feline and canine mammals, weasels, procyoniddae (such as coatimundi and racoon), hooved mammals (tapir, deer, and peccaries), edentates (sloth, anteater, and armadillo), and a variety of rodents, marsupials, and bats (Bennett 1968; Levy and Chong 1977). The marine fauna of the Pacific coast is particularly abundant, especially in the Gulf of Panama and Parita Bay due to a seasonal upwelling that brings about an increase in phytoplankton production and seasonal influxes of shellfish, crustaceans, schools of shallow water fish, and flocks of seabirds (Glynn 1972). This, in addition to mud flats, mangrove swamps, and lagoon estuary systems, makes the Parita Bay region very productive. To the west, along the Pacific

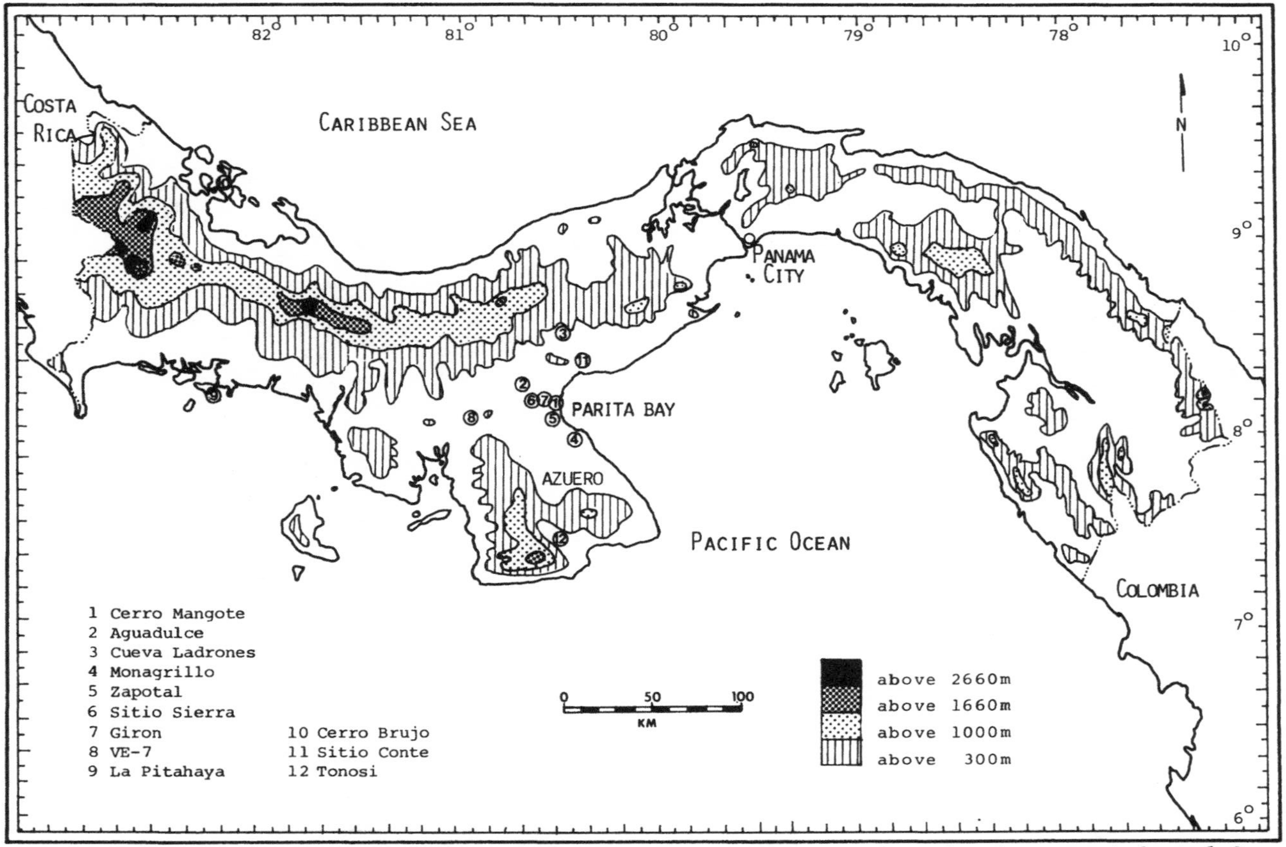

FIGURE 18.1. Relief map of Panama indicating locations referred to in the text (adapted from Bennett 1968).

coast, the Gulf of Chiriquí is a complex embayment of estuaries, with calm waters rich in fish. Mollusks and shellfish are abundant in the adjacent mudflats (Linares 1968).

On parts of the Caribbean coast, stands of mangrove and large flats of turtle grass support green turtle and manatee. Coral and rocky reefs are inhabited by a large number of fish species. Fish biomass is lower in this region than in a comparable environment along the Pacific, but species diversity is quite high (Linares 1980b). Overall, the Isthmus of Panama has excellent natural resource diversity and potential for subsistence production.

BROAD CULTURAL UNITS

The cultural sequence for western and central Panama can be broken down into five major periods of occupation based on artifact assemblage, subsistence base, settlement pattern, and apparent sociopolitical organization.

Paleoindian (?-8000 B.C.)

Surface finds of fluted points and scrapers demonstrate that Paleoindian populations once inhabited the eastern portion of the isthmus, but excavations in rock shelters and caves have not uncovered associated features or skeletal remains (Bird and Cooke 1977, 1978; Cooke 1984; Sander 1964). Excavations in progress in central Panama have recently uncovered what appears to be Paleoindian occupational debris (A. J. Ranere, personal communication).

Preceramic-Archaic (8000-2500 B.C.)

To date, no archaeological remains have been discovered dating to the early part of the Preceramic period (8000-5000 B.C.). The archaeological and skeletal data for the latter portion of this period come from rock shelters in central and western Panama (Bird and Cooke 1978; Cooke 1978; Linares and Ranere 1971; Ranere 1972, 1980) and the Parita Bay coastal shell midden site Cerro Mangote (McGimsey 1956, 1957, 1959; McGimsey et al. 1966; Ranere 1979, 1981; Ranere and Hansell 1978).

Early Ceramic-Early Agriculturalists (2500-300 B.C.)

The initial part of the Early Ceramic period (2500-1000 B.C.) is well known from Monogrillo, a shell midden on the Parita Bay coast (Willey and McGimsey 1954), and from related finds in the central Panama rock shelters La Cueva de los Ladrones and Aguadulce (Bird and Cooke 1978; Cooke 1978; Ranere and Hansell 1978). These cultural deposits are absent from western Panamanian rock shelters (Linares and Ranere 1971).

The latter part of the Early Ceramic period is not well known. Only recently has a site been found in the Parita Bay area that demonstrates *in situ* cultural development from the earliest ceramic sites, through the latter portion of the Early Ceramic period, to the succeeding period of Agricultural Villages (Ranere and Cooke 1982).

Agricultural Villages (300 B.C.-A.D. 500)

Several agricultural villages have been recorded and investigated on the alluvial plains of central Pacific Panama (Cooke 1979, 1984; Ladd 1964; Willey and Stoddard 1954). They provide evidence of the first ceramic and agricultural village occupation of the fertile valleys in the western highlands (Linares and Ranere 1971; Linares et al. 1975; Linares 1977a,b; Linares and Sheets 1980).

Agricultural Chiefdoms (A.D. 500-1550)

Variations in the quantity and quality of burial goods suggest that a rank society was established in the central Pacific region by A.D. 400-500 (Cooke 1984; Helms 1976, 1979). Excavations indicate that a similar level of organization is reached in the western highlands at about the same time (Linares 1977b; Linares and Sheets 1980) and along the Pacific slope of western Panama by A.D. 700. However, chiefdoms never appear to have formed along the Caribbean slopes of western Panama (Linares 1980c).

PREHISTORIC SUBSISTENCE, SETTLEMENT, AND POPULATION GROWTH

A shift in emphasis from hunting and gathering to seed agriculture can be documented along the Pacific slope of central and western Panama. Some form of vegeculture and the tending of fruit and palm trees probably was integrated into the hunting and gathering scheme and remained in practice through the agricultural periods, as it does today (Cooke 1984; Linares 1977b, 1980d; Smith 1980). Due to climatic and geographic variation as well as cultural choices, the transition did not occur uniformly throughout the area.

The Parita Bay region is the only location in all of lower Central America in which there has been a long history of coastal resource utilization, 5000 B.C.-present (Ranere et al. 1980).

Although the rock shelters of western Panama were occupied from circa 5000 B.C., populations did not inhabit the Pacific littoral of western Panama until approximately 1 A.D. (Cooke 1984; Linares 1968). The Caribbean slopes of western Panama were occupied later in the cultural sequence (A.D. 600), and here seed agriculture never replaced root and tree crops as the subsistence base (Linares and Ranere 1971; Linares et al. 1975; Linares 1980d).

Thus, a chronological discussion of trends in economic, subsistence, and settlement data for prehistoric Panama is dependent primarily on the 7000-year occupational sequence from Parita Bay and adjacent regions. Supporting data come from the rock shelters and agricultural villages of the Pacific slopes and highlands of western Panama, while a very brief and different scenario occurred on the Caribbean coast.

Paleoindian (?-8000 B.C.)

Paleoindian populations of the Chagres Valley in eastern Panama presumably were hunting some of the known Late Pleistocene fauna, including a variety of extinct large mammals (Cooke 1984; Gazin 1957) as well as peccary and deer. At present, there is no fossil evidence for terminal Pleistocene mammals in eastern Panama, where Paleoindian lithics are found (Cooke 1984). The degree to which wild fruits and roots of the tropical forest and savanna were utilized in this relatively specialized hunting scheme is not known.

Preceramic-Archaic (8000-2500 B.C.)

The subsistence data for the Preceramic-Archaic period (8000-2500 B.C.) come from rock shelters in western and central Panama and the shell midden site of Cerro Mangote along Parita Bay. The data consist of carbonized plant remains, lithic tool assemblages, faunal remains, pollen, and phytoliths.

Carbonized remains of three plants are common in rock shelters; a tree legume, *Algarrobo (Hymenea courbaril)*; a cherry-like fruit, *nance (Byrsonima crassifolia)*; and fruits of the *corozo* palms *(Acrocomia vinifera* and *Sheelia zonensis* (Ranere and Hansell 1978; Smith 1980). The palms probably contributed more to the diet than the other two products. Botanical remains were not found at the coastal shell midden site of Cerro Mangote, but lithic assemblages suggest a common technology for procurement and processing of food.

The preceramic lithic tool kit suggests "simple extractive technologies" (Ranere 1981) associated with wild plants and possibly with agriculture based on root crops (Linares 1977b). The kit includes edge-ground cobbles or "edge grinders" and boulder milling stones.

Faunal remains from the rock shelters include deer and a variety of medium to small mammals. Remains of reptiles and amphibians were relatively rare, and fish, mollusks, and freshwater turtles were important only at one site (Cooke 1981).

Phytolith and pollen studies indicate that seed crops were present, but perhaps were not a significant part of the subsistence base. Pollen and phytoliths identified as maize have been found in preceramic levels at La Cueva de los Ladrones in the highlands of central Panama (Piperno 1980; Piperno and Clary 1982; Ranere and Cooke 1982). Pollen identified as an early variety or "wild" maize also has been identified from Gatun Lake sediment cores dating to 5350-2280 B.C. Additional palynological evidence for agriculture seen in more recent sediments is absent at this time (Bartlett et al. 1969).

Recent surveys have resulted in preliminary estimates of site density along portions of the Santa Maria River drainage. Open air preceramic sites average about 25 m or less in diameter. Larger sites, elliptical in shape, cover about 450 m^2. Aceramic site density, based on a 2.5 km survey transect, is estimated to be approximately 25 sites/km^2 (Weiland 1982). Based on the carrying capacity of the area, Bennett (1968:31) has attempted a "gross approximation" of the possible densities of human populations. He suggests an overall density of 1.3 persons/km^2 for the Isthmus, with a density of 1.9 and 0.6 persons/km^2 on the Pacific and Atlantic coasts, respectively.

Early Ceramic-Early Agriculturalists (2500-300 B.C.)

During the first part of the Early Ceramic/Early Agriculturalists period (2500-1000 B.C.), settlement continues in the pattern of the previous period (Ranere and Hansell 1978). Use of the rock shelters continues, although new locations are occupied along the Parita Bay, Monagrillo (Willey and McGimsey 1954), and Zapotal (Ranere and Hansell 1978). *In situ* transition from preceramic to ceramic occupation in rock shelters suggests that no appreciable change in resource utilization or technology occurred (Cooke 1984; Linares 1976). Phytolith and pollen analyses from rock shelter contexts show that maize was definitely present in central Panama at the time ceramics were introduced (Piperno 1980; Piperno and Clary 1982); but the continuity in subsistence technology implies that the introduction of a seed crop was no more than a casual addition to the subsistence base.

Preceramic and Early Ceramic period food procurement systems of central Panama involved transhumance among both coastal and inland resources. The annual cycle involved dry season and early wet season exploitation of intertidal, mudflat, mangrove, and estuary resources, including salt, and wet season collection of tree crops and hunting for mammals.

In addition, during the Monagrillo phase maize may have been cultivated. Occupational sites are located on low hills near streams, not on the alluvial plains. Highly mobile groups with a low population density may have cultivated these hill slopes during part of the year (Ranere and Cooke 1982). To date there is no evidence, botanical or otherwise, for the cultivation of root crops during this period.

The last 700 years of the Early Ceramic period (1000-300 B.C.) represent a period of local *in situ* transition into agricultural villages. The presence of large numbers of polished stone tools and large legless "breadboard" rim metates and cylindrical manos after 1000 B.C. suggests an extensive use of maize (Ranere and Cooke 1982). Pollen from the Chagres River valley in eastern Panama is indicative of agriculture 1150 B.C.-A.D. 150. The association of large grains of maize pollen with the scarcity of tree pollen, a large percentage of compositae and graminae pollen, the pollen of herbaceous weeds, and the presence of finely divided charcoal all point toward nearby agricultural activity. The presence of *Manihot esculenta* pollen and *Ipomoea* sp. pollen supports the contention that manioc and possibly sweet potatoes were cultivated during this time (Bartlett et al. 1969).

Agricultural Villages (300 B.C.-A.D. 500)

By 300 B.C., rock shelters and coastal shell middens were abandoned as living sites, and nucleated and permanent villages cultivating maize, beans, and a variety of root and tree crops were established on the alluvial plains along the major rivers of the Pacific lowlands and in the volcanic valleys of the western highlands (Cooke 1979, 1984). Archaeological remains of carbonized seed crops as well as the stone tools used to process them are abundant. The data indicate that by this time, maize had become a staple crop (Cooke 1984; Linares and Cooke 1975; Linares et al. 1975; Linares and Sheets 1980).

The site of Sitio Sierra along the Santa Maria River in central Panama has yielded quantities of carbonized maize from both domestic and burial contexts. Numerous other items indicative of agricultural activities have been found on the floors of small living structures dating 65 B.C.-A.D. 235, including manos and metates as well as polished stone axes. Three varieties of maize are present, and a single fragment of a bean (*Phaseolus vulgarus*) was recovered from the site (Cooke 1979, 1984).

The faunal remains at Sitio Sierra are representative of species from savanna and disturbed habitats, suggesting that the land used by these villagers had been cut repeatedly and cleared for agricultural purposes (Cooke 1979, 1984). White-tailed deer were hunted, but fish (predominantly from fresh water) represent the most common source of protein (Ranere et al. 1980). The faunal assemblage suggests year-round human occupation. Included with the mammalian remains are assorted birds, reptiles, and amphibians (Cooke 1979, 1981; Linares and Cooke 1975). Data collected at sites near the coast indicate that both maize and shellfish were also important components of the diet (Ichon 1980; Ladd 1964).

During this period, the fertile highland valleys of western Panama were settled by agricultural populations that were expanding their subsistence base of palm and root crops to include maize and beans. Carbonized plant remains and ground stone tools are abundant in these highland sites. Remains include charred specimens of beans (*Phaseolus vulgarus*) and maize (Linares et al. 1975; Linares 1977b; Linares and Sheets 1980).

Populations grew rapidly in this area, as they did in the central Pacific region. By the end of this period, the formation of a rank society was well underway, as evidenced by the beginning of a site hierarchy as well as an unequal distribution of elite goods in burials. A similar trend occurred in central Panama (Linares 1977b; Linares and Sheets 1980).

The highland occupation in western Panama was interrupted approximately A.D. 600 when Volcan Baru erupted (Linares and Sheets, 1980; Sheets 1980), prompting migrations to both coasts (Linares 1977a, 1980a,d). It should be noted that the migrations toward the Pacific coast began two or three centuries before the eruption suggesting that increase in population density and a decrease in resource availability may have initiated these migrations (Linares 1977a, 1980a). The chiefdoms on the Pacific coast resembled contemporary chiefdoms in central Panama. The population that migrated to the Atlantic coast became dispersed, and retained an egalitarian sociopolitical organization (Linares and Ranere 1971; Linares 1980c).

Agricultural Chiefdoms (A.D. 500-550)

Much of what is known about diet and population for this period comes from reports by European chroniclers of the sixteenth century (Cooke 1979; de Andagoya 1865; de Espinosa 1873, 1892; Fernandez de Oviedo Valdes 1853; Helms 1979; Lothrop 1937; Sauer 1966). In central and parts of western Panama there existed a number of chiefdoms whose size and location provided access to a wide variety of natural resources. In some cases, territories ranged from the sea to the mountains, usually following a major river valley. Settlements in some areas were nucleated into towns such as Natá in central Panama and Darien in eastern Panama. There were also numerous scattered dwellings near waterways and cultivated fields in the valleys and along the mountain slopes. Estimates of population density by Bennett (1968:37, map 6) for the more populous regions are 4-6 persons/km^2.

Agriculture, hunting, and fishing provided the basic subsistence foods during this period. Crops include maize, manioc, sweet potatoes, and other root crops, peanuts, chili peppers, pineapples, and coconuts. Most early accounts also report an abundance of both terrestrial and marine fauna.

Archaeological knowledge of this period comes from a number of sites in central and western Panama including Sitio Conte (Lothrop 1937), El Hatillo, Delgado, Sixto Pinilla Place (Ladd 1964), several sites near Tonosi (Ichon 1980), and Sitio Sierra (Cooke 1979, 1984), La Pitahaya on Isla Palenque along the Pacific coast (Linares 1980c,e), and Cerro Brujo along the Caribbean coast (Linares 1980b,f).

An analysis of the faunal remains (Cooke 1981, 1984; Linares and Cooke 1974; Linares 1976) shows a regional pattern in resource utilization. Terrestrial faunal remains, principally deer, are quite scarce at the Pacific sites. The few species represented are those inhabiting open savanna and areas cleared for cultivation. In contrast, the abundant terrestrial fauna at Caribbean coastal sites was composed primarily of solitary tropical forest species.

CHEMICAL ANALYSES OF BONE FOR DIETARY RECONSTRUCTION

The chemical analysis of human skeletal remains for mineral composition or stable isotopic composition can be a valuable tool in dietary reconstruction. The ratio of stable carbon isotopes in bone collagen is directly related to the ratio of stable carbon isotopes in the diet (De Niro and Epstein 1978). Similarly, the ratio of stable nitrogen isotopes in bone collagen is directly related to the ratio of stable nitrogen isotopes in the diet (De Niro and Epstein 1981). The ratios of these isotopes vary predictably in nature. Continual consumption of a food source rich in either ^{13}C or ^{15}N will result in a high $^{13}C/^{12}C$ or $^{15}N/^{14}N$ ratio in the body.

Marine fauna are rich in both ^{13}C and ^{15}N compared to terrestrial organisms. There is one exception, however, the $^{13}C/^{12}C$ ratio of plants that have a four-carbon (C_4) photosynthetic pathway is virtually identical to the $^{13}C/^{12}C$ ratio that is found in marine fauna.[1] Some well-known C_4 plants include maize, sorghum, sugar cane, and millet. Ratios of $^{13}C/^{12}C$ and $^{15}N/^{14}N$, expressed in parts per mil (o/oo) and relative to an analytical standard, are written as $\delta^{13}C$ or $\delta^{15}N$ values. The δ values of a sample may be either positive or negative, relative to the analytical standard. The variation of $^{13}C/^{12}C$ ratios in nature, expressed

[1] *A third variation in photosynthetic pathways is the crassulacean acid metabolism (CAM). CAM plants use a metabolic process by which they switch their photosynthetic pathways from C_3-like to C_4-like during night and day. Most CAM plants are succulents and have a $\delta^{13}C$ value somewhere between those of C_3 and C_4 plants (Bumstead 1981). The pineapple is a CAM plant which was eaten in Panama prehistorically.*

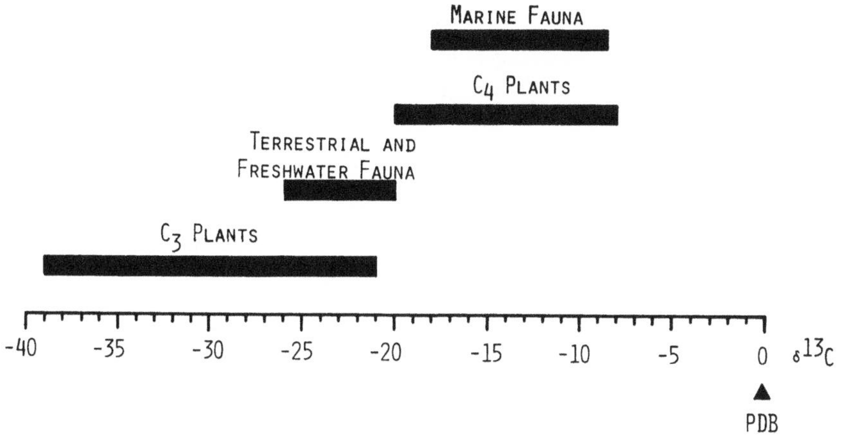

FIGURE 18.2. Variations of $\delta^{13}C$ values in parts per mil (o/oo) in nature (see Norr and Coleman 1982).

as $\delta^{13}C$ values relative to the PDB[2] standard, are shown in Figure 18.2. While all of the $\delta^{13}C$ values are negative, the $\delta^{13}C$ values for marine fauna and C_4 plants are more positive than other terrestrial organisms. Figure 18.3 provides a similar representation showing the variation of $^{15}N/^{14}N$ ratios in nature. These are expressed as $\delta^{15}N$ values relative to the standard, atmospheric nitrogen. The $\delta^{15}N$ values for marine and estuary fauna are more positive than the $\delta^{15}N$ values for terrestrial organisms. Legumes, which utilize nitrogen fixed by symbiotic bacteria, exhibit the most negative $\delta^{15}N$ values.

Applications of stable carbon isotopic analysis of bone collagen are limited to two situations: (1) the interpretation of the contribution of C_4 plants (principally maize in the New World) to the diets of individuals in inland environments, away from marine resources, and (2) the interpretation of the contribution of marine fauna to the diets of coastal individuals who were not potentially consuming C_4 plants or animals that feed on C_4 plants (for a review see Bumstead 1981, 1982). A pilot study using prehistoric skeletal remains from coastal and inland sites in Costa Rica revealed that the $\delta^{13}C$ values of individuals from coastal sites were more positive than those from contemporary inland sites (Norr 1980, 1981a; Norr and Coleman 1982). These results reflect the fact that coastal populations presumably consumed both maize and marine fauna, whereas many inland populations ate little or no marine fauna.

[2]*The PDB standard is a carbon dioxide gas prepared from a crateceous belemnite, Belemnitella americana, from the Peedee formation of South Carolina.*

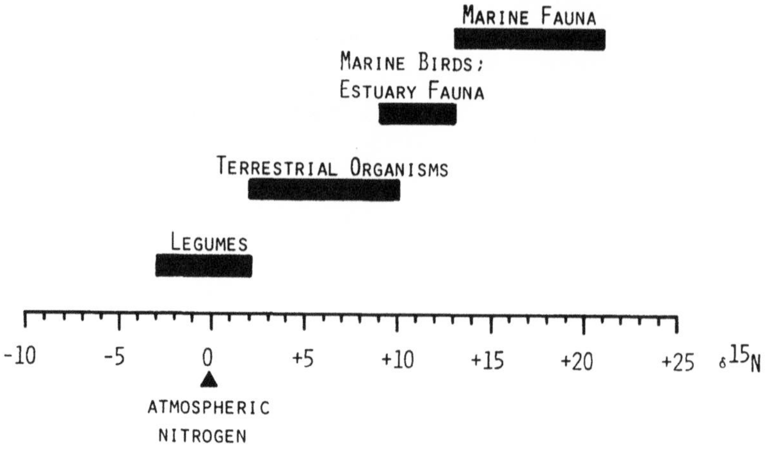

FIGURE 18.3. Variations of $\delta^{15}N$ values in parts per mil (o/oo) in nature (see Norr and Coleman 1982).

The Panamanian example presents a similar situation. However, the Panamanian sample also includes sites such as Cerro Mangote, which is a preceramic-preagricultural coastal population. The stable carbon isotopic composition of bone collagen from preagricultural populations would be indicative of the contribution of marine fauna (not maize) to the diet. Corroborating evidence may be obtained from the stable nitrogen isotopic composition of bone collagen from the same individuals (Norr 1981b; Norr and Coleman 1982; Schoeninger et al. 1983a,b). Although the stable carbon isotope composition of bone collagen from the agricultural populations will be indicative of some combined contribution of maize and marine fauna to the diet, results from stable nitrogen isotope analysis will be suggestive of what portion of the diet consisted of only marine fauna. From this, the maize contribution to the diet may be inferred. While this type of analysis is still in an experimental stage, and estimates of the contribution of a particular resource to the diet may be unreliable, shifts through time in dietary emphasis may be determined by analyses now in progress (L. Norr, unpublished).

SKELETAL REMAINS, PATHOLOGIES, AND STRESS INDICATORS

Human skeletal remains from three of the five major time periods discussed are reported here (Table 18.1). Central and western Pacific Panama are represented by approximately 87 individuals from a Preceramic-Archaic context, and 28 and 32 in-

TABLE 18.1 Sizes of Samples of Individuals from Archaeological Sites in Central and Western Panama

Period	Location	Site	Number of Individuals
Preceramic-Archaic (5000-2500 B.C.)	Central Panama	Cerro Mangote	87
Agricultural Villages (300 B.C.-A.D. 500)	Central Panama	Sitio Sierra	25
		Giron	3
		Tonosi area	38[a]
Agricultural Chiefdoms (A.D. 500-1550)	Central Panama	Sitio Sierra	13
		VE-7	1
		Sitio Conte	?[a]
		Tonosi area	81[a]
	Western Pacific coast	La Pitahaya	18
(A.D. 600-900)	Western Caribbean coast	Cerro Brujo	6

[a]Skeletal remains not analyzed in this report.

dividuals from Agricultural Village and Agricultural Chiefdom contexts, respectively. Six individuals were recovered from the Caribbean coastal region of western Panama. To date, no skeletal remains have been uncovered from either the Paleoindian or the Early Ceramic-Early Agriculturalist periods. Additional skeletal remains have been excavated from the southern Azuero Peninsula (Ichon 1980) and from cemeteries at HE-1 (Ladd 1964) and Sitio Conte (Lothrop 1937), both in the Central Pacific region of Panama. Some of the latter are extremely fragmented and may not be available for analysis.

Burials

Preceramic Archaic (5000-2500 B.C.)

Burials at Cerro Mangote were placed into what appears to have been an actively accumulating shell midden[3] in flexed, bundle, or partially disarticulated positions in single, paired, or group

[3]Excavations in 1979 by Ranere (1979) at Cerro Mangote revealed the fact that some of the burials were quite close to the surface of the shell mound. There is some question as to how early in the preceramic sequence (5000-2500 B.C.) the Cerro Mangote individuals were interred.

contexts, with no clear associations of age or sex. Many were disturbed when new burials were added to the midden, and subsequently fractured from the weight of the overburden. The bundle burials were in a standard arrangement with the skull at one end, the pelvis at the opposite end, the long bones along the two sides, small bones in the center, and the ribs on top. More often than not, the bundles included remains of more than one individual, with no single individual completely represented (McGimsey et al. 1966; Ranere 1981).

Agricultural Villages (300 B.C.-A.D. 500)

A small cemetery dated to circa 240 B.C. was excavated at Sitio Sierra. Adult and child burials were single, flexed, and accompanied by grave goods. Infants were found either in association with an adult or in the household middens (Cooke 1977, 1979, personal communication). Skeletal preservation was good and individual remains (total N = 28, including individuals from Girón) were nearly complete, although occasionally fragmented. An additional 38 individuals excavated on the Azuero Peninsula (Ichon 1980) are not included in the analysis.

Agricultural Chiefdoms (A.D. 500-1500)

Skeletal remains uncovered at Sitio Sierra and La Pitahaya on Isla Palenque in western Panama are combined here for analysis (total N = 32). The Sitio Sierra burials include 13 individuals from single, extended interments in a large cemetery. The small sample is undoubtedly biased (Cooke 1979, personal communication). The Isla Palenque burials include 18 individuals, many associated with an elaborately adorned adult male who probably was a high-ranking individual in the chiefdom. Other remains, often incomplete and fragmented, were encountered throughout the excavations (Linares 1980e). A single, contemporaneous tomb burial from VE-7 (C. R. McGimsey, personal communication) is also included in this analysis. Burials discovered at Sitio Conte (Lothrop 1937) and 81 of the burials from the Azuero Peninsula (Ichon 1980) date to this period, but were not available for analysis.

Caribbean Coastal Region of Western Panama (A.D. 600-900)

A single, partially disarticulated bundle burial, including partial remains of three individuals, was discovered during excavation at Cerro Brujo. The remains of three additional individuals were isolated discoveries scattered throughout the excavations (Linares 1980f).

Methods

The project was initially directed toward determining prehistoric diet through the chemical analysis of bone collagen. Basic demographic information was recorded as bone samples were removed from chemical analysis. Sex and biological age at the time of death were determined by standard macroscopic morphological indicators.

Infectious lesions, either periosteal reactions or osteomyelitis, were recorded for each individual as either systemic or localized, active or healed. Incidence of porotic hyperostosis, either of the cranial vault or of the orbits, was also recorded as active or healed and was graded for severity. Circular caries, as well as cases of hypocalcification, of deciduous teeth also were recorded. Caries, enamel hypoplasias, periodontal disease, and sexual dimorphism in overall robusticity were noted but were not systematically quantified. Any uncertainty in identifying a pathology or in recording has been coded as the absence of data.

Results

Tabulations of age and sex and pathology are presented in Table 18.2. The Agricultural Villages (300 B.C.-A.D. 500) sample was the only one sufficiently complete to permit an estimate of adult ages. The fragmentary information on adult age at death for the other two samples limits the construction of mortality profiles and life expectancy tables to individuals who died before the age of 20 years. The samples are small and the picture is further distorted by practice of interring individuals killed to accompany another in death (Helms 1979; Lothrop 1937). For example, the 18 individuals from La Pitahaya include a proportionally large number of ceremonial or sacrificial burials, primarily infants and children, to accompany a high-ranking individual. Children and infants also accompanied adult male and female burials at the preagricultural site of Cerro Mangote and may have been associated with ritual sacrifice. For these reasons, only information on the age at death is provided in Table 18.2.

The adult male:female ratio for the preagricultural Cerro Mangote sample is nearly 1:1, suggesting that neither sex was preferentially buried in the shell mound. The Agricultural Village component at Sitio Sierra, however, exhibits a biased sex ratio of nearly two adult females for every adult male, suggesting that not all individuals were buried here. It also may be an indication of a polygynous mating system in which certain males may have had more than one female mate. The biases discussed above regarding skewed age compositions apply here as well. The small sample from Sitio Sierra and the burial practices at La Pitahaya may give an atypical sex ratio for that population.

Figure 18.4 shows the percentages of each sample affected by porotic hyperostosis and long bone infections. Twelve percent of

TABLE 18.2 Tabulations of Age, Sex, and Incidence of Infection, Porotic Hyperostosis, and Circular Caries for the Preceramic/Archaic, Agricultural Villages, and Agricultural Chiefdoms Skeletal Samples

Period and age group (years)	Number of individuals	Percentage of total for period	Sex			Long bone infection					Porotic hyperostosis		Circular caries	
						Systemic		Localized						
			Male	Female	?	Active	Healed	Active	Healed	No data	Present	No data	Present	No data
Preceramic-Archaic														
0- 4.9	12	14	--	--	--	1	0	0	0	0	4	4	0	8
5- 9.9	16	18	--	--	--	4	0	0	0	1	2	4	1	7
10-14.9	6	7	--	--	--	0	0	1	0	0	2	0	--	--
15-19.9	3	3	2	1	0	0	0	0	1	0	0	0	--	--
Adult	50	57	23	19	8	1	2	4	7	6	0	11	--	--
	87													
Agricultural Villages														
0- 4.9	3	11	--	--	--	2	0	0	0	1	1	1	1	1
5- 9.9	2	17	--	--	--	0	0	0	0	0	2	0	0	0
10-14.9	0		--	--	--	0	0	0	0	0	0	0	--	--
15-19.9	1	4	0	1	0	0	0	0	0	0	0	0	--	--
20-29.9	2	7	0	2	0	0	0	0	0	1	0	0	--	--
30-39.9	12	43	4	8	0	0	0	0	0	0	2	0	--	--
40-49.9	6	21	1	5	0	0	0	0	0	0	0	0	--	--
50-59.9	2	7	2	0	0	1	0	0	0	0	0	0	--	--
	28													
Agricultural Chiefdoms														
0- 4.9	7	22	--	--	--	3	0	0	0	2	1	1	2	5
5- 9.9	1	3	--	--	--	0	0	0	0	0	0	0	0	0
10-14.9	2	6	--	--	--	0	0	0	0	1	1	0	--	--
15-19.9	1	3	0	0	1	0	0	1	0	0	0	1	--	--
Adult	21	66	12	8	1	1	1	0	5	3	6	6	--	--
	32													
Caribbean Coast														
0- 4.9	1	17	--	--	--	0	0	0	0	0	0	0	0	0
5- 9.9	2	33	--	--	--	0	0	0	0	0	0	0	0	0
10-14.9	0		--	--	--	0	0	0	0	0	0	0	0	0
15-19.9	2	33	0	1	1	0	0	1	0	1	1	1	--	--
Adult	1	17	0	0	1	0	0	0	0	1	0	1	--	--
	6													

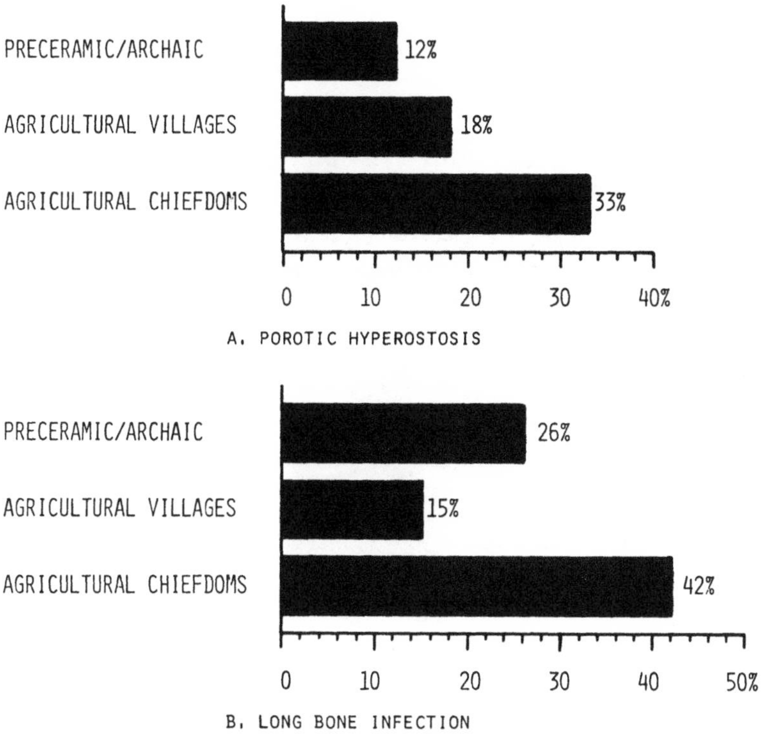

FIGURE 18.4. The percentage of individuals from Preceramic/ Archaic, Agricultural Villages, and Agricultural Chiefdoms that exhibit (a) porotic hyperostosis, and (b) long bone infection.

the Preceramic-Archaic sample, 18% of the Agricultural Village sample, and 33% of the Agricultural Chiefdom sample showed signs of either active or healed porotic hyperostosis. At Cerro Brujo, one of four nearly complete individuals showed indications of a severe case of this deficiency disease.

The incidence of infection in the Cerro Mangote preagricultural sample is rather high (26%), and has been commented on by McGimsey et al. (1966). The frequency of active, chronic, and systemic infection in children under 10 years of age is particularly high, whereas localized periosteal reactions, usually in the tibia and fibula, are more common in adults. Infection is somewhat rarer among the early agriculturalists from Sitio Sierra, affecting only two infants and one older adult male (15%). The adult male had a systemic osteomyelitic infection with numerous lesions affecting principally the tibiae, femora, ulnae and clavicles. The fragmented and partial cranial vault exhibited similar lesions. The distribution, extent, and nature of these lesions are suggestive of a treponemal infection or of chronic and persistent osteomyelitis of staphyloccocal origin. The higher incidence of infection among the Agricultural Chiefdom sample (42%) is consistent with a decrease in health associated with sedentary life and agricultural systems. However, this pattern was not observed among equally sedentary Early Agricultural period populations.

Circular caries and incidences of hypocalcification were found frequently in the deciduous teeth of the children from the Agricultural Village and Agricultural Chiefdom periods. In a process that was probably initially related to prenatally formed enamel hypoplasias, the teeth became carious when exposed to starchy and sticky weaning gruels. This carious variation of enamel hypoplasia is not seen in children of the preceramic, preagricultural sample.

DISCUSSION

Given the abundant natural resources of the Isthmus of Panama, prehistoric populations would be expected to have exhibited several distinct patterns of resource utilization that could provide an adequate and well-balanced diet. Two major dietary patterns can be identified.

The first subsistence pattern is primarily a hunter-gatherer-archaic scheme involving a generalized, wide-ranging pattern of resource utilization. Low population density and high mobility allowed for resource exploitation over a large area. Scheduling made optimal use of seasonal resources such as marine fauna or fruits.

The second subsistence pattern is a more specialized one focusing on an agricultural staple. The high production of a reliable subsistence staple is associated with an increase in population density and a decrease in the diversity of the resource base. As a result of the demand for agricultural production, the environment may be modified in ways that limit the range of resources available to a population. If the agricultural staple is deficient in specific nutrients, and those nutrients are not supplied by other, complementary food sources, a decline in health status can be expected.

In prehistoric Panama, these two subsistence patterns are demonstrated first by the preagricultural Cerro Mangote population, and second by the earlier and later agricultural populations from Sitio Sierra and La Pitahaya in central and western Pacific Panama. For the preagricultural population, there is archaeological evidence documenting a broad-based dietary pattern and the consumption of a wide variety of resources that would have met protein, mineral, and vitamin needs. Root crop vegeculture, which most likely was practiced by the time of the latter portion of the Preceramic-Archaic period, would have provided a good source of carbohydrates.

Incidence of porotic hyperostosis (Figure 18.4a) during the Preceramic-Archaic is quite low, suggesting moderate bioavailability of iron. The infection rate, however, is quite high (Figure 18.4b). It is difficult to relate this high incidence of infection to subsistence and nutritional stress. More detailed information on enamel hypoplasias might identify an annual or seasonal stress that is not yet evident based on the available data, but (except for perhaps a seasonal shortage in resources) there is no obvious deficiency in this pattern of subsistence that might lower resistance and increase susceptibility to infection. The apparently high incidence of infection observed may be associated with injuries or related to poor sanitary habits resulting from the association of a partial degree of sedentism with exploitation of coastal resources.

The agricultural pattern of subsistence apparently was at its peak along the Pacific coast of Panama during the Agricultural Chiefdom period (A.D. 500-1550). Maize was undoubtedly the subsistence staple and provided a high-carbohydrate, high-energy food source that was storable for use during food shortages. Well-known nutritional problems result from a maize-based diet, however. These nutritional deficiencies associated with a maize-based diet can be offset only by either specialized food preparation techniques (such as the use of lime or fermentation) or the addition of a very specific and nutritionally complementary set of food resources (such as beans) to the diet.

The common bean, *Phaseolus vulgaris*, probably was a dietary component of the Pacific coastal chiefdoms and would have complemented the amino acid composition of maize. Unfortunately, besides maize and beans, many other dietary components, such as root crops and marine fauna also exhibit a high phosphorus:calcium ratio, and their inclusion in the diet would do little to contribute to a proper mineral balance. Moreover, much of the phosphorus is in the form of phytates, thereby decreasing further the bioavailability of iron to these populations.

Early Spanish accounts refer to the numerous fermented maize and fruit beverages (*chichas*) consumed by the Pacific coast Agricultural Chiefdom populations (Helms 1979). According to Derman et al. (1980), iron absorption from a fermented beverage can be 12 times that from the same unfermented gruel. This practice may increase iron bioavailability but would be dependent on the degree of fermentation as well as on the assumption that there were no cultural or social restrictions to the consumption of *chichas*. The higher incidence of porotic hyperostosis in the sample from the Agricultural Chiefdom period (33%) (Figure 18.4a) suggests that this population was under some stress for dietary iron.

Requirements for vitamin C could be satisfied by including chili peppers and tropical fruits in the diet. There is no archaeological evidence, however, for *nance* utilization as in preagricultural contexts. In addition, if chili peppers were dried, they would lose approximately 60% of the vitamin C they contain.

Manioc and squash also contain moderate amounts of vitamin C, but the water-soluble vitamin would be lost if these were boiled.

Infection rates for this same late agricultural sample are also high (42%) (Figure 18.4b). A synergistic relationship between iron deficiency and infection has been suggested (Wadsworth 1975; see Goodman et al., Chapter 2, this volume).

While an overall increase in both porotic hyperostosis and infection can be seen relative to the earlier agricultural and preagricultural samples, a breakdown by age categories does not show a close relationship between the two (Figure 18.5). A comparison of these samples reveals a negative correlation. For each age category, when the incidence of porotic hyperostosis increases, there is a decrease in the incidence of infection, and vice versa. The absence of an expected positive relationship between infection and porotic hyperostosis may be a function of the relatively small sample size used in the analysis. If, however, these data are representative of the frequency of skeletal pathologies in these prehistoric populations, then non-dietary factors such as poor sanitation, injury, and parasites may have contributed significantly to the incidence of infectious lesions. The low infection rate in the earlier agricultural population suggests that this later increase in infection is related to an overdependence on a single food source, maize.

It is conceivable that during the Agricultural Chiefdom period (A.D. 500-1550), human populations were changing their environments more rapidly than new complementary resources could be found to supplement the diet. If the resources necessary to complement a maize-based diet were both available and utilized, an identifiable increase in infection and deficiency disease would not be expected. Since we do find indications of nutritional stress, it is reasonable to conclude that the subsistence base of these populations is deficient and affecting health status.

Interestingly, the earlier Agricultural Village (300 B.C.-A.D. 500) sample shows little indication of nutritional stress. The adoption of maize as a dietary staple may have been a long process, begun around 2500 B.C. Smaller amounts of maize in the diet, complemented by abundant game and tropical fruits, probably provided a well-balanced, nutritionally adequate diet for the 240 B.C. sample analyzed from Sitio Sierra. It was not maize per se, that created the problem, but the large-grained South American varieties that were involved in the shift from maize as a dietary component in a mixed economy to maize as a subsistence base (Ranere and Cooke 1982).

The agricultural system that was practiced along the Caribbean coast A.D. 600-900 was very different from the maize agricultural pattern along the Pacific coast, resulting in a reliance on an alternative high-carbohydrate food source, principally manioc. Unlike the Pacific coast agricultural pattern, this was a swidden system and large areas of forest were not destroyed. The environment was changed very little, leaving terrestrial fauna and other forest resources unaltered and relatively abundant.

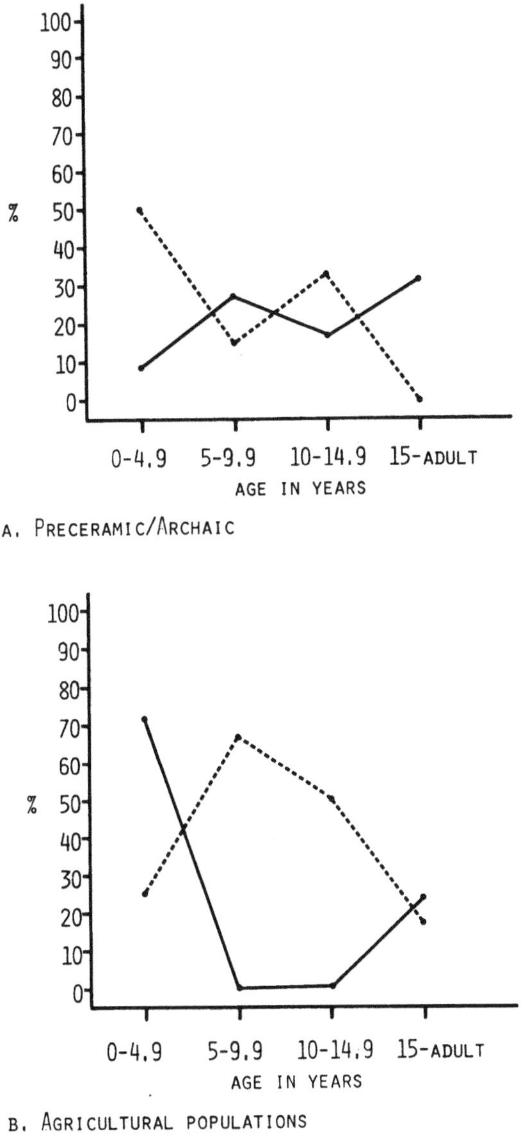

FIGURE 5

FIGURE 18.5. A comparison of the incidence of infection (———) to incidence of porotic hyperostosis (-----) by age category in (a) individuals from preagricultural contexts, and (b) individuals from agricultural contexts.

SUMMARY AND CONCLUSIONS

The infection rate and incidence of porotic hyperostosis for prehistoric coastal populations from the Isthmus of Panama show a general trend to increase in frequency over time. The increase in porotic hyperostosis can be related to the greater dependence on a limited number of dietary resources, primarily maize. The increase in infection rate over time can, in the two agricultural populations, be associated with a greater dependence on fewer dietary resources and a resulting decrease in the nutritional quality of the diet. The somewhat unusually high incidence of infection in the preagricultural sample may be due to injury and unsanitary living conditions.

An in-depth investigation of a greater number of skeletal indicators of nutritional stress is recommended. Those that seem plausible, given the frequently fragmented nature of the skeletal remains, include enamel hypoplasias, caries, periodontal disease, and perhaps growth arrest lines and adult stature. An increase in sample size would greatly increase the reliability of interpretations concerning the relationship between diet and health status in prehistoric Panama.

ACKNOWLEDGMENTS

This research was supported by a Tinker Foundation Field Research Grant and the Department of Anthropology Summer Research Fund at the University of Illinois, Urbana. Skeletal material was provided for analysis by Richard G. Cooke, Charles R. McGimsey III, Olga P. Linares, and Anthony J. Ranere, with the assistance and cooperation of El Museo del Hombre, Panama, and the University of Arkansas Museum, Fayetteville. Research facilities were provided by the Smithsonian Tropical Research Institute, Balboa, Panama, and Jerry Rose, Department of Anthropology, University of Arkansas, Fayetteville.

I wish to thank both Linda L. Klepinger and George R. Milner for the time they devoted to discussions of the skeletal remains. I am deeply indebted to my husband, Paul A. Garber, for his helpful comments on many drafts of this paper.

REFERENCES

Bartlett, A. S., E. S. Barghoorn, and R. Berger
1969 Fossil maize from Panama. *Science 165*:389-390.

Bennett, C. F.
1968 Human influences of the zoogeography of Panama. *Ibero-Americana* No. 51.

Bird, J., and R. Cooke
1977 Los artifactos más antiguos de Panamá. *Revista Nacional de Cultura 6*:7-31.
1978 The occurrence in Panama of two types of Paleo-Indian projectile points. In Early man in the New World from a circum-Pacific perspective, edited by A. L. Bryan. *Department of Anthropology University of Alberta Occasional Papers* No. 1, pp. 263-272.

Bumstead, M. P.
1981 The potential of stable carbon isotopes in bioarchaeological anthropology. In Biocultural adaptation: Comprehensive approaches to skeletal analysis, edited by D. L. Martin and M. P. Bumstead. *Department of Anthropology University of Massachusetts Research Reports* No. 20. Amherst.
1982 The potential of stable carbon isotopes in bioarchaeological anthropology. MS on file, Department of Anthropology, University of Illinois, Urbana.

Cooke, R. G.
1977 El hachero y el carpintero: Dos artesanos del Panamá precolombino. *Revista Panameña de Antropología* No. 2.
1978 La cueva de los ladrones, datos preliminares sobre la ocupación formitiva. *Actos Simposium Nacional de Antropología, Arqueología, y Ethnohistoría de Panamá 4th*, pp. 281-304.
1979 Los impactos de las comumidades agrícolar precolombinas en los ambientes del trópico estacional: Datos del Panamá prehistórico. *Actas Simposium Internacional de Ecología Tropical 4th*, 3:917-973.
1981 Los habitos alimentarios de los indígenas precolombinos de Panamá. *Academia Panameña de Medicina y Cirugía 6*(1):65-89.
1984 Archaeological research in central and eastern Panama: A review of some problems. *School of American Research Advanced Seminar on Lower Central America*, in press.

de Andagoya, P.
1865 *Narrative of the proceedings of Pedrarias Davila*. Translated and edited by C. R. Markhan. Hakluyt Society, London.

de Espinosa, G.
1873 Relacion e proceso quel Licenciado Gaspur Despinosa, Alcalde Mayor, hizo en el viaje...desde esta Ciudad de Panamá a las provincias de Paris e Nata e a las otras provincias comarcanas. *Documentos Ineditos de Indias* Vol. XX.

1892 Relacion hecha por Gaspar de Espinosa, Alcalde Mayor de Castilla de Oro, dada á Pedrarias de Avila, Lugar-Teniente General de aquellas Provincias, de todo lo que sucedió en la entrada que hizo en cellas de orden de Pedrarias. *Documentos Ineditos de Colombia* Vol. II.

De Niro, M. J., and S. Epstein
1978 Influence of diet on the distribution of carbon isotopes in animals. *Geochimica et Cosmochimica Acta 42*:495-506.
1981 Influence of diet on the distribution of nitrogen isotopes in animals. *Geochimica et Cosmochimica Acta 45*:341-351.

Derman, D. P., T. H. Brothwell, J. D. Torrance, W. R. Bezwoda, A. P. MacPhail, M. C. Kew, M. H. Sayers, P. B. Disler, and R. W. Charlton
1980 Iron absorption from maize (*Zea mays*) and sorghum (*Sorghum vulgare*) beer. *British Journal of Nutrition 43*:271-279.

Fernandez de Oviedo y Valdes, G.
1853 *Historia general y natural de las Indias* (Vol. II, part 2; Vol. III). Real Academia de la Historia, Madrid.

Gazin, C. L.
1957 Exploration for the remains of giant ground sloths in Panama. *Annual Report of the Board of Regents of the Smithsonian Institution* 1955-1956, pp. 341-354.

Glynn, P.
1972 Observations on the ecology of the Caribbean and Pacific coasts of Panama. In The Panamic biota: Some observations prior to a sea-level canal, edited by M. L. Jones. *Bulletin of the Biological Society of Washington 2*:13-33.

Helms, M. W.
1976 Competition, power, and succession to office in pre-Columbian Panama. In *Frontier adaptations in lower Central America*, edited by M. W. Helms and F. O. Loveland, pp. 25-35. Institute for the Study of Human Issues, Philadelphia.
1979 *Ancient Panama: Chiefs in search of power*. University of Texas Press, Austin.

Holdrige, L. R., and G. Budowski
1956 Report of an ecological survey of the Republic of Panama. *Caribbean Forester 17*:92-110.

Ichon, A.
1980 Archéologie du sud de la Péninsule d'Azuero, Panama. *Etudes Mésoaméricaines* série II, No. 3.

Ladd, J.
1964 Archaeological investigations in the Parita and Santa Maria zones of Panama. *Smithsonian Institution Bureau of American Ethnology Bulletin* No. 193.

Levy, R., and R. Chong
1977 *Wildlife of Panama*. Special information pamphlet, United States Southern Command, Canal Zone, Panama.

Linares, O. F.
1968 Cultural chronology of the Gulf of Chiriqui, Panama. *Smithsonian Contributions in Anthropology*, Vol. 8.

1976 Garden hunting in the American tropics. *Human Ecology 4*: 331-349.
1977a Adaptive strategies in western Panama. *World Archaeology 8*:304-319.
1977b Ecology and the arts in ancient Panama: On the development of social rank and symbolism in the central provinces. *Dumbarton Oaks Studies in Pre-Columbian Art and Archaeology* No. 17.
1980a Conclusions. In Adaptive radiations in prehistoric Panama, edited by O. F. Linares and A. J. Ranere. *Peabody Museum Monographs* No. 5, pp. 233-249.
1980b Ecology and prehistory of the Aguacate Peninsula in Bocas del Toro. In Adaptive radiations in prehistoric Panama, edited by O. F. Linares and A. J. Ranere. *Peabody Museum Monographs* No. 5, pp. 57-66.
1980c Ecology and prehistory of the Chiriqui Gulf sites. In Adaptive radiations in prehistoric Panama, edited by O. F. Linares and A. J. Ranere. *Peabody Museum Monographs* No. 5, pp. 67-77.
1980d Introduction. In Adaptive radiations in prehistoric Panama, edited by O. F. Linares and A. J. Ranere. *Peabody Museum Monographs* No. 5, pp. 7-14.
1980e La Pitahaya (IS-3) in the Gulf of Chiriqui: Mapping and excavation. In Adaptive radiations in prehistoric Panama, edited by O. F. Linares and A. J. Ranere. *Peabody Museum Monographs* No. 5, pp. 306-315.
1980f The Aguacate sites in Bocas del Toro: Excavations and stratigraphy. In Adaptive radiations in prehistoric Panama, edited by O. F. Linares and A. J. Ranere. *Peabody Museum Monographs* No. 5, pp. 292-305.

Linares, O. F., and R. G. Cooke
1975 *Differential exploitation of lagoon-estuary systems in Panama.* Paper presented at the XL annual meeting of the Society for American Archaeology, Dallas.

Linares, O. F., and A. J. Ranere
1971 Human adaptation to the tropical forests of western Panama. *Archaeology 24*:346-355.

Linares, O. F., and P. D. Sheets
1980 Highland agricultural villages in the volcán Barú region. In Adaptive radiations in prehistoric Panama, edited by O. F. Linares and A. J. Ranere. *Peabody Museum Monographs* No. 5, pp. 44-55.

Linares, O. F., P. D. Sheets, and E. J. Rosenthal
1975 Prehistoric agriculture in tropical highlands. *Science 187*:137-145.

Lothrop, S. K.
1937 Cocle. An archaeological study of central Panama, I. *Memoirs of the Peabody Museum of Archaeology and Ethnology*, Vol. 7.

McGimsey, C. R.
1956 Cerro Mangote: A preceramic site in Panama. *American Antiquity* *22*:151-161.
1957 Further data and a date from Cerro Mangote, Panama. *American Antiquity* *23*:434-435.
1959 A survey of archaeologically known burial practices in Panama. *Actas Congreso Internacional de Americanistas 33rd* *2*:347-356.

McGimsey, C. R., M. B. Collins, and T. W. McKern
1966 *Cerro Mangote and its population.* Paper presented at the XXXVIIth International Congress of Americanists, Mar del Plata.

Myers, C. W.
1969 The ecological geography of cloud forest in Panama. *American Museum of Natural History Novitates* No. 2396.

Norr, L.
1980 *Bone chemistry and prehistoric diet: Initial results from Costa Rica.* Paper presented at the XLVth annual meeting of the Society for American Archaeology, Philadelphia.
1981a *Prehistoric Costa Rican diet as determined from stable carbon isotope ratios in bone collagen.* Hrdlicka prize winning paper presented at the Lth annual meeting of the American Association of Physical Anthropologists, Detroit.
1981b *Prehistoric human diet in lower Central America: The maize vs. marine fauna problem.* Paper presented at the IIIrd annual meeting of the Society for Archaeological Sciences, San Diego.

Norr, L., and D. D. Coleman
1983 Dietary interpretations of $^{13}C/^{12}C$ in prehistoric bone collagen from a tropical coastal environment. Ms. on file, Department of Anthropology, University of Illinois, Urbana.

Piperno, D. R.
1980 *Phytolith evidence for maize cultivation in central Panama during the Early Ceramic.* Paper presented at the XLVth annual meeting of the Society for American Archaeology, Philadelphia.

Piperno, D. R., and K. H. Clary
1982 *Phytolyths and pollen from archaeological sites in central Panama.* Paper presented at the XLIVth International Congress of Americanists, Manchester, England.

Porter, D. M.
1973 The vegetation of Panama: A review. In *Vegetation and vegetational history of northern Latin America*, edited by A. Graham, pp. 167-201. Elsevier, New York.

Ranere, A. J.
1972 *Early human adaptations to New World tropical forests.* Ph.D. dissertation, University of California, Davis. University Microfilms, Ann Arbor.
1979 Cerro Mangote, 1979: Preliminary report. Ms. on file, Department of Anthropology, Temple University.

1980 Preceramic shelters in the Talamancan Range. In Adaptive radiations in prehistoric Panama, edited by O. F. Linares and A. J. Ranere. *Peabody Museum Monographs* No. 5, pp. 16-43.

1981 The re-excavation and reinterpretation of Cerro Mangote: A preceramic shell midden in central Panama. MS. on file, Department of Anthropology, Temple University.

Ranere, A. J., and R. G. Cooke

1982 *The proyecto Santa Maria: A multidisciplinary analyses of prehistoric adaptations to a tropical watershed in Panama.* Paper presented at the XLIVth International Congress of Americanists, Manchester, England.

Ranere, A. J., and P. Hansell

1978 Early subsistence patterns along the Pacific coast of Panama. In *Prehistoric coastal adaptations*, edited by B. L. Stark and B. Voorhies, pp. 43-59. Academic Press, New York.

Ranere, A. J., R. G. Cooke, and P. Hansell

1980 *Food procurement in the Parita Bay region of Panama, 5000 B.C.-500 A.D.* Paper presented at the XLVth annual meeting of the Society for American Archaeology, Philadelphia.

Sander, D.

1964 Lithic material from Panama: Fluted points from Madden Lake. *Actas y Memorias Congreso Internacional de Americanistas 35th 1*:183-192.

Sauer, C. O.

1966 *The early Spanish Main.* University of California Press, Berkeley.

Schoeninger, M. J., M. J. DeNiro, and H. Tauber

1983a $^{15}N/^{14}N$ ratios of bone collagen reflect marine and terrestrial components of prehistoric human diet. *American Journal of Physical Anthropology 60*:252 (Abstr.).

1983b Stable nitrogen isotope ratios of bone collagen reflect marine and terrestrial components of prehistoric human diet. *Science 220*:1381-1383.

Sheets, P. D.

1980 The volcán Barú region: A site survey. In Adaptive radiations in prehistoric panama, edited by O. F. Linares and A. J. Ranere. *Peabody Museum Monographs* No. 5, pp. 267-275.

Smith, C. E.

1980 Plant remains from the Chiriqui sites and ancient vegetational patterns. In Adaptive radiations in prehistoric Panama, edited by O. F. Linares and A. J. Ranere. *Peabody Museum Monographs* No. 5, pp. 151-174.

Wadsworth, G. R.

1975 Nutritional factors in anemia. *World Review of Nutrition and Dietetics 21*;75-150.

Weiland, D.
1982 *Settlement patterns in the Santa Maria drainage: A preliminary analysis.* Paper presented at the XLIVth International Congress of Americanists, Manchester, England.

Willey, G. R., and C. R. McGimsey
1954 The Monagrillo Culture of Panama. *Papers of the Peabody Museum of Archaeology and Ethnology 49*(2).

Willey, G. R., and T. L. Stoddard
1954 Cultural stratigraphy in Panama: A preliminary report on the Giron site. *American Antiquity 19*:332-343.

CHAPTER 19

PREHISTORIC HUMAN BIOLOGY OF ECUADOR: POSSIBLE TEMPORAL TRENDS AND CULTURAL CORRELATIONS

D. H. Ubelaker

Department of Anthropology
National Museum of Natural History
Smithsonian Institution

INTRODUCTION

Ecuador is divided by the north-south-running Andes mountain chain into an eastern lowlands and a coastal strip. The sparsely populated eastern lowland region is largely tropical forest, characterized by "heavy, almost year-round rains and intense heat, with dense forest and vine cover" (Willey 1971:8). Subsistence is traditionally derived from fishing, especially in the larger rivers (Carneiro 1968), hunting and gathering, and horticulture, with manioc the principal product.

The highland area includes some of the highest volcanic peaks in the hemisphere (Chimborazo, 6310 m; Cotopaxi, 5943 m) as well as agriculturally rich mountain valleys at lower elevations. Human exploitation of the highest elevations is mostly restricted to grazing, with the sheep and cattle of today replacing the llama of earlier times. At slightly lower elevations, the potato is the principal crop and apparently dates back to prehistoric times. According to Meggers (1966:23), aboriginal crops of the highland valleys include maize, quinoa (*Chenopodium quinua*), white carrot (*Arracacia esculenta*), squash, beans, and other types of tubers. The lower valleys produced avocados, guavas, chirimoyas, tomatoes and other fruits, and agave (for fiber).

The coastal section of Ecuador shows considerable environmental variety that is largely produced by variation in rainfall, which in turn is influenced by patterns of ocean currents. The northern half of the coastal area benefits from regular rainfall; consequently, agriculture flourishes and many of the sparsely populated areas resemble tropical forest. The southern half (Guayas Province and southern Manabi Province) is semiarid much of the time since rainfall is minimal and irregular. There is no doubt that in prehistoric times as well as today, marine and brackish-water fish and mollusks were a major dietary component for the coastal populations, if not the principal means of subsistence in many areas. Aboriginally, the area supported maize agriculture, especially in the flood plains of the major rivers. Other crops probably included manioc, sweet potato, achira, arrowroot, New World yam, peanuts, and perhaps cotton and the bottle gourd. Deer and smaller mammals were available as a dietary supplement (Lathrap 1976).

CULTURAL HISTORY

Systematic archaeological investigations into Ecuadorean prehistory were initiated by Jacinto Jijón y Caamaño in the early decades of this century and have continued through the efforts of many individuals and institutions. Most of this work has focused on the southern coast, perhaps because this area offers the best preservation of archaeological materials and the most hospitable environment for excavation (Lathrap 1976:15).

Meggers (1966:154) summarized the prehistory of the Oriente region as "almost unknown." Since that time, Porras Garcés has documented more of the prehistoric chronology (1972a,b, 1975) and recently published his startling discovery of a ceremonial center in the area, with radiocarbon dates ranging from 270 B.C. to A.D. 180 (Porras Garcés 1981). Very little data have emerged on settlement patterns, population density, or temporal changes in subsistence. More is known of the cultural chronology of the highlands, but most of the important questions regarding subsistence and settlement patterns in this area also remain unresolved. The most complete archaeological data come from the coast, where most archaeological activity has focused and important research problems are being investigated.

Most archaeologists recognize four developmental periods in Ecuadorian prehistory: Preceramic (before 3000 B.C.); Formative (3000 B.C. to about 500 B.C.); Regional Development (500 B.C. to A.D. 500), and Integration (A.D. 500-1500) (Meggers 1966:25).

As is true for all of the Western Hemisphere, the date of the first human appearance in Ecuador is unknown. The site of El Inga, 22 km east of Quito, in the highlands produced lithic tools dated as early as 9030 years B.P. (Bell 1965). However, the most complete data on subsistence from the Preceramic period come from coastal Preceramic Site 80 (Vegas complex) of the Sta. Elena Peninsula. Radiocarbon dates from this site suggest an antiquity of about 7000 B.C. (Stothert 1976, 1977). Excavation produced a faunal assemblage suggesting the resource utilization of deer, fox, peccary, birds, rabbit, rodents, snakes, lizards, small and medium-sized fish, crab, and mollusks. The presence of the brackish-water fauna suggests that mangrove environments were nearby. Excavation also produced sandstone grindstones (manos), evidence of structures, and a large cemetery of both primary and secondary interments. Collectively, the data suggest a large, semipermanent settlement that relied on hunting, gathering, and fishing for subsistence, and perhaps experimented with horticulture.

The formative period in Ecuador is best known from the Valdivia complex, defined in detail by Meggers et al. (1965). This period marks the introduction of pottery and is the focus of considerable debate on problems of population origins and subsistence. Meggers et al. (1965) felt that stylistic similarities between Early Valdivia pottery and that of Kyushu Jomon period sites in Japan suggested a trans-Pacific Japanese origin for Ecuadorean pottery. Although Willey (1971:276) considers this interpretation "a likely possibility to be kept in mind," others (Lathrap 1976; McEwan and Dickson 1978) have been more skeptical. Bischoff and Viteri Gamboa (1972) report "pre-Valdivia" transitional pottery termed "San Pedro" from site G-31 at Valdivia. Zevallos et al. (1977) and Lathrap (1974, 1976) also argue for a more local origin of Ecuadorean Formative ceramics.

Meggers (1966) suggested that subsistence in early Formative times was primarily sea oriented with some mangrove exploitation, hunting and gathering, and perhaps incipient agriculture. She noted that early Formative sites are distributed near the sea and along what were then mangrove swamps. She felt that the distribution of Chorrera sites along the banks of the major rivers argued for the introduction of agriculture (manioc and/or maize) at that time (1500-500 B.C.).

Lathrap (1976) uses similar arguments for an earlier development of agriculture on the coast. He feels that many early Valdivia sites such as Loma Alta (15 km inland), Azucar (30 km inland), Real Alto, and others are located away from the sea along river floodplains, locations ideal for agriculture. According to Jorge Marcos (personal communication), Valdivia sites have now been found at inland locations throughout Guayas province. Zevallos et al. (1977) introduced such other supportive evidence as the following:

1. Charred organic material included in a Valdivia sherd that appeared to be a kernel of maize
2. Decorations on Valdivia sherds interpreted as stylized cobs of maize
3. Impressions on Valdivia sherds that appear to have been made by stamping with actual corn kernels
4. The presence of hand mills perhaps used to process agricultural products
5. The presence of a brackish water snail that may have been used for lime in food processing
6. The presence of bell-shaped storage pits in Valdivia sites that may have been used for storing dried corn

7. Charred corncobs from the highland site of Cerro Narrio believed to predate 2000 B.C.

Pearsall (1978) claimed to have distinguished maize phytoliths from the Valdivia site of Real Alto and interpreted them as indicators of "on-site cultivation of maize by at least 2450 B.C." (Pearsall 1978:178). In addition, Burleigh and Brothwell (1978) measured carbon isotope ratios in a dog skeleton found at Real Alto and concluded that "about 63% of its diet was derived from maize" (Burleigh and Brothwell 1978:359).

In short, most archaeologists would argue that agriculture was at least "incipient" during the Early Formative and was intensive at least by the Late Formative. In addition, many agree that the circumstantial evidence assembled by Zevallos, Lathrap, and others for intensive agriculture during Early Formative times is convincing. Clearly, additional research is especially needed in comparative phytolith studies (maize versus other native plants), the effects of marine foods on bone collagen carbon isotope ratios in prehistoric Ecuador, and settlement patterns of Early Formative sites.

The Real Alto site has presented not only valuable subsistence information, but a possible ceremonial center as well that attests to the advanced level of social complexity of Early Formative society (Lathrap et al. 1977; Marcos 1978).

Several suggestions for population movement and outside contacts have been offered for the period. Through his analysis of excavated mollusk samples, Sarma (1974) suggested that temporal shifts in pluviality due to changes in the large El Niño-Humboldt ocean current complexes resulted in considerable environmental changes in south coastal Ecuador that influenced human occupation. Sarma's analysis suggested arid conditions on the peninsula from 5000 to 2650 B.C. and from 1600 to 1000 B.C.

Meggers et al. (1965) suggest that the Machalilla phase (1500-1000 B.C. according to Lathrap 1976; or 2000-1500 B.C. according to Meggers 1966) is culturally distinct from the earlier Valdivia ceramics, and they detect a possible northern influence. As mentioned earlier, they postulated a Japanese origin for Valdivia ceramics. Meggers (1966) sees Mesoamerican influence in the Late Formative Chorrera ceramics.

In contrast, Lathrap (1976) feels that Valdivia culture has a local origin that ultimately derives from the eastern lowlands tropical forest. According to Lathrap, (1976:43),

> The economic practices and life style of the early sedentary inhabitants of coastal Ecuador were an extension of Tropical Forest culture, which itself expanded out of the Amazon Basin, first to the Guayas Basin and then on west to the coast. It was a Tropical Forest economy further enriched by the presence of developed races of corn. (Lathrap 1976:43)

Lathrap (1963, 1976) further suggests that Machalilla evolved directly out of Valdivia and sees Machalilla-Valdivia influence in the ceramics of West Mexico. He argues that the Late Formative Chorrera phase exhibits highland, Amazonian, and East Asian influences (Lathrap 1976:37) and in turn may have influenced cultures in Mesoamerica, Peru, and Guatemala.

The Regional Development period in Ecuador (500 B.C. to A.D. 500) was a time of well-developed intensive agriculture and continued exploitation of shellfish and deer on the coast. The period shows evidence of increased population density and the development of metallurgy and has been characterized by Meggers (1966:67) as "the time of differentiation in sociopolitical organization, florescence in art style and elaboration in technology." Meggers sees similarities in ceramics during this period with those from Asia, Mesoamerica, Costa Rica, and Peru. Published reports of skeletal remains from this period are confined to small samples from the Guangala phase (Duckworth 1951; Van Bork-Feltkamp 1965).

Sarma's (1974:122) mollusk analysis and interpretation suggest a pluvial period during the entire regional development period (Guangala phase).

The general trend of population expansion and increased reliance on agriculture continued into the Integration period when, according to Meggers (1966:119), "increasingly reliable agricultural techniques permitted population expansion and habitation sites are more numerous than at any other time. Several are large enough to be classified as urban centres. Occupational division of labour became more extensive and differences in rank more pronounced." Meggers (1966) suggests general Mesoamerican influence in prehistoric Ecuador at this time and Columbian influence in the Cara phase of the Northern highlands. Sarma (1974:122) suggests a return to generalized aridity on the Sta. Elena peninsula during the Integration period.

The Late Integration period culminated in the Inca conquest of Ecuador, which focused primarily in the highlands and began between 1463 and 1471. The Spaniards inaugurated the historic period in the early part of the sixteenth century.

RELEVANT DATA FROM HUMAN SKELETAL BIOLOGY

Since 1973, I have worked closely with officials of the Banco Central del Ecuador, archaeologists, and others in a collaborative attempt to assemble and analyze large samples of human remains from prehistoric Ecuador. The aim of the research is to document prehistoric mortuary behavior in Ecuador and to examine temporal change and spatial variation in prehistoric skeletal biology. Much of the data is relevant to the archaeological problems discussed earlier and offers tentative insight into the relationships between biology and culture within the populations examined. The large, well-documented skeletal samples that have been

APPROXIMATE DATE	SITE	LOCATION	NUMBER OF INDIVIDUALS IN SAMPLE
1230	AYALÁN URN COMPONENT	COAST GUAYAS PROVINCE	384
710	AYALÁN NON-URN COMPONENT	COAST GUAYAS PROVINCE	51
A.D.			
B.C.			
100	GUANGALA OGSE-Ma-172	COAST GUAYAS PROVINCE	30
500	SAN LORENZO	COAST GUAYAS PROVINCE	106
540	COTOCOLLAO	HIGHLANDS PICHINCHA PROVINCE	199
2845	REAL ALTO VALDIVIA III PHASE	COAST GUAYAS PROVINCE	72
6000	STA. ELENA OGSE-80	COAST GUAYAS PROVINCE	192

FIGURE 19.1. Description of human skeletal samples from prehistoric Ecuador.

assembled to date are listed in Figure 19.1. Data published on other skeletal samples (Duckworth 1951; Munizaga 1965; Van Bork-Feltkamp 1965) are not included since either the samples are too small for frequency data or the reported data are not presented in a manner that facilitates comparison. The oldest sample described in Figure 19.1 is that of OGSE-80 from the Sta. Elena Peninsula, excavated by Karen Stothert with support from the Banco Central del Ecuador in Guayaquil. Site 80 represents the Preceramic Vegas complex, with radiocarbon dates clustering at about 7000 B.C. (Stothert 1977). Excavations completed by July, 1978, identified 65 burial features representing at least 192 individuals in an area approximately 200 m^2 in size. Burial features included both primary and secondary interments. One large secondary deposit contained at least 18 adults and 19 subadults. Analysis was limited by the extreme fragmentation of the bones and by the fact that several interments were left in situ for display purposes. Data on bone representation of each feature and of the total sample, artificial modifications of the skeleton, estimates of living stature, measurements and observations, demography, and pathology have been published by Ubelaker (1980a).

The Early Formative site of Real Alto discussed earlier produced another large sample dating from the Valdivia III phase. Excavations between August 1974 and September 1975 (Lathrap et al. 1977) produced 72 individuals dated to the Valdivia III phase (Marcos 1978). The material is well preserved and represents both primary and secondary interments. Biological analysis of the sample by the author is presently in progress.

The only highland sample described in Figure 19.1 is from the Cotocollao site, located just northwest of Quito. Excavations sponsored by the Banco Central del Ecuador culminating in 1978 produced at least 199 human skeletons dated by an overlying layer of volcanic ash and associated radiocarbon dates at about 540 B.C. The remains were very fragmentary and represent both primary and secondary deposits. Biological analysis similar to that of site OGSE-80 was published by Ubelaker (1980b).

Excavations by the author in 1974 at the coastal town of San Lorenzo del Mate produced approximately 106 human skeletons of the Jambelli phase. Cultural materials from the site are still under study; however, tentative ceramic analysis suggests a date of about 500 B.C. No radiocarbon dates are available and analysis of the human skeletons is in progress.

Recent salvage excavations sponsored by the Banco Central del Ecuador at site OGSE-MA-172 in the modern coastal town of Valdivia produced 27 burial features with an early Guangala phase cultural affiliation. The human remains were analyzed by the author from December 1981 to January 1982 in Ecuador and are estimated to date to about 100 years B.C. (Ubelaker, 1983). Analysis revealed the presence of at least 30 individuals of both sexes, ranging in age from newborn to greater than 50 years. Preservation is excellent with little fragmentation.

The remaining large documented human samples from prehistoric Ecuador are from the coastal site of Ayalán in Guayas province. Excavations in the mortuary area of this site were initiated in 1972 and continued by the author in 1973. Of the 81 recognized features, 54 were large funerary urns containing both primary and secondary skeletal remains. The remaining 27 non-urn features consist of primary interments as well as secondary skeletal deposits. Radiocarbon dates and other information suggest that the urn samples date from between A.D. 730 and A.D. 1600 and that the non-urn samples date from between 500 B.C. and A.D. 1155. At least 384 individuals are represented in the urn sample and 51 in the earlier non-urn sample. Detailed biological and cultural information on this material has been published by Ubelaker (1981).

The above-described samples fall short of those ideally needed for a detailed examination of temporal change and spatial variability of biocultural variables in Ecuadorean prehistory. They do, however, allow a tentative look at the emerging pattern and offer directions for additional research. Comparison of biological data from the samples is complicated by the variability among samples in bone preservation and burial customs. Skeletal remains from Ayalán and the Guangala site from Valdivia are so well preserved that histological methods of age determination could be employed and observations could be made on degenerative joint disease, subadult long bone growth, and frequencies of lines of arrested growth. Fragmentation in the Cotocollao and Sta. Elena samples is such that these observations cannot be made reliably.

The manner of interment presents similar comparative problems. In the primary skeletons recovered at the Ayalán non-urn component, Guangala, and San Lorenzo, skeletal data can be correlated with information about the individual (age, sex, cultural inclusions). Such correlations obviously are not possible with samples from the large secondary deposits of the Ayalán urn component, Sta. Elena, and Cotocollao. Thus, to facilitate comparison, I have chosen only those biological traits that can be traced through all of the samples available, and I have presented the comparisons in a manner that allows frequencies to be computed from both primary and secondary interments. Data from the Real Alto and San Lorenzo samples are not included since research on these materials is still in progress.

Stature

Living stature has been estimated from long bone lengths using the formulas of Genovés or Trotter and Gleser (see Ubelaker 1978: 44-45). Table 19.1 summarizes the stature data for five samples in the series. Only those statures that could be correlated with sex are included. Sex was determined from the size of the measured bone or, in the case of primary skeletons, from other associated bones of the individual. In Figure 19.2 the mean stature values are plotted through time for both males and females. Figure 19.2 suggests little, if any, change in stature through time. In fact, the prehistoric statures are close to published values for contemporary Ecuadorean Indian populations (Ubelaker 1981:115).

Demography

Accurate demographic reconstruction from skeletal remains depends on the assumption that the acquired samples are representative of the entire cemetery sample and of the actual deaths in the population, and that estimated ages at death are reasonably accurate. Table 19.2 summarizes relevant demographic data available for five Ecuadorean samples. The most reliable data are those

TABLE 19.1 Mean Values for Estimated Male and Female Living Stature

	Stature			
	Male		Female	
Sample	N	cm	N	cm
Ayalán urns	25	159	31	149
non-urns	9	159	7	149
Guangala	3	161	1	152
Cotocollao	17	159	7	148
Sta. Elena	8	161	14	149

from Ayalán, since those samples were large and preservation was such that the most accurate methods of age determination could be employed. Preservation and age determination were also good for the Guangala material; however, that sample is very small for demographic analysis and may show an unrealistic shortage of adults. Sample size is adequate for the Sta. Elena and Cotocollao samples; however, extreme fragmentation of much of the material may have affected the accuracy of the adult age estimates. Accordingly, the data on maximum longevity described in Table 19.2 and plotted in Figure 19.3 may reflect an increase in longevity with the Ayalán urn sample; however, it also may be only an artifact

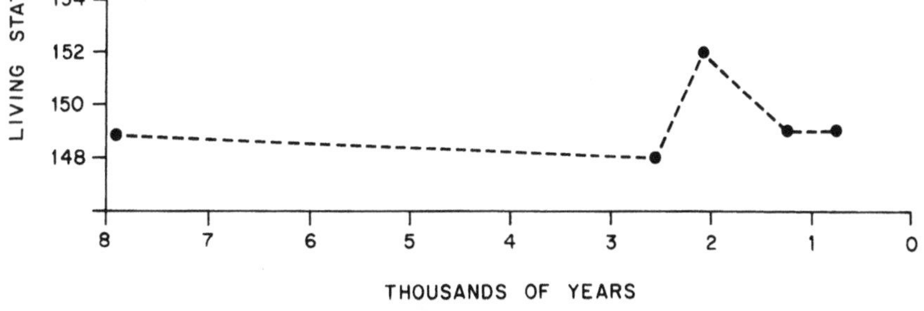

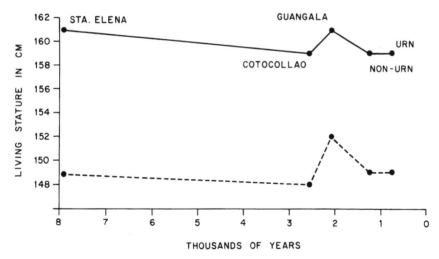

FIGURE 19.2. Estimated male (——) and female (----) living stature through time. In this and all subsequent figures, the plot of years refers to thousands of years B.P., with "0" referring to the present.

TABLE 19.2 Mean Values for Various Demographic Variables

Sample	*Life expectancy (years)*			*Maximum*
	Birth	*Age 5*	*Age 15*	*longevity*
Sta. Elena	*25*	*28*	*22*	*60*
Cotocollao	*28*	*26*	*18*	*60*
Guangala	*13*	*33*	*23*	*60*
Ayalán				
Non-urn	*19*	*27*	*19*	*55*
Urn	*23*	*31*	*26*	*75*

of the variance in procedures used to estimate age at death in the various samples.

The life expectancy values presented in Table 19.2 and Figure 19.4 also may contain errors resulting from sampling problems and variance in age estimation procedures. The one value that seems to show the most temporal change is life expectancy at birth. This value increases from 25 at Sta. Elena to a high of 28 at Cotocollao, drops sharply to only 13 at Guangala, and then recovers to 19 in the Ayalán non-urn and 23 in the Ayalán urn samples. These data generally reflect a temporal increase in infant mortality that peaks in the Guangala sample.

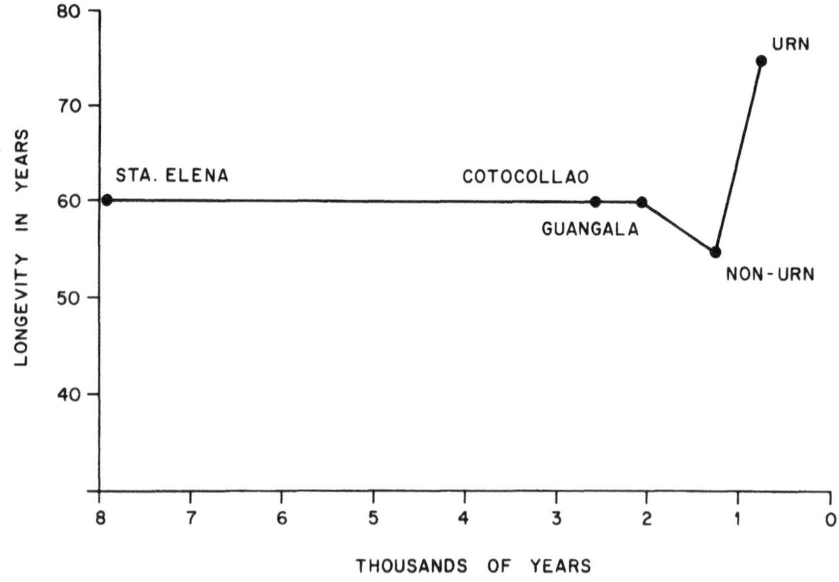

FIGURE 19.3. Maximum adult longevity through time.

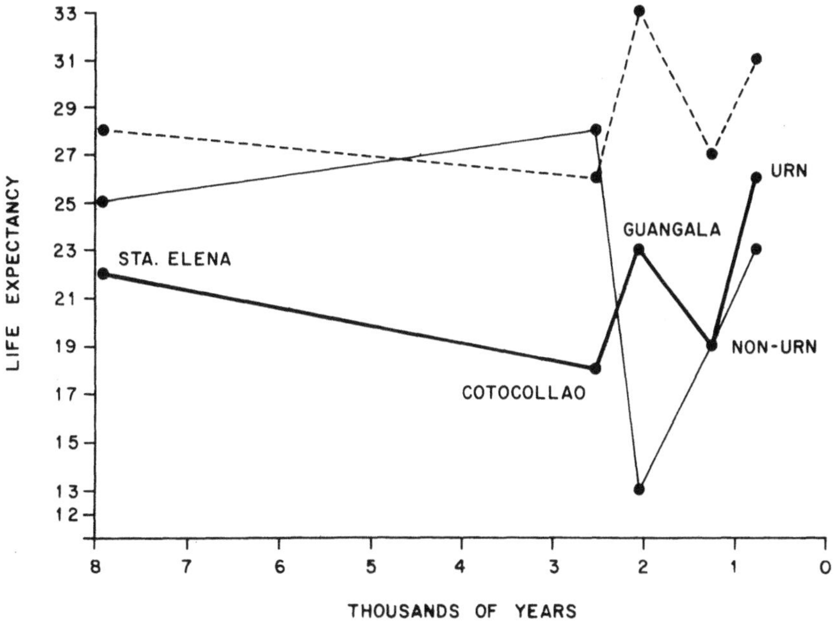

FIGURE 19.4. Life expectancy through time at birth (——), age 5 (----) and age 15 (▬▬).

Trauma

Skeletal indications of trauma also show temporal change in prehistoric Ecuador. Table 19.3 and Figure 19.5 relate the ratio of the number of fractured bones in each sample to the number of individuals in each sample. Ideally, data on trauma should be presented in terms of the frequency of affected individuals; however, that is not possible here since much of the sample is derived from secondary interments. The data suggest a sharp increase in skeletal fractures during Guangala times with a gradual decrease thereafter.

Additional insight is gained by looking at the distribution of fractures on the skeleton through time (Table 19.4). In the Sta. Elena sample, fractures are confined to hand and foot bones and to the mid-shaft area of the long bones. Small, circular depressed fractures of the frontal bone appear in the Cotocollao and Guangala samples and are no longer apparent in the Ayalán samples. In Ayalán, trauma to the skeleton is expanded to include Colles's fractures of the distal ends of the radius and ulna that normally result from falls.

TABLE 19.3. Ratio of the Number of Bones Showing Trauma to the Number of Individuals in Each Sample

Sample	*Number of bones with trauma*	*Number of individuals in sample*	*Ratio*
Ayalán			
Urns	*25*	*199*	*.13*
Non-urns	*5*	*28*	*.18*
Guangala	*3*	*9*	*.33*
Cotocollao	*5*	*164*	*.03*
Sta. Elena	*11*	*127*	*.09*

Infectious Disease

Table 19.5 and Figure 19.6 present the ratio of adult bones showing evidence of infectious disease to the number of adults in the various samples. The data presented are limited to adults since evidence for infectious disease in subadults is confined to only one long bone fragment from the Ayalán urn sample. Again, data on the frequencies of affected individuals are not available since secondary interments are included in the samples. The data show a dramatic increase of periosteal lesions in the Guangala sample followed by an equally dramatic reduction in the Ayalán non-urn sample and a subsequent slight increase in the Ayalán urn sample.

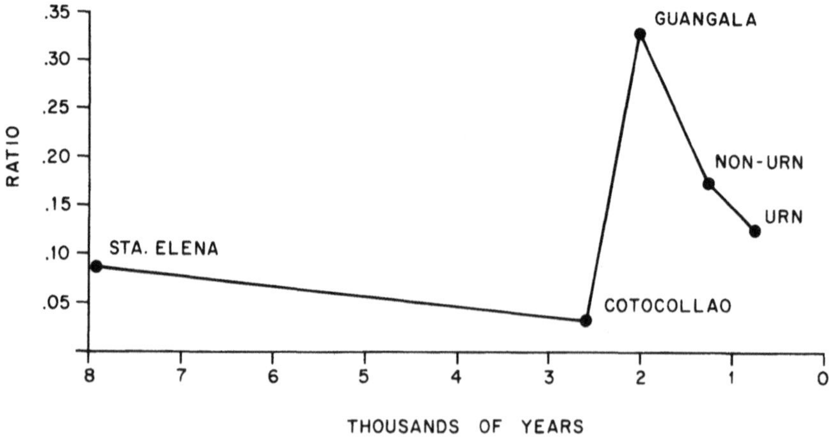

FIGURE 19.5. Ratio of bones showing trauma to the number of individuals in each sample through time.

TABLE 19.4 Skeletal Distribution of the Different Types of Trauma in Each Sample

Sample	Long bones: Colles's fractures		Long bones: non-Colles's fractures		Frontal depressions		Rib fractures		Fractures of hands and feet		Humerus dislocation		Total
	Number	%	Number	%	Number	%	Number	%	Number	%	Number	%	
Ayalán													
Urns	7	28	9	36			3	12	6	24	1	20	25
Non-urns	3	60	1	20									5
Guangala					1	33			2	67			3
Cotocollao			1	20	2	40			2	40			5
Sta. Elena			6	55					5	45			11

TABLE 19.5 Ratio of the Number of Adult Bones with Periosteal Lesions to the Number of Adults in Each Sample

Sample	*Number of bones with lesions*	*Number of adults in sample*	*Ratio*
Ayalán			
Urns	*28*	*199*	*.14*
Non-urns	*1*	*28*	*.04*
Guangala	*4*	*9*	*.44*
Cotocollao	*7*	*164*	*.04*
Sta. Elena	*9*	*127*	*.07*

Porotic Hyperostosis

Data are available from all five samples on types of bony lesions usually called porotic hyperostosis. Frequencies of this pathology, expressed as the ratio of the number of affected bones of the cranial vault to the number of individuals in the sample, are given in Table 19.6. The table shows that such lesions are absent in the Sta. Elena and Cotocollao samples, occur with the greatest frequency in the Guangala sample, and then decrease in frequency in the Ayalán samples.

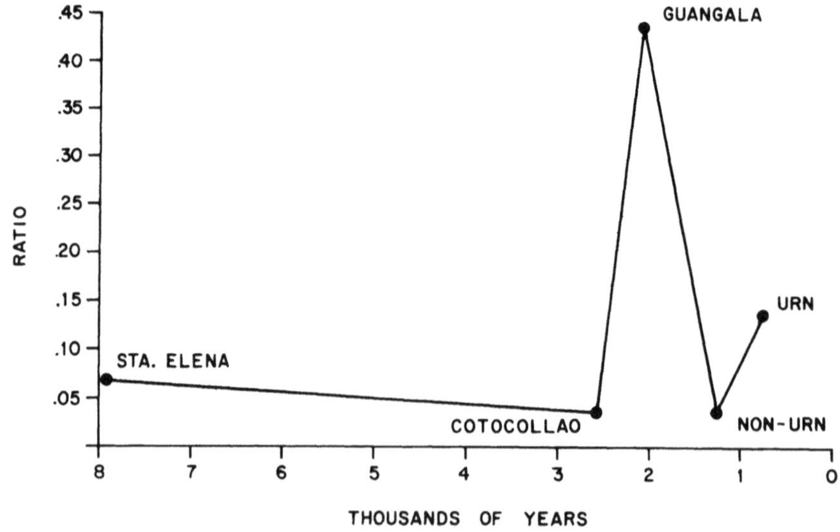

FIGURE 19.6. Ratio of adult bones with periosteal lesions to the number of adults in each sample through time.

TABLE 19.6 Ratio of the Number of Bones of the Cranial Vault Showing Porotic Hyperostosis to the Number of Individuals in Each Sample

Sample	*Number of cranial bones with lesions*	*Number of individuals in sample*	*Ratio*
Ayalán			
Urns	*28*	*384*	*.07*
Non-urns	*4*	*51*	*.08*
Guangala	*7*	*30*	*.23*
Cotocollao	*0*	*164*	*0*
Sta. Elena	*0*	*127*	*0*

TABLE 19.7 Ratio of the Number of Orbits with Cribra Orbitalia to the Number of Individuals in Each Sample

Sample	*Number of orbits with lesions*	*Number of individuals in sample*	*Ratio*
Ayalán			
Urns	*7*	*384*	*.02*
Non-urns	*0*	*51*	*0*
Guangala	*3*	*30*	*.10*
Cotocollao	*0*	*164*	*0*
Sta. Elena	*0*	*127*	*0*

Porotic hyperostosis of the orbits (*cribra orbitalia*) shows a similar pattern. The trait does not appear in the Sta. Elena and Cotocollao samples. Its greatest frequency is in the Guangala sample, followed by a disappearance in the Ayalán non-urn sample and a low frequency in the Ayalán urn sample. The temporal trend in porotic hyperostosis of both the vault and orbits is shown in Figure 19.7 and Table 19.7.

Dental Hypoplasia

Frequencies of dental hypoplasia in the samples are presented in Table 19.8 and Figure 19.8. These data reflect the frequency of affected permanent teeth, not the number of defects or the number of affected individuals. This pathology occurs with relatively low frequencies in the Sta. Elena and Cotocollao samples. The incidence increases sharply in the Guangala sample, followed by a slight decrease in the Ayalán non-urn sample and then a dramatic increase again in the Ayalán urn sample.

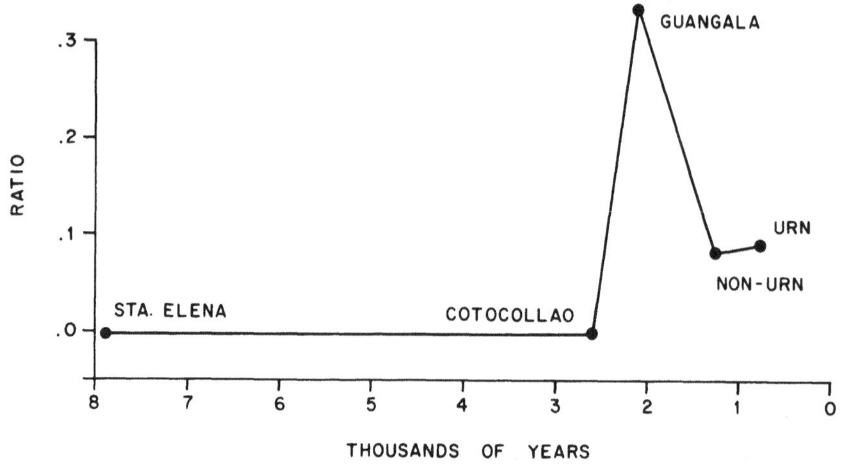

FIGURE 19.7. Ratio of bones with porotic hyperostosis (vault and orbits) to the number of individuals in each sample through time.

Dental Disease

Data are available for the five samples on three indicators of dental disease: carious lesions, alveolar abscesses, and antemortem tooth loss. Carious lesions are defined in this research as cavities in the teeth that show evidence of tissue necrosis with subsequent collapse of the hard tissue, as opposed to alterations resulting from developmental defects or from mechanical abrasion. Observed lesions were about the size of a pinhead or larger. Table 19.9 and Figure 19.9 present the percentage of permanent, fully formed teeth in the sample in which at least one carious lesion is found. Again, data are not available on the percentage of affected individuals since secondary

TABLE 19.8 Percentage of Fully Formed Permanent Teeth with Hypoplasia in Each Sample

Sample	*Number of teeth in sample*	*Number with hypoplasia*	*Percentage*
Ayalán			
Urns	*1966*	*115*	*5.8*
Non-urns	*429*	*6*	*1.4*
Guangala	*73*	*2*	*2.7*
Cotocollao	*1157*	*3*	*.3*
Sta. Elena	*1989*	*7*	*.4*

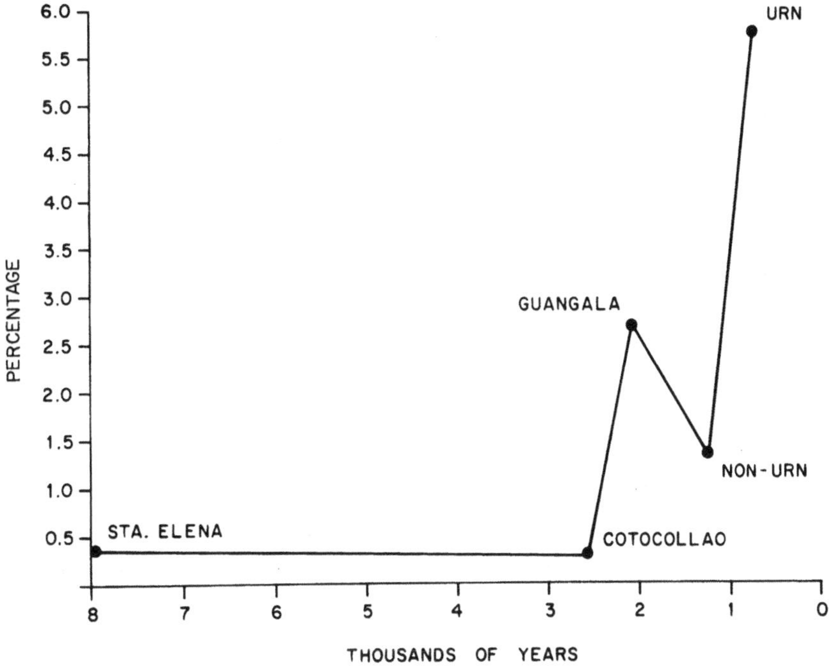

FIGURE 19.8. Percentage of permanent teeth with hypoplasia through time.

interments and loose teeth are included in the samples. The data show a low frequency of carious lesions in the Sta. Elena and Cotocollao samples, an increase in the Guangala and Ayalán non-urn samples, and an even greater increase in the Ayalán urn sample.

Table 19.10 and Figure 19.10 present the ratio of alveolar abscesses to the number of observations on permanent teeth (teeth

TABLE 19.9 Percentage of Fully Formed Permanent Teeth with at Least One Carious Lesion

Sample	Number of teeth in sample	Number carious	Percentage
Ayalán			
Urns	1966	208	11
Non-urns	429	35	8
Guangala	73	6	8
Cotocollao	1157	19	3
Sta. Elena	1989	55	3

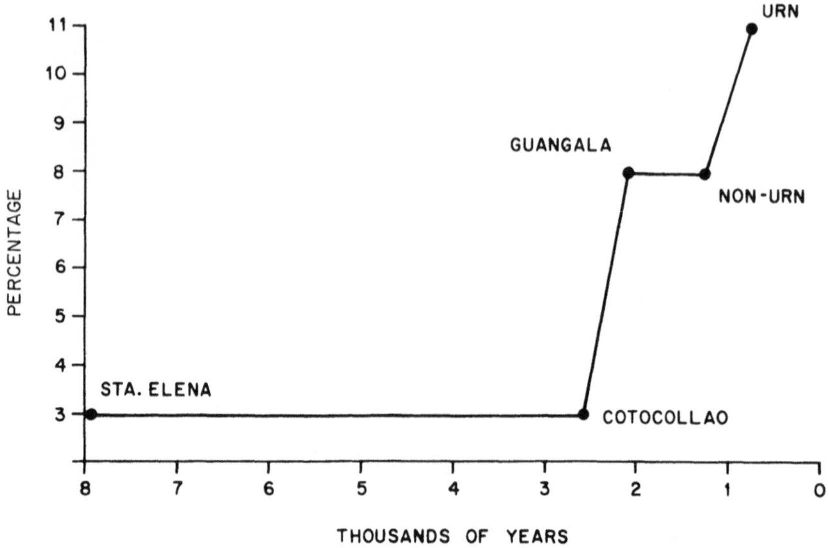

FIGURE 19.9. Percentage of permanent teeth with at least one carious lesion through time.

present plus teeth absent antemortem) in the samples. This ratio shows a temporal increase from Sta. Elena through Cotocollao to Guangala and then a sharp reduction in the Ayalán samples.

The final data set (Table 19.11, Figure 19.11) presents the ratio of permanent teeth lost antemortem to the number of observations on permanent teeth (teeth present plus teeth absent) in the samples. The ratio is low in the two early samples, increases to a peak in the Guangala sample, and then decreases in the Ayalán samples. These data, as well as those on alveolar abscesses, are somewhat inexact since teeth were not always associated with the corresponding maxillae and mandibles.

TABLE 19.10 Ratio of the Number of Alveolar Abscesses in Adults to the Number of Observations (Teeth Present Plus Teeth Absent) on Permanent Teeth in Each Sample

Sample	*Number of dental observations*	*Number of abscesses*	*Ratio*
Ayalán			
Urns	*2302*	*74*	*.03*
Non-urns	*491*	*13*	*.03*
Guangala	*122*	*10*	*.08*
Cotocollao	*1244*	*87*	*.07*
Sta. Elena	*1661*	*10*	*.01*

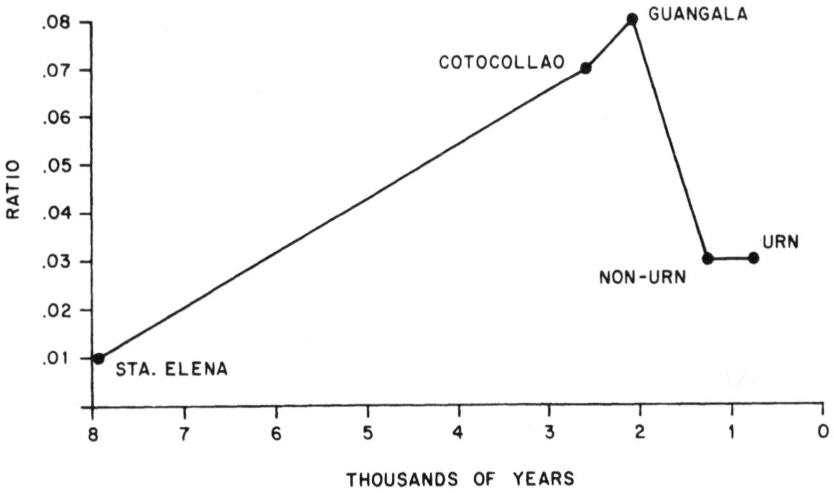

FIGURE 19.10. Ratio of the number of alveolar abscesses to the number of observations of permanent teeth through time.

DISCUSSION

It is not possible at this time to identify exact correlations between temporal changes in subsistence and social organization and changes in skeletal biology. Too little is known of the cultural prehistory of the area, and the skeletal samples still are grossly limited for such generalization. It is possible, however, to suggest some tentative relationships that may be explained with additional data.

TABLE 19.11 Ratio of Permanent Teeth Lost Antemortem to Number of Observations on Presence of Permanent Teeth (Absent and Present)

Sample	*Number of permanent teeth lost antemortem*	*Number of observations*	*Ratio*
Ayalán			
Urns	336	2302	.15
Non-urns	62	491	.13
Guangala	49	122	.40
Cotocollao	87	1244	.07
Sta. Elena	102	1661	.06

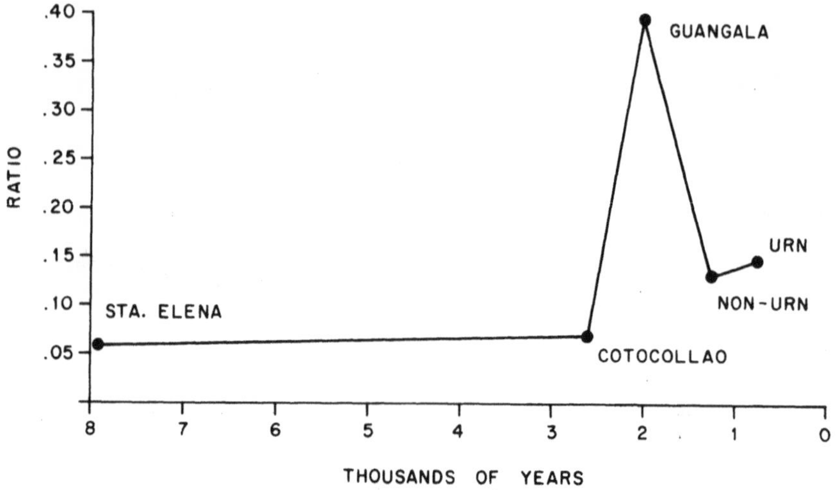

FIGURE 19.11. Ratio of permanent teeth lost antemortem to the number of observations of permanent teeth through time.

Certainly it can be said that subsistence and social structure shifted markedly from the hunting and gathering society of Sta. Elena times to the time of Cotocollao, when intensive agriculture and considerable social stratification must have been present. Yet a curious product of this study is that biological differences between these two samples are confined to an increase in alveolar abscesses. The fact that frequencies of caries and tooth loss remain constant makes even that difference puzzling. Of course, the Cotocollao site is the only highland sample in the series, and the rate and type of biological change may have differed between the highlands and the coast. Also, it is possible that although agriculture was fully developed during Cotocollao times, the population may not have developed a nearly exclusive dependence on agricultural products for subsistence until about the time of the Guangala phase.

Although the sample size is very small, the Guangala data show dramatic increases in nearly all skeletal indicators of stress, especially dental caries, tooth loss, dental hypoplasia, trauma, and infectious disease. Determination of whether this condition is exaggerated in the Guangala sample or represents a generalized condition in the Regional Development period population must await further research.

The trend of increased morbidity continues from the Guangala phase into the Late Integration period with the Ayalán samples showing a regular increase in the frequency of dental caries. Most other skeletal indicators, however, show a decline in frequency between the Guangala and Ayalán urn sample. This may indicate a period of population adjustment after Guangala, followed by renewed problems as the processes of over-reliance on few agricultural products and increased population density continue to intensify.

A more exact appraisal of biocultural associations in prehistoric Ecuador is not possible at this time. However, it is clear that although the acquisition and development of agriculture may have contributed to population expansion and to increased social complexity in prehistoric Ecuador, it also may have had deleterious biological effects that may have reduced the quality of life. More exact statements on the details and timing of this complex relationship must await the analysis of the Real Alto and San Lorenzo material, the acquisition of other large, well-documented skeletal samples, and more archaeological research on prehistoric subsistence and settlement patterns.

ACKNOWLEDGMENTS

I thank Stephanie Damadio and Elizabeth Beard of the Department of Anthropology, Smithsonian Institution, for their assistance in the literature survey and manuscript preparation. Valuable advice on Ecuadorean archaeology was received from Betty J. Meggers of the Smithsonian Institution; Jorge Marcos of the Escuela Politecnica, Guayaquil, Ecuador; and Olaf Holm and Karen Stothert of the Banco Central del Ecuador, Guayaquil, Ecuador.

REFERENCES

Bell, Robert E.
1965 *Archaeological investigations at the site of El Inga, Ecuador.* Casa de la Cultura Ecuatoriana, Quito.
Bischof, Henning, and Julio Viteri Gamboa
1972 Pre-Valdivia occupations on the southwest coast of Ecuador. *American Antiquity 37*;548-551.
Burleigh, R., and D. Brothwell
1978 Studies on Amerindian dogs. I. Carbon isotopes in relation to maize in the diet of domestic dogs from early Peru and Ecuador. *Journal of Archaeological Science 5*:355-362.
Carneiro, Robert L.
1968 The transition from hunting to horticulture in the Amazon Basin. *Proceedings International Congress of Anthropological and Ethnological Sciences 8th 3*:244-248.
Duckworth, W. L. H.
1951 Notes on skulls of the Guangala Period, from La Libertad. Appendix B in the archaeology of the Santa Elena Peninsula

in southwest Ecuador. *Occasional Publications of the Cambridge University Museum of Archaeology and Ethnology* No. 1.

Lathrap, Donald W.

1963 Possible affiliations of the Machalilla Complex of coastal Ecuador. *American Antiquity 29*:239-240.

1974 The moist tropics, the arid lands, and the appearance of great art styles in the New World. *Special Publications of the Museum Texas Tech. Univ. 7*:115-158.

1976 *Ancient Ecuador, culture, clay and creativity, 3000-300 B.C.* Field Museum of Natural History, Chicago.

Lathrap, Donald W., Jorge G. Marcos, and James A. Zeidler

1977 Real Alto: An ancient ceremonial center. *Archaeology 30*:3-13.

Marcos, Jorge Gabriel

1978 *The ceremonial precinct at Real Alto: Organization of time and space in Valdivia society.* Ph.D. dissertation, Department of Anthropology, University of Illinois, Urbana-Champaign.

McEwan, Gordon F., and D. Bruce Dickson

1978 Valdivia, Jomon fishermen, and the nature of the North Pacific: Some nautical problems with Meggers, Evans, and Estrada's (1965) transoceanic contact thesis. *American Antiquity 43*:362-371.

Meggers, Betty J.

1966 *Ecuador*. Praeger, New York.

Meggers, Betty J., Clifford Evans, and Emilio Estrada

1965 Early Formative Period of coastal Ecuador: The Valdivia and Machalilla Phases. *Smithsonian Contributions to Anthropology 1*:1-234.

Munizaga, Juan R.

1965 Skeletal remains from sites of Valdivia and Machalilla phases. Appendix 2 in Early Formative Period of coastal Ecuador: The Valdivia and Machalilla phases. *Smithsonian Contributions to Anthropology 1*:219-234.

Pearsall, Deborah M.

1978 Phytolith analysis of archeological soils: Evidence for maize cultivation in formative Ecuador. *Science 199*:177-178.

Porras Garcés, Pedro I.

1972a Secuencia Seriada de los artefactos de piedra pulida de la Fase de Cosanga en el Oriente (Ceja de Montana) del Ecuador (Suramérica). *Atti Congresso Internazionale Degliamericanisti 40th*, pp. 59-63.

1972b Supervivencia de tradición cerámica común a las culturas del Alto Amazonas y de manera especial a las de la zona oriental del Ecuador en Suramérica. *Atti Congresso Internazionale Degliamericanisti 40th*, pp. 51-57.

1975 Fase Pastaza: El Formativo en el Oriente Ecuatoriano. *Revista de la Universidad Católica* Año III, No. 10.

1981 Sitio Sangay A informe preliminar de la primera etapa. *Numero Monografico de Historia y Geografia de la Revista de la Universidad Catolica* No. 29, pp. 105-145.

Sarma, Akkaraju V. N. Sarma
1974 Holocene paleoecology of South Coastal Ecuador. *Proceedings of the American Philosophical Society 118*:93-134.

Stothert, Karen E.
1976 The early prehistory of the Sta. Elena Peninsula, Ecuador: Continuities between the Preceramic and Ceramic cultures. *Actas del Congreso Internacional de Americanistas 41st*, Vol. 2. pp. 88-98.
1977 Proyecto Paleoindio. *Pubicaciones del Museo Antropológico del Banco Central del Ecuador*.

Ubelaker, Douglas H.
1978 *Human skeletal remains, excavation, analysis, interpretation*. Taraxacum, Washington.
1980a Human skeletal remains from Site OGSE-80, a Preceramic site on the Sta. Elena Peninsula, coastal Ecuador. *Journal of the Washington Academy of Sciences 70*(1):3-24.
1980b Prehistoric human remains from the Cotocollao Site, Pichincha Providence, Ecuador. *Journal of the Washington Academy of Sciences 70*(2):59-74.
1981 The Ayalán cemetery: A Late Integration Period burial site on the South Coast of Ecuador. *Smithsonian Contributions to Anthropology* No. 29.
1983 Human skeletal remains from OGSE-MA-172, an early Guangala cemetery site on the coast of Ecuador. *Journal of the Washington Academy of Sciences 73*(1):16-26.

Van Bork-Feltkamp, A. J.
1965 *Squelettes de Palmar*. Nederlands Museum voor Anthropologie, Amsterdam.

Willey, Gordon R.
1971 *An introduction to American archaeology* (Vol. II). Prentice-Hall, Englewood Cliffs, New Jersey.

Zevallos, M. Carlos, Walton C. Galinat, Donald W. Lathrap, Earl R. Leng, Jorge G. Marcos, and Kathleen M. Klumpp
1977 The San Pablo corn kernel and its friends. *Science 196*: 385-389.

CHAPTER 20

PALEOPATHOLOGY IN PERUVIAN AND CHILEAN POPULATIONS

Marvin J. Allison

Instituto de Antropología
Universidad de Tarapacá, Arica, Chile

This chapter reports on the paleopathology of 16 populations from Peru and Chile (see Tables 20.1 and 20.2). The populations extend geographically from Ancash (Peru) in the North to Tarapaca (Chile) in the south, and they range in time from 6000 to 400 B.P. Both coastal and highland populations are represented, but all of the individuals studied died on the coast. (We have no way of telling where individuals were born or where they spent most of their lives.) Both nomadic and sedentary populations are described as are both politically independent groups and satellite communities (or colonial outposts) of larger political units. One group, the most recent, is a colonial population dating from the period of Spanish rule. The economies represented include intensive marine hunting and foraging economies with incipient agriculture (perhaps primarily for producing raw materials); groups with mixed herding and farming economies; and groups with more intensive agricultural economies. All groups represented employed some agriculture.

Climatic conditions in the coastal desert of Peru and Chile result in the preservation of mummies, often with most of their internal organs intact. These bodies can be autopsied much as modern corpses are, with standard laboratory techniques. A cause of death can often be established, and numerous specific diseases may be identified. One result of such diagnosis is that it is possible to identify a number of specific diseases affecting American Indian populations prior to European contact. (In contrast, skeletal material alone generally reflects less than 20% of the diseases that plague human populations. Most acute

TABLE 20.1 General Information on Peruvian Mummies Studies

Location	Number	Years B.P. (radiocarbon)	Economy	Comments
Huacho Peru	29	4025-4080	Fishing-gatherer	Preceramic with cotton-gourds agriculture for raw materials (?)
Chongos-Pisco Peru	26	2035-2215	Fishing-agriculture	A Paracas culture group living in the Pisco Valley
Ica Peru	16	1045-2045	Farmers	Nazca culture group from different valley
Toquilla Ancash Peru	121	1125	Fishermen	Chima-Casma culture. Small village on beach, questionable farming, but access to agricultural products
Huayuri Peru	59	620-1060	Farmers	Small agricultural community, Wari culture, in Santa Cruz Valley
Ica Peru	42	520	Farmers	Large city, Ica culture, in Santa Cruz Valley
Pisco Peru	54	440-705	Farmers	Inca culture individuals from Pisco Valley
Pisco Peru	71	340-380	Farmers (miners)	Inca and Ica Colonial individuals from Pisco Valley (Murga Hda)

infectious diseases rarely, if ever, leave skeletal lesions. See Allison 1979; Allison et al. 1974a,b,c). Since the skeleton is also present in such individuals, it is possible, using mummified remains, to relate soft-tissue findings to skeletal findings to establish an etiology for skeletal lesions that otherwise could not be diagnosed (Allison and Gerszten 1982). Comparison of

TABLE 20.2 General Information on Chilean Mummies Studied

Location	*Number*	*Years B.P. (radiocarbon)*	*Economy*	*Comments*
Faldas de Morro Arica	*6*	*2855*	*Maritime incipient agriculture*	*Coastal northern Chile--nomads*
Azapa Arica	*31*	*2560-2685*	*Maritime incipient agriculture*	*Probably related to Faldas de Morro people--nomads*
Azapa Arica	*32*	*2400*	*Shepherds, agriculture*	*Alto Ramirez people--nomads, highlanders*
Azapa Arica	*29*	*1600*	*Shepherds, agriculture*	*Cabuza people--villages? Highlanders*
Azapa Arica	*22*	*1360*	*Shepherds, agriculture*	*Classic Tiahuanaco--villages; highlanders spill-over population.*
Azapa Arica	*146*	*910-1070*	*Farmers-shepherds*	*Maitas culture--villages; highlanders*
Arica Chile	*46*	*775-1055*	*Hunters-fishermen-farmers*	*San Miguel culture--sea-oriented villages*
Tarapaca Chile	*49*	*520*	*Farmers-gatherers*	*Atacameno--villages--traders*

skeletal and mummified remains of individuals from the various cultures represented thus provides a particularly good opportunity for assessing the impact of social, economic, and political variables on human health.

THE EVIDENCE OF BONES AND TEETH

One nonspecific measure of the health of a population is mortality, with mortality during the growth phase providing perhaps the most sensitive indicator of nutrition. Table 20.3 lists the

TABLE 20.3 Childhood Mortality (under Age 15) from Six Cultural Groups

Culture	*Childhood mortality (%)*
Azapa	*28*
Alto Ramirez	*50*
Cabuza	*48*
Tiahuanaco	*49*
Huari-Ica	*49*
Colonial Inca-Ica	*45*

childhood mortality (under 15 years of age) for six selected cultural groups spanning roughly 2300 years. The earliest people of the Azapa culture, with essentially a marine economy, had a 28% childhood mortality. All of the other cultures, including the colonial group, had nearly 50% mortality for children under 15 years of age (Ashworth et al. 1976). The latter figure appears to be independent of culture and of region of origin (highland or coast).

Growth is also a nonspecific indicator of health, of which nutrition may be one important component. Table 20.4 shows average stature in cm for adults from the same cultures described in Table 20.3. The Colonial population of Inca and Ica individuals is the only one to show a significant difference from the others in the form of reduced stature. That such a reduction in stature might be of nutritional origin was evident at the time of excavation, since all graves were poor in foodstuffs, clothes were worn and patched, and numerous women were buried with newborn children (another possible indicator of nutritional stress). The other cultures showed no evidence of a shortage of food in the excavations and their stature seems to suggest relatively good nutrition.

Harris lines are another nonspecific measure of disease that may reflect a nutritional etiology (Allison et al. 1974a,b,c). The data in Table 20.5 suggest that fewer individuals from coastal cultures (where agriculture may have been of secondary importance) had lines. Furthermore, the coastal people had fewer lines per person than people from the highland or inland cultures. It would appear that people in a coastal environment had a healthier childhood than people of highland origin. Poor nutrition may be one of the causes of Harris line formation in individual cases; however, Harris lines do not correlate with porotic hyperostosis in this sample, suggesting that malnutrition is not the major cause of line formation here.

Porotic hyperostosis was not common among children even in the Colonial group, where evidence from graves suggests a shortage of

TABLE 20.4 Average Stature of Adults Based on Methods of Trotter and Gleser

Culture	Average stature (cm)
Azapa	166
Alto Ramirez	166
Cabuza	166
Tiahuanaco	169
Huari-Ica	163
Colonial Inca-Ica	156

food: only 9% of the children under 15 years of age displayed the symptoms. Among a pre-Columbian group of Wari-Ica children from around the tenth century, the figure was 6%. (In this latter case there was an abundance of agricultural products in the graves.) In northern Chile, porotic hyperostosis was uncommon in all of the cultures studied. While occasionally seen, it occurs in fewer than 1% of children under 15 years of age in all samples.

A review of data on oral pathology suggests a number of patterns likely to reflect food preparation and oral hygiene as well as nutrition. Elzay et al. (1977) and Sawyer et al. (1978a,b) review individuals from cultures extending from 2600 B.P. to the Colonial period. They found a reduction in jaw size in later cultures, a pattern often attributed to a soft diet requiring little mechanical force to masticate food. In this case, the pattern is complicated by the possibility of gene flow introduced by the Inca invasions since the mandibular body but not the ramus was reduced (Sawyer et al. 1978a,b). The Inca and Colonial period Indians have the highest incidence of missing teeth (antemortem), a finding that parallels the pattern of incidence of dental caries. Groups with high caries rates also displayed high rates of calculus involvement. Osteitis occurred in all populations but was most frequent in the Nazca and Inca groups.

Enamel hypoplasia in these populations seems to be related to an increase in "urban" living since the earlier populations, who presumably lived in small social units, had less enamel hypoplasia than the later people. This may be indicative of a less satisfactory diet as certainly was the case among the colonial populations.

A summary of these nonspecific indicators in bones and teeth reveals that with a more complete agricultural economy, childhood mortality increased (although as discussed later, this is probably explainable on the basis of village life and environment rather than diet). Stature alteration as a response to poor nutrition is seen only in the case of one colonial group. Harris lines reveal a pattern related to geographic location, which may be related in

TABLE 20.5 The Frequency of Harris Lines in Mummies from Six Coastal and Seven Inland Cultures

Cemetery	Culture	No.	Negative No.	Negative %	Positive No.	Positive %	Lines/ positive
Huacho	Preceramic	21	16	76	5	24	2.2
Playa Miller	San Miguel	6	4	67	2	33	1.0
Playa Miller	San Miguel	19	14	74	5	26	1.6
Playa Miller	Tiahuanaco	8	8	100	0		0
Huayuri	Wari	19	10	53	9	47	2.2
Huayuri	Ica	12	7	58	5	42	2.2
Coastal totals		85	59	69.4	26	30.6	1.53
Azapa	Azapa	23	3	13	20	87	6.3
Azapa	Alto Ramirez	8	2	25	6	75	4.6
Pica	Atacameno	16	9	56	7	44	8.7
Azapa	Cabuza	14	6	43	8	57	2.9
Azapa	Tiahuanaco	14	9	64	5	36	6.8
Azapa	San Miguel	8	4	50	4	50	5.5
San Juan	Maitas-Chiri.-Baya	60	13	21.7	47	78.3	9.0
Inland totals		143	46	32.2	97	67.8	6.3

turn to diet (although a dietary etiology is questionable since coastal cultures spanning 2000-3000 years show similar patterns of Harris lines). The low level of porotic hyperostosis in these populations would also tend to argue against diet as a major factor in the pathology. In oral pathology a reduction in mandible size but not in the size of the mandibular ramus suggests a pattern of genetic rather than dietary change. Enamel hypoplasia increased with urbanization. Tooth loss and incidence of caries appeared to be related more to the preparation of foodstuffs than to the selection of foods.

THE EVIDENCE OF SOFT TISSUE

The general conclusions based on pathologic data for bones and teeth can be expanded by reference to soft-tissue studies.

We have discussed the childhood mortality patterns and the fact that among early sea mammal hunters-fishermen-gatherers, this mortality rate was only about half that seen in later agricultural populations. In both groups, however, the major cause

TABLE 20.6 Acute Respiratory Disease in Adults and Children of Six Cultures

Culture	Origin	Incidence (%) of acute respiratory disease Children	Adults
Azapa	Coastal	75	47
Alto Ramirez	Mountain	54	27
Cabuza	Mountain	88	43
Tiahuanaco	Mountain	58	28
Huari	Mountain	50	41
Inca-Ica	Mountain	60	45

of death was acute respiratory disease (striking both sexes equally). From Table 20.6 it is evident that acute respiratory disease in the form of pneumonia was a major cause of death in individuals from both coastal and mountain cultures and indeed was the major cause of death among all people from all time periods independent of diet, involvement, or social organization. It would be no exaggeration to say that for the past 8000 years most Americans have died of the same causes, acute and chronic respiratory diseases. Even today in modern Latin America the major causes of death are pneumonia and tuberculosis. Table 20.7 gives the pathology of acute pulmonary disease seen in 51 pre-Columbian mummies of individuals who died of pneumonia. Nearly 70% of the mummies showed bilateral pneumonia that could be clearly identified grossly as bronchopneumonia or lobar pneumonia. Microscopic examination of the pneumonia seen in the lung showed that most cases produced an abundant exudate containing remains of inflammatory cells and bacteria (Group IV) or an exudate with inflammatory cells and no bacteria (Group III); less than 7% had only edema fluid (Group I) and less than 10% had edema plus bacteria (Group II). The gross diagnosis of pneumonia is based on finding the lungs inflated at the time of autopsy. This signifies that at the time of death they were filled with fluid that evaporated in time, allowing the lung to dry in the expanded position. The lungs of a normal individual who did not die of pulmonary disease are completely deflated and about the thickness of a playing card. Associated with the pneumonia are areas of collapsed lung (atelectasis) as well as areas of hemorrhage and emphysema (local trapping of air in blebs due to dilatation of pulmonary air vesicles), all complications of the pneumonic process. Anthracosis was included in the data given in this table, and its low frequency indicated that cooking was probably done out of doors rather than in a house where the smoke with its carbon particles would be inhaled. This is logical since the climate all along the coast and coastal valleys in the area studied is mild and favors outdoor living. The 44% frequency of pleural adhesions suggests that nearly half of these individuals had had at least one previous

TABLE 20.7 Incidence of Pathologic Findings in 51 Mummies with Acute Pulmonary Disease

Pathologic finding	*Incidence (%)*
Pneumonia	
Gross examination	
Right lung	*13.0*
Left lung	*17.4*
Bilateral	*69.6*
Microscopic examination	
Group I	*6.8*
Group II	*9.1*
Group III	*22.7*
Group IV	*61.4*
Pleural exudate	*14.8*
Atelectasis	*9.3*
Hemorrhage	*13.0*
Emphysema	*41.0*
Anthracosis	*5.6*
Abscess	*3.7*
Granulomas (tubercular?)	*3.7*
Pleural adhesions	*44.4*

bout of pneumonia, but about half of them died of their first attack. The presence of a lung abscess in nearly 4% of the individuals is consistent with a chronic local focus of infection. The granulomas noted are incidental findings of another disease, probably tuberculosis, cases of which have been found in nearly all of the cultures under study here. Extrapulmonary complications seen, in the order of frequency in these mummies, were pleurisy, liver disease, kidney disease, pericarditis, and endocarditis.

Modern laboratory technology makes it possible to identify the specific etiologic agent of many of these pneumonias (Dalton et al. 1976). In one case of bronchopneumonia, numerous streptococci were seen in the sections of the lung; serological techniques revealed this to be a Lancefield group A *Streptococcus*. A Wari man who died of Carrión's disease, Verruga phase, had a bronchopneumonia due to *Bartonella bacilliformis* identified by electron microscopy (Martinez et al. 1975) on the basis of size and flagellum with the characteristic associated pathology (Allison et al. 1974b). An Inca woman with an extensive skin infection died of a bronchopneumonia and both lesions were shown to have a yeast, *Candida* sp. (This individual may have been from the colonial period since its age according to carbon dating overlapped the time of the Spanish conquest. Such a disease today could be associated with diabetes or possibly a nutritional deficiency, but neither possibility can be proven in her case.) At least two cases of bronchopneumonia were associated with a possible salmonellosis group D infection. This particular group of salmonellae includes the agent of typhoid fever (Allison et al. 1982b; Sawicki et al. 1976).

The existence of chronic respiratory disease, mainly in the form of tuberculosis throughout most of pre-columbian America, is now well established. Allison et al. (1973) reported the first case of pre-Columbian tuberculosis with archaeological dating and a ^{14}C date of about A.D. 700. The disease was discovered in an 8-year-old Huari child who died after a long-standing illness that produced, aside from the pulmonary disease, liver and kidney tuberculosis, tuberculous pericarditis, and a psoas abscess with Pott's disease in the lumbar vertebrae. This case had acid-fast bacilli in many different organs and the terminal event was a miliary tuberculosis. Since then more than a dozen such cases have been recorded with numerous different manifestations of this disease in bone and soft tissue (Allison et al. 1981b). The disease as noted in the pre-Columbian Indian is quite similar to that seen in the United States Caucasian population and in no way resembles the rapid, galloping consumption commonly described in the modern Indian population in the pre-antibiotic era. (This rapidly fulminating pulmonary disease is a reflection of a complete disruption of the native American's way of life that results in increased susceptibility to many diseases, among them tuberculosis.)

That the pre-Columbian Indian did not react so differently to disease than the modern person is seen in another chronic pulmonary infection, South American blastomycosis (Paracoccidioidomycosis see Allison et al. 1979). This generalized deep mycotic infection is caused by a fungus, *Paracoccidioides brasiliensis* and is of low frequency, almost exclusively seen in tropical or subtropical rural areas of South America. The present pre-Columbian case was in a 56-year-old woman who died around A.D. 290 with pulmonary and renal lesions. It is probable that this was an imported disease in northern Chile acquired during a trading expedition to a tropical area, since among the grave goods were numerous examples of tropical bird feathers. The age of the individual and the nature of the lesions are all similar to those seen in modern cases of this disease.

Munizaga et al. (1975) reported on pneumoconiosis in a group of mummies of sixteenth century miners from Chile. It is interesting to note that the frequency of chronic infectious pulmonary disease in this group of miners was comparable to that seen in a group of modern sandblasters who also had pneumoconiosis (Bailey et al. 1974). Thus, by all indications the responses of native Americans from Peru or Chile to disease are quite comparable to those of modern white Americans; and we must infer that deviations from this established norm may be due to alterations in the native societies with changes in the economy and nutritional base.

If we consider that respiratory disease is the major cause of death in children of all cultures, it should be relatively easy to measure the relative mortality of different age groups, comparing this to the morbidity as obtained from Harris lines. Table 20.8 presents such data for a group of individuals belonging to the

TABLE 20.8 Maitas-Chiribaya Population Showing Total Mortality and Morbidity

Age of children at death (years)	(A) total population Harris lines	(B) Number of dead children	(A + B = C) Morbidity	$\left(\frac{B}{C} = D\right)$ Percentage Mortality
B- 1	12	28	40	70
1- 5	55	12	67	18
5- 8	66	7	69	10
8-12	221	2	223	<1
12-16	75	11	86	13
	425	60	485	12

Maitas-Chiribaya culture of northern Chile. It is obvious that children from birth to 1 year of age have a low resistance and that 70% of those who become ill will die, while less than 1% of children aged 8-12 will die. Because among most primitive peoples the children are limited to mother's milk at this early age, it is probably sanitation rather than nutrition that causes this mortality.

This problem of poor sanitation as a major cause of disease is further emphasized when we note the change from a nomadic or camp existence to the sedentary life of a village with full agriculture. Table 20.9 shows the effects of a sedentary life on the incidence of gastrointestinal diseases. This table illustrates clearly one problem that arose with a sedentary life in which contamination of food and water probably occurred due to concentration of population. Such population concentration possibly resulted in the ability to feed more people, particularly as irrigation was developed, but it resulted in the introduction of new diseases and a deterioration in health. In the current analysis, gastrointestinal problems were measured by alterations in the volume of feces in the large bowel or changes in its character (blood) or consistency.

The increased frequency of gastrointestinal disease a a valid observation, but the actual etiology of the infectious agents is not easily established. The only positive identification of an agent concerns two cases of salmonella group D, one of which resulted in a generalized infection; the individual died of a peritonitis with extensive hemorrhage into the gastrointestinal tract. It is probable that other salmonellae were also responsible for other cases of gastrointestinal disease since even today this is one of the most common infections of the bowel in modern man.

TABLE 20.9 Incidence of Gastrointestinal Disease in Individuals from Four Cultural Groups of Northern Chile

Culture	*Incidence of gastrointestinal disease (%)*
Azapa	*7*
Alto Ramirez	*2*
Cabuza	*25*
Maitas-Chiribaya	*18*

Fouant, Allison, and Gerszten (1982) completed a preliminary survey of intestinal parasites of Chilean and Peruvian mummies. Although the occasional whipworm, pinworm, and hookworm were found, they were not common enough to produce a serious health problem. This is probably due to the nature of the environment, which does not allow for the completion of the natural cycle of most parasites. The single case of hookworm is of interest (Allison et al. 1974c) in that the finding of *Ancylostoma* has recently been confirmed in pre-Columbian fecal material from Brazil by Gonçalves de Araujo (1980). Thus, it seems certain that ancylostomiasis was a native American disease and that the other hookworm *Necator* was a later import into the Americas, as suggested by Soper (1927).

SOCIAL STRATIFICATION AND HEALTH

The advent of agriculture probably was also responsible eventually for some type of central organization and social stratification. Direct evidence from studies of the Maitas-Chiribaya culture of northern Chile reveal that at least in one case, this was to the detriment of the health of the bulk of the population but to the benefit of the ruling priest class. Table 20.10 presents data on three different classes of people from a Maitas habitational site with what appears to be a temple dated around 1000 B.P. As can be seen from this table, the shamans were a privileged group that had about the same life span as other males, but were taller and had fewer bone lesions. The women are truly a different social group from the commoner males since with the advent of agriculture there has been a separation of duties in Andean society, with women on a lower level than men. (This was not true in the early fishing and sea mammal hunting societies of northern Chile, in which women were buried with harpoons, fish hooks, and lines and used elaborate string turbans that sometimes had silver or copper ornaments, suggesting a sexually egalitarian society.) In the Maitas cemetery were numerous large baskets

TABLE 20.10 Data on Three Socially Stratified Adult Groups from a Maitas-Chiribaya Cemetery

	Number	Age	Height (cm)	Incidence of fractures (%)	Incidence of osteoarthritis (%)		Incidence of osteitis (%)	Bone lesions per person
					Cervical	Lumbar		
Shamans	12	30	165	0	18	18	9	0.4
Commoner males	20	31	162	35	25	30	20	1.3
Commoner females	49	38	159	16	29	39	18	2.1

called "capachos" that were supported by a tumpline to the forehead; this was probably responsible for the cervical vertebral osteoarthritis noted in younger adults in this population. The graves yielded abundant meat, fish, and a wide variety of vegetables, suggesting nutrition was adequate. The shamans were separated from the other males on the basis of the use of ear ornaments, loincloths, and special type of hat, and gold hair clips.

In sum, there is little evidence that farming with subsequent storage of products improved the general health of Andean populations. Rather, the impression is given that sedentary village life was detrimental to health due to crowding and subsequent sanitation problems associated with village living. Similarly, social stratification within an agricultural society only provided an improvement in health for the minority elite priest group. Moreover, colonialism seems to have had a detrimental effect on the health of the colonial people. It would appear that the larger political organizations of pre-Columbian times, the last of which was the Inca, were able to store and distribute agricultural products to provide a less than optimal diet to a large potential labor force, but at the expense of its health.

REFERENCES

Allison, M. J.
1979 Paleopathology in Peru. *Natural History*, Feb. Issue:74-82.

Allison, M. J., and Gerszten, E.
1982 *Paleopathology in South American mummies, application of modern techniques* (third ed.). Medical College of Virginia, Richmond.

Allison, M. J., D. Mendoza, and A. Pezzia
1973 Documentation of a case of tuberculosis in Pre-Columbian America. *American Review of Respiratory Diseases 107*: 985-991.

Allison, M. J., A. Pezzia, E. Gerszten, R. F. Giffler, and D. Mendoza
1974a Aspiration pneumonia due to teeth--A report of two cases, 950 A.D. and 1973 A.D. *Southern Medical Journal 67*:479-483.

Allison, M. J., A. Pezzia, E. Gerszten, and D. Mendoza
1974b A case of Carrion's disease associated with human sacrifice for the Huari culture of southern Peru. *American Journal of Physical Anthropology 41*:295-300.

Allison, M. J., A. Pezzia, L. Hasegawa, and E. Gerszten
1974c A case of hookworm infestation in a Pre-Columbian American. *American Journal of Physical Anthropology 41*:103-105.

Allison, M. J., E. Gerszten, H. J. Shadomy, J. Munizaga, and M. Gonzales
1979 Paracoccidiodomycosis in a mummy. *Bulletin of the New York Academy of Medicine* 55:670-683.

Allison, M. J., E. Gerszten, J. Munizaga, C. Santoro, and D. Mendoza
1981b Tuberculosis in Pre-Columbian Andean populations. In *Prehistoric Tuberculosis in the Americas* edited by Jane Buikstra, pp. 49-61. Northwestern University Archaeological Program, Evanston, Illinois.

Allison, M. J., E. Gerszten, and M. Fouant
1982b Paleopathology, today's laboratory investigates yesterday's diseases. *Diagnostic Medicine*, Sept./Oct. Issue:28-48.

Ashworth, J. T., M. J. Allison, E. Gerszten, and A. Pezzia
1976 The pubic scars of partutition and gestation in a group of Pre-Columbian and colonial Peruvian mummies. *American Journal of Physical Anthropology* 45:85-89.

Bailey, W. C., M. Brown, H. A. Buecher, H. Weill, H. Ichinose, and M. Ziskind
1974 Silicomycobacterial disease in sandblasters. *American Review of Respiratory Diseases* 110:115.

Dalton, H. P., M. J. Allison, and A. Pezzia
1976 The documentation of communicable diseases in Peruvian mummies. *Medical College of Virginia Quarterly* 12:43-48.

Elzay, R. P., M. J. Allison, and A. Pezzia
1977 A comparative study on the dental health status of five Pre-Columbian Peruvian cultures. *American Journal of Physical Anthropology* 46:135-139.

Gonçalves de Araujo, A. J.
1980 Contribucao ao estudo de helmintos encontrados em material arqueologico no Brasil-Tese de Mestrado. Fundacao Oswaldo Cruz, Rio de Janeiro.

Lumbreras, L. G.
1974 *Los origenes de la civilizacion en el Peru.* Milla Batres, Lima.

Martinez, A. J., D. Fults, M. J. Allison, E. Gerszten, and D. C. Stanley
1975 Electron microscopic study of tissues from Pre-Columbian Americans. *Proceedings Electron Microscopy Society of America 33rd Annual Meeting Las Vegas*, pp. 55-60.

Munizaga, J., M. J. Allison, and E. Gerszten
1975 Pneumoconiosis in miners from a 16th century mining community. *Bulletin of the New York Academy of Medicine* 51:1281-1293.

Santoro, C.
1980 Estratigrafia y secuencia cultural funeraria fases: Azapa, Alto Ramirez y Tiwanaku (Arica, Chile). *Chungara* 6:24-45.

Sawicki, V. A., M. J. Allison, H. P. Dalton, and A. Pezzia
1976 Presence of salmonella antigens in feces from a Peruvian mummy. *Bulletin of the New York Academy of Medicine 52*: 805-813.

Sawyer, D. R., M. J. Allison, R. P. Elzay, D. G. Page, and A. Pezzia
1978a Maxillary and mandibular jaw size in Pre-Columbian Peru. *Medical College of Virginia Quarterly 14*(2):101-108.

Sawyer, D. R., M. J. Allison, R. P. Elzay, and A. Pezzia
1978b The dental health status of Pre-Columbian Peruvians: A study of dental caries, missing teeth, attrition, osteitis and calculus and bone loss. *Medical College of Virginia Quarterly 14*:1981-1988.

Soper, F. L.
1927 The report of a nearly pure *Ancylostoma duodenale* infestation in South American Indians and a discussion of its ethnological significance. *American Journal of Hygene 7*: 174-184.

CHAPTER 21

THE CHALLENGES AND REWARDS OF SEDENTISM: THE PRECERAMIC VILLAGE OF PALOMA, PERU

Robert A. Benfer

Department of Anthropology
University of Missouri-Columbia

INTRODUCTION

The Paloma project was designed to provide an interdisciplinary analysis of adaptation to sedentism and food production at the very large preceramic (Archaic) site of Paloma, Chilca Valley, Peru. The site affords relatively rare evidence concerning the prehistory of the Peruvian coast during the period between 8000 and 4500 B.P. when sedentism and food production were evolving. The archaeological and ecological data for the region are reported elsewhere and will be summarized here only briefly (see Benfer 1984a,b; Engel 1980). This chapter provides demographic data and preliminary data from pilot studies on many different skeletal indicators that, in combination, yield a compelling picture of successful adjustment to the challenges and opportunities of sedentism.

ECOLOGICAL BACKGROUND

It is commonly assumed that early Peruvian coastal dwellers emigrated from the Andean highlands (MacNeish et al. 1975; Willey 1971). Upon reaching the coast, they found an extreme desert whose aridity was challenged only by about 50 streams, many of which were not perennial, and by the heavy winter fog or *garua*. In the sea adjacent to the desert they encountered one of the richest biomass concentrations known, quite in contrast to the desert which is one of the most extreme in the world. Lanning (1967) and Moseley (1975) have emphasized the richness of the marine resources that would permit coastal peoples to live in semipermanent villages for at least part of the year. This view has been challenged (Osborne 1977; Raymond 1981; Wilson 1981). Associated short-term climatic cycles may have influenced both subsistence and settlement strategies (Cohen 1975; Dering 1983; Dering and Weir 1979; Vehik 1978; Weir 1978; Weir and Dering 1984).

The modern climate in the vicinity of the Paloma site is homogeneous; winters are extremely foggy and rainfall is nonexistent, except during an El Niño event (failure of the Peruvian current or upwelling). The site of Paloma is only 8.5 km from the Chilca River, which is dry most of the year. Today, floodplain farming is practiced in the middle valley, and wells tap water in the lower valley. Paloma is in a fog oasis, a hilly area near the coast that is dampened by fog from June through November (when the Chilca River is dry). Where there is vegetation to condense the fog, considerable water is captured and vegetation may be lush (Torres and López Ocaña 1981). At the time of Spanish contact, the hills from the north of Peru to Paracas were covered in vegetation (Rostworowski de Diez Canseco 1981); only remnants now exist of this luxuriant environment due to overgrazing and collecting of firewood.

The prehistoric inhabitants were sedentary for at least part of each year. They may have switched their main settlement from Paloma to the nearby river site of Chilca I in the summer when the fog does not nourish the *lomas* but the Chilca River runs.

EXCAVATIONS

Thirteen months of excavation by the University of Missouri team and researchers of the Centro de Investigación de Zonas Áridas (CIZA) of the Universidad Nacional de Agraria of Peru has expanded earlier work by Engel (1980). A total of 2860 square meters have been excavated yielding 55 houses, associated with which were over 200 burials. Of the burials, only two were disturbed to any extent in antiquity and most can be placed in stratigraphic context. No separate cemetery was found at Paloma. The burials were in a good state of preservation; careful excavation produced considerable soft tissue such as hair, skin, and even intestinal contents (Benfer 1984a; Quilter 1979).

The site produced several stratigraphic levels, each of which offered indications of differing subsistence strategies (Benfer 1984a; Engel 1980). Three widespread major stratigraphic zones are recognized, designated numbers 200, 300, and 400-600, in order of increasing depth. The stratigraphic interpretation is supported by both radiometric dates and fluorine analyses (see Appendix and Table 21.A1).

POPULATION CONTINUITY

The site of Paloma is a place, not a population. A breeding population is the proper unit of analysis (Bennett 1969), but it is not possible to know with certainty the limits of a breeding population from human skeletal remains. The 2000 years of occupation at Paloma from which most skeletal remains were obtained is long enough to allow considerable population movement. Recently, C. Turner (personal communication) has found that biological distances between burials from the earlier levels (#400-600) and the later levels, as judged by dental traits, is very large, perhaps too large to be explained by *in situ* change. Analysis of the cranial discrete traits, standard anthropometric measurements, and Cartesian coordinate data (Benfer 1976) is still pending.

The possible effects of genetic drift due to isolation remain to be investigated. However, Page (1974) found evidence of decreased variance in cranial measurements in coastal Peruvian skeletons during the time period of Paloma, supporting Ericksen's (1962) hypothesis that coastal villages experienced breeding isolation that broke down with the beginnings of agriculture. Turner's data may be detecting this breakdown in isolation, since the earlier, smaller samples show decreased variance in many of the 23 dental traits studied. Unequal sample sizes confound this interpretation. Stature is predicted to decrease with inbreeding (Falconer 1960) and contemporary human populations support this prediction (see Schreider 1967). An increase in stature does take place at Paloma, as discussed in the section, "Stature."

SUBSISTENCE

The earlier levels (level 400 and below) indicate mixed hunting and collecting in the *lomas*, nearby river valleys, and western Andean flanks, with exploitation of marine resources important. The middle occupation (level 300, the thickest deposits) show an increase in plant remains, including possible cultivation or management of such plants as the tuberous begonia (*Begonia geraniifolia*), the bottle gourd (*Lagenaria seraria*), and other imported plants such as lima beans (*Phaseolus lunatus*), squash (*Cucurbitaceae* spp.), and possibly others (Weir and Dering 1984). By level 200, a thin but widespread occupation, a greater emphasis on marine resources, and evidence of degradation of the *lomas* are found. Faunal studies are very preliminary and biomass determinations by levels are not yet available. However, sea lions, Andean deer and guanacos, birds, and a variety of fish, including anchovies, are present (Reitz 1983, 1984). Coprolite and intestinal contents studied (N = 276) show that 88% contained shell fragments, 77% bone (fish, mammal, bird, and reptile) fragments, 63% plant fibers; 44% grass fragments, and 23%, various seeds (Weir and Dering 1984).

PALEODEMOGRAPHY AT PALOMA

Several predictions were made before the field work was begun (Benfer et al. 1975). An implicit prediction central to our approach is that successful adaptation to the fog-oasis, riverine, and coastal habitats could be demonstrated by improvements in life expectancy. Specific deductions were also made:

1. Angel (1971) had reported that a decline in the quality of life with adoption of food production in Greece ameliorated as farmers gradually adjusted to sedentism. Patterson (1971) suggested that overexploitation of the fragile habitats of coastal Peru would lead to stress, followed by more emphasis on marine resources (see also Weir and Dering 1984). We predicted that the inhabitants of Paloma would demonstrate stress directly in their demographic profile. We did not predict the expected results of population pressure directly (Cohen 1981; Hayden 1981), but high stress in the earliest inhabitants would be anticipated.

2. We expected to find a high proportion of newborn deaths, detectable due to excellent preservation and the use of houses for burial rather than cemetery areas (where newborns are commonly underrepresented).

3. We expected an excess of newborn females and a deficit of females among early adults if predicted female infanticide was practiced.

4. We predicted an excess of children dying in the 3-5-year age range, due to the lack of adequate transitional diets from mother's milk, if no cultivated plants were available.

Results

The major paleodemographic findings are these:

1. Differences were obtained in the age distributions by stratigraphic levels (Table 21.1). When the analysis included only individuals of documentable stratigraphic placement, significant differences resulted (Table 21.2; chi-square = 18.7, $p < .05$,

TABLE 21.1 *Sex, Age, and Stratigraphic Levels for 201 Paloma Burials*

	#200 (4600–5200 B.P.)			#300 (5200–5500 B.P.)			#400–500 (5500–7000 B.P.)			Unassigned			Totals by sex			Totals by age
Age (years)	M	F	?	M	F	?	M	F	?	M	F	?	M	F	?	
Fetus	0	1	1	0	1	3	2	3	2	0	0	3	2	5	9	16
0– 1	1	0	3	1	4	7	3	7	1	1	0	4	6	11	15	32
1– 4	0	0	2	0	0	2	0	2	0	1	0	2	1	2	6	9
5– 9	0	0	2	0	0	4	0	0	3	0	0	5	0	0	14	14
10–14	1	0	0	0	0	4	0	0	0	0	0	0	1	0	4	5
15–19	1	0	0	1	1	0	0	0	0	0	0	0	2	1	1	4
20–24	0	1	0	2	4	0	3	1	0	0	0	0	5	6	0	11
25–29	5	0	0	4	1	0	4	3	0	1	1	1	14	5	1	20
30–34	1	3	0	1	4	1	4	4	0	0	1	0	6	12	0	18
35–39	2	3	0	2	1	0	1	2	0	0	0	0	5	6	0	11
40–44	1	1	0	5	3	0	0	1	0	0	0	0	6	5	0	11
45–49	1	1	0	1	3	0	0	0	0	1	0	0	3	4	0	7
50–54	1	0	0	0	1	0	0	1	0	0	2	0	1	4	0	5
55+	1	1	1	0	1	0	1	0	0	0	0	0	2	2	1	5
Individuals for whom age is approximate																
Baby (0–5)	0	0	0	0	0	8	0	0	4	0	0	0	0	0	12	12
Child (6–14)	0	0	0	0	0	2	0	0	2	0	0	2	0	0	6	6
Adult (15+)	1	1	0	1	0	4	0	0	5	2	0	1	4	1	10	15
	16	12	9	18	24	35	18	24	17	6	4	18	58	64	79	201

TABLE 21.2 Distribution of Burials by Age and Stratigraphic Levels[a]

Age (years)	Stratigraphic levels #200 (4600-5200 B.P.)	#300 (5200-5500 B.P.)	#400-500 (5500-7000 B.P.)	Total
Fetus-1	6	16	18	40
1- 9	4	6	5	15
10-19	2	6	0	8
20-29	6	11	11	28
30-39	9	9	11	29
40+	8	14	3	25
	35	62	48	145

[a]One hundred forty-five burials with good age and stratigraphic provience from the entire sample of 201 burials.

df = 11). More young died in the earlier levels (48% died before age 10 in levels 400 and below, 35% in level 300, and 28% in level 200). Conversely, fewer people lived to be old (6% > 40 years in levels 400 and below; 23% in both level 200 and level 300). The demographic data are compatible with adaptation taking place from an earlier, extremely stressed population at Paloma to progressively more healthy inhabitants. Figure 21.1 presents individual life expectancies for each level, which have been grouped in 10-year periods and smoothed by running averages in order to produce reliable e_x values with small samples. The trend is quite clear.

2. Over 28% of the Paloma burials were aged 1 year or younger, including fetal and stillborn remains. Excluding fetal remains, 19% were aged 1 year or younger, a figure similar to that reported by Ubelaker (1980) for the preceramic Sta. Elena sample (15%) and by Lovejoy et al. (1977) for the North American Libben site. While a certain stability in the rate of newborn deaths is suggested by these comparative data, it should also be noted that the percentage of infant deaths (including fetuses) decreases at Paloma from level 400 (38%) to 300 (26%) to 200 (17%). The expected high frequency of infant deaths was observed; improved adjustment to the stresses of the coastal habitat is supported by the trend in infant mortality.

3. The prediction of female infanticide is supported; 18 males and 10 females in their 20s were excavated from known stratigraphic levels, while 7 male and 18 female infants less than 1 year of age were found (chi-square = 5.8, $p < .02$ with 1 *df*). This is repeated in levels 300 and 400 and older, while in level 200 only two infant or fetal remains could be sexed (using Weaver's [1980] technique).

4. The prediction of unusually high death rates in the 3-5-year age range is not supported. Only 4% of the remains referable to specific levels were in the 1-4-year range and 6% in the 5-9-

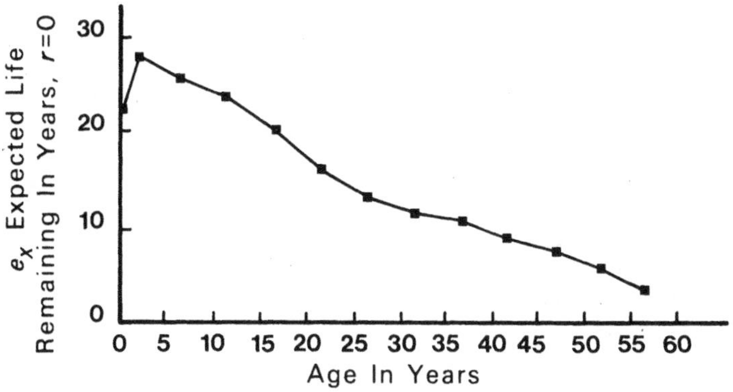

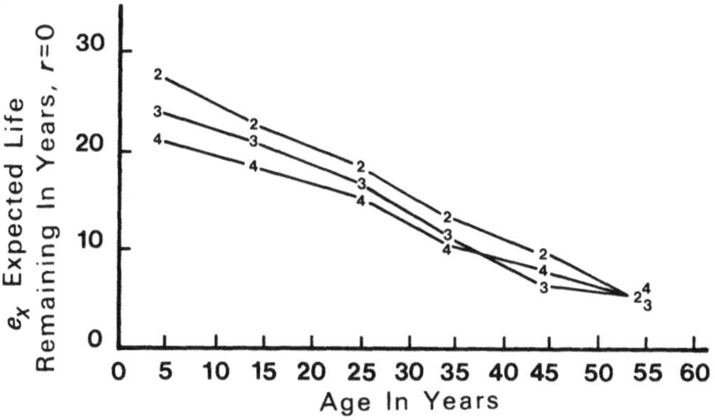

FIGURE 21.1. Life expectancy at Paloma. (a) Total sample (N = 168 males and females for whom accurate age estimates are available; includes 44 individuals lacking precise stratigraphic placement). (b) Sample divided by stratigraphic level; smoothed 10-year age intervals. 2, level 200 only (N = 35); 3, level 300 only (N = 61); 4, level 400 and 500 (N = 48).

year period. Sedentism and transitional foods must have eased this difficult transition from nursing to adult diet. The result would have been to increase population pressure as more children survived childhood, forcing some response in the population.

5. Delaying marriage is a simple response to population pressure. Differential mortality data may show such a response. An unexpected finding, possibly reflecting marriage practice, is reversal of the usual pattern in which female mortality peaks in the 20s and male mortality more commonly peaks in the 30s. The Paloma pattern is the reverse, with 19 males and 11 females dying in their 20s, while 11 males and 18 females died in their 30s (chi-square = 3.8, p = .05, with 1 df). I have not previously

obtained this result in an earlier skeletal study (Benfer 1968) and do not believe it is a consequence of bias in sexing or aging procedures. Instead, delayed marriage is suggested, such as is commonly found where infanticide is practiced. Delayed marriage would result in a delay in female mortality, as the high risks of death in childbirth (see Allison and Gerszten 1982) would be postponed. At Paloma, this reversal of ratio is characteristic of each stratigraphic level (see Table 21.1), suggesting continuing population control.

6. Allison (Chapter 20, this volume) reports five western South American mummy series; four have 45-50% deaths before age 15 (one is anomalous with only 28% before age 15). Paloma, earlier in time, exhibits 45% deaths before age 15. Lower population density may have decreased the effects of infectious diseases that plagued later peoples.

The demographic data suggest a population controlling the production of infants while reducing the mortality of both the very young and the old. However, these findings can also support an alternative hypothesis, that of a reduction in inbreeding depression--very strong heterosis conceivably could explain these data. However, in either case, such extreme social controls as female infanticide and delay of marriage until the 30s suggest considerable competition for available resources on the central coast of Peru between 8000 and 4500 years ago. Skeletal indicators can suggest the mechanisms by which improved adaptation in limited, fragile habitats took place.

DENTAL WEAR--RESULTS

Moore-Jansen (1982) found that microwear on Paloma molars corresponds well to protoagricultural North American specimens, tending to confirm the archaeobotanical data. The presence of a possible cultigen component in the diet was not expected when this work began. The many grinding stones and seeds from coprolites indicate that plants were an important component in the diet, regardless of their degree of domestication.

Edwards (1984) has found that dental wear at Paloma is high overall, in the same range as Scott's (1974) Pacific Littoral groups. Using the principal axis technique for estimating wear (Scott 1979), Edwards found rate of wear increased significantly through time at Paloma for both the mandible and the maxilla. These changes by stratigraphic level fit exactly the prediction obtained by reanalysis of Scott's coastal data of a much longer time span (Edwards 1984), confirming the stratigraphy.

I conclude from Edwards's work that Palomans were responding to stress with increased mastication of abrasive foods. Individuals over 40 years of age had to use roots and gums for mastication. If shellfish were causing much of the wear (see Moore-

Jansen 1982), these data suggest an increasing dependency on marine resources, in compliance with Patterson's (1971) model. Other indicators of dental stress, such as linear enamel hypoplasia, abscessing, tooth size, and pathologies are not yet studied, although data have been gathered by Edwards.

DENTAL ASYMMETRY

On the basis of an assumed adequate and varied diet and a lack of significant stress, we predicted less dental asymmetry at Paloma than in earlier or later populations (Benfer et al., 1975). Gehlert (1979) reported on a pilot study of teeth from Paloma (N = 20) compared with a larger Inca sample from the Sierra (N = 79). She found 10 out of the 12 teeth available for comparison were more asymmetrical at Paloma ($p < .02$). Antúnez de Mayolo (1981) reports that Inca health was quite good overall. In contrast, for 8 of 12 available teeth (excluding canines and the third molar), Palomans showed less asymmetry than Indian Knoll. I conclude from Gehlert's work that the Paloma populations underwent more stress than Incans but less than the Indian Knoll foragers.

SEXUAL DIMORPHISM

We predicted that sexual dimorphism should lessen over time (Benfer et al. 1975) as a consequence of lessening sexual division of labor (Brace and Mahler 1971). It would be expected to increase if inbreeding were reduced.

Results

Diameter of Femoral Head

The average diameter of the head of the femur was examined by stratigraphic level and sex. There is no change in observed sexual dimorphism (males are about 1.1 times larger than females in each time period). Factors that might have affected sexual dimorphism, as indicated by the head of the femur, either were absent or canceled each other.

Selection does not seem to have been strong for this measurement. There is no relationship between the femoral diameter and the age at death for males, and a very weak inverse relationship for females ($r = -.32$, $p < .1$, $N = 33$). However, if real, this

TABLE 21.3 Stature Estimates by Stratigraphic Levels[a]

Level	Male Mean	Male S.D.	Male N	Female Mean	Female S.D.	Female N
#200	168.9	4.02	6	156.9	3.11	3
#300	166.5	3.62	9	154.5	5.98	7
#400-500	164.7	5.01	6	151.9	3.09	4

[a]Estimated from lower limb bones by Genoves's formula; see text.

slight selective differential would explain sexual dimorphism as a consequence of improved survival of more gracile females.

Stature

There is no change in sexual dimorphism for stature either (Table 21.3).

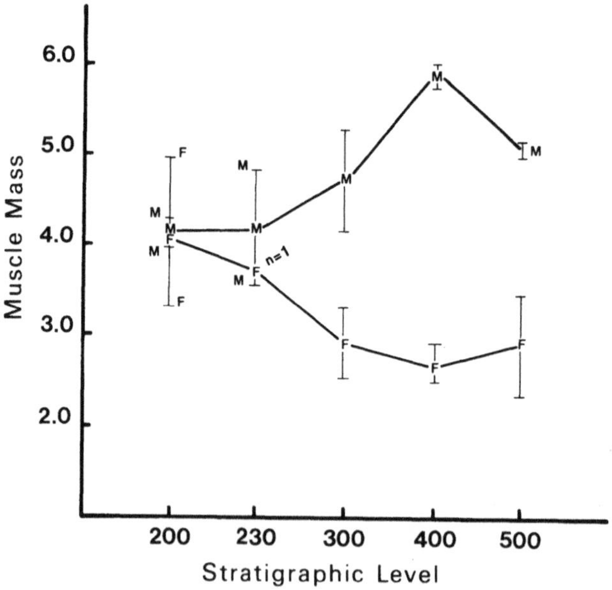

FIGURE 21.2. Total muscle mass (sum of upper and lower muscle masses, each judged on a 1-4 scale; 1, gracile, 4, rugose; vertical lines equal one standard deviation in total length). Average by levels for male and female adults.

Bony Response to Musculature

Figure 21.2 presents the results for specimens coded on a four-point scale indicating bony response to musculature (Brock, personal communication). As can be clearly seen, sexual dimorphism declines noticeably. These results substantiate trends noticed by Page (1974) and Scott (1974). It is plausible to suggest that the earliest inhabitants of Paloma were foragers with very different roles for males and females; as the number of species and the number of niches exploited increased, role division lessened. The obvious alternative explanation, that males decreased in muscle mass due to dietary stresses that affect males more severely than better-buffered females, is contradicted by other data presented here that suggest steadily improving diet and general health.

It should be noted that these data partly contradict my earlier observations and those of Brock (Benfer 1981), that the bones of the earlier inhabitants were the most rugose--this is true for the males only. With respect to sexual division of labor, one clear distinction is the amount of swimming. Sharon Brock has noticed significantly increased amounts of reaction areas on male femora (possibly due to swimming [L. Furbee, personal communication]), as well as frequent auditory osteomas, restricted entirely to males (Benfer 1981).

In sum, skeletal size indicators such as stature and diameter of the head of the femur do not support changes in sexual dimorphism, although over a longer time period, Page observed such changes. Scott found very dramatic reduction in sexual dimorphism in her analysis of a masticatory factor. Here, muscle mass of the postcranial skeleton supports Scott's findings--sexual dimorphism was decreasing between 8000 and 4500 years ago.

STATURE

Theory predicts that stature will decrease in mean size and variance, within lines (Falconer 1960), which we suggested might occur (Benfer et al. 1975) if Ericksen's (1962) hypothesis were correct that there were a breakdown of coastal village breeding isolation after the beginnings of agriculture. We also predicted stature in the tall range due to access to marine protein. It follows that if adaptation was taking place, stature also should have increased as a measure of health (see Nickens 1976).

Results

Table 21.3 presents the mean stature and standard deviations for only specimens with complete lengths of tibia or femora, as estimated by the stature formulas of Genoves as programmed in

Maples's forensic package for the Apple computer (Maples 1981). In order to distinguish the predictions of decreased inbreeding depression from improving diet and health, we must examine the variances. There are no significant differences in variance among levels within sex by Cochren's test. However, variance in stature is greater in the earlier levels among males, although smallest in the earlier levels in females. If the Palomans started as an isolated group, stature variation does not provide evidence of gene flow diluting this isolation.

There is a significant increase in stature through time ($F = 3.43$ with 2 df, $p < .05$, two-way analysis of variance, table not presented). Paloman materials average 3-9 cm shorter than later materials studied by Allison, who used Trotter and Gleser's formulas (Allison, Chapter 20 this volume).

HARRIS LINES

Gehlert (1978) has examined a small sample of 18 tibiae available as of 1976 (a larger sample of 78 is currently under study). Gehlert found that adult males averaged 2.9 and females 2.1 lines/individual; only one specimen lacked lines. Gehlert noted that Paloma demonstrated more lines than all but the Nazca group reported by Allison et al. (1974). Paloma averages 2.8 lines for those with lines, suggesting considerable stress in the preceramic period. Indeed, Gehlert concluded that Palomans were experiencing a great deal of childhood stress.

Harris lines are probably a good indicator of childhood stress in this sample. Significant negative correlations are obtained between tibial length and number of lines for both males ($r = -.65$, $p < .02$) and females ($r = -.48$, $p < .05$). The correlation of number of lines with age at death is positive, as has been reported for other populations, but is not significantly different from zero ($r = .37$, $p > .10$).

Organization of Gehlert's data by stratigraphic zones results in a reduction from an average of 1.1 in levels 500 and 400, to .81 in level 300, to .46 in level 200. These differences are suggestive of reduced childhood stress (Benfer 1981); however, the samples are too small for such comparisons when divided by sex--and males do average slightly more lines than females. Therefore, evaluation of the results of the Harris line data must await completion of study of the sample of 55 additional tibiae.

OSTEITIS AND PERIOSTITIS

Periostitis and osteitis are common at Paloma, indicating high frequencies of infections. There is no significant change in these frequencies by stratigraphic level, where osteitis varies between 10 and 16% and periostitis between 22 and 25%.

HISTOMORPHOMETRICS

Jackson has studied the histomorphometrics of a small sample of 22 rib specimens (Jackson 1981). Comparative studies utilizing these data have also been completed (Stout 1983). Histomorphometrics of a sample of femora and tibiae at Paloma are in progress in Stout's laboratory. Jackson found that none of the five possibly osteopenic specimens, judged by gross appearance, included in her sample produced subnormal rates of bone turnover compared to other Palomans except for one individual, a 55-year-old with a below-average turnover rate.

Jackson also pointed to a higher rate of bone turnover in specimens from the earlier levels (400 and 500) than the later levels (200 and 300), especially in the third and fourth decades. These differences are not statistically significant (t = .53) for the samples. Stout (1983) notes that Paloma resembles the Ray and Gibson (Middle Woodland) populations more than the Ledders Late Woodland sample.

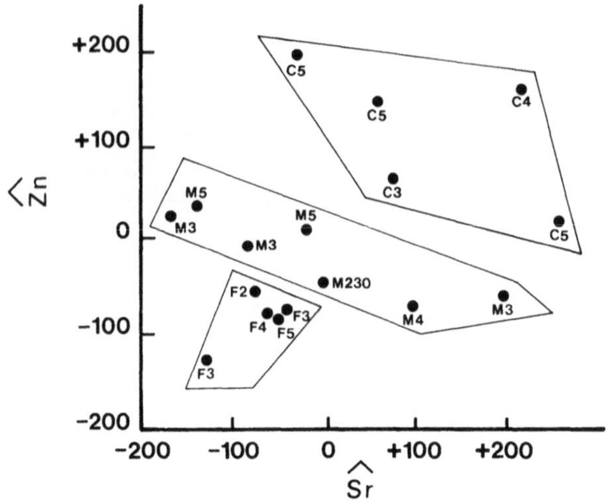

FIGURE 21.3. Strontium and zinc residuals (observed value in ppm minus value predicted from calcium by linear regression). Letters represent sex and age: C, child (less than 7 years); M, male adult; F, female adult. Numbers represent stratigraphic level: 2, #200; 230, #230; 3, #300; 4, #400; 5, #500.

TRACE ELEMENT ANALYSIS OF BONE

Seventeen midshaft sections of femora and 41 samples of soil from the associated tombs have been investigated for trace elements by neutron activation analysis at the Research Reactor of the University of Missouri (Benfer et al. 1981; Benfer 1981). Although 20 elements were considered, only nine were detected reliably in bone in this pilot study: scandium (Sc), chromium (Cr), iron (Fe), cobalt (Co), selenium (Se), zinc (Zn), rubidium (Rb), and strontium (Sr), as well as calcium (Ca), not a trace element. A sample of 35 additional femora plus several camelid bones and teeth (but not bones) of *Carnivora* are under study.

Results

I will present results of analyses for only three elements, zinc, strontium, and calcium. The first two are both important elements due to their behavior in food chains (Edward 1981; Sillen and Kavanagh, 1982). Figure 21.3 presents the results of analyses for calcium, strontium, and zinc. Soil results will not be presented here; we found no correlation between soil concentration and bone concentration of strontium and a low correlation of soil zinc with that of bone ($r = .46$, $.10 > p > .05$). We found no significant relationship between adjacent soil sample and bone sample. Adult females are lower in the levels of both zinc (Zn/Ca × 100; $t = 3.11$ with 10 df, $p < .02$) and strontium (not significantly) than are adult males. Lambert et al. (1979) reported no differences in these elements by sex for the Gibson Middle Woodland site, but similar differences in the Ledders Late Woodland site. These authors argue that increased consumption of carbohydrates in the Late Woodland may have been measured in dietary differences between the sexes. Since Paloma is a sedentary village with considerable evidence of increased carbohydrate availability over earlier hunter-collectors, perhaps the same pattern is present. When the large sample of 35 femora can be added, differences among stratigraphic levels will be evaluated with this hypothesis in mind.

I had reported earlier that strontium was less variable among females than males (Benfer 1981)--for Sr/Ca × 100 ratios, the variance of males (.238) is much greater than that of females (.019) ($F = 23.53$, $p < .05$ with 6 and 4 df). The variance in Zn/Ca × 100 is nearly identical in males (.14) and females (.13). These samples are quite small, and since other investigators have not reported similar findings (for another coastal example see Edward 1984), they must await confirmation with larger samples. It would not seem that female bone, if more porous, has merely changed toward the surrounding soil values. This did not happen with these specimens when compared with adjacent soil strontium values. In any case, females tend to have lower values than males. The reduced division of labor argued for on other grounds might suggest increased similarity of diet for males and females. The present sample is too small to test this conjecture.

Figure 21.3 presents a plot of zinc versus strontium after adjustment for calcium. The values presented are the residuals after linear regression with calcium; a similar plot can be obtained using the ratio of calcium to the two elements, but the picture is less clear. Calcium and zinc show a significant correlation ($r = .64$, $p < .01$) but not calcium and strontium ($r = .34$, $p > .05$). Ratios should not be used to adjust values unless the correlations, as well as the variances, are similar, since simple ratios will not in general remove a correlation between the numerator and denominator (see Atchley et al. 1976). From Figure 21.3 it is apparent that male and female adults and children can be distinguished, suggesting the possible utility of this method in demographic studies. The elevated values for infants could be due to their lower protein intake on a diet of mother's milk, the lesser resistance of their remains to contamination, or both. Edward (1981) found no such clustering by sex. However, the male adults do show consistently higher levels of zinc, perhaps as a result of greater access to land mammals, such as camelids and deer. The strontium levels may be less informative due to elevation in levels due to shellfish eating (Schoeninger and Peebles 1981; also seen Sillen and Kavanagh 1982). However, an interesting finding is that while age at death of adults is not correlated with levels of zinc, age at death has a strong positive relationship with strontium levels, whether measured as a ratio to calcium or as the residual predicted from calcium (r = .69 in the first case, .67 in the second; either is significant [p < .02, with 10 df]). Since these results are at variance with modern data for age classes (Sillen and Kavanagh 1982), one wonders if perhaps older people accumulate more strontium with a high fish and shellfish component to their diet. This suggestion is very speculative, or course, but it should be remembered that in arid preceramic coastal Peru, fish are common and vegetables are not.

TRACE ELEMENT ANALYSIS OF HAIR

Hair is a minor excretory organ, originally investigated for trace element variation for forensic and ^{90}Sr concentration in the 1950s. This work showed that hair reflects, to some extent, body intake, and might be useful for evaluating the body's store of minerals. Blood and urine, by comparison, reflect very temporary conditions. Bone monitors much longer periods. Hair potentially detects mineral changes over the months preceding death (Benfer et al. 1978; Graf 1978).

Results

Cluster analysis of 25 samples from Paloma, Chilca I, and three modern control specimens by 12 elements (Cr, Ca, magnesium [Mg], Zn, copper [Cu], Fe, lead [Pb], cadmium [Cd], manganese [Mn], sodium [Na], potassium [K], and Sr) produced the following results. The Chilca I and modern samples each clustered apart; proximal and distal segments of the same hair clustered together, as did whole hairs not sectioned serially. Reliability is attested to by the fact that multiple hairs from the same individuals also clustered together for both modern control and prehistoric individuals.

Space permits discussion of only a few individual elements. Cadmium did not change over the length of the shaft of the control specimen; however, large proximal-distal fluctuations were detected in the samples from Paloma. Cadmium is very high in salt water Mollusca and Crustacea; it also occurs in deer liver. Perhaps these hairs are monitoring seasonal variation in diet? Cadmium was not detected in soil samples or in bone. But the values for the Paloma hairs are high (1-26 ppm) compared to modern specimens (.3-3 ppm). Excessive cadmium reduces fertility in male rats and slows growth in swine. Is it possible that the shellfish component of the diet may have had a contraceptive effect and account for the evidence for late childbearing age in women? This speculation requires more investigation.

Zinc values were low to normal. Elevated values can indicate kwashiorkor. Chromium approached diabetic values for two specimens, one of which was a 17-year-old, suggesting a high carbohydrate diet (see Wing and Brown 1979:31).

Copper was found to change in our single modern control sample during a period of extreme dietary change. Changes were also detected among proximal, middle, and distal segments of the archaeological specimens. Copper does not vary as a simple function of distance to scalp, that is, to exposure to contaminants, in most modern examples where diet is unchanged. Children maintained too long on mother's milk have elevated levels of copper in hair. Copper levels in hair may also vary with anemia. One other result should be mentioned: strontium in hair was found to be of about the same order of magnitude as in bone, tending to confirm the lack of contamination of bone specimens.

The very small samples analyzed so far suggest the probability of strong seasonal variations in diet that conform to the archaeobotanical analysis of foods present in intestines and coprolites. Further work with a much larger sample, in progress, will be necessary before it is possible to use hair with confidence as a biopsy material (Benfer et al. 1978).

SUMMARY

The results are summarized as follows:

1. Significant differences were observed in age category distributions among stratigraphic levels with later levels exhibiting lower mortality of both the young and the old adults.

2. Microwear studies of dental wear (Moore-Jansen 1982) support a protoagricultural diet.

3. Macrowear studies show that the rate of wear was increasing.

4. With respect to dental asymmetry, Paloma is more asymmetrical than an Inca series, but less asymmetrical than Indian Knoll foragers.

5. No size changes were found in sexual dimorphism, in either stature or the maximum diameter of the head of the femur. However, bony response to musculature showed a regular change toward diminished sexual dimorphism over time.

6. Specimens from the three major stratigraphic divisions increased regularly in stature.

7. Tibial length was found to correlate negatively with the number of Harris lines observed; Harris lines may have decreased in frequency over time.

8. Periostitis and osteitis are frequent and do not change in frequency over time.

9. Histomorphometrics of ribs did not confirm cases of what appear to be osteoporosis.

10. Adult males, females, and children can be readily distinguished at Paloma by analysis of bone for strontium and zinc content. Females are significantly less variable for strontium than are males; age at death increases with increased concentrations of strontium, but not zinc.

11. In human hair, cadmium varied serially along the shafts of hairs, suggesting seasonal variation in shellfish eating. Copper also varied, perhaps due to seasonal shifts in diet and/or transhumanace.

12. The effects of inbreeding/gene flow may confound interpretation; this subject requires additional study for its impact on paleopathological studies.

CONCLUSIONS: DEMOGRAPHY, DIET, AND PALEOPATHOLOGY

The indicators of health and diet on the bones and teeth support the paleodemographic evidence: Early inhabitants of Paloma were stressed, but subsequent generations showed steady improvement in adaptation to the lower western slopes of the Andes. Demography suggests steady improvements in health. Stature and other indicators may provide clues as to their nature. The negative correlation of tibial length with Harris lines, which decrease over time as stature increases, suggest growth is probably increasing due to a reduced number of famine periods, perhaps due to better preservation, storage, and exploitation of alternative food sources rather than a general increase in the adequacy of diet (which was ordinarily abundant in protein and calories), or sanitation.

The seemingly rich and varied diet of Palomans, consisting of sea and land mammals, fish and shellfish, and wild and potentially or actually domesticated plants (Reitz 1983, 1984; Weir and Dering 1984) would lead one to predict excellent health in the arid environment. However, occasional failures of the heavy fogs could have led to periods of great stress. El Niño disruptions of the fishing cycle probably would have been less damaging, because considerable fish would still be available near the shore. Torrential rains might have been destructive but allowed exceptional blooming of the fog oases for some years afterward. Thus adaptations to shortages and radically changing resources were essential.

Adaptation to Food Production

At Paloma, as in other early sites, there is evidence of prolonged experimentation with potential or actual cultigens as an important component of diets. It was not until Paloma was abandoned that we find evidence of early water management (Benfer

1983a; Benfer et al. 1983). The adjustments of Paloma were not studied before and after agriculture, the usual design adopted of necessity. Rather, these adjustments were observed during the centuries plants (and possibly animals) were shaped for domestication in this habitat. Adjustments were strong enough to be detected by paleodemography and skeletal and dental indicators of health and diet. What was their nature?

Presumably, adjustment to sedentism, whether dependent on actual cultigens or not, is not quickly accomplished. The advantages of sedentism, such as food storage possibilities, reduced stress on infants from travel, and intimate knowledge of local resources, are offset somewhat by increased parasite loads from fecal contamination and probably by increases in infectious diseases. Although warfare and competition for better settings might be predicted to occur, there is no evidence of such violence at Paloma. If sedentism is complete, and the option of migration becomes unavailable, occasional periods of resource failure become extremely stressful.

The data presented here argue for the proposition that the early inhabitants were more stressed than the later ones. It is reasonable to assume that the first inhabitants retained greater mobility, so that they may have suffered at times from the stresses of mobility as well as the stresses of sedentism. Living in the nearby Chilca Valley in the summer when it has water (either running or in shallow wells) and in the fog oasis of Paloma in the winter (when it blooms and generates water and plants) would be possible for a fairly large group in this arid stretch of the coast. Radiometric dates from the Chilca I valley site (Engel 1966), less than 9 km away, completely overlap those of Paloma. Mortuary practices are nearly identical (Q. F. M. Viallejos A., personal communication). Detailed comparative studies are required to test this proposition.

The degradation of the *lomas*, which increased gradually as monitored by twig diameter and reduction of suitable species of bushes used for firewood (Weir and Dering 1984), may have pushed the Palomans toward more intensive use of marine resources at the beach 3.5 km from Paloma, as well as more intensive management of water for cultivation in the Chilca Valley.

Such a picture of why Paloma and other alluvial fan fog oasis sites were abandoned in favor of riverine sites does not explain the steadily improving health of the people. Could health have improved at the same time that people were forced to intensify their exploitation of both marine and cultivated plant resources? The answer could be yes if these methods resulted in surpluses of intensively exploited species that could be stored against the occasional failures of the fog or the river, or against changes in the marine species availability, all of which are predictable consequences of the cyclical failure of the Peruvian Current, or upwelling.

The Paloma case illuminates the questions that relate to studies of adaptation to sedentism and food production. Skeletal, dental, and soft-tissue indicators of sex, age, and morbidity provide significant data for these questions. But their utility may vary with the design of the research. Many studies of adaptation to food production employ a "before and after" research design, studying samples from before and after food production was adopted. Also, usually of necessity, samples from a number of archaeological sites often must be combined. There is merit to such approaches, since they average out idiosyncracies of material from different sites, and since they may find strong differences before and after food production. The advantage of study of a single site, occupied over a long period when cultigens were probably an important but not predominant component of the diet, is that many confounding variables are held constant, or are more likely to be held constant.

Paleodemographic studies, of whatever kind of design, are inevitably expensive, since they require large samples. Results presented here suggest that paleopathological indicators, which in general do not require such large samples, may be just as useful, since findings from their study so closely parallel the results of the paleodemographic analysis.

Until the various indicators now in use are perfected, a multidimensional study always must be preferred; unless the bulk of the indicators agree, it is clear that the study will be confounded. However, results presented in this chapter and others in this volume suggest that many of these indicators are more reliable than we might have thought. Taken together, results from the Paloma Project are in remarkable agreement, and seem to describe gradual improvement in life for very early villagers in coastal Peru.

ACKNOWLEDGMENTS

The Instituto Nacional de Cultura of Peru made this work possible by granting me excavation permits, permission to export samples, and extending much-needed help--Hugo Ludeña R. was especially supportive. The National Science Foundation provided major funds for the work (NSF BNF76 12316, NSF BNS78 07727a/b, and NSF BNS-81053940a/b). Additional important funding came from the University of Missouri Research Council and the Swiss Terres Arides Foundation. The Centro de Investigaciones de las Zonas Arides of the Universidad Nacional de Agraria provided laboratories, colleagues, technical assistance, and friends.

Glendon H. Weir, Frederic-Andre Engel, and Alice N. Benfer have been co-investigators; the Paloma Project is largely the sum of their efforts. Another 15 participant investigators and as many student-investigators have invested heavily of their talent, time, and enthusiasm. The results reported here are especially due to the energy and brilliance of a number of graduate students in physical anthropology--especially Sharon Brock, Sarah J. Gehlert, Barbara M. Jackson, and Daniel S. Edwards. Without the participation of these and other students, the project would not have achieved its goals.

The work of some participants is mentioned in this paper--but their credit deserves more space than is available here. This manuscript has been improved by helpful comments from Glen Weir, Louanna Furbee, James A. Gavan, and Mark Cohen.

APPENDIX

Space does not permit a full discussion of the stratigraphic evidence. Table 21.A1 presents all the radiometric determinations available for the site. The results indicate exceptional stratification for a preceramic site. Later reoccupation was confined to one small area. No animals, other than insects, had disturbed the site. No recent pothunters had bothered a preceramic site. However, living activities of the inhabitants, the construction of habitations, storage pits, burials, and the growth of middens naturally disturbed the stratigraphy somewhat. See Engel (1980) for a review of the stratigraphy as it was known up to 1976. Currently the Peruvian archaeologist, Bernardino Ojeda (see Ojeda, 1982), and the 1976 field season director, John W. Greer, and I, are working toward producing a final analysis of the stratigraphy based on the excavations of 1973, 1975, 1976, 1979, and 1982.

REFERENCES

Allison, M. J., and E. Gerszten
1982 *Paleopathology in South American Mummies: Application of Modern Techniques*. Virginia Commonwealth University, Richmond.

Allison, M. J., D. Mendoza, and A. Pezzia
1974 A radiographic approach to childhood illness in Pre-Columbian inhabitants of southern Peru. *American Journal of Physical Anthropology 40*:409-415.

Angel, J. L.
1971 *The People of Lerna*. Smithsonian Institution Press, Washington, D.C.

Antúnez de Mayolo R., Santiago E.
1981 *La Nutricion en el Antiguo Peru*. Banco Central de Reserva del Peru, Lima.

Atchley, W. R., C. T. Gaskings, and D. Anderson
1976 Statistical properties of ratios. I. Empirical results. *Systematic Zoology 25*:137-148.

TABLE 21.A1 Radiocarbon Determinations: Archaic Site of Paloma, Chilca Valley, Peru (12B-VII-613)

Number	Provience	Material	Laboratory	Submitted by	Radiocarbon years	Stratigraphic Level	Notes
1.	N85 E120 H136 UNIT I	Bone, skin of dog	UGa 4207	UMC	1830 ± 85	#230	Intrusive dog, maize
2.	N80 E120 H137 UNIT I	Burned cane	UGa 4206	UMC	4780 ± 100	#220	
3.	General level	Fish bones	Birm-515	CIZA	4900 ± 130	#200	Level not subdivided
4.	N180 E0 Unnumbered house, PROBABILITY SAMPLE	Wood	UGa 4118	UMC	5000 ± 200	#230	See footnote 1
5.	N80 E115 H13 UNIT I	Gynerium	UGa 4120	UMC	5020 ± 85	#400	Bad date; UGa 4211 from same house gives anticipated date
6.	N215 W10 CIZA test	Wood	UGa 4205	UMC	5055 ± 85	#230	
7.	N95 E130 T83 UNIT I	Grass/cane	UGa 4210	UMC	5110 ± 125	#300	
8.	N75 E120 UNIT I	Compositae	UGa 4119 UGa 4120	UMC	5210 ± 85	#300	Mean of split sample (4119 = 5, 400 ± 75; 4120 = 5, 020 ± 85)
9.	N75 E95 H42 UNIT I	Wood	UGa 4208	UMC	5435 ± 110	#400	

10.	N85 E120 H136 UNIT I	Compositae	UGa 4117	UMC	5535 ± 95	#400	
11.	N105 E65 H101 UNIT I	Burned cane	UGa 4121	UMC	5636 ± 360	#230/300?	Ojeda-#300; Benfer--#230; probably #300, but standard error high
12.	N80 E115 H13 UNIT I	Tilandsia	UGa 4211	UMC	6000 ± 150	#400	
13.	N100 E115 H29 T12 UNIT I	Vegetable	Ny-242	CIZA	6030 ± 180	#400	
14.	N90 E40 Quebrada test trench	Burnt twigs	UGa 4204	UMC	6165 ± 810	#300/400?	Standard error too high
15.	N90 E45 T1 CIZA test	Human feces	I-3126	CIZA	6310 ± 340	#400	
16.	N50 E115 H22 UNIT I	Charcoal	Birm-516	CIZA	6410 ± 140	#400	Submitted incorrectly as #300; #400 in Fig. 16 in Engel (1980)
17.	N95 E115 T11 H11 Unit I	Cordage	Ny-243	CIZA	6510 ± 180	#500	
18.	N105 E115 H103 F252 UNIT I	Wood	UGa 3892	UMC	7735 ± 100	#600	Submitted as #700
19.	N120 E65	Charcoal	UGa 4212	UMC	9895 ± 4380	#300	Standard error is too large

[a] #300 was assigned by P. Dering, who in his field notes wrote that he used levels merely as an ordering device, that his levels did not necessarily correspond to those in UNIT I. In 1982, it was necessary to reexamine the probability squares. Accordingly, I asked B. Ojeda to recheck this square, without informing him of the radiocarbon determination. His profile shows the house as level #230, with which I concur, and which Dering also considered.

Benfer, R. A.
1968 *An Analysis of a Prehistoric Skeletal Population, Casas Grandes, Mexico.* Unpublished Ph.D. dissertation, Department of Anthropology, University of Texas, Austin.
1976 Morphometric analysis of cartesian coordinates of the human skull. *American Journal of Physical Anthropology 42*: 371-382.
1981 Adaptation to sedentism and food production: The Paloma Project, II. *Paleopathology Newsletter 37*:6-8.
1983 Preceramic fields in the lower Chilca Valley. Paper presented to the Conference on Andean and Amazonian Archaeology and Ethnohistory, Bloomington, Indiana.
1984a Holocene coastal adaptations. In *Andean Archaeology*, edited by R. Matos M. *University of California Monographs in Archaeology*, in press.
1984b El Proyecto Paloma de la Universidad de Missouri y el Centro de Investigaciones de Zonas Aridas. *Zonas Aridas*, in press.

Benfer, R. A., Frederic Engel, and Alice N. Benfer
1975 The people of Paloma: A prefarming village from coastal Peru. Research proposal submitted to the National Science Foundation; see also report to the National Science Foundation submitted as appendix A to 1978 research proposal "Human-Environment Interactions in Arid Coastal Peru."

Benfer, R. A., J. W. Typpo, V. B. Graff, and E. E. Pickett
1978 Mineral analysis of ancient Peruvian hair. *American Journal of Physical Anthropology 48*:277-282.

Benfer, R. A., J. A. Vogt, and S. Schlagel
1981 Instrumental neutron activation analysis of ancient Peruvian bone: The effects of soil, strata, demography, diet, and disease. Paper presented to Symposium on Biogeochemistry in Archaeology, Society for American Archaeology and Society of Archaeological Science Meetings, San Diego.

Benfer, R. A., G. F. Weir, and B. Ojeda E.
1983 Water management in preceramic coastal Peru. Paper presented to the International Congress of Anthropological and Ethnological Sciences, Vancouver, Canada, 1983.

Bennett, K. A.
1969 The typological versus the evolutionary approach in skeletal population studies. *American Journal of Physical Anthropology 30*:407-414.

Brace, C. L., and P. E. Mahler
1971 Post-Pleistocene changes in the human dentition. *American Journal of Physical Anthropology 34*:191-204.

Cohen, N. M.
1975 Population pressure and the origins of agriculture: An archaeological example from the coast of Peru. In *Population, Ecology, and Social Evolution*, edited by S. Polgar, pp. 167-190. Mouton, The Hague.

1981 Comment on research and development in the Stone Age: Technological transitions among Hunter-Gatherers, by Brian Hayden. *Current Anthropology* *22*:532.

Dering, P., and G. H. Weir
1979 Analysis of plant remains from the Preceramic site of Paloma, Peru. In Report to the National Science Foundation, pp. A67-A76.

Edward, J.
1984 *Analysis by neutron activation of human bone from the Hellenistic cemetery in Asine, Greece. Journal of Field Archaeology 11*:37-46.

Edwards, D. S.
1984 Dental attrition and subsistence of the Preceramic site of Paloma, Peru. Unpublished M.A. thesis, Department of Anthropology, University of Missouri, Columbia.

Engel, Frederic-Andre
1966 *Geografia Human Prehistorica y Agricultura Precolombina de la Quebrada de Chilca.* Universidad Nacional de Agraria, Lima, Peru.
1980 Paloma: Village 613. In *Prehistoric Andean Ecology*, edited by Frederic-Andre Engel, pp. 103-135. Humanities Press, New York.

Ericksen, M. F.
1962 Undeformed Pre-Columbian crania from the North Sierra of Peru. *American Journal of Physical Anthropology 20*:209-222.

Falconer, D. S.
1960 *Introduction to Quantitative Genetics.* Ronald Press, New York.

Gehlert, S. J.
1978 Harris lines of Paloman tibia. In Report to the National Science Foundation, pp. A185-A189.
1979 *Dental asymmetry in two Peruvian archaeological samples.* Unpublished M.A. paper, Department of Anthropology, University of Missouri, Columbia.

Graf, V. B.
1978 *Trace element levels in human hair at childbirth.* Unpublished M.A. thesis, Department of Human Nutrition, University of Missouri, Columbia.

Hayden, B.
1981 Research and development in the Stone Age: Technological transitions among hunter-gatherers. *Current Anthropology 22*:519-531.

Jackson, B.
1981 Histomorphometric analysis of ribs from three archaeological populations. Unpublished M.A. thesis, Department of Anthropology, University of Missouri, Columbia.

Lambert, J. G., C. B. Zpuznar, and J. E. Buikstra
1979 Chemical analyses of excavated human bone from Middle and Late Woodland sites. *Archaeometry 21*:115-129.

Lanning, E. P.
1967 *Peru before the Incas.* Prentice-Hall, Englewood Cliffs, New Jersey.

Lovejoy, C. O., R. S. Meindl, T. R. Pryzbeck, T. S. Barton, K. G. Heiple, and D. Knotting
1977 Paleodemography of the Libben site, Ottaw County, Ohio. *Science 198*:291-293.

MacNeish, R. S., T. S. Patterson, and D. L. Browman
1975 The central Peruvian prehistoric interaction sphere. *Papers of the Robert S. Peabody Foundation for Archaeology* Vol. 7.

Maples, W. R.
1981 Bones and teeth: A program for forensic anthropology (revised version). Available from author, Florida State Museum, Gainesville.

Moore-Jansen, P. H.
1982 *Observations of human dental enamel using light and scanning electron microscopy as means for dietary reconstruction in prehistoric populations.* Unpublished M.A. thesis, Department of Anthropology, University of Arkansas.

Moseley, M. E.
1975 *The Maritime Foundations of Andean Civilization.* Cummings, Menlo Park, California.

Nickens, Paul R.
1976 Stature reduction as an adaptive response to food production in Mesoamerica. *Journal of Archaeological Science 3*:31-41.

Ojeda, E. B.
1982 Informe de la estratigraphia del sitio de la Paloma. Ms. on file, Paloma Project files, Department of Anthropology, University of Missouri-Columbia, Columbia, Missouri.

Osborne, A. J.
1977 Strandloopers, mermaids, and other fairy tales: Ecological determinants of marine resource utilization--the Peruvian case. In *For Theory Building in Archaeology*, edited by L. R. Binford, pp. 157-206. Academic Press, New York.

Page, J. W.
1974 *Human Evolution in Peru: 9,000-1,000 B.P.* Unpublished Ph.D. dissertation, Department of Anthropology, University of Missouri, Columbia.

Patterson, R. C.
1971 The emergence of food production in central Peru. In *Prehistoric Agriculture*, edited by S. Struever, pp. 181-207. Natural History Press, New York.

Quilter, J.
1979 *Paloma: Mortuary practices and social organization of a Preceramic Peruvian village.* Unpublished Ph.D. disserta-

tion, Department of Anthropology, University of California, Santa Barbara.

Raymond, J. S.
1981 The maritime foundations of Andean civilization: A reconsideration of the evidence. *American Antiquity 46*:806-821.

Reitz, E. J.
1983 Vertebrate Fauna from Paloma, Peru, 12B-VII-613. Manuscript of the Paloma Project, Department of Anthropology, University of Missouri-Columbia, Columbia, Missouri.
1984 Informe preliminario sobre La Paloma. Appendix in El Proyecto Paloma de la Universidad de Missouri y El Centro de Investigaciones de Zonas Aridas. *Zonas Aridas*, in press.

Rostworowski de Diez Canseco, M.
1981 *Recursos naturales renovables y pesca, siglos XVI y XVII.* Instituto de Estudios Peruanos, Lima, Peru.

Schoeninger, M. J., and C. S. Peebles
1981 Effect of mollusc eating on human bone strontium levels. *Journal of Archaeological Science 8*:391-397.

Schreider, E.
1967 Body-height and inbreeding in France. *American Journal of Physical Anthropology 26*:1-4.

Scott, E. C.
1974 *Dental variation in Precolumbian coastal Peru.* Unpublished Ph.D. dissertation, Department of Anthropology, University of Missouri, Columbia.
1979 Principal axis analysis of dental attrition. *American Journal of Physical Anthropology 51*:203-212.

Sillen, A., and M. Kavanagh
1982 Strontium and paleodietary research: A review. *Yearbook of Physical Anthropology 25*:67-90.

Stout, S.
1983 The comparative cortical bone histomorphometrics of several ancient human populations. *ANTHROPOS*, in press.

Torres, G., J., and C. López Ocaña
1981 Productividad primaria en las lomas de la Costa Central del Peru. *Boletin de Lima 14*:2-11.

Ubelacker, D. A.
1981 Human skeletal remains from site OGSE-80, a Preceramic site of Sta. Elna Peninsula, coastal Ecuador. *Journal of Washington Academy of Science 70*:3-24.

Vehik, S. C.
1978 Climate, population, subsistence, and the central Peruvian Lomas between 8,000 and 2,500 B.P. Appendix in Report to the National Science Foundation, pp. A112-A136.

Weaver, D. S.
1980 Sex differences in the ilia of a known sex and age sample of fetal and infant skeletons. *American Journal of Physical Anthropology 52*:191-195.

Weir, G. H.
1978 Preliminary fossil pollen and macrofossil analyses of coprolites and sediments from the La Paloma Village site (12b-VII-613) area, Chilca Valley Drainage, Peru. In Report to the National Science Foundation, pp. A138-A182.

Weir, G. H., and J. P. Dering
1984 The Lomas of Paloma: Human-environment relations in a central Peruvian fog oasis--Archaeobotany and palynology. In *Andean Archaeology*, edited by R. Matos M. *University of California Monographs in Archaeology*, in press.

Willey, G. R.
1971 *An Introduction to American Archaeology* (Vol. II). Prentice-Hall, Englewood Cliffs, New Jersey.

Wilson, D. J.
1981 Of maize and men: A critique of the maritime hypothesis of state origins on the coast of Peru. *American Anthropologist 83*:93-120.

Wing, E. S., and A. B. Brown
1979 *Paleonutrition: Methods and theory in prehistoric foodways*. Academic Press, New York.

CHAPTER 22

POPULATION, HEALTH, AND THE EVOLUTION OF SUBSISTENCE: CONCLUSIONS FROM THE CONFERENCE

Anna Curtenius Roosevelt

Museum of the American Indian
New York, New York

INTRODUCTION

The evolutionary history of human ecology has become a subject of broad theoretical interest. Historians, economists, demographers, biologists, and anthropologists have speculated extensively about the causes and consequences of changes in early human population, subsistence, and health, despite the fact that there has been little detailed evidence with which to evaluate their theories. In the last few decades, however, techniques to collect and analyze relevant archaeological data have improved. Studies of settlement patterns, archaeological food remains, and human osteology have begun to create a considerable body of relevant data. In order to bring some of this new evidence together and review its theoretical significance, Mark Cohen and George Armelagos organized a Wenner-Gren-funded conference in Plattsburgh, New York, in March of 1982. At that conference, physical anthropologists specializing in different world regions summarized their sequences. Their findings, which are published in this book, are significant for evaluating theories of cultural ecological evolution.

BOSERUP'S POPULATION PRESSURE THEORY

One of the major theories about the causes and consequences of economic change is the population pressure theory. The best-known early statement of this theory is Ester Boserup's short book *The Conditions of Agricultural Growth: The Economics of Agrarian*

Change under Population Pressure, published in 1965. Boserup attributes the development of intensive agriculture to the impetus given by population pressure on subsistence resources. According to the theory, a growing population puts pressure on its food sources and, in response, people step up labor inputs to produce more food per unit of land. The increasingly intensive land use is supposed to lead to a drop in labor productivity due to declining soil fertility, which in turn leads to the use of methods such as plowing and fertilization to increase productivity. Boserup argues that agricultural intensification would not have occurred without the stimulus of population pressure, because of its greater labor costs. She reasoned that stable populations would follow the principle of least effort and choose less extensive subsistence systems with higher labor productivity. Boserup did not explain why some populations might grow and others might not, but denied that environmental differences in agricultural potential were responsible.

POPULATION PRESSURE AND THE RISE OF AGRICULTURE

Mark Cohen has applied Boserup's population pressure theory to human prehistory in the book *The Food Crisis in Prehistory: Overpopulation and the Origins of Agriculture* (1977). Cohen and other scholars, such as Marvin Harris (1977), believe that human population growth is a more general phenomenon than supposed by Boserup and that it has occurred frequently throughout human history. According to this version of the population pressure theory, cultural subsistence systems will continually evolve toward higher and higher carrying capacity in order to accommodate recurrent population growth. Cohen points out that by late Pleistocene times, growing populations of *Homo sapiens* has spread over much of the earth and could have begun to put pressure on local food resources. Cohen believes that increasingly intensive resource use and human selection of resources to increase food supplies led to the development of agriculture in the early Holocene.

According to Cohen, the earliest subsistence economies of modern humans would have been focused on abundant game species that afforded palatable, easily available foods in convenient packages. He feels that as populations grew and put pressure on food resources, people would have expanded their subsistence to include less favored foods of greater abundance, such as plant products, invertebrates, and aquatic faunas, a process that has been called "the Broad-Spectrum revolution" (Flannery 1969, 1973). Ecological logic suggests that higher carrying capacity subsistence systems will emphasize species with "r" reproductive strategies, which are highly productive in calories per hectare, and concurrently will deemphasize "K" selected food sources which, although more balanced nutritionally, are lower in productivity per hectare. Plants, in particular, being low in the trophic pyramid, would have furnished support for larger numbers of people than game and would have been more storable in most climates than flesh.

Cohen envisions the development of agriculture as the result of intensified exploitation of the more productive plant species, some of which changed genetically in the process, as Flannery (1969, 1973) has pointed out, eliciting further selection by humans for greater caloric value, storability, and productivity. This process of positive feedback is supposed to have led to agriculture as subsistence systems came to rely more and more on the plants with the greatest capability for intensive harvesting.

Systems that focus on a few productive, highly caloric plant species, although able to support more people per hectare, are inherently less stable and less favorable nutritionally than more broadly based ones and would be more subject to periodic failures. Cohen argues that such systems would not have developed in the absence of population pressure. He points out that this theory predicts not only a characteristic history of subsistence economy but also a particular history of health. Early hunter-gatherers would be relatively well nourished and free of disease. The buildup of population pressure among later hunter-gatherers would have led to a phase of poorer nutrition and greater susceptibility to disease. The theory also predicts, although Cohen does not actually say so, that the instability and nutritional poverty of intensive, focal subsistence systems would create a pattern of chronic malnutrition and severe periodic famines during later prehistoric times.

ALTERNATIVE THEORIES

The logic of the population pressure theory has been challenged by a varied group of competing theories, which have contrasting predictions for the archaeological record (Asch et al. 1972; Binford 1968; Bronson 1975; Earle and Christenson 1980; Flannery 1969, 1973; Ford 1977; Hassan 1975, 1978, 1981; Hayden 1981; Jochim 1976). It is argued that population pressure could not have been an important causal factor in the history of subsistence because it has been absent for much of prehistory, due either to limitations on growth through high infant mortality and low adult life expectancy, or to the cultural control of population growth. Many scholars see population growth as a phenomenon restricted to recent times, caused mainly by health improvements brought by the industrial revolution. They argue that, in the absence of population pressure, adaptive evolutionary change in human subsistence is likely to minimize effort and maximize subsistence quality and reliability.

By this argument, successful cultural adaptation is expected to produce small-scale, equilibrium subsistence systems that are increasingly stable, cost effective, and favorable to human health. Contrary evolutionary developments, such as the rise and expansion of agriculture and the growth of population, are attributed to disequilibria caused by environmental fluctuations or changes in social organization. It is assumed that human population size will remain in equilibrium with carrying capacity unless disturbed by factors in the environment.

Several scholars explain the development of agriculture in the early Holocene as the consequence of a period of unusual environmental change. Binford, followed by Flannery, has theorized that favorable environmental changes occurring at the end of the Pleistocene allowed increasing sedentism of settlement in areas of rich, concentrated resources. Sedentary settlement is supposed to have led to a higher birth rate by making it easier for women to stay home to care for closely-spaced children. The resulting population growth put pressure on subsistence resources in neighboring marginal areas, inspiring the intensification of subsistence and the rise of agriculture. Others hypothesize that unfavorable environmental changes made subsistence unstable, and they interpret the rise of agriculture as an attempt to increase the reliability of subsistence (e.g., Ford 1977). They suggest that sociopolitical elites came into being because of the greater management needs of agricultural economies.

These theories might usefully be grouped under the category of "equilibrium" theories, for they stress human subsistence systems as equilibrium-seeking systems. Cultural change is often viewed as occurring to "regulate" the human ecosystem, an approach that Flannery, an early enthusiast, has irreverently called the "Serutan" hypothesis. The approach seems derived ultimately from two sources: traditional structural-functionalist ethnology and equilibrium-oriented systems theory. Cohen (1977) has summarized some of the problems of the equilibrium theories, which overestimate post-Pleistocene climate change and ignore the widespread evidence for hunter-gatherer population growth. These theories also tend to attribute inexplicable goal-seeking behavior to systems as wholes, and they tend to view control by elites as benign, even necessary "regulation" for the benefit of the whole population, despite evidence to the contrary. In addition, despite their rejection of population as a prime causal factor, the equilibrium theorists often build population growth into their explanations without explicitly accounting for its presence and effects.

These theories have somewhat different predictions for the archaeological record than Cohen's, and it is clear that to evaluate the empirical validity of the different theoretical formulations we need longitudinal data about prehistoric and early historic population growth, subsistence, and health. To provide such data, the participants in this conference were asked to summarize the relevant evidence from their regions of study. The regions covered in this review are the West Coast, Southwest, Midwest, and Southeast of the United States, lower Central America, Northwestern South America, Western Europe, the Eastern Mediterranean, East Asia, and South Asia. Because of the importance of population pressure and growth in theoretical arguments, the organizers chose physical anthropologists to summarize the regional data and asked them to present in detail the osteological evidence for demographic patterns and physiological stress, an expected correlate of population pressure.

POPULATION GROWTH AND SEDENTISM

In most of the regions reviewed, regardless of whether agriculture was ever developed, population growth seems to occur throughout the sequence, starting with the earliest occupations. This growth manifests itself in period-by-period increases in the sizes and numbers of known archaeological sites and in the numbers of osteological remains recorded. Although there is always a possibility that the apparent growth is an artifact of a greater destruction rate for earlier remains, the magnitude of the growth and its widespread occurrence seem unarguable evidence for a distinctive, worldwide trend of population expansion.

Knowledge about changes in the numbers and sizes of sites in the different regions is the by-product of decades of general archaeological reconnaissance rather than the product of systematic site surveys, and the numbers of known sites in a region seems to reflect more closely the amount of archaeological work that has been done in a region than the absolute number of sites occupied in prehistoric times. Thus, in order to get comparative information about changing population size from region to region, it will be necessary to carry out planned site surveys. Until that is done, it is difficult to say whether or not there were periods of simultaneous rapid population growth throughout the world at certain times, such as during the rise of agriculture.

In a few regions, such as the Midwest and Southwest in the United States, drops in population size occurred late in prehistoric times, apparently due to environmental changes that decreased the productivity of resources for human subsistence. And in one region, Peru, resource overuse and exogenous environmental change seem to have reduced the carrying capacity for humans over time in some biomes, such as the fog meadows. Such cases, however, are exceptions to the general picture of growth, a finding that supports the view of past human demography espoused by Cohen and Harris. The predictions of the equilibrium view, which include long periods of static population size, are not supported. (Discussion of the demographic processes that caused the growth, whether decreased mortality, increased fertility, or a combination of both, will be found in the section on the paleopathological osteological evidence, where the evidence for health and activity patterns is summarized.)

Contrary to equilibrium theories, there seems to be no deterministic relationship between population growth and sedentism, for population growth occurs throughout the sequence whether or not there was sedentary settlement, and the rate of growth during the Paleolithic and Mesolithic, as best as can be determined, seems independent of permanence of settlement, which varies greatly from one region to another.

ARCHAEOLOGICAL ECONOMY

In order to evaluate the role of population pressure in subsistence change, we need to know in detail how subsistence actually changed in prehistoric times. The predictions of the population pressure theory contrast with the opposing theories in the changes that it envisions in the exploitation of species and consumption of different nutrients. Unfortunately, period-by-period reconstruction of the development of prehistoric subsistence economies has been the most difficult part of this review. And yet this exercise is important for the information it yields about the causes of subsistence change, as Cohen has pointed out. The problem is that, for most of the regions under study, there has been no systematic collection or study of archaeological food remains, especially at sites dating either end of the sequence: the Paleolithic and the late Neolithic[1]. The richly documented sequences of the Midwest and Southwest in the United States, Central Mexico, Panama, Peru, and West Asia are rare exceptions. The small amount of food remains that have been recovered elsewhere were for the most part collected fortuitously during excavations aimed mainly at recovery of artifacts, and these chance finds do not furnish a very good idea of the spectrum of species used for subsistence, not to speak of the quantities in which different foods were eaten. Thus, for many of these regions at present there is little reliable basis for inferring prehistoric subsistence patterns because archaeologists have not purposefully collected food remains.

In systematic sampling for archaeological food remains, it is important to control for different size classes of material. If

[1] *For most writers, the terms Paleolithic, Mesolithic, and Neolithic have come to have a nonchronological, stage-like meaning in terms of subsistence, as follows: Paleolithic--early, extensive hunting-gathering; Mesolithic--late, intensive hunting-gathering and incipient agriculture; and Neolithic--effective subsistence agriculture.*

only large pieces of animal bone are collected, such as those that can be recognized during troweling or shoveling, as is the common method, then the consumption of large animals will be greatly overestimated. At the same time plant consumption will be grossly underestimated since carbonized plant remains are almost impossible to detect and collect by troweling and shoveling alone. In order to collect small, light remains such as seeds, small bones, and fish scales, it is necessary to use soil flotation or dry fine-screening of standard soil measures so that the quantity by weight of the different food remains may be compared. Larger remains are the most easily recovered in the absence of screening and flotation, but these remains often are not the predominant foods in the diet. Payne (1972a,b) has shown through flotation and screening experiments that the smaller, more difficult to retrieve remains often make up the bulk of the food remains, and proper sampling changes dramatically the estimate of the importance of different foods in the diet. Other experiments support this conclusion (Ford 1979; Struever 1968).

Even where food remains have been assiduously collected, there still may be no secure basis from which to infer their proportion in the diet, because food remains often are not preserved in the ground in proportion to their abundance in the diet. Most food is destroyed by being eaten and digested; what remains is often a poor representation of what was eaten, as Buikstra points out (Chapter 9 this volume). In addition, some archaeological foods (such as root crops and delicate fish bones) do not preserve readily, while others (such as nuts, seed crops, and large pieces of animal bone) do, so it can be difficult, if not impossible, to compare dietary importance on the basis of the food remains alone.

To determine levels of consumption, other methods are necessary, such as studies of bone chemistry and of dental caries, calculus, and abrasion. Incidence of gum and tooth disease and damage is often related to diet content and texture and may be used to reconstruct ancient diets. Much has been done to trace levels of carbohydrate consumption through study of calculus and caries, which are clinically associated with the consumption of sticky, carbohydrate-rich food, but there have been few studies that take into consideration microscopic tooth wear (Rose et al., Chapter 15 this volume, is an exception). Chemistry has the potential to reveal levels of food consumption during prehistory through analysis of the element composition of archaeological human bone. This is possible because some elements and their isotopes are incorporated into the body in a determinable relation to the amounts in food. By calculating the amounts of certain elements in ancient human bone and comparing the results with the archaeological food remains, one can sometimes determine what foods were eaten in what quantities (for a brief summary of this field see Wing and Brown 1979).

This procedure works with stable carbon isotopes, which vary in diet and thus in human bone collagen (and possibly in bone mineral also) according to the amounts of dietary carbon derived from different plant groups. In many regions, land food and seafood also contrast strongly in carbon isotope ratios. Tauber (1981), for example, found a shift from high to low $^{13}C/^{12}C$ ratios in ancient Danish skeletons, indicating that the average Mesolithic diet among coastal inhabitants was heavily dependent on seafood, which has a high ratio, whereas the Neolithic diet depended mainly on terrestrial food, which has a low ratio. This conclusion would not have been possible through study of the archaeological food remains, which did not accurately reflect the quantitative changes. As another example, the New World food crop maize contrasts in $^{13}/C^{12}C$ ratio with most other aboriginal foods, making it possible to trace the intensification of this important cereal through the chemical analysis of ancient human bones (Bender et al. 1981; van der Merwe and Vogel 1978; van der Merwe et al. 1981). Some elements occur in contrasting quantities in plant versus animal food. A useful element in this regard is strontium, which is far more abundant in plants than in land animals, making it possible to estimate relative proportions of plant and animal food in a person's diet from chemical analysis of the skeleton and associated animal bones (Brown 1973; Smith et al. Chapter 5, this volume). Such studies are directly relevant to evaluation of the population pressure theory, which predicts changing proportions of animal and plant food in human diets through time.

The fields of archaeobotany, archaeozoology, dental pathology, and bone chemistry are becoming increasingly important in archaeology due to the theoretical importance of questions about quantitative and qualitative diet change. Money to carry out relevant technical studies can be built into grant proposals, and many laboratories will carry out chemical analyses free of charge. In the future these methods can fill many of the gaps and uncertainties in existing knowledge about the history of human subsistence.

SUBSISTENCE CHANGE

Despite the deficiencies of present evidence, the results of the survey carried out in the conference tend to show that, as Cohen predicted, intensification is a much broader phenomenon than the rise of agriculture, occurring among mobile as well as sedentary people, in both agricultural and preagricultural subsistence systems, and in egalitarian, ranked, and state societies. Most regions seem to experience progressive intensification of subsistence exploitation throughout prehistory. During the Upper Paleolithic stage, subsistence seems focused on relatively easily available foods of high nutritional value, such as large herd animals and migratory fish. Some plant foods seem to have been eaten, but they appear not to have been quantitatively important in the diet. Storage of foods appears early in many sequences, even during the Paleolithic, apparently to save seasonal surpluses for consumption during seasons of low productivity.

As hunting and gathering economies evolve during the Mesolithic, subsistence is expanded by exploitation of increasing numbers of species and by increasingly heavy exploitation of the more abundant and productive plant species. The inclusion of significant amounts of plant food in prehistoric diets seems to correlate with increased use of food processing tools, apparently to improve their taste and digestibility. As Cohen suggests, there is an increasing focus through time on a few starchy plants of high productivity and storability. This process of subsistence intensification occurs even in regions where native agriculture never developed. In California, for example, as hunting-gathering populations grew, subsistence changed from an early pattern of reliance on game and varied plant resources to one with increasing emphasis on collection of a few species of starchy seeds and nuts. In the Near East, cereals became the dietary staple even before they were domesticated, and this may prove to have been true in other regions with abundant stands of wild seeds. In most regions, the intensification of plant gathering led to the development of effective agriculture in the Neolithic. Most early Neolithic economies seem to have been mixed economies based mainly on agriculture but supplemented with food from hunting and gathering. Late Neolithic intensive agriculture typically focused on a few productive cereal and legume crops, and, in some areas, on starchy root crops.

This widespread prehistoric intensification of subsistence seems to have produced changes in carrying capacity, whether through exploitation of wild or domestic species, but agricultural intensification had a significantly greater capacity for economic growth and is historically associated with a much greater magnitude of population growth than most hunting-gathering economies. What seems to have happened in many regions is that intensive use of wild plants produced changes in the genetic and physiological characteristics of the plants. These changes in turn elicited increasingly intensive use of the plants, until some species became irrevocably altered from the wild state. Whether or not this happened in a particular region seems to depend partly on the species present (Cohen 1977) and partly on the environmental capacity to support intensive land use. In many regions seeds were important in the intensification effort, and the intensive use of seeds frequently led to agriculture, probably due in part to the reproductive characteristics of the various species. The more successful crops spread rapidly from region to region, but there also is evidence that some species were independently domesticated in more than one region.

Cohen's thesis is also supported by evidence of change in diet content, as can be judged from bone chemistry studies and knowledge of the nutritional characteristics of the changing spectrum of species used in subsistence. As he predicts, evolutionary change in prehistoric subsistence has moved in the direction of higher carrying capacity foods, not toward foods of higher-quality nutrition or greater reliability. Early nonagricultural diets appear to have been high in minerals, protein, vitamins, and trace nutrients, but relatively low in starch. In the development toward agriculture there is a growing emphasis on starchy, highly caloric food of high productivity and storability, changes that are not favorable to nutritional quality but that would have acted to increase carrying capacity, as Cohen's theory suggests.

Comparing developments in prehistoric subsistence with those in population size, we see that the two are definitely correlated in time. As populations have grown, subsistence has increased in carrying capacity. The two processes seem to track one another. The rate of population growth seems to be determined by temporary technoenvironmental limitations on the rate of economic intensification. For example, growth is slow when based on exploitation of wild species but speeds up as domesticated species are developed or diffused. A possible mutually causal relationship is further suggested by the tendency of economic deintensification to follow drastic drops in population size and density, as if the level of intensification were responsive to the level of population. This correlation does not establish causality by itself, but it conforms to the predictions of the population pressure theory.

The sequence appears to refute the suggestion that prehistoric intensification of subsistence occurred only where sedentism fostered population growth, for the intensification process proceeded whether populations were sedentary or not. And contrary to those who suppose that intensification is only a response to the development of stratified social systems, intensification clearly occurs in many diverse social contexts. It is a more general phenomenon than any particular process of social evolution, occurring in some regions long before chiefdoms and states developed. This is not to say that changes in social organization did not interact with the intensification process. It will be clear from the following discussion that, under states, intensification was carried out with less regard for human health than it was in populations independent of elite control. The process of population growth and intensification apparently also had effects on the trajectory of sociopolitical evolution, for it was only in regions with the ecological capacity to support massive population growth through agricultural intensification that the development of bureaucratic states occurred, although chiefdoms came into being in several regions where there was no indigenous system of agriculture.

PALEOPATHOLOGY AND POPULATION PRESSURE

Given that prehistoric population growth and subsistence seem to have interacted basically in concordance with Cohen's version of the population pressure theory, it is crucial to investigate the incidence of population pressure during this time. Without this information, we cannot tell whether population pressure inspired the economic changes or the economic changes merely permitted population growth and arose independently of population pressure.

Until now, it has been a problem to detect the existence of population pressure in archaeological populations. Archaeologists have commonly inferred pressure indirectly, from archaeological evidence of population growth in the form of increases in the sizes and numbers of archaeological sites. This approach is invalid, however, because it ignores the problem of the relationship of population growth to expansion in economy. Although population growth may put pressure on a subsistence system, economic growth may free a population from pressure and allow unfettered population growth for a time. The simple observation that growth has occurred does not identify which process has gone on. In other words, changes in the size of a population may or may not reflect population pressure, since population pressure is defined as an unfavorable imbalance between a population and its means of support, and so far knowledge of the productivity of prehistoric subsistence systems and the size of prehistoric populations is insufficiently precise to tell us whether a given population supported by a given economy in a given region would or would not have put pressure on resources.

Cohen recognized that direct evidence of prehistoric population pressure exists in the data of physical anthropology, although archaeologists generally have not used it. This direct evidence is the paleopathological and demographic data embodied in ancient human skeletons from archaeological sites throughout the world. By recording past survival rates and osteological responses to physiological stress, these skeletons have the potential to provide primary evidence of nutritional stress, an expected result of severe population pressure. Although it is often not possible to determine the causes of bone pathologies, comparative, population-level study of certain kinds of pathologies nevertheless may reveal the frequency and degree of physiological stress as a general phenomenon. Even without knowing exact causes, it is possible to create a history of stress for the population of a given region, and thus to learn how changes in health correlate with changes in population, economy, and social organization.

The population pressure and equilibrium theories have different predictions in this regard. Cohen's theory predicts that physiological stress should be recurrent and persistent, with particularly severe stress possibly occurring during incipient agriculture. In contrast, the equilibrium theory predicts that physiological stress should occur only rarely and that cultural adaptation should increasingly buffer people from stress. In addition, the demographic effects of the change to sedentary settlement are interpreted differently in the different theories, so that most equilibrium theorists expect a decrease in mortality at this time, whereas the population pressure proponents expect an increase. Study of the paleopathological data can shed light on these different interpretations of the evolutionary relationship of human health and economic development, and, in addition, can yield evolutionary socioeconomic information about health differences between individuals within the population.

METHODOLOGY

Among the pathologies considered useful for recording physiological stress are the following: Harris lines, tooth enamel hypoplasias, stature reduction, cortical bone loss, porotic hyperostosis/cribra orbitalia, and bone lesions caused by the infectious diseases (Buikstra and Cook 1981). Each type of pathology yields a slightly different kind of information. Studied together rather than in isolation, they tell more through the complementation of information, as Angel points out (Chapter 3 this volume). A major problem, however, is that of determining whether pathologies are related to nutritional stress or other disease stress (Buikstra, Chapter 9 this volume; Cook, Chapter 10 this volume. Nutrition and disease are integrally and synergistically related with one another, and, while malnutrition can lower an individual's resistance to disease, so also can disease cause malnutrition by increasing the body's need for certain nutrients. Thus, it is possible that pathologies might arise in a skeleton in response to a particular disease and not because of any deficiency in the diet. However, since malnourished people are more subject to disease than well-nourished people, the pathologies still are useful indicators of the degree of nutritional stress. It is commonplace in community health studies to infer nutritional status from general health status, and the use of paleopathological indicators is a parallel usage.

Because the growth rate of the young is considered a useful indicator of the nutritional status of a living population, some of the most useful paleopathological indicators of stress are those that record a suspension of growth during the development of fetuses, infants, and children. Stress in adults is less detectable due to the lessened susceptibility of the adult body to both stress and bone remodeling. Commonly studied indicators of suspended growth include enamel hypoplasias, Harris lines, and stature reduction. Hypoplasias, which are horizontal linear tooth enamel defects, are useful diagnostically because they mark episodes that can be dated quite precisely in the development of the individual. They also correlate well with mortality patterns, indicating that the conditions that cause hypoplasias are often life threatening. Although hypoplasias do not in themselves reveal whether a stress stemmed from disease or from dietary stress, there is potential in the future for trace element analysis of the enamel to determine whether the hypoplasias correlate with nutrient deficiencies (Gilbert 1975). With these, as with other stress indicators, it has not been possible to tie stress episodes down securely in a temporal sense, but perhaps this will be possible in the future. It is thought that hypoplasias record chronic stress occurring on an annual basis or more frequently.

Harris lines, which record a suspension of growth followed by catch-up growth at the epiphyses of long bones during childhood, have given problems in interpretation. Unlike enamel hypoplasias, the incidence of Harris lines does not correlate well with higher mortality rates. Previously, scholars have assumed that individuals with more Harris lines were those in poorer health, but the lines do not necessarily appear in the bones of the people most subject to stress. The lines' formation seems to record a good period of recovery from a stress, something that may not befall a person who is poorly fed or sick. Thus, it may be that the healthier people in a stressed population are more subject to Harris lines than the less healthy people. Another problem with Harris lines is that they can be effaced by remodeling, unlike hypoplasias. The absence of Harris lines, then, does not tell whether or not a person was subject to physiological stress, but their presence does mark the occurrence of some kind of physiological stress in a person who recovered well. It is thought that Harris lines record episodic stress, such as famines or epidemics.

Chronic physiological stress during childhood growth causes stature reduction or stunting (Stini 1975). In addition, the stunting of growth due to nutritional or disease stress is known to affect the shape of the head and pelvis, because portions of these structures do not expand as they would with normal growth (R. A. Benfer, personal communication; Angel, Chapter 3 this volume). For secure identification of such stress-related changes in a regional sequence, it is necessary to employ biological distance studies to control for population replacement by migration, for gene flow could mimic the physiological changes (Buikstra, Chapter 9 this volume; Cook, Chapter 10 this volume). Our understanding of changes in stature throughout prehistory is as yet unclear due to the lack of knowledge in most regions about patterns of gene flow.

Severe physiological stress can also produce loss of cortical bone in long bones, both among children and adults, and study of thin sections by age and sex can illuminate the patterning of stress in a prehistoric population. This pathology, however, has not been studied much archaeologically, and it can be caused by changes in a person's activity levels as well as in nutritional status. Armelagos and Martin (Martin and Armelagos 1979) have shown how valuable this stress indicator can be, and it should be a useful area for future study.

Two useful pathologies reviewed by the participants in this conference are porotic hyperostosis and cribra orbitalia, which mark heightened production of red blood cells in the fact of chronic iron-deficiency anemia. These pathologies are notable indicators of nutritional stress, because high carrying capacity agricultural diets are often low in iron. If one can control for incidence of genetically- or parasitically-caused anemias, the frequency of porotic hyperostosis and cribra orbitalia can be interpreted quite securely, as evidence of the degree of nutritional stress (Buikstra, Chapter 9 this volume; Cook, Chapter 10 this volume).

Occurrence of infectious disease is recorded by the incidence of both specific and generalized bone lesions. The frequency of these pathologies is expected to increase with the rise of sedentary settlement and with increased nutritional stress, which would synergistically increase the infectious disease rate.

A final potential indicator of population pressure is the overall mortality rate, which presumably will show increased rates during times of severe population pressure. Mortality rates are determined by quantitative study of different age and sex classes of human skeletons within cemeteries. It is complicated by the problem of ascertaining whether a group of ancient skeletons fairly represent the living population from which they came. Differential disposal and preservation of skeletons of certain ages, such as infants or people of very high status, and difficulties of sexing infant skeletons or aging those of old people, may skew the reconstructed proportions. Nevertheless, determining mortality rates from skeletons is a routine method with which to obtain a basic idea of rates of survival in ancient populations.

HISTORY OF MORTALITY AND PHYSIOLOGICAL STRESS

Although there is a relative lack of evidence for the Paleolithic stage, enough skeletons have been studied that it seems clear that seasonal and periodic physiological stress regularly affected most prehistoric hunting-gathering populations, as evidenced by the presence of enamel hypoplasias and Harris lines. What also seems clear is that severe and chronic stress, with high frequency of hypoplasias, infectious disease lesions, pathologies related to iron-deficiency anemia, and high mortality rates, is not characteristic of these early populations. There is no evidence of frequent, severe malnutrition, and so the diet must have been adequate in calories and other nutrients most of the time. During the Mesolithic, the proportion of starch in the diet rose, to judge from the increased occurrence of certain dental diseases, but not enough to create an impoverished diet. At this time, diets seem to have been made up of a rather large number of foods, so that the failure of one food source would not be catastrophic. There is a possible slight tendency for Paleolithic people to be healthier and taller than Mesolithic people, but there is no apparent trend toward increasing physiological stress during the Mesolithic. Thus, it seems that both hunter-gatherers and incipient agriculturalists regularly underwent population pressure, but only to a moderate degree.

During the periods when effective agriculture first comes into use there seems to be a temporary upturn in health and survival rates in a few regions: Europe, North America, and the Eastern Mediterranean. At this stage, wild foods are still consumed periodically and a variety of plants are cultivated, suggesting the availability of adequate amounts of different nutrients. Based on the increasing frequency of tooth disease related to high carbohydrate consumption, it seems that cultivated plants probably increased the storable calorie supply, removing for a time any seasonal or periodic problems in food supply. In most regions, however, the development of agriculture seems not to have had this effect, and there seems to have been a slight increase in physiological stress.

Stress, however, does not seem to have become common and widespread until after the development of high degrees of sedentism, population density, and reliance on intensive agriculture. At this stage in all regions the incidence of physiological stress increases greatly, and average mortality rates increase appreciably. Most of these agricultural populations have high frequencies of porotic hyperostosis and cribra orbitalia, and there is a substantial increase in the number and severity of enamel hypoplasias and pathologies associated with infectious disease. Stature in many populations appears to have been considerably lower than would be expected if genetically-determined height maxima had been reached, which suggests that the growth arrests documented by pathologies were causing stunting. Accompanying these indicators of poor health and nourishment, there is a universal drop in the occurrence of Harris lines, suggesting a poor rate of full recovery from the stress. Incidence of carbohydrate-related tooth disease increases, apparently because subsistence by this time is characterized by a heavy emphasis on a few starchy food crops. Populations seem to have grown beyond the point at which wild food resources could be a meaningful dietary supplement, and even domestic animal resources were commonly reserved for farm labor and transport rather than for diet supplementation.

It seems that a large proportion of most sedentary prehistoric populations under intensive agriculture underwent chronic and life-threatening malnutrition and disease, especially during infancy and childhood. The causes of the nutritional stress are likely to have been the poverty of the staple crops in most nutrients except calories, periodic famines caused by the instability of the agricultural system, and chronic lack of food due to both population growth and economic expropriation by elites. The increases in infectious disease probably reflect both a poorer diet and increased interpersonal contact in crowded settlements, and it is, in turn, likely to have aggrevated nutritional problems.

Thus, it seems that Cohen is correct in supposing that population pressure was present through most of prehistory except possibly during the beginning of effective agriculture in a few regions. Although population pressure is common in preagricultural populations and thus does precede the development of agriculture, it is not particularly severe at this time, contrary to Cohen's expectations. The origin of agriculture, then, cannot accurately be attributed to the existence of unusually high levels of pressure at the time. Severe population pressure occurs only after the development of highly intensive agriculture, when populations are dense and sedentary, and sociopolitical organization is stratified.

It seems significant that population growth speeds up at the very time that health and mortality worsen. In order for growth to occur in such a situation, there would have had to be a substantial simultaneous increase in natality. In part, this pattern contradicts the expectations of the equilibrium theorists who hold that agriculture and sedentism bring an improvement in health. On the other hand, the indirect evidence for an increase in natality, probably through closer child spacing, is consonant with both groups of theories. To better understand the causal implications of these patterns, we need to know more about the etiology of the various physiological stresses that these prehistoric populations were experiencing. It seems that the nature of population pressure is different at different times and places, at different levels of economic and sociopolitical development, and in different demographic situations. In addition, the rates, types, severity, and causes of physiological stresses vary among the different age, sex, and social classes of a population, and further work is required to elucidate the relationships that produce these patterns.

CHANGES IN ACTIVITY AND LABOR PRODUCTIVITY

An important assumption in most theories is that labor productivity declines with intensive food production. An interesting by-product of this review of paleopathology is evidence for a marked change in human activity patterns during the transition to agriculture. This pattern of change shows up in many sequences, including the Midwest and Southeast in the United States, Western Europe, the Eastern Mediterranean, the Near East, East Asia, and South Asia. During the Paleolithic and the Mesolithic, both bones and teeth seem to have received much greater use than in later times, and the result was extensive tooth wear and the development of large, rugged bony structures and considerable osteoarthritis.

In the transition from the Mesolithic to Neolithic in these regions there is a definite drop in skeletal robusticity, osteoarthritis, and dental attrition. It seems that the development of sedentary agriculture eased mechanical stress on the body and teeth, to judge from these changes, which seem to have been achieved both through evolutionary genetic change and through physiological processes taking place during the lives of individuals. Significantly, it seems to be a response to much lessened physical activity after the development of agriculture. Cohen (Chapters 1 and 23 this volume) interprets these changes mainly as evidence of stunting due to nutritional stress in a context of increased population pressure, but, as Larsen (Chapter 14 this volume), points out, many of the physical changes relate to a reduction in muscular activity. (Both the hunting-gathering lifeway and the habitual actions of plant cultivation and food preparation put strains on the human skeletal frame, however, and osteoarthritis continued to occur in agricultural populations, though at a lower rate.)

Change in bone remodeling patterns as an indicator of changing activity patterns seems a fruitful area to look into in the future, both for a better understanding of the causes and consequences of the rise of agriculture and for investigating occupational specialization (Buikstra, Chapter 9, and Larsen, Chapter 14, this volume). To improve our understanding of the relationship of stress to bone remodeling, we may need to pursue further laboratory studies of bone remodeling under known stresses, to improve our understanding of the mechanical and physical processes that cause the bone pathologies.

The paleopathological evidence for decreased mechanical stress suggests that one of the things that the rise of agriculture might have brought is an improvement in the cost-benefit ratio of subsistence labor. As subsistence productivity per hectare was going up, the land exploited for subsistence became more concentrated spatially, and so there was a drop in labor costs per unit gained. This finding is contrary to most recent theoreticians' expectations. Only Bronson (1975) seems to have predicted it.

SUMMARY

The data gathered together and summarized in this conference give a picture of widespread, recurring prehistoric population growth, based on increases through time in sizes and numbers of archaeological sites and in numbers of human skeletal remains. Concurrent with this growth, there is a definite trend in most regions toward subsistence intensification for increased production.

During the Upper Paleolithic stage, subsistence seems to have been based predominantly on the explcitation of larger game species of high nutritional value and easy availability, such as herd animals or anadromous fish. During the Mesolithic stage, however, subsistence was progressively altered to include more foods such as plants, which are abundant and storable but of relatively low digestibility and palatability. The cost-effectiveness of subsistence labor during both periods seems to have been low, for the bodies of most individuals exhibit signs of extensive remodeling and wear under mechanical stress, and there also seems to have been selective pressure on the genome for the maintenance of large and robust bones and teeth. During both periods, also, subsistence adaptation was apparently ineffective at preventing periods of want, for most populations seem to have regularly experienced periods of nutritional stress, to judge from the presence of skeletal pathologies of the type that record episodes of physiological stress. Nonetheless, throughout the long period before effective agriculture, there is no evidence for chronic or severe nutritional or disease stress. During this period, sedentism is rare or absent, and yet populations grew during almost every period of occupation.

By the end of the Mesolithic, in the early Holocene, the process of intensification had produced diets increasingly focused on a few highly productive plant food sources that were relatively starchy and low in protein, minerals, and vitamins. This pattern is inferred from changes in the archaeological food remains, artifacts, patterns of tooth disease, and bone chemistry. By early Neolithic times effective agricultural crops had been developed or borrowed in most regions, and these provided a greatly increased potential for economic and demographic expansion and sedentary settlement later in the stage. In a few regions, the rapid economic expansion of the early Neolithic produced an upturn in health contemporary with a rapid increase in population growth. This seems to be one of the few instances when population pressure may have been absent--due, apparently, to the rapid expansion in subsistence permitted by the inception of agriculture.

In contrast, during the later Neolithic, when systems of intensive agriculture had developed and dense, sedentary settlement was the rule, there was a widespread, marked increase in rates of physiological stress and mortality, apparently due both to lessened diet quality, adequacy, and stability, and to increased rates of infectious disease. This change is evident in the paleodemographic patterns and the high frequencies of paleopathological indicators of chronic stress. Since population growth continued unabated, it seems that there must have been a large increase in birth rates to balance the increased mortality. Despite the adverse long-term effects of Neolithic developments on health and nutrition, the period brought a clear increase in the labor efficiency of subsistence. Throughout most of the world, the rise of efficient, sedentary agriculture correlates with a substantial drop in dental and skeletal robusticity and wear that is due, apparently, to a decrease in the amount of physical activity needed for subsistence.

It is clear that none of the different theories are completely confirmed or falsified by these patterns of prehistoric data. Cohen's version of the population pressure theory comes off better than most, in that population growth, pressure, and economic growth occur continuously throughout most sequences. The considerable intrinsic potential of human populations for growth is evidenced by the substantial growth that took place even among mobile hunter-gatherers and by the rapid growth of population even in the face of the heightened mortality rates characteristic of intensive agriculturalists. Cohen's interpretation of the causal role of population pressure is also supported by the universal progression of subsistence systems toward greater carrying capacity, rather than toward improved nutrition or economic stability.

The equilibrium theories fare less well. Contrary to these theories' expectation of human adaptation, human subsistence becomes less stable and lower in nutritional quality as adaptation proceeds, and there is a prevalence of population growth and nutritional stress that the theories do not provide for. In contrast to such theories, early hunter-gatherers did not control their populations well below carrying capacity, for the pathologies of their bodies show repeated experience of nutritional stress. On the other hand, their methods of population management were sufficient to keep them from chronic starvation, for which there is absolutely no evidence in preagricultural populations.

Several theories, including Cohen's, posit a period of greater population pressure occurring just as incipient agriculture begins, but it seems clear that there was no period of increased population pressure at that juncture. Agriculture probably developed at this time not because pressure was any more severe than before but because previous population growth and subsistence change had fostered a number of species that were able to respond to increased labor inputs with increased outputs, attracting increasingly heavy reliance on them for food in the face of continued population pressure. Another tenet common to most theories about the rise of agriculture was that agriculture had greater labor costs than hunting and gathering. From the evidence of pathology, it seems that labor costs did not increase but decreased with the implementation of effective agriculture. This finding adds a second impetus to the development of agriculture: the principle of least effort.

To some degree most tenets of the different theories can be accommodated by specifying different environmental, demographic, and sociological contexts for them (this approach is explained in greater detail in Roosevelt 1980). Thus, although population pressure might be accepted as a major force for subsistence intensification in human prehistory, there will be times and places where there will be either no population pressure or no potential for intensification. So, in the absence of population pressure, after an epidemic or when populations enter an unpopulated region, humans would act as the equilibrium theory predicts, to minimize effort and to maximize nutritional quality and reliability. In such a context, demographic potential could also be optimized by relaxing population controls. Larger population size could have given a group an advantage in the face of intergroup warfare and competition for resources.

When population pressure developed through the inevitable growth of population, people would have intensified subsistence as far as was technoenvironmentally possible. Where environmental potential is limited, people would have had to control their population growth culturally until some way to intensify production could be found. In regions of high subsistence potential, population pressure would encourage subsistence intensification, which is a quicker, more cost-effective response to stress than population control, which is only a long-range solution because of the inevitable time lag between a change in family planning and the resulting change in the size of the population.

The spatial concentration and productivity of agriculture and its favorable labor costs make it susceptible to takeover by elites, who could use their control of resources to ensure their own nutrition and health in the face of population pressure. The burden of centralized expropriation in effect would have increased population pressure on all but the elite, and it may be that this phenomenon, along with urban crowding, produced the widespread increase in poor nutrition and health among populations subsisting by intensive agriculture in preindustrial states.

PALEOPATHOLOGY AND ANTHROPOLOGY FOR THE FUTURE

The papers in this volume illustrate the great value of archaeological-physical anthropological studies for the elucidation of theories about human evolution, and they show how important it is to collect, preserve, and analyze prehistoric osteological remains. These papers also demonstrate that to gain really useful data requires goal-oriented field collection. Where physical anthropologists have been involved from the start, the research has produced really useful and sophisticated results based on high-quality and abundant data. Where the physical anthropologists have had only the leavings of projects with other aims, it has been very difficult to make useful inferences because remains frequently were not systematically collected in the field and were not preserved for analysis in museums or research laboratories, as Palkovich points out (Chapter 16 this volume). Because of the lack of recognition of their interpretive potential, archaeologists have often relegated the report on skeletal remains to an appendix in their reports, or they have not bothered to have them analyzed. Museums, in turn, have not valued these remains and often have not properly curated and conserved them. There seems to be a lesson to archaeologists in this: take care over the excavation, conservation, analysis, and curation of the human remains from your excavations. Bone have not been of very high priority among archaeologists, but the rigor of inferences about many aspects of prehistoric life depends on these remains.

It should be obvious why osteological remains are integral to the study of prehistoric human ecology, but they also have a contribution to make to studies of prehistoric social organization. For example, almost all anthropological definitions of sociopolitical organizational types and processes include human-ecological causes and consequences. Fried's (1967) famous definition of differential access to life-sustaining resources as a key to social stratification is just one example. Just a few of the aspects of life that might be expected to be affected by differences in status and rank are housing, clothing, diet, health care, and occupation. Significant differences in the quality of these aspects of life within a population can be expected to have effects on the health and nutrition of people. Health and dietary differences, as shown in this symposium, are reflected in the bones and can be studied in archaeological populations. Thus, paleopathology is a primary method for the study of prehistoric socioeconomic organization as Buikstra (Chapter 9 this volume) and others have pointed out. Paleopathology can define the health and dietary correlates of sociopolitical structures and can lead to a better understanding of the processes of social differentiation. For example, without information about health, archaeologists might detect a system of differential ranking, but they would be unable to say much about the nature of the ranking because, without paleobiological information from the skeletons, there would be no information on differences in health or diet or age and sex between and within the social units.

Ethnographers also could do more in the study of health, diet, and demography. We need ethnographic studies of the various pathologies relevant to the explanation of prehistoric change. There is a gap in information between the laboratory studies of animals and the studies of the prehistoric dead. To better understand the relationship of the bone pathologies to living physiological and genetic systems we need to study them in the flesh, and many of the pathological states and processes found among the ancient populations are still occurring now, but general ethnographers often seem to be uninterested or unaware of them. Basic ethnographic studies of nutrition and disease need to be done to test the causal relationship between physiological stress and bone pathology and chemistry. For example, we need to know what levels of nutritional stress cause hypoplasias and other pathologies among pre-industrial populations. The relationships of stable carbon isotope patterns to diet need to be investigated among living people of known diet, as do the relationships among levels of strontium in the body, the environment, and food.

We also need to learn more about the relationship of stress to stature depression. It is common for ethnographers to assert that "their" populations are healthy and well nourished because the male adults appear so. It is usual, however, for the adults in such populations to have very low stature, and the few ethnographic studies that have been done of maternal and infant health and diet document the presence of nutritional stress, a probable cause of stature reduction. If more were known about the relationship of physiological stress and stature reduction, stronger inferences could be made on the basis of archaeological stature variation.

We also need ethnographic information about the human ecological consequences and correlates of different forms of social and political organization. Most of the causal processes that scholars envision are assumed; they are not demonstrated. Thus, we think that there are different patterns in access to life-sustaining resources within different types of societies, but this conclusion needs to be assessed with studies of living populations. It is a particular problem that traditional ethnographers have not been as interested in the life of women and children as they are in men, and the health status of the community is often inferred from knowledge of adult males. This practice often yields an inaccurate view because women and children often have lower status than men, and, as a consequence, they may have less favorable health due to restricted access to some resources. Variation within even egalitarian populations needs to be recognized and studied before we really understand the meaning of mean or average health. The study of social organization seems incomplete if we do not know what are the consequences to health and nutrition of membership in different classes, whether age-grade, genealogical, achieved, or ascribed. If archaeologists are going to infer the nature of social organization from the health correlates of rank and status, then we need to know more about the causal relationships among living peoples.

These epistemological problems and gaps in knowledge illustrate the inescapable interdependence of the subfields of anthropology. Interpretations of ethnology require a knowledge of the past, to understand the similarities and differences between the past and the present and the reasons for them. Conversely, the field of archaeology is dependent on studies of living people, since we must model many vanished processes of the past on knowledge of the present nature of humans. And any study of humans as cultural beings, whether past or present, eventually will run up against the need to know the physical human, for culture and the body continually interact, and to explain one without consideration of the other seems impossible.

REFERENCES

Asch, N. B., R. I. Ford, and D. L. Asch
1972 Paleoethnobotany of the Koster Site: The archaic horizons. *Illinois State Museum Research Papers* Vol. 6, *Reports of Investigations* No. 6.
Bender, M. M., D. A. Barreis, and R. L. Steventon
1981 Further light on carbon isotopes and Hopewell agriculture. *American Antiquity 46*:346-353.
Binford, L. R.
1968 Post-Pleistocene adaptations. In *New perspectives in archaeology*, edited by S. R. Binford and L. R. Binford, pp. 313-341. Aldine, Chicago.
Boserup, E.
1965 *The conditions of agricultural growth: The economics of agrarian change under population pressure.* Aldine, Chicago.
Bronson, B.
1975 The earliest farming: Demography as a cause and consequence. In *Population, ecology, and social evolution*, edited by S. Polgar, pp. 53-78. Mouton, The Hague.
Brown, A.
1973 *Bone strontium as a dietary indicator in human skeletal populations.* Ph.D. dissertation, University of Michigan, Ann Arbor.
Buikstra, J., and D. C. Cook
1981 Paleopathology: An American account. *Annual Review of Anthropology 9*:933-970.
Cohen, M. N.
1977 *The food crisis in prehistory: Overpopulation and the origins of agriculture.* Yale University Press, New Haven.
Earle, T. K., and A. L. Christenson (editors)
1980 *Modeling change in prehistoric subsistence economies.* Academic Press, New York.
Flannery, K. V.
1969 Origins and ecological effects of early domestication in Iran and the Near East. In *The domestication and exploitation of plants and animals*, edited by P. J. Ucko and G. W. Dimbleby, pp. 73-100. Aldine, Chicago.
1973 The origins of agriculture. *Annual Review of Anthropology 2*:271-310.
Ford, Richard I.
1977 Evolutionary biology and the evolution of human ecosystems: A case study from the Midwestern U.S.A. In *Explanation of prehistoric change*, edited by J. M. Hill, pp. 153-184. University of New Mexico Press, Albuquerque.
1979 Paleoethnobotany in American archaeology. In *Advances in archaeological method and theory* (Vol. 2), edited by M. B. Schiffer, pp. 285-336. Academic Press, New York.

Fried, M.
1976 *The evolution of political society.* Random House, New York.
Gilbert, R. I.
1975 *Trace element analysis of three skeletal Amerindian populations at Dickson Mound.* Ph.D. dissertation, Department of Anthropology, University of Massachusetts, Amherst.
Harris, M.
1977 *Cannibals and kings: The origins of cultures.* Random House, New York.
Hassan, F. A.
1975 Determination of the size, density, and growth ratio of hunting-gathering populations. In *Population, ecology, and social evolution,* edited by S. Polgar, pp. 27-52. Mouton, The Hague.
1978 Demographic archaeology. In *Advances in archaeological method and theory* (Vol. 1), edited by M. B. Schiffer, pp. 49-103. Academic Press, New York.
1981 *Demographic archaeology.* Academic Press, New York.
Hayden, B.
1981 Research and development in the Stone Age: Technological transitions among Hunter-Gatherers. *Current Anthropology 22*(5):519-548.
Jochim, M. A.
1976 *Hunter-Gatherer subsistence and settlement: A predictive model.* Academic Press, New York.
Martin, P. L., and G. J. Armelagos
1979 Morphometrics of compact bone: An example from Sudanese Nubia. *American Journal of Physical Anthropology 51*: 571-578.
Payne, S.
1972a Partial recovery and sample bias: The results of some sieving experiments. In *Papers in economic prehistory,* edited by E. S. Higgs, pp. 49-64. Cambridge University Press, Cambridge.
1972b On the interpretation of bone samples from archaeological sites. In *Papers in Economic Prehistory,* edited by E. S. Higgs, pp. 65-82. Cambridge University Press, Cambridge.
Roosevelt, A. C.
1980 *Parmana: Prehistoric maize and manioc subsistence along the Amazon and Orinco.* Academic Press, New York.
Stini, W. A.
1975 Adaptive strategies of human populations under nutritional stress. In *Biosocial interrelations in population adaptation,* edited by E. S. Watts, F. E. Johnston, and G. W. Lasker, pp. 19-41. Mouton, The Hague.
Struever, S.
1968 Flotation techniques for the recovery of small-scale archaeological remains. *American Antiquity 33*:353-362.

Tauber, H.
1981 ^{13}C evidence for dietary habits of prehistoric man in Denmark. *Nature 292*:332-333.

van der Merwe, N. J., and J. C. Vogel
1978 ^{13}C content of human collagen as a measure of prehistoric diet in Woodland North America. *Nature 276*:815-816.

van der Merwe, N., A. C. Roosevelt, and J. C. Vogel
1981 Isotopic evidence for prehistoric subsistence change at Parmana, Venezuela. *Nature 292*:536-538.

Wing, E. S., and A. B. Brown
1979 *Paleonutrition: Method and theory in prehistoric food-ways.* Academic Press, New York.

CHAPTER 23

PALEOPATHOLOGY AT THE ORIGINS OF AGRICULTURE: EDITORS' SUMMATION

Mark Nathan Cohen

Department of Anthropology
State University of New York
College at Plattsburgh

George J. Armelagos

Department of Anthropology
University of Massachusetts-Amherst

INTRODUCTION

Despite the limitations of individual studies and the problems of interpopulation and inter-regional comparability discussed in the introductory chapter, the studies in this volume collectively describe a number of clear trends in data. Many of these trends have a significant bearing on discussions of comparative health and of economic and technological "progress" associated with the Neolithic Revolution. The data contribute significantly to the resolution of one long-standing controversy in anthropology concerning the relative health of hunter-gatherers and farmers. They also address a second controversy concerning the role of population growth in instigating economic change, but provide no clear resolution of the latter. Finally, the techniques reported demonstrate *approaches* (but as yet no aggregated data) to a number of other long-standing issues in anthropology and prehistory.

MAJOR TRENDS IN DATA ON HEALTH

The Incidence of Infection

The clearest major trend in the collected data concerns the incidence of infections as measured by the frequency of nonspecific skeletal lesions of infectious etiology as well as by the frequency of certain specific diseases. Twelve studies report on the incidence of infection (Buikstra/Cook [Chapters 9 and 10]; Angel [Chapter 3]; Goodman et al. [Chapter 11]; Norr [Chapter 18]; Allison [Chapter 20]; Cassidy [Chapter 12]; Rathbun [Chapter 6]; Rose et al. [Chapter 15]; Larsen [Chapter 14]; Meiklejohn et al. [Chapter 4]; Perzigian et al. [Chapter 13]; Ubelaker [Chapter 19]). Most conclude that infection was a more common and more serious problem for farmers than for their hunting and gathering forebears; and most suggest that this resulted from some combination of increasing sedentism, larger population aggregates, and the well-established synergism between infection and malnutrition. As exceptions, Rose et al. note a relatively high rate of infections in a hunting and gathering population in one of the three subzones of the Mississippi Valley that they discuss; and Norr notes a decline in infections from a hunting and gathering population to an early farming population followed by a rise to new, much higher levels with more intensive farming in Panama. Meiklejohn et al. report an increase in cranial infections, but not in postcranial lesions, with the Neolithic in Europe. Rathbun reports a higher rate of infection for Neolithic and Chalcolithic populations than for pre-Neolithic groups in Iran, but, surprisingly, notes that Bronze and Iron Age samples showed the lowest rates.

In addition to reporting on generalized lesions of infection, two studies (Perzigian et al. and Buikstra and Cook) note an increase in the frequency of mycobacterial (tubercular) infections identifiable in the skeletons of farming or later populations; and one study (Allison) working with mummies documents an increase in rates of gastrointestinal infections with sedentism and agriculture, although no trend in respiratory diseases was found. Where it was possible to document several stages of agricultural development, some studies (Goodman et al.; Angel) found a progressive increase in the frequency of infections while others noted an initial surge of infection rates accompanying the adoption of agriculture with later rebound suggestive of a more successful adjustment to the new living conditions (Ubelaker; Rose et al.; Rathbun). In contrast, Cassidy suggests that infections, and most other health problems, were more commonly found in late, maize-dependent farming sites than in either hunter-gatherer or transitional groups.

Chronic Malnutrition

The studies also suggest fairly consistently that the adoption of farming was accompanied by a decline in the overall quality of nutrition. The clearest indicator of this is provided by the incidence of porotic hyperostosis and cribra orbitalia (porosity of the skull and orbits) considered indicative of anemia. Sixteen studies (Allison; Buikstra and Cook; Goodman et al.; Martin et al. [Chapter 8]; Norr; Smith et al. [Chapter 5]; Kennedy [Chapter 7]; Angel; Cassidy; Rathbun; Rose et al.; Larsen; Meiklejohn et al.; Palkovich [Chapter 16]; Perzigian et al.; Ubelaker) note rates of porotic hyperostosis and most conclude that the lesions appear or increase with farming, suggesting that anemia is primarily a disease of agricultural groups. (Such anemia is most commonly attributed to poor nutrition but may also be genetic or parasite-related.) Martin et al., however, report no comparative hunter-gatherer data; Allison, Meiklejohn et al., and Larsen report generally low rates of porotic hyperostosis with no clear trend, as do Rose et al. for one of their study areas. Palkovich reports no temporal trend but does note that, geographically, porotic hyperostosis correlates with dependence on maize farming. Rathbun notes that orbital lesions clearly increase through time but that cranial lesions are high in the Neolithic and decline thereafter.

Other indicators of chronic malnutrition (slowing of growth, thinning of longbone cortices, changes in skull base and pelvic inlet) are more sporadically reported, and, in some cases, less certain of interpretation, but appear generally to support a similar conclusion. Palkovich suggests that chronic malnutrition became an increasingly severe problem in the American Southwest with the intensification of agriculture, and she provides data indicating severe stress in later (Pueblo) groups, largely in the form of signs of infantile malnutrition; but she offers no good comparative data on earlier periods. Goodman et al. report that a slowing of growth in childhood (as measured by attained length and circumference of bone for age) suggests that growth dampening from malnutrition was most marked in their later agricultural groups. Cook similarly argues that the slowing of growth and the thinning of long bone cortices may be signs of relative malnutrition in groups first adopting maize agriculture in Illinois. Cassidy suggests that cortical thinning of bone is indicative of poorer nutrition in a late farming group than in an earlier hunting and gathering group in Kentucky.

In the Old World, Smith et al. report that bone cortical thickness is greater for Middle Paleolithic and Epipaleolithic Natufian populations than for later agricultural groups in the Levant, suggesting better nutrition for the earlier groups; and they cite a study of cortical hypertrophy suggestive of calcium deficiency in early farming groups. For the Mediterranean, Angel uses measurements of skull base height and pelvic inlet depth as indices of nutritional quality and finds a decline in the overall quality of nutrition from Paleolithic through Mesolithic to Neolithic farming groups.

Several of the studies also suggest that a decline in adult size, stature, and skeletal robusticity as hunter-gatherers became farmers might be indicative of declining quality of nutrition (Kennedy for India; Angel for the Mediterranean; Larsen for Georgia; Meiklejohn et al. for Europe), but this was a point of contention in the discussions. Not all of the studies agree on the significance of this indicator and not all show similar trends. Meiklejohn et al. report a decrease in stature from the Paleolithic through the Mesolithic to the Neolithic in Europe followed by a rebound, but cautiously conclude that the trend might reflect either dietary stress or altered activities. Smith et al. show a decline in stature from Paleolithic to Mesolithic groups in the Levant with a rebound in some Neolithic groups, but argue against considering the decline in stature an index of declining nutrition, since there are no accompanying stress indicators (although they do consider the rebound in one Neolithic group a reflection of improved diet). (It was noted at the conference, however, that dietary limitations might select for small individuals who would not, then, necessarily display signs of stress in their own skeletons although their populations were evolving to meet stringent dietary conditions.) Allison, while using declining stature as an index of poor nutrition, saw no trend in time in Peru other than a decline in stature among groups subject to colonial domination. Cassidy and Ubelaker report no clear trends in stature through time. Perzigian et al. report an increase in stature from hunter-gatherers to transitional groups in Ohio followed by a decrease from transitional to fully agricultural groups. Rose et al. suggest that an increase in size in the Caddoan region of the Lower Mississippi Valley might reflect an *increase* in available protein with farming, while noting that a decline in size, reflecting declining nutrition, occurred in the Lower Mississippi Valley proper. Buikstra and Cook note an increase in stature for women, but not for men, at the transition in Illinois despite the fact that other indicators lead them to conclude that the quality of nutrition was declining.

Changes in sexual dimorphism, sometimes considered indicative of changing nutrition, show no consistent trend. Several different patterns of changing dimorphism are noted. Moreover, a decline in dimorphism (once equated with poor nutrition) consists in some cases of a relative decrease in male size and in others of an increase in female size. Hence, the meaning of dimorphism itself as an index appears to be ambiguous.

Indicators of Episodic Stress

One of the most interesting and, in some ways, most problematic sets of data is provided by skeletal indicators of the disruption of childhood growth. Two such indicators are commonly reported with surprisingly conflicting results. Harris lines are reported in seven studies comparing hunter-gatherers and farmers (Goodman et al.; Buikstra and Cook; Allison; Cassidy; Rathbun; Rose et al.; Perzigian et al.). Most conclude that the frequency of lines is higher in hunter-gatherers than in the farmers who follow them, possibly suggesting more frequent growth-disrupting stresses in the earlier groups. Rathbun, in contrast, reports an increase through time; and Allison primarily offers a geographic rather than a temporal comparison. Cook notes that the lowest frequency of Harris lines occurs in her transitional group.

Linear enamel hypoplasias (LEH) and enamel microdefects of teeth tell a very different story. In one study, Rose et al.[1] report (in the version of their paper presented to the conference) that in the Caddoan region of the Mississippi Valley, late hunter-gatherers and well-established farmers had comparable rates of hypoplasias; but they note that no data are available from transitional populations that on other grounds they believe to be the most stressed. Ten other studies (Goodman et al.; Buikstra and Cook; Allison; Smith et al.; Kennedy; Angel; Cassidy; Perzigian et al.; Ubelaker; and, very tentatively, Rathbun) all report that the frequency and/or severity of this indicator of growth disruption increases in farming and later populations in comparison to hunter-gatherers, suggestive of more frequent and/or more severe episodes of stress in later groups. Three studies (Cassidy; Smith et al.; Perzigian et al.) also note that hypoplasias of deciduous teeth (indicating episodes of prenatal stress presumably reflecting poor maternal health) are more common in later agricultural groups than in hunting and gathering groups. In addition, Norr states that carious enamel hypoplasias and hypocalcification of deciduous teeth are common in her later populations but not in her hunter-gatherers; and Buikstra and Cook note that while the incidence of deciduous hypoplasias does not increase through time in their sample, the tendency of stressed infants to die early increases in later groups. Palkovich also suggests that episodic stress would have been an increasingly severe problem for increasingly dense and immobile farming groups in the American Southwest, but she offers no data on LEH to support the suggestion.

The apparent contradiction in the patterns of Harris lines and enamel defects may be resolved in various ways. One possibility is that the two represent stresses of differing etiology. Both are considered general indicators of stress sufficient to cause growth disruption, but in neither case is the range of possible stressing agents well defined. Hence, it is possible that the contradictory trends indicate a trade-off of one form of stress

[1]*Rose et al. have eliminated aspects of their discussion in this volume in response to space constraints. However, they have informed us (personal communication) that their interpretation of this point has not changed.*

for another. One study (Cassidy) suggests that minor, regular hunger periods among hunter-gatherers may have been traded for more irregular and more severe stresses of farming life involving bouts of infection and more serious famine associated with crop failure. It was also pointed out in several of the chapters and in discussion that, of the two, enamel hypoplasias are almost certainly the more valid and reliable indicator of general stress. Harris lines are subject to subsequent erasure during growth, while enamel hypoplasias are not. Moreover, Harris lines record not so much the cessation of growth as the subsequent compensatory acceleration of growth. It was argued by some at the conference that the lower frequency of Harris lines in farming populations might reflect chronic malnutrition and the resulting failure of the acceleration phase as much the actual incidence of growth arrest. This interpretation is strongly supported by research reported by Murchison et al. (1983) suggesting that protein-deprived Rhesus monkeys develop fewer Harris lines than those fed a healthier diet. At best, therefore, the two indicators taken together suggest that no relaxation of episodic stress resulted from the adoption of farming in most regions. They may indicate the trade-off of one type of stress for another; more probably, they indicate a net increase in such episodes.

It should be noted, however, that both hypoplasias and Harris lines reflect not just the incidence of stress episodes but the incidence of such episodes *that were survived* by the individuals in question. One possible interpretation of a low incidence of hypoplasias among hunter-gatherers is that individuals commonly failed to survive any stresses sufficient to produce lesions. (The possibility must also be entertained that changes in tooth structure associated with the adoption of farming somehow made it increasingly likely that childhood stresses would be reflected in hypoplastic lesions.) However, hypoplasias are known to occur commonly in wild animals including other primates and they are reported among the Australopithecines (White 1978). Moreover, they are known to occur in fairly high frequencies in the teeth of recent and modern Australian aborigines (Smith et al., Chapter 5, this volume). Hence, their relative scarcity among reported prehistoric hunter-gatherers suggests a real, relative scarcity of major stress episodes and supports the contention that episodic stress was as much, or more commonly, felt by farming populations than by their hunting and gathering forebears.

Physical Stress

The data on physical stress as measured by arthritis, skeletal robusticity and physical injury) are more mixed, but seem to argue, on balance, for a reduction in physical stress and therefore a probable reduction in work load associated with the adoption of agriculture. It should be pointed out that both arthritis and muscular robusticity are likely to reflect the severity of peak or intermittent demand on muscles and joints rather than simply the number of hours of work involved in the two economies. The data thus suggest that in most regions such *peak* demand was greater for hunter-gatherers than for farmers; but it does not necessarily indicate that farming resulted in a reduction in the time invested in the food quest. The arthritis data are also complicated by the fact that the hunter-gatherers discussed commonly displayed *higher* average ages at death (see below) than did the farming populations from the same region. The hunter-gatherers would therefore be expected to display more arthritis as a function of age even if workloads were comparable.

Smith et al. suggest that the greater robusticity of pre-Neolithic populations in the Levant is suggestive of greater functional demand on the skeleton. Kennedy concludes that pre-farming groups in India were subject to more physical stress than farming groups as evidenced by skeletal robusticity and degenerative arthritis. Meiklejohn et al. suggest that slightly greater rates of arthritis indicate greater functional demands on the skeleton in the European Mesolithic than in the Neolithic. Rathbun's figures for Iran suggest that high arthritis levels among (a relatively aged sample of) Neanderthals was followed by higher levels for late pre-farming groups and by Neolithic (farming) levels equal to or greater than that of the Neandertals (but in a generally younger population). Only after the Neolithic did rates of arthritis decline in this region.

In the New World, Larsen suggests that Amerindian groups in Georgia also display a decline in robusticity and in arthritis accompanying the adoption of farming; and Perzigian et al. note a decline in physical stress in agricultural populations in Ohio. Rose et al., however, note a decrease in arthritis from hunter-gatherer to transitional populations followed by an increase to new, higher levels with intensive agriculture in the Caddoan region of the lower Mississippi Valley. Osteophytosis shows a similar pattern in the Lower Mississippi Valley proper, whereas osteoarthritis simply declines through time. Cassidy notes that arthritis is most marked in late agricultural populations in Kentucky, but she suggests an infectious etiology for the arthritis in question; and Goodman et al. argue for a progressive increase in various kinds of arthritis as agriculture was adopted and intensified in Illinois.

The incidence of trauma, both accidental and violence-related, shows a similarly mixed picture, generally decreasing in some study regions with the adoption of agriculture (Rathbun; Meiklejohn et al.; Perzigian et al.) while increasing in others (Goodman et al.; Kennedy). Rose et al. see no trend in their trauma data but do suggest that interpersonal violence was highest early in one of their sequences and highest very late in another. For the most part, however, the reporting of trauma and the resolution of accidental and violence-related trauma is not sufficient to permit statements about trends in the two classes. There is as yet no clear resolution to the debate about hunter-gatherer non-violence; but the evidence does not seem to suggest any simple pattern of change.

Mean Age at Death

Perhaps the most interesting results concern changes in the mean age at death associated with the transition to agriculture. Thirteen of the regional studies provide data (of varying quality) bearing on this issue. These data are presented in a variety of forms and are therefore difficult to summarize. Moreover, the translation of ages-at-death from skeletal populations to the actual dynamics of living populations is complex (Howell 1982; Sattenspiel and Harpending 1983). Nonetheless it is of interest, and counter to prevailing wisdom, that 10 of these sequences either conclude, or provide fragmentary evidence suggesting, that mean age at death (and/or life expectancy at various ages) *declined* with the adoption of farming. Working with relatively good, well-controlled samples (*N* = 114, 224, 219, respectively) from a single well-defined location, Goodman et al. suggest that there was a progressive decline in life expectancy for all age classes as hunter-gatherers first adopted and then intensified agriculture in Illinois. With larger samples (*N*s = 300-800) (Cook, personal communication) Cook finds some increase in life span as cultigens were added to a hunting and gathering diet, but an increase in age-specific mortality as maize agriculture was adopted (followed by a partial rebound in life expectancy in a later, intensive maize farming group). Cassidy finds that a maize-farming group in Kentucky (*N* = 296) had a lower life expectancy for both sexes and for all age groups than did an earlier hunting and gathering group (*N* = 295). Ubelaker notes that life expectancy at birth was relatively high in an early hunter-gatherer group (*N* = 192), rose slightly in what may be a transitional group (*N* = 199) (which, however, still exhibited a low caries rate, leading him to question their degree of reliance on agriculture) and then fell sharply in an intensive agricultural group (*N* = 30) before a partial rebound occurred (*N* = 435). He suggests that there was a trend toward increasing infant mortality through his sequence. Life expectancies at more advanced ages (E_5 and E_{15}) fluctuated more irregularly over time, but the earliest, clearly hunting and gathering, population had life expectancies at both ages comparable to the average of later groups.

Larsen, while cautioning that available samples (*N* = 152, 177) are unlikely to be truly representative (because both show too high a percentage of survivors to adulthood), nonetheless notes that the age distribution of the available sample of farmers is lower than that of the earlier hunter-gatherers in Georgia. He reports higher percentages of farmers dying in all age classes below 25 and higher percentages of hunter-gatherers dying in all age classes over 25 with the exception of the 30-35 year age bracket. Even if subadult mortality is discounted, the preagricultural adults have the higher average age at death. In the version of their chapter presented to the conference, Rose et al.[1] working with samples of similar size, suggest that in the Caddoan region of the lower Mississippi, hunter-gatherers had a lower probability of dying both as children and as young adults than did later farmers. In the Lower Mississippi Valley proper, they also suggested that the lowest mortality was associated with a dispersed hunter-gatherer group.

Working with more fragmentary and/or scattered data, a number of other studies report similar trends. Angel notes a decrease in adult life expectancy from Paleolithic (N = 59) to Mesolithic (N = 120) and Neolithic (N = 106) for males in the Mediterranean. For females he reports an increase in adult life expectancy from Paleolithic (N = 53) to Mesolithic (N = 63) followed by a decline to levels at or below that of the Paleolithic for the Neolithic (N = 200). Kennedy notes that the aggregate preagricultural sample from India (N = ±100) displays higher ages at death than do later agricultural populations. Rathbun, who claims no trend because his samples are so small, cites figures on average age at death of known adult specimens that are higher for preagricultural individuals (N = 9) than for early agricultural (Neolithic) groups (N = 69). In his tables, 10 small samples of Neolithic burials generally have average ages at death for adults below those of the Shanidar Neandertals and the pre-Neolithic Hotu population (although the latter may be select groups.) And Allison suggests that childhood mortality was lowest in his earliest population (although recovery bias is probably involved in this sample).

These latter studies, which suffer from very poor sampling of early hunting and gathering populations, mean relatively little individually; but collectively, in combination with the larger and better controlled samples discussed above, and bolstered by the evidence of other indicators of health, they begin to suggest a fairly widespread pattern of declining mean age at death with the adoption of farming. Certainly the data at least challenge the prevailing reverse assumption. It must be pointed out that these data may reflect changes in fertility and population growth rates as well as in mortality (Sattenspiel and Harpending 1983). However, several of the studies report a downward trend in life expectancy even when only adults are considered.

Three studies do suggest an increase in mean age at death with farming. Smith et al. report a general increase in life expectancy from late preagricultural (Natufian) populations in the Levant through the Bronze age; Perzigian et al. cite a comparison

[1]*Rose et al. have eliminated aspects of their discussion in this volume in response to space constraints. However, they have informed us (personal communication) that their interpretation of this point has not changed.*

suggesting better survivorship for an agricultural (N = 44) group in Ohio than for preagricultural groups (N = 1327), but they note that the later, smaller sample almost certainly underestimates subadult mortality accounting at least in part for the difference in life expectancy. Finally, figures provided by Norr might also be read as suggesting greater survivorship to adulthood in agricultural populations compared to preagricultural populations in Panama, but she adds several disclaimers, both about the size (N = 87, 28, 32) of her samples and about probable age biases related to known burial practices.

THE RELATIVE HEALTH OF HUNTER-GATHERERS AND FARMERS

Taken as a whole, these indicators fairly clearly suggest an overall decline in the quality--and probably in the length--of human life associated with the adoption of agriculture. This decline was offset in some regions, but not in others, by a decline in physical demands on the body. The studies support recent ethnographic statements and theoretical arguments about the relatively good health and nutrition of hunter-gatherers. They also suggest that hunter-gatherers were relatively well buffered against episodic stress. These data call in question simplistic popular ideas about human progress. They also call in question models of human population growth that are based on assumed progressive increases in life expectancy. The data suggest that the well-documented expansion of early farming populations was accomplished in spite of general diminution of both child and adult life expectancy rather than being fueled by increased survivorship.

It should be stressed that the hunter-gatherer/farmer comparison lumps together a number of separate adaptive shifts whose importance in accounting for the changes in health is not always clear. The effects of population growth, of new foods, of farming as an activity, of sedentism, of the dispersal or nucleation of settlements, and of changing politics all need to be evaluated separately. Several of the chapters allude to the effects of some of these variables but the task of sorting out their individual effects on health is approached most scientifically in this volume by Rose et al., who use a comparison of their three subregions of the Mississippi Valley to isolate the effects of individual variables, noting particularly the effects of population nucleation.

THE POPULATION PRESSURE MODEL

Although the data point fairly clearly to a decline in health associated with the origins of agriculture, it is not yet clear whether they confirm the particulars of the (Boserupian) population pressure model of agricultural origins. The generally negative slope of health and nutrition do conform to the model. Moreover, population growth is identified as a concomitant of changes in health and economy in most of the sequences (although not in all portions of all sequences); and the sequence of preagricultural economic changes in most regions discussed is consistent with predictions about economic changes associated with increasing population density and/or declining resources (Christenson 1980; Cohen 1977; Earle 1980; Hespenheide 1980; O'Connell and Hawkes 1981; Winterhalder 1981).

On the other hand, the data, though mixed, suggest an overall decline in work load and physical stress that may have helped to motivate the economic transition, reducing the necessity to postulate declining resources and/or growing populations as a necessary stimulus to economic change. In some of the studies, therefore, it is possible to interpret pathology trends in terms of the scenario described by Reidhead (1980) in which populations are seduced by declining labor costs associated with agriculture (rather than being forced to adopt it) but incur unanticipated health problems associated with sedentism, nucleation, protein shortage, and crop failure that result from the transition.

Moreover, some of the studies in question suggest that stress (whether or not it occurs in a pattern of progressive increase as a population pressure model might suggest) may occur without concomitant evidence of population growth (Angel) or may be more readily explained by other factors such as population nucleation (Rose et al.) or political exploitation (Martin et al.; Allison; Goodman et al.).

The interpretation of health trends *before* the adoption of agriculture is particularly important for evaluation of the population pressure hypothesis, which predicts declining (or at least steady) levels of health and nutrition rather than improvements in health (compare Hayden 1981) as hunter-gatherers approach the transition. Unfortunately, these trends are particularly hard to unravel in the absence of good early ("Paleo") hunter-gatherers. As noted, several of the Old World studies (Meiklejohn et al.; Angel; Smith et al.; Kennedy) suggest that there is a decline in size beginning in the Upper Paleolithic and extending through the Mesolithic. Such a widespread trend could be offered as evidence of a decline in nutrition or selection for reduced nutritional needs among hunter-gatherers before the adoption of agriculture, supporting a population pressure model; but, as discussed above, this interpretation is controversial. One study shows the trend paralleled by other indicators of increasing nutritional stress (Angel) while two others do not (Smith et al.; Meiklejohn et al.).

Decreasing size and robusticity might also be considered evidence of declining labor demands, supporting the Hayden model.

Changes in the frequencies of episodes of growth arrest prior to the adoption of agriculture would be, perhaps, the most important data for resolving this controversy. A population pressure model would predict increasing or at least steady rates of such indicators among hunter-gatherers associated with growing populations and changing economic strategies, since it would suggest that new food economies wrought no net improvement in economic homeostasis. The Hayden hypothesis predicts the decline of such indicators because it assumes an increase in economic buffers. Unfortunately, although good comparisons can be made between hunter-gatherers and farmers with respect to the incidence of growth arrest episodes (as discussed above), there are relatively few data on which to measure changes in their frequencies among preagricultural populations. One pioneering study in Europe with very small samples (Brothwell 1963) did report an increase in hypoplasias in the Mesolithic compared to the Paleolithic. In this volume, Smith et al. find no trend in the incidence of hypoplasia from Upper Paleolithic to Epipaleolithic in the Levant.

Two other studies in the symposium, not yet discussed because they involve no fully agricultural populations, are worthy of note in this discussion. Dickel et al. (Chapter 17) report on the relative health of early and late hunting and gathering populations of California, the latter employing a very intensive hunting and gathering strategy involving the processing of acorns in a manner reminiscent of agricultural production to support increasingly dense populations. By their report, population growth and the concomitant intensification of the hunting and gathering economy were accompanied by a mixed bag of changing indicators of stress. Harris lines decreased through time, suggesting a decline in episodic stress, possibly indicative of increased hunger-buffering capabilities of the acorn economy (but as discussed above, possibly indicative only of a decline in the overall quality of the diet). Enamel hypoplasias, as elsewhere, had an irregular pattern showing a net increase in frequency through time (or, possibly, no net trend if the confounding effects of European-introduced diseases during a portion of their late period are considered). Porotic hyperostosis was generally rare in this group and showed no trend. Stature declined slightly early in the sequence but generally showed no significant trend and overall life expectancy decreased through time for most age classes. Taken together, these indicators suggest no net improvement over time in health or economic homeostasis.

Data from a second study (Benfer, Chapter 21) of a "proto-agricultural" population in Peru with some incipient cultivation seems to suggest a progressive improvement in health over time. The sequence documents a series of quantitative shifts in economy among populations that first moved toward increasing dependence on manipulated or cultivated plant species and then shifted back toward increasing dependence on seafood. The shifts were accompanied by an overall improvement in survivorship (total *N* = 168), an increase in stature, and a decrease in Harris line formation. (Benfer considers the latter a good indicator of relative stress in these populations since there is a negative correlation between Harris lines and stature among individuals.) On the other hand, Benfer also proposes that several means were being adopted to curtail population growth, speaks of population pressure and intense competition for resources, and notes that his Peruvians were living in a progressively degraded environment. All of the latter suggest that population pressure played a role in instigating economic changes by a population more successful than most at maintaining the biological well-being of individuals amidst declining resources.

In sum, these data provide some suggestive evidence but no clear indication of declining health and nutrition among later hunter-gatherers as a population pressure model might suggest. Conversely, the data may show a declining workload among late hunter-gatherers, but otherwise, with the exception of the Benfer study, they provide little indication of any general, progressive improvement in hunter-gatherers' lifestyles and economic homeostasis.

APPROACHES TO OTHER PROBLEMS OF ANTHROPOLOGICAL INTEREST

Although the conference was primarily designed to address the theoretical issues discussed above, it was also designed to alert anthropologists/prehistorians and skeletal biologists to the potential for cross-fertilization between their respective fields. *The Food Crisis in Prehistory* (Cohen 1977), although expressly dealing with predictions about changing diet, nutrition, and health, was written largely in ignorance of the potential (and even of the existing) contribution of skeletal pathology to the issues under discussion. And, in recent years, much of the continuing discussion of these and other related issues has continued to ignore the skeletal data. On the other side, much of the work in skeletal pathology, derived from a tradition focusing on specific diseases and their diagnosis, has not been designed with anthropological issues in mind; and, as became clear in the process of designing and holding the conference, even many skeletal biologists interested in prehistory have not been aware of the full potential of their techniques for resolving anthropological issues. In many cases they have not been aware of the issues themselves. Therefore, it seems important to call attention to some additional examples of approaches to anthropological problems offered by the studies in this book, even though those problems are tangential to our main goals and the data are not yet systematically available or systematically reported in the volume.

Several chapters (Buikstra; Smith et al.; Martin et al.; Benfer) discuss the use of skeletal data as a means of determining the degree of genetic continuity and genetic isolation among groups spanning the economic transition in particular regions. As Buikstra points out, there is a significant difference between the appearance of a new group that coincidentally brings new technology and new diseases to a region and the appearance of new stresses in an indigenous population contingent on adoption of a new economy. Moreover, the meanings of certain skeletal indices such as altered stature, when they occur within a population are very different from when they occur with replacement of one population by another. Skeletal data are also an important supplement to artifact studies in assessing models of cultural transmission, diffusion, and trade, as well as in assessing models of population "flux," population movement, and breeding isolation. (See Cavalli-Sforza 1983; Wobst 1974).

Several chapters in the volume (Smith et al.; Rathbun; Norr; Benfer; Angel) directly or indirectly employ data from new techniques of trace element and isotope analysis of skeletons to supplement archaeological refuse in reconstructing human diets. Smith et al. cite one study by Schoeniger (which they consider controversial) suggesting a decline in the percentage of animal protein in the diet from Upper Paleolithic to Epipaleolithic in the Levant, a result that, if correct, adds support to archaeological identification of the "Broad-Spectrum revolution" and to the population pressure model. Smith et al. also use strontium analysis to suggest that animal protein may have increased in importance in the diet over late hunter-gatherer levels in at least some parts of the Levant during the Neolithic coinciding with the adoption of animal husbandry. In addition, Smith et al. cite a study using strontium analysis as a means of determining the age of weaning and diet supplementation in archaeological populations, an application that could help resolve a major ongoing controversy about the effects of the Neolithic Revolution on nursing practices and the relation between altered nursing and the apparent increase in human fertility that accompanied the adoption of farming (cf. Cohen 1980; Hassan 1980; Konner and Worthman 1980; Lee 1980). Benfer notes the potential of trace element analysis, using hair, to determine seasonal trends in diet, supplementing data on longer-term trends obtained from bone. Finally, implicit in several of the studies is the potential for using trace element and isotopic analysis to determine the age and sex distribution of food consumption patterns within a population (and the changing pattern of this distribution through time), data rarely available from other archaeological refuse.

Several of the chapters, studying other indicators of health discussed above, also provide data on age and sex distribution of particular stresses and their changes over time that can be used to test anthropological theories about the structure of social groups and about changes in society related to major economic shifts. Larsen, for example, uses the distribution of infectious lesions, dental caries, and skeletal robusticity to measure the differential effects of the adoption of farming on males and females, and it is clear that the potential exists more broadly to determine the effects of economic change on the relative health, nutrition, workload, and, indirectly, status of the sexes.

The age and sex distributions of various stressors (particularly episodic rather than chronic stressors) are used in several of the studies (see especially Cassidy; Goodman et al.; Martin et al.; Benfer) as a means of determining not only the "natural" distribution of health problems, but also the culturally determined focus of stress. Cassidy and Benfer are perhaps most explicit in suggesting that social strategies intentionally focus biological stress and even death on particular age or sex classes as a matter of adaptive policy; but other studies (Goodman et al.; Martin et al.) describe methods for identifying the distribution of chronic malnutrition through age classes; and, of course, mortality profiles for many populations display the distributions of deaths, just as the studies of Harris lines and enamel hypoplasias (see especially Cassidy; Goodman et al.) provide data on age and sex distributions and periodicity of episodic stressors.

The combined health indicators are also used in several of the chapters to assess the importance of high social rank in affording real economic privileges as measured by health and nutrition (Palkovich; Allison; Angel; Buikstra and Cook). Such studies add a dimension to the archaeological recognition of the distinction between mere rank and real class privilege (see Fried 1967). One chapter (Buikstra) discusses the uses of skeletal data to distinguish ascribed and achieved status. And several chapters (Martin et al.; Goodman et al.; Allison) comment on the effects of political centralization on health. (The impact is largely negative in these studies.) These data provide one approach for testing theories that view early centralized political systems alternately as supportive homeostatic mechanisms (Service 1975) or as systems essentially exploitive of subject populations (Fried 1967).

This is necessarily a highly selective list from among a potentially rich array of arenas in which anthropology, prehistory, and skeletal biology might benefit from better communication. We hope that this volume will serve not only to stimulate new work on the central issues discussed but also to promote creative exploration of new avenues of joint research among these fields.

REFERENCES

Brothwell, Don

1963 The macroscopic dental pathology of some earlier populations. In *Dental anthropology*, edited by D. R. Brothwell, pp. 271-288. Pergamon, Oxford.

Cavalli-Sforza, L. L.
1983 The transition to agriculture and some of its consequences. *How humans adapt*, edited by D. Ortner, pp. 103-120. Smithsonian Institution, Washington, D.C.

Christenson, Andrew
1980 Changes in the human niche in response to population growth. In *Modeling prehistoric subsistence economies*, edited by T. Earle and A. L. Christenson, pp. 31-72. Academic Press, New York.

Cohen, M. N.
1977 *The food crisis in prehistory.* Yale University Press, New Haven.
1980 Speculations on the evolution of density measurement and population regulation in Homo sapiens. In *Biosocial mechanisms of population regulation*, edited by M. N. Cohen, R. S. Malpass, and H. G. Klein, pp. 275-304. Yale University Press, New Haven.

Earle, Timothy
1980 A model of subsistence change. In *Modeling prehistoric subsistence economies*, edited by T. Earle and A. L. Christenson, pp. 1-29. Academic Press, New York.

Fried, Morton
1967 *The evolution of political society.* Random House, New York.

Hassan, Fekri
1980 The growth and regulation of human population in prehistoric times. In *Biosocial mechanisms of population regulation*, edited by M. N. Cohen, R. S. Malpass, and H. G. Klein, pp. 305-320. Yale University Press, New Haven.

Hayden, Brian
1981 Research and development in the Stone Age. *Current Anthropology 22*:519-548.

Hespenheide, H. A.
1980 Ecological models of resource selection. In *Modeling prehistoric subsistence economies*, edited by T. Earle and A. L. Christenson, pp. 73-78. Academic Press, New York.

Howell, Nancy
1982 Village composition implied by a paleodemographic life table: the Libben site. *American Journal of Physical Anthropology 59*:263-270.

Konner, Melvin, and Carol Worthman
1980 Nursing frequency, gonad function, and birth spacing among !Kung Hunter-Gatherers. *Science 207*:788-791.

Lee, R. B.
1980 Lactation, ovulation, infanticide and women's work: A study of hunter-gatherer population regulation. In *Biosocial mechanisms of population regulation*, edited by M. N. Cohen, R. S. Malpass, and H. G. Klein, pp. 321-348. Yale University Press, New Haven.

Murchison, M. A., D. W. Owsley, and A. J. Riopelle
1983 *Transverse line formation in protein deprived rhesus monkeys*. Paper presented to the annual meeting of the Paleopathology Association, Indianapolis.

O'Connell, J. F., and Kristen Hawkes
1981 Alyawara plant use and optimal foraging theory. In *Hunter-Gatherer foraging strategies*, edited by B. Winterhalder and E. A. Smith, pp. 99-125. Aldine, Chicago.

Reidhead, Van
1980 The economics of subsistence change: A test of an optimization model. In *Modeling prehistoric subsistence economies*, edited by T. Earle and A. L. Christenson, pp. 141-186. Academic Press, New York.

Sattenspiel, Lisa and Henry Harpending
1983 Stable populations and skeletal age. *American Antiquity 48*:489-498.

Service, Elman
1975 *Origins of the state and civilization*. Norton, New York.

White, Tim D.
1978 Early hominid enamel hypoplasias. *American Journal of Physical Anthropology 49*:79-84.

Winterhalder, Bruce
1981 Optimal foraging strategies and Hunter-Gatherer research in anthropology: theories and models. In *Hunter-Gatherer foraging strategies*, edited by B. Winterhalder and E. A. Smith, pp. 13-35. Aldine, Chicago.

Wobst, M.
1974 Boundry conditions for paleolithic social systems: A simulation approach. *American Antiquity 39*:147-177.

Index

D

N

O

P

Contributors

Numbers in parentheses indicate the pages on which the authors' contributions begin.

Marvin J. Allison (515), *Instituto de Antropología, Universidad de Tarapacá, Arica, Chile*

J. Lawrence Angel (51), *Department of Anthropology, National Museum of Natural History, Smithsonian Institution, Washington, D.C. 20560*

George J. Armelagos (13, 193, 271, 585), *Department of Anthropology, University of Massachusetts, Amherst, Massachusetts 01003*

Ofer Bar-Yosef (101), *Institute of Archaeology, Hebrew University, Mt. Scopus Campus, Jerusalem, Israel*

Robert A. Benfer (531), *Department of Anthropology, University of Missouri–Columbia, Columbia, Missouri 65211*

Mark W. Blaeuer (393), *Department of Anthropology, University of Arkansas, Fayetteville, Arkansas 72701*

Donna J. Braun[1] (347), *Department of Anthropology, University of Cincinnati, Cincinnati, Ohio 45221*

Jane E. Buikstra (215), *Department of Anthropology, Northwestern University, Evanston, Illinois 60201*

Barbara A. Burnett (393), *Department of Anthropology, University of Arkansas, Fayetteville, Arkansas 72701*

Claire Monod Cassidy (307), *Division of Behavioral and Social Sciences, Department of Anthropology, University of Maryland, College Park, Maryland 20742*

George Clark (13), *Department of Anthropology, University of Massachusetts, Amherst, Massachusetts 01003*

Mark Nathan Cohen (1, 585), *Department of Anthropology, State University of New York College at Plattsburgh, Plattsburgh, New York 12901*

Della Collins Cook (235), *Department of Anthropology, Indiana University, Bloomington, Indiana 47405*

[1]Present address: Department of Anthropology, University of Pennsylvania, Philadelphia, Pennsylvania 19104.

David N. Dickel (439), *Department of Anthropology, University of California, Davis, Davis, California 95616*

Alan H. Goodman[2] (13, 193, 271), *Department of Anthropology, University of Massachusetts, Amherst, Massachusetts 01003*

Kenneth A. R. Kennedy (169), *Ecology and Systematics, Division of Biological Sciences, Department of Anthropology, Cornell University, Ithaca, New York 14853*

Patrick Key (75), *The KEY Company, Inc., Williston, North Dakota 58802-2690*

John Lallo (271), *Department of Anthropology, Cleveland State University, Cleveland, Ohio 44115*

Clark Spencer Larsen (367), *Department of Anthropology, Northern Illinois University, DeKalb, Illinois 60115*

Debra L. Martin (13, 193), *School of Natural Science, Hampshire College, Amherst, Massachusetts 01002*

Henry M. McHenry (439), *Department of Anthropology, University of California, Davis, Davis, California 95616*

Christopher Meiklejohn (75), *Department of Anthropology, University of Winnipeg, Winnipeg, Manitoba R3B 2E9, Canada*

Michael S. Nassaney (393), *Department of Anthropology, University of Massachusetts, Amherst, Massachusetts 01003*

Lynette Norr (463), *Department of Anthropology, University of Illinois at Urbana—Champaign, Urbana, Illinois 61801*

Ann M. Palkovich (425), *Anthropology Program, George Mason University, Fairfax, Virginia 22030*

Anthony J. Perzigian (347), *Departments of Anthroplogy and Anatomy, University of Cincinnati, Cincinnati, Ohio 45221*

Ted A. Rathbun (137), *Department of Anthropology, University of South Carolina, Columbia, South Carolina 29208*

Anna Curtenius Roosevelt (559), *Museum of the American Indian, New York, New York 10032*

Jerome C. Rose (271, 393), *Department of Anthropology, University of Arkansas, Fayetteville, Arkansas 72701*

Catherine Schentag (75), *Department of Anthropology, University of Winnipeg, Winnipeg, Manitoba R3B 2E9, Canada*

Peter D. Schulz[3] (439), *Department of Anthropology, University of California, Davis, Davis, California 95616*

Andrew Sillen (101), *National Museum of Natural History, Smithsonian Institution, Washington, D.C. 20560*

[2]Present address: Department of Orthodontics, University of Connecticut Health Center, Farmington, Connecticut 06032.

[3]Present address: Resource Protection Division, California Department of Parks and Recreation, Sacramento, California 95811.

Patricia Smith (101), *Department of Anatomy, Hebrew University—Hadassah School of Dental Medicine, Jerusalem, Israel*
Patricia A. Tench[4] (347) *Department of Anthropology, University of Cincinnati, Cincinnati, Ohio 45221*
D. H. Ubelaker (491), *Department of Anthropology, National Museum of Natural History, Smithsonian Institution, Washington, D.C. 20560*
Dennis P. Van Gerven (193), *Department of Anthropology, University of Colorado, Boulder, Colorado 80309*
Alexandra Venema (75), *Department of Anthropology, University of Winnipeg, Winnipeg, Manitoba R3B 2E9, Canada*

[4]Present address: Department of Anthropology, Indiana University, Bloomington, Indiana 47405.

Bioarchaeological Interpretations of the Human Past: Local, Regional, and Global Perspectives
Edited by Clark Spencer Larsen

This series examines the field of bioarchaeology, the study of human biological remains from archaeological settings. Focusing on the intersection between biology and behavior in the past, each volume will highlight important issues, such as biocultural perspectives on health, lifestyle and behavioral adaptation, biomechanical responses to key adaptive shifts in human history, dietary reconstruction and foodways, biodistance and population history, warfare and conflict, demography, social inequality, and environmental impacts on population.

Ancient Health: Skeletal Indicators of Agricultural and Economic Intensification, edited by Mark Nathan Cohen and Gillian M. M. Crane-Kramer (2007; first paperback edition, 2012)
Bioarchaeology and Identity in the Americas, edited by Kelly J. Knudson and Christopher M. Stojanowski (2009; first paperback edition, 2010)
Island Shores, Distant Pasts: Archaeological and Biological Approaches to the Pre-Columbian Settlement of the Caribbean, edited by Scott M. Fitzpatrick and Ann H. Ross (2010)
The Bioarchaeology of the Human Head: Decapitation, Decoration, and Deformation, edited by Michelle Bonogofsky (2011)
Bioarchaeology and Climate Change: A View from South Asian Prehistory, by Gwen Robbins Schug (2011)
Violence, Ritual, and the Wari Empire: A Social Bioarchaeology of Imperialism in the Ancient Andes, by Tiffiny A. Tung (2012)
The Bioarchaeology of Individuals, edited by Ann L. W. Stodder and Ann M. Palkovich (2012)
The Bioarchaeology of Violence, edited by Debra L. Martin, Ryan P. Harrod, and Ventura R. Pérez (2012)
Bioarchaeology and Behavior: The People of the Ancient Near East, edited by Megan A. Perry (2012)
Paleopathology at the Origins of Agriculture, edited by Mark Nathan Cohen and George J. Armelagos (2013)

CPSIA information can be obtained
at www.ICGtesting.com
Printed in the USA
LVHW090101290119
605567LV00001B/5/P

9 780813 044897